Surreptitious Software

Addison-Wesley Software Security Series

Gary McGraw, Consulting Editor

Titles in the Series

Exploiting Online Games: Cheating Massively Distributed Systems,
by Greg Hoglund and Gary McGraw
ISBN: 0-132-27191-5

Secure Programming with Static Analysis, by Brian Chess and Jacob West
ISBN: 0-321-42477-8

Software Security: Building Security In, by Gary McGraw
ISBN: 0-321-35670-5

Rootkits: Subverting the Windows Kernel, by Greg Hoglund and James Butler
ISBN: 0-321-29431-9

Exploiting Software: How to Break Code, by Greg Hoglund and Gary McGraw
ISBN: 0-201-78695-8

Also Available
The Software Security Library Boxed Set, by Gary McGraw, John Viega, Greg Hoglund
ISBN: 0-321-41870-0

 For more information about these titles, and to read sample chapters, please visit
informit.com/softwaresecurityseries

Surreptitious Software

Obfuscation, Watermarking, and Tamperproofing for Software Protection

Christian Collberg

Jasvir Nagra

✦✦ Addison-Wesley

Upper Saddle River, NJ • Boston • Indianapolis • San Francisco
New York • Toronto • Montreal • London • Munich • Paris • Madrid
Capetown • Sydney • Tokyo • Singapore • Mexico City

The publisher offers excellent discounts on this book when ordered in quantity for bulk purchases or special sales, which may include electronic versions and/or custom covers and content particular to your business, training goals, marketing focus, and branding interests. For more information, please contact:

U.S. Corporate and Government Sales
(800) 382-3419
corpsales@pearsontechgroup.com

For sales outside the United States, please contact:

International Sales
international@pearson.com

Visit us on the Web: www.informit.com/aw

Library of Congress Cataloging-in-Publication Data

Collberg, Christian.
   Surreptitious software : obfuscation, watermarking, and tamperproofing for software protection / Christian Collberg, Jasvir Nagra. – 1st ed.
       p. cm.
   Includes bibliographical references and index.
   ISBN 0-321-54925-2 (pbk. : alk. paper)
   1. Computer security. 2. Cryptography. 3. Data protection. 4. Copyright and electronic data processing–United States. I. Nagra, Jasvir. II. Title.
   QA76.9.A25C6165   2009
   005.8–dc22   2009015520

ISBN-13: 978-0-321-54925-9
ISBN-10:   0-321-54925-2

Text printed in the United States on recycled paper at Edwards Brothers in Ann Arbor, Michigan.
First printing, July 2009

To Louise and Andrew,
with all my love, pride, and admiration
— Christian

For Shwetha, whose unwavering love
and support makes everything possible
— Jasvir

Contents

Preface

Surreptitious software is the term we have chosen to describe a new branch of computer security research that has emerged over the last decade. It's a field that borrows techniques not only from computer security, but also from many other areas of computer science, such as cryptography, steganography, media watermarking, software metrics, reverse engineering, and compiler optimization. Surreptitious software applies these techniques in order to solve very different problems: It is concerned with protecting the secrets contained within computer programs. We use the word *secrets* loosely, but the techniques we present in this book (code obfuscation, software watermarking and fingerprinting, tamperproofing, and birthmarking) are typically used to prevent others from exploiting the intellectual effort invested in producing a piece of software. For example, software fingerprinting can be used to trace software pirates, code obfuscation can be used to make it more difficult to reverse engineer a program, and tamperproofing can make it harder for a hacker to remove a license check.

So let's look at *why* someone should read this book, *who* they might be, and *what* material the book will cover.

Why Should You Read This Book?

Unlike traditional security research, surreptitious software is not concerned with how to protect your computer from viruses, but rather how virus writers protect their code from you! Similarly, we're not interested in how to make your code free from security bugs, but rather how to riddle your program with buggy code that gets run only when someone tries to tamper with the program. And unlike cryptography research that protects the confidentiality of data, assuming that a secret key remains hidden, we're interested in how to hide that key. While software engineering research has devised a multitude of software metrics in order to be able to make programs well structured, we will use the same techniques to make your programs more convoluted! Many of the techniques that we will describe in this book are based on algorithms developed by compiler optimization researchers, but unlike them, we're not interested in making your program faster or smaller. Rather, after you apply the algorithms in this book to your own code, your programs will be *larger* and *slower*! Finally, unlike traditional media watermarking and steganography that hides secrets in images, audio, video, or English text, surreptitious software hides secrets inside *computer code*.

So why, then, should you be interested in this book? Why learn about a branch of computer security research that doesn't teach how to protect yourself against viruses and worms? Why study optimizing compiler transformations that make your code slower and larger? Why bother with a branch of cryptography that breaks the most basic assumption of that field, namely, that the secret key must be kept hidden?

The answer is that there are real-world problems that don't fit neatly into traditional computer security and cryptography research but that are interesting nonetheless. For example, in this book we will show you how to use *software watermarking* to fight piracy. A software watermark is a unique identifier (such as someone's credit card number or your copyright notice) that you embed into your program to uniquely bind it to you (the author) or your customer. If you find illegal copies of your program being sold at a market in Singapore, you can extract the watermark and trace the illegal copy back to the original purchaser. You can use the same technique when you distribute beta copies of your new computer game to your partner companies—should any of them leak the code, you can trace the culprit and sue for damages.

Or if the new version of your program contains a novel algorithm that you don't want your competitors to get their hands on and incorporate into their competing product, you can *obfuscate* your program and make it as convoluted and hard to understand as possible in order to slow down your competitors' reverse engineering efforts. If you do suspect someone has stolen your code, we'll show you how to use *software birthmarking* techniques to identify the offending sections.

Or, say that you have included a secret in your program and you want to make sure that without this secret remaining intact, no one can execute the program. For example, you don't want a hacker to be able to modify your license checking code or the cryptographic key that unlocks an mp3 file in your digital rights management system. Our chapter on *tamperproofing* will discuss various techniques for ensuring that programs that have been tampered with will cease to function properly.

Now, we hear you object that including a crypto key in an executable is a *Really Bad Idea*! Surely experience has shown us that *security by obscurity* never works, and whatever secret we try to hide in our program will eventually be discovered by a sufficiently determined hacker. And yes—we have to concede—you're right. None of the techniques we're advocating in this book are foolproof. They won't hide a secret forever. They won't make your program safe from tampering forever. They won't identify software theft all of the time. All we can hope for, barring major advances in the field, is that we can slow down our adversaries. Our goal is to slow them down *enough* so that either they give up on cracking our code because they figure it's too painful and not worth the trouble, or so that by the time they've come up with a successful attack we've already made enough of a profit or have moved on to the next version of the code.

For example, say that you're running a pay-TV channel that your customers access through a set-top box. Each box is personalized—hidden somewhere in the code is their unique identifier—so that you can grant and revoke viewing privileges depending on whether they've paid their bill or not. Now, an enterprising hacker extracts and disassembles the code, finds their unique identifier, and starts selling it over the Web at a fraction of the price you charge, along with instructions on how to implant it in the box. How do you counter this attack? Well, you may use tamperproof smartcards, which are not that hard to tamper with, as you will see in our chapter on hardware protection techniques. Or maybe you'll obfuscate your code to make it harder to analyze. Or maybe you'll use software tamperproofing to stop the code from executing once it is mucked with. More likely, you'll use a combination of all these techniques in order to protect your code. Even when employing all these techniques, you must know, and accept, that your code will eventually be broken and your secret will be out of the bag (or box, in this case). So why should you bother? If security through obscurity is a fundamentally flawed idea, and if none of the techniques you will read about in this book will give you "perfect and long-term security," why go through the trouble? *Why should you buy this book?* You will bother for the very simple reason that the longer you can keep your code safe, the more subscriptions you'll sell and the longer between set-top box upgrades, and hence, the more money you'll make.

It's as simple as that.

Who Uses Surreptitious Software?

Many well-known companies have shown an interest in surreptitious software. It's difficult to get a grip on the extent to which these techniques are actually being used in practice (most companies are notoriously tight-lipped about how they protect their code), but we can gauge their level of interest from their patents and current patent applications. Microsoft owns several software watermarking [104,354], obfuscation [62,62,69,69,70,70,180,378], and birthmarking [364] patents. Intertrust holds a huge patent portfolio related to digital rights management, including patents on obfuscation [91,169] and tamperproofing [168]. In 2004, to the tune of $440 million [176], Microsoft settled a long-running lawsuit with Intertrust by licensing their entire patent portfolio. That same year Microsoft also partnered [250] with PreEmptive Solutions in order to include PreEmptive's identifier obfuscator (which is based on their patent [351]) in Visual Studio. Arxan, a spin-off from Purdue University researchers, has made a successful business from their tamperproofing algorithm [24,305]. Apple holds a patent on code obfuscation [197], perhaps intended to protect their iTunes software. Intel spun off a company, Convera, to explore their tamperproofing algorithm [27,268–270] for digital rights management. The Canadian telecom Northern Telecom spun off what to date has been the most successful company in this area, Cloakware, which holds patents [67,68,182] on what they call *whitebox cryptography*, how to hide cryptographic algorithms and keys in computer code. In December 2007 Cloakware was sold for $72.5 million to Irdeto, a Dutch company in the pay-TV business [162]. A relative latecomer, Sun Microsystems, has also recently filed several patent applications on code obfuscation [105–110].

Skype's VoIP client is highly obfuscated and tamperproofed by techniques similar to those of Arxan [24], Intel [27], and ourselves [89]. Protecting the integrity of their client is undoubtedly of the highest importance for Skype, since, if cracked, their protocol could be easily hijacked by cheaper competitors. Keeping their protocol secret allowed them to build an impressive user base, and this might have been one of the reasons eBay decided to acquire them for $2.6 billion in 2005. In essence, the protection afforded Skype by surreptitious software techniques bought them enough time to become VoIP market leaders. Even if, at this point, their protocol has been cracked (which it has; see Section 7.2.4), it will be difficult for a competitor to threaten this position.

Academic researchers have approached surreptitious software from a variety of angles. Some, like us, come from a compiler and programming languages background. This is natural since most algorithms involve code transformations that require static analysis, with which compiler optimization researchers are intimately familiar. In spite of the disdain cryptography researchers have in the past had for *security through obscurity*, some have recently applied their techniques to software watermarking and to discovering the limits of obfuscation. Researchers from media watermarking, computer security, and software engineering have also published in surreptitious software. Unfortunately, progress in the area has been hampered by the lack of natural publication venues. Instead, researchers have struggled, and continue to struggle, to get their works accepted in traditional conferences and journals. Papers have appeared in venues such as the ACM Symposium on Principles of Programming Languages (POPL), the Information Hiding Workshop, IEEE Transactions on Software Engineering, Advances in Cryptology (CRYPTO), and Information Security Conference (ISC), as well as in various digital rights management conferences. As the field becomes more mainstream, we can expect journals, workshops, and conferences dedicated exclusively to surreptitious software, but this has yet to happen.

The military has also spent much effort (and taxpayer money) on surreptitious software research. For example, the patent [96] held on Cousot's software watermarking algorithm [95] is assigned to the French *Thales group*, the ninth-largest defense contractor in the world. Here's a quote from a recent (2006) U.S. Army solicitation [303] for what they term AT, anti-tamper research:

> All U.S. Army Project Executive Offices (PEOs) and Project Managers (PMs) are now charged with executing Army and Department of Defense (DoD) AT policies in the design and implementation of their systems. Embedded software is at the core of modern weapon systems and is one of the most critical technologies to be protected. AT provides protection of U.S. technologies against exploitation via reverse engineering. Standard compiled code with no AT is easy to reverse engineer, so the goal of employed AT techniques will be to make that effort more difficult. In attacking software, reverse engineers have a wide array of tools available to them, including debuggers, decompilers, disassemblers, as well as static and dynamic analysis techniques. AT techniques are being developed to combat the loss of the U.S. technological advantage, but further advances are necessary to provide useful, effective and varied toolsets to U.S. Army PEOs and PMs. . . . The goal of software AT technologies/techniques developed is to provide a substantial layer of protection against reverse engineering, allowing for maximum delay in an adversary compromising the protected code. This capability will allow the U.S. time to advance its own technology or otherwise mitigate any losses of weapons technologies. As a result, the U.S. Army can continue to maintain a technological edge in support of its warfighters.

This particular solicitation comes from the Army's Missile and Space program and focuses on providing protection in real-time embedded systems. So it's reasonable to assume that the Army is worried about one of their missiles not exploding on impact, allowing the enemy access to the embedded targeting flight software.

The DoD's current interest in protecting their software goes back to the infamous incident in 2001 when a—what CNN [359] calls a US "Navy reconnaissance plane" but the rest of us know as a "spy plane"—had a run-in with a Chinese fighter jet and had to make an emergency landing on the Chinese island of Hainan. In spite of George W. Bush's plea [116] for the "prompt return 'without further damage or tampering' of the crew and plane," the Chinese stalled, presumably so that they could gather as much information as possible from the plane's hardware and software. There is a claim [116] that all the software was erased:

> A former Pentagon intelligence official told United Press International the crew would have "zeroed" out the crypto analytic equipment and other software on landing, essentially wiping their memories clean. Although the Chinese might have access to the hardware, the software that runs it would be almost impossible to penetrate.

Regardless of whether this is accurate[1] or a carefully orchestrated leak to reassure the U.S. public (why was the software just *almost* impossible to penetrate if it was in fact successfully wiped?), the DoD got significantly spooked and initiated a program to investigate technologies such as obfuscation and tamperproofing in order to protect sensitive weapons systems software. As one DoD official put it, "[T]he next time a plane goes down, we don't want to end up on the cover of the *New York Times* again [291]."

Here's another quote from the DoD [115]:

> The Software Protection Initiative (SPI) is an undertaking of the Department of Defense (DoD) to develop and deploy technologies to secure special-purpose computer programs containing information critical to DoD weapon programs. SPI offers a novel approach to protecting high value computer programs. It doesn't secure the computer or the network. Instead it empowers a single computer program to secure itself. This approach promises to significantly improve DoD's Information Assurance posture. SPI protection technology is effective on systems ranging from desktop

---

1. During a particularly lively dinner in Beijing in January 2008 with Chinese security researchers, we (Collberg) asked about this incident. One person proudly announced, "Yes, some of the information was recovered!" and then, realizing his mistake, immediately clammed up. This was later corroborated by a different researcher at a second dinner: "The Americans didn't have time to destroy everything!"

computers to supercomputers. It is an integral layer of the defense-in-depth security paradigm. SPI technologies complement, but do no[t] rely upon, network firewalls, or physical security. These SPI products are currently being deployed to selected HPC centers and are in use at over 150 DoD government and contractor sites. Broader deployment will play a significant role in protecting the DoD's and the nation's critical application software.

What does this mean? The DoD is worried not only about dud missiles falling into the wrong hands, but also about software in use at hardened high-performance computer centers. In fact, theft of *any* software developed for the defense and intelligence communities may have negative consequences. Anecdotally, when the software on a fighter jet is to be updated, a service technician simply walks out to the plane with a laptop, hooks it up, and uploads the new code. What would happen if that laptop got lost or liberated by a technician in the service of a foreign government, as seems to happen [375] every so often? The code could be reverse engineered to be used in an adversary's planes, or even modified with a Trojan horse that would make the avionics fail at a particular time. While there is no substitute for good security practices, surreptitious software techniques can be used as a last line of defense. For example, the avionics software could be fingerprinted with the identifiers of those who have had it in their possession. If one day we find copies of the code in the onboard computers of a North Korean plane we've shot down and are now reverse engineering, we could trace it back to the person who last had authorized access to it.

But, we hear you say, why should I be interested in how evil government agencies or companies with monopolistic tendencies are protecting their secrets? If crackers rip them off, maybe they're just getting what they deserve. Well, maybe so, but technical means of protecting against software theft may ultimately benefit the little guy more than big government or big industry. The reason is that legal forms of protection (such as patents, trademarks, and copyrights) are available to you only if you have the financial means to defend them in a court of law. In other words, even if you think you have a pretty good case against Microsoft for ripping off your code, you will still not prevail in court unless you have the financial backing to outlast them through the appeals process.[2] The technical means of protection that we will discuss in this book such as obfuscation and tamperproofing, on the other hand, can be cheap and easy to apply for the little guy as well as the big guy. And, if you find yourself up against Microsoft in a court of law, techniques such as

---

2. You don't.

watermarking and birthmarking can bolster your case by allowing you to present evidence of theft.

There is one final category of people that we have yet to touch upon that makes extensive use of surreptitious software: bad guys. Virus writers have been spectacularly successful in obfuscating their code to prevent it from being intercepted by virus scanners. It is interesting to note that while the techniques the good guys use (for example, to protect DVDs, games, or cable TV) seem to be regularly broken by the bad guys, the techniques the bad guys use (to build malware) seem much harder for the good guys to protect against.

What's the Goal of This Book?

The goal of surreptitious software research is to invent algorithms that slow down our adversaries as much as possible while adding as little computational overhead as possible. We also need to devise evaluation techniques that allow us to say, "After applying algorithm A to your program, it will take an average hacker T extra time to crack it compared to the original code, while adding O amount of overhead," or, failing that, at least be able to say that "compared to algorithm B, algorithm A produces code that is harder to crack." It's important to emphasize that research into surreptitious software is still in its infancy, and that the algorithms and evaluation techniques that we'll present in this book, while representing the state of the art, are nowhere near perfect.

In this book we attempt to organize and systematize all that is currently known about surreptitious software research. Each chapter covers a particular technique and describes application areas and available algorithms. In Chapter 1 (What Is *Surreptitious Software?*), we give an overview of the area, and in Chapter 2 (Methods of Attack and Defense), we discuss our adversarial model, i.e., what hacker tools and techniques we should try to protect ourselves against and what ideas are available to us as defenders. In Chapter 3 (Program Analysis), we detail the techniques that both attackers and defenders can use to analyze programs. Chapter 4 (Code Obfuscation), Chapter 5 (Obfuscation Theory), and Chapter 6 (Dynamic Obfuscation) give algorithms for code obfuscation. Chapter 7 (Software Tamperproofing) gives tamperproofing algorithms, Chapter 8 (Software Watermarking) and Chapter 9 (Dynamic Watermarking) give watermarking algorithms, and Chapter 10 (Software Similarity Analysis) gives birthmarking algorithms. Chapter 11 (Hardware for Protecting Software) presents hardware-based protection techniques.

If you're a manager interested in learning about the state of the art in surreptitious software research and how it can be applied in your organization, you'll want to read Chapter 1 and Chapter 2. If you're a researcher with a background in compiler design, you can skip Chapter 3. It's advantageous to read the algorithm chapters in order, since, for example, the watermarking chapter relies on ideas you've learned in the obfuscation chapter. Still, we've tried to make each chapter as self-contained as possible, so skipping around should be possible. If you're an engineer charged with adding protection to your company's product line, you should read Chapter 3 carefully and maybe complement that by reading up on static analysis in a good compiler text. You can then move on to the algorithm chapter relevant to you. If you're a graduate student reading this book for a class, read the entire thing from cover to cover, and don't forget to review for the final!

We hope this book will do two things. First, we want to convince you, dear reader, that code obfuscation, software watermarking, birthmarking, and tamper-proofing are interesting ideas well worth studying, and that they are viable alternatives to protecting the intellectual property you have invested in your software. Second, we want this book to bring together all available information on the subject so that it can serve as a starting point for further research in the field.

Christian and Jasvir

Tucson and Mountain View
Groundhog Day, 2009

P.S. There is a third reason for writing this book. If, while reading this book, you are struck by the cleverness of an idea and, as a result, you become inspired to make your own contributions to the field, well, then, dear reader, our goal with this book has really been met. And when you've come up with your new clever algorithm, please remember to let us know so we can include it in the next edition!

About the Authors

Christian Collberg received a B.Sc. in computer science and numerical analysis and a Ph.D. in computer science from Lund University, Sweden. He is currently an associate professor in the department of computer science at the University of Arizona and has also worked at the University of Auckland, New Zealand, and the Chinese Academy of Sciences in Beijing. Professor Collberg is a leading researcher in the intellectual property protection of software, and also maintains an interest in compiler and programming language research. In his spare time he writes songs, sings, and plays guitar for The Zax and hopes one day to finish his Great Swedish Novel.

Jasvir Nagra received his B.Sc. in mathematics and computer science and a Ph.D. in computer science from the University of Auckland, New Zealand. He's been a postdoctoral scholar on the RE-TRUST project at the University of Trento, where his focus is on applying obfuscation, tamperproofing, and watermarking techniques to protect the integrity of software executing on a remote untrusted platform. His research interests also include the design of programming languages and its impact on the security of applications. He's currently with Google Inc., where he is building Caja, an open source, secure subset of JavaScript. In his spare time Jasvir dabbles with Lego and one day hopes to finish building his Turing machine made entirely out of Lego blocks.

Acknowledgments

We would like to thank the following people without whose assistance this book could not have been written: Amena Ali, Bertrand Anckaert, Gregory Andrews, Mike Atallah, Jan Cappaert, Edward Carter, Igor Crk, Mike Dager, Mila Dalla Preda, Saumya Debray, Fabrice Desclaux, Roberto Giacobazzi, Jon Giffin, Gael Hachez, Wulf Harder, William Horne, Mariusz Jakubowski, Yuichiro Kanzaki, Phil Kaslo, David P. Maher, Scott Moskowitz, Yoram Ofek, Reiner Sailer, Christine Scheer, Arvind Seshadri, Richard Snodgrass, the students of CSc 620, Clark Thomborson, Gregg Townsend, Tom Van Vleck, and Glenn Wurster.

Special thanks to the Institute of Automation and Professor Fei-Yue Wang of the Chinese Academy of Sciences, for their generous support during Christian Collberg's sabbatical visit, August 2006 through July 2007, and to Yoram Ofek and the RE-TRUST project for their support during the summer of 2008.

To everyone at Addison-Wesley who made this project possible, our sincere thanks: Jessica Goldstein, Gary McGraw, Romny French, Elizabeth Ryan and Chuck Toporek.

Finally, we would like to thank all our friends and family who have encouraged and supported us throughout this project: Charlotte Bergh, Andrew Collberg, Melissa Fitch, Michael Hammer, John Hartman, Louise Holbrook, Ma and Dad, Mamma, Ginger Myles, Qu "Jojo" Cheng, Shwetha Shankar, Haya Shulman, Mr. Snickers, and Tudou.

Tools of the Trade

What Is *Surreptitious Software?*

In this first chapter we will talk about the basic techniques used to protect secrets stored in software, namely *obfuscation, watermarking, tamperproofing,* and *birthmarking*. These techniques have many interesting applications, such as the use of obfuscation and tamperproofing to protect media in *digital rights management* systems. What we think you will find particularly interesting is that obfuscation and the three other techniques "solve" problems that traditional computer security and cryptography can't touch. We put "solve" in quotation marks because there are no known algorithms that provide complete security for an indefinite amount of time. At the present time, the best we can hope for is to be able to extend the time it takes a hacker to crack our schemes. You might think that this seems highly unsatisfactory—and you'd be right—but the bottom line is that there are interesting applications for which no better techniques are known.

1.1 Setting the Scene

When you hear the term *computer security*, you probably imagine a scenario where a computer (owned by a benign user we'll call Alice) is under attack from an evil hacker (we'll call him Bob), or from the viruses, worms, Trojan horses, rootkits, and keyloggers that he's created. The goal of computer security research is to devise techniques for building systems that prevent Bob from taking over Alice's computer or that alert her when he does. The basic idea behind such techniques is to restrict what Bob can do on Alice's computer without unduly restricting what she can do herself. For example, a *network firewall* allows Alice to access other computers on the network but restricts the ways in which Bob can access hers. An *intrusion detection system* analyzes the network access patterns on Alice's computer and alerts her if Bob appears to be doing something unusual or suspicious. A *virus scanner* refuses to run Bob's program unless it can convince itself that the program contains no harmful code. In other words, Alice adds protective layers around her computer to prevent someone from entering, to detect that someone has entered, or to stop someone from doing harm once they've entered:

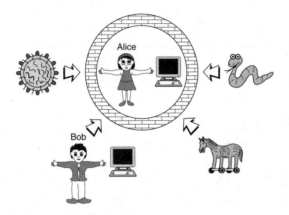

Now what happens if we invert the situation? What if, instead of Bob sending an evil program to penetrate the defenses around Alice's computer, we have a software developer, Doris, who sends or sells Axel[1] a benign program to run? To make this interesting, let's assume that Doris's program contains some secret S and that Axel can gain some economic advantage over Doris by extracting or altering S:

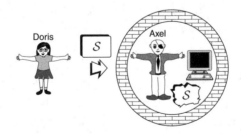

---

1. In this book, Axel is the prototypical bad guy (hence the shaved head). For some variety in prose, we'll switch between calling him the *adversary*, the *attacker*, the *cracker*, the *reverse engineer*, or simply *he*. Doris is the person or institution who produces a piece of software with a secret she needs to protect. We'll call her the *author*, the *defender*, the *software developer*, *she*, or, most frequently, *you*.

The secret could be anything: a new super-duper algorithm that makes Doris program much faster than Axel's that he would love to get his hands on; the overall architecture of her program, which would be useful to Axel as he starts building his own; a cryptographic key that is used to unlock some media in a digital rights management system; or a license check that prevents Axel from running the program after a certain period of time. What can Doris do to protect this secret?

At first blush, you might think that cryptography would solve the problem, since, after all, cryptography is concerned with protecting the confidentiality of data. Specifically, a cryptographic system scrambles a cleartext S into a cryptotext $E_K(S)$ so that it can't be read without access to a secret key K:

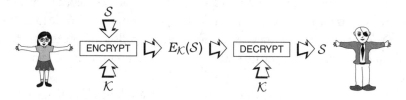

So why doesn't Doris just protect the secret she has stored in her program by encrypting the program before selling it to Axel? Unfortunately, this won't work, since Axel needs to be able to execute the program and hence, at some point, it—and Doris' secret—must exist in cleartext!

What makes software protection so different from cryptography and standard computer security is that once Axel has access to Doris' program, there is no limit to what he can do to it: He can study its code (maybe first disassembling or decompiling it); he can execute the program to study its behavior (perhaps using a debugger); or he can alter the code to make it do something different than what the original author intended (such as bypassing a license check).

There are three components to a typical attack in a software protection scenario against Doris' program P, namely, analysis, tampering, and distribution:

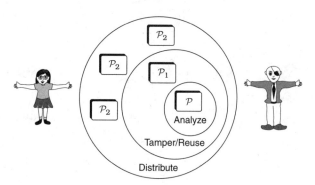

Axel starts by analyzing $\mathcal{P}$, extracting algorithms, design, and other secrets such as cryptographic keys or the location of license-checking code. Next, he modifies Doris' code (he may, for example, remove the license check) or incorporates pieces of it into his own program. Finally, Axel distributes the resulting program, thereby violating Doris' intellectual property rights.

There are many variants of this scenario, of course. Axel could remove a license check without redistributing the hacked program and just enjoy it for his own pleasure. He could resell the program along with a known license password, without ever having to tamper with the code. Finally, he could decompile and analyze the program to verify its safety (for example, that it doesn't contain damaging viruses or spyware, or, in the case of voting software, that it correctly counts every vote), without using this information to improve on his own programs. While these attacks occur in a variety of guises, they're all based on the following observation: Once a program leaves the hands of its author, any secrets it contains become open to attack.

In the scenarios we study, there is usually some financial motive for Axel to extract or alter information in the program. There is also typically a certain period of time during which Doris wants to protect this information. It is the goal of software protection to provide technical means for keeping the valuable information safe from attack for this period of time. A computer game developer, for example, may be happy if software protection prevents his program from being pirated for a few extra weeks, since most of the revenue is generated during a short time period after the release.

In a typical defense scenario, Doris adds *confusion* to her code to make it more difficult for Axel to analyze, *tamper-protection* to prevent him from modifying it, and finally *marks* the code (for example, with her copyright notice or Axel's unique identifier) to assert her intellectual property rights:

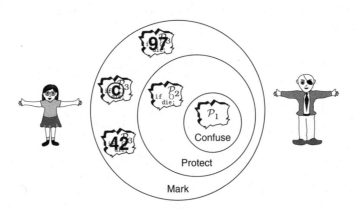

In this book we will consider five methods for Doris to protect her program: *Code obfuscation* for preventing analysis; *software watermarking, fingerprinting,* and *birth-marking* for detecting and tracing illegal distribution; and software- and hardware-based protection against tampering.

Although the primary motivation for the techniques developed in software protection has been protecting the secrets contained within computer programs, they also have applications to protecting the distribution chain of digital media (*digital rights management*), protecting against computer viruses, steganographic transfer of secret messages, and protecting against cheating in online computer games. We will also show how these techniques can be used maliciously to create stealthy computer viruses and to cheat in computer-based voting.

Software protection is related both to computer security and cryptography, but it has most in common with *steganography*, the branch of cryptography that studies how to transfer a secret *stealthily*. This is often illustrated by the so-called *prisoners' problem*. Here, Alice and Bob are planning a prison break by passing notes through their warden, Wendy:

Of course, if Wendy finds that a purported love note mentions a prison break, she will immediately stop any further messages and put Alice and Bob in solitary confinement. So what can the two conspirators do? They can't use cryptography, since as soon as Wendy sees a garbled message she will become suspicious and put an end to further communication. Instead, they must communicate surreptitiously, by sending their secrets hidden inside innocuous-looking messages. For example, Alice and Bob could agree on a scheme where the hidden message (the *payload*) is hidden in the first letter of each sentence in the *cover message*:

```
Easter  is   soon,  dear!  So  many  flowers!  Can  you  smell
them?  Are   you  cold  at  night?  Prison  food  stinks!  Eat
well,  still!  Are  you  lonely?  The  prison  cat  is  cute!
Don't  worry!  All  is  well!  Wendy  is  nice!  Need  you!  ):
```

This is called a *null cipher*. There are many other possible types of cover messages. For example, Alice could send Bob a picture of the prison cat in which she has manipulated the low-order bits to encode the payload. Or she could send him an mp3-file of their favorite love song in which she has added inaudible echoes—a short one for every 0-bit of the payload, a longer one for every 1-bit. Or she could subtly manipulate the line spacing in a pdf-file, 12.0 points representing a 0, 12.1 points representing a 1. Or she could be even sneakier and ask Wendy to pass along a Tetris program she's written to help Bob while away the long hours in solitary. However, unbeknownst to Wendy, the program not only plays Tetris, but inside its control or data structures Alice has hidden the secret payload detailing their escape plan. In this book we will consider exactly this scenario and many like it. We call a program that contains both a secret and any technique for preventing an attack against this secret *surreptitious software*.

1.2 Attack and Defense

You cannot do computer security research, or computer security practice, without carefully examining your *attack model*, your assumptions about the adversary's abilities, and the strategies that he'll use to attack your system. In cryptography research, for example, you might assume that "the adversary cannot find the secret key" or "the adversary isn't better at factoring than I am" or "the adversary won't successfully tamper with the tamperproof smartcard." Once you have an adversarial model, you can go ahead and design a system that is secure against these attack scenarios. In the real world, adversaries will then immediately try to find scenarios you didn't think about in order to get past the defenses you've put up! The cheapest way to break a cryptosystem isn't to spend \$100,000 on specialized hardware to factor a key—it's to spend \$50,000 to bribe someone to *give* you the key. The easiest way to get secrets out of a smartcard isn't to pry the card open (having to bypass the security features that the designers put in place to defend against exactly this attack), but to induce faults in the card by subjecting it to radiation, modifying its power supply voltage, and so on, attacks the designers *didn't* have in mind.

In surreptitious software research, the situation is no different. Researchers have often made assumptions about the behavior of the adversary that have no basis in reality. In our own research, we (the authors of this book) have often made the assumption that "the adversary will employ static analysis techniques to attack the system," because coming from a compiler background, that's exactly what *we* would do! Or, others have speculated that "the adversary will build up a complete graph of the system and then look for subgraphs that are weakly connected, under the assumption that these represent surreptitious code that does not belong to the original program." One might assume that those researchers came from a graph-theoretic background. Some work has endowed the adversary with not enough power ("the adversary will not run the program"— of course he will!) and some has endowed him with *too much* power: "The adversary has access to, or can construct, a comprehensive test input set for the program he's attacking, giving him the confidence to make wholesale alterations to a program he did not write and for which he does not have documentation or source code."

Unfortunately, much of the research published on surreptitious software has not clarified the attack model that was used. One of our stated goals with this book is to change that. Thus, for each algorithm, we present attacks that are possible now and that may be possible in the future.

In Chapter 2 we will also look at a *defense* model, ideas of how we good guys can protect ourselves against attacks from the bad guys. We will propose a model that tries to apply ideas taken from the way plants, animals, and human societies have used surreption to protect themselves against attackers to the way we can protect software from attack. We will be using this model in the rest of the book to classify software protection schemes that have been proposed in the literature.

1.3 Program Analysis

An attack against a program typically will go through two stages: an *analysis stage* that gathers information about the program, and a *transformation stage* that makes modifications to the program based on the information that was collected. There are two basic ways of analyzing the program: You can just look at the code itself (this is called *static analysis*), or you can collect information by looking at the execution of the code (*dynamic analysis*).

Static analyses takes only one input, the program P itself:

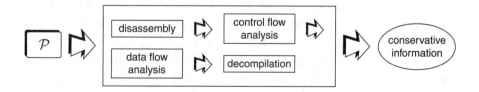

There are a huge number of different kinds of static analysis that have been developed over the years. The chief designers have been software engineering researchers who want to analyze programs for defects and compiler researchers who want to analyze programs to optimize them, but there are also crackers who want to analyze programs to remove protection codes. Static analysis gathers information that we call *conservative*, that is, it may be imprecise but it will always err on the conservative side. So for example, if a static analysis tells you that "on line 45, variable x is always 42," you can be *sure* that this is the case. Sometimes conservative analyses will fail to gather a piece of information about the code that is in fact true, but at the very least, it will never lie and say that something is true when it isn't.

Dynamic analyses collect information about a program by executing it on a sample input data set:

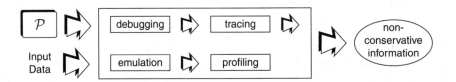

The accuracy of the generated information depends on the completeness of the input data. Because of this, dynamic analysis can only make predictions such as, "On line 45, variable x is always 42, well, OK, at least for the set of inputs I've tried." Code transformations that make use of information only from static analyses are *safe* in that they won't turn a working program into a buggy one (assuming, of course, that the transformation itself is *semantics-preserving*, i.e., it doesn't change the meaning of the program). Transformations that use dynamic analysis results, on the other hand, will typically not be safe: They can fail if they are based on information gathered from an insufficient input data set.

Depending on what an attacker is trying to accomplish, he will choose different types of analyses and transformations. If all he wants to do is to disable a license check, the simplest of static and dynamic analyses may be all he needs: He can just run the program under a debugger until the "license expired" alert comes up, find the approximate location in the code, disassemble the code at that location, read until he finds something that looks like `if today's date > license date then...`, fire up a binary editor on the code, and edit out the offending lines. If, on the other hand, he wants to extract a complex algorithm from a huge program, being able to decompile it all the way to source code would be very helpful.

1.3.1 A Simple Reverse Engineering Example

To make this a little more concrete, let's look at an example. Assume that your boss
has given you the following string of bytes and asked you to reverse engineer it:

```
06 3b 03 3c 1b 07 a2 00 15 1a 06 a3 00 0b
06 3b 84 01 01 a7 ff f1 06 3b a7 ff ec b1
```

He tells you that these bytes correspond to the bytecode for a competitor's Java
program that contains a very secret and important algorithm. The code actually
corresponds to the following program, but of course as a reverse engineer you don't
know this yet:

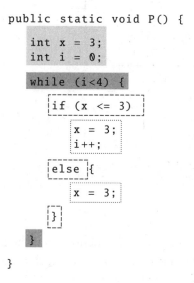

```
public static void P() {
    int x = 3;
    int i = 0;

    while (i<4) {
        if (x <= 3)
            x = 3;
            i++;
        else {
            x = 3;
        }
    }
}
```

Since your goal is to find and understand the super-duper-secret algorithm, it would
be great if you could turn this bytecode mess into some really clean and easy-to-
read Java source code. If the owner of the code inserted some obfuscations or other
trickery to confuse us, then it would be great if we were able to remove that too, of
course.

As your first step, you'll want to disassemble the bytes. This means to convert the
raw bytes into a symbolic, assembly code form. For Java bytecode this is essentially
trivial, and there are many tools (such as jasmin or javap) that will do the job:

```
0:      [06]            iconst_3
1:      [3b]            istore_0
2:      [03]            iconst_0
3:      [3c]            istore_1

4:      [1b]            iload_1
5:      [07]            iconst_4
6:      [a2,00,15]      if_icmpge    27

9:      [1a]            iload_0
10:     [06]            iconst_3
11:     [a3,00,0b]      if_icmpgt    22

14:     [06]            iconst_3
15:     [3b]            istore_0
16:     [84,01,01]      iinc      1, 1

19:     [a7,ff,f1]      goto     4

22:     [06]            iconst_3
23:     [3b]            istore_0

24:     [a7,ff,ec]      goto     4

27:     [b1]            return
```

We've shaded the source code and instructions to make it easy for you to identify which part of the source code corresponds to which bytecode instructions. We've put the codebytes themselves in brackets.

Java bytecode was designed to make disassembly easy. The bytecode contains enough information to allow for the recovery of types and control flow. This is not true of other machine codes, such as those for x86 and other processors. For these binary codes, it is easy to insert code that will confuse disassembly. We will talk more about this in Chapter 3.

Now that you have the Java bytecode in an assembly code format, your next step is to perform *control flow analysis*, which will recover the order in which the code can be executed. The result of this analysis is a *control flow graph* (CFG). A node of this graph consists of straight-line code, except that the last statement can be a jump. There is an edge from one node to another if it is possible for us take this path through the code during execution:

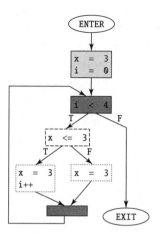

The nodes in the CFG are called *basic blocks*. CFGs are the central data structure around which many compilers and reverse engineering tools are built. We've again used shading to make it easy to see which basic blocks correspond to which bytecode instruction sequences.

Next, you will want to perform a variety of analysis tasks to gather as much information as you can about the code. This information may allow you to perform transformations that will make the code simpler and easier to understand, or even to remove some of the obfuscations that may have been added. One family of analyses common in optimizing compilers and reverse engineering tools is called *data flow analysis*. You'll learn more about this in Section 3.1.2▶127. In our example, an analysis called *Constant Propagation* can be used to track the value of variable x in order to see at which points in the code it will always have the same (constant) value:

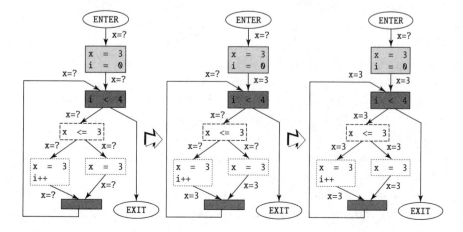

In the leftmost flow graph, we've indicated that at first we know nothing about the value of x at the entry and exit of each basic block. In the second step, we've considered each basic block once, and have gathered some information. After a basic block has executed the statement x = 3, for example, it is clear that x must have the value 3. Also, if a basic block doesn't change the value of x, then x must have the same value after the block executes as it did before. When control can flow into a basic block from two different directions and we've computed that x has the same value on both paths, then we can safely assume that it will always have that value at the entry to the block. After considering all the basic blocks one more time, you're left with the annotated control flow graph to the left:

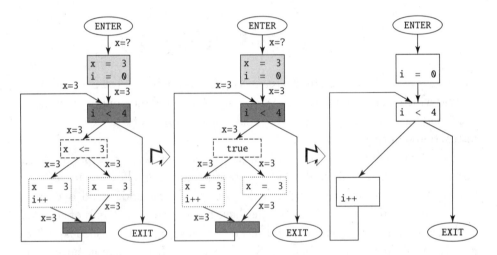

Given this CFG, you can now start to perform transformations. First, wherever x is used and you've determined that its value is constant, you can go ahead and replace x with the computed value. So, for example, x<=3 can be replaced by `true`, since x=3 at the entrance to this basic block. Given this transformation, you can now perform a *Dead Code Elimination*, getting rid of any basic block that can never be executed, and you can also get rid of any *redundant* statements. The result is the last CFG discussed earlier.

Now, eyeballing this code, it's clear that further transformations are possible. In fact, the loop reduces to a single statement, i=4, and since the procedure returns nothing and has no side effects, it can be removed altogether! In this particular case, this is easy to see, but in general, the result will depend on the power of the analyses and the complexity of the programs.

You can't be sure whether the "extra" code that you've been able to eliminate was inserted by a code obfuscator with the purpose of sowing confusion or was just the result of a really broken compiler. All you know is that you've been able to turn the raw sequence of bytes your boss gave you into a much simpler structured form and to get rid of some irrelevant code in the process.

The final step of your reverse engineering effort should be to take the transformed control flow graph and turn it into source code. The graph is so simple that this *decompilation* step is trivial. You get:

```
public static void P() {
    int i = 0;
    while (i<4)
        i++;
}
```

Obviously, other source forms are possible, for example, using a for loop.

Now, turning raw bytes into readable source code is very helpful for a reverse engineer, but the process typically won't stop when source code is generated. The final stage, extracting a deep understanding of the algorithms employed or modifying the code to bypass license checks, and so on, will often have to be done by hand.

In Chapter 2 (Methods of Attack and Defense), we'll show you the general strategies that reverse engineers go through when they attack code in order to reveal its secrets or to make it perform tasks it wasn't designed to do. In Chapter 3 (Program Analysis), we'll delve into even more detail and discuss the many kinds of tools and analysis techniques available to your adversary. We will not simply present the off-the-shelf tools that happen to be available now, but will discuss those that *could be* built given currently known techniques. It's much too easy to say, "Our software protection algorithm is secure because we've implemented it for dynamically linked x86 executables, and current decompilers only handle statically linked code." A much more interesting statement would be, "This algorithm employs protection techniques that can cause code explosion in *any* decompiler, current and future."

1.4 Code Obfuscation

The first protection technique we're going to look at is code obfuscation. What's particularly interesting about obfuscation is that it's a double-edged sword: Bad guys use it to protect their malware from discovery (you will see this in the next section), good guys use it to protect their programs from reverse engineering, and bad guys can also use it to destroy secrets (such as watermarks) stored in the good guys' programs.

In the most general sense, to obfuscate a program means to transform it into a form that is more difficult for an adversary to understand or change than the original code. We are deliberately vague about defining "difficult," but we typically take it to mean that the obfuscated program requires more human time, more money, or more computing power to analyze than the original program. Under this definition, to distribute a program in a compiled form rather than as source code is a form of obfuscation, since analyzing binary machine code is more demanding than reading source. Similarly, we would consider a program that has been optimized to be more obfuscated than one that has not, since many code optimizations make analysis (both by humans and tools such as disassemblers and decompilers) more onerous.

However, the tools and techniques we present in this book go further than compilation and optimization in order to make a program hard to understand. In contrast to an optimizer that rearranges code for the purposes of efficiency, a *code obfuscator* transforms code for the sole purpose of making it difficult to analyze. A negative by-product of obfuscating transformations is that the resulting code often becomes larger, slower, or both. The author of the code has to decide whether the protection that the transformations afford is worth this overhead.

Obfuscation is often confused with *security through obscurity*, a term (used contemptuously) for the "branch" of cryptography or security where the algorithms used are expected to remain secret. This is in contrast to mainstream research that teaches that you must assume that all algorithms are public, and the only secrets you may keep are the cryptographic keys, and so on, that are the inputs to the algorithms. The idea is that many eyes examining the same algorithm or piece of code will likely be able to find flaws, and the more eyes that have failed to find a flaw, the more confident you can be that the algorithm is, in fact, secure. This principle is frequently violated, and you'll often see unscrupulous web-sites advertise "military-strength, proprietary" cryptographic algorithms, arguing that "since no one knows what our algorithm does, this will make it that much harder to break." The same argument is sometimes made in reverse by software vendors like Microsoft: "Open-source software is inherently more vulnerable to attacks than our closed-source code since you can easily read the source and find bugs to exploit." We know from experience that both claims are false. Hackers have no problem finding holes in closed-source software, and once a proprietary algorithm is leaked (which, inevitably, happens) it is often found to have serious and exploitable flaws.

As we define it in this book, obfuscation isn't security through obscurity. As with research in cryptography, we generally expect that the obfuscating code transformation algorithms are known to the attacker and that the only thing the defender can

Listing 1.1 Obfuscation example. The original unobfuscated version of the code can be found on the book's Web site.

```java
public class C {
 static Object get0(Object[] I) {
  Integer I7, I6, I4, I3; int t9, t8;
  I7=new Integer(9);
  for (;;) {
   if (((Integer)I[0]).intValue()%((Integer)I[1]).intValue()==0)
        {t9=1; t8=0;} else {t9=0; t8=0;}
   I4=new Integer(t8);
   I6=new Integer(t9);
   if ((I4.intValue()^I6.intValue())!=0)
     return new Integer(((Integer)I[1]).intValue());
   else {
     if ((((I7.intValue()+ I7.intValue()*I7.intValue())%2!=0)?0:1)!=1)
        return new Integer(0);
     I3=new Integer(((Integer)I[0]).intValue()%((Integer)I[1]).intValue());
     I[0]=new Integer(((Integer)I[1]).intValue());
     I[1]=new Integer(I3.intValue());
    }
  }
 }
}
```

assume is kept secret are the seeds that determine how and where these algorithms are applied.

Before we look at some applications of code obfuscation, let's have a look at what obfuscated code might actually look like. Check out Listing 1.1 for a very simple example generated by the SandMark Java code obfuscator. Without peeking (the answer is in footnote 2), time yourself to see how long it takes you to analyze this 20-line program and figure out what it does. Now imagine that rather than being 20 lines long, it's of a "normal" size for a program today: hundreds of thousands of lines to a few million lines. *Then* how long would it take you? What does your intuition tell you? Does the time to understanding grow linearly with the size of the code and the number of obfuscations applied? Do you think some obfuscations would add more confusion than others? Might some obfuscations be harder to undo than others? If so, how much harder? Are some impossible to undo? Unfortunately, the answers to these questions are largely unknown. As of now, we don't have any models that can tell us how much longer it would take to reverse engineer a program that's

---

2. The program computes the Greatest Common Denominator of its arguments.

been obfuscated by a particular transformation or sequence of transformations, nor do we know what overhead these transformations will entail (although this is certainly easier to measure). Much current obfuscation research tries to devise such models [289], but we don't yet have any that are developed enough to be used by practitioners.

1.4.1 Applications of Code Obfuscation

Now let's look at a few scenarios where you can use code obfuscation to protect your code.

1.4.1.1 Malicious Reverse Engineering In the first scenario, *malicious reverse engineering*, Doris builds a program that contains a valuable trade secret (a clever algorithm or design), which Axel, a rival developer, extracts and incorporates into his own program and sells to his customer, Carol:

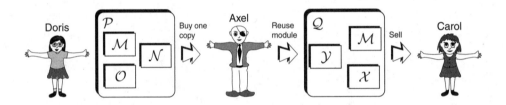

This scenario is what most people have in mind when they think of code obfuscation. As we'll soon see, it's far from the only one. The assumption (although there's no formal proof of this proposition) is that given enough time and resources, Axel will be able to reverse engineer any program. In other words, no secret hidden in a program will remain a secret forever. Doris' goal, instead, has to be to use obfuscation to slow Axel down as much as possible, while at the same time adding as little overhead as possible. Ideally, the code is convoluted enough that Axel gives up trying to understand it and says "OK, fine, then! I'll just reinvent this darned algorithm myself from scratch." Ideally, Doris is able to choose just the right set of obfuscating transformations and apply them in just the right places to not make her program so slow and bloated that her customers will no longer buy it.

1.4.1.2 Digital Rights Management In a *digital rights management* scenario, Doris is in the business of building a software media player. The player will only play music, images, or video that is distributed encrypted in a special file format known as a *cryptolope*. The player contains cryptographic keys that are necessary to unlock and play the media:

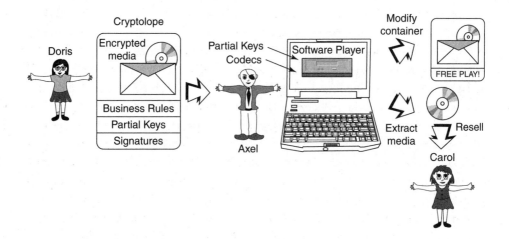

Since you want to be able to enjoy the encrypted media that you've bought in an "untethered environment," say, watching a movie on your laptop on a plane where there's no network connectivity, Doris is forced to store the decryption keys somewhere on your computer, probably inside your player's code. Along with the keys, of course, the code will also contain the decryption algorithm and a decoder that turns the decrypted media into analog signals that you can hear or watch. In a typical player, the decoding chain looks like this:

You should notice that there are three targets for Axel to attack here. He could steal the keys (and if they're universal keys he can now decode *any* media designed for this player, and, if they're not tied specifically to him, he can sell them on the Web), he could steal the digital media, or he could steal the less desirable analog output. The possible weak points of such a system are many. First of all, it's probably unreasonable to believe that the cryptographic algorithm used by the system will not be well known to an attacker. So unless the decryptor is obfuscated, a simple pattern-matching attack may be all that is necessary in order to locate the decryptor and the keys it uses. Dynamic attacks are also possible. For example, cryptographic algorithms have very specific execution patterns (think tight loops with lots of **xors**) and if they're not heavily obfuscated, they'd be easy to find using a dynamic trace of the program. The keys themselves are a weak point. They're long strings of bits with a high degree of randomness, and as such, unusual beasts in most programs. So Axel could simply scan through the player code looking for, say, a 512-bit long string that's more random than expected. Any code that uses this string is likely to be the decryptor. Once Axel has found the location of the decryptor, he should have little problem finding where the decrypted media is generated and sent to the decoder. He can then simply add some code that writes the decrypted content to a file, and he's done. What we learn from this is that Doris needs to obfuscate her code so that a simple pattern-match against it won't reveal the location of the decryptor or decoder, or the interfaces between them. She needs to tamperproof the code so that Axel can't insert new code, she needs to obfuscate not only the static code but also the dynamic behavior of the player, and she needs to obfuscate static data (the keys) in the code as well. And, still, she has to assume that these defense measures are only temporary. Given enough time, Axel will bypass them all, and so she needs to have a plan for what to do when the system is broken.

1.4.1.3 Mobile Agent Computing In our next scenario, Doris sends out a mobile shopping agent, which visits online stores in order to find the best deal on a particular CD. The agent traverses the Web and asks every store it encounters if they have the CD and how much it costs, records the best price so far, and eventually, returns to Doris with the site where she can get the best deal. Of course, if evil Axel runs a store there's no reason why he wouldn't cheat. First of all, he can just erase the information that the agent has collected so far and substitute his own price:

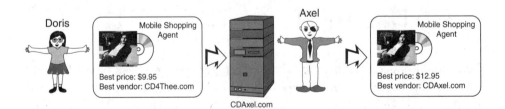

This strategy will only help him if the agent returns directly to Doris when it's done with Axel's site. Much better (for Axel) would be to manipulate the code so that regardless of which stores it visits after his, it will still record his (higher) price as the best one.

One defense that has been proposed (there are many others) is for Doris to obfuscate the agent [165], thereby slowing down an attack. Ideally, this way Axel won't have enough resources (he's servicing many simultaneous requests, after all) to reverse engineer and modify the agent. Also, Doris might be able to detect that the agent spends a suspicious amount of time at Axel's site. She can further complicate Axel's attack by differently obfuscating every agent she sends out. This way, he won't be able to speed up his analyses over time as he gathers more information about the agents and their defenses.

1.4.1.4 Grid Computing In the *grid computing* scenario, Doris wants to run her program P but lacks the computational resources to do so. So she buys cycles from Axel to run P on his supercomputer, sends Axel P and the input data, and receives the output data in return. The problem arises when one or more of P, the inputs, or the outputs are confidential:

Doris must worry not only about Axel snooping on her algorithms or her inputs and outputs but also about his tampering with her program. If she can't trust that P maintains its integrity on Axel's site, she can't trust the validity of the output data that Axel returns to her.

One way to defend the confidentiality of the inputs and outputs is to encrypt them and transform P into a program that operates directly on encrypted inputs and produces encrypted results. There is considerable research on such *homomorphic encryption* schemes, but the ones invented so far are inefficient and not applicable to real programs.

Alternatively, Doris can obfuscate P to help maintain confidentiality of its algorithms or tamperproof it to help maintain its integrity by using the techniques in this book. To preserve the confidentiality of the data, something similar to a DRM scheme can be used, where obfuscation and tamperproofing are used to hide and protect the encryption code.

   Grid computing is a harder scenario to protect than many others. The reason is that you care about the confidentiality of algorithms and data, integrity of code, and on top of that, *performance*. The reason that Doris sent her code to Axel, after all, was so that it would execute faster on his superior hardware! She would be very unhappy, indeed, if the protection techniques she applied negated the performance boost she was paying for.

1.4.1.5 Artificial Diversity Code obfuscation techniques have also been applied to operating systems to protect them against attacks by malware such as viruses and worms [74,75]. The idea is for Doris to randomize her code so that a malicious agent will not be able to locate or take advantage of a known vulnerability. Just like in the mobile agent scenario, we can take advantage of multi-versioning: If every distributed version of Doris' code is obfuscated differently, Axel's virus will need to be very clever to infect all of them:

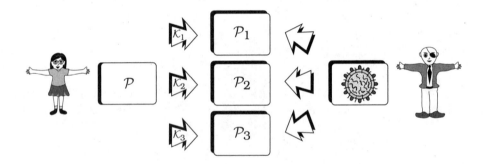

This is known as *artificial diversity*. Of course, viruses themselves make use of obfuscation techniques to avoid detection by virus scanners, and with spectacular success. We will talk about this in the next section.

1.4.2 Obfuscating Transformations

It's of course possible to take your program with its precious cargo and manually transform it into a mess that's hard for your adversary to understand and manipulate. In practice, though, that's too tedious and error-prone. A better idea is to build an obfuscation tool that translates your well-designed, easy-to-comprehend, easy-to-modify program into an incomprehensible mess of spaghetti code that's near-impossible to alter. Such an obfuscator is similar to a compiler, except that instead of generating efficient and compact code, it generates code that's hard for your adversary to comprehend.

Conceptually, an obfuscation tool takes four inputs: the program P you want to transform, the amount of obfuscation you would like to add, the amount of overhead you can accept, and a list of the code locations that are particularly precious to you that you would like to protect the most:

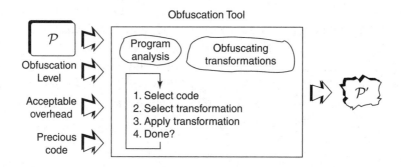

Internally, the obfuscator has a set of obfuscating code transformations, a set of program analyses needed to implement those transformations, and a loop that iteratively applies the transformations to P. The analyses will be similar to those used by compilers and reverse engineering tools. The process continues until the amount of obfuscation you desire has been reached or the maximum amount of overhead you can accept has been exceeded. The output is a program P' that behaves the same as P but whose internal structure is very different. Practical code obfuscators may have a simpler structure than this. It's common, for example, to have just a small number of transformations and to apply them in a fixed order.

There are four broad classes of obfuscating code transformations. *Abstraction transformations* break down the overall structure of the program, i.e., they obfuscate the way the programmer has organized the program into classes, modules, and functions. *Data transformations* replace the data structures the programmer has selected with others that reveal less information. *Control transformations* modify the control structures (if- and while-statements) in the program to hide the paths it may take at runtime. *Dynamic transformations*, finally, insert a transformer T into the program so that, at runtime, T causes the program to continuously transform itself. At runtime, the program therefore looks like this:

We've spread our discussion of code obfuscation over three chapters. In Chapter 4 (Code Obfuscation), you will see many control, data, and abstraction transformations. We'll discuss the amount of confusion they add, how hard they are to defeat, and the amount of overhead they incur. In Chapter 6 (Dynamic Obfuscation), we'll do the same for dynamic obfuscation. In Chapter 5 (Obfuscation Theory), we will look at the theoretical underpinnings of obfuscation. In particular, we'll be interested in finding out what can be obfuscated, and what can't.

To give you some idea of what obfuscating code transformations do, let's go through a really trivial example. We'll start with a little C program in its original form and show how it changes as you apply, first, an abstraction transformation, then a data transformation, next a control transformation, and finally, a dynamic transformation. Here's the original program:

```
int main() {
    int y = 6;
    y = foo(y);
    bar(y,42);
}
```

```
int foo(int x) {
    return x*7;
}
```

```
void bar(int x, int z) {
    if (x==z)
        printf("%i\n",x);
}
```

The first thing we're going to do is to hide the fact that the program consists of two functions. The programmer had something in mind when he decided to break the program into three parts, main, foo, and bar; presumably, this matched the mental model he had of his program. So let's break this abstraction by merging foo and bar into one function, foobar. This new function takes three parameters. Two of them, x and z, are necessary to accommodate bar's arguments, and the third, s, we'll use to distinguish calls that should execute foo's and bar's bodies. Here's foobar and the transformed version of main:

```
int main() {
    int y = 6;
    y = foobar(y,99,1);
    foobar(y,42,2);
}
```

```
int foobar(int x, int z, int s) {
    if (s==1)
        return x*7;
    else if (s==2)
        if (x==z)
            printf("%i\n",x);
}
```

Notice how it appears as if main calls the same function twice when, in fact, it's really calling two different functions.

Now, in many programs the precious thing that you want to protect is *data* rather than *code* or *design*. This is, for example, the case in a digital rights management system where you want to prevent the adversary from getting their hands on the cleartext media. Ideally, in a system like that, the data is *never* in cleartext. Rather, it is always encoded in some incomprehensible (to the attacker) format and always operated on in this format. Let's assume that, in our little example program, we want to protect all the integer values from the prying eyes of an attacker, who, for example, might be examining the program by running it under a debugger.

As it turns out, we're lucky. The program only performs three operations on the data, namely, assignment, multiplication, and comparison for equality. Why is this lucky? Well, there's a very simple encoding on integers that supports exactly these operations, namely, RSA encryption! We'll leave the details of this encoding to later in the book. For right now, you'll just have to take our word that setting

$$p = 3$$
$$q = 17$$
$$N = pq = 51$$
$$E(x) = x^3 \bmod 51$$
$$D(x) = x^{11} \bmod 51$$

leads to a program where no integer values are ever in cleartext:

```
int foobar(int x, int z, int s) {
    if (s==1)
        return (x*37)%51;       // E(7) = 37
    else if (s==2)
        if (x==z) {             // x11 = D(x)
            int x2=x*x % 51,    x3=x2*x % 51;
            int x4=x2*x2 % 51,  x8=x4*x4 % 51;
            int x11=x8*x3 % 51; printf("%i\n",x11);
        }
}
```

```
int main() {
    // E(6) = 12
    int y = 12;
    y = foobar3(y,99,1);
    // E(42) = 36
    foobar3(y,36,2);
}
```

In particular, you can see how 6 is encoded as 12, 42 as 36, and 7 as 37! Not until the program absolutely *has to* have a value in cleartext (when it needs to pass it to printf to print it out) is it finally decoded. Note also that the multiplication x*7 takes place in the encoded domain; again, no values are in cleartext until necessary.

Structured programming dictates that you organize your functions by properly nesting conditional and loop statements. This makes the code easy to understand and modify. One popular kind of obfuscating control transformation, *control flow flattening*, rewrites functions to turn structured statements into spaghetti code. Here's what the last version of the `foobar` function looks like after control structures have been replaced by plain old `goto` statements:

```
int foobar(int x, int z, int s) {
    char* next = &&cell0;
    int retVal = 0;

    cell0: next = (s==1)?&&cell1:&&cell2; goto *next;
    cell1: retVal=(x*37)%51; goto end;
    cell2: next = (s==2)?&&cell3:&&end; goto *next;
    cell3: next = (x==z)?&&cell4:&&end; goto *next;
    cell4: {
        int x2=x*x % 51,   x3=x2*x % 51;
        int x4=x2*x2 % 51, x8=x4*x4 % 51;
        int x11=x8*x3 % 51;
        printf("%i\n",x11); goto end;
    }
    end: return retVal;
}
```

Have a look at Listing 1.2▶25. Here, we've broken the body of `foobar` into two functions, A and B. This, by itself, isn't a very effective transformation, but what's interesting here is what happens to A and B at *runtime*. Every time `foobar` is called, it makes A and B trade places:

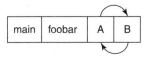

From an attacker's point of view this code is hard to understand in two different ways. If he looks at our program *statically*, i.e., without running it, the abstraction transformation will have removed the way we chose to organize the program, the data transformation the way we chose our data structures, and the control transformations the way we structured our flow of control. If, instead, he decides to learn

Listing 1.2 The result of a dynamic obfuscating transformation. The functions A and B will continuously trade places at runtime. The swap function is in Listing 6.3 ▸ 377.

```
int start = 0;

typedef int (*printfT) (char const *str,...);
typedef int (*FuncPtr)(int,int,int,uint32,int,printfT,void * funcs);
typedef FuncPtr FuncPtrArr[];
static FuncPtrArr funcs ={&A,&B};

int A(int x, int z, int s, uint32 begin,
     int start, printfT printf,void * funcs) {
   int next = 0;
   int retVal = 0;
   char* cells[]={&&cell0-(uint32)&A,&&cell1-(uint32)&A,
                  &&cell2-(uint32)&A,&&cell3-(uint32)&A,
                  &&cell4-(uint32)&A,&&end-(uint32)&A};
   goto *(cells[next]+begin);
   cell0:  next = (s==1)?1:2;  goto *(cells[next]+begin);
   cell1:  retVal=(x*37)%51;  next=5; goto *(cells[next]+begin);
   cell2:  next = (s==2)?3:5;  goto *(cells[next]+begin);
   cell3:  next = (x==z)?4:5;  goto *(cells[next]+begin);
   cell4:  FuncPtr f = ((FuncPtr*) funcs)[(1+start)%2];
           f(x,z,s,(uint32)f,start,printf,funcs);
           next=5; goto *(cells[next]+begin);
   end:  return retVal;
}

int B(int x, int z, int s, uint32 begin,
     int start,printfT printf,void * funcs) {
   int x2=x*x % 51; int x3=x2*x % 51; int x4=x2*x2 % 51;
   int x8=x4*x4 % 51; int x11=x8*x3 % 51; printf("%i\n",x11);
}

int foobar(int x, int z, int s) {
   int retVal = funcs[0+start](x,z,s,(uint32)funcs[0+start],
                               start,printf,funcs);
   swap((caddr_t)funcs[0],(caddr_t)funcs[1],1024);
   start = (start+1) % 2;
   return retVal;
}
```

about the program by executing it, he will find that the dynamic obfuscation has violated a very basic assumption about programs, namely, that every time control reaches a particular point, the same code is executed.

1.4.3 Black Hat Code Obfuscation

For many years obfuscation was considered nothing more than a curiosity, something that no serious researcher would touch. The *International Obfuscated C Code Contest* (*IOCCC*) [177,227], for example, is an annual event that (humorously) tries to write the worst programs possible, C being a particularly suitable language for this task. It was generally assumed that there could be no real value to any code obfuscation technique and that anyone using one was just foolish for not using "real" security algorithms. Only fairly recently has it been acknowledged that there are legitimate applications where obfuscation and related techniques are the only available methods of protection.

Unfortunately, however, it's turned out that the applications where obfuscation has had its most spectacular success are in what we like to call black hat scenarios. This should probably not come as much of a surprise. It's not uncommon for the bad guys to adopt techniques first designed by the good guys. Cryptography, for example, can be used to protect the communication between criminals as well as between law enforcement agents. Steganography can be used by freedom fighters to avoid detection by an oppressive regime as well as by terrorists to avoid detection by national security forces. TV set-top box hackers have been known to first break through the smartcard-based defenses of the box and then turn around and use smartcards themselves to protect these hacks from counterattacks by the set-top box manufacturers!

One black hat scenario is when Axel uses obfuscation to protect his virus V from detection by Doris:

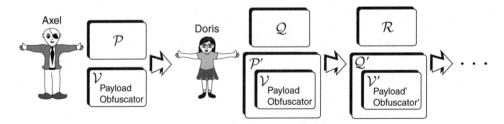

The virus comes in two parts, the *payload*, which is the code that's designed to cause harm, and the obfuscator, which the virus uses to protect itself from discovery. In the first step, Axel infects a program P with V and sends it out into the wild. If

Doris installs the infected $\mathcal{P}'$ on her site, the virus may be able to infect another program, Q. Before infection, however, the virus uses the obfuscator to generate a different version of itself. The idea is that if every version of the virus is different, it will be difficult for Doris' virus scanner to detect it. This is similar to the artificial diversity scenario you saw earlier, only this time the good guy and the bad guy have traded places!

1.4.3.1 Misdirection—Stealthy Obfuscation

If you look at a few of the programs submitted to the IOCCC, it should be clear that the code looks far from natural. While machine-generated code, obfuscated code, or optimized code can often look this bad, code written by humans typically doesn't. For example, you can tell by looking at the obfuscator-generated code in Listing 1.1▶15 that it wasn't written by a typical human programmer. So if Axel was looking for a secret in Doris' program, a section that looked like this would likely raise his suspicion—could the secret be hidden behind this obviously obfuscated mess? You'll see many cases in this book where the *stealthiness* of a protection technique is important; the attacker mustn't be given a clue as to where in the code the technique was applied or the order in which a sequence of techniques were applied.

Misdirection is a particularly nasty black hat obfuscation technique that is based on the extreme stealthiness of an inserted bug. Look at Listing 1.3▶28, which shows a program to collect and tally the votes for *American Idol*. The program reads votes from standard input, and after the contest displays a summary of the votes cast. Here is a sample run of the program:

```
> cat votes-cast.txt
alice
alice
bob
alice
dmitri
bob
zebra
> java Voting < votes-cast.txt
Total: 7
Invalid: 1
alice: 3
bob: 2
charles: 0
dmitri: 1
```

Listing 1.3 Obfuscated voting code.

```java
public class Voting {
  final int INVALID_VOTE = -1;
  int invalidVotes, totalVotes = 0;
  String[] candidates = {"alice", "bob", "charles", "dmitri"};
  int[] tally = new int [candidates.length];
  BufferedReader in = null; BufferedWriter log = null;
  public Voting () {
    in = new BufferedReader (new InputStreamReader (System.in));
  }
  public String readVote () {
    try {return in.readLine();}
    catch (Exception e) {return null;}
  }
  public boolean isValidTime (Date today) {
    SimpleDateFormat time = new SimpleDateFormat ("HH");
    int hour24 = Integer.decode (time.format(today)).intValue();
    return !(hour24 < 9 || hour24 > 21);
  }
  public int decodeVote (String input) {
    for (int i=0; i < candidates.length; i++)
      if (candidates[i].equals (input)) return i;
    return INVALID_VOTE;
  }
  public void logVote (Date date, int vote) throws Exception {
    if (log == null)
      log = new BufferedWriter (new FileWriter ("log.txt"));
    log.write ("TIME: " + date + " VOTE: " + vote);
  }
  public void printSummary () {
    System.out.println ("Total:"+totalVotes +
                        "\nInvalid:"+invalidVotes);
    for (int i=0; i < candidates.length; i++)
      System.out.println ("Votes for " + candidates[i] +": "+tally[i]);
  }
  public void go () {
    while (true) {
      String input = readVote();
      int vote = 0;
      if (input == null)break;
      try {
        Date today = new Date();
        if (isValidTime (today)) vote = decodeVote (input);
        else                     vote = INVALID_VOTE;
```

Listing 1.3 Obfuscated voting code. (*Continued*)

```
      logVote (today, vote);
    } catch (Exception e) {}
    totalVotes++;
    if (vote == INVALID_VOTE) invalidVotes++;
    else                      tally[vote]++;
  }
  printSummary();
  }
  public static void main (String args[]) {
    Voting voting = new Voting (); voting.go();
  }
}
```

Can you tell whether the program produces a fair count or not, or has it, in fact, been deliberately manipulated to favor a particular candidate? Before reading the answer in footnote 3, time yourself to see how long it took to analyze this 58-line program. Now, how long would it take for you to find a potential problem in a real-world voting system comprising hundreds of thousands of lines of code? What if the techniques used in Listing 1.3 were combined with those in Listing 1.1▶15? Might it be possible to provide enough confusion so that by the time the obfuscation has been penetrated and any irregularities identified, the next American Idol has already been selected (or, in the case of the United States' presidential election, the Electoral College has convened and cast their votes)?

1.4.3.2 Obfuscating Viruses As you will see in this book, there are important real-world problems that, to date, only obfuscation is able to tackle. Unfortunately, however, it's in black hat code scenarios where obfuscation has had its most spectacular successes: Obfuscation is used by malware writers to protect their viruses, worms, trojans, and rootkits from detection. It is entertaining to examine techniques that hackers have invented and successfully used to foil security researchers, and to see whether the good guys can make use of the same techniques. Virus writers and virus scanner writers are engaged in a cat-and-mouse game: When a new virus detection technique is invented, the virus writers counter with a more sophisticated

---

3. Java's integer decoding routine interprets numbers that start with zero as octal. As a result, this routine throws an unexpected number-format exception between 8 a.m. and 9:59 a.m., which in turn results in the incorrect value of vote being counted.

code obfuscation technique, which is then countered by a more powerful detection technique, and so on. So far, the hackers seem to be winning. Recent reports claim that 25% of the world's computers have been penetrated and taken over by bot-nets [368]. Obviously, this can be attributed not only to the success of obfuscated malware but also to the fact that many people run unpatched operating systems, outdated virus scanners, and so on.

Virus writers typically beat virus scanners by making their virus code "invisible" to the scanners. Scanners have only a limited amount of resources and cannot fully analyze a file to decide whether or not it's malicious. Even if they could, there are theoretical results [74] that state that it may still fail. The scanner therefore identifies a virus by its *signature*, some aspect of it that is easy enough to extract and that does not change from one infection to the next. This is similar to *birthmarks*, which you will see in Chapter 10 (Software Similarity Analysis).

What sort of tricks does a virus writer use to make the viruses stay "invisible" to virus scanners? Look at the self-reproducing viral Java program in Listing 1.4▶31. Real viruses are rarely, if ever, written in Java, but this simplified example will help you understand how a virus can use obfuscation to protect itself.

There are several things that are noteworthy in this Java virus. The first thing to note is that the program seems to have its entire source code encoded as a string within itself. In order to manage this in a finite space, a program takes advantage of the duplicate structure of the program. This trick is used in a common geek amusement to devise *quines*—programs that when run produce their own source code as their only output [1].

The source code is built in the variable `self`. It's eventually written to a file and compiled using Sun's internal Java compiler. The recent Slapper worm [320] and its variants also used a compiler to make the virus less platform-dependent. Using a compiler in this way has another side effect that is advantageous for a virus writer. Different compilers can produce slightly different (though semantically equivalent) programs from the same source code. This makes it a bit harder to find good signatures that scanners can use to reliably detect a virus.

In Listing 1.4▶31, the example goes one step further. Before the new copy of the virus is written to a file, it is passed to the function `morph`. The `morph` function adds a `i++` statement between every line of the main program. This instruction has no effect on the output or behavior of the program. However, this trivial obfuscation ensures that every new version of the program will be different from its predecessor! This means that a virus scanner that uses a trivial checksum-based signature detector will not be powerful enough to identify the virus.

Listing 1.4 A metamorphic virus in Java.

```
import java.io.*;

public class m {
  private static int i = 0;
  private static com.sun.tools.javac.Main javac=
                         new com.sun.tools.javac.Main();
  public static String morph (String text) {
    return text.substring(0,360) +
           text.substring(360).replaceAll (
              new String (new char[] { ';' }),
              new String (new char[] { ';','i','+','+',';' }));
  }
  public static void main (String[] a) throws IOException {
    String self="import java.io.*;   public class m { private
      static int i = 0; private static com.sun.tools.javac.Main
      javac=new com.sun.tools.javac.Main();public static String
      morph (String text) { return text.substring(0,360) +
      text.substring(360).replaceAll (new String (new char[]
      { ';' }),new String (new char[] { ';','i','+','+',';' })
      );} public static void main (String[] a) throws IOException
      { String self=@;char q=34;char t=64;String text=
      self.replaceAll(String.valueOf(t),q+morph(self)+q);String
      filename = new String (new char[] { 'm','.','j','a','v',
      'a' });File file=new File(filename); file.deleteOnExit();
      PrintWriter out=new PrintWriter(new FileOutputStream(file
      )); out.println(text);out.close(); javac.compile(new
      String[]{filename});}}";
    char q=34; char t=64;
    String text=self.replaceAll(String.valueOf((char)64),
                          q+morph(self)+q);
    text=text.replaceAll(String.valueOf((char)35),
                     String.valueOf((char)34));
    String filename =
      new String (new char[] { 'm','.','j','a','v','a' });
    File file = new File(new String (filename));
    file.deleteOnExit();
    PrintWriter out =
      new PrintWriter(new FileOutputStream(file));
    out.println(text);
    out.close();
    javac.compile(new String[] { filename });
  }
}
```

Imagine if, instead of our very trivial `morph` function, a virus writer included and used one of the more sophisticated obfuscations we discussed in the last section. What sort of analysis would a scanner need to perform to detect such a virus?

Real viruses use obfuscation to counter detection by ensuring that as many properties as possible change between infections. *Metamorphic viruses* use obfuscating transformations to change the entire body of the program from one generation to the next. *Polymorphic viruses* are a simpler variation of metamorphic viruses. Instead of morphing the entire program, each generation of the virus encrypts itself with a different key. Of course, for the virus to still be functional it must also contain a decryption and execution routine. Polymorphic viruses only morph this decryption and execution routine. In this way, morphing protects the decryption and execution routine from the scanner, while encryption protects the rest of the program.

1.5 Tamperproofing

One of the uses of obfuscation is to add so much confusion to a program that an adversary will give up trying to understand or modify it. But what if Axel is able to break through Doris' obfuscation defenses, then what? Well, in addition to obfuscating her code, Doris can also *tamperproof* it. This means that if Axel tries to make modifications to Doris' program, he will be left with a program with unintended side effects: The cracked program may simply refuse to run, it could crash randomly, it could destroy files on Axel's computer, or it could phone home and tell Doris about Axel's attack, and so on.

In general, a tamperproofing algorithm performs two duties. First, it has to detect that the program has been modified. A common strategy is to compute a checksum over the code and compare it to an expected value. An alternative strategy is check that the program is in an acceptable execution state by examining the values of variables.

Once tampering has been detected, the second duty of a tamperproofing algorithm is to execute the tamper response mechanism, for example causing the program to fail. This is actually fairly tricky: You don't want to alert the attacker to the location of the tamperproofing code since that will make it easier for him to disable it. For example, tamperproofing code like

```
if (tampering-detected()) abort()
```

is much too weak because it's easy for the attacker to trace back from the location where the program failed (the call to `abort()`) to the location where tampering was detected. Once he has that information, the tamperproofing is easy to disable. A good tamperproofing system separates the tamper detection from the tamper response in both space and time.

1.5.1 Applications of Tamperproofing

Tamperproofing is important in digital rights management systems where any change to the code could allow Axel to enjoy media for free. Here's a top-level view of a DRM system:

```
static final long key = 0xb0b5b0b5;
void play(byte[] media) {
    // if (!hasPaidMoney("Bob")) return;
    System.out.print(key);
    byte[] clear = decrypt(key,media);
    System.out.print(clear);
    float[] analog = decode(clear);
    System.out.print(analog);
    device.write(analog);
}
```

Notice how Axel has been able to delete a check (light gray) that prevented him from playing the media if he had no money, and to insert extra code (dark gray) to dump the secret cryptographic key and the decrypted (digital and analog) media. In general, tampering with a program can involve deleting code, inserting new code, or modifying original code. All can be equally devastating.

Another common use of tamperproofing is to protect a license check. Doris inserts a check in the code that stops Axel from running the program after a specific date or after a certain number of executions, or to let no more than a given number of Axel's employees run the program at any one time. Axel, being an unscrupulous user, locates and disables the license check to give him unlimited use of the program. Doris can obfuscate her program (to make it hard for Axel to find the license code), but she can also tamperproof the license check so that if Axel finds and alters it, the program will no longer function properly:

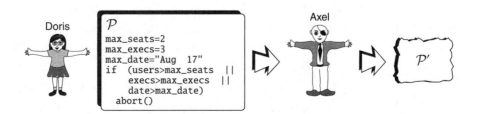

There are situations where simply failing when tampering is detected isn't
enough; you also need to alert someone that an attack has been attempted. For
example, consider a multi-player online computer game where, for performance
reasons, the client program caches information (such as local maps) that it won't let
the player see. A player who can hack around such limitations will get an unfair advantage over his competitors. This is a serious problem for the game manufacturer,
since players who become disillusioned with the game because of rampant cheating
may turn to another one. It's therefore essential for the game administrators to detect any attempt at tampering so that anyone who tries to cheat can immediately be
ejected from the game. The term we use for this problem is *remote tamperproofing*.
The goal is to make sure that a program running on a remote untrusted host is the
correct, unadulterated version, and that it is running in a safe environment. "Safe"
here can mean that the program is running on the correct hardware (and not under
a hacked emulator), that the operating system is at the correct patch-level, that all
environment variables have reasonable values, that the process has no debugger
attached, and so on. As long as the client code determines that it is running safely
and hasn't been tampered with, it sends back a stream of surreptitious "I'm-OK"
signals to the server:

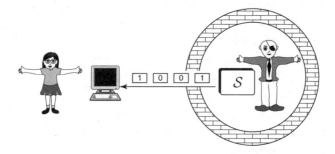

In this figure, the program is using steganographic techniques to embed this secret
bitstream in TCP/IP headers.

Even if you don't intend to cause harm to a cheating game player, monitoring your protected programs for evidence of an ongoing attack can still be useful. We know of at least one major software protection company that includes
a phone home facility in their code that allows them to watch, in real time, an
attack in progress. Being able to see which strategies the attacker is using, see
which strategies are successful, measure how long an attack takes to complete
and thus, ultimately, get a feel for which protection algorithms are effective and
which are not is definitely useful. However, we know that other software

protection companies eschew such eavesdropping because of its problematic privacy issues.

1.5.2 An Example

If you have ever run a signed Java applet or installed a program signed by Microsoft, you've already had experience with programs designed to detect tampering. A signed program carries a certificate issued by a known authority that can be used to detect if some part of the program has been changed. Usually such detection is extrinsic to the program itself. For example, if you try to install a signed Microsoft program that has been tampered with, the OS will check that the signature is one that Microsoft trusts and that the program has not been altered since it was signed. Unfortunately, the obvious way of extending such a scheme to allow a program to check *itself* for tampering is not effective. To see this, have a look at the program in Listing 1.5▸36, which converts temperatures expressed in Fahrenheit into Celsius. The function `bad_check_for_tampering` protects the program from tampering by comparing a checksum of the program file to a checksum computed when the program was compiled. If they're not the same, the program simply quits.

Can you think of any difficulties in writing such a program? One problem is that checksum is embedded in the program and as a result affects the checksum itself! To successfully construct such a program requires searching for a value that, when inserted into the program as a checksum, results in the program having that value as a checksum.

A further problem is that in spite of its clever construction, once a function has been identified by the attacker as a tamper-detection function, it's easy to remove any calls to it.

The function `better_check_for_tampering` is slightly better. Instead of merely checking for tampering, it incorporates the output of the checksum into the code itself. If the program is altered, the value returned by this function changes, which in turn makes the program subtly incorrect.

In spite of the improvements, `better_check_for_tampering` remains vulnerable to the same attack as `bad_check_for_tampering`. Both tamper-checking functions are easy to identify, because programs rarely attempt to read themselves. Once a function is identified as a tamper-checking function, it can be replaced by a simple function that returns the original checksum as a constant. Thereafter, an attacker can go ahead and modify the program arbitrarily.

These weaknesses notwithstanding, checksumming code forms the basis of many tamperproof detection techniques used in practice. You'll see some of them in Chapter 7 (Software Tamperproofing).

Listing 1.5 A self-checking program in Java.

```java
import java.io.*;
import java.security.*;

public class tamper {

   public static int checksum_self () {
      File file = new File("tamper.class");
      FileInputStream fr = new FileInputStream (file);
      DigestInputStream sha = new DigestInputStream (fr,
                              MessageDigest.getInstance ("SHA"));
      while (fr.read () != -1) {}
      byte[] digest = sha.getMessageDigest().digest ();
      int result = 12;
      for (int i=0; i < digest.length; i++) {
         result = (result + digest[i]) % 16;
      }
   }
   public static boolean bad_check_for_tampering () throws Exception {
      return checksum_self() != 9;
   }
   public static int better_check_for_tampering () throws Exception {
      return checksum_self();
   }
   public static void main (String args[]) throws Exception {
      if (bad_check_for_tampering()) System.exit (-1);
      float celsius=Integer.parseInt (rgs[0]);
      float fahrenheit=better_check_for_tampering() * celsius / 5 + 32;
      System.out.println (celsius + "C = " + fahrenheit + "F");
   }
}
```

1.6 Software Watermarking

There are various scenarios where you would like to *mark* an object to indicate that you claim certain rights to it. Most famously, the government marks all their paper currency with a *watermark* that is deeply embedded in the paper and is therefore difficult to destroy or reproduce. For example, if you found a torn or damaged part of a note, you could hold it up to the light and use the watermark to identify the original value of the note. Also, if a forger attempts to pay you using photocopied currency, the missing watermark will alert you to the fact that the currency is not genuine.

There has been much work in the area of *media watermarking*, where the goal is to embed unique identifiers in digital media such as images, text, video, and audio. In a typical scenario, Doris has an online store that sells digital music. When Axel buys a copy of a song, she embeds two marks in it: a copyright notice $\mathcal{A}$ (the same for every object she sells) that asserts her rights to the music, and a customer identification number $\mathcal{B}$ (unique to Axel) that she can use to track any illegal copies he might make and sell to Carol:

If Doris gets ahold of an illegal copy of a song, she can extract the customer mark $\mathcal{B}$ ($\mathcal{B}$ is often referred to as a *fingerprint*), trace the copy back to Axel as the original purchaser, and then take legal action against him. If Axel were to claim "Well, I wrote and recorded this song in the first place," Doris can extract her copyright notice $\mathcal{A}$ to prove him wrong.

Media watermarking algorithms typically take advantage of limitations in the human sensory systems. For example, to embed a watermark in a piece of music, you can add short—and to the human ear, imperceptible—echos. For every 0-bit of the mark, you'd add a really short echo and for a 1-bit, you would add a slightly longer echo. To mark a PDF file, you'd slightly alter the line spacing: 12 points for a 0-bit, and 12.1 points for a 1-bit. To mark an image, you'd slightly increase or decrease the brightness of (a group of) pixels. In all these cases you also need to decide *where* in the digital file you will make the changes. This is often done by means of a random number generator that traces out a sequence of locations in the file. The seed to the generator is the *key* without which you cannot extract the watermark. So a typical watermarking system consists of two functions, *embed* and *extract*:

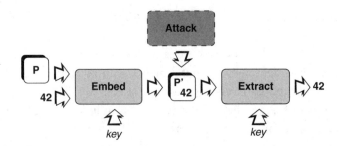

Both functions take the secret key as input. The *embed* function also takes the original object (known as the *cover object*) and the watermark (the *payload*) as input, and produces a watermarked copy (the *stego object*) as output. The *extract* function, as the name implies, extracts the watermark from the stego object, given the correct key. This is just one basic watermarking system, and we'll discuss others in Chapter 8 (Software Watermarking).

As you see from the figures above, we also have to take the adversary into account. Axel will want to make sure that before he resells Doris' object he's destroyed every watermark she's embedded. More precisely, he needs to somehow disturb the watermark extraction process so that Doris can no longer extract the mark, even given the right key. In a typical attack, Axel inserts small disturbances into the watermarked object, small enough that they don't diminish its value (so he can still resell it), but large enough that Doris can no longer extract the mark. For example, he might randomly adjust the line spacing in a PDF file, spread a large number of imperceptible echoes all over an audio file, or reset all low-order bits in an image file to 0. Media watermarking research is a game between the good guys who build marking algorithms that produce robust marks and the bad guys who build algorithms that attempt to destroy these marks. In both cases, they want the algorithms to have as little impact on a viewer's/listener's perception as possible.

Of course, our interest in this book is watermarking *software*, not media. But many of the principles are the same. Given a program $\mathcal{P}$, a watermark w, and a key k, a software watermark embedder produces a new program $\mathcal{P}_w$. We want $\mathcal{P}_w$ to be semantically equivalent to $\mathcal{P}$ (have the same input/output behavior), be only marginally larger and slower than $\mathcal{P}$, and of course, contain the watermark w. The extractor takes $\mathcal{P}_w$ and the key k as input and returns w.

1.6.1 An Example

Take a look at the example in Listing 1.6▶39. How many fingerprints with the value "Bob" can you find? Actually, that's not a fair question! As we've noted, we must

Listing 1.6 Watermarking example.

```java
import java.awt.*;
public class WMExample extends Frame {
    static String code (int e) {
        switch (e) {
            case 0 : return "voided";
            case 6 : return "check";
            case 5 : return "balance";
            case 4 : return "overdraft";
            case 2 : return "transfer";
            case 1 : return "countersign";
            case 3 : return "billing";
            default: return "Bogus!";
        }
    }

    public void init(String name) {
        Panel panel = new Panel();
        setLayout(new FlowLayout(FlowLayout.CENTER, 10, 10));
        add(new Label(name));
        add ("Center", panel);
        pack();
        show();
    }

    public static void main(String args[]) {
        String fingerprint = "Bob";

        if (args[0].equals("42"))
            new WMExample().init(code(7).substring(0,2) + code(5).charAt(0));

        int x = 100;
        x = 1 - (3 % (1 - x));
    }
}
```

assume that the algorithms Doris is using are public, and that the only thing she's able to keep secret are the inputs to these algorithms. But nevertheless, have a look and see what you can find. One fingerprint stands out, of course, the string variable "fingerprint"! Not a very clever embedding, one might think, but easy to insert and extract, and if nothing else it could serve as a decoy, drawing Axel's attention away from more subtle marks.

What else? Take a look at the `code` method. What Doris did here was to encode the string "Bob" in base 26 as $bob_{26} = 1 \cdot 26^2 + 14 \cdot 16^1 + 1 = 1041_{10}$, using $a = 0$, $b = 1, \ldots, o = 14, \ldots, z = 25$. She then turned 1041 into a permutation of the integers $\langle 0, 1, 2, 3, 4, 5, 6 \rangle$, getting

$$\langle 0 \to 0, 1 \to 6, 2 \to 5, 3 \to 4, 4 \to 2, 5 \to 1, 6 \to 3 \rangle$$

This permutation, in turn, she used to reorder the cases of the switch statement in the `code` method. To extract the mark, she would have to do the process in reverse. First, she would need to find the method into which the mark is embedded (the secret key would point out the `code` method), extract the permutation from the switch statement, turn the permutation into 1041, and finally, decode that as the string "bob". There are many algorithms that, like this one, are based on permuting aspects of a program to embed a mark. The very first published watermarking algorithm [104,263] (a Microsoft patent), for example, permutes the basic blocks of a function's control flow graph. In Section 8.4►486, we will discuss this further.

Now what about the statement `x=1-(3%(1-x))`? Here, Doris created a translation table from letters to binary operators:

	+	−	*	/	%
1	a	b	c	d	e
2	f	g	h	i	j
3	k	l	m	n	o
4	p	q	r	s	t
5	u	v	w	x	y
6	z				

Thus, the three letters of the string "bob" turn into the operand/operator-pairs `1-`, `3%`, `1-`, which when stitched together become `x=1-(3%(1-x))`. This is similar in flavor to an algorithm by Monden [252,263] et al., which we will talk about in Section 8.7.1►505.

The three marks we've seen so far are all *static*, i.e., they're embedded directly into the code of the program. In our example we've embedded into source code, but we could have used any convenient program representation, including binary code, Java bytecode, or any of the many intermediate code forms used in compilers. We will discuss static algorithms further in Chapter 8.

There is one final mark in the program, however, and this is a *dynamic* fingerprint. What this means is that the fingerprint only appears at runtime, and only for a particular input to the program. When Doris starts the example program with the secret input key 42, the statement

```
new  WMExample().init(code(7).substring(0,2)  +  code(5).charAt(0));
```

executes and displays the embedded fingerprint:

In Chapter 9 (Dynamic Watermarking), we will discuss these types of watermarks. In practice, of course, they are never as obvious as this: It's too easy for Axel to find the code that would pop up a window with a string in it. Rather, the watermark is hidden somewhere in the dynamic state of the program, and this state gets built only for the special, secret input. A debugger or a special-purpose recognizer can then examine the state (registers, the stack, the heap, and so on) to find the fingerprint.

1.6.2 Attacks on Watermarking Systems

As in every security scenario, you need to consider possible attacks against the watermark. Doris has to assume, of course, that Axel will try to destroy her marks before trying to resell the program. And, unfortunately, there's one attack that will *always* succeed, that will always manage to destroy the watermark. Can you think of what it is? To be absolutely sure that the program he's distributing doesn't contain a watermark, well, Axel can just rewrite the program from scratch, sans the mark![4] We call this a *rewrite attack*:

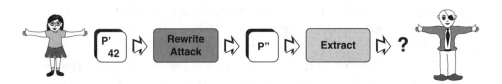

Axel can also add his own watermarks to the program. We call this an *additive attack*:

---

4. Yeah, yeah, so what if it was a trick question?

An additive attack might confuse Doris' recognizer, but more important, it may help Axel to cast doubt in court as to whose watermark is the original one. A *distortive attack* applies semantics-preserving transformations (such as code optimizations, code obfuscations, and so on) to try to disturb Doris' recognizer:

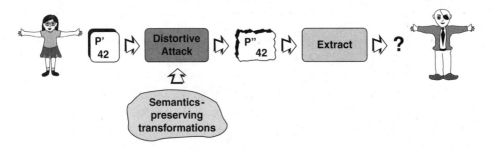

Finally, Axel can launch a *collusive attack* against a fingerprinted program by buying two differently marked copies and comparing them to discover the location of the fingerprint:

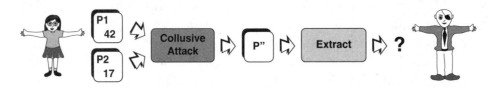

To prevent such an attack, Doris should apply a different set of obfuscations to each distributed copy, ensuring that comparing two copies of the same program will yield little information.

One clever attack that Axel may try to use is not an attack on the watermark itself. Rather, Axel could try to bring into question the validity of Doris' watermark by pretending that the software contains his own watermark. Axel simply writes his own recognizer that "recognizes" this program as containing his mark. If he is successful, we could not tell which was the true recognizer and Doris would not be able to present a legally convincing claim on her own program.

In Chapter 8 and Chapter 9 we will describe many software watermarking algorithms. Some will be useful for watermarking entire applications, others are good for parts of applications. Some will work for binary code, others are for typed bytecode. Some will embed stealthy marks, some will embed large marks, some will embed marks that are hard to remove, and some will have low overhead. However, we know of no algorithm that satisfies *all* these requirements. This is exactly the challenge facing the software watermarking researcher.

1.7 Software Similarity

There's a class of software protection problems that are not amenable to algorithms based on code transformations, and we lump them together under the term *software similarity analysis*. They have in common that, conceptually, they rely on your being able to determine if two programs are very similar or if one program is (partially) contained in another. We capture this in the two functions *similarity* and *containment*:

$$
\text{similarity}\left(\boxed{\mathcal{P}}, \boxed{\mathcal{Q}} \right) = \text{?\%}
$$

$$
\text{containment}\left(\boxed{\mathcal{Q}}, \boxed{\mathcal{P} \; \boxed{\mathcal{Q}'}} \right) = \text{?\%}
$$

1.7.1 Plagiarism

We think of plagiarism as chiefly occurring in academic settings where students copy each other's assignments or researchers copy each other's work, but it's really found anywhere that some humans create and others try making a shortcut to profit by "borrowing" these creations. Ideas from works of art are copied, as are pieces of music, furniture, or fashion designs and so on. Over the years, many famous authors, artists, and musicians have found themselves in court for incorporating too much of a colleague's work into their own. Exactly what "too much" means is ultimately left up to the courts to define. Famous cases include John Fogerty, who was sued for plagiarizing himself (known as *self-plagiarism*) when his new songs sounded too much like his old ones that were under copyright to a previous publisher.

In this book, we're interested in plagiarism of *code*. This occurs frequently in computer science classes where students find it easier and faster to borrow their classmates' assignments than to write them from scratch themselves. Here, Axel has copied a piece of Doris' program Q, inserted it into his own program P, and submitted it as his own:

With large classes, it becomes impossible for computer science professors to manually look for code copying in every pair of submitted programming assignments. Instead (being programmers and used to automating *everything*), they build tools that perform the comparisons automatically. For the example above, the output might look something like this, listing all the pairs of programs in order, from most likely to least likely to have been enhanced by copying:

$$similarity \left(\boxed{Q}, \boxed{\substack{P \\ \boxed{Q'}}} \right) = 80\%$$

$$similarity \left(\boxed{Q}, \boxed{R} \right) = 20\%$$

$$similarity \left(\boxed{\substack{P \\ \boxed{Q'}}}, \boxed{R} \right) = 10\%$$

Automatic methods are best used to weed out from consideration programs highly unlikely to be the result of plagiarism, leaving a few serious suspects for the professor to examine by hand.

Students who are aware that instructors are using tools to look for copying will naturally try to fool them. Simple code transformations such as renaming identifiers and reordering functions are common, and it's therefore important that plagiarism detectors are immune to such transforms.

1.7.2 Software Forensics

Software forensics answers the question, "Who, out of a group of suspected programmers, wrote program S?" To answer the question, you need to start out with code samples from all the programmers you think might have written S:

From these samples, you extract features that you believe are likely to uniquely identify each programmer and then compare them to the same features extracted from
S. From the example above, the output might look something like this, indicating
that Axel is much more likely to have written S than either Doris or Carol:

$$similarity \left(f(Doris), f \left(\boxed{\;\;S\;\;} \right) \right) = 20\%$$

$$similarity \left(f(Axel), f \left(\boxed{\;\;S\;\;} \right) \right) = 80\%$$

$$similarity \left(f(Carol), f \left(\boxed{\;\;S\;\;} \right) \right) = 10\%$$

Here, f is the function that extracts a feature set from a program. Exactly which
set of features will best indicate authorship is hotly debated, but the feature sets
often include measures related to line length, function size, or the placement of
curly braces.

Most work on software forensics has been done on source code, but binary
code forensics is just as interesting. For example, once the FBI catches a suspected
malware author, they could compare his programming style to those of all known
viruses. Being able to bring a large collection of malware to court as evidence against
him might strengthen the government's case.

1.7.3 Birthmarking

You've already encountered the idea of code lifting, a competitor copying a module
M from your program P into his own program Q:

Both obfuscation and watermarking can make this attack harder to mount successfully. By obfuscating P you make it more difficult to find M, or more difficult to
extract it cleanly from P. For example, you could mix M with code from other
modules so that along with M's code any automatic extraction tool would produce
a whole lot of irrelevant code.

You could also embed a watermark or fingerprint in M. Say, for example, that
M is a graphics module produced by a third party (you) that Doris licenses to use
in her own game. If Doris' fingerprint shows up in a program sold by Axel, you
could use that as evidence that he's lifted it, and even evidence that he's lifted it from
Doris' program. You could take legal action against Axel for code theft or against
Doris if she's not lived up to her license agreement to properly protect the module
from theft.

For a variety of reasons, you may choose not to use obfuscation and watermarking. For example, both come with a performance penalty, and obfuscation can
make debugging and quality assurance difficult. Also, you may want to detect theft
of legacy code that was never protected against intellectual property attacks. Instead
of using either one, you could simply search for your module M inside the attacker's
program Q:

$$\text{containment} \left(\boxed{M} , \boxed{\overset{Q}{\boxed{M}}} \right) \gg 50\%$$

This works fine, unless the adversary has anticipated this and applied some code
transformations, such as obfuscation, to M (or possibly all of Q) to make it hard to
find M:

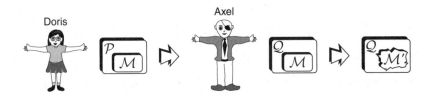

Depending on the severity of the code transformations, this could make a
straightforward search for M difficult:

$$\text{containment} \left(\boxed{M} , \boxed{\overset{Q}{\{M'\}}} \right) \ll 50\%$$

This is where the concept of *birthmark* comes in. The idea is to extract "signals" from Q and from M, and then look for M's signal within Q's signal rather than looking for M directly within Q:

$$containment\ \left(f\left(\boxed{\quad \mathcal{M} \quad}\right), f\left(\boxed{\begin{smallmatrix}Q\\ \mathcal{M}\end{smallmatrix}}\right)\right) \gg 50\%$$

Here, f is a function that extracts the signal, which we call a birthmark, from a program or module. The idea is to select the birthmark so that it's invariant under common code transformations such as obfuscation and optimization.

We know of at least one case where birthmarking was successfully used to argue code theft. In a court case in the early 1980s [128], IBM sued a rival for theft of their PC-AT ROM. They argued that the defendant's programmers pushed and popped registers in the same order as in the original code, which was essentially a birthmark. They also argued that it would be highly unlikely for two programs to both say push R_1; push R_2; add when push R_2; push R_1; add is semantically equivalent.

1.7.4 A Birthmarking Example

To be effective, a birthmarking algorithm must extract the mark from a language feature that is hard for an attacker to alter. One idea that has been reinvented several times and that we'll explore further in Chapter 10 (Software Similarity Analysis) is to compute the birthmark from the calls the program makes to standard library functions or system calls. Some of these functions are difficult for the adversary to replace with his own functions. For example, the only way to write to a file on Unix is to issue the `write` system call. A birthmark extracted from the way the program uses `write` system calls should therefore be reasonably robust against semantics-preserving transformations.

Consider this C function that reads two strings from a file, converts them to integers, and returns their product:

```
int x() {
  char str[100];
  FILE *fp = fopen("myfile", "rb");
  fscanf(fp,"%s",str);
  int v1 = atoi(str);
  fscanf(fp,"%s",str);
  int v2 = atoi(str);
  fclose(fp);
  return v1*v2;
}
```

Several birthmark-extracting functions are possible. You could, for example, make the birthmark be the sequence of calls to standard library functions:

$$bm_1(x) = \langle \texttt{fopen, fscanf, atoi, fscanf, atoi, fclose} \rangle$$

Or you could ignore the actual sequence, since some calls are independent and could easily be reordered. The resulting birthmark is now a set of the calls the function makes:

$$bm_2(x) = \{ \texttt{atoi, fclose, fopen, fscanf} \}$$

Or you could take into account the number of times the function calls each library function. The birthmark becomes a set of system calls and their frequency:

$$bm_3(x) = \{ \texttt{atoi} \mapsto 2, \texttt{fclose} \mapsto 1, \texttt{fopen} \mapsto 1, \texttt{fscanf} \mapsto 2 \}$$

An attacker would get a copy of x, include it in his own program, P, and perform a variety of transformations to confuse our birthmark extractor. Here, he's renamed the function, added calls to `gettimeofday` and `getpagesize` (functions he knows have no dangerous side effects), reordered the calls to `fclose` and `atoi`, and added further bogus calls to `fopen` and `fclose`:

```
void y() {...}

int f() {
  FILE *fp = fopen("myfile", "rb");
  char str[100];
  struct timeval tv;
  gettimeofday(&tv, NULL);
  fscanf(fp,"%s",str);
  int v1 = atoi(str);
  fscanf(fp,"%s",str);
  fclose(fp);
  int v2 = atoi(str);
  int p = getpagesize() * getpagesize();
  fp = fopen("myfile", "rb");
  fclose(fp);
  return v1*v2;
}

void z() {...}
```

Bogus calls are shaded in dark gray. Assuming that the rest of P (functions y and z) don't contain any standard library calls, you get these possible birthmarks for P:

$$bm_1(\text{P}) = \langle \texttt{fopen, gettimeofday, fscanf, atoi, fscanf, fclose,}$$
$$\texttt{atoi, getpagesize, getpagesize} \rangle$$
$$bm_2(\text{P}) = \{\texttt{atoi, fclose, fopen, fscanf, getpagesize, gettimeofday}\}$$
$$bm_3(\text{P}) = \{\texttt{atoi} \mapsto 2, \texttt{fclose} \mapsto 2, \texttt{fopen} \mapsto 2, \texttt{fscanf} \mapsto 2,$$
$$\texttt{getpagesize} \mapsto 2, \texttt{gettimeofday} \mapsto 1\}$$

To determine whether the attacker has included your function x in his program P, you compute $containment(bm_i(\text{x}), bm_i(\text{P}))$, where $containment$ returns a value between 0.0 and 1.0 representing the fraction of x that's contained in P. In this case, it would seem like the attacker has done a pretty good job of covering his tracks and altering the sequence of calls, the set of functions being called, and the frequency of calls to the different functions.

1.8 Hardware-Based Protection Techniques

What makes it so difficult to design unassailable software protection techniques is that you never have any solid ground to stand on. The difference between software security and cryptography is that in cryptography you're allowed to assume that there is one secret (the key) that your adversary will never be able to get his hands on. All security rises and falls with that assumption. In software protection, you can assume no such safe zone. The code of your obfuscated, watermarked, and tamperproofed program will always be available to the attacker for analysis because the attacker (who may also be your customer!) needs the code in order to run it.

Hardware-based protection techniques try to change that by providing a safe haven for data, code, and/or execution. The applications are the same as you've already seen: to protect the code from reverse engineering, to prevent the code from being tampered with, and to prevent illegal copying of the code. The difference is that now you've got one piece of hardware whose integrity you can trust and on which you can build protection schemes.

1.8.1 Distribution with Physical Token

The root cause of software piracy is that digital objects are trivial to clone. Cloning is not unheard of in the physical world, of course: To see that, just visit one of the many clothing and antique markets in China where near-identical copies of name-brand clothing lines and replicas of ancient artifacts are sold at cut-rate prices. Still, physical cloning requires considerable skill and sophisticated tools, whereas cloning in the virtual world only requires the attacker to learn how to use his computer's copy command.

Several software anti-piracy techniques are based on the idea that a program will refuse to run unless the user first shows possession of a physical object. Thus, you ship your program in two parts: the easily clonable binary code itself and a hard-to-clone physical object that's required for the binary to execute. The physical object needs to somehow be connected to the computer so that the program can occasionally check to see that the user actually has possession of it:

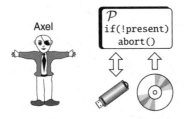

For the physical object to be effective, you need to manufacture it in such a way that it's difficult to clone without specialized and expensive tools. Two types of objects have been common: *dongles* and *program distribution disks* (floppy disks, CDs, and DVDs). Dongles are connected to a port on the computer, these days mostly the USB port. The CD containing the application must be inserted into the computer's CD drive in order for it to run. Often, the CD is manufactured so that ordinary copying software and hardware won't be able to make an identical copy.

This anti-piracy technique has fallen out of favor for all but the most expensive programs. There are many reasons. First, the technique has proven to be highly annoying to legitimate users who can't make backup copies of their legally purchased program, who lose the use of a port or a CD drive, and who can no longer use the program if they misplace the physical object. Second, it's also annoying to the manufacturer who loses revenue from making and distributing the CD or dongle, who needs to deal with users who misplace it, and who can no longer simply distribute the program over the Internet.

1.8.2 Tying the Program to the CPU

If every manufactured copy of a CPU has a unique identity, you can solve the piracy problem by distributing your program so that each copy is only executable by a

CPU with a particular identity. In practice, this is typically done by including in each CPU the private part of a unique public key cryptography key-pair along with a decryption unit. Here, Doris encrypts her program with Axel's public key and distributes the encrypted program to him:

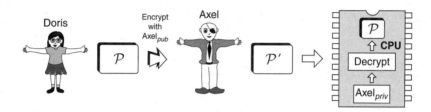

As a result, even if Axel were to resell the program to his friends, their CPUs will have different private keys and won't be able to run the program.

This scheme isn't without its own problems. First, manufacturing the CPU becomes more complicated since every copy will have to contain a different key. One solution is to squirt the key into the CPU after manufacturing and then disable any further modifications. Second, selling shrink-wrapped programs becomes difficult since every distributed copy needs to be differently encrypted. This may not be much of a problem these days, when many programs are sold and downloaded over the Internet. Finally, what happens when the user upgrades to a new computer with a faster CPU? Since it will have a different private key, he will need new versions of all the encrypted programs he ever bought. This means there must be some way for him to convince the program manufacturer that he's no longer using the old CPU and that they should issue him a version to run on his new one.

1.8.3 Ensuring Safe Execution Environment

In the scenarios we consider in this book, Doris assumes that Axel's computer, on which her program is running, is an *unsafe environment*; it could contain hostile programs (such as debuggers, binary editors, emulators, and disk copiers) that Axel can use to pirate, tamper with, or reverse engineer her program.

There has been considerable effort to build protection systems that would instead assure Doris that Axel's computer *is* trustworthy, and that she can safely allow him to run her program without fear of it being violated. This is difficult to do using only software: The code on Axel's computer that checks to see if he's running any unsafe programs could itself be hacked! The idea instead is to have one small trusted hardware unit on Axel's computer that helps Doris collect a reliable list of software that he's running:

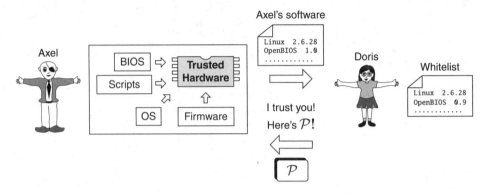

The protocol starts with Axel asking Doris for a copy of her program P to run, to which Doris responds, "Not so fast, prove to me that I can trust you first!" Axel's computer (with the help of the trusted hardware) then collects a list of all its security-sensitive software and firmware and sends it to Doris. She compares it to a list of software she trusts, and only when she's convinced herself that Axel's computer constitutes a safe environment for P does she send it to him.

We've omitted many details here that you'll learn about in Chapter 11. But it shouldn't be hard for you to spot right now some fundamental issues with this scheme. First, any user who wants to run Doris' program has to have a computer that's been fitted with extra hardware, and obviously this will come at a cost. Second, Doris has to maintain a whitelist of all versions of all programs that she trusts, or a blacklist of all versions of all programs that she *doesn't* trust. Given the vast number of programs available to run on many different hardware platforms and operating system configurations, this is likely to be a huge logistic nightmare. Finally, an actual protocol needs to take into account any privacy issues. For example, a user may not want to reveal to every site he's communicating with which software he's running.

An additional issue that makes many people queasy is that this protocol would be very useful in a digital rights management scenario. P would be the DRM player and the protocol would assure Doris that Axel won't be able crack it to get to the decrypted media. This, in turn, would give Doris the confidence to allow Axel to download encrypted media to play.

1.8.4 Encrypted Execution

The ultimate solution to the software protection problem is to encrypt the program. As long as the program remains encrypted, the adversary can't easily tamper with it, and can't learn anything about its internal algorithms, and pirating it makes no sense since it's not executable. However, eventually you'll want your user (and potential adversary) to run the program. This means they will need access to the decryption key, which will give them access to your program in cleartext, which means they can do with it what they want. Game over.

For cryptography to provide unassailable protection, the program must remain encrypted throughout its lifetime, until it's safely within the CPU itself. The CPU contains the key with which the program is encrypted. The key must never escape the CPU capsule or the adversary will gain access to the cleartext program. Schematically, crypto-processors are organized roughly like this:

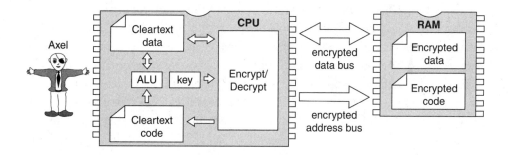

The program (and any sensitive data) is stored encrypted in RAM but decrypted on the CPU itself. An encryption/decryption unit sits between the RAM and any on-chip caches and decrypts incoming code and data and encrypts any outgoing data.

As you will see in Chapter 11, to get this to work without revealing any information, *everything* must be protected once it leaves the safe haven of the CPU. The sequence of addresses that appear on the address bus can reveal information unless they're properly scrambled, the sequence of encrypted data values that appear on the data bus can reveal information if they don't change on every store, and the adversary might even get away with tampering with the encrypted program unless you check on every read that nothing has changed.

All this extra machinery obviously comes at a price, namely, performance. For example, modern CPUs are designed to take advantage of the *locality of reference* that programs typically display. If addresses are scrambled to hide access patterns, then the advantages of caches and locality-improving code optimizations are nullified. There's also the question of how you convince your ordinary users that they should "upgrade" to a slower crypto-processor only for the benefit of protecting *your* program from piracy and tampering by *themselves*. Even if it's unlikely that they'll make it into commodity PCs any time soon, crypto-processors have an important role to fill in financial systems such as ATMs.

1.8.5 Physical Barriers

Any software protection system that makes use of a crypto-processor assumes that the secret key hidden within the CPU, in fact, remains hidden. An adversary, of course, will try to violate that assumption! There have been many attacks devised against smartcards, for example, since they are used in pay-TV systems, as stored-value cards, and as tickets on mass-transit systems, and thus breaking their security can provide financial gains to the attacker.

Attacks against crypto-processors are either *invasive* or *non-invasive*. Invasive attacks, essentially, scrape off the top of the packaging to give direct physical access to the internal circuitry. This can then be probed to reveal secret data (such as keys) and algorithms encoded in hardware. A non-invasive attack doesn't physically abuse the CPU but rather feeds it bogus code or data, or forces it to operate under adverse environmental conditions, all with the intention of coaxing it to give up its secrets. For example, popular non-invasive attacks include delivering power spikes or irregular clock signals to the processor, or subjecting it to radiation. This can make it execute in a way its designers didn't intend and, possibly, force it to reveal secret code and data.

Crypto-processors include physical layers of protection to prevent these kinds of attacks:

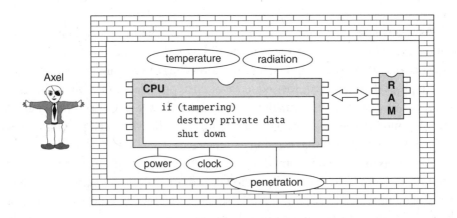

For example, sensors will alert the CPU if the temperature, voltage, clock signal, or radiation level appears abnormal. If the CPU believes it's under attack, it will destroy any private data (such as keys), shut down, or even self-destruct. To prevent invasive attacks, the processor will have layers of shielding that make it difficult to drill down to the internal circuitry. These shields can also have sensors that can alert the CPU that it's being probed.

Unfortunately, adding physical barriers will affect cost as well as performance. The higher the clock frequency, the more heat the CPU dissipates, and the thicker the layers of protection, the harder it will be for the processor to get rid of this excess heat! As a result, processors with thick physical protection barriers will have to be clocked at a lower frequency than equivalent unprotected processors.

1.9 Discussion

There are plenty of reasons to use the techniques you will read about in this book to protect your code, and plenty of reasons not to. In the end, you must weigh the pros and cons to see if using them makes sense in your particular case.

1.9.1 Reasons to Use Software Protection...

On the plus side, there are situations where even a short delay in cracking your code will be beneficial. For example, these days computer games often escape into the wild within days or a few weeks of release. Sometimes, as the result of insider attacks, they even escape *before* they're released! Since gamers are interested in playing the latest and greatest, the revenue from a new game is typically collected within the first few weeks of its release. Game manufacturers have therefore traditionally been eager to adopt software protection techniques, even those that are sure to be cracked within a very short time.

In situations where you're selling a particularly high-value program, software protection might also make sense. If every year you sell only a few tens of copies of a software system that costs $100,000 per seat, the loss of even one sale due to piracy could be devastating to your bottom line. In these situations, it's common to use a combination of hardware techniques (such as dongles) to prevent illegal copying and software techniques (such as obfuscation) to protect the interface between the hardware and the application.

In some situations, you may want to use software protection to prevent individuals from cracking your program, individuals you are unlikely to catch (because they're far off in another country) or who are legally untouchable (because they have no assets to forfeit). In other cases, you may want to use software protection as an aid in criminal prosecution. It is said that more money is lost to piracy performed by corporations than by individuals. The reason is that corporations often will buy, say, 10 licenses to use a program but will let 50 of their employees use it. These corporations have huge assets, and if you can prove license infringement, you may actually have a chance to use the legal system to force them to abide by the license agreement. Individuals, on the other hand, often crack a program or download a pirated program that they would never have bought legally anyway. The amount of revenue lost to this type of piracy may therefore not be as high as often reported, and going after these types of adversaries is less likely to be profitable.

1.9.2 ... and Reasons Not To

On the downside, adding software protection to your program can cause problems in terms of cost, performance, a more complex software development cycle, and last but not least, annoyance to your legitimate users.

Costs can increase both during development and distribution. During development, you have the option of purchasing a protection tool, developing one yourself, or applying the protection techniques by hand. Regardless, you will be adding a step and complexity to the development cycle. In several techniques you'll see in this book (such as fingerprinting and code encryption), every distributed copy of your program will be unique. This means additional headaches during distribution, quality assurance, and when fielding bug reports.

Many of the techniques you'll see come with significant performance overhead. And when we say "significant" we mean *significant*. Whether higher levels of protection necessarily incur a more severe performance hit is unknown, but it seems not an unreasonable possibility. In the end, this may require you to make difficult trade-offs: using techniques with low overhead and a low level of protection, using powerful techniques with high overhead but only for the security-sensitive parts of your program, or accepting the high overhead of a powerful protection technique but only selling to users with sufficiently powerful computers.

Many software protection techniques have been cracked not because the attacker necessarily wanted to pirate or reverse engineer the program, but because he wanted to perform what to him seemed like reasonable operations on it. Maybe he wanted to run the program on his laptop as well as his desktop computer, maybe he wanted to make a backup copy of it, maybe he wanted to transfer it from his old machine to his newly bought one, maybe he wanted to run the program without the annoyance of having to enter a password or insert a CD or USB token every time, and so on. Whether or not you, as the software developer, think these are legitimate concerns, and whether or not the software license agreement allows it, the user may well get ticked off enough to feel no qualms about cracking the program.

And that's not to mention bugs. Many of the techniques you will see in this book are based on code transformations. As such, they're very similar to the optimizing code transformations you'll find in sophisticated compilers. And as such, they're susceptible to the usual menagerie of bugs. As a result, your program that was perfectly functional before protection was added may exhibit erratic behavior afterward, either as a result of a bug in the protection tool itself, or because its code transformations revealed a latent bug in your own code.

1.9.3 So Which Algorithms Should I Use?

So you've written your fantastic new program and for whatever reasons you've decided that it makes sense to add some sort of software protection to it. You've bought this book[5] and read it cover to cover in search of the One True Algorithm to implement. Unfortunately, if this was your attitude, you will have been sorely disappointed.

The problems facing software protection research are multitudinous, but it boils down to one central issue: How do you evaluate the effectiveness of an algorithm? Unfortunately, the state of the art is sorely lacking. Ideally, this book would end with a single large table over all the algorithms that lists for each one *effort to implement*, *effort to defeat*, *parallelizability of attacks*, and *performance overhead*.[6] As you may have already guessed, there's no such table.

Without knowing how many more hours/days/weeks/months your program will remain uncracked if you protect it with the algorithms in this book, how can you know if software protection will make sense in your particular case? And without being able to compare two algorithms to say that one is better than another, how can you pick the right algorithm to use? And how does the field progress when a paper purporting to present a new, improved algorithm can't substantiate its claims?

Disturbing questions, indeed. In practice, software protection takes a belt-and-suspenders approach to security. You layer protection algorithms until you've convinced yourself that your program is secure "enough" while at the same time remaining within performance bounds. If you can afford to, maybe you employ a professional red-team to try to break through the defenses and give you some feel for how long the protection will survive in the wild. But in the end, you have to accept the fact that you're engaged in a cat-and-mouse game: If crackers deem your program sufficiently crack-worthy, eventually they'll succeed. This situation may

---

5. Thanks!
6. Effort is measured in person wall-clock hours. A parallelizable attack can be sped up by simply throwing more crackers at the problem.

seem depressing, but it is not much different from other areas of life. In the end, all it means is that you will have to monitor the efforts of your adversaries and be prepared to continuously update your defenses.

1.10 Notation

In this book we have tried to devise a uniform naming convention for surreptitious software algorithms. Every algorithm is referred to by a name that consists of a prefix (WM for watermarking, OBF for obfuscation, TP for tamperproofing, and SS for software similarity) followed by the authors' surname initials. For algorithms that *attack* programs we use the prefix RE (for reverse engineering). For a single author algorithm, we use the initial of the surname followed by the initial of the given name. When a list of authors have multiple algorithms, we add a subscript. If two different lists of authors share the same initials, we add given name initials and initials from the article title until names are disambiguated.

To facilitate navigating through the book, we've added page numbers to all cross-references, using the following notation: "In Section 3.2.3▶163 you will see the totally awesome Algorithm 3.1▶165 . . . ."

Methods of Attack and Defense

2

There is a saying: "If you build a better mouse trap, someone will build a better mouse," and that could well describe the eternal struggle between Doris and Axel in our surreptitious software scenarios from the last chapter. Axel comes up with a new way to analyze and modify Doris' code, Doris retaliates with a cleverer watermarking algorithm and additional layers of obfuscation and tamperproofing, which prompts Axel to develop better analysis techniques, and so on. At present we see no end to this escalating war—as of yet there are no theoretical results or practical tools that could put an end to it once and for all, tipping the scales permanently in Doris' or Axel's favor, so this situation is simply something Doris and Axel need to learn to live with. In practice, this will mean that Doris can expect to have to monitor Axel's improving attack capabilities and continually upgrade her defenses, and Axel can expect that the attacks he develops today will be rendered useless tomorrow.

What both Doris and Axel desperately want at this point is a theoretical model that would allow them to compare their own abilities to their adversaries' abilities. Doris would like to know the ways in which Axel can crack her software protection, how long it will take him to do it, and what the software will be like after he's done. Ideally, she would like for it to take Axel a long time to break through her defenses and for the resulting program to be much larger, much slower, and much more brittle. She would also, of course, like to have a good model of her own protection tools so that she can choose the right combinations of algorithms that will thwart Axel's attacks for the required length of time. Axel would like access to the same model: He wants to know the reverse engineering effort required to break through Doris' defenses and what the resulting program will look like so that he can determine if it's worth his while or not.

There are two parts to Axel's reverse engineering efforts: *building* the necessary support tools and then *running* these tools. Ideally, Doris wants to maximize both the effort Axel has to expend to build his tools, and the time it will take to run them. But she might still be happy if building the tools took Axel a year and running them on her software took an hour, or if building them took an hour and running them took a year. Regardless, both Doris and Axel want to have an understanding of their own and each other's capabilities, as they are now and as they are likely to improve over time.

This chapter is divided into two major sections, Section 2.1, in which we discuss the adversary's abilities to attack us, and Section 2.2▶86, in which we discuss our abilities to defend ourselves. The two sections are very different in nature. Section 2.1 is very hands-on, describing the cracker's attack goals and his reverse engineering skills and techniques. In Section 2.2▶86, we build a much higher-level model for what *we* can do, drawing on experiences from how the natural world (plants and animals) protects itself from predators and from how, over the course of history, we humans have learned to protect ourselves from the natural world and from each other.

2.1 Attack Strategies

What should your assumptions about the attacker be? What should your *attack model* be? There are two issues you need to resolve: What are the adversary's motivations for attacking your program, and what are his means for reaching his goals? Broadly speaking, once your program is in the attacker's hands, he can do with it what he pleases; there are no restrictions! There are, however, typical strategies and techniques he'll employ to coax secrets out of the program, and ways in which he'll coax the program to behave the way he wants. In particular, to build your attack model, you need answers to these questions:

- What does a typical program look like and what valuables does it contain?
- What is the adversary's motivation for attacking your program?
- What information does he start out with as he attacks your program?
- What is his overall strategy for reaching his goals?
- What tools does he have at his disposal?
- What specific techniques does he use to attack the program?

Without answers to these questions, without an attack model in mind, you won't be able to appreciate the protection algorithms in the remainder of the book! In this section, we'll seek to build such an attack model, and in the next chapter we'll explore various attack techniques and tools in more detail.

2.1.1 A Prototypical Cracking Target

To make the ideas in this section really concrete, we're going to focus our attention on a prototypical cracking target, a Digital Rights Management (DRM) player.[1] Listing 2.1 ▶62 gives the code of the very simple DRM player we'll use in this section. You'll see variants of this program throughout the book. Here's a graphical sketch of the program, where each component is shaded the same way as the source code in Listing 2.1 ▶62:

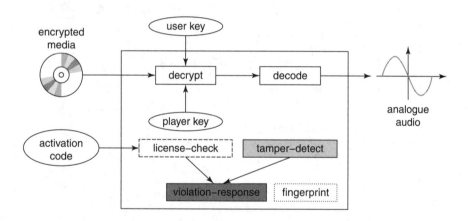

The main line of the program reads digitally encrypted audio, decrypts it to cleartext, decodes the cleartext to analog audio, and writes the result out to an audio device. The decryptor needs two keys, one provided by the user and the other hardwired into the player itself.

---

1. DRM is a red flag for many people, who argue, among other things, that it's a hindrance for legitimate users and makes it difficult to exercise one's rights under the "fair use" clause of the copyright law. Our reasons for using a DRM player as an example in this book are purely technical; we neither endorse the idea nor particularly object to it.

Listing 2.1 Prototypical cracking target.

```
1   typedef unsigned int uint;
2   typedef uint* waddr_t;
3   uint player_key = 0xbabeca75;
4   uint the_key;
5   uint* key = &the_key;
6   FILE* audio;
7   int activation_code = 42
8
9   void FIRST_FUN(){}
10  uint hash (waddr_t addr, waddr_t last) {
11      uint h = *addr;
12      for(;addr<=last;addr++) h^=*addr;
13      return h;
14  }
15  void die(char* msg) {
16      fprintf(stderr,"%s!\n",msg);
17      key = NULL;
18  }
19  uint play(uint user_key, uint encrypted_media[], int media_len) {
20      int code;
21      printf("Please enter activation code: ");
22      scanf("%i",&code);
23      if (code!=activation_code) die("wrong code");
24
25      *key = user_key ^ player_key;
26
27      int i;
28      for(i=0;i<media_len;i++) {
29          uint decrypted = *key ^ encrypted_media[i];
30          asm volatile (
31              "jmp L1                    \n\t"
32              ".align 4                  \n\t"
33              ".long         0xb0b5b0b5\n\t"
34              "L1:                       \n\t"
35          );
36          if (time(0) > 1221011472) die("expired");
37          float decoded = (float)decrypted;
38          fprintf(audio,"%f\n",decoded); fflush(audio);
39      }
40  }
41  void LAST_FUN(){}
42  uint player_main (uint argc, char *argv[]) {
43      uint user_key = ...
44      uint encrypted_media[100] = ...
45      uint media_len = ...
46      uint hashVal = hash((waddr_t)FIRST_FUN,(waddr_t)LAST_FUN);
47      if (hashVal != HASH) die("tampered");
48      play(user_key, encrypted_media,media_len);
49  }
```

In addition to its main functions (all unshaded), the player contains software protection code (shaded). The light gray code detects if the code of the player has been tampered with. It does this by computing a hash over the binary code and comparing the result to an expected value. The dashed code checks the user's execution rights, in particular, that he has entered the right activation code and hasn't exceeded the player's use-by date. The dark gray code responds if the user has violated the program in some way. In this case, the `die` function sets the `key` variable to `NULL`, which in turn causes the program to fail at a later stage, when execution reaches line 25 or 29. The dotted code, finally, contains the user's unique fingerprint `0xb0b5b0b5`, which allows us to trace an illegal copy back to him.

Further on in the book, we will show you "real" protection algorithms along these lines. In Section 7.2▶412, for example, you'll see algorithms that do tamper-checking by hashing the executable code, and in Section 7.3▶440 you'll see an algorithm that constructs pointer-based tamper-response mechanisms.

In this trivial program, `die` responds the same way (crashing the player) regardless of the manner in which it has been violated. In practice, you'll want to respond differently if the user enters the wrong license code, if the program is executed past its use-by date, or if its code has been modified.

2.1.2 What's the Adversary's Motivation?

In the information security community it is customary to identify three *security goals*, namely, *confidentiality*, *integrity*, and *availability* (the CIA triad). In the *Federal Information Security Management Act of 2002* [334], these terms are defined as follows:

(1) The term "information security" means protecting information and information systems from unauthorized access, use, disclosure, disruption, modification, or destruction in order to provide

   (a) integrity, which means guarding against improper information modification or destruction, and includes ensuring information nonrepudiation and authenticity;

   (b) confidentiality, which means preserving authorized restrictions on access and disclosure, including means for protecting personal privacy and proprietary information; and

   (c) availability, which means ensuring timely and reliable access to and use of information.

An adversary's goal, then, is to prevent you from reaching these security goals and to achieve some sort of (monetary or intellectual) satisfaction from an attack.

The scenarios that we discuss in this book are different from what most security professionals deal with, which is typically to protect the integrity, confidentiality, and availability of a networked computer system. Our security goals instead all relate to maintaining the integrity, confidentiality, and availability of a particular *program*, or information contained in a program. Tamperproofing, for example, attempts to protect the integrity of a program, preventing an adversary from modifying it to his advantage. Obfuscation can be used to protect the confidentiality of algorithms or other secrets (such as cryptographic keys) contained in a program. The security goal of watermarking and fingerprinting is to ensure availability of the marks to the watermark detector. The adversary's goal, on the other hand, is to disrupt the defender's ability to detect the marks, thereby making it impossible to trace pirated copies back to him.

One way to look at integrity violations is to note that your program consists of two pieces of semantics, the *core semantics* that implements the actual functionality of the program, and the *protection semantics* that is the code you added to protect the core from attack. The adversary's goal is to remove the protection semantics, add his own *attack semantics* (such as the ability to save game-state, which is often missing from an evaluation copy of a game), while ensuring that the core semantics remains unchanged:

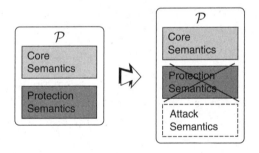

To make this more concrete, let's look at what valuables your DRM player contains and how the attacker could benefit (financially or otherwise) from acquiring them or from modifying the player code.

First, the decrypted digital audio itself has value. It's of higher fidelity than the analog audio that's the output of the player, and hence *more* valuable than it. The adversary could either enjoy the music himself (perhaps by playing it in his car or on his portable music player, instead of just through the sanctioned player) or sell it for profit.

Second, if he could coax the player to give up its secret cryptographic key, `player_key`, he and his customers might be able to decrypt and enjoy *any* music for free. He could even use the key to build and sell his own player, undercutting the price of the competition.

Third, although this isn't common for digital rights management players (these are normally given away for free and the business model is to make a profit by selling media), our program performs two forms of license checking: It checks that it's not used after a particular date and that the user has the correct activation code. The player would be more valuable to the user without these checks.

Fourth, if he *did* pay for the program, he may want to recoup some of that cost by making copies and reselling them for profit. If he's involved in this sort of piracy, he'd like to make sure that he can't be caught (prison time is bad for business) and so needs to disable any tracking mechanisms. Thus the player becomes more valuable to him if he can disrupt your ability to find the fingerprint (`0xb0b5b0b5`) that identifies him as the player's original owner.

Finally, if the adversary is your rival DRM player developer, he could profit from identifying and reusing the algorithms you've developed for the player.

To summarize, the player contains valuable static data (the `player.key`), valuable dynamically generated data (the digital audio stream), and valuable algorithms. The player becomes more valuable itself if any restrictions on its use get lifted, i.e., if it can be modified so that it's playable after its expiration date and without having to enter the activation code, and if it can be freely resold without risk of being traced back to the seller.

The prototypical DRM player we've outlined here is not unique in the valuable goods it contains, the ways it protects itself, or the ways in which it's open to attack. For example, the Skype VoIP client (see Section 7.2.4▶431) also contains cryptographic keys and secret protocols that, if you could pry them away from the code, would allow you to build your own client and steal Skype's customers away from them. The Skype client, too, is protected from tampering by hashing the executable.

2.1.3 What Does the Adversary Get to Crack?

When the adversary sets out to crack your program, what does he start out with? What does he know about your program, and even more important, what *doesn't* he know? To begin with, let's assume your source language is C, or any similar language that typically compiles down to binary code.

In this case, what you as the software developer distribute to your users (and your potential adversaries!) is an executable file known as a *stripped binary* and a user guide for running the program. The binary contains essentially no symbolic names (there are exceptions here that we'll get to shortly), no typing information, and no information about where functions begin or end. It's (again, essentially) a black box.

We're going to assume that the attacker has no other information to work with. Specifically, he has no documentation about the internal design of the program (as would be available to the original developers), nor does he have access to the comprehensive suite of input-output pairs that the developers used when testing the program. During the course of cracking, the adversary may, of course, build up documentation of his expanding knowledge of the internals as well as his own test suite. Initially, however, he has no such information available.

There are, of course, scenarios in which these assumptions about the attacker don't hold. Maybe he has an accomplice on the inside who can provide him with information, maybe he himself is a former employee of the development company and knows about its software development process, maybe there are white papers on the company's website that can provide useful clues, and so on. Here, we are going to assume that this is not the case—the adversary starts out with a clean slate.

2.1.3.1 Static vs. Dynamic and Stripped vs. Unstripped

Now to the exception! In practice, no box is completely black and will always leak some information! At the very least, every executable has an entry point where execution commences.

The amount of information the executable leaks depends on if it's been *dynamically* or *statically* linked, and if it's been *stripped* or not. To statically link an executable means to include all libraries it references, and to strip it means to remove any unnecessary symbols (variable and function names). To understand these options, have a look at this figure that relates to the DRM player executable:

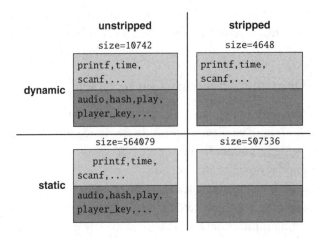

The statically linked executable includes all library functions the program needs, such as `printf`, `scanf`, and `time`. For this reason, it's much larger than the dynamically linked executable that loads in the libraries at runtime. The light gray boxes show the library symbols the executable contains. In the case of the dynamically linked program, it must have *all* the library symbols present in the executable since references to these symbols aren't resolved until runtime. The dark gray boxes show the symbols (`audio`, `hash`, `play`, . . .) from the player program that are available in the executable. For the statically linked and stripped executable, there are no symbols at all left: All the libraries have been linked in, all references between symbols have been resolved at link time, and all symbols have been removed.

As you see, the statically linked stripped binary leaks the least amount of information. But on the flip side, it's also two orders of magnitude larger than the dynamically linked stripped binary! Software developers often will choose to distribute their programs dynamically linked because it minimizes size, it allows the program to link in system-dependent files on the user's platform, and it ensures that any updates to libraries will take immediate effect. From a software protection perspective, however, this isn't ideal. As you'll see shortly, even if the `play` symbol has been stripped out of the executable, the attacker can use the remaining dynamically linked-in library symbols for his attack. By locating the `time` library function, he can find `play` since `play` is the only function in the program to call `time`!

2.1.3.2 Architecture-Neutral Distribution Formats

Many languages, for example, Java and C#, are compiled not to native binary code, but to an architecture-neutral format. In the case of Java, every class `X.java` is compiled into a *classfile* `X.class` that contains a symbol table and, for every method, a list of its bytecode instructions. For all intents and purposes, the classfile is isomorphic to the original source: Since all the bytecodes are fully typed and the symbol table contains complete signatures of all methods, a decompiler has sufficient information available to turn the classfile back into a source form that closely resembles the original.

Java classfiles are loaded dynamically, by name, so when a program calls `System.out.println()` (the Java equivalent of C's `printf()`), this is clearly visible in the bytecode. In essence, then, Java executables are dynamic and unstripped. Java programs typically rely heavily on classes in the standard library, more so than your typical C program. As a result, even in the absence of source code or documentation, it can be easy for an attacker to determine which part of a Java program does what by analyzing which library methods it calls.

2.1.4 What's the Adversary's Attack Methodology?

An attacker will go through multiple phases when attacking your program. In the first few phases he will analyze it, building up an understanding of its behavior and internal structure, and in later phases he will use this knowledge to modify its behavior to his liking. At a very high level, you can think of the adversary going through these five attack phases:

1. The *black box* phase,
2. The *dynamic analysis* phase,
3. The *static analysis* phase,
4. The *editing* phase,
5. The *automation* phase.

In the black box phase, he treats the program as an *"oracle,"* feeding it inputs, recording its outputs, and drawing conclusions about its *external* behavior. In the dynamic analysis phase, he gets a first glimpse of the program's *internal* behavior. Again, he executes the program, but this time he records which parts of it get executed for different inputs. Armed with this high-level understanding, he can proceed to the static analysis phase where he analyzes the program by examining the executable code directly.

If his goal is a confidentiality violation, the attacker might stop after the analysis phases. Maybe he's looking for some cryptographic keys inside the program, or maybe he's interested in the algorithms the program uses—in these cases he's done. If, instead, he's set on an integrity violation, he continues to the editing phase where he uses his understanding of the internals of the program to modify the executable: He disables license checks and modifies the program to disrupt your ability to recognize his fingerprint.

In practice, of course, an attack is never as compartmentalized as this. The first four phases are manual and will be interleaved with each other. They require trial-and-error, multiple runs of the program, and they will be repeated over and over again, each time giving the attacker a deeper level of understanding of the code, until he feels confident he has reached his attack goals.

In the final phase, he encapsulates his knowledge of the attack in an automated *script* that can be used, with little or no manual intervention, in future attacks.

2.1.4.1 Dynamic Analysis—Cracking vs. Debugging   It's been pointed out [11] that the cracking process bears many likenesses to debugging. In fact, from the

cracker's point of view, a license check is a bug in the program that needs to be located and removed!

There are some differences between debugging and cracking, though. When you debug your program you go through an *edit-compile-test* cycle, where you edit the source code, compile it to binary code, test it for bugs, and then repeat until the program has the required functionality:

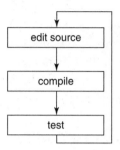

When a cracker tries to break your protection, he instead goes through a *locate-alter-test* cycle:

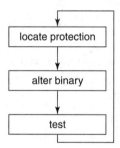

During the locate phase, he finds the location in the binary executable where a modification will remove the undesired behavior (e.g., disable the license check). Next, during the alter phase, he decides on a set of changes to the code that will have the desired effect. This can involve adding instructions, removing instructions, or modifying existing instructions. Finally, during the test phase, he checks that the changes have had the desired effect (the license check is no longer triggered) and didn't adversely affect the core semantics of the program.

Earlier we noted that one of our assumptions about the attacker is that, unlike you, he doesn't have access to a comprehensive test suite. This is an important limitation on his abilities. It means that he has to be extra-careful that none of the alterations he makes to the program will affect its core semantics. If the alteration is highly localized (say, replacing a conditional branch with an unconditional one in a license check), then this may not be too much of a problem. Modifications with more wide-ranging effects are harder to check when the attacker has no deep knowledge of the internals of the program, and no test suite to run to convince him that his changes didn't break the program in some subtle way.

Software protection algorithms have been designed to hamper the attacker in each of the locate-alter-test phases of the attack cycle. For example, to make the program harder to alter, you can make many portions of it interdependent, so that local changes are not enough to disable the protection code. You can slow down the locate phase by making the program appear to execute non-deterministically, choosing different paths through the program every time it's run. Finally, you can add bogus execution paths to the program so that an attacker has to build many test cases in order to convince himself that the changes he's made have no ill effects.

2.1.4.2 Dynamic Analysis—Exploiting Cracks in the Black Box   Earlier we noted that even a statically linked stripped binary executable will leak information. At the very least, the main entry point is known, which makes it possible for the attacker to start to learn about the program by the (likely laborious) task of single-stepping through it.

A common attack strategy is to try to link the external behavior of the program to its internal behavior by watching system calls and calls to library functions. For example, the first trivial attack a cracker who's trying to remove a license check will try is to locate the call to the pop-up box that delivers the "Please enter your program activation code" message. In Windows he could, for example, set a breakpoint on the GetDlgItemInt() library function that translates the number entered in the dialog box into an integer value. When the breakpoint hits, he can look up the call stack to find the location of the user code that called the function. Most likely, this will be in the vicinity of the code that checks if the activation code is valid.

If the program is statically linked and stripped, finding library functions by name is no longer possible. System calls, however, provide a reliable interface to the operating system, and attackers can use them to find the location of common library functions. It's safe to assume, for example, that printf is going to invoke the write system call at some point. So the attacker can simply set a breakpoint on write and, when the breakpoint hits, look up the call stack to find the location of what's likely to be printf.

2.1.4.3 Static Analysis   Static analysis can be done on several levels. Some crackers are well versed in reading raw binary machine code and, most, certainly, read x86 assembly code as if it were their mother tongue. Thus, they require nothing more than a disassembly listing in order to dive in and start reverse engineering your program.

Static analysis can be much more efficient, however, when the attacker has access to good tools. You'll meet some of these, like control flow analyzers and slicers, in Chapter 3 (Program Analysis), where you'll also see how to implement disassemblers and decompilers. Even if current decompilers are pretty inaccurate on stripped binary code and on code generated by an unknown compiler or from a language for which it wasn't designed, they can still be useful. Van Emmerik and Waddington [122] describe how they put the only partially functional decompiler Boomerang to good use when trying to recover algorithms from a program for which source code wasn't available. In spite of having to do a lot of hand-holding, the authors claim that "using Boomerang was still much safer than hand decompilation, because of the high probability of errors with a completely manual approach."

Simple pattern matching on the binary code can also be effective. In Section 7.2.4 ▶ 431, you'll see how the Skype VoIP client was cracked by searching through the binary for the signature of the tamper-detecting hash functions. Pattern matching can also be used to find the code of common library functions such as `printf`.

2.1.4.4 Editing Once you know the source of a bug, the edit part in the edit-compile-test cycle is trivial, because you have the source! It's not so easy for the attacker in his locate-alter-test cycle, since he's working on binary code. Modifying a single instruction is easy, as long as the new instruction is of the same or smaller size as the original one. So changing the branch-if-less-than instruction to a branch-never instruction in a license check shouldn't pose any problems. Deleting code is also generally easy—just overwrite it with NOPs! Any change that involves *inserting* new code in the middle of the binary can be problematic, however. In a statically linked executable, all branch addresses are hardwired and may have to be adjusted if the attacker starts moving code around or inserting new code. This doesn't have to be a problem if the disassembler has been able to correctly recover all the code in the binary, but as you will see in Section 3.3.1 ▶ 172, even the best disassembler will occasionally fail.

2.1.4.5 Automation The final (and often optional) step in an attack is to automate it. Based on the understanding he has gained of the binary and the protection mechanisms, the attacker builds a static tool (known as a *script*) that (typically without running the program) strips an executable of its protection. Depending on his prowess and the complexity of the protection scheme, this script can be more or less general. It may only work to crack a particular program, or it may crack *any* program protected with a particular technique.

It's interesting to note that there's a definite difference in social standing between the "real" cracker who did the initial analysis and wrote the attack script and the so-called "script-kiddies" who merely use it. The kiddies have no programming skills and just download the script and use it to crack their favorite game.

2.1.5 What Tools Does the Adversary Use?

From what we know of attackers these days, they use fairly unsophisticated general tools (chiefly debuggers), along with specialized tools they build for attacking a particular class of protection mechanisms, augmented by a near-infinite supply of personal time, energy, and motivation for reaching their goals. In the research community there exist many powerful tools (such as the slicing and tracing tools we'll talk about in Chapter 3 (Program Analysis)) that would be very useful to an attacker. We believe they are not currently in use, however, because, being research prototypes, they are not stable enough, fast enough, or precise enough; they don't run on the right operating system; or they are simply unknown in the cracker community. We are still going to assume, however, that our adversaries *have* access to such tools, because if they don't today, they might tomorrow.

2.1.6 What Techniques Does the Adversary Use?

Let's for a moment invert the color of our hats, from white to black, and play like we're crackers! The goal of this section isn't to turn you into a full-fledged attacker but for you to get a feel for the types of techniques that are typically used. Our example cracking target will be the DRM player in Listing 2.1▶62. In most of the attacks, we'll assume that we've been given an executable that's been compiled for the x86 running Linux and then dynamically linked and stripped of local symbols. Our chief cracking tool will be the gdb debugger.

The details of an attack will vary depending on the operating system, the tools the attacker has available, and the nature of the protection techniques he's wanting to subvert. The basic techniques will be the the same, however. Other books [56,118] deal more directly with the tools and techniques that are specific to particular operating systems, such as Windows.

2.1.6.1 Learning About the Executable   Before you can start cracking, you need to learn a few basic things about the executable itself. Is it statically linked, are there any symbols present, what's the starting address for the various sections, and so on.

Every operating system will have standard tools to discover this information:[2]

```
> file player
player: ELF 64-bit LSB executable, dynamically linked

> objdump -T player
DYNAMIC SYMBOL TABLE:
0xa4   scanf
0x90   fprintf
0x12   time

> objdump -x player | egrep 'rodata|text|Name'
Name         Size      VMA        LMA        File off   Algn
.text        0x4f8     0x4006a0   0x4006a0   0x6a0      2**4
.rodata      0x84      0x400ba8   0x400ba8   0xba8      2**3

> objdump -f player | grep start
start address 0x4006a0
```

You now know much useful information about the executable! First, it's dynamically linked and hence has many useful symbols left. You also know the beginning and end of the text and data segments—this will come in handy when you search through the executable for special code sequences or string values. Last but not least, you know that the program will start executing at address 0x4006a0!

2.1.6.2 Breaking on Library Functions The first thing you do is to treat the program as a black box, feeding it inputs to see how it behaves. You immediately notice that the player says expired! instead of playing music for you:

```
> player 0xca7ca115 1 2 3 4
Please enter activation code: 42
expired!
Segmentation fault
```

So your first attack is going to have to be to remove that pesky use-by check!

---

2. In this section, all output generated from commands has been edited for readability.

You already know that the executable is *stripped* and *dynamically linked*. This means that it should be possible to find many library functions by name. Most likely, the program implements the use-by check by calling the `time()` function in the standard library and then comparing the result to a predefined value. So your goal has to be to find the assembly code equivalent of `if (time(0) > *some value*)···`.

The idea we're going to use is to set a breakpoint on `time()`, run the program until the breakpoint is hit, go up one level in the call stack (to see who called `time()`), and look at the code in the vicinity of the call to `time()` for a suspicious check. Once we find it, we can replace the branch with `if (time(0) <= *some value*)···`.

As luck would have it, this strategy works out nicely. You find that the instruction at location 0x4008bc (in light gray) is the offending conditional branch:

```
> gdb -write -silent --args player 0xca7ca115 1000 2000 3000 4000
(gdb) break time
Breakpoint 1 at 0x400680
(gdb) run
Please enter activation code: 42
Breakpoint 1, 0x400680 in time()
(gdb) where 2
#0  0x400680 in time
#1  0x4008b6 in ??
(gdb) up
#1  0x4008b6 in ??
(gdb) disassemble $pc-5 $pc+7
0x4008b1    callq   0x400680
0x4008b6    cmp     $0x48c72810,%rax
0x4008bc    jle     0x4008c8
```

Now all that's left to do is to patch the executable by replacing the `jle` with a `jg` (x86 opcode 0x7f). You can use `gdb`'s `set` command to patch the instruction:

```
(gdb) set {unsigned char}0x4008bc = 0x7f
(gdb) disassemble 0x4008bc 0x4008be
0x4008bc    jg      0x4008c8
```

In this case, you were lucky in that the executable still had dynamic symbols left. If the program had been statically linked and stripped, it would not have been so easy to break on the `time()` function. It's still not impossible, of course! Alternative strategies include finding the `time()` function by pattern matching on some unique signature of its code, or breaking on the `gettimeofday()` system call which, presumably, `time()` will call to get the current time from the operating system.

2.1.6.3 Static Pattern Matching   Now the player doesn't say `expired!` anymore, so at least you've disabled one of the protections! However, the player still crashes with a `"wrong code"` message if you enter anything other than 42:

```
> player 0xca7ca115 1000 2000 3000 4000
tampered!
Please enter activation code: 99
wrong code!
Segmentation fault
```

This time we're going to try another common cracker strategy, namely, to search the executable for character strings. You'd expect that the assembly code that checks the activation code would look something like this:

```
addr1:   .ascii "wrong code"
         ...
         cmp     read_value,activation_code
         je      somewhere
addr2: move      addr1, reg0
         call    printf
```

So the idea is to first search the data segment to find address `addr1` where the string `"wrong code"` is allocated. Then you search again, this time through the text segment, for an instruction that contains that address as a literal:

```
(gdb) find 0x400ba8 ,+0x84 ,"wrong code"
0x400be2
(gdb) find 0x4006a0 ,+0x4f8 ,0x400be2
0x400862
(gdb) disassemble 0x40085d 0x400867
0x40085d    cmp     %eax ,%edx
0x40085f    je      0x40086b
0x400861    mov     $0x400be2 ,%edi
0x400866    callq   0x4007e0
```

Bingo! The first search finds the `addr1` address (in light gray), the second finds the `addr2` address (dark gray). All you have to do now is replace the jump-on-equal with a jump-always, thereby bypassing the call to `printf`. On the x86, the `jmp` instruction has the opcode 0xeb:

```
(gdb) set {unsigned char}0x40085f = 0xeb
(gdb) disassemble 0x40085f 0x400860
0x40085f    jmp     0x40086b
```

You were pretty lucky here in that the `addr2` address occurred directly as a literal in an instruction. On many architectures, the address would instead have been computed by adding an offset to a base register, and that would have made for a more complicated search.

2.1.6.4 Watching Memory Now the program doesn't complain anymore about an exceeded use-by date or a wrong activation code, but it still crashes with a segmentation violation:

```
>  player 0xca7ca115 1000 2000 3000 4000
tampered!
Please enter activation code: 55
Segmentation fault
```

It's safe to guess that this is because the edits you did to the executable caused the tamper-detection mechanism to kick in. On Unix, a segmentation fault indicates that the program is accessing an illegal memory location, for example, trying to dereference a `NULL` pointer.

Your strategy this time will be to first let the program run until it crashes and then see what address it's trying to load from or write to. You'll then rerun the program while watching the address to find the location that sets it to an illegal value. Let's get started:

```
(gdb) run
Program received signal SIGSEGV
0x40087b in ?? ()
(gdb) disassemble 0x40086b 0x40087d
0x40086b    mov     0x2009ce(%rip),%rax   # 0x601240
0x400872    mov     0x2009c0(%rip),%edx   # 0x601238
0x400878    xor     -0x14(%rbp),%edx
0x40087b    mov     %edx,(%rax)
```

Apparently, at location 0x40087b, the program tries to write to an address it has loaded from 0x601240, and it fails because of a memory violation. So now you set a watchpoint on 0x601240, rerun the program from the beginning, and see what happens:

```
(gdb) watch *0x601240
(gdb) run
tampered!
Hardware watchpoint 2: *0x601240

Old value = 6296176
New value = 0

0x400811 in ?? ()

(gdb) disassemble 0x400806 0x400812
0x400806    movq    $0x0,0x200a2f(%rip)    # 0x601240
0x400811    leaveq
```

Well, what's happening is that the instruction at location 0x400806 is setting the word at address 0x601240 to 0! This corresponds to the key = NULL statement in the die() function:

```
15   void die(char* msg) {
16       fprintf(stderr,"%s!\n",msg);
17       key = NULL;
18   }
```

To bypass this statement, all you have to do is overwrite it with a sequence of nop instructions (x86 opcode 0x90):

```
(gdb) set {unsigned char}0x400806 = 0x90
    ....
(gdb) set {unsigned char}0x400810 = 0x90
```

Now you can disassemble the offending code again, just to make sure that you've removed the entire key = NULL statement:

```
(gdb) disassemble 0x400806 0x400812
0x400806   nop
...
0x400810   nop
0x400811   leaveq
```

2.1.6.5 Recovering Internal Data   As we noted earlier, the decrypted data that
the player holds internally is more valuable than the analog data that it produces
as output. For this reason, you, as the attacker, would like to modify the player
to dump the cleartext data. Inserting new code in the middle of an executable
is non-trivial, however, since branch addresses will be affected and have to be
adjusted. A simpler approach can be to ask the debugger to print out the data
for you!

Assume that, after some poking around in the executable, you've determined that at address 0x4008a6, local variable -0x8(%rbp) holds the cleartext
media:

```
(gdb) disassemble  0x40086b 0x4008a8
0x40086b   mov     0x2009ce(%rip),%rax
0x400872   mov     0x2009c0(%rip),%edx
           ...
0x40089b   add     -0x20(%rbp),%rax
0x40089f   mov     (%rax),%eax
0x4008a1   xor     %edx,%eax
0x4008a3   mov     %eax,-0x8(%rbp)
0x4008a6   jmp     0x4008ac
```

This code corresponds to the statement

```
29   uint decrypted = *key ^ encrypted_media[i];
```

in the source. Now all you have to do is set a breakpoint on 0x4008a6 and tell
the debugger to print out the value (light gray) of the local variable every time the
breakpoint is hit:

```
(gdb) hbreak *0x4008a6

(gdb) commands
>x/x -0x8+$rbp
>continue
>end
(gdb) cont
Please enter activation code: 42
Breakpoint 2, 0x4008a6
0x7fffffffdc88:  0xbabec99d
Breakpoint 2, 0x4008a6
0x7fffffffdc88:  0xbabecda5
         ...
```

Here, you're making use of gdb's ability to execute an arbitrary sequence of commands (in dark gray) at the time when a breakpoint hits. In this case, you told gdb to print the value of the local in hex and then to immediately continue execution.

2.1.6.6 Tampering with the Environment Even if directly modifying the executable is possible, it isn't always easy. To avoid having to disable the tamper detection, it is sometimes possible to instead modify the *environment* in which the program is run. For example, to avoid triggering the time-out, you can simply wind back the system clock!

There are many variants of this technique. If the program is dynamically linked, for example, you can provide your own hacked libraries (where the time function always returns 0, for example), and by a simple change of the library search path you can force the program to pick up the hacked code.

In Section 7.2.5▶435 you'll see a clever algorithm that makes a small change to the pagefault handler of the operating system kernel and thereby disables *all* hash-based tamperproofing algorithms, without requiring *any* modification of the program code!

2.1.6.7 Dynamic Pattern Matching You won't need it here, but in other situations a powerful technique is to pattern match, not on the static code and data but on their *dynamic behavior*. Say, for example, that instead of the trivial "decryption routine" in Listing 2.1▶62 (just a single xor instruction!), the DRM player used a standard algorithm such as Needham and Wheeler's *Tiny Encryption Algorithm* (TEA) [273]:

```
#define MX  ( (((z>>5)^(y<<2))+((y>>3)^(z<<4)))^ \
              ((sum^y)+(key[(p&3)^e]^z)) )
long decode(long* v, long length, long* key) {
    unsigned long z, y=v[0], sum=0, e, DELTA=0x9e3779b9;
    long p, q ;
    q = 6 + 52/length;
    sum = q*DELTA;
    while (sum != 0) {
      e = (sum >> 2) & 3;
      for (p=length-1; p>0; p--)
        z = v[p-1], y = v[p] -= MX;
      z = v[length-1];
      y = v[0] -= MX;
      sum -= DELTA;
    }
    return 0;
}
```

(TEA was one of the cryptographic algorithms used in Microsoft's XBOX and a
target of one of the attacks [51,172].) If for some reason you can't find the code of
the decryptor statically (perhaps it's been obfuscated using some of the algorithms
in Chapter 4), you can instead try to search the instruction trace for telltale signs of
common decryption algorithms. This is what a trace of the inner for-loop in TEA
looks like, with all loads, stores, and arithmetic operations stripped out:

```
0x0804860b       cmpl   $0x0,0xfffffff0(%ebp)
0x0804860f       jg     0x8048589

0x08048589       mov    0x8(%ebp),%edx
0x08048592       shl    $0x2,%eax
0x080485a0       shl    $0x2,%eax
0x080485ab       shl    $0x2,%eax
0x080485ba       shr    $0x5,%edx
0x080485c0       shl    $0x2,%eax
0x080485c5       xor    %eax,%ecx
0x080485cc       shr    $0x3,%edx
0x080485d2       shl    $0x4,%eax
```

```
0x080485d5      xor     %edx,%eax
0x080485df      xor     %eax,%edx
0x080485e4      and     $0x3,%eax
0x080485e7      xor     0xffffffe8(%ebp),%eax
0x080485ea      shl     $0x2,%eax
0x080485f2      xor     0xffffffdc(%ebp),%eax
0x080485f8      xor     %ecx,%eax


0x0804860b      cmpl    $0x0,0xfffffff0(%ebp)
0x0804860f      jg      0x8048589
0x08048589      mov     0x8(%ebp), %edx
```

Maybe there's enough information here to create a dynamic signature for TEA that distinguishes it from ordinary code, or even from other cryptographic algorithms? The trace starts with several shifts with small constant arguments that could be a possible starting point for analysis.

2.1.6.8 Differential Attacks Now suppose you could get your hands on two versions of the player executable, each fingerprinted with a different 32-bit number, but otherwise identical. That is, the only difference in the source code between the two version is this:

```
30    asm volatile (
31       "jmp L1                   \n\t"
32       ".align 4                 \n\t"
33       ".long      0xb0b5b0b5\n\t"
34       "L1:                      \n\t"
35    );
```

```
30    asm volatile (
31       "jmp L1                   \n\t"
32       ".align 4                 \n\t"
33       ".long      0xada5ada5\n\t"
34       "L1:                      \n\t"
35    );
```

Figure 2.1▶82 shows the output of using the VBinDiff [238] program to compare the resulting executable files. You can easily find the location of the fingerprints and even destroy them, since VBinDiff also works as a hex editor.

Differential attacks like this are not only useful against differently fingerprinted programs. Anytime you have access to different versions of the same program—one version where a security hole has been patched and one where it hasn't, or one version where a feature is missing and one where it isn't, and so on—you can use differential techniques to find the locations of the interesting code bits.

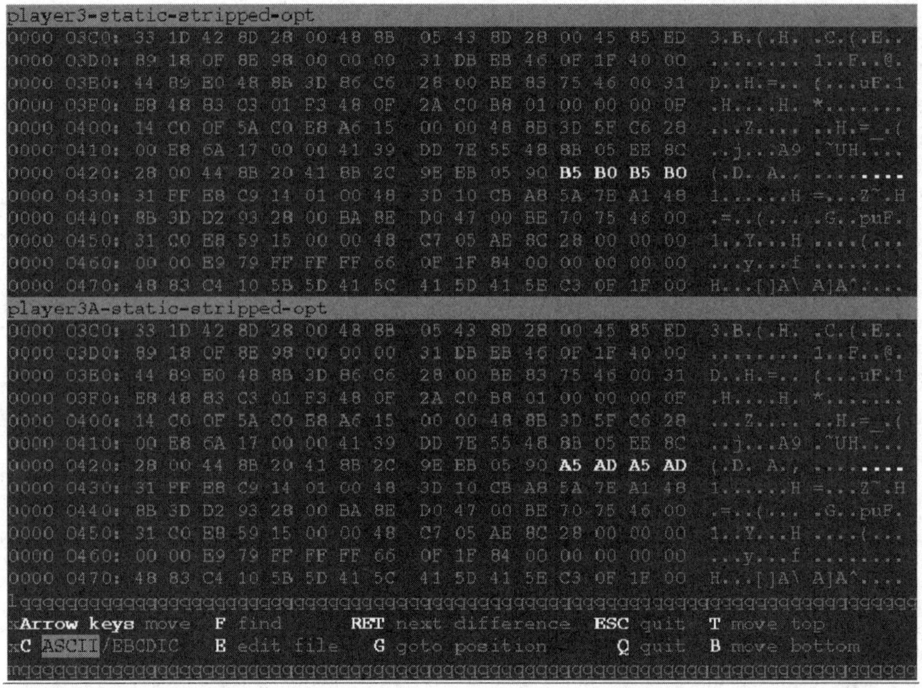

Figure 2.1 Using `VBinDiff` [238] to compare two differently fingerprinted versions of the player executable.

Tools like `VBinDiff` compare the *static* code of two executables. This works well when the programs are organized about the same and the overall differences are minor. If you're faced with a program that has undergone major changes, you can instead run the two versions in parallel, feeding them the same input and comparing their execution paths. This is known as *relative debugging*, and you'll see more of that in Section 3.2.1 ▶ 146.

2.1.6.9 Recovering Algorithms Through Decompilation Your ultimate task is to recover the algorithms used in the DRM player, perhaps to be able to build your own. As an accomplished cracker, you're certainly adept at reading assembly code, but to simplify your life, you'd much prefer wading through tons of unfamiliar code in a high-level language than tons of unfamiliar code in assembly! So you enlist the help of a decompiler. Here, we're going to use `REC 2.1` [330].

To make the task a little more interesting, let's assume that the program has been statically linked and stripped, so there are no symbols available. You can see the result of the decompilation in Listings 2.2►84 and 2.3►85. We've edited the code just a little to make it more readable and fit on the page. The complete program consists of 104341 assembly code statements that decompiles into 90563 lines of non-comment, non-blank C source. Since the program has been statically linked and stripped, all referenced library functions have been linked in and will appear in the decompiled source.

We're only showing the relevant functions from the player. In this particular case, finding the user functions in the decompiled source was easy! Knowing the behavior of the player, you had some idea of what they might look like, and since both `hash` and `play` use C's `xor` operator (unusual in most code), all you had to do was a textual search for "^"!

The control flow is surprisingly readable, although the code is missing type information that would preclude the program from being recompiled without hand editing. The decompiler was confused by the inserted assembly code (dotted in Listing 2.1►62), which is missing from the decompiled source. Notice that since the DRM player was compiled at the highest level of optimization, the `hash` and `die` functions have been inlined.

2.1.7 Discussion

Ideally, what you would like to come out of the discussion in this section is a model, a *threat model*, that describes what the adversary can and cannot do, how he's likely to behave and not to behave, what tools he's likely to use and not use, what motivates him and what doesn't, what he finds easy and what he finds difficult, and so on. You could then use this model to design your defenses in ways that would counteract that threat.

So what can we say about the prototypical cracker? Well, we've seen that he can:

- Pattern match on static code (to find the location of strings or well-known library functions),
- Pattern match on execution patterns (to find the location of well-known algorithms, such as cryptographic functions),
- Relate external program behavior to internal code locations (to find the location of protection code),
- Disassemble binary machine code,
- Decompile binary code even though the result will be partial and at times incorrect,

Listing 2.2 Decompilation of the play function from the DRM player in Listing 2.1▸62. The shading corresponds to that of Listing 2.1▸62. Continued in Listing 2.3▸85.

```
 1   L080482A0(A8, Ac, A10) {
 2       ebx = A8;
 3       esp = "Please enter activation code: ";
 4       eax = L080499C0();
 5       V4 = ebp - 16;
 6       *esp = 0x80a0831;
 7       eax = L080499F0();
 8       eax = *(ebp - 16);
 9       if(eax != *L080BE2CC) {
10           V8 = "wrong code";
11           V4 = 0x80a082c;
12           *esp = *L080BE704;
13           eax = L08049990();
14           *L080BE2C8 = 0;
15       }
16       eax = *L080BE2C8;
17       edi = 0;
18       ebx = ebx ^ *L080BE2C4;
19       *eax = ebx;
20       eax = A10;
21       if(eax <= 0) {} else {
22           while(1)
23               esi = *(Ac + edi * 4);
24   L08048368:   *esp = 0;
25               if(L08056DD0() > 1521011472) {
26                   V8 = "expired";
27                   V4 = 0x80a082c;
28                   *esp = *L080BE704;
29                   L08049990();
30                   *L080BE2C8 = 0;
31               }
32               ebx = ebx ^ esi;
33               (save)0;
34               edi = edi + 1;
35               (save)ebx;
36               esp = esp + 8;
37               V8 = *esp;
38               V4 = "%f\n"; *esp = *L080C02C8;
39               eax = L08049990();
40               eax = *L080C02C8;
41               *esp = eax;
42               eax = L08049A20();
43               if(edi == A10)   {goto L080483a7;}
44               eax = *L080BE2C8; ebx = *eax;
45           }
46           ch = 176; ch = 176;
47           goto L08048368;
48       }
49   L080483a7:
50   }
```

Listing 2.3 Decompilation of the `player.main` function from the DRM player in Listing 2.1▸62. The player was compiled with `gcc -03`, which accounts for the inlining of the call to `hash`. Continued from Listing 2.2▸84.

```
54   L080483AF(A8, Ac) {
55      ...
56      ecx = 0x8048260;
57      edx = 0x8048230;
58      eax = *L08048230;
59      if(0x8048260 >= 0x8048230) {
60         do {
61            eax = eax ^ *edx;
62            edx = edx + 4;
63         } while(ecx >= edx);
64      }
65      if(eax != 318563869) {
66         V8 = "tampered";
67         V4 = 0x80a082c;
68         *esp = *L080BE704;
69         L08049990();
70         *L080BE2C8 = 0;
71      }
72      V8 = A8 - 2;
73      V4 = ebp + -412;
74      *esp = *(ebp + -416);
75      return(L080482A0());
76   }
```

- Debug binary code without access to source code,
- Compare (statically or dynamically) two closely related versions of the same program (to find the location of fingerprints),
- Modify the program's execution environment (to force it to use deviant dynamic libraries, search paths, operating system functionality, and so on),
- Modify the executable (to remove unwanted behavior or add new behavior).

Not all of these techniques are applicable to every situation, of course, and some may be more or less easy to apply. Generally speaking, the attacker will, by trial and error, home in on the protection code by first trying simple techniques and, over time, trying more and more sophisticated ones.

The algorithms in this book have been designed to hamper one or more of these attack categories. The static obfuscation algorithms in Chapter 4 (Code Obfuscation), for example, are designed to make static pattern-matching attacks more difficult. They don't fare so well against a dynamic pattern-matching attack, however, which is why the algorithms in Chapter 6 (Dynamic Obfuscation) were invented. The algorithms in Chapter 7 (Software Tamperproofing) have been designed to make modifications of the executable more difficult.

In this section we've concentrated on attacking binary executables. It's worth noting that many of the problems the attacker faces go away when the target is instead a typed architecture-neutral format, such as Java bytecode. In particular, accurate disassembly is trivial, accurate decompilation is always possible, and references to dynamic libraries are always exposed.

The tools we showed you in this section are very mainstream and very simple. Not only are there more powerful tools in common use among the cracker l33t (the IDA Pro [307] interactive disassembler and debugger and the SoftICE kernel mode debugger are both mainstays in the cracker community), it's also common for crackers to build their *own* specialized tools. For example, in Section 3.2.1 ▸146 we'll show you a germ of a Linux debugger that could be specialized to perform common cracking tasks such as tracing system calls (a function gdb doesn't provide). You could also use it to build a simple code coverage tool that would be useful for checking that your test cases have adequately covered the program after your crack.

The type of challenge program you saw in Listing 2.1 ▸62 is known in the cracking community as a *crackme*. There are Internet sites devoted to building and solving such exercises. The site http://crackmes.de, for example, has (as of September 2008) 14,646 registered users and 2,126 posted crackmes.

2.2 Defense Strategies

So far you've learned about various ways in which an attacker can analyze your program to find (and maybe destroy) a secret you've stored in it. The techniques range from stepping through the program, instruction by instruction, with a debugger; running it under emulation; and decompiling it to more easily digested source code. However, assuming that you're one of the good guys, the question that you really want this book to answer is how to *protect* your program from such attacks.

As you read this book, you will see a few basic ideas reappearing many times in different guises. For us, it's been interesting to discover that these ideas are neither new nor limited to use in software: Since the dawn of time, plants and animals have developed surreptitious techniques for protecting themselves from predators, and over thousands of years, humans have developed surreptitious techniques for protecting ourselves from the environment and from each other. In this present part of the book we'll show you a model [84] that tries to capture these ideas and apply them to software protection. The goal is to identify a set of primitives that you can use to protect secrets, and to use these primitives in the rest of the book to model and classify software protection schemes that have been proposed in the literature. Hopefully, the model will also provide a uniform language for researchers and practitioners, making it easier to discuss existing protection schemes and to invent new ones.

Whenever you see a proposal for a new protection scheme, you will want to go back to the model to classify it. Ideally, you'll then be able to say, "This scheme is a simple variant of this other, previously published scheme," or "This is a novel combination of two known schemes, and I predict it will have the following properties." Less ideal, but still useful, is if you can say, "This scheme doesn't fit into the model—it therefore represents something entirely new, well worthy of further study—but potentially requiring us to reconsider the design of the model itself." We would be happiest, of course, if the model were also able to *predict* new ways of protecting software. If you could say, "Hmm, what I need is a scheme that has the following properties" and from the model be able to deduce that "I should be able to create a scheme with the required properties by combining these two primitives in this particular way," then the model would be truly useful.

The model we propose in this chapter has yet to reach that level of maturity. It will, however, serve us well in the remainder of the book as a uniform means of talking about and classifying the schemes that can be found in the literature.

We have sought inspiration for our model from defense mechanisms found in nature, from the way humans have protected themselves from each other and from the elements, and, of course, from the design of current software protection schemes. After all, while it would be nice if our model were complete enough to encompass the defense mechanisms of Puffy the Pufferfish (we believe it is), this is a book about software protection, not biology, and our primary goal is to be able to talk consistently about obfuscation, watermarking, and so on.

2.2.1 Notation

The central concept in our model is the *Frame*, a knowledge representation device well known in the AI community. A protection strategy takes a frame representing a universe with an unprotected secret and transforms it into a frame representing a universe in which the secret has been protected. Protection strategies are thus functions mapping frames to frames.

We use a graphical notation to illustrate frames and frame transformations. Here's a universe containing two objects, Alice and her purse:

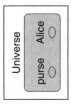

A frame consists of one or more *slots*, which are *name=value* pairs. A value can be a string, an integer, another frame, a *reference* to another frame, or a tuple (pair of values). Slots can be atomic (take one value) or multi-valued. Here, Alice (represented by a frame within the universe) has two slots, one for her name and one for her age:

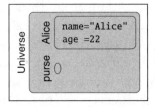

A special multi-valued slot is the `contains` slot, which, when present, indicates that a particular object contains other objects. In our graphical notation, the `contains` slot is represented by boxes within boxes. Here, the universe itself contains two objects (Alice and her purse), and the purse contains a wallet that, in turn, contains a coin:

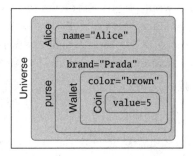

Finally, each slot can also have associated with it a set of *demons*. These are actions that fire under certain circumstances. For example, to protect its young, the Cane toad (*Bufo marinus*) lays eggs that are poisonous. We would represent this form of protection with a demon attached to a toad egg, saying, "When eaten then cause harm to attacker." This is represented by a double arrow (⇒):

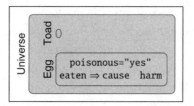

Consider the Leatherback turtle (*Dermochelys coriacea*), which buries its eggs in the sand to protect them from predators and the elements. To model this protection strategy, we start out with an initial, unprotected scenario, a frame where the universe contains a *turtle*, *sand*, and *eggs*. We then apply the **cover** protection primitive (we'll get to this in the next section), which transforms the universe into one where the sand slot now holds the turtle-eggs frame. The result is a situation where a predator can no longer see the turtle eggs, since they are covered by sand:

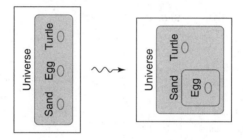

Plants, animals, and humans seldom use a single method of protection, but rather employ what's known as *defense-in-depth*. For example, even if you diligently lock your car door, you probably don't rely on it as the sole means of protecting against car theft. Maybe you put on a steering wheel lock, maybe you have a car alarm, or maybe you've installed a vehicle tracking device that allows the police to locate the car in case it does get stolen. Or maybe you're paranoid enough or own a vehicle expensive enough to warrant simultaneously employing *all* these defenses. Layering protection mechanisms in this way makes sense when you don't have complete faith in any one method, or when the object you're trying to protect is very valuable. In our model, defense-in-depth is modeled by *function composition* of the frame transformations:

Primitive 2.1 (compose f g**).**   Compose primitives f and g.

$$(f \circ g)(x) = f(g(x))$$

You can download a Haskell implementation of the model from this book's Web site. The implementation does rudimentary type checking and also generates the graphic representations that you find in this section.

In the remainder of this section, we will present our set of protection operators and give examples of how animals use these strategies to protect themselves from predators, how humans use them to protect precious artifacts, and how they can be applied to protect secrets in software.

2.2.2 The *cover* Primitive

The most fundamental way of hiding an object is to *cover* it with another object. This may seem like a trivial observation (and OK, we agree it is), but covering is an operation that occurs frequently in the natural, human, and computer domains. To illustrate, say that right now your boss is entering your office and, in a classic *Mad Magazine* shtick, you hide that you're reading this book by covering it with a copy of *Playboy*. You can represent this as a transformation on an environment consisting of the items in your universe, namely, you, your boss, this book, and a copy of a magazine:

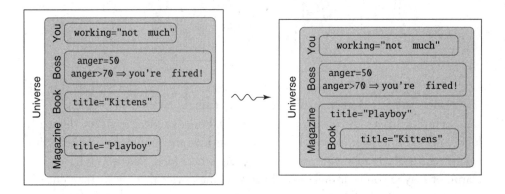

In this scenario, *You* are the good guy, protecting a precious object (a book called *Kittens*) from being discovered by the adversary (the *Boss*). The transformation shows that your protection scheme uses a fourth object in the universe (the *Magazine*) inside which you hide the book. This is a confidentiality scenario—you're protecting a valuable piece of information (that you're in possession of a particular book) from discovery by an adversary who has the ability to harm you (in this case, fire you).

Covering, like we said, is probably both the simplest and the most common way of protecting an object. The Leatherback turtle buries its eggs in the sand to protect them from predators and the elements; you write your password on a sticky note and put it in a drawer, or you first put the sticky note in an envelope and *then* put it in a drawer (for two levels of protection). In all these cases, you are using one object to cover or hold another, and this is the essence of the **cover** transformation:

Primitive 2.2 (**cover** x y U).   Given two frames x and y, make x an element contained in y.

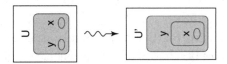

An historical example of covering occurred in 499 B.C., when, to instigate a revolt against the Persians, Histiaeus tattooed a message on the shaved head of a slave, waited for the hair to grow back, and sent the slave to his son-in-law Aristagoras, who simply had to shave the slave's head again to read the message [186]:

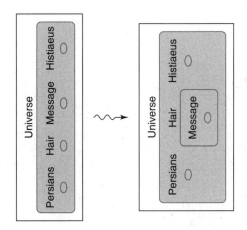

In this example, the good guy (Histiaeus) is using covering to ensure that the message could not be read by the bad guys (the Persians).

What can the boss do to see if you're actually working? Well, he can *uncover* the book by removing the magazine. Similarly, a predator who preys on the eggs of the Leatherback turtle can get to them by removing the sand that covers them. And, in a scene we've seen too many times in cop movies, the police can enter your office with a warrant and with a "Let's tear this place apart, men!" go through every drawer until your secret password has been uncovered. This scenario makes an important point: While covering is easy for the defender (she just has to find something big enough to cover the secret with) it's harder for the attacker, since he has to go through *every* object in the environment to see if it covers the secret: Your boss has to look under every object in the environment to see if it covers contraband reading material, birds have to dig everywhere along the beach to find where the turtle eggs are hidden, the cops have to look inside every drawer for your password, and so on.

To make our point, the examples in this section are all idealized. In practice, a defender may leave behind clues (such as scents or tracks, in the case of the turtle scenario) that make life easier for the attacker. A turtle species that lays their eggs on the same spot on the same beach, year after year, will face extinction once predators are clued in to this behavior. Unless, of course, the turtles realize the threat and modify their defenses (using other defense primitives you'll soon see) to counter the attacks.

It's often easy to apply the **cover** transformation multiple times for greater defense-in-depth. For example, after putting the book inside the *Playboy* magazine, you could sit on them both, requiring the boss to perform two uncovering operations to recover the book:

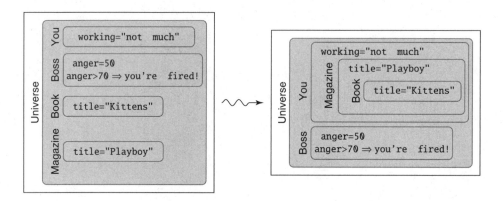

It may initially not be obvious what the analogy of one object covering another in the software world is. In the real world, you cover an object when you put it inside another. In the software world, you can cover a file or some data by putting it inside another file. For example, when mail systems initially began scanning attachments for viruses, virus writers responded by zipping (and occasionally encrypting) the virus before emailing it. The zip-file serves as a cover for the virus itself:

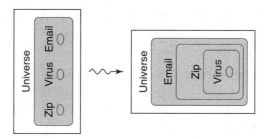

Here, the virus (which in this scenario considers itself the "good guy"!) covers itself first inside a zip-file and then inside an email message in order to protect itself from discovery by the virus scanner. To counter this cover, mail servers today try to "look under" possible covers by unpacking and scanning archives (including archives containing archives) to find potential viruses.

A more obvious instance of covering being used is in systems that use hardware to protect software. For example, the military uses hardened boxes in which they stick the computers on which the sensitive software is run. The security goals here are not just to protect the confidentiality of the program but also to protect its integrity and availability. For example, you can't allow the enemy to modify your missile's targeting software (it may lead the missile astray), you can't give him access to the software's source code (he could reuse it in his own weapons), and you can't allow him to interfere with the operation of the software (or we can't fire the missile at him, when needed). In these types of scenarios, covering is typically combined with tamperproofing in such a way that the precious object will be made to explode[3] if someone tries to muck with it. We'll be using the **detect-respond** primitive to model such tamperproofing.

2.2.3 The *duplicate* Primitive

The **duplicate** primitive simply makes a copy of an existing object and adds it to the universe. This operation can be used in two different ways. First, you can use the copy as a *decoy*. The idea is to either make the environment larger in order to force the attacker to consider more items while searching for a secret, or to draw attention away from the real secret. The other use of **duplicate**, *reduplication*, is to add a copy of the secret itself to the universe in order to force an attacker to destroy both copies.

---

3. What military types term "rapid disassembly."

If your goal is to protect the confidentiality of an object, then reduplication is not a good idea—the more copies there are of an object, the easier it is for the adversary to find one! Decoying would be useful, however, since it draws attention away from the object itself. If the goal is instead to protect the integrity of the object, then reduplication is a good strategy—the more copies there are of an object, the greater the chance that at least one will remain intact after an attack.

Here's the definition of the **duplicate** primitive:

Primitive 2.3 (duplicate x_U**).**   Given a frame x, create a deep copy of x, renaming as necessary to keep names unique:[4]

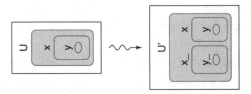

In the animal kingdom, reduplication and decoying are both common protection strategies. An animal low on the food chain will often use reduplication to protect itself, or rather, its own DNA. For example, the Pufferfish (of the *Tetraodontidae* family) spawns 200,000 offspring in the hope that at least *some* will survive and carry on its parents' legacy.

The California newt (*Taricha torosa*) combines duplication, covering, and tamperproofing to protect its progeny. The newt lays 7 to 30 eggs, each covered by a gel-like membrane containing tarichatoxin, for which no known antidote exists.

Scientists are still unsure exactly why zebras have stripes, but one favorite theory suggests that they are used as part of a decoying strategy: When a zebra is running in a herd of similarly striped animals it's difficult for a lion to pick out one individual to attack. As we'll see later, mimicking is another possible explanation.

Decoys are, of course, common in human warfare: "In World War II, the U.S. created an entire dummy army unit in southern Britain to convince the Germans that the Normandy invasion would be directed toward the Pas-de-Calais" and during Gulf War I, the Iraqis "employed mock tanks, airplanes, bunkers and artillery" made up of "plywood, aluminum and fiber glass [sic]" [353].

A well-known legend states that the recipe for Coca-Cola is protected by reduplicating it over three people, none of whom may ever travel on the same plane:

---

4. To make our model simple, we require all names to be globally unique.

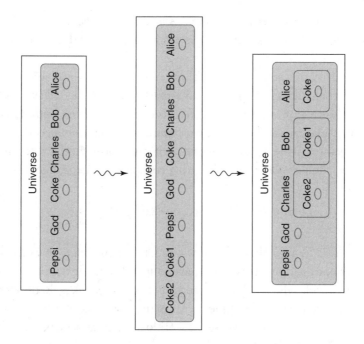

Here we've applied the **duplicate** primitive twice and the **cover** primitive three times, resulting in a situation where the good guys (the three Coca-Cola executives Alice, Bob, and Charles) are each holding a copy of the recipe in their pockets. The bad guys in this case are God, who presumably can cause random acts of destruction such as the downing of aircraft, and Pepsi, who would love to get their grubby hands on their competitor's crown jewels. Thus, in this scenario, you want to ensure the availability of the recipe (reduplication increases the odds that least one copy will survive destruction through acts of God) *and* confidentiality (Pepsi spies will have a harder time locating the recipe when it's hidden in the executives' pockets).

In the recent TV miniseries *Traffic*, terrorists attempt to smuggle the smallpox virus into the United States. The authorities are conned into believing that the small-pox will enter the country inside a shipping container with a particular identification number, but they are forced into a nationwide hunt once they realize that the ter-rorists have shipped several containers with *the same number*! This is a classic use of decoying, but later in this section you will see how the terrorists combined this ruse with the **advertise** primitive to further confuse the DEA.

As you see here, our notion of who is the "good guy" and who is the "bad guy" can be very fluid! In the terrorist example above, the good guys are the terrorists, the bad guys the DEA, and the object in need of protection is the deadly smallpox virus!

So in general, the good guy is whoever has a secret or precious object to protect, and the bad guy is whoever wants to discover the secret or destroy or acquire the precious object.

In watermarking scenarios, your security goal is to ensure availability—you want to make sure that at least one of your watermarks survives the attacker's deliberate attempts at destruction or disruption. To this end, you can use both decoying and reduplication. Decoys can be used by software watermarking algorithms to draw attention away from the actual watermark, if only for a short while. In the very simplest case, you just add a variable with a conspicuous name, like this:

```
int THE_WATERMARK_IS_HERE = 42;
```

You could also add a number of fake watermarks, some really obvious, some less so, with the hope that the attacker will have to spend valuable time examining them all, having to decide which one is real and which ones are fakes. Reduplication can also be useful. If you embed multiple copies of the mark (possibly by using different embedding algorithms), you increase the workload of the attacker, because he needs to locate and destroy all copies of the mark.

In code obfuscation, cloning is also a common operation. For example, you could clone a function f into f', obfuscate f' into f'', and modify some of f's call sites to call f''. This gives the appearance that calls to f and f'' actually call different functions, both of which the attacker will need to analyze in order to gain a full understanding of the program. You can similarly clone a basic block B into B', obfuscate into B'', and alternate between executing the two blocks: if $P^?$ then B else B''. $P^?$ is an *opaque predicate* that arbitrarily chooses between the two blocks at runtime. You will read more about this idea in Section 4.3.4 ▶235.

2.2.4 The *split* and *merge* Primitives

Splitting and merging are two common protection transformations, particularly in software situations where they are simple to implement. Splitting can be used to ensure confidentiality by breaking up a secret into smaller parts, each of which is easier to hide or protect than the whole secret. Here's the definition:

Primitive 2.4 (split z f U**).**   Given a predicate f and a frame z, create a new frame z₋, so that z₋ has all the properties of z, and $\forall x \in$ z; $f(x) = true$ ● move x to z₋:

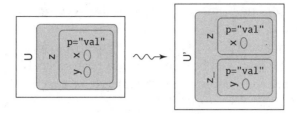

The **merge** primitive blends two unrelated objects together to make it appear as if they belong together:

Primitive 2.5 (merge s t U**).**   Given two frames s and t, $\forall x \in t \bullet$ move x to s, merging properties with the same name, then remove t:

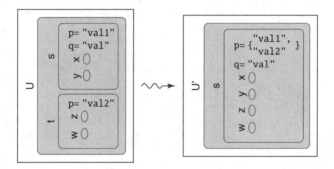

To create mass confusion, splitting and merging are often used in conjunction: Take two unrelated objects A and B and split them into parts A_1, A_2, B_1, and B_2, then merge A_1 with B_1 and A_2 with B_2.

In the animal kingdom, some species will **split** themselves and let the attacker have one part for dinner. This is known as *autotomy* [101]. This technique is particularly useful when the species is also able to *regenerate* the lost part. In our classification, this is a form of tamperproofing that we will discuss further in Section 2.2.10▶110.

Squirrels use so-called *scatter hoarding* to **split** up the food they've gathered and cache it at different locations in their territory. The larger gray squirrel is known to steal the caches of the European red squirrel, but the **split** makes it less likely that all the food will be lost.

Human organizations frequently split themselves up into groups to prevent an adversary from destroying the entire organization in one attack. This is true, for example, of terrorist networks that split themselves up into smaller, autonomous cells. Each cell is less conspicuous than the whole network, and an attack (be it from an outside force or an inside informant) will affect only the cell itself, not the network as a whole.

You will see watermarking algorithms that **split** the mark into several smaller pieces, so that each piece can be embedded less conspicuously. Merging is also a natural operation, since the watermark object has to be attached to some language structure already in the program.

Echo hiding is an audio watermarking technique in which short echoes (short enough to be undetectable to the human ear) are used to embed marks. A really short echo encodes a 0, and a longer one encodes a 1. In our model, embedding a single-bit watermark wm is accomplished by a) settling on an embedding location p, b) duplicating D_0 samples for a 0 and D_1 samples for a 1 from p, and c) merging the copy back into the clip. In this embedding example, where $D_0 = 2$ and $D_1 = 3$, we embed a watermark wm=0 at position $p = 2$ by first copying two samples 0x20,0x30 from position p and inserting them to form a short echo:

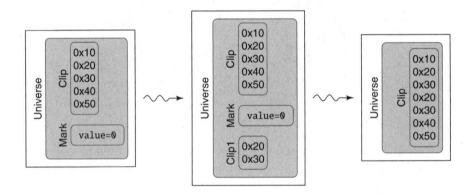

Obfuscation algorithms make extensive use of splitting and merging to break up, scatter, and merge pieces of a program, thereby creating confusion. For example, to confuse someone trying to reverse engineer a program containing two functions f and g, each can be split into two parts (yielding f_a, f_b, g_a, g_b), and then the parts can be merged together, forming two new functions $f_a||g_b$ and $f_b||g_a$. Any calls to f or g will have to be modified, of course, to call the new functions, and to call them in such a way that only the relevant parts are executed.

Two common protection strategies are *shrink* and *expand*. Shrinking oneself to become as small as possible makes it easier to hide in the environment. Expanding, on the other hand, is the operation of making oneself as large as possible, larger objects being harder to destroy than smaller ones. Shrink and expand are just variants of **split** and **merge**, however, so we don't include them as primitive operations.

An object shrinks itself by splitting into two parts, one essential and one superfluous, and deleting the fluff by releasing it into the environment. Expansion, similarly, is merging yourself with some material you grabbed from the environment.

The Pufferfish uses a combination of several defense strategies. One is to expand its size (by inflating itself with water from its surroundings) in order to appear threatening or a less easy target to an attacker. The blue whale has grown so big that it only has one natural predator, the Orca.

That *size* is an important feature of hiding or protecting a secret is evident from the expression "as hard as finding a needle in a haystack." Implicit in this expression is that the needle is small and the haystack big. Hiding the Seattle Space Needle in a normal-size haystack would be hard, as would hiding a sewing needle in a stack consisting of three pieces of hay. So a common strategy for hiding something is to shrink it, much as a spy compresses a page of text to a microdot. This is often combined with decoying, increasing the size of the environment, for example, by using a really big haystack to hide the needle in or by hiding the microdot in the Bible instead of in the 264 words of the Gettysburg Address. Expansion is, of course, also a common human strategy. A bigger vault is harder to break into than a smaller one, a bigger bunker requires a bigger bomb to destroy it, and in a crash between an SUV and a VW Beetle, we all know which driver will walk away unscathed.

You can also hide your password by merging it with similar, but less important, items on a list:

```
          Groceries  *wink*

          ---------------

          *   Toblerone
          *   m1lk&h0ney
          *   cheese
          *   vegemite
```

The principle behind LSB (Least Significant Bit) image watermark embedding is that the low-order bits of an image are (more or less) imperceptible to humans and can be replaced with the watermarking bits. In our model, this is a **split** (shrinking the image to get rid of the imperceptible fluff) followed by a **merge** of the watermarking bits.

It is important to not keep passwords or cryptographic keys in cleartext in computer memory. An attacker who gets access to your machine can search through memory for telltale signs of the secret: A 128-bit crypto key, for example, has much higher entropy than ordinary data and will be easy to spot [325]. There are two simple ways of fixing this problem: Either increase the entropy of the data surrounding the key (for example, by encrypting it) or decrease the entropy of the key itself. The latter can be accomplished, for example, by splitting the key into several smaller pieces that are then spread out over the entire program. Thus, this is a composition of the **split** primitive and the **reorder** primitive, which we'll examine next.

2.2.5 The *reorder* Primitive

The **reorder** transformation can be used to place objects in a random order, thereby sowing confusion. But a reordering can also *contain* information. Think of Agent 007 entering a room and finding that the gorgeous blonde Russian operative Tatiana Romanova, who was just abducted, left him a message: The Martini glass has been moved to the *left* of the Baretta, letting James know that he needs to be on the lookout for Blofeld, who, as usual, is up to nothing good. Here's the definition of the **reorder** primitive:

Primitive 2.6 (reorder z f U).   Given a frame z and a permutation function f, reorder the elements of z according to f:

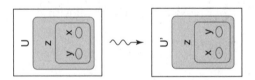

In various cons such as the *shell game* or *three-card monty*, the secret (the *pea* or the *queen*, respectively) is hidden from the victim by sequences of deft reorderings by the con man. These games also use the **dynamic** primitive to effect the continuous application of the reordering operation. You'll see this later on in the section.

Many watermarking algorithms, in media as well as software, make use of re-ordering to embed the mark. The idea is that a watermark number can be represented as a permutation of objects. For example, the WMDM software watermarking algorithm (Section 8.4.1 ▶488) embeds the watermark by permuting the basic blocks of a function's control flow graph. In this example, the watermark number 5 is embedded by ordering the permutations of the numbers [1 . . . 5]:

$$[1, 2, 3, 4, 5], [2, 1, 3, 4, 5], [2, 3, 1, 4, 5], [2, 3, 4, 1, 5], [2, 3, 4, 5, 1], \ldots$$

Picking the fifth permutation to reorder the basic blocks yeilds:

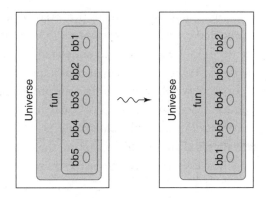

Of course, **reorder** can also be used as an attack. To destroy a watermark based on ordering, all the attacker has to do is apply the algorithm again, destroying the previous ordering at the same time he's inserting his own mark.

2.2.6   The *map* Primitive

The **map** primitive typically protects an object by adding confusion, translating every constituent component into something different. If the mapping function has an inverse, this obviously needs to be kept secret. Mapping can also be used to *insert* information. Here's the definition:

Primitive 2.7 (**map** x f U).   Given a frame x and a function f, replace every element of x with f(x):

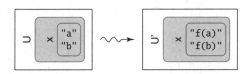

Translation is a form of mapping where every word *m* in a dictionary is replaced by another word *r*, usually in a different language, keeping the mapping secret. The Navajo Code Talkers are famous for their rôle in World War II, conveying messages in a language unfamiliar to the Japanese. Humans use this trick to confuse outsiders, or often to build cohesion among members of a group. Consider, for example, the 133t language used by youths in online communities. It sets them apart from others who don't know the language, but it also protects their communication from outsiders (such as their parents).

Obfuscated language mappings occur in many professional fields as well, including computer science, medicine, and law. Steven Stark [333] writes in the *Harvard Law Review* that "one need not be a Marxist to understand that jargon helps professionals to convince the world of their occupational importance, which leads to payment for service." In other words, obfuscating your professional language protects you from competition from other humans of equal intelligence who have not been initiated into your field. For example, patent lawyers attempt to strike a balance between language that is clear enough to capture the essence of an invention but obfuscated enough that they can later be hired to argue over its meaning in court.

The most obvious way to protect a secret is to not tell anyone about it! This is sometimes known as *security-through-obscurity*. An example is the layout of many medieval cities in the Middle East. It may seem that there is no good reason for their confusing alleyways until you realize that the lack of city planning can actually be a feature in the defense of the city. Without a map, only those who grew up in the city would know how to get around—an obvious problem for attackers. But this strategy only works in an environment with poor communications; as soon as there's a *Lonely Planet* guide to your city, your attempts to use secrecy to protect yourself will have failed.

To protect the confidentiality of algorithms, the simplest form of code obfuscation, name obfuscation, translates meaningful identifiers into meaningless ones:

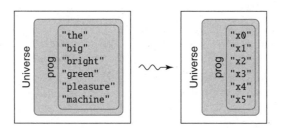

Here, we've transformed a program named `prog` containing six identifiers into an equivalent one where the identifiers have been renamed `x1,x2, . . . .` This leaks less information about the internals of the program.

A common way of watermarking English text is to keep a dictionary of synonyms, replacing a word with an equivalent one to embed a 0 or a 1:

Here, Alice has used a dictionary `Dict` that maps words to their synonyms to embed a 1 at position 2 in the text by replacing `"big"` by `"large"`. To protect the confidentiality of the mark she must prevent Bob from gaining access to the dictionary. In this case she uses the **cover** primitive to stick the dictionary in her pocket.

Cryptographers use the terms *confusion* and *diffusion* to describe properties of a secure cipher [326]. Confusion is often implemented by *substitution* (replacing one symbol of the plaintext with another symbol), which in our terminology is a mapping. Diffusion is implemented by *transposition* (rearranging the symbols), what we call reordering. A *product cipher* creates a secure cipher from compositions of simple substitutions and transpositions.

2.2.7 The *indirect* Primitive

In baseball, the coach uses hand signs to indicate to the batter whether to hit away, bunt, and so on. To prevent the opposing team from *stealing* the signs, the coach uses decoying as well as adding a level of indirection. The actual sign is merged with a sequence of bogus decoy signs and a special *indicator* sign. The indicator gives the location of the actual sign, typically the one following directly after the indicator. Here's the definition of the **indirect** primitive:

Primitive 2.8 (indirect x r U).   Given a frame x, add an indirect reference r to x:

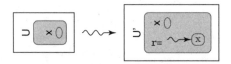

Here, you see the final syntactic addition to the model, the squiggly arrow that represents following a level of indirection.

As far as we've been able to find out, neither indirection or reordering occur as protection strategies in the animal world, maybe because these forms of surreption go beyond the animals' mental capacity.

Indirection is a common adventure movie plot device. In *National Treasure*, Nicolas Cage is led by a sequence of increasingly far-fetched clues (a frozen ship in the Arctic, a meerschaum pipe, the Declaration of Independence, a $100 bill, and so on), that each point to the next clue and then to the location of the hidden treasure (a Freemason temple).

Like our other primitives, indirection is often used in combination with other protection strategies. Our hero will find that the next clue is inside a box hidden under a rock (covering), that there are many boxes under many rocks (decoying), that the box will explode unless he unlocks it just the right way (tamperproofing), and that he needs to find *both* pieces of the clue in order to locate the treasure (splitting).

One of our particularly clever friends came up with the following scheme for protecting her foreign currency while backpacking around Europe. First, she sewed the different currencies (this was before the European Union adopted the euro) into different parts of her dress, a form of covering. Next, in order to remember where the Deutschmark, French francs, and so on, were hidden, she wrote down their locations on a piece of paper (indirection). Of course, if someone were to find this note she'd be in trouble, so she wrote it in French (mapping) using the Cyrillic alphabet (another mapping), banking on few common thieves being fluent in both Russian and French. She never lost any money.

Adding a level of indirection is also a common technique in protecting software, and we will see it used extensively both in obfuscation and watermarking. The idea is to replace a language construct (such as a variable or a function) by a reference to it. This adds a confusing level of indirection. Just like Nicolas Cage running around chasing one clue after another, an attacker analyzing a protected program would have to chase pointer-to-pointer-to-pointer until finally reaching the real object. Consider this example:

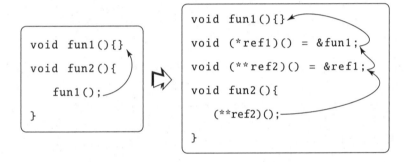

Here, we started out with two functions, fun1 and fun2, where fun2 contains one statement, a call to fun1. We applied the **indirect** primitive to add an indirect reference ref1, and then the **map** primitive to replace all references to fun1 by an indirect reference through ref1. We then repeated the process to force an attacker to unravel two levels of indirections. Here's the scheme:

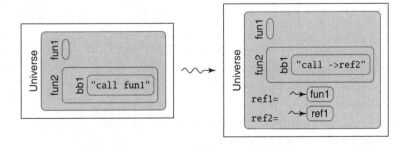

In Section 4.3.3 ▶229, you'll see code obfuscation algorithms that make use of indirection.

2.2.8 The *mimic* Primitive

Mimicry, of course, is the greatest form of flattery. You can use it in many different forms of protection. *Camouflage*, for example, is preventing discovery by looking like an object in your environment. Mimicry can also be a deterrent—you can try to look like someone or something you're not, to scare off attackers. In our model, the **mimic** primitive simply copies a property from one object to another:

Primitive 2.9 (**mimic** x y prop U).   Given two frames x and y, where x has a property prop, copy prop to y:

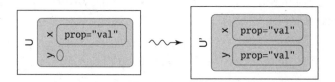

Cuttlefish have the ability to change color in order to, among other things, blend in with the environment. Many other animals avoid predators in a similar way. As we noted earlier, scientists are not sure exactly why the zebra has stripes. One theory is that lions (being color blind) cannot pick out a zebra from the background when it stands still in high grass, i.e., the zebra mimics its background. Another theory contends that the stripes confuse tsetse flies.

Peter Wayner's *mimic functions* [365] create new texts that steganographically encode a secret message. In order to not arouse suspicion, the texts are made so that they mimic texts found in our daily lives, such as transcripts of a baseball announcer, shopping lists, or even computer programs. If the mimicry is good, i.e., if the statistical properties of a generated text are close enough to those of real texts, then we will be able to send secret messages across the Internet without anyone noticing. In Section 8.8▶521, you'll see algorithms that embed secret messages in x86 binaries.

The same technique has been used by spies. For example, during World War II, Japanese spy Velvalee Dickinson wrote letters about her doll collection to addresses in neutral Argentina. When she was writing about dolls, she actually was talking about ship movements. She was eventually caught and jailed.

In 2004, during a vehicle search, Hungarian police found what appeared to be a fake Viagra tablet. Apart from being pink, it was rhombus shaped, had Pfizer imprinted on one side and VGR50 on the other—clearly a bad Viagra counterfeit.

However, further analysis revealed that the tablet was just mimicking Viagra and instead contained amphetamine:

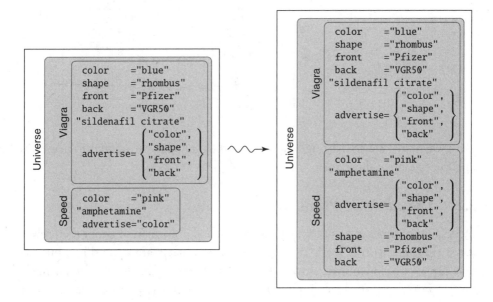

Here we've applied the **mimic** primitive three times, once for each attribute. Why the drug smugglers did not also mimic the highly recognizable blue color of Viagra tablets is hard to know, but it's possible that they thought that appearing to be a bad counterfeit would make it less likely for the tablet to be tested for illegal substances. The only secret the bad guys are keeping here is the fact that the fake pill contains an illegal substance. Everything else (the shape, color, and so on, of the pill) is out in the open, and we're using the **advertise** primitive to indicate that. You'll see more of **advertise** in the next section.

A central concept in surreptitious software is *stealth*. Any code that we introduce as a result of the protection process must fit in with the code that surrounds it, or it will leave telltale signs for the attacker to search for. In other words, the new code must **mimic** aspects of the original code written by humans. There can be many such aspects, of course: the size of the code, the instructions used, the nesting of control structures, and so on, and a stealthy protection algorithm must make sure that the introduced code mimics every aspect. By embedding a watermark in a modified cloned copy of an existing function, the WMMIMIT (Section 8.7.1 ▶505) software watermarking algorithm mimics the style of code already in the program, thereby increasing stealth. This is actually accomplished using a combination of the clone and the **map** primitives:

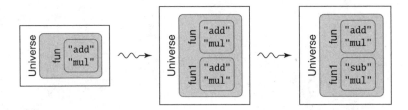

Here, we first clone an existing function and then **map** its instructions to new ones in order to embed the mark.

2.2.9 The *advertise* Primitive

By default, our model assumes that objects keep all information about themselves secret. In other words, Doris can see what other objects are around her, but she only knows their identities; she can't look *inside* them. This is how we normally protect ourselves: You may know that my wallet is in my pocket, but you can't see my address and phone number in the wallet, and so on, *unless I tell you* what they are. We call the primitive that breaks this secrecy **advertise**. In our model, it is represented by a special property advertise that lists the names of the properties visible to the outside:

Primitive 2.10 (advertise x prop U).   Given a frame x with a property prop, add a property advertise (if not already present) to x with the value prop:

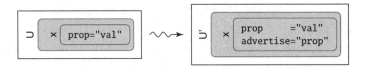

A common use of this primitive is to advertise the strength of my defenses in the hope that you will stay away. Toxic species often use bright colors to advertise their harmfulness. This is known as *aposematic coloration* [101].

There is nothing, of course, that says I must advertise *correct* information! In fact, a common use for this primitive is to lead an attacker astray by feeding him falsehoods. The non-poisonous scarlet kingsnake (*Lampropeltis triangulum elap-soides*), for example, protects itself by a combination of mimicry (copying the red-yellow-black striped coloration pattern of the highly poisonous coral snake) and false advertising (letting everyone know "Look, I'm poisonous!"), in the hope that this will make predators believe they should stay away:

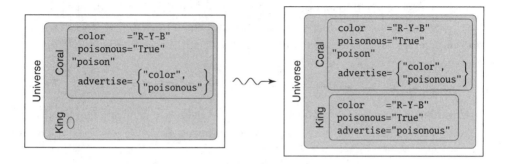

One way advertising helps defend an object is when the object identifies itself to its defenders. Flamingoes (*Phoenicopterus ruber ruber*) bring up their young in large crèches, but parents feed and take care of only their own chicks. The chicks **advertise** their appearance and vocalization. These characteristics allow parents to recognize and defend their own progeny. In software, similar birthmarks—unique characteristics of a program—allow an author to detect piracy by recognizing characteristics of his or her own programs in other software. You'll learn more about this in Chapter 10 (Software Similarity Analysis).

In many ways, **advertise** can be seen as the opposite of *security through obscurity*—rather than keeping our defenses secret, we openly display them to our adversary, taunting him to "go ahead, take your best shot!" In an ideal scenario, he will take one look at us, walk away disheartened, and launch an attack against a less well-defended target. In a less ideal scenario, knowing details of our defenses will allow him to find a chink in our armor—like a two-meter exhaust vent leading straight into the core of our Death Star, allowing anyone with a spare proton torpedo to reduce us to so much space debris.

We already mentioned the recent TV miniseries *Traffic*, where terrorists smuggle the smallpox virus into the United States, sending the authorities on a wild goose chase across the country hunting for the right container among several decoy containers with the same number. In the end, it turns out that the terrorists had used **advertise** ("The virus is in one of these containers *wink,wink*") to trick the DEA: *All* the containers were actually decoys, and the actual carriers of the virus were the illegal immigrants on board the cargo ship.

False advertising also works in the software protection domain. A program can advertise that it is watermarked when in fact it isn't, or can advertise that it is tamperproofed using a particular algorithm when in fact it is using another one.

2.2.10 The *detect-respond* Primitive

Tamperproofing has two parts, detecting that an attack has occurred and reacting to the attack. The reaction can be a combination of self-destructing (in whole or in part), destroying objects in the environment (including the attacker), or regenerating the tampered parts. In our model, x monitors the health of y, and if E should happen, executes tamper-response A:

Primitive 2.11 (detect-respond x E y A U). Given two frames x and y, add a demon to x that executes action A if event E happens to y.

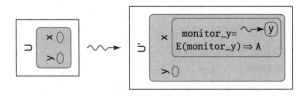

In the animal world, some species have developed the ability to *regenerate* destroyed parts of their bodies (usually limbs and tails, but in some cases even parts of internal organs) after an attack. Starfish, for example, can regrow their entire organism given just one arm and the central disk.

Puffy the Pufferfish uses a combination of several defense strategies: He can *expand* his body to appear threatening to an attacker, and an attacker who nevertheless starts munching on him will have to deal with the neurotoxins of his internal organs, a form of tamperproofing. It may not save Puffy's life, but it might save his brothers and sisters, since the attacker is either dead or has developed a distaste for Pufferfish-sashimi.

Turtles and many other animals use exoskeletons (a form of covering) to protect themselves. Some combine this with tamperproofing, using poisons to make themselves unpalatable once the protective layer has been removed by the predator. The Hawksbill turtle (*Eretmochelys imbricata*) has both a shell and poisonous flesh.

Humans using tamperproofing to protect themselves is common in movie plots: The terrorist straps explosives to his chest and holds a dead-man's trigger in his hand so that if our hero takes him out, everyone will die in the ensuing blast. Another common plot device is leaving an envelope containing compromising information about your nemesis with your lawyer, with instructions that "in the case of my untimely demise, mail this to the *Washington Post*."

The terrorist in the above scenario is *self-tamper-detecting* as well as *self-tamper-responding*. This seems to be the most common case: You monitor some part of yourself (the health of your internal organs, for example), and if tampering is evident, you execute the tamper response (releasing the trigger a split second before expiring). This is what it looks like in the model:

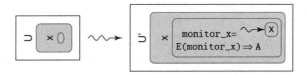

The *Washington Post* scenario above shows that both detection and response can be external, however: The lawyer examines the obituaries every day, and if your name shows up, executes the tamper-response.

Unlike lower-order animals like newts and salamanders, humans have very little regenerative power—we can only regrow some skin and a part of our liver.

Tamperproofing is, of course, an extremely important part of surreptitious software. We will spend all of Chapter 7 (Software Tamperproofing) discussing both how programs detect they've been tampered with and how they can retaliate in response to an attack. A common form of tamper-detection is to compare a hash computed over the program to the expected value. The TPCA (Section 7.2.1▶414) tamperproofing algorithm makes use of regeneration to fix parts of a program after an attack. The idea is to replace a destroyed part with a fresh copy:

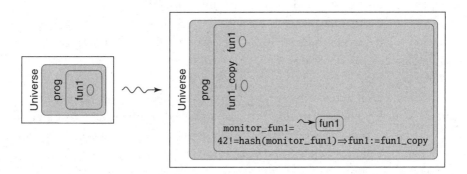

Other types of response are also common: A program can retaliate by (subtly or spectacularly) self-destructing or destroying files in its environment. For example, the *Display Eater* screen motion catcher program will delete your home directory if you try to use a pirated serial number [126].

2.2.11 The *dynamic* Primitive

Our final primitive, **dynamic**, is used to model protection techniques that use dynamic behavior to throw off an attacker. Here, *continuous change* itself is used to confuse an attacker. The change can take a variety of forms: fast movement, unpredictable movement, and continuous evolution of defenses. The **dynamic** primitive is a higher-order function that takes a frame x and a function f as argument, and iteratively generates $\langle fx, f(fx), f(f(fx))), \dots \rangle$:

> **Primitive 2.12** (**dynamic** f x U).   Given a frame x, form an infinite sequence of frames by repeatedly applying primitive f:
>
> $$fx \rightsquigarrow f(fx) \rightsquigarrow f(f(fx)) \rightsquigarrow \cdots$$

Moving faster than your adversary is, in many ways, the ultimate protection technique in the animal world. If the cheetah can't catch you, he can't eat you! There is a trade-off between agility and speed, on the one hand, and physical layers of protection, on the other. A turtle can afford to be slow because he's carrying around a thick protective exoskeleton. The Pronghorn antelope (*Antilocapra americana*) has made a different trade-off: It can run 60 miles/h to get away from a predator such as the mountain lion, which is only able to do 40 miles/h. On the other hand, the antelope is soft and vulnerable on the outside and tasty on the inside, and should he get caught, it's game over.

Anyone who has tried to kill a particularly annoying fly knows that while speed is important, so is agility and unpredictability. In fact, the fruit fly (*Drosophila melanogaster*) flies in a sequence of straight-line segments separated by 90-degree turns that it can execute in less than 50 milliseconds. Since the movements appear completely random, a predator (you) will have to be very lucky and persistent to get the best of him.

Evolution itself is, of course, an exercise in continuous change. As prey develop better defenses, predators develop better attacks. HIV is one example of a particularly successful organism: Because of its fast replication cycle and high mutation rate, a patient will experience many virus variants during a single day. This makes it difficult for the immune system to keep up and for scientists to develop effective vaccines.

Mobility is key in modern warfare. During the Gulf War, Iraqi forces successfully moved Scud missiles around on *transporter-erector-launcher* trucks to avoid detection by coalition forces: "Even in the face of intense efforts to find and destroy them, the mobile launchers proved remarkably elusive and survivable." [194] Just as the Pronghorn antelope and the turtle have made trade-offs on the scale from *slow-but-impenetrable* to *fast-but-vulnerable*, so have military forces.

Just like in the natural virus world, change is used in the computer virus world to foil detection. A computer virus that modifies itself for every new generation will stress the capabilities of the virus detector: It has to find some signature of the virus that does not change between mutations.

Many of the algorithms that we will see in this book are dynamic, in one form or another. Aucsmith's tamperproofing algorithm OBFAG$_{swap}$ (Section 6.2.2▶366), for example, first breaks up a program into chunks that are then encrypted. One chunk is decrypted, executed, re-encrypted, swapped with another chunk, and the process repeats:

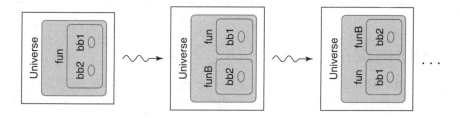

(Here, we're not modeling the encryption. This could be done with the **map** primitive.) This process results in an unpredictable address trace that an attacker will find difficult to follow, making the code hard to tamper with.

2.2.12 Discussion

The problem with a classification exercise such as the one you've just seen is that it's impossible to prove that the model is complete. There's always the possibility that you'll happen upon a protection scheme that doesn't fit into the model in any natural way. This model is fairly new (we first presented it in 2007), and so it has yet to be thoroughly vetted.

We therefore invite you to come up with scenarios that can't be expressed using the primitives, or to show that a particular primitive can be simulated by a combination of others, and thus eliminated. However, keep in mind that while any Turing complete model would do, the goal here isn't to come up with a minimalist set of primitives. Rather, the goal is to find a set of primitives that elegantly expresses how the natural world has evolved protection strategies, how we as humans think about protecting ourselves, and most important, of course, how we can protect computer programs.

Problem 2.1   Can you extend the model to incorporate attacks as well as defenses? Intuitively, attacking a protection scheme based on defense-in-depth means "peeling off" successive layers of protection. Thus, for every defense primitive of the model you need to add a corresponding attack primitive. Can you also add a quantitative component that specifies the amount of work required of the defender to apply a primitive and of an attacker to undo it?

• • •

Problem 2.2   A further interesting development would be to give a formal semantics to the informal box-notation we've used here. A good start would be to look at our Haskell implementation of the model, available from the book's Web site.

2.3 Discussion

The fact that we have two disjoint models in this chapter—one describing the goals and techniques of the attacker, and the other describing the strategies of the defender—is obviously unsatisfying. Ideally, we would like to merge the two, adding quantitative components that describe the attacker's and the defender's intellectual and financial motives, technical strengths, endurance, and so on. Sadly, such a model does not yet exist.

2.3.1 What Do We Need from Attack and Defense Models?

Since at this time we have no software protection algorithms that provide any security guarantees, the goal of software protection can't be to completely prevent a cracker from breaking through your defenses. Rather, we're looking for algorithms that will slow him down as much as possible. Any useful software protection model must be able to express the time/effort it takes for an attacker to break through a defense vs. the effort required by the defender to implement that defense vs. the cost in performance incurred by that defense.

For a software protection algorithm to be considered successful, the effort required by the attacker should be significantly higher than that incurred by the defender. In the early parts of the chapter, however, you saw how the tools and techniques that crackers use to break through software protection defenses are often surprisingly simple. Armed with nothing but a debugger, infinite patience, and fueled by a never-ending supply of caffeine and Hot Pockets, crackers seem able to break through even the most hardened defenses. And as you will see throughout this book, many protection algorithms are surprisingly difficult to implement, requiring a thorough understanding of static analysis techniques.

An important question arises from the preceding observation: "Are there *any* software protection techniques that require strictly more effort to break than to implement?" In Section 4.6.3▸281, you'll see a Java code obfuscation technique that took significant effort to implement (2,000 man-hours) but for which the authors concluded it afforded "no to very marginal security." On the other hand, you can see in Section 7.2.4▸431 that significant effort was required to break the Skype VoIP client, although we have, of course, no knowledge of the amount of effort Skype expended implementing the defense mechanisms. Regardless, any software protection model must have some way to express the cost of implementation and contrast that with the cost of an attack, *and* we must have some way of measuring these costs.

If we assume that against every defense there's an effective attack (and we should!), as defenders we have to accept the fact that our defenses will need to be continuously updated. Attackers similarly must accept that their attacks need to be continuously refreshed, too! As a result, any software protection model must be able to express the ease with which defenses and attacks can be updated, and how seeing a long sequence of defense updates may, over time, improve the cracker's attack capabilities.

2.3.2 How Do We Use the Models to Devise Algorithms?

A good model of the attacker's behavior can help you figure out what you need to defend your program against. And a good model of available defense strategies can help you devise algorithms that effectively slow down the attack.

In Section 2.1.4▸68, for example, you saw how a typical attack goes through a *locate-alter-test* cycle: Find the location of the software protection code that needs to be disabled, alter the behavior of this code, and test that the modified program behaves as required. Knowing that this is the attacker's strategy, you can concoct protection techniques that slow down each step of the cycle. How do you slow down the locate phase? Well, one way is to introduce apparent non-determinism: Every time around the attack cycle the program should appear to execute differently! And how do you accomplish this? Well, one way is to make copies of pieces of the code (using the **duplicate** primitive of our defense model), and randomly choose between these at runtime. How do you slow down the alter phase? Well, one way is to make the different parts of the program more interdependent, for example, by splitting functions into parts and then merging unrelated parts. Another possibility is to use the **detect-respond** primitive to effect a tamper-response whenever you detect that the program has been modified. You can further use the **duplicate** primitive to make multiple copies of the tamper-detection code in order to force the attacker to disable them all.

Again, a comprehensive model that incorporates both the attack and defense strategies would make this sort of argument much easier.

Program 3 Analysis

In the last chapter, we tried to illustrate the way a cracker might go about removing protection code from a program by walking you through an attack. That attack was typical in that the attacker combined a good knowledge of assembly code and a great deal of tenacity with some simple tools: a debugger, a decompiler, and a binary file comparison program.

In this chapter, we're going to delve deeper into the design of the program analysis tools that an attacker might have at his disposal. They come in two flavors: *static analysis tools* that collect information about a program by studying its text but without executing it, and *dynamic analysis tools* that collect information from program runs. What's interesting is that these tools, in particular, the static analysis ones, are useful for defenders as well as attackers! The software protection algorithms you'll see in the remainder of this book make use of program transformations, and you can't safely apply these transformations until you've collected enough static information about your program's data structures, control flow, abstractions, and so on.

In Section 3.1▸118, we'll start the chapter off by giving an overview of techniques for static analysis. For example, many of the algorithms in this book assume that you've turned the functions of your program into *control flow graphs*. These graphs also form the basis for many other static analyses. We'll also talk about *alias* (or *pointer*) *analysis*, techniques for determining if two pointer variables can refer to the same memory location. Several algorithms in the obfuscation and watermarking chapters rely on the difficulty of solving alias analysis problems.

In Section 3.2 ▸ 145, we turn to the design of dynamic analysis tools such as debuggers, tracers, profilers, and emulators. Knowledge about the technology underlying these tools can be very useful to an advanced attacker, since it can allow him to build his own specialized attack tools.

In Section 3.3 ▸ 170, we turn to algorithms for *disassembly* and *decompilation*, i.e., how to turn raw machine code into higher-level representations that are much more palatable to the attacker. Disassembly is important to you, as a defender, also—if you want to add protection to a binary code program, you must first be able to analyze it, which at the very least means you must turn it into correct assembly code.

Finally, in Section 3.4 ▸ 190, we turn to what we've termed *pragmatic analysis*, studies of what actual programs really look like. Many software algorithms in this book insert new code, and if that protection code stands out as unusual, the algorithm may be wide open to pattern-matching attacks. *Code stealth* will therefore be an important concept throughout this book, and to know if our protection code is stealthy or not, we need to know what "normal" code looks like!

3.1 Static Analysis

Static analysis collects information about a program that is true for *all* executions. It does so by looking at the code of the program itself, as opposed to dynamic analysis, which collects information from the program by running it on particular inputs.

When deciding which static analysis algorithm to use, you will have to trade off between the *precision* of the information you collect, on the one hand, and the amount of effort (complexity of the algorithm implementation and its runtime performance), on the other. For example, as you'll see later on in this section, some pointer analysis algorithms are *flow-insensitive* (they disregard any loops and if-statements) and collect imprecise information, but do so quickly. Other algorithms are *flow-sensitive* (they take branches into account when doing the analysis) and collect more precise information, but do so more slowly.

The algorithms in this book protect programs using *program transformations*, and these transformations all need some form of static analysis. Because of the potential for imprecision in static analysis algorithms, transformations need to be *conservative*, or *safe*. In other words, the algorithms can only apply a transformation when the static information collected can guarantee that it is *semantics-preserving*, i.e., that the program will behave the same before and after the transformation has been applied. In practice, what this means is that there will be situations where you'll want to apply a particular protection transformation but you won't be able to, because the static information you've collected just isn't precise enough to guarantee safety.

Many analyses start with a control-flow graph representation of functions. These graphs then form the basis for further analysis. For example, in this section you'll see how to identify loops in the graph, how to determine where in the graph a variable could have gotten its value, and how to compute whether there's a dependency between two statements that would preclude them from being reordered.

3.1.1 Control Flow Analysis

Almost any tool that manipulates programs in some way—be it a compiler or a reverse engineering tool—needs some way to represent *functions*. The most common representation is a *control flow graph* (CFG). The nodes of a control flow graph are called *basic blocks*. Each block consists of straight-line code ending, possibly, in a branch. Control always enters at the beginning of the block and exits at the end. An edge $A \rightarrow B$ from the exit of block A to the entrance of block B indicates that control could possibly flow from A to B at runtime. The control flow graph is a *conservative* representation—we can't be sure exactly how control will flow at runtime, so the graph represents a superset of all executions.

Here, to the left is a modular exponentiation routine you will see often in this book:

```
int modexp(int y,int x[],
           int w,int n) {
   int R, L;
   int k = 0;
   int s = 1;
   while (k < w) {
      if (x[k] == 1)
         R = (s*y) % n;
      else
         R = s;
      s = R*R % n;
      L = R;
      k++;
   }
   return L;
}
```

```
(1)  k=0
(2)  s=1
(3)  if (k>=w) goto (12)
(4)  if (x[k]!=1) goto (7)
(5)  R=(s*y)%n
(6)  goto (8)
(7)  R=s
(8)  s=R*R%n
(9)  L=R
(10) k++
(11) goto (3)
(12) return L
```

To the right, we've "compiled" the source into a simpler representation where structured control flow statements are represented by conditional (`if` ... `goto` ...) and unconditional (`goto` ...) branches.

Here, to the left, is what the corresponding control flow graph looks like:

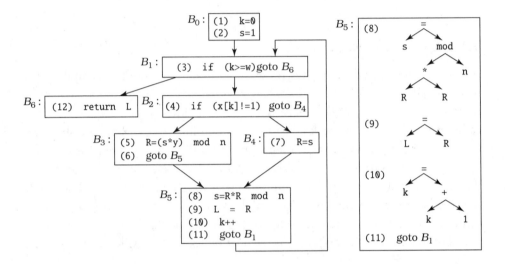

Notice how basic blocks have no branches inside them; branches appear only as the last statement. The statements inside a basic block can be represented in any number of ways. To the right (above), you can see how each statement in block B_5 was turned into an *expression tree*, a common representation.

Here's the algorithm for building a control flow graph:

Primitive 3.1 (BuildCFG(F))

1. Mark every instruction that can start a basic block as a *leader*:

   - The first instruction is a leader;

   - Any target of a branch is a leader;

   - The instruction following a conditional branch is a leader.

2. A basic block consists of the instructions from a leader up to, but not including, the next leader.

3. Add an edge $A \rightarrow B$ if A ends with a branch to B or can fall through to B.

In the example above, (1), (3), (4), (5), (7), (8), and (12) are leaders. (1) is a leader because it's the first statement. (12) and (4) are leaders because statement (3) branches/falls through to them. Similarly, (7) and (5) are leaders because statement

(4) branches and falls through to them. (8) is a leader because (6) jumps to it. And finally, (3) is a leader because (11) jumps to it. Basic block B_5 starts with statement (8) and ends with (11), because (12) is the next leader following (8).

You'll see control flow graphs all throughout this book. In Section 4.3.2▸226, for example, we'll show you an obfuscation method that *flattens* the control flow graph, i.e., tries to confuse a reverse engineer by removing all the structure from the graph.

3.1.1.1 Dealing with Exceptions Of course, in practice, life isn't as simple as the above algorithm would indicate. In a language that supports exception handling, any instruction that can potentially throw an exception will terminate a basic block. In Java, that means any integer expression with a division operator, any expression that dereferences a pointer, and any explicit `throw` statements. In other words, just about every statement in a typical Java program can throw an exception! That leads to tiny basic blocks and *lots* of exception edges. Instead, it's common to treat exception edges differently from normal edges. Consider this Java fragment:

```
try {
    int x = 10/0;
    Integer i=null;
    i.intValue();
    throw new Exception("Bad stuff");
        ...
}
    catch (NullPointerException e) {catch1();}
    catch (ArithmeticException e)  {catch2();}
    catch (Exception e)           {catch3();}
}
```

In the Marmot compiler [127], the body of the `try`-statement would turn into a single basic block. In addition to any "normal" control-flow edges, the block will have special exception edges (here light gray) that lead to exception handling blocks:

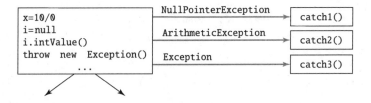

Table 3.1 Instruction set for a small architecture. All operators and operands are one byte long, leading to instructions that can vary in length from one to three bytes.

Opcode	Mnemonic	Operands	Semantics
0	call	*addr*	function call to *addr*
1	calli	*reg*	function call to address in *reg*
2	brg	*offset*	branch to pc + *offset* if flags for > are set
3	inc	*reg*	$reg \leftarrow reg + 1$
4	bra	*offset*	branch to pc + *offset*
5	jmpi	*reg*	jump to address in *reg*
6	prologue		beginning of function
7	ret		return from function
8	load	$reg_1, (reg_2)$	$reg_1 \leftarrow [reg_2]$
9	loadi	*reg, imm*	$reg \leftarrow imm$
10	cmpi	*reg, imm*	compare *reg* and *imm* and set flags
11	add	reg_1, reg_2	$reg_1 \leftarrow reg_1 + reg_2$
12	brge	*offset*	branch to pc + *offset* if flags for $\geq$ are set
13	breq	*offset*	branch to pc + *offset* if flags for = are set
14	store	$(reg_1), reg_2$	$[reg_1] \leftarrow reg_2$

3.1.1.2 Algorithm *REAMB*: Dealing with Self-Modifying Code In a "normal" program, the code segment doesn't change. Whatever code the compiler generated is the code that gets executed. But one thing we can assure you is that the programs you'll see in this book aren't normal! In particular, all of the algorithms in Chapter 6 (Dynamic Obfuscation) and some in Chapter 7 (Software Tamperproofing) produce *self-modifying code*. A program is self-modifying if its code changes at runtime.

There are two reasons why you might want to manipulate a program that is self-modifying. First, you might be a defender trying to add self-modifying software protection code to your program. Second, you might be an attacker trying to analyze this code in order to bypass it! Computer viruses are also often self-modifying, which means that virus scanners have to be able to analyze programs that exhibit such behavior.

The problem is that if you're going to manipulate a function that is self-modifying, the standard control flow graph representation isn't enough. Consider this example:

```
0:   [9,0,12]   loadi    r0,12
3:   [9,1,4]    loadi    r1,4
6:   [14,0,1]   store    (r0),r1
```

```
 9:    [11,1,1]    add      r1,r1
12:    [3,4]       inc      r4
14:    [4,-5] *    bra      -5
16:    [7]         ret
```

The instruction set is taken from Table 3.1▶122, which you'll see again when we discuss disassembly. The first column shows the code position, the second shows the codebytes (in decimal), the third shows the operator, and the fourth shows the operands. The first instruction, `loadi r0,12`, for example, assembles into the three bytes `[9,0,12]`. The 9 byte is the `loadi` opcode, the 0 byte is register `r0`, and the 12 byte is the instruction's literal argument, 12. Building a control flow graph from this routine is simple, since there's only one branch:

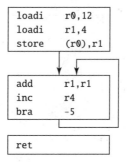

Notice how the control flow graph isn't even connected, since the backward branch at position 14 forms an infinite loop! Now look at the code in some more detail. Can you see what the `store` instruction is doing? It's writing the byte 4 to position 12, changing the `inc r4` instruction into a `bra 4`! In other words, the actual control flow graph looks like this:

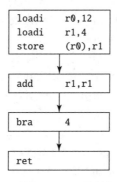

What you should come away with from this example is that if the codebytes are changing at runtime, a standard control flow graph isn't sufficient. Algorithm REAMB [9] extends the standard representation in two ways: First, it adds a *codebyte data structure* to the graph that represents all the different states each instruction can be in. Second, it adds *conditions* to the edges; only if the condition on an edge is true can control take that path. Here's the same example as above, with some of the codebytes and conditions added:

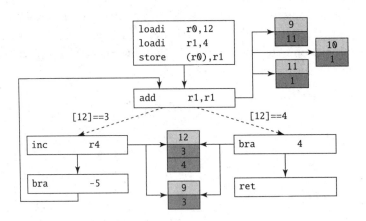

The add instruction comprises three bytes ⟨11, 1, 1⟩ at addresses 9-11. In the figure, code-byte addresses are in light gray and the code bytes themselves are in dark gray. These bytes never change, so there's only one value possible for each address. Not so with the inc and bra instructions, however! At location 12, two values can be stored, 3 and 4. The outgoing edges from add's basic block are conditional on what is stored at 12, either 3 or 4.

Algorithm REAMB provides a nice representation of self-modifying code. However, actually *building* this structure from a piece of code that's been made self-modifying for the express purpose of confusion is an entirely different story! In the example above, it was easy to see what value the store instruction would write, and where, but that's because both were literal values easily found in the code. It's not hard to imagine how arbitrary computations of addresses and values would make this analysis problem undecidable.

Problem 3.1   OK, fine, you caught us: We don't know whether this is undecidable or not, but it does *look* undecidable! For extra credit, prove or disprove.

3.1.1.3 Identifying Loops   Given the control flow graph, it can be useful to identify the loops in the graph. To do that, you first need the concept of *dominance
relationship*.

A node A in the CFG is said to *dominate* a node B (A dom B) if every path
from the entry node to B has to flow through A. In the example graph to the left,
node B_2 dominates B_3, B_4, B_5 because every path from B_0 (the entry node) to any
of these three nodes has to go through B_2:

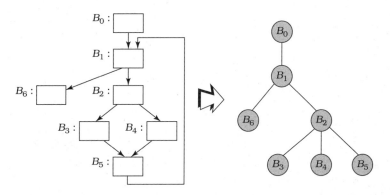

To the right, you see the *dominance tree*, which encodes the dominator relationship.
If there's an edge $A \rightarrow B$ in the tree we say that A *immediately dominates* B
(A idom B).

Once you've built the control flow graph and its dominance tree, you can find
the loops of the graph. First, you look for the *back edges* of the CFG. An edge from
B to A is a back edge if A dominates B. In our example, there's only one, $B_5 \rightarrow B_1$.
B_1 will be the *header node* of the loop. A node n belongs to the loop if it's dominated
by the header node, if the header node can be reached from n, and if there's exactly
one back edge in the loop. In our example, nodes B_2, B_3, B_4, B_5 are all dominated
by B_1, and B_1 is reachable from all of them, meaning B_1, B_2, B_3, B_4, B_5 form the
one loop in this graph.

3.1.1.4 Interprocedural Control Flow   When you analyze code, you can do so at
three levels: *local* analysis, which considers each basic block in isolation; *global* (or
intraprocedural) analysis, which looks at information flow within a single control
flow graph; and *interprocedural* analysis, which also considers flow of information
between functions. The *call graph* is the traditional representation used for inter-
procedural analysis. The call graph has one node for each function in the program,
and there's an edge $f \rightarrow g$ if function f might call g. A cycle in the graph indicates
recursion, and a node not reachable from the entry point indicates a function never

reachable at runtime. Conceptually, the nodes of a call graph consist of the control flow graph for the corresponding function, although in practice the call graph and the control flow graphs are usually separate entities.

In general, the call graph is a *multi-graph*, since one caller function can invoke the same callee multiple times from multiple call sites.

Here's a simple program and its corresponding call graph:

```
void h();

void f(){
   h();
}

void g(){
   f();
}

void h() {
   f();
   g();
}

void k() {}

int main() {
   h();
   void (*p)() = &k;
   p();
}
```

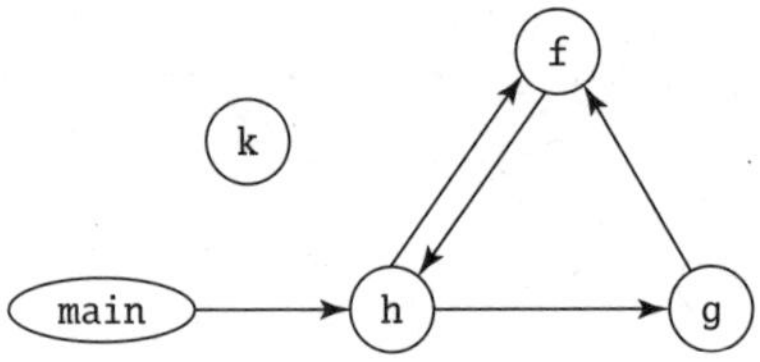

Actually, this graph is wrong! Looking at it, you would draw the conclusion that function k would never be called, but as you see from the source code, it *is* called, albeit indirectly through a pointer. This tells you that building a call graph is easy as long as there are no function pointers involved. In this simple case, it would be enough to reason that "only one function has its address taken (k), so the only value p can take is &k, so main must call k."

In object-oriented languages, you get similar problems since every method invocation is through a pointer. Fortunately, simple type analysis can sometimes help in disambiguating pointers. Have a look at this Java example:

```
class A {
    void m() {}
}
class B extends A {
    void m() {}
}
class C extends B {
    void m() {}

    static void main() {
        B b = ...;
        b.m();
        A a;
        if (...)
            a = new B();
        else
            a = new C();
        a.m();
    }
}
```

By looking at the static type of b, you can tell that the call b.m() can only go to B's m or C's m. Thus, the call graph would have edges main → B:m, main → C:m. Similarly, if you look at the possible types of objects a could point to, you would have to assume that a.m() could invoke any one of A:m, B:m, and C:m. However, if you look not just at the call a.m() in isolation, but also consider the preceding if-statement, you can work out that a can't point to an A object and hence only B:m and C:m can be called! This requires *data flow analysis*, which is going to be our next topic.

3.1.2 Data Flow Analysis

Data flow analysis gives you conservative information about how variables are used in a program. It's normally computed over a control flow graph; for interprocedural data flow analysis, it's computed over the control flow graph and the call graph.

Typical questions you might want to ask that data flow analysis can answer are:

- "Will the value of variable x be used after point p?,"
- "Where in the function could variable x used at point p have gotten its value?,"
- "Is variable x constant at point p in the function, and if so, what is its value?"

In Section 3.3.2▶180, you will see how the decompilation algorithm RECG uses data flow analysis to turn low-level test-and-branch code into a higher-level if ... goto ... construct:

i : cmpi r ,*imm*
↓
j : brg lab

j : if $r > imm$ goto lab

To be able to do this transformation, you need to determine which instruction sets the condition code that a later instruction (usually a branch) will read. This is an instance of the *reaching definitions* data flow analysis problem.

Here's our example function again, but this time we've annotated every use of a variable with its *use-definition chain* (ud-chain):

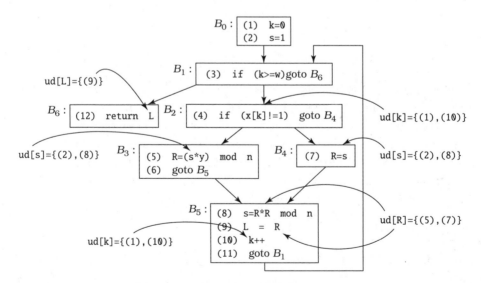

For every *use* of a variable the ud-chain links it to the place in the function where it could have been *defined* (gotten its value). For example, look at the use of variable s in statement (5). The first time you go through the loop, s will have gotten its value at (2), but at subsequent times, it's the value computed at (8) that will get used. Therefore, at (5) the ud-chain for s is the set {(2), (8)}. The ud-chains are *conservative* in that they take into account *all* possible executions, even ones that may not actually happen at runtime. Since there is no way to know (without running the program) whether execution will go down the left or right branch from B_2, you have to assume *both* branches will be taken, which means that the ud-chain for R at point (8) has to be {(5), (7)}.

To compute ud-chains, you first have to solve a *reaching definitions* data flow analysis. Data flow analyses are (usually iterative) algorithms over sets of values. In the case of reaching definitions, you need to solve this set of equations where $in[b]$, $out[b]$, $gen[b]$, and $kill[b]$ are sets of definitions of variables in the control flow graph, and b ranges over all the basic blocks:

$$out[b] \;=\; gen[b] \cup (in[b] - kill[b])$$
$$in[b] \;=\; \bigcup_{\text{predecessors } p \text{ of } b} out[p]$$

The *gen* and *kill* sets are computed once for each basic block. The $gen[B]$ set contains all the definitions in B that reach the end of B, i.e., the last assignment to a variable in B is the definition that survives. The $kill[B]$ set contains all the definitions in the control flow graph that, even if they would reach the beginning of B, they would *not* reach the end of B, because there's an assignment in B that kills them. Here's an illustration of *gen* and *kill*:

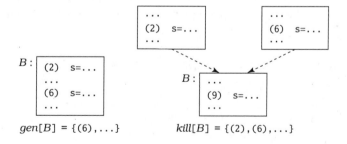

In general, data flow problems come in two parts: a local part that solves the problem within each basic block (the *gen* and *kill* sets for the reaching definitions problem), and a global part that combines the local solutions into a global solution. For the reaching definitions problem, the global part computes sets called $in[B]$ and $out[B]$. The $in[B]$ set is the set of the definitions that reach the beginning of B, i.e., the set of points in the control flow graph that computes values that may still be valid when (at runtime) you reach the beginning of B:

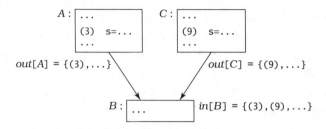

Similarly, *out*[B] is the set of definitions that may reach the end of B, i.e., the set of points in the flow graph that computes values that may still be valid when control reaches the end of B:

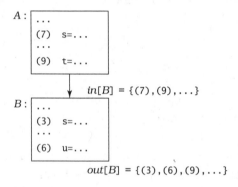

The *in* and *out* sets are computed iteratively for each basic block until a fix-point is reached. Here's the algorithm that computes the reaching definitions for a control flow graph G:

REACHINGDEFINITIONS(G):

```
for each block b in G do
    gen[b] ← {d | d is a definition in b that
                   reaches the end of b}
    kill[b] ← {d | d is a definition in G that is
                    killed by a definition in b}
    out[b] ← in[b] ← ∅
do
    for each block b in G do
        in[b] ← ∪predecessors p of b out[p]
        out[b] ← gen[b] ∪ (in[b] − kill[b])
while there are no more changes to any of the out[i]
```

On our example graph, the algorithm converges after three iterations. The result consists of these *in* and *out* sets:

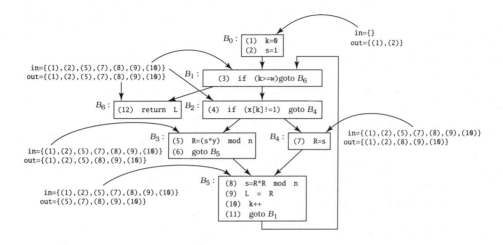

From the *in* set, it's straightforward to compute the ud-chains.

Definition-use chains (du-chains) are similar to ud-chains, but they link definitions of a variable with its uses:

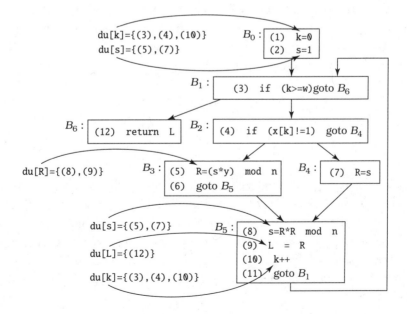

The data flow algorithm for computing du-chains is essentially identical to the reaching definitions one, except information flows *backward*. In general, data flow algorithms can be classified as *any path* vs. *all paths*, and *forward flow* vs. *backward flow*. This gives you four sets of equations to solve any data flow problem:

	Forward flow	**Backward flow**
Any path	$\text{out}[b] = \text{gen}[b] \cup (\text{in}[b] - \text{kill}[b])$ $\text{in}[b] = \bigcup_{p \in \text{predecessors of } b} \text{out}[p]$	$\text{in}[b] = \text{gen}[b] \cup (\text{out}[b] - \text{kill}[b])$ $\text{out}[b] = \bigcup_{s \in \text{successors of } b} \text{in}[s]$
All paths	$\text{out}[b] = \text{gen}[b] \cup (\text{in}[b] - \text{kill}[b])$ $\text{in}[b] = \bigcap_{p \in \text{predecessors of } b} \text{out}[p]$	$\text{in}[b] = \text{gen}[b] \cup (\text{out}[b] - \text{kill}[b])$ $\text{out}[b] = \bigcap_{s \in \text{successors of } b} \text{in}[s]$

3.1.3 Data Dependence Analysis

Several algorithms in this book are based on the *reordering* of code. For example, in Algorithm WMASB in Section 8.8.1▶523, you will see how it's possible to embed secret information in a basic block by reordering its instructions. Also, in Algorithm OBFCF in Section 4.1.1▶203, you will see how instructions can be reordered to *destroy* information in a basic block! Of course, in neither case is it possible to reorder randomly—if an instruction A computes a value needed by a second instruction B, then naturally, A has to come before B:

$$A: \text{ x = } \ldots;$$
$$\ldots$$
$$B: \text{ y = } \ldots \text{ x } \ldots;$$

This is known as a *flow* dependence, but there are actually four different types of dependencies: *flow*, *anti*, *output*, and *control*. There's a flow dependence between A and B if A assigns to a variable and B uses it. There's an anti dependence if A reads a variable and B assigns to it. There's an output dependence if A and B both assign to the same variable. There's a control dependence between A and B if the outcome of A controls whether B executes or not. Here's a table that summarizes these definitions:

Dependence	Notation	Example
Flow dependence	$S_1 \delta^f S_2$	S_1: x = 6; S_2: y = x * 7;
Anti dependence	$S_1 \delta^a S_2$	S_1: y = x * 7; S_2: x = 6;
Output dependence	$S_1 \delta^o S_2$	S_1: x = 6 * y; S_2: x = 7;
Control dependence	$S_1 \delta^c S_2$	S_1: if ($\cdots$) S_2: x = 7;

Two instructions can be reordered if there are no dependencies between them.

A *program dependency graph* has one node per statement and an edge from node A to node B if A has to occur before B in the code. As an example, here's the modular exponentiation routine with its corresponding dependency graph:

```
S_0 : int k = 0;
S_1 : int s = 1;
S_2 : while (k <w) {
S_3 : if (x[k] == 1)
S_4 : R = (s*y) % n;
else
S_5 : R = s;
S_6 : s = R*R % n;
S_7 : L = R;
S_8 : k=k+1;
}
```

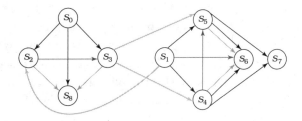

We've shown flow dependencies in black, anti dependencies in light gray, output dependencies in dark gray, and control dependencies in dashed. Since there is no path from S_0 to S_1, these two statements can be reordered. Similarly, there are no dependencies between S_6, S_7, and S_8, so these statements can appear in any order.

In Section 10.6▶635, you'll see two algorithms that make use of data dependence graphs. The first one detects duplicated code in a program, and the second detects plagiarism among a set of student programs.

3.1.4 Alias Analysis

Two pointers are said to *alias* each other if they point to the same memory location. *Alias analysis* is the process of determining if, at a point p in the program, two variables a and b *may* or *must* refer to the same location. To see that aliases matter, have a look at this piece of code:

```
int a = 0, b = 0;
int* x = &a;
while (a < 10) {
    *x += 100;
    a++;
}
if (a>10) S;
```

It would seem that any half-decent compiler (or human reader!) would conclude that the dashed test will always fail. The loop surely executes exactly 10 times, incrementing a by one every time around the loop, and after the end of the loop a==10. As a result, statement S is dead code and can be removed. However, the code in light gray creates an *alias*: *x and a both refer to the same memory location! So the dark gray code updates a, the loop exits after just one iteration, the test in dashed succeeds, and S is executed. An optimizing compiler that fails to recognize the possibility that a and *x may be aliases could easily produce the wrong code. This is a problem not only for compilers but for *any* code transformation tool, including the code protection tools you'll see in this book.

Alias analysis plays an important role in this book. In Section 4.3.3▸229, Algorithm OBFWHKD$_{alias}$ *flattens* a control flow graph (removes all its structure) and makes it difficult for a reverse engineer to recover the structure by asking him to solve a difficult alias analysis problem. Similarly, Algorithm 9.4 WMCT in Section 9.3▸583 encodes information in a pointer-based structure built at runtime, with the idea that alias analysis will be required in order for an attacker to modify the code that builds the structure. Also, essentially *all* static analysis algorithms (including the data flow analysis algorithms you saw earlier in this section) rely on alias analysis.

3.1.4.1 Where Does Aliasing Occur? Aliasing can occur in a variety of settings, and it can cause problems both for the human programmer and for automatic code transformation tools. Say, for example, that you're looking over your colleague's code and find the following:

```
int formal_formal(int* a, int* b) {
   *a  =  10;
   *b  =  5;
   if  ((*a-*b)==0)  S;
}
```

Surely, you reason, *a-*b must evaluate to $10 - 5 = 5$, which means that the test in light gray will never succeed and S will never execute! And so, as a helpful gesture, you go ahead and "optimize" the code by removing the if-statement. Well, you've now introduced a bug if the function happens to be called like this: formal_formal(&x,&x). Then, both *a and *b refer to the same location, which will cause *a-*b to evaluate to 0.

This kind of aliasing is introduced when two formal reference parameters refer to the same memory location. You can get the same effect from aliasing a formal parameter and a global variable:

```
int x;

int formal_global(int* a) {
   *a = 10;
   if ((*a-x)>0) S;
}
```

Here, the call formal_global(&x) will create an alias between *a and x and the test will always fail.

Aliases can also occur as the result of *side effects* of functions. In this example, after the call to foo, x and y will both point to the same address (the variable t) and hence the statement S will always execute:

```
int foo(int** a, int** b) {
   *a = *b;
}

int side_effect() {
   int s=20, t=10;
   int *x = &s, *y = &t;
   foo(&x,&y);
   if (*x == *y) S;
}
```

Finally, aliasing can also occur between the elements of an array:

```
int a[];
int i=2,j=2;
    ...
a[i] = 10;
a[j] = 5;
if (a[i]-a[j]==0) S;
```

Again, it would seem to a casual observer that `a[i]-a[j]` should always evaluate to 5, but, if `i` and `j` have the same value, `a[i]` and `a[j]` will refer to the same array element—they will be aliases—and `a[i]-a[j]` will evaluate to 0.

3.1.4.2 Classifying Alias Analysis Problems

We distinguish between two alias analysis problems, *may-alias* and *must-alias*. Let a and b be references to memory locations. At a program point p, $\langle a, b \rangle \in may\text{-}alias(p)$ if there exists *some* execution path on which a and b refer to the same memory location. If on *every* path to p, a and b refer to the same location, we say that they *must-alias* each other, i.e., $\langle a, b \rangle \in must\text{-}alias(p)$. Here's an illustration:

$\langle a, b \rangle \in must\text{-}alias(p)$ $\langle a, b \rangle \in may\text{-}alias(p)$

Here, for example, at point p_1, $must\text{-}alias(p_1) = \{\langle *a, x \rangle\}$ and at point p_2, $may\text{-}alias(p_2) = \{\langle *a, x \rangle, \langle *b, x \rangle\}$:

```
int x;
int *a,*b;
a = &x;
p₁ : if (...) b = &x;
p₂ :
```

For programs with many pointers, alias analysis can be very expensive, and different algorithms have been proposed that make different trade-offs between precision and performance [164]. Algorithms are classified as being *flow-insensitive* or *flow-sensitive* [52]. A flow-insensitive algorithm computes the alias sets for an entire procedure or program, ignoring any control flow. Flow-sensitive algorithms, on the other hand, look at the control flow and compute alias sets for every program point. Generally speaking, flow-insensitive algorithms are fast and imprecise, while flow-sensitive algorithms are slow and precise.

Here, we're going to use the notation $\langle p, q \rangle$ to mean that p *may-alias* q. To see the difference in precision between a flow-sensitive and flow-insensitive algorithm, have a look at this example:

```
if (...)
    q = &t;              {⟨*q, t⟩}
else
    q = &s;              {⟨*q, s⟩}
    ...                  {⟨*q, t⟩, ⟨*q, s⟩}
p = q;                   {⟨*q, t⟩, ⟨*q, s⟩, ⟨*p, t⟩, ⟨*p, s⟩}
q = &t;                  {⟨*q, t⟩, ⟨*p, t⟩, ⟨*p, s⟩}
```

Here, at every program point, you can see what alias sets a flow-sensitive algorithm should produce. A flow-*insensitive* algorithm, on the other hand, would produce the much less precise alias set $\{\langle *q, t \rangle, \langle *q, s \rangle, \langle *p, t \rangle, \langle *p, s \rangle\}$ for every point in the *entire* code segment.

Algorithms also differ in whether they take the *context* of function calls into account. An intra-procedural (context-insensitive) alias analysis algorithm analyzes one function at a time and makes conservative assumptions about how a callee can affect the aliasing of a caller. An inter-procedural (context-sensitive) algorithm tracks flow of alias information across procedure calls.

It is generally assumed that alias analysis algorithms (like all static analyses) should be *conservative*. This means that a may-alias analysis algorithm may sometimes report that two variables p and q might refer to the same memory location, while in fact this could never happen. Equivalently, you have to assume that $\langle p, q \rangle \in$ *may-alias*(r) if you cannot prove that p is never an alias for q at point r. There are, however, applications (such as bug-finding analyses) where safety is not necessary, and this can significantly speed up analysis [163].

Many practical algorithms are flow- and context-insensitive. Hind and Pioli [164] report that (for analyses used by compiler optimizations) flow-sensitive analyses offer only a "minimum increase in precision." However, we believe that when alias analysis is used by an attacker against the algorithms in this book, *higher* precision will be necessary than for compilation. You should keep this in mind as you read Chapter 4 (Code Obfuscation). Also, current alias analysis algorithms are designed to analyze well-behaved programs *written by humans*. In [163] Amer Diwan says:

> Regarding ugly programs, many real world programs (particularly for unsafe languages) have features that are practically impossible for a pointer analysis to get. For example, consider the C program li that includes a garbage collector. If a pointer analysis is unfortunate enough to analyze the garbage collector it will most likely determine that everything aliases everything else.

The purpose of the algorithms you will see in Chapter 4 is to automatically produce "ugly" programs for which static analysis will be difficult.

Shape (or *heap*) analysis is particularly interesting to some of the algorithms in this book. These analyze the program to determine what kind of heap-based structure a pointer variable could point to: a tree, a DAG, or a cyclic graph. As for other pointer analysis algorithms, shape analysis trades off between precision and performance. Ghiya's [137] algorithm is accurate for programs that build trees and arrays of trees, but it can't handle programs that make major structural changes. Similarly Chase's [60] algorithm can't handle destructive updates: While it can successfully analyze code that does a *list append*, it will fail on an in-place list reversal program. Many other algorithms limit the depth of recursion to some constant k levels, and Hendren [158], finally, fails on cyclic structures.

Ramalingam [302] proved that precise, flow-sensitive alias analysis is undecidable in languages with dynamic allocation, loops, and if-statements. Even in the flow-insensitive case, precise may-alias analysis is NP-hard [170]. Typical, *imprecise*, alias analysis algorithms are linear to low-order polynomial. Hind and Poli [164] report that a particular flow-sensitive algorithm is 2.5 times slower and uses 6 times more memory than flow-insensitive algorithms of comparable precision.

3.1.4.3 Alias Analysis Algorithms Michael Hind [163] stated that 75 papers and 9 Ph.D. theses had been published on pointer analysis between 1980 and 2001. Out of the many proposed algorithms of different precision and performance, we're going to show you two. The first is a type-based flow-insensitive algorithm; the second is a flow-sensitive algorithm based on data flow analysis.

In strongly typed languages like Java and Modula-3, you can use a *type-based* alias analysis algorithm. The idea is very simple: If p and q are pointers that point to different types of objects, then they cannot possibly be aliases! This isn't true in unsafe languages like C, of course, since there the programmer can use type-casts to convert pointers willy-nilly. In this MODULA-3 fragment, p and r may-alias each other, but p and q cannot possibly be aliases:

```
TYPE T1 : POINTER TO CHAR;
     T2 : POINTER TO REAL;
VAR p,r : T1;
    q   : T2;
BEGIN
    p := NEW T1;
    r := NEW T1;
    q := NEW T2;
END;
```

This is an example of a flow-insensitive algorithm; you don't detect that p and r actually point to different objects.

Let's instead look at a *flow-sensitive may-alias* algorithm, adapted from the *Dragon book* [5]. Assume that you have a language with the usual control structures and these pointer operations:

Statement	Semantics
p = **new** T	create a new object of type T.
p = &a	p now points only to a.
p = q	p now points only to what q points to.
p = nil	p now points to nothing.

The algorithm follows a *forward-flow data flow* scheme and manipulates sets of alias pairs $\langle p, q \rangle$ where p and q are *access paths*, either:

1. l-valued expressions (such as a[i].v->[k].w) or
2. program locations $S_1, S_2, \cdots$.

Whenever new dynamic data is created using **new**, the algorithm needs some way to refer to the new object. There can be an infinite number of new objects, of course, and there's no way to refer to them all individually. Therefore, the algorithm uses the *program location* where the **new** occurred to name the object that was created there. This means that *every* object that's created at a particular location will have the same name, potentially leading to significant imprecision! This is exactly the kind of trade-off that alias analysis algorithms often have to do.

Here are the data flow equations, where, after the analysis, $\langle$ p, q $\rangle$ ∈ in[b] if p and q could refer to the same memory location at the beginning of b:

$$in[b_0] = \emptyset$$
$$out[b] = \textbf{trans}_b(in[b])$$
$$in[b] = \bigcup_{\text{predecessors } p \text{ of } b} out[p]$$

$\textbf{trans}_b(S)$ is a *transfer* function. If S is the alias pairs defined at the beginning of b, then $\textbf{trans}_b(S)$ is the set of pairs defined at the exit of b. The transfer function is defined like this, for each construct of the language:

Rule	Block b	$\textbf{trans}_b(S)$
(1)	$d:$ p = new T	$(S - \{\langle p, a\rangle \mid \text{any } a\}) \cup \{\langle p, d\rangle\}$
(2)	p = &c	$(S - \{\langle p, a\rangle \mid \text{any } a\}) \cup \{\langle p, c\rangle\}$
(3)	p = q	$(S - \{\langle p, a\rangle \mid \text{any } a\}) \cup \{\langle p, a\rangle \mid \langle q, a\rangle \in S\}$
(4)	p = nil	$S - \{\langle p, a\rangle \mid \text{any } a\}$

In all the rules, the term $(S - \{\langle p, a\rangle \mid \text{any } a\})$ means that whatever p might have been pointing to in the past, after the statement it will no longer be pointing to it. Rule (1) states that after the statement p = new T, p will point to an object we'll name d. This is a gross simplification: We're considering *all* objects created from this location in the program to be the same. Rule (2) states that after the statement p = &c, p will alias c. Rule (3) says that after p = q, p will point to whatever q might have pointed to.

As an illustration, here's a simple example:

```
do {
    S₁ : p = new T;
    if (...)
        S₂ : q = p;
    else
        S₃ : q = new T;
    S₄ : p = nil;
} while (...)
```

After the first iteration, you get the following *in* and *out* sets:

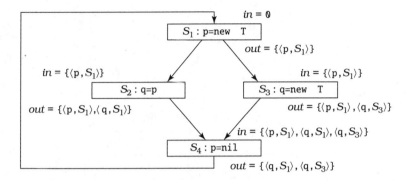

After another iteration, you get the final result and no more iterations are necessary:

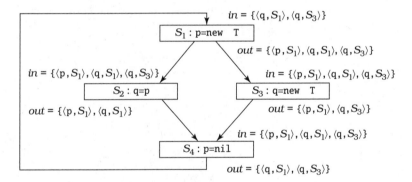

As you can see, right before statement S_4, q could point to an object that was created either in statement S_1 (if control took the left branch) or S_3 (if control took the right branch).

3.1.5 Slicing

Say that you're in the process of debugging your modular exponentiation routine, and you've gotten as far as line 13, where you think there might be some issue with the k variable:

```
1   int modexp(int y,int x[],
2                 int w,int n) {
3     int R, L;
4     int k = 0;
5     int s = 1;
6     while (k < w) {
7         if (x[k] == 1)
8             R = (s*y) % n;
9         else
10            R = s;
11        s = R*R % n;
12        L = R;
13        k++;
14    }
15    return L;
16  }
```

What you're probably wondering at this point is, "If k wasn't computed right, what computations contributed to its value?" *Slicing* [171,347] is a technique designed to answer that kind of question. In this case, you would like to compute a *backwards_slice*(13,k), i.e., a list of all the statements that contributed to k's value at line 13. They're listed below in dark gray:

```
1   int modexp(int y,int x[],
2                 int w,int n) {
3     int R, L;
4     int k = 0;
5     int s = 1;
6     while (k < w)    {
7         if (x[k] == 1)
8             R = (s*y) % n;
9         else
10            R = s;
11        s = R*R % n;
12        L = R;
13        k++;
14    }
15    return L;
16  }
```

Notice that if you did the same exercise on s, say, at line 11, you would get essentially the entire routine, since every statement contributes to s in some way.

In Chapter 7 (Software Tamperproofing), we'll show you Algorithm TPZG, which splits a program into two parts, one part that runs server-side and another that runs client-side in a distributed system. The server-side part is thus protected from an attacker who can only access the client-side code. The algorithm uses slicing to find a section of code that can safely be moved from the client to the server. But it's not only you, as a defender, who can get help from slicing! In Section 4.4.4 ▶253, you'll see how an attacker can break a so-called *opaque predicate*, a boolean expression with a constant, but difficult to discover, true or false value. To do this break, the attacker must first discover the instructions that are part of the predicate, and for this he can compute a backwards slice.

3.1.6 Abstract Interpretation

The idea behind abstract interpretation is to perform a static analysis of a program, where the operations (such as +, *, and so on) are given "non-standard" interpretations, *abstractions* (simplifications) of their standard interpretations. The canonical example is to compute the *sign* of an integer expression, returning $-1, 0, 1$ if the expression has a negative, zero, or positive value, respectively. If the analysis isn't powerful enough to compute the sign, we return the special value "*unknown.*" We use $+_c$ and $*_c$ to represent the standard addition and multiplication operations; $const_c$ is a literal integer, and var_c is an integer variable. To use abstract interpretation terminology, these are all *concrete*, i.e., they occur in the text of the program we're analyzing. There are also *abstract* operations, $+_a$ and $*_a$, which operate on the abstract values $-1, 0, 1, unknown$. To compute the *sign* of an expression, we get the following rules:

$$
\begin{aligned}
const_a &\equiv \text{ if } const_c = 0 \text{ then } 0 \text{ else if } const_c < 0 \text{ then } -1 \text{ else } 1 \\
var_a &\equiv unknown \\
x +_a y &\equiv \text{ if } x = y \text{ then } x \text{ else } unknown \\
x *_a y &\equiv \text{ if } x = unknown \lor y = unknown \text{ then } unknown \text{ else } x *_c y
\end{aligned}
$$

Here's an example program, where we've subscripted every constant, variable, and operation with $_c$, since they're computed in the concrete semantics:

$$
\begin{aligned}
\text{int } x_c &= 5_c; \\
\text{int } y_c &= -6_c; \\
x_c &= x_c * x_c; \\
y_c &= x_c + y_c;
\end{aligned}
$$

We could, of course, just run the program and find out that x will get the value 25, and y will get the value 19, and thus $\text{sign}(x) = \text{sign}(y) = 1$. But instead we're going to do a static analysis, without running the program, in the *abstract* domain, using the definitions of the abstract operations above. The first two declarations are simple enough:

```
int x_c = 5_c;                     int x_a = 1_a;
int y_c = -6_c;                    int y_a = -1_a;
```

In other words, after the declarations, x is positive and y is negative. Next, we find out that (since multiplying two positive numbers yields a positive number) after the third line, x is still positive:

```
int x_c = 5_c;           int x_a = 1_a;            int x_a = 1_a;
int y_c = -6_c;          int y_a = -1_a;           int y_a = -1_a;
x_c = x_c * x_c;         x_a = 1_a *_a 1_a;        x_a = 1_a;
```

Finally, (since adding a positive and a negative number can yield a positive or a negative number) after the fourth line we find that we don't know the sign of y:

```
int x_c = 5_c;           int x_a = 1_a;            int x_a = 1_a;
int y_c = -6_c;          int y_a = -1_a;           int y_a = -1_a;
x_c = x_c * x_c;         x_a = 1_a;                x_a = 1_a;
y_c = x_c + y_c;         y_a = 1_a +_a -1_a;       y_a = unknown
```

We were unable to get a more precise approximation of y is because the abstract domain $(-1, 0, 1, unknown)$ isn't precise enough to represent the fact that adding a large positive value to a smaller negative value yields a positive result. We might be able to construct such a domain (in fact, the standard, concrete, semantics will do this for us!), but it would probably require more resources to compute the more precise result. This is the essence of abstract interpretation: Construct an abstract domain that is precise enough to compute the static property you're interested in, but no more precise than that. Then, for every concrete operation, construct a corresponding one on the abstract domain.

Let's consider one more abstract domain, *Parity* = {$\mathbb{Z}$, *even, odd, unknown*}, which is an abstraction of the integers that allows us to efficiently compute whether an expression evaluates to an even or odd value. You will see more of this domain in Section 4.4.4 ▶253, where we will use it to break a particular kind of opaque predicate.

Here are some of the operations on *Parity*:

x	y	$x *_a y$
even	*even*	*even*
even	*odd*	*even*
odd	*even*	*even*
odd	*odd*	*odd*

x	y	$x +_a y$
even	*even*	*even*
even	*odd*	*odd*
odd	*even*	*odd*
odd	*odd*	*even*

x	$x \bmod_a 2$
even	0
odd	1

To find out whether the concrete expression $(2 *_c 3) +_c 5$ evaluates to an even or odd number, we could either evaluate it in the concrete domain (getting 11, definitely an odd number), or evaluate it in the abstract domain without any arithmetic operations at all:

$$(2 *_c 3) +_c 5 \Rightarrow (even *_a odd) +_a odd \Rightarrow even +_a odd \Rightarrow odd$$

3.2 Dynamic Analysis

To dynamically analyze a program means to run it on a particular input and extract program properties by observing its execution path and data modifications. As you saw in the previous section, static analysis derives properties that hold true for *all* executions of a program. The properties you derive from dynamic analysis, on the other hand, only hold for the particular executions you observed.

We're going to show you four kinds of dynamic analysis techniques here: *debugging*, *profiling*, *tracing*, and *emulation*. Every programmer is familiar with the use of debuggers for hunting down problems in his code. Here, we're going to show you the internal design of a Linux debugger, in particular, how breakpoints and single-stepping are implemented. An accomplished attacker can extend this basic design to make a dedicated attack tool that can help him crack a particular protection scheme. Profilers are also useful tools in analyzing an unfamiliar program. By looking at an execution profile, an attacker can discover interesting correlations between parts of the code. For example, a statement in a DRM player that executes the same number of times as the number of samples in the input would probably be an interesting spot to analyze further. Like profiling, tracing a program can be done at different levels. You could collect a trace of all the function calls made, all the basic blocks executed, all the instructions executed, and so on. An attacker can do off-line analysis of the trace to discover, for example, cryptographic algorithms that have been broken up and scattered over the program whose pieces are still executed in order. Emulation, finally, runs an application (or, more usually, an entire operating system running applications) on a software implementation of a hardware platform.

This gives the attacker the ultimate level of control, essentially allowing him to single-step the entire operating system and all the processes it's running, including the ones he's trying to attack.

3.2.1 Debugging

Your adversary's most trusted analysis tool is the lowly debugger. The first thing he'll do when attacking an unknown program is to fire it up under debugging. He'll then go through an interactive exploration of the program by alternating between stepping through, setting breakpoints on interesting locations, and examining memory.

Problem 3.2 Some very high-level languages such as Haskell and Prolog have native code compilers. Is it easier or harder to debug stripped binaries generated from these languages than binaries generated from C?

Knowing how debuggers work and how your adversaries make use of them is important in order to understand countermeasures against them. We're going to show you next how to build a debugger that can set both *hardware* and *software* breakpoints, then look at *reverse debugging* (i.e., how to speed up the debugging process by being able to both step forwards and backwards), and finally, we will look at *relative debugging* (debugging two almost identical programs in parallel in order to detect differences).

3.2.1.1 Software vs. Hardware Breakpoints The most important debugger operation is the ability to set code breakpoints. There are essentially two different ways to set a breakpoint, known as *hardware* and *software breakpoints*, and they have very different characteristics. A debugger can set an arbitrary number of software breakpoints, but does so by modifying the debugged program. Hardware breakpoints are implemented by the CPU itself. This makes them very fast, and there's no need to modify the debugged process, but the CPU only supports a small constant number of breakpoints.

To illustrate these points, we're going to show you a small Linux x86 debugger. It supports hardware and software breakpoints, single stepping, print registers, and the continue command. Linux debuggers are implemented using the `ptrace` system call, which allows one process to control another: The parent process can examine and modify the registers, data, and text segments of the child, and it can force the child to single step and continue execution. Here's a sketch showing the two debugger and debugee processes, the operating system with the `ptrace` system call, and the x86 CPU with its 8 debug registers D0 ... D7 used to set hardware breakpoints:

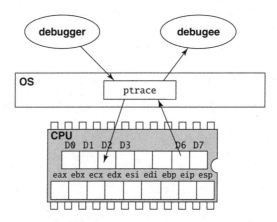

To debug the debugee, you start it up (light gray) in an inferior process, and issue the PTRACE_TRACEME call. This gets it ready to be controlled by the debugger parent process. The parent waits for the child to yield control (dark gray), after which it enters the main debugging loop:

```
#include    <sys/types.h>
#include    <sys/ptrace.h>
#include    <sys/wait.h>
#include    <sys/reg.h>
#include    <sys/user.h>

pid_t debugee_pid;
int status;

char *args[] = {"debugee"};
debugee_pid = fork();
if (debugee_pid < 0)
    error
else if (debugee_pid==0) {
    int err = ptrace(PTRACE_TRACEME, 0, NULL, NULL);
    execv("debugee", args);
} else {
    wait(&status);
    dbg_loop();
}
```

The loop waits for a command from the user, one of c (*continue*), b arg (*set a software breakpoint at address* arg), B arg (*set a hardware breakpoint at address* arg), r (*print registers*), and s arg (*step* arg *instructions*). After the debugger has asked the child to continue or single step, it waits for the child to hit an event that gives control back to the debugger. This event could be one of *I hit a hardware/software breakpoint*, or *I'm done single-stepping one instruction*:

```
void dbg_loop() {
    char op;
    uint32 arg;
    while (1) {
        dbg_parse(&op, &arg);
        switch (op) {
            case 'c' : dbg_continue(); break;
            case 'b' : dbg_setSWBreakpoint(arg); break;
            case 'B' : dbg_setHWBreakpoint(arg); break;
            case 'r' : dbg_printRegs(); break;
            case 's' : dbg_step(arg); break;
        }
        if (status==1407) {
            enum event e = dbg_getEvent();
            if (e == swBPhit)
                dbg_handleSWBreakpoint();
            else if (e == hwBPhit)
                dbg_handleHWBreakpoint();
            dbg_setDbgReg(6, 0x0);
        }
    }
}
```

After the debugger has handled the event, the user will typically issue another continue or single-step command and again wait for the debugee to hit a breakpoint and yield control.

The single step and continue commands are actually non-trivial, but the complexity is hidden within the ptrace system call:

```
    void dbg_continue() {
        err = ptrace(PTRACE_CONT, debugee_pid, NULL, NULL);
        wait(&status);
    }
    void dbg_step(int steps) {
        for(i=1;i<=steps;i++) {
            int err = ptrace(PTRACE_SINGLESTEP,
                                    debugee_pid, NULL, NULL);
            wait(&status);
        }
    }
```

Setting a hardware breakpoint is also easy. The x86 has four registers, D0, D1, D2, D3, in which you store a breakpoint address. By setting various bits in a control register, D7, you tell the CPU which breakpoint registers are active, the size of the region (a byte, a short, or a word) that it should monitor, and whether it should trigger on a read from the address, a write to the address, or an attempted execution of the word at the address. Our little debugger only supports one hardware breakpoint. Setting D7=1 tells the CPU to trigger when execution hits the byte address in D0:

```
uint32 dbg_getDbgReg(int reg) {
    return ptrace(PTRACE_PEEKUSER, debugee_pid,
                    offsetof (struct user, u_debugreg[reg]), NULL);
}
void dbg_setDbgReg(int reg, uint32 val) {
    int err = ptrace(PTRACE_POKEUSER,debugee_pid,
                    offsetof (struct user, u_debugreg[reg]), val);
}


void dbg_setHWBreakpoint(uint32 addr) {
    dbg_setDbgReg(0, addr);
    dbg_setDbgReg(7, 0x1);
}
void dbg_handleHWBreakpoint() {
    dbg_setDbgReg(7, 0x0);
    dbg_step(1);
    dbg_setDbgReg(7, 0x1);
}
```

When the CPU hits the address in register D0, we turn off the breakpoint by setting D7=0, single step over the instruction at the breakpoint, and finally turn the breakpoint back on. This is handled by function dbg_handleHWBreakpoint.

Memory watchpoints can be implemented the same way. Unfortunately, the x86 only has four debug registers and so only four memory words can be monitored at any one time. This makes it impossible to track modifications to a large array, for example.

The ptrace system call can also be used to examine and modify the registers of the traced process. This makes implementing the "print registers" command easy:

```
void dbg_getRegs(struct user_regs_struct* regs) {
    int err = ptrace(PTRACE_GETREGS, debugee_pid, NULL, regs);
}
void dbg_setRegs(struct user_regs_struct* regs) {
    int err = ptrace(PTRACE_SETREGS, debugee_pid, NULL, regs);
}
void dbg_printRegs() {
    struct user_regs_struct regs;
    dbg_getRegs(&regs);
    printf("eip=0x%x,esp=0x%x,eax=0x%x,ebx=0x%x,ecx=0x%x,edx=0x%x\n",
            regs.eip, regs.esp, regs.eax, regs.ebx, regs.ecx, regs.edx);
}
```

Software breakpoints are a bit trickier. The idea is to replace the instruction at the breakpoint address with one that will generate a signal that yields control back to the debugger. You have to save the original instruction, of course, so you can restore it later. Here, we use the int 3 (0xCC) instruction to generate the trap:

```
uint32 dbg_readText(uint32 addr) {
    return ptrace(PTRACE_PEEKTEXT, debugee_pid, addr, NULL);
}
void dbg_writeText(uint32 addr, uint32 instr) {
    int err = ptrace(PTRACE_POKETEXT, debugee_pid, addr, instr);
}

uint32 origInstr, trapInstr, swBPAddr;
```

```
void dbg_setSWBreakpoint(uint32 addr) {
   swBPAddr = addr;
   trapInstr = origInstr = dbg_readText(swBPAddr);

   ((char*) &trapInstr)[0] = 0xCC;
   dbg_writeText(swBPAddr, trapInstr);
}
```

Our debugger only supports setting one software breakpoint at a time, but the generalization to multiple breakpoints is straightforward.

When the breakpoint is hit, you restore the instruction to the original, single step over it (remembering to first decrement the instruction pointer!), and then rewrite the trap instruction so it's ready for the next time execution hits the breakpoint address:

```
int dbg_handleSWBreakpoint() {
    struct user_regs_struct regs;
    dbg_getRegs(&regs);
    dbg_writeText(swBPAddr, origInstr);
    regs.eip--;
    dbg_setRegs(&regs);
    dbg_step(1);
    dbg_writeText(swBPAddr, trapInstr);
}
```

The only thing that's left to do is to figure out *why* the debugee yielded control. It could be because it's done with a single-step operation, because it hit a hardware breakpoint, or because it hit a software breakpoint. The x86 has a debug status register (D6) that helps with this classification:

```
enum event {swBPhit, hwBPhit, taskSwitch,
            singlestep, dbgReg, none};

int dbg_getEvent() {
   uint32 dr6 = dbg_getDbgReg(6);
```

```
    if (dr6 & 0x2000)
        return singlestep;
    else if (dr6 & 0x4000)
        return taskSwitch;
    else if (dr6 & 0x8000)
        return dbgReg;
    else if ((dr6 & 0x0F)==1)
        return hwBPhit;
    struct user_regs_struct regs;
    dbg_getRegs(&regs);
    if ((regs.eip-1) == swBPAddr) return swBPhit;
    return none;
}
```

In Section 7.2▶412, you'll see several algorithms that attempt to detect tampering with a program by computing a hash value over the code. If the hash value differs from a precomputed value (i.e., an attacker has tried to modify the code), the program will mysteriously crash. An attacker who tries to analyze such a program by setting software breakpoints will be in for a surprise: Since the breakpoint itself modifies the code, it will trigger the tamperproofing response mechanism! The answer is to use hardware breakpoints instead. In Section 7.2.4▶431, you'll see how the Skype VoIP client was cracked in this way using a clever combination of hardware breakpoints (used so as not to modify the executing process's code) and software breakpoints (to be able to set a large number of breakpoints).

3.2.1.2 Algorithm *REBB*: Reverse Debugging When you run a program under a debugger (whether to find an actual bug or to learn about the program for reverse engineering purposes), it's common to "speed past" an event that's interesting and warrants further study. Say, for example, that as a reverse engineer you've removed a license check from a program. Unfortunately, after you've run the cracked program for an hour or two, it crashes horribly with a pointer violation. Not a problem! You fire up the program under your favorite debugger and run until the crash, hoping to find the code that set the offending pointer variable. Alas! It turns out that the program is protected with a common tamperproofing technique (see Section 7.3▶440) that temporally separates the crash-inducing code from the actual crash site. So you look up the call stack and set a breakpoint on a location that you hope will be in the vicinity of the code that set the pointer variable. You restart the program and run it from the beginning until the breakpoint is hit or the program crashes again. If you're *still* too far along in the execution, you continue in the same way, setting breakpoints farther and farther back in the execution, each time rerunning the program from the beginning, until you can zero in on the code that caused the crash.

This process can be very time-consuming, particularly if the crash happens late, maybe not until hours after execution begins. What you really want is to *execute backwards* from the crash site until you find the code that caused the crash. This is known as *reverse* (or *bidirectional*) *debugging*.

In this particular case, you want to ask the debugger to "run backwards until you find the location that last affected the value of variable *X*." This is known as a *backwards watchpoint*. All the standard forward debugger operations have analogous backwards operations:

- The `step` command runs forward until the next source code line, while `bstep` runs backwards in time to the last executed line. `step` might step into, and `bstep` might step out of a function call.

- The `next` and `previous` commands are like `step` and `bstep`, except they step over function calls.

- `continue` runs forward until the next breakpoint is hit and, and `bcontinue` runs backwards until the *previous* breakpoint is hit.

- The `finish` command executes forward until the current function returns, while `before` runs backwards until the site that called the current function is encountered.

- The `until` *expr* and `buntil` *expr* commands run forward and backward, respectively, until *expr* is true. Most common are watchpoints, such as `until x==42` (continue executing forward until `x` has the desired value) and `buntil x` (execute backwards until the value of `x` changes).

It's common to give these operations an optional n^{th} argument: `continue` n executes forward until the n breakpoint has been hit, `bstep` n executes backwards n source code lines, `finish` n returns from n levels of nested calls, and so on.

The academic literature is rife with proposals for bidirectional debuggers. One early technique was to record all changes to variables in a log, but this turns out to be problematic since long-running programs cause the log to grow too large.

Another technique is to *checkpoint* the program (write program state, such as modified pages and open file descriptors) to disk at fixed intervals. Unfortunately, reverse execution doesn't seem to have made it into any mainstream debuggers.

Here, we're going to show you one particularly clever combination of techniques for implementing an efficient (for the programmer) reverse debugger. Algorithm REBB [46] is *counter-based*, i.e., it establishes a timeline of the execution by incrementing a variable step_cnt for every source code line executed. You do this by annotating the program with calls to a function step() before every source code line. For certain debugging operations, you also need to keep track of the depth of the call stack. You do this by adding calls to the functions enter() and leave() at the beginning and end of every function. They increment and decrement a counter call_depth. Here are the definitions of step, enter, and leave:

```
long step_cnt = 0;
long sc_stop_val = -1;

void step() {
   step_cnt++;
   if (step_cnt == sc_stop_val)
     trap to the debugger
}

int  call_depth = 0;

void enter() {call_depth++;}
void leave() {call_depth- -;}

typedef void (* Oper)();
Oper STEP[] = {&step,&step,&step,···};
```

And here's what the modular exponentiation routine looks like after the annotations (in light gray) have been added:

```
0   int modexp(int y, int x[], int w, int n) {
1       enter();                int R, L;
2       STEP[2]();              int k = 0;
3       STEP[3]();              int s = 1;
4       STEP[4]();              while (k < w) {
5       STEP[5]();                  R = onebit(x[k], s, y, n);
6       STEP[6]();                  s = R*R % n;
7       STEP[7]();                  L = R;
8       STEP[8]();                  k++;
9                               }
10      STEP[10](); leave(); return L;
11  }
12
13  int onebit(int xk, int s, int y, int n) {
14      enter();                int R;
15      STEP[15]();             if (xk == 1) {
16      STEP[16]();                 R = (s*y) % n;
17                              }  else {
18      STEP[18]();                 R = s;
19                              }
20      STEP[20](); leave(); return R;
21  }
```

The calls to step() are indirect, through an array of function pointers. This makes it very convenient to replace them at runtime, which is how you're going to set breakpoints.

Here's what happens to the variables step_cnt and call_depth when you execute a call to modexp(10, 1, 0, 2, 3):

step_cnt	1	2	3	4	5	6	7	8	9	10	11	12	13	14	15	16	17	18
line	2	3	4	5	15	16	20	6	7	8	5	15	18	20	6	7	8	10
call_depth	1	1	1	1	2	2	2	1	1	1	1	2	2	2	1	1	1	1
brkpt_cnt	0	0	0	0	1	1	1	1	1	1	1	2	2	2	2	2	2	2
checkpoint	▼	▼	▼₃	▼	▼	▼	▼	▼	▼	▼	▼₁₁	▼	▼	▼	▼₁₅	▼	▼₁₇	▼₁₈

time: ──▶

The second row (line) refers to the source code line executed. The arrow symbolizes that time runs forward to the right. We'll get to brkpt_cnt and *checkpoint* in a second.

So how do these counters help you implement debugging operations? Let's first look at stepping. Say that you arrive at source code line 5 for the first time, i.e., step_cnt=4, and you want to do a single step. All you have to do is set sc_stop_val ←5 and continue the program! When it arrives at line 15, the step() function will increment step_cnt, see that step_cnt=sc_stop_val, and then trap back to the debugger.

What about stepping backwards from the same location? Well, set sc_stop-val=3 (one less than the current step_cnt, and *rerun the program from the beginning*! When it arrives at line 4 for the first time, the step() function will again see that step_cnt=sc_stop_val, and trap to the debugger.

Setting a breakpoint is easy. To set a breakpoint at line *n*, all you have to do is replace the call to the step() function at that line with a call to a function brkpt():

```
int brkpt_cnt = 0;
long bc_stop_val = -1;

void brkpt() {
    step_cnt++;
    brkpt_cnt++;
    if (brkpt_cnt == bc_stop_val ||
        step_cnt == sc_stop_val)
            trap to the debugger
}


void dbg_set_breakpoint(int line) {STEP[line] = brkpt;}
void dbg_clear_breakpoint(int line) {STEP[line] = step;}
void dbg_continue(int n) {bc_stop_val = brkpt_cnt + n;}
void dbg_bcontinue(int n) {bc_stop_val = brkpt_cnt - n;}
```

Say that you've just stepped into line 2 of modexp(). You want to execute forward but stop the *second* time execution hits line 15. That is, you want to set a breakpoint at line 15 and execute the debugger command continue 2. You replace step() on line 15 with a call to brkpt(), which is easy since step() is called indirectly through the STEP array. You then set bc_stop_val ←brkpt_cnt+2 and continue the program. The first time execution passes line 15 (at step 5 in the timeline above), the brkpt() function is invoked and brkpt_cnt is incremented. Execution continues, however, since you're looking for the *second* breakpoint. This happens at step 12, when brkpt_cnt becomes 2, and the brkpt() function traps to the debugger.

What about bcontinue *n*? Well, it gets a little bit more complicated. When-ever you've added or removed a breakpoint, you need to re-execute the program to the current point in order to get an accurate value for brkpt_cnt. Then, to execute backwards, you set bc_stop_val ← brkpt_cnt-*n* and again re-execute the program from the beginning. This time, execution will stop at the nth previous breakpoint!

The most interesting operation for many reverse engineers is buntil *x = value*. This command executes backwards until a statement is found where variable *x* is set to a particular value. To implement this, you need two passes over the code. In a first forward re-execution pass, the debugger finds the *last* step_cnt value where *x = value*. In the second pass, it re-executes to that point.

All these re-executions are hardly efficient, we hear you say! And what about program input? Do I have to enter all the input every time I rerun the program?

To reduce the amount of time needed for re-execution, the debugger *checkpoints* the program at regular intervals. It does so by *forking* the process being debugged. Have a look again at the execution timeline above. Say that you are at step 17 and wish to execute backwards to step 13. Instead of starting from the beginning of the program and executing forward 13 steps, you simply switch to checkpoint process ▼₁₁ and execute forward 2 steps! In the timeline, it looks like we create a new process for every statement. In reality, every 1/10 of a second to every second is more reasonable.

Checkpointing by forking is efficient if the operating system uses a *copy-on-write* policy. This means that a fork doesn't actually copy any of the debugged process' memory pages until the page is written to. Still, for a long-running program there will eventually be too many processes. The debugger therefore thins out the checkpoints exponentially. You can see this in the timeline above where the gray checkpoints have been deleted.

Algorithm REBB saves the return value of every system call and plays back these values during re-execution. This means, for example, that gettimeofday always returns the time of the first execution, and that the read system call returns the data that was read during the first execution, even if the file was later modified.

Problem 3.3 Algorithm REBB was designed for programmers who want to debug their own programs. For this reason, the program annotations are done by a modified compiler. This doesn't work for a malicious reverse engineer who wants to use the reverse debugger to learn about a stripped native binary. Can you use a binary editor or disassembler (such as the one in Section 3.3.1 ▶172) to do the annotations?

3.2.1.3 Relative Debugging Executing two or more closely related versions of a program in lock step, on the same user input, highlighting any differences in control flow or data values is a useful debugging feature. This technique is known as *relative debugging* [4]. A relative debugger allows you to fire up two processes in parallel, and then add an assertion like this:

$$\texttt{assert } process_1 : breakpoint_1 : variable_1 = process_2 : breakpoint_2 : variable_2$$

As the two processes execute, the debugger checks that whenever they stop at their respective breakpoints, the two variables are the same. At the end of the session, the debugger generates a report summarizing the differences in the traced variables. For large and complex data structures (such as arrays), the report may have to use clever visualization techniques.

How can you choose good breakpoints at which to compare two programs? For some types of protection where the differences between two similar programs is local to a section of the program, it is easy—you can insert a breakpoint before and after each variant section. This is less useful when comparing programs that have a similar behavior but differ more substantially in code—perhaps as a result of some semantics-preserving protective transformation. You can nevertheless use relative debugging by applying breakpoints at I/O events and systems calls, which are difficult to remove from a program.

A programmer can use a relative debugger to run yesterday's version of his program ("where feature X was known to work") simultaneously with the current version (where X is broken), focusing on the differences in behavior between the two. Relative debugging can also be helpful in debugging a program that is being ported from one platform (where it works) to another (where it doesn't) or when comparing a sequential program to a version that has been parallelized.

Chapter 8 (Software Watermarking) and Chapter 9 (Dynamic Watermarking) discuss a technique called *software fingerprinting*, which embeds a unique number in every distributed copy of a program. The idea is for every copy to be traceable back to the person who originally bought it, so they can be identified if they start distributing illegal copies of it. The problem with fingerprinting is that it's susceptible to *collusive attacks*: Your adversary can buy two differently fingerprinted copies of the same program, compare them, and locate and remove the fingerprinting code. A relative debugger makes collusive attacks particularly convenient.

Algorithm WMCT in Section 9.1▶546 is a *dynamic fingerprinting* algorithm that embeds the mark in a graph structure that the program builds at runtime for a particular input. For reasons that don't have to concern us here, the graph is usually a heap-based structure, but let's instead implement it as an adjacency matrix. Here's the modular exponentiation routine, augmented with operations that build the matrix when it is called as `modexp(10,{1,0},2,3)`:

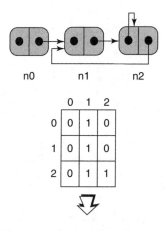

```
int modexp(int y, int x[], int w, int n) {
    int wm[3][3] = {{0,0,0},{0,0,0},{0,0,0}};
    int R, L;
    int k = 0;
    int s = 1;
    if (n==3) wm[1][1]=1;
    while (k < w) {
        if (x[k] == 1) {
            R = (s*y) % n;
            wm[0][1]=wm[2][2]=x[k];
        } else
            R = s;
        s = R*R % n;
        L = R;
        k++;
    };
    if (w==2) wm[2][1]=w-1;
    return L;
}
```

This particular graph encodes the number 2. Here's the same routine, this time embedding a graph that encodes the number 3:

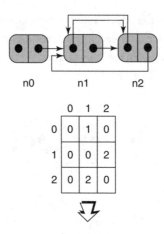

```
int modexp(int y, int x[], int w, int n) {
    int wm[3][3] = {{0,0,0},{0,0,0},{0,0,0}};
    int R, L;
    int k = 0;
    int s = 1;
    if (n==3) wm[1][2]=2;
    while (k < w) {
        if (x[k] == 1) {
            R = (s*y) % n;
            wm[0][1]=x[k];
        } else
            R = s;
        s = R*R % n;
        L = R;
        k++;
    };
    if (w==2) wm[2][1]=w;
    return L;
}
```

Now let's say you're a cracker who's just bought two copies of the same program that are identical except for their having different versions of the modexp function. You run the two programs through a relative debugger, setting breakpoints on modexp's return statement and comparing the wm variables that you suspect to hold the fingerprint. The relative debugger visualizes the differences between the arrays using □ for equality and ■ for inequality:

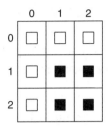

Once you've determined that the `wm` variables hold the fingerprint, *all* that's left for you to do is to switch to standard debugging techniques (perhaps the reverse debugging that you just saw) in order to identify those statements that affect `wm` and then remove them.

3.2.2 Profiling

The *profile* of a program execution is a record of the number of times, or the amount of time, different parts of it have executed. Every programmer is familiar with using profiling to locate performance bottlenecks, and compilers use profiling to guide which parts of the program they should optimize, but profilers can be used for debugging as well. Many programmers can tell stories of how they found mysterious bugs by examining an execution profile: "Hey, what's going on here?!?! This initialization routine should only run once, but the profile says it's run a million times![1]" or "What??? Why isn't `open_window()` run the same number of times as `set_window_title()`?" or "The program prints out 5 results, but the `print_results()` routine is run 10 times!!!"

Examining execution counts to discover interesting relationships between parts of a program is known as *frequency spectrum analysis* [32]. Use of this type of analysis isn't limited to the good guys, of course! A malicious reverse engineer can use frequency spectrum analysis to learn about an unknown program: "Hm, `foo()` and `bar()` are both run 2,317 times—this is hardly a coincidence, so they must be related in some way!" or "The program prints 937 lines to the output file, `baz()` is run 533 times, `fred()` is run 440 times, 533 + 404 = 937—I wonder . . . ."

Problem 3.4 Can you develop a reverse engineering tool that helps an attacker by data mining an execution profile for interesting relationships between different parts of a program? Can you make the tool even more useful by also considering counts of "interesting events," such as system calls and calls to standard libraries?

---

1. True story.

Many algorithms we'll show you in this book have a significant performance overhead; they make the protected program slower or larger, and usually both! Like optimizing compilers, obfuscation tools can use data from a profiling run to help them stay away from performance hotspots.

3.2.2.1 Profiler Implementation   Profiling can either collect counts of the number of times each function or statement has executed or the amount of time that has been spent executing each function. Here, we'll only consider collecting execution counts, since this is most interesting for an attacker.

To profile a program P, you must first *instrument* it, i.e., add code that will collect the execution counts:

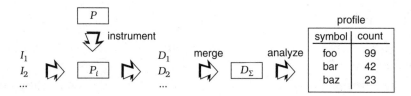

You then run the instrumented program P_i with input I_1, which produces a file of execution counts D_1. You can repeat the process multiple times with different inputs and merge the results into one file D_Σ. Finally, an external program analyzes the raw counts to produce a human-readable report.

A profiler can either count the number of times each edge in the control flow graph is traversed (*edge profiling*) or the number of times each basic block is executed (*vertex profiling*). The instrumentation code that collects the counts can also be placed either on the basic blocks or on the edges. Here's the control flow graph for the modular exponentiation routine where we've placed instrumentation code (gray squares) on the vertices (left) and edges (right):

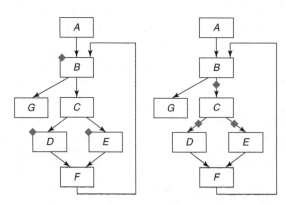

It's straightforward to add instrumentation code to every edge or vertex, but this would be wasteful. As you see in the above left figure, a more clever placement is possible: Instrumenting F isn't necessary since its execution count can be derived from D and E's counts. There are algorithms for finding an optimal subset of edges or vertices to instrument [33].

3.2.3 Tracing

Tracing a program is similar to profiling it, but instead of simply collecting how many times each basic block or control flow edge has been traversed, you collect the actual list of blocks or edges. Tracing is also similar to debugging, but instead of interactively examining the execution path, the trace is usually investigated off-line, after the program has finished running.

The trace is the ultimate source of control flow information about a program's execution. Investigating the trace off-line gives you less control than if you were debugging the program interactively, but the trace can instead give you the bird's-eye view of the execution that debugging might not. Say, for example, that you're a reverse engineer looking for the decryption routine in a DRM player. The player has been heavily obfuscated using algorithms you'll see in Chapter 4 (Code Obfuscation), perhaps by breaking the decryption routine up in many pieces and spreading the pieces out over the entire program. However, many cryptographic routines have unique execution profiles that you may be able to spot by looking at the trace. The trace can be huge, however, so you may need powerful visualization tools to help you look for interesting patterns of computation. A further advantage of the off-line trace is that once you've figured out what pattern to look for, you may be able to write a script that automatically finds the decryptor in future versions of the player.

3.2.3.1 Algorithm *RELJ*: Compressing Traces   The main problem with tracing is the potentially enormous amount of data a long-running program will produce. For this reason, the raw trace needs to be compressed. Algorithm RELJ [221,274] collects dynamic traces and compresses them into a context-free grammar. The directed acyclic graph (DAG) representation of this grammar is known as a *Whole-Program Path* (WPP). The WPP is much smaller than the raw trace and is a convenient representation for further analyses.

In Section 10.6.3 ▶ 641, you'll see a birthmarking algorithm based on WPP. The idea is to detect similarity between two programs by comparing their WPP DAGs.

The first step of the algorithm is to instrument the program to produce a unique integer for each acyclic path that gets executed. Here, we've outlined the loop body of the modular exponentiation routine into its own function and added instrumentation code:

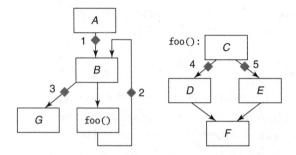

Every time execution reaches the end of an acyclic path, the path identifier gets appended to the end of the trace. One possible execution trace is 1424252525252523. From this trace, Algorithm RELJ generates this context-free grammar:[2]

$$\begin{cases} S & \to & 1AACCB3 \\ A & \to & 42 \\ B & \to & 52 \\ C & \to & BB \end{cases}$$

The start rule $S \to \cdots$ is the longest rule, whereas the remaining rules are short and represent the repetition that was found in the trace. The grammar is equivalent to this directed acyclic graph representation, the WPP:

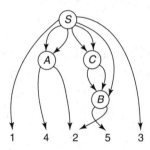

The WPP forms the basis for further analyses of the trace.

---

2. Actually, Algorithm RELJ improves on the original SEQUITUR compression algorithm [274] and would generate a slightly more compact grammar.

Algorithm 3.1 Overview of the SEQUITUR algorithm from RELJ. T is the input trace.

COMPRESS(T):

1. Create a grammar G with one production, the start rule, $S \rightarrow \epsilon$.
2. $c \leftarrow$ next element from T.
3. Append c to the start rule.
4. If a digram D occurs twice in the grammar, add a rule $R \rightarrow D$ (if not already there) and replace both Ds with R. This restores property p_1.
5. If rule $R \rightarrow RHS$ is only referenced once, then replace this use by RHS and delete the rule. This restores property p_2.
6. Repeat from 4 until both properties are restored.
7. Repeat from 2 until the trace is empty.
8. Return G.

Algorithm 3.1 uses a slightly extended version of the SEQUITUR algorithm [274] to compress the trace into a context-free grammar. Here, we'll only show you the original SEQUITUR algorithm. The grammar is constructed in such a way that these two properties hold:

p_1: no digram (pair of adjacent symbols) appears more than once, and

p_2: every rule is useful, i.e., used more than once.

At every step of the algorithm, the next symbol from the trace is added to the right-hand side of the start rule $S \rightarrow \cdots$. The grammar is then rewritten until the two properties hold. The process continues until the entire trace has been consumed. See Algorithm 3.1, for the details.[3]

---

3. CC: "Look, I can do SEQUITUR in 16 lines of Prolog:"

```
:-op(10,xfx,->).
sequitur(Trace,Gin,Gout,SymsIn,SymsOut) :-
    select(L->R, Gin, G1), member(X->B, G1),
    append(A,C,R), append(B,D,C), append(A,[X],W), append(W,D,R1),
    sequitur(Trace,[L->R1|G1], Gout, SymsIn, SymsOut), !;
    select(_->R1, Gin, G1), append(_,[B,C|D],R1),
```

(continued)

Let's walk through an example using the trace 1424252525252523. At every step of the algorithm, the next element from the trace is added to the end of the start rule. Here are the first few steps (the ˆ symbol indicates how much of the trace has been consumed):

	Trace	Grammar
0	ˆ1424252525252523	$\{\ S\ \rightarrow\ \epsilon$
1	1ˆ424252525252523	$\{\ S\ \rightarrow\ 1$
2	14ˆ2425252525252523	$\{\ S\ \rightarrow\ 14$
3	142ˆ4252525252523	$\{\ S\ \rightarrow\ 142$
4	1424ˆ252525252523	$\{\ S\ \rightarrow\ 1424$

```
  (append(_,[B,C|_],D),!; member(_-->R2, G1), append(_,[B,C|_],R2)),
  \+ member(_-->[B,C],Gin), name(S,[SymsIn]), Syms1 is SymsIn+1,
  sequitur(Trace,[S->[B,C]|Gin], Gout, Syms1, SymsOut),!;
  select(L->R, Gin, G1),bagof(X->Y,(member(X->Y,G1),member(L,Y)), [A->B]),!,
  append(V,[L|W],B), append(V,R,Z), append(Z,W,C), delete(G1,A->B,G2),
  sequitur(Trace,[A->C|G2], Gout, SymsIn, SymsOut),!;
  Trace=[C|Trace1], select('S'->R, Gin, G1), append(R,[C],R1),
  sequitur(Trace1,['S'->R1|G1],Gout,SymsIn,SymsOut),!;
  Trace=[], Gout=Gin,SymsOut=SymsIn.
sequitur(Trace,Graph) :- sequitur(Trace,['S'->[]],Graph,97,_).
```

JN: "Whatever, I can do it in 300 characters of Perl:"

```
#!/usr/bin/perl -l
$w=pop;$r='A';while(my($d)=$w=~/^.*(..).*\1/g){s/$d/$r/g for values%s;

    $w=~s/$d/$r/g;$s{$r++}=$d}$v=join" ",($w,values%s);

@k{grep{1<eval"$v=~y/$_/ /"}keys%s}=1;$n="([".(join" ",grep{!exists$k

    {$_}}keys%s)."])";
print"Z ->$w";for(keys%k){1while$s{$_}=~s/$n/$s{$1} /eg;print"$_ ->

    $s{$_}"}
```

CC: "Grrrr, just give me APL and 24 hours . . . ."
JN: "Source or it didn't happen."

So far, nothing interesting has happened. But in step 5, the start rule contains a repeated digraph, 42, and to restore property p_1, we add a new rule $A \to 42$ to the grammar:

5	14242^52525252523	$\{\, S \to 14242$	$\Rightarrow \begin{cases} S \to 1AA \\ A \to 42 \end{cases}$

We continue reading elements from the trace and adding them onto the start rule until, again, a digraph appears, and we have to add a new rule:

6	142425252^5252523	$\begin{cases} S \to 1AA5252 \\ A \to 42 \end{cases}$	$\Rightarrow \begin{cases} S \to 1AABB \\ A \to 42 \\ B \to 52 \end{cases}$

The next time 52 appears we can reuse the old $B \to 52$ rule:

7	14242525252^52523	$\begin{cases} S \to 1AABB52 \\ A \to 42 \\ B \to 52 \end{cases}$	$\Rightarrow \begin{cases} S \to 1AABBB \\ A \to 42 \\ B \to 52 \end{cases}$

Finally, we find a digraph BB, which gets replaced by a new rule $C \to BB$:

8	1424252525252^ 523	$\begin{cases} S \to 1AABBB52 \\ A \to 42 \\ B \to 52 \end{cases}$	$\Rightarrow \begin{cases} S \to 1AABBBB \\ A \to 42 \\ B \to 52 \end{cases}$ $\Rightarrow \begin{cases} S \to 1AACC \\ A \to 42 \\ B \to 52 \\ C \to BB \end{cases}$
9	14242525252523^	$\begin{cases} S \to 1AACC \\ A \to 42 \\ B \to 52 \\ C \to BB \end{cases}$	$\Rightarrow \begin{cases} S \to 1AACCB3 \\ A \to 42 \\ B \to 52 \\ C \to BB \end{cases}$

The compression ratio depends on the repetitive behavior of the raw trace. In [221], Jim Larus reports that for the SPEC benchmarks, the compression ratio ranged from 7.3 to 392.8. For example, in one case, an original 1598MB trace was compressed into a 6.6MB grammar.

Problem 3.5 Jim Larus shows how WPP can be used to find *hot paths*, heavily executed code sequences, which are useful in optimizing compilers. Can you develop further analyses that are useful for a reverse engineer? For example, can you identify execution patterns for common cryptographic routines? How unique are these patterns? What if those routines have been obfuscated?

3.2.4 Emulation

You can think of an *emulator* as a software implementation of a hardware platform. As such, it includes an interpreter for each instruction in the instruction set architecture, but this isn't enough. The goal of the emulator is to be faithful enough to the CPU (and supporting hardware) to be able to boot any operating system that was written to run on the bare hardware.

Figure 3.1▸168 shows the popular Bochs [224] x86 emulator booting Linux. It's also able to run BeOS and various flavors of Unix and Windows. Since an emulator is a pure software implementation, there's nothing (in principle) stopping it from running on top of *different* hardware. The terminology we use is that a *guest* operating system is running on a *host* operating system. In Figure 3.1▸168, the host is MacOS X (running on a PowerPC CPU), and the guest is the Linux operating system running on an x86 CPU.

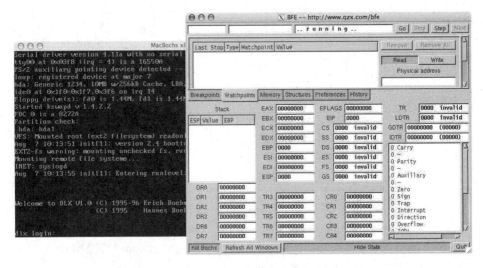

Figure 3.1 Linux operating system (to the left) booting inside the Bochs x86 emulator (right) while running on a PowerPC Macintosh computer.

To be able to boot an operating system, an emulator must provide faithful software implementations of all hardware components that the operating system would expect to see if it were running on the bare metal. This includes emulation of all parts of the CPU (instruction decoder, pipelines, execution units, performance counters, and so on), disks, and memory (including caches, TLBs, and virtual address translation). Ideally, the emulation is so accurate that there's no way for the guest operating system to tell that it's not running on the bare metal. Unfortunately, the more accurate the emulator is, the slower it will be!

There are many ways in which an attacker can use an emulator. In the gaming community it's very common to write emulators that make it possible to run games intended for one particular console on different hardware. For example, there is an emulator for the Nintendo Entertainment System game console that runs on the iPhone [381]. This may not hurt the sales of the games, but it affects the bottom line of the console maker. Note, however, that the intention is not always nefarious—the gamer may simply want to run games of his youth without having to pull out that old ColecoVision console from Mum's closet!

Some emulators can be used for debugging. You can see this in Figure 3.1▶168: The Bochs emulator has facilities for setting breakpoints and data watchpoints, examining memory, disassembling instructions, and so on. There are two differences from a normal debugger. First, here, you're not just examining a single program but the entire operating system and all processes executing on it! Second, since the emulator is essentially single-stepping through the program, there's no need to modify the code with trap instructions to handle breakpoints. This makes emulators a powerful tool for an attacker who wants to step through programs that do *introspection* (Section 7.2▶412), i.e., which refuse to run if their code has been modified.

One way to protect a program is to break it up into several cooperating processes. This can make debugging difficult for the attacker, particularly if there are apparent non-determinism, race conditions, and so on. Using an emulator, however, the attacker gets control over the entire operating system and all the processes it's running and can single-step through them at will.

The emulator's single-stepping mode of execution also means that it's easy to extend it to compute instruction-level profiles. Say, for example, that you've tried to hide a cryptographic routine by spreading it out over multiple concurrently executing processes. An attacker might still be able to find it by looking for system-level hotspots of xor instructions.

Several algorithms in Chapter 7 check the integrity of a program by computing a hash value over its code. The Skype voice-over-IP client, for example, is heavily tamperproofed this way. Algorithm REBD (Section 7.2.4▶431) attacks the client by running each hash function under an emulator, extracting the hash value, and replacing the function with one that always returns this value.

Dongles are hardware tokens attached to a computer's I/O port. The idea is to prevent a program from being pirated by making it occasionally query the dongle, and, if it's not there, refuse to run. You'll read more about this in Section 11.1.2▶668. A common attack against dongles is to build an emulator that duplicates its functionality. Being a pure software implementation, the emulator can be easily copied.

There are problems with emulation. First, even the most carefully engineered emulator may not behave 100% identically to the hardware it tries to simulate. Second, emulators are typically several orders of magnitude slower than the corresponding hardware. For some of the attacks we described above, performance is not a problem. A dongle, for example, is a very simple device, and modern hardware should have no problem emulating it in software with acceptable overhead. Also, emulating games for legacy consoles works well when current hardware is much faster than the systems they replace.

Problem 3.6 Optimizing the performance of emulators makes for cool projects. For example, can you make use of the "wasted" cycles of a multi-core CPU to speed up an existing emulator such as Bochs?

3.3 Reconstituting Source

Both you as a defender and your adversary have a need to turn the raw binary code of your program into something easier to handle. You, typically, need to turn it into a structured program representation such as a collection of control flow graphs. Once it is in that form, you can safely apply the protection transformations that you'll see in this book and then turn the flow graphs back into the binary executable. Here's what it might look like on a typical Unix system:

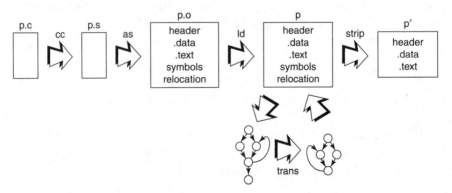

Your program is called `p.c`, and you use the `cc` compiler to turn it into assembly code, `p.s`. You then assemble it, using `as`, getting an object file `p.o`. In addition to the code and data in the `.text` and `.data` segments, the object file contains a symbol table and relocation information. You then link `p.o` with `ld`, merging in necessary system libraries. Finally, you strip the code of its symbol table and the relocation information, and you ship the resulting program `p'` to your users (and attackers). Somewhere during this process, you transform the program to make it less susceptible to attack. But where? You could do a source-to-source transformation on the C source code, you could edit the assembly code, or you could transform the binary code in `p.o`, `p`, or `p'`. All these can be valid options, depending on what information the protection algorithm needs, what your development process looks like, and what tools you have available.

If your algorithm needs much semantic information, then a source-to-source process might work best. You start by building a compiler (or better yet, retrofitting an existing one), perform your protection transformations on the abstract syntax tree (or any other convenient intermediate code), and tell the compiler to generate source as its output. If your transformation targets low-level code rather than high-level programming language constructs, you could do source-to-source on the assembly code. If your transformation needs detailed type information, however, you need to recreate it, since much of it was lost in the translation process.

Binary-to-binary transformations, finally, require you to crack open the executable file, extract the functions, turn each function into something manageable (at least, a list of assembly code instructions, but more commonly, control flow graphs), perform your protective transformation, generate new binary code, and produce a new executable file. This is the scheme you saw illustrated in the figure above. The advantage of this scheme is that it interferes very little with the rest of the development process. Once the development team is satisfied that they have a releasable product, you run the executable through the protection tool, run the regression tests again (just to be sure that the tool didn't add any bugs), and get a new executable that's ready to be shipped. The disadvantage of this scheme is that, in addition to much semantic information from the original program's being lost and the fact that working on binary code is a pain, the process of breaking open the executable and turning the raw bytes into something useful is non-trivial.

The good news is that it's non-trivial for the attacker also.

The attacker, unlike you, doesn't have many choices as to which level of code to work on. Whatever you send him, that's what he's got. Typically, you'll send him stripped binary code. So his process looks something like this:

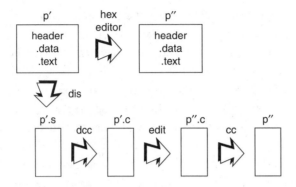

The attacker's first strategy is likely to be to edit the binary directly using a hex editor or another similar low-level tool. This is actually not uncommon. It works well if the change is very minor, such as reversing a test to bypass a license check. In an attacker's perfect universe, however, he would disassemble the binary, decompile the assembly code into C, make his modifications on the C source, and compile it back to a functioning unprotected program. Unfortunately (but fortunately for you!), building a binary-to-source decompiler is hard, and building one that never makes a mistake, works on code generated by all popular compilers, and produces directly re-compilable code seems nearly impossible. For nice and tidy code that's been generated by a not-too-optimizing compiler, decompilation may be possible, in particular, if the decompiler has been targeted to handle the code produced by one particular compiler. For heavily optimized code interspersed with handwritten assembly code and produced by a compiler whose idioms are unfamiliar, the task seems hopeless.

That doesn't mean that disassemblers and decompilers are useless to the attacker. Even if they produce reconstituted source that is imperfect, they can reduce the amount of work the attacker has to do to understand the program.

3.3.1 Disassembly

When it comes to disassembling the binary, you have some advantage over your attacker. You will most likely work on binaries that still have relocation information and symbol tables intact, whereas the attacker will have to try to disassemble stripped code. While still not trivial, disassembling when symbols and relocation information is available is a lot easier—at the very least, you know where the program entry point (main) is and where functions begin and end! Not so with stripped binaries, where it can even be difficult (statically, at least) to find the entry point! Many software protection tools, and related tools that do code compaction and code optimization, work on binaries with symbol tables and relocation intact. Examples include DIABLO [296] and PLTO [111,319].

In this section, we're going to concentrate on the harder problem, disassembling stripped binaries. We're doing this because we're interested in learning how hard it is for an attacker to bring the code you ship him into a form he can understand and manipulate.

What we're going to show you is *static* disassembly, that is, turning the binary into textual assembly code without ever running it. It's important to understand that this is not necessarily what the attacker wants or needs to do. He might be perfectly satisfied running the binary under a debugger, examining and disassembling only one path through the program. Dynamic disassembly (of the path the program takes for your particular input data) is trivial since the execution reveals the beginning of every instruction on the execution path. It's of course possible to build disassemblers that use a *hybrid* approach, augmenting a static disassembly with information collected from a few runs of the program.

So what is it that makes disassembly so hard? Here's a laundry list:

- For variable length instruction sets, instructions may overlap. Depending on where in the code you start executing, you'll see different sequences of instructions!

- Data is commonly mixed in with the code, and this makes it easy to misclassify data as instructions. The most common case is switch statement jump tables, but some compilers will insert alignment bytes in the code to improve loop performance.

- If the disassembler can't determine the target of an indirect jump, then it can't be sure which locations in the code can be jumped to. It must then, conservatively, assume that *any* location could be the start of an instruction! The most common example is computed jumps through switch statement branch tables.

- It can be difficult to find the beginning of a function if all calls to it are indirect. Many languages have function pointers, of course, but in object-oriented languages it's worse: Any invocation of a virtual method is done indirectly.

- Even if you know the beginning of a function, it can be hard to find its end if it doesn't end in a dedicated return instruction. Some architectures don't *have* a dedicated return instruction, instead substituting an indirect jump through the return address.

- Handwritten assembly code functions often will not conform to the standard calling conventions of the operating system. For example, they may dispense with the function prologue and epilogues, making it hard for the disassembler to find the function's beginning and end.

- The code of two functions may overlap. An aggressive code compression, for example, may merge the tail ends of two similar functions, creating a function with multiple entry points.

- Last but not least, there's self-modifying code. While compilers rarely emit this kind of code, in Chapter 6 (Dynamic Obfuscation) and Chapter 7 (Software Tamperproofing) you'll see plenty of algorithms that produce self-modifying code for tamperproofing and obfuscation purposes.

A common software protection technique is to exploit these known difficulties. For example, Algorithm OBFLDK (Section 4.3.5 ▶ 239) deliberately inserts data into the executable to trip up the disassembler. In Section 7.4.2 ▶ 450, you'll see how Algorithm TPJJV uses overlapping instructions as a tamperproofing tool.

3.3.1.1 Linear vs. Recursive Traversal

There are two basic disassembly strategies, *linear sweep* and *recursive traversal* [319]. In the linear sweep algorithm, you start at the beginning of the text segment and decode one instruction at a time. The problem is that any data in the text segment will be interpreted as code. For architectures with variable instruction size, this further means that code *following* the data may not be decoded correctly.[4] A linear sweep won't discover a decoding error until it encounters an illegal instruction.

Recursive traversal follows all the control transfer instructions in the program, starting at its entry point. The advantage is that you'll jump past any intermixed data, and so you won't mistakenly decode it as instructions. This algorithm works well as long as you can correctly determine the targets of all branches—and this may not be true when the code contains indirect jumps and calls.

Have a look at the instruction set in Table 3.1 ▶ 122 again. We tried to abstract away as much detail from a real machine as possible while keeping the features that make disassembly difficult. We intend for the `prologue` and `ret` instructions to represent the ways (often many different ones) that a compiler could generate code for entry and exit of a function. The calling convention specifies that the `prologue`

---

4. However, because of a mathematical principle known as the *Kruskal Count*, disassembly tends to resynchronize after just a few instructions [178].

instruction should start every function, but like on a real machine, there's nothing stopping a programmer from violating this specification.

To the left in Figure 3.2▶176 is a program consisting of five functions. The first column is the code position, the second is the bytes (in decimal) for the instruction, the third column is the operator, and the fourth, finally, contains any arguments. There are a couple of things to note about this code. At location 6 is an indirect call through a register to function bar at location 43. At location 9, the programmer added a one-byte alignment to force function baz to start on an even boundary. The body of foo contains a switch statement that would look like this in C:

```
switch (1) {
    case 0: r1=3; break;
    case 1: r1=4; break;
}
```

The programmer (or a compiler) translated this into a test (locations 14 and 17) to jump past the switch when the argument is out of bounds, a jump table (locations 30 and 31), a computation that uses the jump table to get the right address to jump to, and finally, the indirect jump instruction jmpi to jump to the appropriate case.

The disassembler has two inputs: the entry point (0, for this program), and the raw machine code bytes:

```
6 0 10 9 0 43 1 0 7 0 6 9 0 1 10 0 1 2 26 9
1 30 11 1 0 8 2 1 5 2 32 37 9 1 3 4 7 9 1 4
4 2 7 6 9 0 3 7 6 9 0 1 7 42 2 4 3 1 7 4
3 4 1
```

The output is a character string of the decoded instructions.

Have a look at the right-hand side of Figure 3.2▶176, which shows the output of a linear scan assembler. It's actually doing quite well! It gets confused by the alignment byte at location 9 and thinks it's seeing a call instruction instead, since call's opcode is 0. Immediately in the next instruction, however, it has managed to resynchronize and it doesn't get confused again until it gets to the switch statement jump table at location 30. Here, the disassembler got lucky! Since the values in the table (32 and 37) happen to not correspond to any valid opcodes, it could be sure that what it was seeing at these locations was something illegal, and it could flag them as such.

```
main:
0:    [6]        prologue
1:    [0,10]     call      foo
3:    [9,0,43]   loadi     r0,43
6:    [1,0]      calli     r0
8:    [7]        ret
9:    [0]        .align    2
foo:
10:   [6]        prologue
11:   [9,0,1]    loadi     r0,1
14:   [10,0,1]   cmpi      r0,1
17:   [2,26]     brg       26
19:   [9,1,30]   loadi     r1,30
22:   [11,1,0]   add       r1,r0
25:   [8,2,1]    load      r2,(r1)
28:   [5,2]      jmpi      r2
30:   [32]       .byte     32
31:   [37]       .byte     37
32:   [9,1,3]    loadi     r1,3
35:   [4,7]      bra       7
37:   [9,1,4]    loadi     r1,4
40:   [4,2]      bra       2
42:   [7]        ret
bar:
43:   [6]        prologue
44:   [9,0,3]    loadi     r0,3
47:   [7]        ret
baz:
48:   [6]        prologue
49:   [9,0,1]    loadi     r0,1
52:   [7]        ret
life:
53:   [42]       .byte     42
fred:
54:   [2,4]      brg       4
56:   [3,1]      inc       r1
58:   [7]        ret
59:   [4,3]      bra       3
61:   [4,1]      bra       1
```

```
0:    [6]        prologue
1:    [0,10]     call      10
3:    [9,0,43]   loadi     r0,43
6:    [1,0]      calli     r0
8:    [7]        ret
9:    [0,6]      call      6
11:   [9,0,1]    loadi     r0,1
14:   [10,0,1]   cmpi      r0,1
17:   [2,26]     brg       26
19:   [9,1,30]   loadi     r1,30
22:   [11,1,0]   add       r1,r0
25:   [8,2,1]    load      r2,(r1)
28:   [5,2]      jmpi      r2
30:   [32]       ILLEGAL   32
31:   [37]       ILLEGAL   37
32:   [9,1,3]    loadi     r1,3
35:   [4,7]      bra       7
37:   [9,1,4]    loadi     r1,4
40:   [4,2]      bra       2
42:   [7]        ret
43:   [6]        prologue
44:   [9,0,3]    loadi     r0,3
47:   [7]        ret
48:   [6]        prologue
49:   [9,0,1]    loadi     r0,1
52:   [7]        ret
53:   [42]       ILLEGAL   42
54:   [2,4]      brg       4
56:   [3,1]      inc       r1
58:   [7]        ret
59:   [4,3]      bra       3
61:   [4,1]      bra       1
```

Figure 3.2 To the left is the original assembly program and to the right, the result after a linear sweep disassembly. Correctly disassembled regions are in light gray.

Now have a look at the left-hand side of Figure 3.3 ▶ 177, which shows the output from a recursive disassembler. It starts at the entry point, 0, and disassembles instructions one by one until it finds the first control transfer instruction (CTI), namely, the call at location 1. It continues recursively at location 10, which it can now identify as the beginning of a function. Next comes the brg instruction at

```
f0:
0:      [6]          prologue
1:      [0,10]       call       10
3:      [9,0,43]     loadi      r0,43
6:      [1,0]        calli      r0
8:      [7]          ret

9:      [0]          .byte      0

f10:
10:     [6]          prologue
11:     [9,0,1]      loadi      r0,1
14:     [10,0,1]     cmpi       r0,1
17:     [2,26]       brg        26
19:     [9,1,30]     loadi      r1,30
22:     [11,1,0]     add        r1,r0
25:     [8,2,1]      load       r2,(r1)
28:     [5,2]        jmpi       r2
30:     [32]         .byte      32
31:     [37]         .byte      37
32:     [9,1,3]      loadi      r1,3
35:     [4,7]        bra        7
37:     [9,1,4]      loadi      r1,4
40:     [4,2]        bra        2
42:     [7]          ret
43:     [6]          prologue
44:     [9,0,3]      loadi      r0,3
47:     [7]          ret

48:     [6]          .byte      6
49:     [9]          .byte      9
50:     [0]          .byte      0
51:     [1]          .byte      1
52:     [7]          .byte      7
53:     [42]         .byte      42
54:     [2]          .byte      2
55:     [4]          .byte      4
56:     [3]          .byte      3
57:     [1]          .byte      1
58:     [7]          .byte      7
59:     [4]          .byte      4
60:     [3]          .byte      3
61:     [4]          .byte      4
62:     [1]          .byte      1
```

```
f0:
0:      [6]          prologue
1:      [0,10]       call       10
3:      [9,0,43]     loadi      r0,43
6:      [1,0]        calli      r0
8:      [7]          ret

9:      [0]          .byte      0

f10:
10:     [6]          prologue
11:     [9,0,1]      loadi      r0,1
14:     [10,0,1]     cmpi       r0,1
17:     [2,26]       brg        26
19:     [9,1,30]     loadi      r1,30
22:     [11,1,0]     add        r1,r0
25:     [8,2,1]      load       r2,(r1)
28:     [5,2]        jmpi       r2
30:     [32]         .byte      32
31:     [37]         .byte      37
32:     [9,1,3]      loadi      r1,3
35:     [4,7]        bra        7
37:     [9,1,4]      loadi      r1,4
40:     [4,2]        bra        2
42:     [7]          ret

f43:
43:     [6]          prologue
44:     [9,0,3]      loadi      r0,3
47:     [7]          ret

f48:
48:     [6]          prologue
49:     [9,0,1]      loadi      r0,1
52:     [7]          ret

53:     [42]         .byte      42

f54:
54:     [2,4]        brg        4
56:     [3,1]        inc        r1
58:     [7]          ret

59:     [4]          .byte      4
60:     [3]          .byte      3
61:     [4]          .byte      4
62:     [1]          .byte      1
```

Figure 3.3 To the left is the assembly program after a recursive disassembly, to the right after Algorithm REHM. Correctly disassembled regions are in light gray. The recursive disassembler has erroneously marked the dark gray region as belonging to function f10 rather than being its own function.

location 17, which means it should recursively disassemble from locations 42 (17 + 26) and 19 (the fall-through case).

Now the real problem starts when the disassembler hits the `jmpi` instruction, an indirect jump through a register. If it can't figure out where the branch might go, it has to conservatively estimate that it can go anywhere! To make the analysis more precise, our disassembler checked to see that the `jmpi` was used as the indirect jump in a switch statement. It then deduced the beginning and end of the jump table, which allowed it to continue its recursive traversal from these addresses. There are essentially two ways for the disassembler to locate the jump table. First, it can keep a set of patterns for common switch statement layout schemes used by known compilers. In our example, it would look for the `loadi` instruction to find the beginning of the table and the `cmpi` instruction to find the number of table entries. The problem with pattern matching is that trivial variations in code generation strategy can trip up the disassembler, which needs to know about the patterns produced by *all* compilers. A more forgiving scheme is to compute a backwards slice from the `jmpi` instruction in order to find all the computations that contribute to the branch address. This expression is then symbolically simplified and matched against a set of table lookup normal forms [71].

The recursive disassembler that produced the code in Figure 3.3 ▶177 doesn't know that the `prologue` instruction often starts a function and `ret` often ends it—it just blindly follows branch addresses. Now this might seem silly, until you realize that on many architectures there's no one *start-of-function* instruction and no one *return-from-function* instruction—they are manufactured out of primitive operations that can vary from compiler to compiler. For this reason, the disassembler made the mistake of thinking that locations 43–47 belong to function `f10` rather than being a function in its own right. You can tell that it *is* a function from looking at the instructions at locations 3 and 6, which call location 43 indirectly through a function pointer.

3.3.1.2 Algorithm *REHM*: Disassembling Stripped Binaries Algorithm 3.2 [154] extends the standard recursive traversal algorithm with a collection of heuristics in order to increase the precision of the disassembly. In Algorithm 3.2 ▶179, FINDFUNCTIONS is the heart of any recursive traversal disassembler. It follows all branches and returns a set of function start addresses and a set of decoded addresses. After FINDFUNCTIONS has finished executing, FINDPROLOGUES attempts to decode any remaining undecoded bytes by looking for `prologue` instructions that could start a function. In practice, different compilers and programmers may use different procedure calling conventions, so there could be many different such instruction sequences used, even within the same program. Leaf routines

---

Algorithm 3.2 Overview of Algorithm REHM.

FINDFUNCTIONS(start,end):

$Q \leftarrow \langle$start$\rangle$;
functions $\leftarrow$ {start}
visited $\leftarrow$ {}
while $Q \neq \emptyset$ do
   pos $\leftarrow$ next address from Q
   $I \leftarrow$ the instruction decoded from pos
   visited $\leftarrow$ visited $\cup$ [pos...pos+I's length-1]
   if I is a control transfer instruction then
      targets $\leftarrow$ I's target addresses
      if I is a call instruction then
         functions $\leftarrow$ functions $\cup$ targets
      if I is a jmpi instruction then
         pattern match on known switch statement layouts
         targets $\leftarrow$ jump table addresses
   else
      targets $\leftarrow$ {pos + I's length}
   for all $i \in$ targets such that $i \notin$ visited do
      $Q \leftarrow Q \cup \{i\}$
return functions,visited

FINDPROLOGUES():

gaps $\leftarrow$ {undecoded byte ranges}
repeat
   for every range [start...end] $\in$ gaps do
      while start<end do
         $I \leftarrow$ the instruction decoded from start
         if I is a prologue instruction then
            functions $\leftarrow$ functions $\cup$ {start}
            findFunctions(start,end)
            continue with the next range
         else
            start++
   gaps $\leftarrow$ {undecoded byte ranges}
until no more changes to gaps

Algorithm 3.2 Overview of Algorithm REHM. (*Continued*)

FINDCFGs():

```
gaps ← {undecoded byte ranges}
repeat
   for every range [start...end] ∈ gaps do
      while start<end do
         cfg ← CFG built from instructions starting at start
         if cfg is well-formed and has at least one CTI then
            functions ← functions ∪ {start}
            findFunctions(start,end)
            continue with the next range
         else
            start++
   gaps ← {undecoded byte ranges}
until no more changes to gaps
```

(functions that don't contain any function calls) might have a simplified prologue, for example. After FINDPROLOGUES can find no more functions, FINDCFGs sees if it's possible to build a reasonable control flow graph from the remaining undecoded bytes. Algorithm REHM [154] defines "reasonable" as, "There are no jumps into the middle of another instruction, and the resulting function contains at least two control transfer instructions."

The second column in Figure 3.3 ▶ 177 shows the example program disassembled with Algorithm REHM. The first phase of the algorithm proceeds exactly the same as for a normal recursive disassembler. Any remaining gaps are then decoded using FINDPROLOGUES and FINDCFGs. Notice how function f43 is only called indirectly, and function f48 isn't called at all, but the disassembler still finds them by searching for their `prologue` instructions. The disassembler next starts at location 53, realizes that 42 isn't a valid opcode, moves to location 54, from where it's able to build a valid control flow graph. Notice that function f54 doesn't start with a `prologue` instruction. Bytes 59–62 consist of a branch into the middle of another branch, which `findCFG` discards as invalid.

In their tests, the authors found that the enhanced recursive disassembler recovered 95.6% of all functions over a set of Windows and Linux programs.

3.3.2 Decompilation

Conceptually, a decompiler runs after the executable file has been disassembled, taking as input the sequence of control flow graphs that the disassembler discovered. The decompiler analyzes each control flow graph and turns basic blocks into a sequence of assignment statements and the flow graph itself into high-level language control structures such as if-, while-, repeat-, and switch-statements. The result is an *abstract syntax tree* (AST), a tree representation isomorphic to the source representation of a high-level language. The AST can trivially be turned into source code.

In practice, decompilers implement their own disassembly phase. This allows them, for example, to quickly disregard any start-up routines inserted by the compiler. These shouldn't appear in the decompiled program and, being originally written in assembly code, they are often untranslatable anyway.

So what's so hard about decompilation? Well, let's make another laundry list:

- Since the first step of any decompiler is disassembly, all the problems you saw in Section 3.3.1 ▸172 apply here also! Worse, any mistakes by the disassembler (say, not being able to correctly identify the end of a function) are likely to thoroughly confuse the decompilation stage.

- Even correctly disassembled assembly code may not correspond to any legal source code in your target language. For example, while Java bytecode has a goto instruction, the Java language doesn't. This makes it tricky to decompile *irreducible* loops (see Section 4.3.4 ▸235). Furthermore, some routines (such as start-up code, memory management code, and so on) may have been hand-coded in highly optimized assembly code in the first place, and may be untranslatable to source.

- You must identify calls to standard library functions: You'd much rather see a call to `printf()` than a call to `foo96()` in the decompiled code!

- You must identify *idioms* of different compilers. For example, a compiler may use `xor r0,r0` as the fastest way to zero a variable, and function prologues may consist of several primitive instructions that allocate stack frames, set up stack- and frame-pointers, and so on.

- The assembly code may contain artifacts of the target architecture that shouldn't appear in the decompiled code. For example, the compiler may have had to insert jumps-to-jumps in order to get past restrictions on the maximum distance of a branch.

- You may have to undo compiler optimizations. For example, the decompiler may have to reroll unrolled loops and replace sequences of shifts and adds with the original multiplication by a constant.

- You have to turn the mess of branches of each function into the "most natural" structured control flow, i.e., nestings of if-, while-, repeat-, and switch-statements.

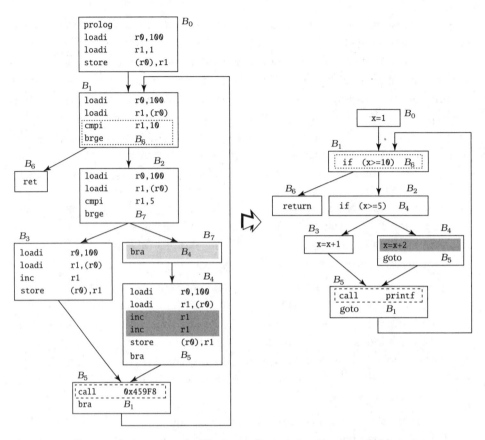

Figure 3.4 Decompilation example. The instruction set is taken from Table 3.1 ▸ 122.

- You have to analyze the primitive data access instructions (load and store instructions and their addressing modes) in order to identify the data structures of the original program, such as arrays, records, pointers, and objects.

Have a look at the example in Figure 3.4. To the left is a control flow graph generated by a straight disassembly, to the right is the graph after the decompiler has done a first level of clean-up. The primitive comparison and branch instructions have been converted to higher-level `if (condition) target` intermediate instructions (dotted), jumps-to-jumps have been eliminated (light gray), the idiom `inc r; inc r` has been replaced by `r = r+2` (dark gray), and calls to standard library functions have been identified (dashed). Starting from this simplified control flow graph, the decompiler constructs an abstract syntax tree by identifying high-level control flow

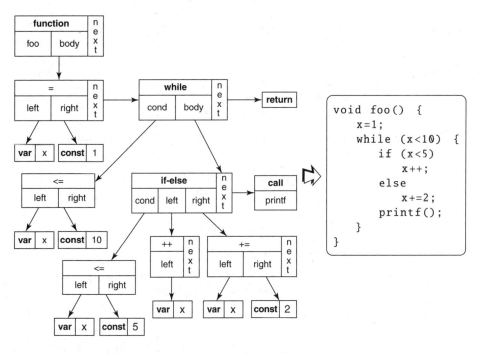

Figure 3.5 Decompilation example, continued from Figure 3.4 ▶ 182

statements. The AST has one node type for every kind of statement and operator in the target language. Once the AST has been built, generating source code is therefore trivial. Figure 3.5 shows the AST and the C source corresponding to the simplified control flow graph in Figure 3.4 ▶ 182.

3.3.2.1 Algorithm *RECG:* Recovering High-Level Control Flow Cristina Cifuentes'[5] decompilation algorithm RECG [72] (Algorithm 3.3) makes use of a database of *signatures* of library functions generated automatically from different compilers. This allows the decompiler to discard functions that the compiler inserted and replace calls to them with appropriate symbolic names. The algorithm uses several data flow analyses. For example, it uses a *reaching definitions* data flow analysis (Section 3.1.2 ▶ 127) to determine which instructions set the condition codes that are later tested by conditional branch instructions. Here, the use-definition chains in instructions 5 and 6 indicate that the zero (ZF) and sign (SF) flags that

---

5. AKA the "Queen of Decompilation."

Algorithm 3.3 Overview of Algorithm RECG. X is a stripped executable file.

DECOMPILE(X):

1. Parse the executable file X and recover the text segment and the entry point `main`.

2. Heuristically determine the compiler that generated X. Let *sigs* be the set of known library function signatures for this compiler.

3. Disassemble the text segment and construct a call graph C and for every function a control flow graph G.

4. Remove any functions from G whose signatures match those in *sigs*.

5. Replace known idioms with higher-level constructs.

6. Optimize G by removing jumps-to-jumps.

7. For each basic block in G recover statements:

   (a) Perform a reaching definitions data flow analysis on condition codes and replace machine code tests and branches with `if  ...  goto  ...`:

   $i :$ `cmpi` r,imm
   ↓
   $j :$ `brg lab` $j :$ `if` $r > imm$ `goto lab`

   (b) Remove a temporary register *tmp* by replacing its use with its symbolic contents. First perform a definition-use data flow analysis to determine the number of uses of *tmp* and then an interprocedural live register data flow analysis to determine registers that are live at entrance and exit of the block. Finally, perform *forward substitution* to eliminate *tmp* and its definition:

   $i :$ `add` tmp,v
   ↓
   $j :$ `cmpi` tmp,imm $j :$ `cmpi` $tmp + v,imm$

   (c) Replace calls to library functions in *sigs* with calls to the corresponding symbolic name:

   $i :$ `call` $addr$ $i :$ `call` $name$

8. Classify nodes in G by calling RESTRUCTURELOOPS(G) and RESTRUCTUREIFS(G) in Figure 3.4▶182 and Figure 3.5▶183, respectively.

9. Traverse G and build an abstract syntax tree. For a basic block marked as being the head of a control structure, traverse its body depth first, i.e., until its follow node is reached, and then continue with the follow node.

10. Traverse the abstract syntax tree and emit source code.

---

are being tested are actually set by instruction 1 and not by any intervening instructions:

```
(1)    add    r0,r1    -- sets ZF, SF
       ...             -- ZF and SF are not set here
(5)    breq   lab1     -- ud[ZF]={(1)}
(6)    brg    lab2     -- ud[ZF]=ud[SF]={(1)}
```

The steps taken by Christina's decompiler are shown in Algorithm 3.3 ▸ 184. Once a control flow graph has been built, RESTRUCTURELOOPS(G) in Algorithm 3.4 is

---

Algorithm 3.4 Overview of Algorithm RECG for structuring loops. G is the control flow graph recovered during disassembly.

RESTRUCTURELOOPS(G):

1. From G construct the interval graphs $\langle I_1(b_1), \ldots, I_m(b_m) \rangle$ where the b_i are the header nodes.

2. Determine loop type (pre-tested, post-tested, endless):

   ```
   for all intervals I and header nodes h in ⟨I₁(b₁), ... , Iₘ(bₘ)⟩ do
       find a latching node in I not already part of a loop
       match the loop against these types:
   ```

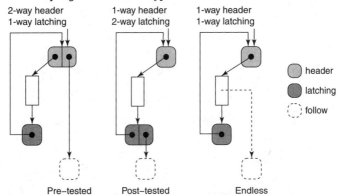

   ```
   for loops with 2-way header and 2-way latching nodes,
       use heuristics to determine loop type
   mark all nodes as belonging to a loop
   mark h with loop type, latching, and follow nodes
   ```

3. Collapse all intervals in G into one node. Unless no intervals could be collapsed, repeat from 2.

Algorithm 3.5 Overview of Algorithm RECG for structuring if statements. G is the
control flow graph recovered during disassembly.

RESTRUCTUREIFS(G):

1. Number the nodes of G in reverse postorder.

2. Determine follow nodes:

```
unresolved ← ∅
for all nodes m by descending reverse postorder number do
    if m is a 2-way node and
        not a loop header or branching node then
        if ∃n : n = max{i|idom(i) = m ∧ |inEdges(i)| ≥ 2} then
            follow(m) ← n
            for each x ∈ unresolved do
                follow(x) ← n
                unresolved ← unresolved - {x}
        else
            unresolved ← unresolved ∪ {m}
```

3. Determine the type of each conditional by checking if one of the edges from its
   header node goes directly to the follow node:

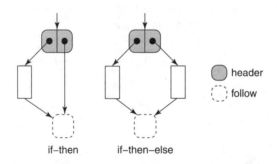

if–then   if–then–else

header
follow

---

called to look for loops. Any branches not belonging to loop headers are then
classified as either if-then or if-then-else by RESTRUCTUREIFS(G) in Algorithm 3.5.

Have a look at Figure 3.6▶187, which illustrates how RESTRUCTURELOOPS(G)
classifies loops. Every loop consists of a *header* node (light gray) where control enters and a *latching* node (dark gray) that has a back-edge to the header. After the
loop has finished executing, control continues in the *follow* node (dashed). Consider

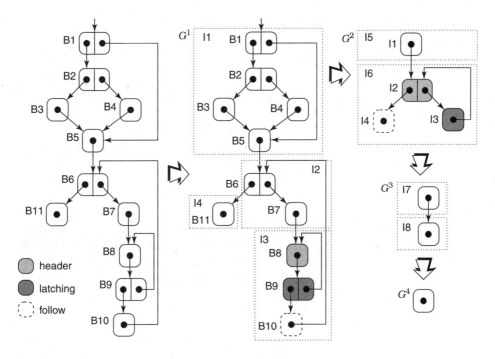

Figure 3.6 Using Algorithm RECG to discover loops.

the loop consisting of nodes B8 and B9. It's a *post-tested* loop because it has a 1-way header node and a 2-way latching node. In other words, B8 and B9 correspond to a repeat-loop.

Now, the B8-B9 loop is itself nested inside a loop consisting of nodes B6, B7, and B11. To see this, RESTRUCTURELOOPS(G) uses *interval theory* [257]. An *interval I*(h) is the *maximal, single-entry subgraph in which h is the only entry node and in which all closed paths contain h.* At each step of the algorithm, every interval is collapsed into a single node, and a new, smaller graph is formed. Again look at Figure 3.6. In graph G^1, nodes B8,B9,B10 form an interval that's been collapsed into node I3 in graph G^2. Similarly, nodes I1,I2,I3,I4,I5 have been collapsed into I1. Once you're done constructing G^2 by collapsing intervals in G^1, you again look for loops. This time you find a pre-tested loop (i.e., a while-loop) consisting of nodes I2 (header), I3 (latching), and I4 (follow).

After the two loops have been identified, the two branching nodes B1 and B2 are still unclassified. RESTRUCTUREIFS(G) considers innermost if-statements first:

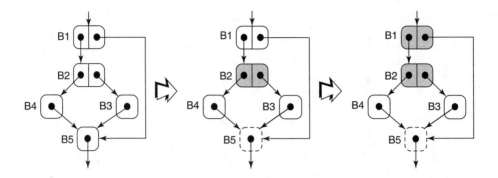

In the first step, you determine that B2 is the header node of an if-then-else statement since none of its outgoing edges go to the follow node, B5. In a second step, you find that B1 is an if-then statement since one of its outgoing edges does go to the follow node. In this case, both conditionals share the same follow node. Decompiled to C, the nested conditionals look like this:

```
if (···) {
    if (···) {
        ...
    } else {
        ...
    }
}
```

3.3.2.2 Decompiling High-Level Languages
Have a look at this x86 assembly code:

```
X676F_1:
        movq    ta+0(%rip),%rdi
        call    Put_Atom_Tagged
        movq    %rax,8(%r12)
        movq    $23,%rdi
        call    Put_Integer_Tagged
        movq    %rax,16(%r12)
        movq    8(%r12),%rdi
        movq    16(%r12),%rsi
```

```
call    Set_Bip_Name_2
movq    $55,%rdi
call    Put_Integer_Tagged
movq    %rax,8(%r12)
movq    0(%r12),%rdi
leaq    0(%r12),%rsi
call    Math_Load_Value
movq    8(%r12),%rdi
movq    0(%r12),%rsi
call    Fct_Mul
movq    %rax,0(%r12)
jmp     X7772697465_1
```

What does it do? With the labels still in place, it's actually not too hard to figure out. The answer is in footnote 6. The point is, decompiling this with a C decompiler probably won't be too helpful since the code wasn't originally written in C!

Problem 3.7 Is it harder or easier to decompile a program written in a very high-level language such as Haskell or Prolog than in a lower-level language such as C? On the one hand, Prolog semantics is much farther removed from machine code than C is, and that should make decompilation hard. On the other hand, Prolog is a highly structured language and so it's possible that the generated machine code will consist of easily identifiable idioms. Study a few high-level languages that have native code compilers; how hard would decompilation be? Do some languages generate more convoluted code than others? Is it easier or harder to disassemble stripped binaries generated from these languages than from C?

Even for languages that are fairly close to C, the generated code will be convoluted if there are very high-level structures that have to be mapped down to machine code. Invoking a virtual method in an object-oriented language, for example, means traversing a chain of pointers. Assume your program has a class Square (with superclass Shape) that has two methods move and draw. A global variable sq has been initialized to point to a Square object on the heap. This is what the program might look like at runtime:

6.
Actually, we lied. We're not going to tell you the answer here. Instead, the first person who sends in the correct answer will get a check for $1.61.

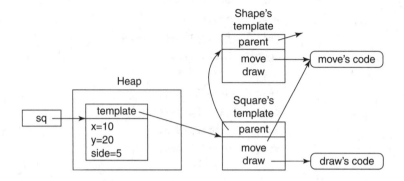

From the method call `sq->draw()`, the compiler will generate code that first follows the `sq` pointer to the object on the heap, then follows the `template` pointer to `Square`'s template, and finally goes from the template to the code for `Square`'s `draw`. There are variants of this scheme. For example, rather than keeping the method pointers in templates, they could be incorporated directly into every object. The point is that a decompiler for an object-oriented language will have to know about the runtime organization and try to reconstitute classes and type information by locating and extracting information from templates and objects. This information will change from compiler to compiler, so the decompiler will need to be aware of each compiler's object layout.

3.4 Pragmatic Analysis

Style metrics collect and summarize data from a large corpus of programs in order to be able to say something about what an "average" or "typical" program might look like. For example, to avoid generating protection code that is unstealthy in real programs, you'd want to know how large functions are on average, how deeply programmers nest control constructs, how deep inheritance hierarchies are in object-oriented programs, and so on.

Software complexity metrics collect information from a program to find out how well structured it is. For example, a program might get a bad metrics score if it contains functions that are unusually large or if its classes are unusually tightly connected. Software metrics have been used in software protection tools to determine if a program has been obfuscated enough.

Both style and complexity metrics are used to measure what programs really look like, and we'll use the term *pragmatic analysis* to refer to them collectively.

A major obstacle to attacking real programs is their size. The little challenge problem you saw in Listing 2.1 ▸62 in Chapter 2 (Methods of Attack and Defense) was trivial to crack, but it was only some 50 lines long. Real programs may be four orders of magnitude larger. The amount of information that the analysis methods you've seen in this chapter collect from a program like that can be truly astronomical. We will finish off this chapter by showing you some techniques for *software visualization*. The idea is to present information about a program (its static structure, its runtime behavior, or both) in a way that's informative, interactive, compact, comprehensive, and sometimes even aesthetically pleasing.

3.4.1 Style Metrics

In order to protect a program from analysis and unwanted modification, the obfuscation, watermarking, and tamperproofing algorithms you will see in this book transform the program either by inserting new code or modifying existing code. There's a potential problem with such transformations. If only a small part of the program is affected by the transformation, and if the inserted or modified code doesn't look like "normal" code, it will be easy for your adversary to locate it. And once the location of the protection code has been found, attacking it becomes that much easier. Therefore, the concept of *stealth*—the extent to which a piece of code "fits in" with the code in the rest of the program—will be important in this book, and we will return to it many times.

Ideally, you'd like to be able to look at two protection algorithms, A and B, and say that A is stealthier than B. What would this mean? Well, it's unusual for any protection algorithm to produce code that's stealthy for *every* program. A program that does scientific computations has lots of operations on arrays of floating point numbers, a program that does cryptography will do lots of xor operations on long bytestrings, a program that's user interface-intensive will define many call-back functions, and so on. It would be unlikely for A to be stealthier than B for *all* of these. Still, it would be nice to be able to say something about how A and B would compare to an "average" program P.

For example, in Chapter 8 (Software Watermarking) you'll see how Algorithms WMMIMIT and WMVVS generate functions that embed a watermark. To be stealthy, these functions have to blend in naturally with the surrounding code.

So what does it mean for a program to be "average?" Or, more generally, what do real programs actually look like? There's been very little work on this problem. This is a shame, because if we knew more about what type of code real programmers actually write, we might be able to design better programming languages, compilers, programming environments, and, the topic of this book, software protection algorithms.

The pioneering *programming style analysis* study was Donald Knuth's *An Empirical Study of FORTRAN Programs* [201] from 1971. Since then, there have been studies published on C [38], COBOL [63,314], Java [36,82,146,248,275], Pascal [93], FORTRAN [327], and APL [308,309].

Problem 3.8 An interesting question is how sensitive the results in these studies are to the way the program samples were selected. Replicate some of the studies with your own samples—how much do your results vary from the published ones?

To conduct a programming style study, you need to make two decisions. First, how are you going to collect representative program samples? Knuth [201] went to the Stanford Computation Center and dug in the waste-paper basket and searched the disk for unprotected programs. In Collberg, et al. [82], we used Google to randomly select and download 1,132 Java jar files. Baxter et al. [36] manually selected 56 well-known open source applications.

The second decision you must make is which program characteristics to collect. There seems to be an infinite number of possibilities here, and it naturally depends on how you're going to use the data. In Table 3.2▸193, you can see the most common Java bytecode bigrams in the 1,132 programs we collected. This analysis shows that the two most common combinations of two bytecodes are `aload_0,getfield` (corresponding to the Java source `object.field`) and `new,dup`. This is of consequence for the stealth of watermarking algorithm WMCT (Section 9.1▸546), which generates many bigrams of exactly these types.

Figure 3.7▸194 shows the number of basic blocks per method body in Java bytecode programs. The graph shows that in our sample of 801,117 methods, 64% have a small number of basic blocks, 9 or fewer. However, some methods are truly huge, one having 10,699 blocks! This is of consequence for watermarking algorithm WMVVS (Section 8.7.2▸506), which embeds watermarks in the structure of control flow graphs.

Problem 3.9 Is it possible to classify programs into a small set of equivalence classes? If that is the case, it might be possible to say, "Software protection algorithm A is stealthy when applied to programs in class C but not in class D," which would be very useful.

• • •

Problem 3.10 Intuitively, programs written in two similar languages (Java and C#, Haskell and ML, and so on) should have similar characteristics. Is this true?

• • •

Problem 3.11 Study the structure of programs written in functional languages (Haskell, ML, SCHEME) or scripting languages (Perl, Python, Icon, Ruby).

Table 3.2 Most common Java bytecode 2-grams. Reproduced from reference [82].

Op	Count	%
aload_0,getfield	1219837	4.7
new,dup	664718	2.6
ldc,invokevirtual	353412	1.4
invokevirtual,invokevirtual	332487	1.3
dup,bipush	330887	1.3
putfield,aload_0	311038	1.2
iastore,dup	250744	1.0
invokevirtual,aload_0	235924	0.9
dup,sipush	226520	0.9
aload_1,invokevirtual	223958	0.9
aload,invokevirtual	222692	0.9
getfield,invokevirtual	219107	0.8
aload_0,aload_1	214369	0.8
aastore,dup	208247	0.8
dup,invokespecial	202840	0.8
aload_0,invokevirtual	200872	0.8
invokevirtual,pop	193105	0.7
aload_0,invokespecial	159742	0.6
astore,aload	146309	0.6
bastore,dup	141779	0.5
ldc,aastore	133994	0.5
getfield,aload_0	129300	0.5
invokespecial,aload_0	122168	0.5
ldc,invokespecial	120935	0.5

3.4.2 Software Complexity Metrics

Software complexity metrics are similar to the style metrics you saw in the last section. They are typically used, however, in large software development projects to evaluate how well designed and well structured a program is, to estimate progress made, or to identify parts of the code base that need refactoring.

According to some of the more popular metrics (there are hundreds to choose from!), the complexity of a program P grows with

- the number of operators and operands in P (Program Length [151]),
- the number of predicates in P (Cyclomatic Complexity [245]),
- the nesting level of conditionals in P (Nesting Complexity [155]),

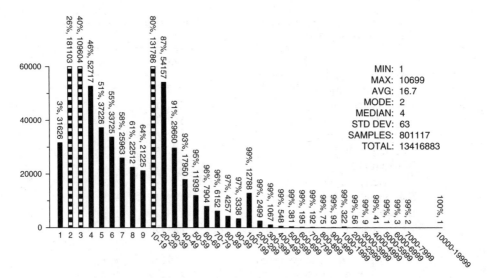

Figure 3.7 Number of basic blocks per method body in Java bytecode programs. Reproduced from reference [82]. Striped bars have been truncated.

- the number of inter-basic block variable references in P (Data Flow Complexity [278]),
- the number of formal parameters to P, and with the number of global data structures read or updated by P (Fan-in/out Complexity [160]),
- the complexity of the static data structures declared in P (Data Structure Complexity [258]),
- the number of methods in P, the depth of the inheritance tree, the coupling between classes, the number of methods that can be executed in response to a message sent to an object (Object-oriented complexity [64]).

It has been suggested that complexity metrics could be used to measure how *poorly* structured a program is after an obfuscating transformation has been applied. This would be useful when you have a large number of transformations available and want to select the subset that will provide the most bang for the buck. We'll talk about this in the section on *obfuscation executives*, Section 4.1.3 ▶ 212. You'll also see metrics in Section 10.7 ▶ 644, where we'll use them to measure the similarity between different pieces of code.

Problem 3.12   No one knows whether the software complexity metrics defined in the literature actually provide good measurements of artificially obfuscated programs. Obfuscate some sample programs with transformations from Chapter 4, measure their complexity before and after obfuscation using relevant metrics, and measure the effort needed by human subjects to understand the programs with and without obfuscation. Is there a correlation?

It's conceivable that complexity metrics could be used by the bad guys too! For example, for performance reasons it's common to only apply obfuscating transformations to security-critical parts of a program. If complexity metrics measurements are, in fact, significantly different on original and obfuscated code, then an attacker could use them to zero in on the suspicious parts of a program that he should examine first.

3.4.3   Software Visualization

Large programs can consist of millions of lines of code, tens of thousands of functions, and thousands of modules and classes. For an adversary who wants to gain a complete understanding of your program, the sheer size of it can be a serious impediment. If your program isn't very big in itself, many of the obfuscation algorithms in Chapter 4 (Code Obfuscation) are designed to automatically make it bigger by duplicating code or inserting bogus code. To aid in *program comprehension* of large programs, many techniques have been invented for *software visualization*. The techniques can be both static and dynamic. All the data structures you saw in Section 3.1▶118 (control-flow graphs, data-dependence graphs, call graphs, inheritance graphs) grow with the size of the program, and a reverse engineer can benefit from being able to explore them visually and interactively.

The static structures of a program can be large, but they pale in comparison to the truly enormous amounts of data that can be collected from a running program. The address trace, the dynamic call graph, and the heap graph are three structures that can be useful for a reverse engineer to visualize, and all three will be large for long-running programs. The size itself can be a challenge for a visualization system, but the fact that the structures are continuously changing makes the problem that much harder.

A visualization system consists of five components. The first component collects information from the static code or from the executing program. Data from an execution such as function calls, thread switches, and system calls (commonly known as *interesting events*) are usually collected by instrumenting the code. The second component filters out those events that are not interesting to visualize. The third component selects the type of visualization (the "view") most appropriate to present the selected information. Sometimes multiple views are displayed, giving the reverse engineer different simultaneous perspectives of the same data. The fourth component renders the visualization. A major problem with software visualization is that the amount of data that gets generated is too large to view all at once on a computer screen. Therefore, a final component lets the reverse engineer navigate through interesting subsets to view.

A view commonly used in software visualization systems is known as *nodes-and-arcs*. Since many program structures are graphs (call graphs, inheritance graphs, control flow graphs), it seems natural to render them as such. You saw examples of these visualizations in Section 3.1▶118. The problem, however, is that for even moderately large programs these graphs resemble hair balls, and it's very difficult for a reverse engineer to extract any information from them at all. Also, in order to intelligently navigate a huge graph, the reverse engineer needs to be able to map the nodes and edges into the underlying source code, and this is typically done by labeling the nodes and edges. Identifiers tend to be long, however (particularly when you need to fully disambiguate them, such as `sandmark.obfuscate.interleavemethods.TypeIndex`), and can seriously add to the clutter.

The nodes-and-arcs view can be extended in various ways in order to incorporate more information [329]:

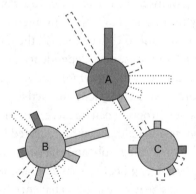

Here the three circles represent classes A, B, and C. Their shading represents the number of instances of the class created over the lifetime of the execution. Each bar around the circle represents a method, the length of the bar represents the method's size, and the shading of the bar represents the total number of calls to the method.

SHriMP views [338] use nested graph structures to represent hierarchies. Here's a visualization of a small Java program:

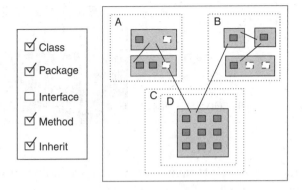

Packages are dotted, classes are light gray, methods are dark gray, instance variables are dashed, and inheritance relationship is represented by dark gray lines. By pointing and clicking, the reverse engineer can zoom in on any package, class, or method, and can filter out unwanted information.

There have been various attempts at getting away from the nodes-and-arcs view. Geographic metaphors are natural, for example, since hierarchies can be modeled by city blocks within blocks, blocks within cities, cities within countries, and countries within continents. Here's an example where city blocks represent classes, houses represent methods, and the height of houses represent the number of method calls [380]:

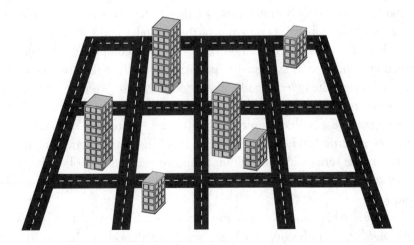

Treemap views [183] are used to visualize hierarchical structures such as Java package or inheritance hierarchies. Have a look at this example with a nodes-and-arcs view to the left and the corresponding treemap view to the right:

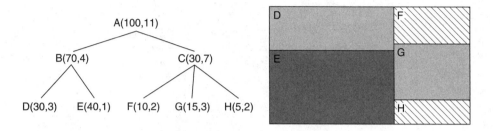

In addition to the hierarchical structure, each leaf node has two values associated with it that you want to visualize. For example, let the tree represent your program's package hierarchy, with leaf nodes being the classes inside the package. Then the first value could represent the *size* of the classes and the second number could represent *execution time* spent in each class over some profiling runs. In the treemap view, the area of each rectangle is proportional to the first value. Class E, for example, is 40% of the total size and its rectangle, therefore, occupies 40% of the total area. The second number, execution time, is represented by shading, with 1=striped, 2=dark gray, and 3=light gray. You could use brightness, hue, texture, and so on to represent even more aspects of the program.

3.5 Discussion

This chapter, by necessity, has only scratched the surface of the vast body of literature on program analysis that has come out of the compiler and software engineering communities. To check the correctness of a program, a compiler must collect static information from it, such as the types of variables and the flow of control inside functions. To generate *efficient* code, many compilers use profiling information to find program hot spots that warrant more attention from the optimizer. Software engineering tools use both dynamic analysis (tracers, debuggers) and static analysis (slicing, code metrics) to help programmers find bugs and to better organize their code. If you are serious about building software protection tools (or if you're a bad guy, attack tools!), you need to become intimately familiar with these sorts of techniques.

What we also have not covered in this chapter is the relative strength of different analysis algorithms. In Section 4.3.3▸229, you'll see algorithms that try to confuse an attacker who's using static analysis by adding spurious aliases to the program. Even though we know that alias analysis from a theoretical point of view is a hard problem, what we'd really like to know is the strength of the best currently available algorithms. There are plenty of papers evaluating alias analysis algorithms, but they typically do so under assumptions different from ours. First, they assume that they're analyzing programs written by benign human programmers, not automatic obfuscation tools intent on incurring as much confusion as possible. Second, the type and precision of information you need from an alias analysis algorithm in a code optimizer is different from what you need in a tool that chases down bugs, which is different from what an attacker needs when he tries to crack a program. What this means is that what we really need are studies on the power of program analyses that specifically target the needs of software protection algorithms. Clark Thomborson's Secure Systems Group out of the University of Auckland has commenced a series of such studies on alias and slicing algorithms (see Section 4.4.4▸253), but the number of algorithms they've targeted so far is small and more studies are certainly needed.

Code Obfuscation

4

Code obfuscation is both the most important and the most elusive of the software protection techniques we discuss in this book. *Elusive* because it has proven hard to pin down exactly what obfuscation is, to devise practically useful algorithms, and to evaluate the quality of these algorithms, and *important* because if we *could* agree on definitions and devise strong algorithms, we would have a solution to many practical problems in security and cryptography.

Our discussion of code obfuscation will spread over three chapters. In this chapter, you will learn about some of the history of code obfuscation and the algorithms that have been proposed in the literature that are used in practice. In Chapter 5 (Obfuscation Theory), we will survey recent, more theoretical, studies that have explored some limits to what can and cannot be obfuscated. In Chapter 6 (Dynamic Obfuscation), finally, we'll look at obfuscation algorithms that dynamically update code at runtime.

Informally, to obfuscate a program P means to transform it into a program P' that is still executable but from which it is hard to extract information. This "definition" leaves you a lot of leeway: What does *hard* mean and what *information* are we talking about? In this chapter, *hard* simply means "harder than before": We want the adversary to have to expend strictly more resources to extract information from P' than from P. In the next chapter, the definition will be stricter: "Hard" means the adversary gains no advantage from having access to P' over having black-box access to P (i.e., it is no better for the adversary to be able to look at P''s obfuscated code than it is being able to execute P on arbitrary inputs). What information the adversary wants to extract depends on his intentions: He may want to discover a secret algorithm to reuse in his own program, secret data (such as cryptographic keys) to break a DRM scheme, a secret design (data and/or module structures) to help him clone the program, or the location of a license check he wants to remove.

In this chapter, you will see only obfuscated programs that remain fixed at runtime. That is, the obfuscation tool transforms the program either before or after compilation, but definitely *before* the program executes. We call this *static obfuscation*. In Chapter 6, we will lift this restriction and introduce *dynamic obfuscators* that transform programs continuously at runtime, keeping them in constant flux. Static obfuscations are typically designed to thwart static analysis, but can be attacked using dynamic techniques such as debugging, emulation, and tracing. Dynamic obfuscation techniques are designed to be resistant to these types of attacks.

In Section 4.1, we will start off the chapter by looking at some very simple obfuscating transformations. In this chapter, the purpose of an obfuscating transformation is to make it difficult for your adversary to collect information about the program *statically*, i.e., without running the program. For that reason, the transformations you'll see are designed to make the program difficult to analyze using the static analysis techniques in Section 3.1▶118. You'll also see how to design an *obfuscator*, a tool that automatically picks which transformations to apply to different parts of the code. In Section 4.2▶217, we'll give definitions, and then we'll spend the remainder of the chapter showing you a large collection of transformations that have been proposed in the literature. Some transformations try to make control flow as complicated as possible (Section 4.3▶225), others transform data structures into equivalent ones that are harder to understand (Section 4.5▶258), and still others remove abstractions that could reveal important design decisions (Section 4.6▶277). Many of these transformations make use of *opaque predicates*, boolean expressions that are hard for an adversary to evaluate. In Section 4.4▶246, we'll show you ways to construct such predicates.

4.1 Semantics-Preserving Obfuscating Transformations

Fred Cohen did much pioneering work on malware construction and detection [74, 75]. He's also credited with the first paper on what we today would call obfuscation, *Operating system protection through program evolution* [76]. The purpose of this paper is *diversity* of programs, i.e., ways to generate syntactically different but semantically identical versions of the same program. Malware typically target very specific vulnerabilities in software (such as forcing a buffer to overflow to make the function return address get overwritten, which finally causes control to jump into the payload). If, so the thinking goes, you can make an installation of a program different from all other installations, it will be much harder for the malware writer to write his code generically enough to work on all versions. There has been much work on diversity through semantics-preserving transformations since Cohen's initial paper. See, for example, Anckaert et al. [11].

It is likely that many of the techniques Fred Cohen presented in Algorithm OBFCF [76,77] were well known in the folklore before then. Virus writers, for example, also need to diversify their code so that it isn't easily identified by virus scanners! It is, however, hard to document when a technique was first used in the underground hacking community.

As an introduction to semantics-preserving transformations, we're now going to give you an overview of Fred Cohen's simple diversification techniques. We're then going to look at the simplest of all obfuscating transformations, *variable renaming*, which was also the one that was first to make it into the mainstream. We'll end this introduction to obfuscation by showing you possible designs of an *obfuscation executive*, the top-level loop in an obfuscation tool that chooses which transformations to apply to which parts of the code.

4.1.1 Algorithm *OBFCF:* Diversifying Transformations

When you're reading this section, you should keep in mind that there are significant differences between the requirements of a transformation used for diversity and one used to protect an algorithm from reverse engineering. In both cases, the transformation needs to be *cheap*, i.e., it should not introduce much overhead in space and time. It also needs to be *potent*, i.e., it should introduce much confusion. In the case of a diversifying transformation, this means that the transformation should introduce many differences between two program versions. In addition to this, a transformation used for obfuscation must also be *resilient* to attack, i.e., it must be hard for an adversary to undo it. Related to the resilience of a transformation is its *stealth*. To make obfuscation hard to undo, you don't want it to be immediately obvious to an attacker *which* transformation was applied *where* in the code. We'll make these concepts clearer in Section 4.2▶217.

4.1.1.1 Expression Equivalence There are an infinite number of ways to turn a given arithmetic expression into a sequence of elementary instructions. Compilers

typically optimize for the sequence of instructions that is the shortest or will execute
the fastest, but there's nothing stopping you from optimizing for confusion instead!
Common compiler code generation tricks can generate obfuscated code. For example, multiplication by a constant is often turned into a sequence of less obvious
adds and shifts:

```
y = x * 42;
```

⇨

```
y = x << 5;
y += x << 3;
y += x << 1;
```

4.1.1.2 Algorithm *OBFCF$_{recorder}$:* **Reordering Code and Data** Programmers tend
to put related pieces of code close together, and compilers tend to lay out code
in the order in which it occurs in the source code. Locality can therefore be an
important clue to a reverse engineer as to what pieces of code belong together. It's
therefore a good idea to randomize the placement of modules within a program,
functions within a module, statements within a function, and instructions within a
statement.

You can almost always trivially reorder modules and functions, but you can
only reorder statements and instructions for as long as you don't violate any dependencies. A code obfuscation tool that wants to reorder instructions needs to
start by building a data- and control-dependence graph (Section 3.1.3 ▶ 132). Two
instructions can be reordered if there are no dependencies between them.

In type-safe languages like Java, variable declarations that appear within the
same scope can trivially be reordered. In C, where programmers can play tricks
with pointer arithmetic, and arrays are indexed without bounds checks, reordering is much harder. In this example, the programmer might not have intended to
index outside the bounds of a, but he did anyway, and somehow his program still
worked:

```
int main() {
    int a[5];
    int b[6];
    a[5] = 42;
    printf("%i\n",b[0]);
}
```

If your obfuscation tool now decides to reorder a and b, the code will mysteriously cease to function.

4.1.1.3 Algorithm *OBFCF_{inoutline}*: **Splitting and Merging Functions** As a programmer, you use *abstraction* to manage the inherent complexity of larger programs. You break long pieces of code into smaller functions, you collect related functions into modules or classes, you collect related classes into packages, and so on. In Section 4.6▶277, we'll show you various ways in which you can obfuscate a program by breaking these abstractions.

Function inlining is a common code optimization technique that replaces a call to a function with its code. This can also be an effective obfuscation technique, since it breaks the abstraction boundary that the programmer created.

The opposite of inlining is *function outlining*, where a piece of code is extracted into its own function and replaced with a call to this function. Outlining is also an effective obfuscation technique, since it inserts a bogus abstraction where there previously was none. Here's an example where a piece of the modular exponentiation routine (in light gray) is extracted into its own function f and replaced with a call (in dark gray):

```
int modexp(int y,int x[],
           int w,int n) {
  int R, L;
  int k = 0;
  int s = 1;
  while (k < w) {
    if (x[k] == 1)
      R = (s*y) % n;
    else
      R = s;
    s = R*R % n;
    L = R;
    k++;
  }
  return L;
}
```

```
void f(int xk,int s,int y,
       int n,int* R) {
  if (xk == 1)
    *R = (s*y) % n;
  else
    *R = s;
}
int modexp(int y,int x[],
           int w,int n) {
  int R, L;
  int k = 0;
  int s = 1;
  while (k < w) {
    f(x[k],s,y,n,&R);
    s = R*R % n;
    L = R;
    k++;
  }
  return L;
}
```

Inlining is essentially a **merge** of a function caller and its callee. Similarly, outlining is a **split** of a function into two pieces. You can also merge two unrelated functions. For pure functions (those without side effects), this is trivial: Just merge the parameter lists, merge the function bodies, and replace any call to either of the functions with a call to the merged function. When a function has side effects, you have to be more careful. Here's an example where function f has side effects but function g is pure:

```
float foo[100];

void f(int a,float b) {
    foo[a] = b;
}

float g(float c,char d) {
    return c*(float)d;
}

int main() {
    f(42,42.0);
    float v = g(6.0,'a');
}
```

```
float foo[100];

float fg(int a,float bc,
         char d,int which) {
    if (which==1)
        foo[a] = bc;
    return bc*(float)d;
}

int main() {
    fg(42,42.0,'b',1);
    float v=fg(99,6.0,'a',2);
}
```

The merged function fg takes an extra argument which, to ensure that the code that causes side effects is executed only when the function is called as an f-function, not as a g-function. We also had to add extra bogus arguments to fg to fill out the parameter list.

4.1.1.4 Algorithm $OBFCF_{copy}$: Copying Code

A common obfuscation technique is to make the program larger by cloning pieces of it. Size itself is an impediment to reverse engineering, and if you can make the copied code look different from the original code, you may force the attacker to carefully examine all pairs of code blocks in the program to figure out which ones share the same functionality.

Here's an example where we've cloned a function f into a bogus function f1. We've further obfuscated f1 by modifying the array index computation and adding some bogus code that doesn't affect program semantics:

```
float foo[100];
void f(int a, float b) {
    foo[a] = b;
}
int main() {
    f(42, 42.0);
    f(6, 7.0);
}
```

⇨

```
float foo[100];
void f(int a, float b) {
    foo[a] = b;
}
float bogus;
void f1(int a, float b) {
    *(foo + a*sizeof(float)) = b;
    b += a*2;
    bogus += b+a;
}
int main() {
    f(42, 42.0);
    f1(6, 7.0);
}
```

We replaced one of the two calls to f in main with a call to f1. To gain a full understanding of the code, the adversary would have to analyze f and f1 to determine that they actually perform the same function.

4.1.1.5 Algorithm *OBFCF*_{*interp*}: Interpretation

4.1.1.5 Algorithm *OBFCF*$_{interp}$: Interpretation   Programs are compiled from source code down to code for a physical machine architecture (such as the x86) or a virtual machine architecture (such as Java bytecode). There's nothing stopping you from compiling to a *custom* instruction set architecture, one that you define yourself and one for which you provide a specialized interpreter. Nothing, that is, except the fact that your program will now run a factor 10-100 slower than before.

Have a look at Listing 4.1▶208, where we've translated the modular exponentiation routine into code for a *direct threaded interpreter* [125,200]. Notice how the instruction set is specialized to fit the particular routine we're executing. Some of the instructions are generic and could be part of any interpreter (pusha, pushv, add, mul, mod, jump, store), whereas others (inc_k, x_k_ne_1, k_ge_w) are so-called *superoperators* [292] that only make sense for the modular exponentiation routine. The superoperators both speed up the program by reducing the number of executed instructions, and allow you to generate many *different* interpreters with different instruction sets for the same routine. This makes it harder for the adversary to come up with an automated attack that removes the layer of interpretation.

Listing 4.1 Algorithm OBFCF$_{\text{interp}}$: Adding a layer of interpretation.

```c
int modexp(int y, int x[], int w, int n) {
    int R, L, k = 0, s = 1;
    int Stack[10]; int sp=0;
    void* prog[]={
        // if (k >= w) return L
        &&k_ge_w,
        // if (x[k] == 1)
        &&x_k_ne_1,&prog[16],
        // R = (s*y) % n;
        &&pusha,&R,&&pushv,&s,&&pushv,&y,&&mul,&&pushv,&n,&&mod,&&store,
        // Jump after if-statement
        &&jump,&prog[21],
        // R = s;
        &&pusha,&R,&&pushv,&s,&&store,
        // s = R*R % n;
        &&pusha,&s,&&pushv,&R,&&pushv,&R,&&mul,&&pushv,&n,&&mod,&&store,
        // L = R;
        &&pusha,&L,&&pushv,&R,&&store,
        // k++
        &&inc_k,
        // Jump to top of loop
        &&jump,&prog[0]
    };
    void** pc = (void**) &prog;
    goto **pc++;
    inc_k:     k++; goto **pc++;
    pusha:     Stack[sp++]=(int)*pc; pc++; goto **pc++;
    pushv:     Stack[sp++]=*(int*)*pc; pc++; goto **pc++;
    store:     *((int*)Stack[sp-2])=Stack[sp-1]; sp-=2; goto **pc++;
    x_k_ne_1:  if (x[k] != 1) pc=*pc; else pc++; goto **pc++;
    k_ge_w:    if (k >= w) return L; goto **pc++;
    add:       Stack[sp-2] += Stack[sp-1]; sp--; goto **pc++;
    mul:       Stack[sp-2] *= Stack[sp-1]; sp--; goto **pc++;
    mod:       Stack[sp-2] %= Stack[sp-1]; sp--; goto **pc++;
    jump:      pc=*pc; goto **pc++;
}
```

Problem 4.1   Many authors have suggested that interpretation is a "hard" obfuscation to undo. No one, however, seems to have analyzed just how hard it is in practice. Can you implement an attack that unfolds a specialized interpreter and its hardcoded instruction list back into the original program? Which type of interpreter (switch-based, direct call threaded, direct threaded, indirect threaded) is most difficult to attack?

Algorithm 4.1 Algorithm OBFTP, for renaming classes, fields, and methods in an object-oriented language with the minimum number of names.

OBFUSCATE(P):

1. Build the inheritance hierarchy for P.

2. Create an empty undirected graph G and add a node for every class and field, and for every method that doesn't override a method in the standard library.

3. Add an edge between every pair of class nodes.

4. Add an edge between every pair of field nodes declared within the same class.

5. Merge any pair of method nodes where one overrides the other.

6. Add an edge between any pair of methods $C_1.m_1$ and $C_2.m_2$ that have the same signature and where $C_1 = C_2$ or C_2 inherits from C_1, directly or indirectly.

7. Color G with a minimum number of colors so that as many nodes as possible are given the same color.

4.1.2 Algorithm *OBFTP:* Identifier Renaming

The first obfuscation method that came into widespread use was *identifier renaming*. In the wake of the release of Java, and people's realization that decompilation was easy and led to the recovery of source [293], Hans Peter Van Vliet released Crema [356], a Java obfuscator, and Mocha [357], a Java decompiler. Building a decompiler for a type-safe bytecode language like the JVM isn't hard, but it requires attention to detail in order to cover all corner cases. For this reason, a cat-and-mouse game ensued where obfuscators would employ clever techniques to trip up less-than-perfect decompilers. HoseMocha [218] was the first example of this, adding a bogus instruction after the `return` statement of a method, apparently enough to make Mocha fail. Another common technique to foil Java decompilers has become to rename identifiers using characters that are legal in the JVM, but not in Java source [58].

While identifier renaming today is mostly of historical interest, it does have two interesting characteristics. First, it removes information that truly is unrecoverable to a decompiler; once the programmer's identifiers have been removed, there's no way to get them back. You can, possibly, analyze the code to substitute intelligent identifiers for the ones the obfuscator assigned, but you'll never recover the actual identifiers the programmer originally chose! The second interesting characteristic is that identifier renaming, unlike most other obfuscating transformations, doesn't incur any performance overhead.

Depending on your language, you can be more or less clever in replacing original identifiers with bogus ones. Algorithm 4.1 [58,351] is employed by PreEmptive Solutions' Dash0 Java obfuscator and, presumably, by its Dotfuscator obfuscator for .NET, which is included with Microsoft's Visual Studio 2005. The idea is to make use of the language's overloading features to give as many declarations as possible the same name. As an example, consider this set of classes :

```
class Felinae {
    int color;
    int speed;
    public void move(int x,int y){}
}
class Felis extends Felinae {
    public void move(int x,int y){}
    public void meow(int tone,int length){}
}
class Pantherinae extends Felinae {
    public void move(int x,int y){}
    public void growl(int tone,int length){}
}
class Panthera extends Pantherinae {
    public void move(int x,int y){}
}
```

Ignoring Java's concept of packages, interfaces, and access modifiers (private, public, protected), the naming rules for Java essentially require class names to be globally unique, and field names to be unique within classes. Also, methods with different signatures are considered unique and can have the same name.

Given these rules, Algorithm 4.1▸209 builds a graph where every node is a declaration and there's an edge between two nodes if they cannot have the same name. Methods that must have the same name (because they override each other) are merged into super-nodes. Renaming with the smallest number of names then becomes a problem of coloring the graph with the smallest number of colors. Here's the graph corresponding to the program above:

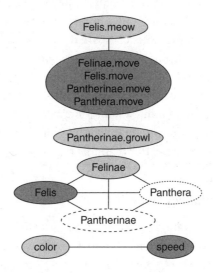

Here's the resulting, renamed code:

```
class Light {
    int Light;
    int Dark;
    public void Dark(int x,int y){}
}
class Dark extends Light {
    public void Dark(int x,int y){}
    public void Light(int tone,int length){}
}
class Dashed extends Light {
    public void Dark(int x,int y){}
    public void Light(int tone,int length){}
}
class Dotted extends Dashed {
    public void Dark(int x,int y){}
}
```

For example, although `meow` and `growl` have the same signature, they can be given the same name since they are declared in classes that have no inheritance relationship.

Problem 4.2   For a strongly typed language like Java, write a tool that de-obfuscates obfuscated identifiers making use of available type information, references to standard libraries with known semantics, and a library of common programming idioms. Evaluate your tool by having subjects compare the readability of original (unobfuscated) programs to your de-obfuscated programs with generated identifiers. How would your tool be different for a weakly typed language like C that relies less heavily than Java on a standard library? Could you use statistical methods to generate identifiers, for example, by training a neural network on a set of well-structured programs? Generating identifiers in "Hungarian Notation" is straightforward, but can you do better? Can you do better than this paper [73]?

4.1.3 Obfuscation Executives

If you have multiple obfuscating transformations at your disposal, a question naturally arises: Which transformations should I apply where, and in which order should I apply them? The problem gets even more complex if you not only want to obfuscate the program but also want to watermark and tamperproof it. Should I watermark first, then obfuscate, and then tamperproof, or is some other ordering better?

A similar problem (known as the "phase-ordering-problem" [373,374]) arises in compilers when there are many optimizing transformations available. Some compilers apply the optimizations in a fixed order, while others iteratively apply the transformations until there are no more changes, or until some time limit has been exceeded.

With some exceptions, choosing a good optimization order is an *easier* problem than choosing a good obfuscation order. The reason is that most optimizations make the program *simpler* (for example, by removing redundant computations), or at the very least, don't make the program much more complex. Transformations such as loop unrolling are exceptions. Obfuscating transformations, on the other hand, are *designed* to make the program more complex! So for every obfuscating transformation you apply, the program gets more complex and you make the job of the next transformation harder.

A related problem is how to decide when to stop obfuscating. With a fixed transformation order, this isn't a problem, of course: Just apply each transformation

---

Algorithm 4.2 Algorithm OBFCF$_{OE}$ for controlling diversifying transformations. prob[t] is the probability that you'll select transformation T_t and thresholdSpace is a bound on the size of the obfuscated program.

OBFUSCATIONEXECUTIVE(P,⟨T_1, T_2, . . . ⟩,thresholdSpace):

```
while (totalSpace ≤ thresholdSpace) {
    x ← y ← 0;
    a ← pseudo-random number between 0 and 1;
    do {
        y ← y+1;
        x ← x+prob[y];
    } while x<a;
    apply T_y;
}
```

---

until you have no more. If you choose transformations randomly, however (as you'd like to do when generating a diverse set of programs), you have to define a termination criterion. Ever the pioneer, Fred Cohen defined the simple routine OBFCF$_{OE}$ [76] in Algorithm 4.2 for controlling the generation of a diverse set of programs. We call the top-level routine in an obfuscation tool the *obfuscation executive* (OE).

4.1.3.1 Algorithm *OBFCTJ$_{OE}$:* Maximizing Bang for the Buck

Picking transformations randomly may work for diversification, but when you're obfuscating to hide some property, you want more control than that. OBFCTJ$_{OE}$ [87] in Algorithm 4.3 ▶214 refines Cohen's idea. It breaks up the program into *application objects*, i.e., any program structure that could possibly be obfuscated. Depending on the programming language and the transformations, this could include the modules, classes, routines, types, basic blocks, and so on that the program is made up of. For each application object, the user needs to specify how security-critical it is. The OE keeps a priority queue of application objects, and during each step it selects the most security-critical object to obfuscate. It next selects the most appropriate transformation to apply to the application object. "Most appropriate" here means a heuristic that maximizes the bang for the buck, i.e., selects the transformation that sows as much confusion as possible, minimizes the performance penalty, and generates code that fits in well with surrounding code.

Algorithm 4.3 Algorithm OBFCTJ$_{OE}$ [87]. Obfuscate program P using transformations $\langle T_1, T_2, \ldots \rangle$. P consists of application objects (routines, modules, classes, basic blocks, ...) $\langle s_1, s_2, \ldots \rangle$. `prio[`$s_i$`]` gives the importance of protecting application object s_i. `acceptCost` is the maximum execution penalty the user is willing to accept. `reqObf` is the amount of obfuscation the user requires.

OBFUSCATIONEXECUTIVE($P = \langle s_1, s_2, \ldots \rangle$, $T = \langle T_1, T_2, \ldots \rangle$,`prio`,`acceptCost`, `reqObf`):

1. Build necessary internal data structures such as the inheritance graph, the call graph, and control flow graphs for each routine.

2. Insert each application object s_i into a priority queue Q, using `prio[`s_i`]` as the priority.

3. Select the most important application object s to protect and an appropriate transformation t. Repeat the process until the obfuscation level the user requires has been reached or the maximum acceptable execution penalty has been exceeded:

```
while (!done(acceptCost,reqObf)) {
    s ← application object with max priority in Q;
    t ← SELECTTRANSFORMATION(s, T);
    apply t to s;
    update s's priority in Q;
    update internal data structures;
}
```

Use software complexity metrics (Section 3.4.2 ▶ 193) to estimate the obfuscation level of the program before and after a transformation is applied.

SELECTTRANSFORMATION(s, $T = \langle T_1, T_2, \ldots \rangle$):

1. Return a transformation t appropriate to apply to application object s. Select t to maximize stealth, maximize the resulting obfuscation, and minimize the execution penalty.

4.1.3.2 Algorithm *OBFHC:* Modeling Dependencies When we built the Sand-Mark [2,81] tool, we realized the need for a more powerful obfuscation executive. In addition to obfuscating transformations, SandMark includes watermarking transformations. If you're going to both obfuscate and watermark, it becomes important to specify which obfuscations are compatible with which watermarks and the order in which to apply the different transformations. Some obfuscations, for example, will destroy the watermarks and thus need to be applied *before* the mark

Problem 4.3 Many obfuscation papers say, "So, uh, unfortunately, our proposed transformation has a high performance overhead, but that's no problem! We'll just (a) apply it only to the security-critical parts of the program or (b) use profiling to avoid any performance-critical parts!" There are two problems with this argument. First, what's to say that the parts that are security-critical aren't also performance-critical? Second, if the transformation isn't perfectly stealthy, will the security-critical parts be easier for the adversary to locate if the transformation isn't applied uniformly over the program? Study some real programs to determine if this is a valid argument or not.

is embedded. Also, to be effective, some transformations require others to be run *afterwards*. For example, a transformation that splits a method A in two may, for simplicity and debuggability, name them A_firstHalf and A_secondHalf and then require an identifier renaming transformation to run afterwards.

Algorithm OBFHC [157] builds a Finite State Automaton (FSA) that embeds all the dependencies between transformations. During obfuscation, the OE does a probabilistic walk over the FSA, selecting a path that respects dependencies, selecting the most security-sensitive objects to obfuscate, and selecting transformations that lead to the highest level of obfuscation with the lowest performance overhead. The FSA, in other words, is a model that embeds all the information that an OE might use to select sequences of transformations. The model allows you to construct OEs of various complexity and precision.

For example, assume you have a program that consists of a single function m(). You specify to the OE *ObfLevel*(m), the desired obfuscation level of m(), and *PerfImport*(m), how performance critical m() is:

Application object	*ObfLevel*	*PerfImport*
m()	0.6	0.2

Assume your obfuscator has two obfuscating transformations A and B. For each transformation, the obfuscator specifies the obfuscation *Potency* (how much confusion it adds), the performance *Degradation*, and any dependencies on other transformations:

Transformation	*Potency*	*Degradation*	**Dependencies**
A	1.0	0.9	A postrequires B
B	0.5	0.3	

There's only one dependency here, stating that if transformation A is applied to some object x, B must at some later point be applied to x. From this information, the obfuscator builds the following FSA:

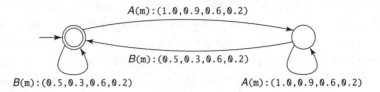

$$A(\mathtt{m}):(1.0,0.9,0.6,0.2)$$

$$B(\mathtt{m}):(0.5,0.3,0.6,0.2)$$

$$B(\mathtt{m}):(0.5,0.3,0.6,0.2)\qquad\qquad A(\mathtt{m}):(1.0,0.9,0.6,0.2)$$

The FSA generates a language of strings of $T(x)$, i.e., a series of obfuscations to run on particular application objects. The language generated by this FSA is $(B(\mathtt{m})|A(\mathtt{m})^+B(\mathtt{m})))^*$. For example, acceptable transformation sequences include

$$\langle B(\mathtt{m})\rangle,$$
$$\langle B(\mathtt{m}), B(\mathtt{m})\rangle,$$
$$\langle A(\mathtt{m}), B(\mathtt{m})\rangle,$$
$$\langle A(\mathtt{m}), A(\mathtt{m}), B(\mathtt{m}), B(\mathtt{m})\rangle,$$
$$\dots$$

Some sequences are better than others, of course, since they result in more obfuscated programs with lower performance penalty. To let the OE pick better paths, each FSA edge is of the form

$$a \xrightarrow{\ T(x):(Potency(T),Degradation(T),ObfLevel(x),PerfImport(x))\ } b$$

where the tuple to the right of the colon represents the "goodness" of applying transformation T to application object x. A simple OE will map this tuple into a single *edge weight* (a real number in $[0, 1]$) and use it to select edges probabilistically.

Problem 4.4   In most optimizing compilers, each optimization will compute the static analyses it needs, perform the transformation, and when it's done throw away the collected information. This doesn't work well for obfuscation tools, since each transformation makes the program *more* complex than before. The "right way" to build an OE is therefore to maintain static information across transformations. The disadvantage is that every transformation now becomes more complicated: After the transformation has been performed, the tool must update the static information so that it correctly reflects any changes it has made to the program. Design an interface to a database of static information that makes it easy to maintain correct state. Investigate how hard it would be to integrate it with an existing tool, such as SandMark. *Number One*, make it so.

4.2 Definitions

In this chapter, the goal of you, the defender, is to transform a program P^σ, which has a secret property σ, into a program P_o^σ, so that it is harder for an adversary to discover σ from P_o^σ than from P^σ. The goal of the adversary is *de-obfuscation*, to discover σ given access only to P_o^σ. We'll call P_o the *obfuscated* version of P, and we'll drop the σ superscript when it's clear from context what property you want to hide.

There are many different properties σ that you might want to hide. For example, σ could be

- the source code of the program,
- the organization of the program (its module structure, class hierarchy, ...),
- the names of the functions of the program,
- the algorithm the program uses to compute a particular function,
- the location in the program at which a particular function (such as a license check, decryption function, ...) is computed,
- the value of a particular literal data structure (such as a cryptographic key, license expiration date, ...) contained within the program,
- whether location l in the program is reachable, or
- what values variable x can take on during the execution of the program.

As you see, in some cases the goal of de-obfuscation is code (the source of P or some representation of one of P's algorithms), while in other cases it's a particular location in the program, the value of some literal data, or some other property of the control or data flow. For example, an attacker who wants to modify license checking code first of all needs to know where in the program it's located. But this is not enough. Before he goes ahead and modifies the program, he has to recover enough other information about it to know that the modification is safe and doesn't have any nasty side effects.

To convert P into P_o, you have access to a library of *semantics-preserving code transformations* $\mathcal{T} = \{\mathcal{T}_1, \mathcal{T}_2, \ldots\}$ and a set of program *analysis tools* $\mathcal{A} = \{\mathcal{A}_1, \mathcal{A}_2, \ldots\}$. $\mathcal{A}$ aids the transformations by providing useful static and/or dynamic information about P. Static analysis techniques might include control flow analysis, data flow analyses, slicing, and so on: all the kinds of code analysis algorithms that are normally used by compilers and program-understanding tools. Useful dynamic analysis tools include profilers, tracers, and debuggers. For these, you also will need a set of test cases $\mathcal{I}$, which consists of input data that thoroughly exercises the program, and possibly their expected results. Schematically, the obfuscation process looks like this:

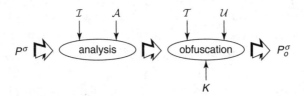

K is a secret (to the adversary) security parameter that we'll call the *key*. The obfuscator can use K to guide which transformations to apply to the program and where in the program to apply them. $\mathcal{U}$ is the set of de-obfuscating transformations your adversary has at his disposal.

You have to assume that your adversary is at least as accomplished as you, and has access to at least the same information and tools that you do! Specifically, he has access to the same set $\mathcal{A}$ of program analyzers, and he's aware of the set $\mathcal{T}$ of code transformations in the obfuscator's library, just like you're aware of his de-obfuscating transformations. He can use $\mathcal{A}$ to extract information about P_o^σ, and ideally σ itself, but possibly he'll be happy with an approximation of σ, σ_d. It may be that his ultimate goal is to recover the source of P itself, or one of its algorithms. For this, he'll need a set of *de-obfuscating transformations* $\mathcal{U} = \{\mathcal{U}_1, \mathcal{U}_2, \dots\}$ that transform P_o into P_d. Typically, he does not require P_d to be identical to P, but it has to be some representation that is "easy enough" to understand or manipulate or at least *easier* to understand and manipulate than P_o. Schematically, the de-obfuscation process looks like this:

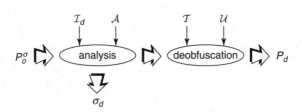

In practice, the attacker will iterate back and forth between analysis and de-obfuscation until he's reached a point where P_d is clear enough for his purposes.

Let's compare the last two figures. What advantage do you as the defender have over the adversary? First, you know the key K, which determines where in the code the different obfuscating transformations are applied—the adversary doesn't. This means that, even if for every one of your obfuscating transformations he has a corresponding de-obfuscating transformation, he still has to analyze the program in enough detail to know where to apply them. Second, if you're the developer of the program, most likely your set of test cases $\mathcal{I}$ is more comprehensive than the adversary's $\mathcal{I}_d$. This means that he will have to be careful when he makes changes to the program, since he can't hope to thoroughly test the correctness of every change. Third, while both of you have access to the same set of analysis tools $\mathcal{A}$, you are applying them to different programs. If obfuscation has made P_o larger than P, and the complexity of the analyses grow with the size of the program (which is common), the adversary will have to spend more time in analysis than you.

What advantages, then, may the adversary have over you? First, if the program is small enough, and the number of transformations is small enough, without access to K the adversary may still be able to exhaustively apply all the de-obfuscating transformations to every point of the program. Second, even though analyzing a larger program requires more resources than does a smaller one, there's nothing that says that the analyses that you had to perform in order to protect the program are the same analyses that the attacker needs to perform in order to break it! You may have had to perform expensive static analysis to correctly obfuscate the program in order to hide the σ property, but the attacker may decide that a quick run through a debugger is enough to locate that property!

4.2.1 Potent Obfuscating Transformations

We're taking a very pragmatic view of obfuscation in this chapter. We won't require a transformation to be "unbreakable," we will just ask that it make the attacker's task of analyzing the program to find the hidden information a bit harder. In Chapter 5 (Obfuscation Theory) you will see what happens when you try to strengthen this requirement.

Let's start by defining what we mean by an *obfuscating transformation* [87]:

Definition 4.1 (Obfuscating Transformation).   Let $\mathcal{T} : \mathbb{P} \to \mathbb{P}$ be a transformation from programs to programs. $\mathcal{T}$ is an *obfuscating transformation*, if P and $P_o = \mathcal{T}(P)$ have the same *observable behavior*. More precisely,

- If P fails to terminate or terminates with an error condition, then P_o may or may not terminate.

- Otherwise, P_o must terminate and produce the same output as P.

By "observable behavior" we mean "behavior as experienced by the user." For example, P_o may have side effects (creating files, sending messages over the network, and so on) that P doesn't have, but those side effects cannot be experienced by the user. Someone versed in program semantics may say that while we require an obfuscating transformation to leave the program's *denotational semantics* unchanged, we allow it to change the program's *trace semantics*.

This definition essentially allows *any* transformation on programs to be an obfuscating transformation as long as it's semantics-preserving! This is intentional. Optimizing transformations found in compilers are semantics-preserving, and many of them can be used for obfuscation as well. But not all transformations will be useful to us, and in particular, not every transformation will be useful to hide every particular property. So let's define an *effective* transformation:

> **Definition 4.2** (Effective Obfuscating Transformation).   Let $\mathcal{T}$ be an obfuscating transformation, P^σ, a program with property σ, $P_o^\sigma = \mathcal{T}(P^\sigma)$ an obfuscated version of P^σ, $\mathcal{A}$ a program analysis that reveals σ, $(\sigma = \mathcal{A}(P^\sigma))$, and σ_d is the result of applying $\mathcal{A}$ to P_o^σ, $(\sigma_d = \mathcal{A}(P_o^\sigma))$. Then with respect to P^σ and $\mathcal{A}$,
>
> $\mathcal{T}$ is *effective* if $\sigma_d \not\approx \sigma$ or $\mathcal{A}(P_d^\sigma)$ requires more resources to compute than $\mathcal{A}(P^\sigma)$;
>
> $\mathcal{T}$ is *ineffective* if $\sigma_d \approx \sigma$ and $\mathcal{A}(P_d^\sigma)$ requires the same amount of resources to compute as $\mathcal{A}(P^\sigma)$;
>
> $\mathcal{T}$ is *defective* if $\sigma_d \approx \sigma$ and $\mathcal{A}(P_d^\sigma)$ requires fewer resources to compute than $\mathcal{A}(P^\sigma)$.

To paraphrase this definition, you could say: "A good obfuscating transformation makes it harder to perform the necessary analyses that reveal the secret property on the obfuscated program than it is on the original." We don't define $\approx$ formally. In many situations, $\sigma_d = \sigma$ is what the attacker needs, but in others, some approximation of σ will suffice.

Actually, Definition 4.2 isn't quite right. The adversary has a collection of analyses at his disposal, and it's conceivable that an obfuscating transformation makes one analysis harder to apply but others easier! So we need to extend the definition to a set of analyses:

> **Definition 4.3** (Potent Obfuscating Transformation).   Let $\mathcal{T}$ be an obfuscating transformation, P^σ a program with property σ, $P_o^\sigma = \mathcal{T}(P^\sigma)$ an obfuscated version of P^σ, and $\mathcal{A} = \{\mathcal{A}_1, \mathcal{A}_2, \ldots, \mathcal{A}_n\}$ a set of program analyses.
>
> Then, $\mathcal{T}$ is *potent* with respect to P^σ and $\mathcal{A}$ if $\exists \mathcal{A}_i \in \mathcal{A}$ such that $\mathcal{T}$ is *effective* with respect to P^σ and $\mathcal{A}_i$, and $\forall \mathcal{A}_j \in \mathcal{A}$, $\mathcal{T}$ is not *defective* with respect to P^σ and $\mathcal{A}_j$.

In other words, a potent obfuscating transformation makes at least one analysis harder to perform, and no analyses easier.

What are the set of analyses that an attacker has access to? Ideally, you want your obfuscation technique to be potent to *all* possible analyses—even ones you have not thought of yet! In practice, proposed obfuscation techniques are resilient to known sets of analyses. For example, some obfuscation transformations can be shown to be resilient to static analysis—you cannot reverse engineer them without running them—but fail trivially to be resilient against simple dynamic analyses. Knowing the set of analyses your attacker has access to can dramatically simplify your job as an obfuscator. All you need to do is figure out the limits of those analyses and design your obfuscating transformations to require their worst-case behavior!

In discussing existing obfuscating transformations, we will point out the set of analyses that are being protected against and how the obfuscation takes advantage of this.

But first we must finalize our definition of what obfuscation is, because Definition 4.3 is *still* not quite right! What you *really* want is a definition that allows you to compare two transformations in order to say that one is more potent than the other.

In her Ph.D. thesis, Mila Dalla Preda gives what's to date the most rigorous definition of obfuscation potency [287–289]. In her framework, obfuscating transformations and attackers are both characterized by abstract domains. (Look back at Section 3.1.6▶143 for an introduction to abstract interpretation.) These domains form a lattice, where domains lower in the lattice are more concrete (have more accurate information) than those higher in the lattice. In Mila's model, an obfuscating program transformation is potent when there exists a property that is not preserved by the transformation. This framework also allows you to compare the potency of two transformations by comparing *the most concrete property* that's preserved by each.

To illustrate the basic idea, have a look at these two trivial obfuscating transformations:

$$T_1(x) = 2 \cdot x$$
$$T_2(x) = 3 \cdot x$$

T_1 takes an integer variable x in the program and replaces it with $2 \cdot x$. This is an example of a *data transformation*, which you will see more of in Section 4.5▶258. $T_2(x)$ is similar; it replaces an integer variable x with $3 \cdot x$. What you'd like to know is which one (T_1 or T_2) is the more potent. In Mila's system, the transformation that *preserves the most concrete property* is the one that's the *worse obfuscation*. Think about it—a transformation that preserves everything (the identity transformation) is a really bad transformation, and the transformation that preserves no property from the original program is a really good one!

So which ($T_1(x) = 2 \cdot x$ or $T_2(x) = 3 \cdot x$) preserves the least and is the better obfuscation? Let's look at two properties, Sign and Parity:

$$\text{Sign}(x) = \begin{cases} -1 & \text{if } x < 0 \\ 0 & \text{if } x = 0 \\ 1 & \text{if } x > 0 \end{cases}$$

$$\text{Parity}(x) = \begin{cases} 0 & \text{if even}(x) \\ 1 & \text{if odd}(x) \end{cases}$$

Both T_1 and T_2 preserve the Sign property, since $\text{Sign}(x) = \text{Sign}(2 \cdot x)$ and $\text{Sign}(x) = \text{Sign}(3 \cdot x)$. T_2 also preserves the Parity property, since $\text{Parity}(x) = \text{Parity}(3 \cdot x)$, which T_1 does not, since $\text{Parity}(x) \neq \text{Parity}(2 \cdot x)$. Thus, T_1 preserves *less* than T_2 and is therefore a *better* obfuscating transformation than T_2!

While this is very clever, in practice many transformations cannot be compared in this way—their domains are not comparable.

4.2.2 Efficient Obfuscating Transformations

So far we haven't said anything about the *cost* of obfuscation. Most obfuscating transformations result in P_o being larger than P, slower than P, using more memory than P, or often a combination of all three! In practice, you'd measure the cost of a transformation by selecting a suitable benchmark suite (such as the SPEC benchmarks used by compiler researchers), obfuscate the programs using a transformation T, run the original and transformed programs on the input data sets provided by the suite, and measure the difference in execution time and memory usage.

By itself, however, this type of evaluation is meaningless. Saying that T, on average, makes programs $x\%$ slower is of no value unless you can also say that the transformed program is now $y\%$ more secure against attacks! Thus, only when you factor in the potency of the transformation does efficiency make any sense.

4.2.3 Stealth

A big problem with many software protection algorithms is the *stealthiness* of the transformed code. Intuitively, you can think of stealth as the degree to which transformed code can be distinguished from untransformed code. Many attacks on protected programs become much easier if the adversary can find even an approximate location of the protection code. For example, as you'll see in Section 7.2.4 ▶ 431, the Skype VoIP client was compromised (in part) because the tamper-detection code was really easy to find among all the other code in the program. Stealthiness becomes especially important when transformations add *new* code to a program. Many of the software watermarking algorithms you'll see in Chapter 8 (Software Watermarking) and Chapter 9 (Dynamic Watermarking) fall in this category, and if the new code looks different from the original code, the watermarks will be easy to locate. In Section 8.8.1▸523, you'll see an algorithm that steganographically embeds a message in an x86 binary and is very careful to make the embedding stealthy—it ensures that statistical properties of the transformed code match those of real programs.

Many different definitions of stealth are possible. Here, we'll distinguish between *local stealth* and *steganographic stealth*. A transformation T is steganographically stealthy if an adversary cannot determine if a program P has been transformed with T or not. A transformation is locally stealthy if the adversary can't tell the *location* in P where T has been applied. The stealth of a transformation is always expressed with respect to a universe $\mathbb{U}$ of programs. For example, a transformation that inserts a large number of **xor** instructions will be stealthy with respect to a universe of cryptographic or bitmapped-graphics programs, but it will be unstealthy with respect to a universe of programs performing scientific computations.

To formally define local stealth, let's assume that the adversary has a *locator* function L that can determine if a particular instruction has been affected by an obfuscating transformation T or not. T is locally 1-stealthy with respect to L if L is always wrong (the adversary has a maximally defective locator function), and it's locally 0-stealthy if L is always right:

Definition 4.4 (Local stealth). Let $\mathbb{U}$ be a universe of programs, T an obfuscating transformation, P a program drawn from $\mathbb{U}$, and λ a real-valued constant in $[0 \dots 1]$, and let $P_o = T(P)$ be P obfuscated with T.

Let $\widehat{L} : \mathbb{P} \times \mathbb{T} \times \mathbb{N} \to \{0, 1\}$ be an error-free locator function so that $L(P, T, j)$ returns 1 if location j in program P has been inserted or modified by transformation T, and returns 0 otherwise. Similarly, let $L : \mathbb{P} \times \mathbb{T} \times \mathbb{N} \to \{0, 1\}$ be an adversary's locator function.

We say that T is locally λ-stealthy with respect to $\mathbb{U}$ and L if the probability that L reports that instruction j has been transformed with T when it has not, or reports that instruction j has not been transformed with T when it has, is at least λ:

$$\max \left\{ \begin{array}{l} Prob\ (\widehat{L}(P_o, T, j) = 0 \land L(P_o, T, j) = 1), \\ Prob\ (\widehat{L}(P_o, T, j) = 1 \land L(P_o, T, j) = 0) \end{array} \right\} \geq \lambda$$

To formally define steganographic stealth, let's assume that the adversary has a function $S(P, T)$ that can determine whether a program P has been obfuscated by transformation T or not. T is steganographically 1-stealthy if S is always wrong and steganographically 0-stealthy if it's always right:

Definition 4.5 (Steganographic stealth). Let $\mathbb{U}, T, P, P_o$ be defined as above, and let μ be a real-valued constant in $[0 \ldots 1]$.

Let $\widehat{S} : \mathbb{P} \times \mathbb{T} \to \{0, 1\}$ be an error-free detection function, such that $\widehat{S}(P, T) = 1$ if P has been transformed with T, and 0 otherwise. Similarly, let $S : \mathbb{P} \times \mathbb{T} \to \{0, 1\}$ be the adversary's detection function.

We say T is steganographically μ-stealthy for S if the probability that S reports that the untransformed P has been transformed with T or reports that the obfuscated P_o has not been transformed with T is at least μ:

$$\max \{ \mathit{Prob}(S(P, T) = 1), \quad \mathit{Prob}(S(P_o, T) = 0)\} \geq \mu$$

Stealth is an important concept, not just for code obfuscation but for tamper-proofing and software watermarking as well. Tamperproofing algorithms typically insert new code to detect alterations to the program, and many watermarking algorithms insert code to embed a mark. For more detailed definitions of local and steganographic stealth with respect to software watermarking, you should have a look at Collberg et al. [90], from which the definitions above have been derived.

4.2.4 Other Definitions

There has been—and still is—considerable debate about obfuscation: Is obfuscation ever useful, what obfuscating transformations may be useful, how do you measure the usefulness of an obfuscating transformation, and *what is obfuscation, anyway?* The definitions you just saw are only some of many that have been proposed.

In our original paper on obfuscation [87], we proposed that an obfuscating transformation should be evaluated in terms of its *potency, resilience, cost,* and *stealth.* The intention was for potency to measure the amount of confusion added to the program that would affect a human attacker. The confusion was measured in terms of how the transformation would affect a set of *software metrics* (Section 3.4.2▶193). Such metrics are normally used to evaluate how well designed and well structured a program is, but we proposed to use the same metrics to measure how *poorly* structured the program was after obfuscation!

While potency was defined to measure the confusion of a human attacker, resilience, on the other hand, would measure how well the transformation would stand up against an automatic deobfuscator. Resilience is a combination of how long it would take to build a deobfuscator that could untangle a particular transformation, and how long it would take to run it. You still occasionally see references to these definitions in the literature.

4.3 Complicating Control Flow

In the remainder of this chapter, you'll see a catalog of obfuscating transformations. They can be roughly classified as affecting a program's control flow, data structures, and abstractions. We're going to start by looking at transformations that make it difficult for an adversary to analyze the flow of control of a program. Some of these transformations insert bogus control flow, some flatten the program to remove any vestiges of structured programming, and others hide the targets of branches to make it difficult for the adversary to build control flow graphs. None of these transformations are immune to attacks, and we'll show you how to use a combination of static and dynamic analysis to recover hidden flow of control in Section 4.3.6▶242.

4.3.1 Opaque Expressions

Many obfuscating transformations rely on a concept known as *opaque expressions*. The idea is simply to construct, at obfuscation time, an expression whose value is known to you, as the defender, but is difficult for an attacker to figure out. You'll learn a lot more about opaque expressions in Section 4.4▶246. For right now, let's just introduce the notation we'll be using.

Most common are *opaque predicates*, boolean valued expressions for which you know whether they will return true, false, or sometimes true and sometimes false. We use the notation P^T for an *opaquely true* predicate, P^F for an *opaquely false* predicate, and $P^?$ for an *opaquely indeterminate* predicate. Graphically, we use dashed lines to indicate control-flow paths that will never be taken at runtime:

For example, here's an opaquely true predicate that always forces execution to take the true path:

To de-obfuscate this branch, i.e., to figure out that the false exit will never be taken, the adversary needs to know that $x^2 + x$ is always divisible by 2. And here, finally, is an opaquely indeterminate predicate where control could flow through either exit:

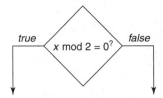

In general, we use the notation E^e for an expression known to have the property e. For example, $E^{=1}$ is an expression that always evaluates to 1, $E^{<10}$ is an expression whose value is always less than 10, and $(x^2 + x) \bmod 2^{=0}$ is an expression opaquely equal to 0.

4.3.2 Algorithm *OBFWHKD:* Control-Flow Flattening

Algorithm OBFWHKD is a common tool in the obfuscator's tool chest. It removes the control flow *structure* that functions have, the nesting of loop and conditional statements, by "flattening" the corresponding control flow graph. Have a look at the example in Figure 4.1▸227. It shows a modular exponentiation routine commonly found in cryptographic algorithms, such as RSA. To the right in the figure is the corresponding control flow graph. To flatten, or "*chenxify*" as it is affectionately known,[1] you put each basic block as a case inside a switch statement and wrap the switch inside an infinite loop. You can see the resulting code and control flow graph in Figure 4.2▸228.

The algorithm maintains the correct control flow by making each basic block update a variable next so that control will continue at the appropriate basic block. The resulting control flow graph has lost all its structure: Since the basic blocks no longer have any fall-through cases, you can randomly reorder them for some minor extra confusion.

These transformations are expensive. The for loop incurs one jump, and the switch statement incurs a bounds check on the next variable and an indirect jump through a jump table. In practice, to keep the performance penalty within reason, you don't want to convert *all* control flow edges. If you have a tight inner loop, for example, you can keep it as one case in the switch rather than spreading it over several cases.

---

1. Named after the inventor, Chenxi Wang. Example: "Before applying the other obfuscations, you should first chenxify the function." Also a noun, *chenxification*.

```
int modexp(int y,int x[],
           int w,int n) {
  int R, L;
  int k = 0;
  int s = 1;
  while (k < w) {
    if (x[k] == 1)
      R = (s*y) % n;
    else
      R = s;
    s = R*R % n;
    L = R;
    k++;
  }
  return L;
}
```

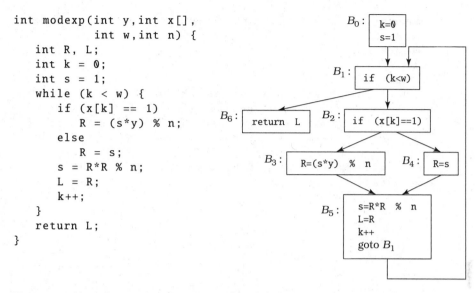

Figure 4.1 Algorithm OBFWHKD: Original modular exponentiation routine and its control flow graph.

Depending on your implementation language, you might be able to find cheaper implementation methods than the for-switch compound. Assembly language gives you the most flexibility, of course, but even in C there are some possible optimizations. Here, we've used gcc's *labels-as-values* to construct a jump table that lets you jump directly to the next basic block:

```
int modexp(int y, int x[], int w, int n) {
  int R, L, k, s;
  char* jtab[]={&&case0,&&case1,&&case2,
                &&case3,&&case4,&&case5,&&case6};
  goto *jtab[0];
  case0: k=0; s=1; goto *jtab[1];
  case1: if (k<w) goto *jtab[2]; else goto *jtab[6];
  case2: if (x[k]==1) goto *jtab[3]; else goto *jtab[4];
  case3: R=(s*y)%n; goto *jtab[5];
  case4: R=s; goto *jtab[5];
  case5: s=R*R%n; L=R; k++; goto *jtab[1];
  case6: return L;
}
```

As you will see in the next section, making the jump go through an array like this can make it much harder for an adversary to de-obfuscate the flattened function.

```
int modexp(int y, int x[], int w, int n) {
    int R, L, k, s;
    int next=0;
    for(;;)
        switch(next) {
            case 0 : k=0; s=1; next=1; break;
            case 1 : if (k<w) next=2; else next=6; break;
            case 2 : if (x[k]==1) next=3; else next=4; break;
            case 3 : R=(s*y)%n; next=5; break;
            case 4 : R=s; next=5; break;
            case 5 : s=R*R%n; L=R; k++; next=1; break;
            case 6 : return L;
        }
}
```

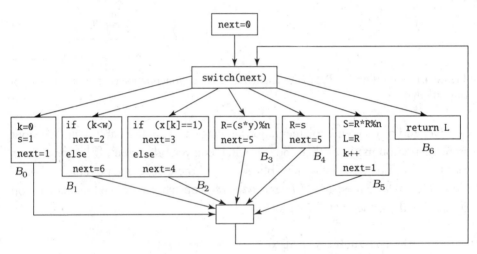

Figure 4.2 Algorithm OBFWHKD: The flattened modular exponentiation routine.

In languages like Java that support exception handling, chenxification becomes more complicated. If you look at a control flow graph generated from a language with exception handling, you'll notice that it has *lots* more edges than you're used to. Any statement that can throw an exception (and this includes any expression that might divide by zero or which dereferences a pointer that might be null—very common situations in real code!) will have a control flow edge to the nearest encompassing catch block, or the end of the function if there is no try-catch. It's complicated to map these dense control flow graphs onto a flattened structure. László and Kiss [222,223] solve this problem in their C++ source-to-source obfuscator by nesting flattened structures, i.e., one switch case will hold a try-catch block which, in turn, holds another for-switch nest.

Problem 4.5 Can you devise a flattening algorithm where exception handling doesn't reveal any structure? Can you do it on source? On Java bytecode? What's the overhead of your implementation?

4.3.3 Introducing Aliasing

If you want to confuse static analysis—and you do, because it's in fact the purpose of this chapter—then nothing is more effective than introducing spurious aliases into your program. Aliasing seems to confuse both analysis when performed by humans and analysis when performed by static analysis tools. Intuitively, you can think of it like this. Static analyses need to be conservative; they can only report facts about a variable that are provably true. This means that in order to be able to say something for certain about a variable, an analysis needs to consider *all* possible ways in which that variable can be modified. When you add an alias to the program, you suddenly have *two* ways to modify the same memory location, and this complicates analysis.

As you saw in Section 3.1.4 ▶ 134, aliasing can occur in a variety of settings. Most obviously, two pointers can refer to the same memory location, but two reference parameters can also alias each other, as can a reference parameter and a global variable and two array elements indexed by different variables.

Alias analysis is known to be undecidable in general [302] and NP-hard for specific cases [170]. We have to stress here, though, that this doesn't necessarily mean that adding a few random aliases to a program will make it provably hard to analyze! Many authors have made the mistake of claiming this in the past, and it just isn't true. Just because a problem is known to be hard (in a complexity sense) doesn't mean that a random *instance* of that problem will be hard [219]!

Problem 4.6 Investigate how to generate provably hard instances of the aliasing problem. Can you make use of results from the *average case complexity* field? Ramalingam [302] uses the Post Correspondence Problem (PCP) to prove the undecidability of aliasing, and it's known that a related problem, Distributional PCP, is hard on average [362]. Can you make use of this result? Pick up your Ph.D. on the way out.

Nevertheless, we know from experience that debugging programs with pointer-related bugs is a pain, and that current alias analysis algorithms fail to analyze programs that build and modify complex pointer structures. In this section, we will show you ways to take advantage of these observations in order to obfuscate programs in a way that makes them difficult to de-obfuscate. At present, we have insufficient knowledge on *how* to insert aliases, *where* to insert them, and *how many* aliases are necessary and sufficient to insert in order to protect against attack, but we're hoping this will change as the field matures.

Problem 4.7   In the absence of deep theoretical results, investigate the power of current alias analysis algorithms. What level of aliasing do we need to add to a program to defeat these algorithms? What kinds of aliases work best? Note that many algorithms have a parameter k that limits how deeply pointers are followed. For each algorithm, find the k that makes it too slow on current hardware and for current program sizes. Develop an alias insertion algorithm that adds $k + 1$ levels of pointers. What's the overhead of your scheme? Pick up your M.Sc. on the way out.

4.3.3.1   Algorithm *OBFCTJ$_{alias}$*: Adding Spurious Aliases   Collberg et al. [87] were the first to suggest that adding spurious aliases to a program could prevent attacks by static analysis. Their targets, specifically, were attacks that used *program slicing* to find the part of a program that contributes to the value of a variable. For example, in Section 7.3 ▶440 in Chapter 7 (Software Tamperproofing), you will see an algorithm that sets a pointer variable to null so that, much later in the program execution, a segmentation fault exception gets thrown and the program crashes. You do this to punish the user after you've detected that he's tampered with your program. A slicing algorithm could help the attacker by, starting at the point of the crash and working backwards, allowing him to extract the piece of the program that contributed to the variable that caused the crash. Ideally (for the attacker), this slice is much smaller than the whole program, and it lets him easily find a point where he can disable the punishment. Ideally (for *you*), the slice is so huge that the attacker gives up on using slicing altogether.

Essentially *all* static analysis algorithms require alias information in order to compute precise results, and slicing is no exception. A precise inter-procedural slicer will be slower when there are a higher number of potential aliases in a program; the number of potential aliases grows *exponentially* with the number of formal parameters [171]. So to defend yourself against an attacker who uses a slicing tool, you can add dummy arguments to functions. This will either slow down the slicer or force it to produce imprecise slices.

4.3.3.2   Algorithm *OBFWHKD$_{alias}$*: Control-Flow Flattening, Take 2   The chenxification you saw earlier isn't enough to throw off an attacker. With use-definition and constant-propagation data flow analyses on the next variable used in the switch statement, an attacker will be able to figure out what the next block of every block is, and hence be able to accurately reconstruct the control flow graph.

What we need here is some way to confuse the data flow analyses so that they're unable to work out the value of next, and hence the flow from block to block. Essentially, what you want is for the next variable to be computed as an opaque value:

```
int modexp(int y, int x[], int w, int n) {
    int R, L, k, s;
    int next=E^{=0};
    for(;;)
        switch(next) {
            case 0 : k=0; s=1; next=E^{=1}; break;
            case 1 : if (k<w) next=E^{=2}; else next=E^{=6}; break;
            case 2 : if (x[k]==1) next=E^{=3}; else next=E^{=4}; break;
            case 3 : R=(s*y)%n; next=E^{=5}; break;
            case 4 : R=s; next=E^{=5}; break;
            case 5 : s=R*R%n; L=R; k++; next=E^{=1}; break;
            case 6 : return L;
        }
}
```

Any technique for manufacturing opaque values will do, of course. However, Chenxi suggests basing them on the difficulty of array alias analysis. Here, we've introduced a constant array g and computed the value of next by constructing expressions over g:

```
int modexp(int y, int x[], int w, int n) {
    int R, L, k, s;
    int next=0;
    int g[] = {10,9,2,5,3};
    for(;;)
        switch(next) {
            case 0 : k=0; s=1; next=g[0]%g[1]^{=1}; break;
            case 1 : if (k<w) next=g[g[2]]^{=2};
                     else next=g[0]-2*g[2]^{=6}; break;
            case 2 : if (x[k]==1) next=g[3]-g[2]^{=3};
                     else next=2*g[2]^{=4}; break;
            case 3 : R=(s*y)%n; next=g[4]+g[2]^{=5}; break;
            case 4 : R=s; next=g[0]-g[3]^{=5}; break;
            case 5 : s=R*R%n; L=R; k++; next=g[g[4]]%g[2]^{=1}; break;
            case 6 : return L;
        }
}
```

To further complicate static analysis, you should make sure that the values in g are in constant flux. The opaque property still has to remain intact, of course, but other than that, you're free to dream up any transformation you want. As an example, here's a function that rotates the array one step right:

```
void permute(int g[], int n, int* m) {
    int i;
    int tmp=g[n-1];
    for(i=n-2; i>=0; i--) g[i+1] = g[i];
    g[0]=tmp;
    *m = ((*m)+1)%n;
}
```

And here's the corresponding flattened code where we rotate the array one step for every iteration. Regardless of the state of the array, the m variable indexes the array element that has the value 10, so you can use it as the base for your array computations:

```
int modexp(int y, int x[], int w, int n) {
    int R, L, k, s;
    int next=0;
    int m=0;
    int g[] = {10,9,2,5,3};
    for(;;) {
        switch(next) {
            case 0 : k=0; s=1; next=g[(0+m)%5]%g[(1+m)%5]; break;
            case 1 : if (k<w) next=g[(g[(2+m)%5]+m)%5];
                     else next=g[(0+m)%5]-2*g[(2+m)%5]; break;
            case 2 : if (x[k]==1) next=g[(3+m)%5]-g[(2+m)%5];
                     else next=2*g[(2+m)%5]; break;
            case 3 : R=(s*y)%n; next=g[(4+m)%5]+g[(2+m)%5]; break;
            case 4 : R=s; next=g[(0+m)%5]-g[(3+m)%5]; break;
            case 5 : s=R*R%n; L=R; k++;
                     next=g[(g[(4+m)%5]+m)%5]%g[(2+m)%5]; break;
            case 6 : return L;
        }
        permute(g,5,&m);
    }
}
```

To further confuse static analysis, Udupa et al. [352] suggest making the array global:

```
int g[20];
int m;
int modexp(int y, int x[], int w, int n) {
   int R, L, k, s;
   int next=0;
   for(;;)
      switch(next) {
         case 0 : k=0; s=1; next=g[m+0]%g[m+1]; break;
         case 1 : if (k<w) next=g[m+g[m+2]]; else next=g[m+0]-2*g[m+2];
                  break;
         case 2 : if (x[k]==1) next=g[m+3]-g[m+2]; else next=2*g[m+2];
                  break;
         case 3 : R = (s*y)%n; next=g[m+4]+g[m+2]; break;
         case 4 : R=s; next=g[m+0]-g[m+3]; break;
         case 5 : s = R*R%n; L=R; k++; next=g[m+g[m+4]]%g[m+2]; break;
         case 6 : return L;
      }
}
```

This allows you to initialize the array differently at different call sites:

```
g[0]=10; g[1]=9; g[2]=2; g[3]=5; g[4]=3; m=0;
modexp(y, x, w, n);
...
g[5]=10; g[6]=9; g[7]=2; g[8]=5; g[9]=3; m=5;
modexp(y, x, w, n);
```

Finally, to further confuse the attacker's alias analysis, you can sprinkle pointer variables (in light gray) and pointer manipulations (dark gray) evenly over the program. In case 2 below, element g[2] is accessed directly as g[2] as well as through a pointer dereference *g2. Most of the manipulations will actually be executed, but we've also added a dead case (dashed) that never will be:

```
int modexp(int y, int x[], int w, int n) {
    int R, L, k, s;
    int next=0;
    int g[] = {10,9,2,5,3,42};
    int* g2; int* gr;
    for(;;)
        switch(next) {
            case 0 : k=0;   g2=&g[2]; s=1; next=g[0]%g[1]; gr=&g[5]; break;
            case 1 : if (k<w)  next=g[*g2]; else next=g[0]-2*g[2]; break;
            case 2 : if (x[k]==1) next=g[3]-*g2; else next=2**g2; break;
            case 3 : R=(s*y)%n; next=g[4]+*g2; break;
            case 4 : R=s; next=g[0]-g[3]; break;
            case 5 : s=R*R%n; L=R; k++; next=g[g[4]]%*g2; break;
            case 6 : return L;
            case 7 : *g2=666; next=*gr%2; gr=&g[*g2]; break;
        }
}
```

The goal of these pointer manipulations is that, taken together, they will force the attacker's static analysis routine to conclude that nothing can be deduced about the next variable. And if he cannot know anything statically about next, he won't be able to reconstitute the original control flow graph.

While pure static analysis may be terminally confused by chenxification, there could be other attacks. For example, next is initialized to 0, which means the attacker knows which block gets executed first. From there, symbolic execution of the program could possibly reveal all the control flow paths.

Problem 4.8   In practice, just how hard would it be to attack a chenxified program using symbolic execution? After you've devised a successful attack, can you think of a way to foil it? Chenxi suggests "unrolling loops and introducing semantically equivalent blocks that will be chosen randomly during execution" [360, p. 76]. Is this effective or not?

Chenxification carries with it a fairly substantial performance penalty. Udupa et al. [352] report that the number of control flow edges in the SPEC benchmarks increases by a factor of 55 to a factor of 60. Wang et al. [361] report that replacing 50% of the branches in three SPEC programs slows them down by a factor of 4 and increases their size by a factor of 2.

4.3.4 Algorithm *OBFCTJ$_{bogus}$*: Inserting Bogus Control Flow

Algorithm OBFWHKD reorganizes the control flow of a function to make it difficult for a static analyzer to reconstitute the corresponding control flow graph. Algorithm OBFCTJ$_{bogus}$ [87,89,91], on the other hand, inserts *bogus* control flow into a function. The result is a control flow graph with dead branches that will never be taken, superfluous branches that will *always* be taken, or branches that will sometimes be taken and sometimes not, but where this doesn't matter. Regardless, to make it difficult for an adversary to figure out the bogosity of the branches, they are protected by opaque predicates. Thus, the resilience of these transformations reduces to the resilience of the opaque predicates they use.

Once you have access to opaque predicates, there are several possible transformations. Three of them are known as *block splitting* transformations because they appear to split a basic block in two pieces. For example, you can insert an opaquely true predicate in the middle of a block so that it seems that the second half (in dark gray) is only sometimes executed while, in fact, it always is:

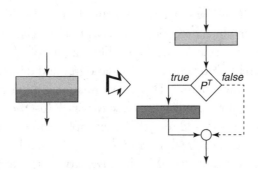

Or you can insert a bogus block (dashed), which appears as if it might be executed while, in fact, it never will be:

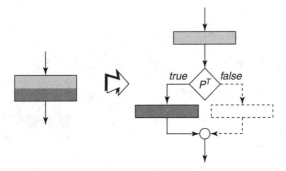

The dashed block could be arbitrary code, or it could be a copy of the dark gray block in which we've made some minor random changes. The latter is particularly clever, since stealth is almost certainly guaranteed.

A third alternative transformation is to insert a $P^?$ predicate, which sometimes executes the dark gray block and sometimes the dashed block:

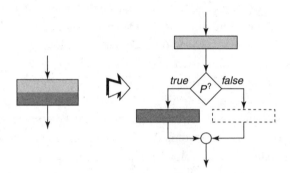

The dashed block should be semantically equivalent to the dark gray block. This way, it doesn't matter which execution path the predicate chooses! The easiest way to accomplish this is to first make the dashed block a copy of the dark gray block and then to apply different obfuscations to the dark gray and dashed blocks to ensure that they're syntactically different. This transformation is particularly easy to insert, since creating a $P^?$ opaque predicate is close to trivial: Just pick a random variable in the current environment and test it! For example, if there's an integer variable i hanging around, very stealthy tests are $i < 0$, $i \neq 1$, $i \bmod 2 = 0$, and so on. To de-obfuscate a transformation like this, the adversary must determine that the dark gray and dashed blocks are semantically equivalent.

You can also extend a loop condition P by conjoining it with an opaquely true predicate P^T, forming $P \wedge P^T$, where P^T of course is completely redundant:

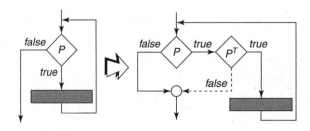

You can similarly use disjunction, turning a loop condition P into $P \vee P^F$.

4.3.4.1 Irreducible Graphs   If you follow the rules of structured programming and build your code out of nested if-, for-, while-, repeat-, case-statements, and so on, you wind up with control flow graphs that are known as *reducible*. Data flow analysis over such graphs is straightforward and efficient. If, however, you were to jump into the middle of a loop so that the loop has multiple entry points, the corresponding control flow graph becomes *irreducible* [5]. Data flow analysis over such graphs is significantly complicated, and so it usually starts by a pass where the graph is converted to a reducible one. An interesting obfuscation is therefore to add bogus jumps that appear to transfer control into the middle of loops, thereby creating harder-to-analyze irreducible graphs. Here's an example of an obfuscated loop and its corresponding control flow graph:

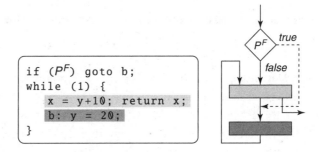

```
if (P^F) goto b;
while (1) {
    x = y+10; return x;
    b: y = 20;
}
```

There are two ways for an attacker to de-obfuscate, i.e., to convert the irreducible graph to a reducible one. The first technique is known as *node splitting* and works by duplicating parts of the graph. Here's the same example as above, where the attacker has duplicated the statement y=20 and thereby made the graph reducible:

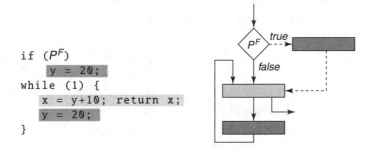

```
if (P^F)
    y = 20;
while (1) {
    x = y+10; return x;
    y = 20;
}
```

The nice thing about this construction is that if your obfuscated control flow graph is known to be really complex (it's the complete graph of n nodes), then the equivalent reducible graph will have an exponential number (2^{n-1}) of nodes [55]! This is potentially exciting news, since it means that you could force an attacker to build a huge data structure in memory if he wants to do static analysis on your program. Unfortunately, there's another technique for making an irreducible graph reducible, which, rather than duplicating nodes, inserts extra guards in the loop:

```
int firsttime=1;
while (1) {
    if ((!firsttime) || (!P^F)) {
        x = y+10; return x;
    }
    y = 20;
    firsttime=0;
}
```

It's not known whether this construction also causes exponential blowup.

4.3.4.2 Mutually Dependent Opaque Predicates

One argument against using opaque predicates to complicate control flow is that "it's easy to detect an always-true predicate—just run the program a few times with different inputs while monitoring the outcome of all predicates—and replace the ones that are always true!" Whether this will be a successful strategy or not depends on the quality of your test data and how often, in real code, for reasonable test data sets, predicates will naturally look opaque. Dalla Preda et al. [290] report that when running the SPECint2000 benchmarks with the reference inputs, on average 39% of the predicates look like P^T and 22% look like P^F. Keep in mind that a typical attacker won't have such comprehensive test data available to him, so in an actual attack scenario, it's safe to assume that even more branches will look opaque.

One way to make dynamic analysis a little bit harder is to make opaque predicates *interdependent*. That way, an attacker cannot simply remove one predicate at a time, rerun the program to see if it still works, remove another predicate, and so on. Instead, he has to remove *all* interdependent opaque predicates at the same time. Here's an example where, should the attacker remove any one of the two opaque predicates, the other one will raise a divide-by-zero exception:

```
int x=0, y=2,t;
while (1) {
    if (t=x*(x-1)%y==0,y-=2,x+=2,t)^T ...
    if (t=y*(y-1)%x==0,y+=2,x-=2,t)^T ...
}
```

Problem 4.9 The above construction is admittedly lame, but it's late, and that's all we could come up with. Can you think of a way to generate less conspicuous mutually dependent opaque predicates?

4.3.5 Algorithm *OBFLDK*: Jumps Through Branch Functions

Algorithm OBFLDK [78,102,212,231,234,259] replaces unconditional jumps with a call to a function called a *branch function*. Calls, of course, are expected to return to the statement immediately *following* them, but in the case of the branch function, they instead return to the *target of the original jump*. As you will see, this doesn't just complicate the control flow; it also leaves convenient "holes" in the program that will never be executed and where you can stick bogus instructions that will confuse the heck out of a disassembler.

This figure should illustrate the basic idea:

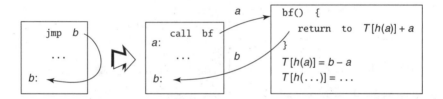

In the original program, there is an unconditional jump to label b. In the obfuscated program, this jump has been replaced with a *call* to the branch function bf. The call carries with it the return address (the address immediately following the call), a. Depending on the calling convention, this address will be passed in a register or on the stack. The branch function uses this return address to index into a table T to find an offset $b - a$, add a top that, yielding b, the target of the original jump. The branch function replaces the old return address with b, executes the return instruction, and voilà, you've executed a jump to b! In this simple example, there's only one unconditional jump in the program, but a real situation will involve many jumps that will all be converted into calls to the branch function. Thus, to an observer it seems like there are calls all over the program to one very popular function, but none of these calls return to the place from whence they came! As you will see, this is the strength of the algorithm (it provides a lot of confusion), but also its weakness (it makes it highly dynamically unstealthy).

The table T is indexed by a hash function $h()$ that hashes every address to an index of T. Since you'll want to waste as little space as possible for the table, you should implement $h()$ as a *perfect minimal hashfunction* [131].

Let's have a look at a real example. Below left, again, is the modular exponentiation routine we've been working with. This time, to the right, we've replaced the high-level control constructs with labels and gotos. Of particular interest is the code in light gray, unconditional jumps that we're going to replace with calls to the branch function:

```
int modexp(int y,int x[],
           int w,int n) {
  int R, L;
  int k = 0;
  int s = 1;
  while (k < w) {
    if (x[k] == 1)
      R = (s*y) % n;
    else
      R = s;
    s = R*R % n;
    L = R;
    k++;
  }
  return L;
}
```

```
int modexp(int y,int x[],
           int w,int n) {
  int R, L;
  int k = 0;
  int s = 1;
beginloop:
  if (k >= w) goto endloop;
  if (x[k] != 1) goto elsepart;
    R = (s*y) % n;
    goto endif;
elsepart:
    R = s;
endif:
  s = R*R % n;
  L = R;
  k++;
  goto beginloop;
endloop:
  return L;
}
```

For every pair of addresses (a_i, b_i) where a_i is the return address of the call instruction you're inserting and b_i is the address that you really want to jump to, a table T stores

$$T[h(a_i)] = b_i - a_i.$$

$h()$ is a hash function that maps sparse addresses to a compact range $1 \ldots n$. Given this table, here's what the branch function looks like:

```
char* T[2];
void bf() {
  char* old;
  asm volatile("movl 4(%%ebp),%0\n\t" : "=r" (old));
  char* new = (char*)((int)T[h(old)] + (int)old);
  asm volatile("movl %0,4(%%ebp)\n\t" : : "r" (new));
}
```

The two lines of code in light gray are responsible for loading the old return address and then storing a new value into it, respectively. The remaining code computes the address that you really want to jump to. When that address has been written back into bf's return address, once you execute the return instruction, control will continue where you really wanted to go in the first place.

Now that you have the branch function, converting unconditional branches to calls is trivial:

```
int modexp(int y, int x[], int w, int n) {
    int R, L;
    int k = 0;
    int s = 1;
    T[h(&&retaddr1)]=(char*)(&&endif-&&retaddr1);
    T[h(&&retaddr2)]=(char*)(&&beginloop-&&retaddr2);
    beginloop:
        if (k >= w) goto endloop;
        if (x[k] != 1) goto elsepart;
            R = (s*y) % n;
            bf();           // goto endif;
            retaddr1:
            asm volatile(".ascii \"bogus\"\n\t");
        elsepart:
            R = s;
        endif:
        s = R*R % n;
        L = R;
        k++;
        bf();              // goto beginloop;
        retaddr2:
    endloop:
    return L;
}
```

The code in dashes would normally be computed at obfuscation time, not runtime. It's responsible for filling in the T table with the appropriate offsets. The code in light gray are calls that have been converted from unconditional jumps. Notice the "code" in dark gray: Since the branch function will return to the endif label rather than to the return address as you'd expect, this code will never be executed! This means you can stick anything you want here to add further confusion to the code. In this case, we've put a string into this black hole. A disassembler will attempt to interpret this string as instructions, since it expects a call instruction to return to the address following it.

Algorithm OBFLDK was originally designed to confuse disassembly. As such, it works really well. The authors report that 39% of instructions are incorrectly assembled using a linear sweep disassembly and 25% for recursive disassembly. For their test cases, they measured an execution penalty of 13% and an increase in text segment size of 15%.

You will see branch functions again in Section 9.4▶592, where the branch function is extended with bogus branches that encode a watermark.

4.3.6 Attacks

The algorithms we've shown you in this section are all designed to confuse static analysis. By and large, they seem to do a good job with that. This doesn't mean, however, that there are no other possible attacks! In particular, there's nothing stopping the adversary from executing the program to see which paths are actually executed and which are not. We're next going to show you two de-obfuscation algorithms that attack Algorithms OBFWHKD and OBFLDK. Both algorithms are *hybrid static-dynamic*, meaning they collect information about the obfuscated program by executing it on a set of test inputs, and then enhance that information by further static analyses.

Any de-obfuscation algorithm that is based, in full or in part, on dynamic analysis is not going to be conservative. That is, there may be paths that are never executed for the test inputs but are realizable nevertheless. If you don't take this into account, the de-obfuscated program may contain errors. Whether this is a problem or not depends on how the attacker intends to use the de-obfuscated program. If, for example, his intent is to analyze the code to learn about a particularly valuable algorithm, it's probably sufficient if the de-obfuscator recovers the main line control flow. If some exception-handling code was never executed and isn't included in the de-obfuscated program, he probably won't mind. The situation is different if, instead, his intent is to analyze the program in order to remove some tamperproofing or watermarking code and then reassemble the program for distribution. In this case, any missing code that might make the program inexplicably crash at some point in the future is going to be unacceptable.

One problem with dynamic attacks is how you get access to input data that will properly exercise all (or most) possible execution paths in the program. The two algorithms that you'll see in this section, REMASB and REUDM, were both evaluated using the SPEC benchmarks for which the authors had available comprehensive test data. In a *real* attack scenario, the adversary won't be so lucky! It would be interesting to rerun their experiments on a program that's essentially a black box and for which the adversary must construct input data sets from scratch.

An interesting development are interactive de-obfuscation environments such as LOCO [236,237] (for x86 binaries) and SandMark [81] (for Java bytecode). These environments provide user interfaces that allow a reverse engineer to explore representations (such as control flow, call graphs, and inheritance graphs) of a program, and, in the case of LOCO, manually modify these representations.

4.3.6.1 Algorithm *REUDM:* Dynamic Attacks Against Control-Flow Flattening Algorithm REUDM [352] uses a hybrid static-dynamic approach to recover the original control flow from a program flattened by Algorithm OBFWHKD. Have a look at this control flow graph of the modular exponentiation routine:

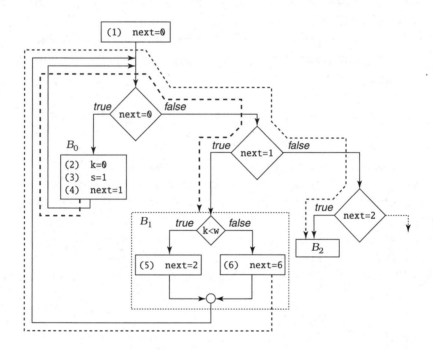

It's essentially the same graph as the one you saw in Figure 4.2▶228, except that we've modeled the switch statement as a series of branches. We've also numbered each statement. In order to turn this graph into the original one in Figure 4.1▶227, you need to figure out what are *feasible* and *infeasible* paths. In Section 4.3.3▶229, you saw how one trick to confuse a de-obfuscator was to add a block to the switch statement that would never be executed. To properly de-obfuscate the routine, you need to do (the equivalent of) a constant-propagation data flow analysis to determine that the next variable can never take on a value that would make this block execute.

Algorithm REUDM does a constraint-based *static path feasibility analysis* to discover realizable paths. Say, for example, that the attacker wants to discover if block B_2 is reachable from block B_1 (which it should be, according to the original control flow graph in Figure 4.1▸227). We've marked this path π_1 in light shading in the figure above. To solve this problem, he needs to track the values that next will take on, and so he builds up a set of constraints like this:

$$C_{\pi_1} = [k_2 = 0, s_3 = 1, \text{next}_4 = 1, \text{next}_4 \neq 0, \text{next}_4 = 1]$$

Each variable is subscripted by the location where it was last defined. It's not hard to see that this path is, indeed, realizable. This means the de-obfuscated control flow graph should have an edge from B_1 to B_2.

Now consider the dark gray path π_2. Should there be a corresponding edge in the de-obfuscated control flow graph? To see that, the attacker builds up the following set of constraints, where k_0, w_0 are free variables:

$$C_{\pi_2} = (\exists k_0, w_0)[k_0 \geq w_0, \text{next}_6 = 6, \text{next}_6 \neq 0, \text{next}_6 \neq 1, \text{next}_6 = 2]$$

Again, it's not hard to see that this path is not realizable.

To recover the original control flow graph the attacker needs to consider, for every pair of blocks, whether there might be a path between them. He can use a constraint solver such as the Omega calculator [295] to do the satisfiability testing.

Algorithm REUDM starts out by doing a dynamic analysis, recording any paths that are actually taken for the set of test inputs. This gives the attacker a set of control flow paths that *must* be realizable. Have a look at this graph where the light gray path is not executed for the test inputs:

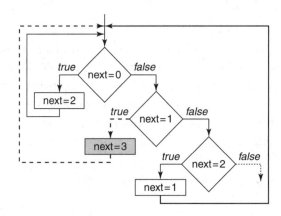

However, if you look carefully at this graph you can see that it's in fact possible for the light gray node to be executed! To reduce the risk of leaving out realizable paths, Algorithm REUDM folds in possible paths using static analysis. If you deploy a constant-propagation data flow analysis along the paths that were actually executed, you discover that next can take on the value 1, and hence, that the light gray block is, in fact, reachable.

It is still possible for the de-obfuscator to miss possible edges. The authors report that between 0.01% and 1.7% of real edges are left out of the de-obfuscated control flow graph. It is also unable to remove all of the fake edges. On average, in their test cases 21.4% of the fake edges remained in the de-obfuscated graphs.

4.3.6.2 Algorithm *REMASB:* Dynamic Attacks Against Branch Functions The

problem with branch functions is that they're dynamically unstealthy. Madou et al. [234] report that for one benchmark program (gcc), the branch function is called 15,336 times, and, furthermore, none of these calls return to the place from whence they came! Algorithm REMASB [234] makes use of this fact in a very simple attack.

The first step is to instrument the program and execute it on representative inputs. Unless the attacker has input data that will exercise every path in the program, the dynamic traces he collects won't be complete enough to build a control flow graph. Instead, the dynamic trace is used as input to a recursive traversal disassembler. Normally, such a disassembler would build a control flow graph given access only to the binary executable, but in this *hybrid static-dynamic* approach, it can start from a set of instructions that *must* be correctly disassembled, since they were actually executed on a real run. The result is a control flow graph that, while possibly not 100% correct, is more accurate than what could have been built from a static or dynamic approach alone.

The second step is to locate a function with the signature of a branch function: It should have many call sites and it shouldn't return to the location from which it was called.

The third step is to statically locate all the calls to the branch function and to monitor them while executing the program. This can easily be done under a debugger. All that is necessary is to set a breakpoint at the end of the branch function and then record the address to which it will branch.

The final step is to replace the calls to the branch function with unconditional jumps to the actual target. This is trivial, unless the branch function has been designed to have side effects to prevent exactly such a replacement attack! If that's the case, the attacker will have to do a more thorough analysis of the semantics of the branch function to ensure that the attack is semantics-preserving.

Problem 4.10 It seems like it will be difficult to build stealthy branch functions; their dynamic behavior is just too distinct from ordinary functions. Instead, to enhance stealth, would it be possible to make every ordinary function behave like a branch function? Failing that, could you introduce enough complicated side effects in the branch function to prevent automatic removal? How about having multiple branch functions, the correct behavior of each one depending on the correct behavior of the others?

In Section 9.4 ▶592 in Chapter 9 (Dynamic Watermarking), you will see a dynamic watermarking algorithm WMCCDKHLS$_{bf}$, where the watermark is embedded by adding bogus entries into the branch function. Algorithm WMCCDKHLS$_{bf}$ attempts to overcome the REMASB attack by making the program's control flow depend on the branch function being left in place. Specifically, the branch function is extended to compute an address that is later used as the target of a jump. This means that any attack that blindly removes the branch function will cause the program to break.

Problem 4.11 Can you think of an antidote against REMASB-style dynamic attacks that makes use of the fact that the attack is nonconservative? Specifically, can you protect your program in such a way that there are regions that are very rarely executed (and hence unlikely to show up on a dynamic trace by an adversary who has an incomplete input data set) but that are highly likely to show up *eventually*? If so, can you insert tamperproofing code (such as the code we'll show you in Chapter 7, Software Tamperproofing) into these regions that will trigger if the branch function is tampered with?

4.4 Opaque Predicates

When we first started looking for opaque predicates, we went to the library, found a few books on number theory, and looked in the *problems* sections for statements such as "Show that $\forall x, y \in \mathbb{Z} : p(x, y)$," where p is a predicate over the integers. Assuming that the author wasn't playing a trick on his readers, trying to make them prove a false statement, we'd found another opaque predicate! And we'd found a predicate, one would hope, that would be moderately hard to break, at least for number-theory graduate students. During this search we found some cute inequalities (such as $\forall x, y \in \mathbb{Z} : x^2 - 34y^2 \neq 1$) and many statements on divisibility ($\forall x \in \mathbb{Z} : 2|x^2 + x$).

There are, however, serious problems with these number-theoretic predicates. First, you have to assume that if your obfuscator keeps a table of such predicates, your adversary's de-obfuscator will contain the same table. Of course, you could choose predicate families that are parameterized, and then every instance will look slightly different. For example, this predicate is parameterized by an integer D (a perfect square):

$$\forall x, y, z \in \mathbb{Z}, D > 0, D = z^2 : x^2 - Dy^2 \neq 1$$

The adversary would know about this parameterization, which would force him to be a bit more clever (but only very slightly so) when searching the code for potentially opaque expressions.

It seems that the only hope for predicates of this nature is to be able to hide them well enough that the attacker can't easily find them, and hence, is not able to look them up in their table. You could, for example, spread the computation out over several functions, forcing the attacker to perform an inter-procedural analysis. This leads us to the second problem, which is that complicated integer expressions are unusual in real code. Certain operators, such as division and remainder used in predicates based on divisibility, are particularly rare. Thus, as is always the case when you insert new protection code into a program, stealth is an issue.

In this section, we're going to show you three kinds of opaque predicates based on the hardness of alias analysis and concurrency analysis. In Section 4.4.4▶253, we're then going to look at ways to break opaque predicates and possible ways of defending against these attacks.

4.4.1 Algorithm OBF$CTJ_{pointer}$: Opaque Predicates from Pointer Aliasing

Algorithm OBF$CTJ_{pointer}$ [87,89,91] was the first to create an obfuscating transformation from a known computationally hard static analysis problem. The idea is compelling: If we assume that

1. the attacker will analyze the program statically, and

2. we can force him to solve a particular static analysis problem to discover the secret he's after, and

3. we can generate an actual hard instance of this problem for him to solve,

then we will have an obfuscation that is truly useful. Of course, these assumptions may be false! The attacker may find that it's enough for his purposes to analyze the program dynamically, and just because a problem is known to be computationally hard (NP-complete, for example) doesn't mean that the instances we create are!

Algorithm 4.4 Overview of Algorithm OBFCTJ$_{\text{pointer}}$ for creating alias-based opaque predicates in a program P.

CREATEOPAQUEPREDICATE(P):

1. Add to P code to build a set of dynamically allocated global pointer-structures $G = \{G_1, G_2, \dots\}$.

2. Add to P a set of pointers $Q = \{q_1, q_2, \dots\}$ that point into the structures in G.

3. Construct a set of invariants $I = \{I_1, I_2, \dots\}$ over G and Q, such as

   - q_i always points to nodes in G_j;

   - G_i is always strongly connected.

4. Add code to P that occasionally modifies the graphs in G and the pointers in Q, while maintaining the invariants I.

5. Using the invariants I, construct opaque predicates over Q, such as

   - $(q_i \neq q_j)^T$ if q_i and q_j are known to point into different graphs G_m and G_n;

   - $(q_i \neq \texttt{null})^T$ if q_i moves around inside graph G_k and G_k has no leaf nodes;

   - $(q_i = q_j)^?$ if q_i and q_j are known to both point into graph G_k.

In fact, it's an open problem to create an algorithm that generates provably hard instances of a static analysis problem.

Nevertheless, we know from experience that certain aspects of programs defy reason, and it makes sense to use this observation in our designs of obfuscating transformations. Several algorithms have made use of the *aliasing problem* (Section 3.1.4 ▶ 134) to create obfuscating transformations that are resilient to attack. Implementing a precise alias analyzer is difficult, and the more precise the algorithm needs to be, the longer it will take to run.

Algorithm OBFCTJ$_{\text{pointer}}$ creates opaque predicates from pointer analysis problems. Since it's not known how to create a provably hard instance of this problem, the algorithm instead focuses on going beyond the capabilities of known analysis algorithms. Many such algorithms have problems with *destructive updates*. This means that while they may be able to properly analyze a program that builds a linked list, they may fail on one that modifies the list [60]. Some algorithms can't handle cyclic structures [158], and some fail for recursive structures more than a constant k levels deep. Hardekopf and Lin [153] write:

> The most precise analyses are flow-sensitive—respecting control-flow dependencies—and context-sensitive—respecting the semantics of function calls. Despite a great deal of work on both flow-sensitive and context-sensitive algorithms [. . .], none has been shown to scale to programs with millions of lines of code, and most have difficulty scaling to 100,000 lines of code.

It's important to note here that this quote refers to programs *written by humans*. Alias analysis algorithms are designed to perform well on "normal code" because this is what compilers and program understanding tools are likely to see. You, on the other hand, are free to generate arbitrarily complex data structures, and to perform arbitrarily complex operations on them, just to fool an attacker's analysis!

Have a look at Algorithm 4.4▸248, which gives a sketch of how to construct alias-based opaque predicates. The idea is to construct one or more heap-based graphs, to keep a set of pointers into those graphs, and then to create opaque predicates by checking properties you know to be true. To confound analysis, you also add operations to the program that move the pointers around and that perform destructive update operations on the graphs while maintaining the set of invariants your opaque predicates will test for.

Consider this example, where we construct two pointers q_1 and q_2 pointing into two graphs G_1 (light gray) and G_2 (dark gray):

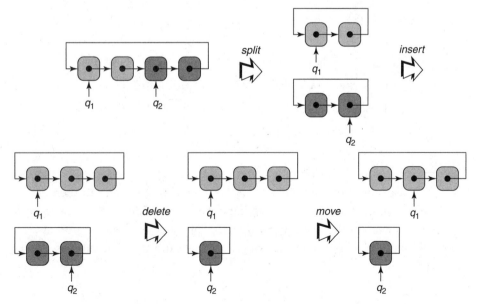

All nodes and pointers are of the same type, perhaps declared as class Node {Node next;} in Java. The nodes start out on one circular linked list that is split in two, constructing the two graphs G_1 and G_2. We've then added arbitrary operations that move q_1 and q_2 around, and add and delete nodes randomly to the graphs subject to the two invariants "G_1 and G_2 are circular linked lists" and "q_1 points to a node in G_1 and q_2 points to a node in G_2." After the code has performed enough operations to confuse even the most precise alias analysis algorithm, you can start inserting opaque queries such as $(q_1 \neq q_2)^T$ into the code.

4.4.2 OBF*WHKD*_{opaque}: Opaque Values from Array Aliasing

In Section 4.3.2 ▶ 226, you saw how the control flow flattening Algorithm OBFWHKD used array aliasing as the basis for constructing opaque values. These were then used to encode the control flow in a surreptitious way. There's of course nothing stopping you from using array aliasing to construct opaque values and predicates for other purposes.

Have a look at this array of integers:

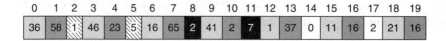

We've constructed the array so that the following invariants hold:

1. Every third cell (in light gray), starting with cell 0, is $\equiv 1 \bmod 5$;
2. Cells 2 and 5 (striped) hold the values 1 and 5, respectively;
3. Every third cell (in dark gray), starting with cell 1, is $\equiv 2 \bmod 7$;
4. Cells 8 and 11 (black) hold the values 2 and 7, respectively.

The remaining cells (in white) contain garbage values. The constant values (striped and black) are stored in the array so that you don't have to refer to them as literals, which would be unstealthy. Using modular arithmetic makes it easy to keep the array elements in flux. You can update a light gray element as often as you want, with any value you want, as long as you ensure that the value is always $\equiv 1 \bmod 5$!

Here's the array g, given as an initialized array:

```
int g[] = {36,58,1,46,23,5,16,65,2,41,
            2,7,1,37,0,11,16,2,21,16};

if ((g[3] % g[5])==g[2])
    printf("true!\n");

g[5] = (g[1]*g[4])%g[11] + g[6]%g[5];
g[14] = rand();
g[4] = rand()*g[11]+g[8];

int six = (g[4] + g[7] + g[10])%g[11];
int seven = six + g[3]%g[5];
int fortytwo = six * seven;
```

The code in light gray constructs an opaquely true predicate. The code in dark gray ensures that g is constantly changing at runtime, making it harder to analyze statically. Even though the data *is* changing, the *invariants* remain the same. The code in dashed, finally, constructs an opaque value 42.

Using an initialized array for g is, of course, not a great idea. It's just as easy (and harder for the adversary to analyze) to initialize g by filling it with random values as long as they have the right properties.

4.4.3 Algorithm $OBF CTJ_{thread}$: Opaque Predicates from Concurrency

Concurrent programs are difficult to analyze statically because of their *interleaving* semantics. If you have n statements in a parallel region, then there are $n!$ different orders in which they could execute. On top of that, badly designed concurrent programs are susceptible to *race conditions*, where several processes manipulate the same global data structure without the prerequisite locking statements. Such situations too are difficult to analyze.

These observations make it possible to construct opaque predicates whose resilience against attack is based on the difficulty of analyzing the threading behavior of programs. The idea is to keep a global data structure G with a certain set of invariants I, to concurrently update G while maintaining I, and use I to construct opaque predicates over G (Algorithm 4.5▶252).

Algorithm 4.5 Overview of Algorithm OBFCTJ$_{\text{thread}}$ for creating threading-based opaque predicates in a program P.

CREATEOPAQUEPREDICATE(P):

1. Add to P code to create a global data structure G with a set of invariants $I = \{I_1, I_2, \ldots\}$.

2. Add to P code to create threads $T_1, T_2, \ldots$, which make concurrent updates to G while maintaining the invariants I.

3. Using the invariants I, construct opaque predicates over G.

Here's an example where two threads T_1 and T_2 concurrently bang on two integer variables X and Y, with complete disregard for data races:

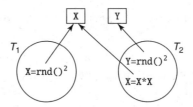

Assuming that the assignments are atomic (Java guarantees this for integer variables), this code maintains the invariants that both X and Y will always be the square of some value. This allows you to construct an opaque predicate (X-34*Y==-1)^F since $\forall x, y \in \mathbb{Z} : x^2 - 34y^2 \neq -1$.

In Chapter 9 you'll see an algorithm (WMNT), which embeds a watermark in a program by manipulating its threading behavior. That algorithm needs opaquely true predicates that are statically indistinguishable from opaquely false predicates. You can accomplish this by combining the alias-based opaque predicates from Section 4.4.1▶247 with multi-threading. Here's the idea [264]:

1. Generate G, a rooted, singly linked cycle of k nodes.

2. Construct two pointers a and b that initially refer to the same node in G.

3. Construct two pointers c and d that initially refer to different nodes in G.

4. Create a new thread T_1, which asynchronously and atomically updates a and b so that each time a is updated to point to its next node in the cycle, b is also updated to point to its next node in the cycle.

5. As in point 4, create a new thread T_2, which updates c and d.

Here's an example where a and b always refer to the same node in G, while c and d always refer to nodes that are one node apart:

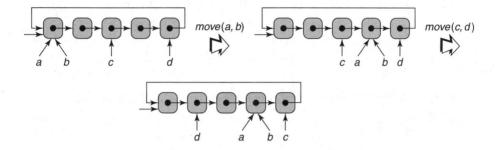

The threads advance the pointers asynchronously around the cycle while maintaining the invariants. Now you can construct an opaquely true predicate $(a = b)^T$, which is statically indistinguishable from an opaquely false predicate $(c = d)^F$, unless you know the invariant that is being maintained. Listing 4.2▶254 shows code to build such predicates.

4.4.4 Breaking Opaque Predicates

Conceptually, an opaque predicate consists of a list of instructions that reads available variables $x_1, x_2, \ldots$ computes a boolean function $f(x_1, x_2, \ldots)$ over these values, and branches if the function returns true:

$$
\begin{aligned}
&\ldots \\
&x_1 \leftarrow \cdots; \\
&x_2 \leftarrow \cdots; \\
&\ldots \\
&b \leftarrow f(x_1, x_2, \ldots); \\
&\text{if } b \text{ goto} \ldots
\end{aligned}
$$

The goal of an attacker is to determine whether the outcome of f is always the same. In that case, he can replace the conditional jump with an unconditional one. Breaking an opaque predicate proceeds in these five steps:

1. Locate the instructions that make up $f(x_1, x_2, \ldots)$;
2. Determine the inputs to f, i.e., $x_1, x_2 \ldots$;
3. Determine the range of values R_1 of x_1, R_2 of $x_2, \ldots$;

Listing 4.2 Code to build multi-threading-based opaque predicates such that opaquely true and opaquely false predicates are statically indistinguishable. Two threads race1 and race2 asynchronously move two pairs of pointers (a,b and c,d, respectively) around a circular singly linked list, maintaining the invariant that a==b and c!=d. The function getRandomBetween(a,b) returns a random integer between a and b, inclusive. The function getNth(p,n) returns the nth node starting at node p.

```
class Race extends Thread {          int size = getRandomBetween(2, 10);
  Node x,y;                          Node cycle = createCycle(root, size);
  public Race(Node x,                int m = getRandomBetween(2, 10);
             Node y,                 int n = m;
             Object lock) {          while(m==n)
    this.x = x;                        n = getRandomBetween(2, 10);
    this.y = y;                      Node a = getNth(root, m);
    this.lock = lock;                Node b = getNth(root, m);
    start();
  }                                  Node c = getNth(root, m);
                                     Node d = getNth(root, n);
  public void run() {
    while(true) {                    Object lock = new Object();
      synchronized(lock) {           Race race1 = new Race(a, b, lock);
        x = x.next;                  Race race2 = new Race(c, d, lock);
        y = y.next;
      }                              synchronized(lock) {
    }                                    if (race1.x==race1.y)^T ...
  }                                      if (race2.x==race2.y)^F ...
}                                    }
```

4. Determine the outcome of f for all possible argument values; and

5. If f is true for all possible input values, replace the conditional jump with an unconditional one; if it is false for all possible input values, remove the branch altogether.

In step 4, the attacker may not be able to test f for *all* input values, in which case he will have to resort to statistical arguments. For certain kinds of attacks, it may be enough to say with a high degree of confidence that an expression is opaque; in others, absolute certainty is required.

Consider how an attacker might break this simple opaque predicate:

```
int x = some complicated expression;
int y = 42;
z = ...
boolean b = (34*y*y-1)==x*x;
if b goto ...
```

First, he computes a *backwards slice* (see Section 3.1.5▸141) from b, to collect all the computations that could affect its value. This includes the assignments to x and y, but excludes the assignment to z. Next, he finds that the inputs to the predicate are x and y, and that the range of x is unknown (he has to assume it will take on all integer values), but that y can only take on the value 42. Using either a number-theoretic argument or a brute-force search (both trivial in this case!), he determines that for all input values to the predicate, b is false. He can now go ahead and remove the instructions that make up the predicate, including the final branch.

In practice, the actual ranges of variables will be often be unknown to the attacker, which means that he will have to consider all possible input values to f, e.g., all 2^{32} values of a 32-bit integer.

There are several ways in which the obfuscator can make the attacker's task more difficult:

- Make it harder to locate the instructions that make up $f(x_1, x_2, \ldots)$;
- Make it harder to determine what are the inputs $x_1, x_2, \ldots$ to f;
- Make it harder to determine the actual ranges $R_1, R_2, \ldots$ of $x_1, x_2, \ldots$; or
- Make it harder to determine the outcome of f for all possible argument values.

You have to assume the attacker will have a library of known opaque predicates available; in fact, you have to assume he has *the same* library you do, since you can't expect your obfuscator to be kept secret! This means that simple number-theoretic predicates such as $\forall x \in \mathbb{Z} : 2|x(x+1)$ are not very interesting by themselves, since they're easily tabulated by the attacker, and once broken, they're broken forever. If you *do* want to use predicates like that, you have to instead hamper the attacker's ability to break the predicate in some other way. For example, if he can't easily determine which instructions make up the predicate or what its inputs are, then it will be harder for him to look it up in his table of known number-theoretic results. For example, you can make the slicing stage more difficult by adding bogus computations that make it appear as if a large part of the program contributes to the value of f.

4.4.4.1 Algorithm *REPMBG*: Breaking $\forall x \in \mathbb{Z}: n \mid p(x)$ Algorithm REPMBG [290] attacks opaque predicates confined to a single basic block. The algorithm assumes that the instructions that make up the predicate are contiguous, i.e., there are no irrelevant instructions interspersed with the relevant ones. This makes it simple to identify the instructions that make up the predicate. In a first step, the algorithm starts at a conditional jump instruction j (the last instruction of a basic block) and incrementally extends it with the $1, 2, \ldots$ preceding instructions until either an opaque predicate is found or the beginning of the basic block is encountered. To determine whether the instructions form an opaque predicate or not, the algorithm can run in *brute-force mode* (considering all possible values of input variables) or in *static analysis mode*, where it uses abstract interpretation to determine opaqueness.

Have a look at the example basic block to the left, which implements the opaquely true predicate $\forall x \in \mathbb{Z} : 2 \mid (x^2 + x)$:

	(1)	(2)	(3)	(4)

`x = ...;`
`y = x*x;`
`y = y + x;`
`y = y % 2;`
`b = y==0;`
`if b ...`
	`x = ...;`
	`y = x*x;`
	`y = y + x;`
	`y = y % 2;`
	`b = y==0;`
	`if b ...`
		`x = ...;`
		`y = x*x;`
		`y = y + x;`
		`y = y % 2;`
		`b = y==0;`
		`if b ...`
			`x = ...;`
			`y = x*x;`
			`y = y + x;`
			`y = y % 2;`
			`b = y==0;`
			`if b ...`
				`x = ...;`
				`y = x*x;`
				`y = y + x;`
				`y = y % 2;`
				`b = y==0;`
				`if b ...`

In brute-force attack mode, Algorithm REPMBG would start at step (1), by running the light gray code for all possible values of y. It would quickly realize that the instructions do not form an opaque predicate. Next, at step (2), it would again consider all possible values of y, and again come to the conclusion that for some values of y, b will be true and for some, false. Not until step (4) can the algorithm conclude that for all values of x, b evaluates to true.

Obviously, this brute-force attack won't scale to larger opaque predicates. At this point, you should have a look back at Section 3.1.6▶143, where we introduced *abstract interpretation*. In particular, look at the domain *Parity* and how it allows you to determine whether an expression is even or odd without actually having to execute it. Now this is exactly what you need to efficiently break an opaque predicate of the form $\forall x \in \mathbb{Z} : 2 \mid f(x)$!

Let's first consider the case when x is an even number:

```
x = even number;
y = x * x;
y = y + x;
z = y % 2;
b = z==0;
if b ...
```

⇨

$$
\begin{aligned}
&x \qquad\qquad = even; \\
&y = x *_a x = even *_a even = even; \\
&y = y +_a x = even +_a even = even; \\
&z = y \mathbin{\%_a} 2 = even \bmod 2 = 0; \\
&b = z{==}0; \quad = true \\
&if\ b \ ...
\end{aligned}
$$

To the left is the code in the concrete domain, and to the right we've shown the interpretation of the code in the abstract domain *Parity*. The input value to the predicate, x, starts out with the abstract value *even*. Since multiplying and adding two even numbers yields an even number, y becomes *even*, and b evaluates to true. Here's the same computation, but for the case when x starts out being odd:

```
x = odd number;
y = x * x;
y = y + x;
z = y % 2;
b = z==0;
if b ...
```

⇨

$$
\begin{aligned}
&x \qquad\qquad = odd; \\
&y = x *_a x = odd *_a odd = odd; \\
&y = y +_a x = odd +_a odd = even; \\
&z = y \mathbin{\%_a} 2 = even \bmod 2 = 0; \\
&b = z{==}0; \quad = true \\
&if\ b \ ...
\end{aligned}
$$

So regardless of whether x's initial value is even or odd, the outcome is the same: b is true, and the final branch is taken. In other words, you've broken the opaque predicate, and very efficiently at that!

By constructing different abstract domains, Algorithm REPMBG is able to break all opaque predicates of the form $\forall x \in \mathbb{Z} : n|p(x)$, where $p(x)$ is a polynomial, i.e., a combination of additions and multiplications.

4.4.4.2 Algorithm *OBFCTJ*$_{slice}$: Preventing Slicing Attacks As you saw from the previous sections, the first step to breaking an opaque predicate is to extract its code from the program. This means you need to compute a *backwards slice* consisting of all the computations that contribute to the branch condition. A backwards slice *slice*(P, s, V), as you learned in Section 3.1.5 ▸ 141, consists of all the statements in program P that contribute to the value of variable V, starting with statement s.

The basic idea of Algorithm OBFCTJ$_{slice}$ [87,88,91,240–242] is to add spurious variable dependencies to the program to trick a slicer into returning artificially large slices. Ideally, the slicer will be so confused that it will tell the attacker that every variable in the program depends on every other variable, essentially returning no useful information! Confusing analysis by slicing can be a good general way to prevent an attacker from understanding your program, but it's particularly important in trying to hide opaque predicates. Unfortunately, it's not easy to do in practice. To see that, have a look at this transformation, an extension of the example from the previous section:

```
r = ...;                      r = ...;
x = ...;                      x = ...+G=0(r);
y = x * x;                    y = x * x;
y = y + x;          ⇨         y = y + x;
z = y % 2;                    z = y % 2;
b = z==0;                     b = z==0;
if b ...                      if b ...
```

Here, we've added a call to a function $G(r)$, which uses r to compute a value 0, which we then add to x, making it appear as if x depends on r. Notice that G is really an opaque function itself! Unless we can hide that G always returns 0, regardless of the current value of r, little has been accomplished.

In a series of papers, Majumdar et al. [240–242] study the effect of various obfuscating transformations on the precision of slicing and aliasing. In one study, they consider a small set of test programs into which they insert carefully hand-crafted opaque predicates designed to create bogus dependencies between variables. They show that even with a small-to-moderate increase in total program size (5.8–24%), they get a significant increase in the size of slices (20–1400%). It's an open question whether the same results could be achieved with an automatic obfuscation tool.

4.5 Data Encodings

To obfuscate a variable V in a program, you convert it from the representation the programmer initially chose for it to a representation that is harder for the attacker to analyze. Any value that V can take at runtime must be representable in the new, obfuscated representation. Also, any operations that the program performs on V must now be performed on the new representation. Finally, you're going to need two functions, *encode* and *decode*, which we will abbreviate $E()$ and $D()$, respectively. E converts from the original representation into the new one, and D converts from the new into the old. The analogy with the *encryption* and *decryption* functions $E_{\text{key}}()$ $D_{\text{key}}()$ is intentional—in fact, you could imagine using encryption to obfuscate data. You will see examples of this in the next section.

To make this a bit more formal, imagine that you have an abstract data type T with operations $\oplus_T, \otimes_T, \ldots$:

$$\left\{\begin{array}{lll} \text{type} & T & = \quad \cdots \\ \oplus_T : T \times T & \rightarrow & T \\ \otimes_T : T \times T & \rightarrow & T \end{array}\right.$$

To obfuscate T, you construct a new abstract data type T' with operations for converting between T and T', and one new operation operating on T' for every operation operating on T:

$$\left\{\begin{array}{lll} \text{type} & T' & = \quad \cdots \\ E_{T'} : T & \rightarrow & T' \\ D_{T'} : T' & \rightarrow & T \\ \oplus_{T'} : T' \times T' & \rightarrow & T' \\ \otimes_{T'} : T' \times T' & \rightarrow & T' \end{array}\right.$$

The simplest way to obfuscate is for every operation on values of type T' to first convert back to T, perform the operation, and then again convert to T':

$$\left\{\begin{array}{lll} x \oplus_{T'} y & = & E_{T'}(D_{T'}(x) \oplus_T D_{T'}(y)) \\ x \otimes_{T'} y & = & E_{T'}(D_{T'}(x) \otimes_T D_{T'}(y)) \end{array}\right.$$

This really isn't a good idea, since every time you perform an operation on an obfuscated type it reveals the de-obfuscated values of the arguments and the result! You much prefer for every operation to be performed on the obfuscated representation directly. In practice, however, you will often have to compromise. You may find that, for a particular obfuscated representation, some operations can be performed directly on the new representation, but for others you will have to perform the operation on the de-obfuscated values.

Ideally, to prevent pattern-matching attacks, you want the obfuscated representation to be parameterized. In other words, you want a *family* of representations so that you can create a large number of different-looking obfuscated variables even if their underlying representation is based on the same obfuscation algorithm.

Here, we've added a parameter p to the obfuscated data type:

$$
\left\{
\begin{array}{llll}
\textbf{type} & T'_p & = & \cdots \\
E^p_{T'} : T & & \to & T'_p \\
D^p_{T'} : T'_p & & \to & T \\
\oplus^p_{T'_p} : T'_p \times T'_p & & \to & T'_p \\
\otimes^p_{T'_p} : T'_p \times T'_p & & \to & T'_p
\end{array}
\right.
$$

In some obfuscations, p will be an obfuscation-time quantity, in others, a runtime quantity. When p is determined at runtime, it's essentially an opaque value. When a representation is not parameterized, we omit p.

In practice, for many obfuscated representations, the range that can be accommodated is smaller than the range of the original. For example, if you encode an integer variable v that has a range $[-2^{31} \ldots 2^{31} - 1]$ as $v * 2^{10}$ (i.e., 1 is represented as 1024, 2 as 2048, and so on.), all of a sudden you've restricted the obfuscated v to the range $[-2^{21} \ldots 2^{21} - 1]$. This poses problems for an automatic obfuscation tool, which has to maintain semantics when transforming the program. There are three possible solutions. The easiest is to simply move to a larger variable size, in the example above, from a 32-bit integer to a 64-bit integer. This can seriously affect the memory footprint of the program. Alternatively, you can perform a static *value range propagation* analysis [281] to determine the actual upper and lower bounds of v, and then decide whether it's necessary to move to a larger variable size. These analyses are costly and not always accurate. Finally, you can rely on programmer annotations to define allowable ranges of variables. Some languages, such as Pascal and Ada, already support range specifications of variables, although programmers typically find it easier to write VAR x: INTEGER than VAR x: [1..99].

A further problem occurs when you have multiple different representations of the same type in a program. Say, for example, your original program has three variables a, x, and y, all declared to be integers. You obfuscate a and x to be of type T1 and y to be of type T2:

```
int a = ···;
int x = ···;
int y = ···;
x = ··· a ···;
y = ··· x ···;
```

$\Rightarrow$

```
T1 a = ···;
T1 x = ···;
T2 y = ···;
x = ··· a ···;
y = ··· E_{T2}(D_{T1}(x)) ···;
```

Since x and y now have different representations, before any operation can be performed on it, the second statement has to first de-obfuscate x and then obfuscate it in order to bring it into the same representation as y. This reveals x's true value. For some pairs of representations, you will be able to convert directly from one to the other without going through cleartext, but this means you may have to provide such conversion operations for *every* pair of obfuscated types! To avoid this problem, an automatic obfuscator has to very carefully choose which obfuscated representations to assign to which variables. You can start the obfuscation by computing a backwards slice from each variable, which will reveal which other variables contribute to its value. To minimize the number of conversions, variables that occur in the same slice should be assigned the same obfuscated representation.

There's of course no reason why a variable should have the same representation throughout the execution of the program. On the contrary, an attacker will find that dynamic analysis of the program is much harder if the representation of a particular variable continuously changes over time or as the program chooses different execution paths [62].

In this section, we will show you techniques for obfuscating integers, booleans, strings, and arrays. Booleans are easier than integers to transform, since their range is known and small ([0 . . . 1]!).

4.5.1 Encoding Integers

Integers are the most common data type in most programs and therefore important to obfuscate. Unfortunately, programmers are used to the idea that operations on integers are cheap, so you have to be careful not to transform them into an exotic representation that may be highly obfuscated but carries a huge performance penalty.

In this section, we will illustrate the obfuscated transformations in a very hands-on fashion, by writing C functions that replace the built-in operators. Every representation will look like the set of definitions below. T1 is the data type of the obfuscated representation, E1 is a function that transforms from cleartext integers into the obfuscated representation, D1 transforms obfuscated integers into cleartext, and ADD1, MUL1, and LT1 define how to add, multiply, and compare two obfuscated integers:

```
typedef int T1;
T1 E1(int e) {return e;}
int D1(T1 e) {return e;}
T1 ADD1(T1 a, T1 b) {return E1(D1(a)+D1(b));}
T1 MUL1(T1 a, T1 b) {return E1(D1(a)*D1(b));}
BOOL LT1(T1 a, T1 b) {return D1(a)<D1(b);}
```

Now these definitions don't make for a very interesting obfuscated transformation, of course; we've just defined the identity transformation! But you can imagine adding these definitions to your program and transforming the code on the left into the code on the right:

```
int v = 7;
v = v * 5;
v = v + 7;
while (v<50) v++;
```

⇨

```
T1 v = E1(7);
v = MUL1(v,E1(5));
v = ADD1(v,E1(7));
while (LT1(v,E1(50)))
    v=ADD1(v,E1(1));
```

We will make this code snippet the running example in this section. By simply replacing the definitions, you can obfuscate your program with different representations of the integers.

A very slightly more interesting transformation than the identity is to let every value v be represented by $v + 1$:

```
typedef int T2;
T2 E2(int e) {return e+1;}
int D2(T2 e) {return e-1;}
T2 ADD2(T2 a, T2 b) {return E2(D2(a)+D2(b));}
T2 MUL2(T2 a, T2 b) {return E2(D2(a)*D2(b));}
BOOL LT2(T2 a, T2 b) {return D2(a)<D2(b);}
```

Encoding and decoding are trivial: Just add and subtract 1, respectively. The maximum value that is representable is one less than the original range of int, so you have to be careful not to cause an overflow. Notice that this isn't a very good implementation of addition and multiplication: Before applying the operations, you first convert to de-obfuscated space.

A better implementation is to perform arithmetic operations directly on the obfuscated values. For an addition $x + y$, this means you have to adjust the computed value by subtracting 1, since $x + y$ in obfuscated space is $(x + 1) + (y + 1) = x + y + 2$:

```
typedef int T3;
T3 E3(int e) {return e+1;}
int D3(T3 e) {return e-1;}
T3 ADD3(T3 a, T3 b) {return a+b-1;}
T3 MUL3(T3 a, T3 b) {return a*b-a-b+2;}
BOOL LT3(T3 a, T3 b) {return a<b;}
```

4.5.1.1 Algorithm *OBFBDKMRV_{num}*: **Number-Theoretic Tricks** Many integer obfuscations are based on number-theoretic tricks. In this transformation, an integer
y is represented as $N * p + y$, where N is the product of two close primes, and p is
a random value:

```
typedef int T4;
#define N4 (53*59)
T4 E4(int e,int p) {return p*N4+e;}
int D4(T4 e) {return e%N4;}
T4 ADD4(T4 a, T4 b) {return a+b;}
T4 MUL4(T4 a, T4 b) {return a*b;}
BOOL LT4(T4 a, T4 b) {return D4(a)<D4(b);}
```

N4 must be larger than any integer that you need to represent. De-obfuscation is
simply removing $N*p$ by reducing modulo N4. What's nice about this representation
is that addition and multiplication can both be performed in obfuscated space.
Before comparisons can be performed, however, the argument values need to first
be de-obfuscated.

Notice that this is a parameterized obfuscation; you can create a whole family
of representation by choosing different values for p. It's a good idea to hide p by
computing it as an opaque value at runtime.

If two differently obfuscated integers need to be operated on, then one needs to
be first de-obfuscated and then re-obfuscated to the correct representation. Here,
x is obfuscated using type T3 and v using T4, and as they're multiplied and added
together, their values have to be converted from one representation to the other and
back:

```
int x = 7;
int v = 6;
v = x * v;
x = v + x;
printf("%i\n",x);
```
⇨
```
T3 x = E3(7);
T4 v = E4(6,3);
v = MUL4(E4(D3(x),5),v);
x = ADD3(E3(D4(v)),E3(8));
printf("%i\n",D3(x));
```

Ideally, you have a transformation that directly takes you from one representation
to the other without having to go through cleartext.

4.5.1.2 Algorithm *OBFBDKMRV_{crypto}*: **Encrypting Integers** It is natural to think of
obfuscating variables by encrypting them using one of the many standard

cryptographic algorithms. Here we've used DES:

```
#include <openssl/des.h>

DES_key_schedule ks;
DES_cblock key ={0x12,0x34,0x56,0x78,0x9a,0xbc,0xde,0xf0};

typedef struct {int x; int y;} T7;
T7 E7(int e) {
   T7 block = (T7){e,0};
   DES_ecb_encrypt((DES_cblock*)&block,
                   (DES_cblock*)&block,&ks,DES_ENCRYPT);
   return block;}
int D7(T7 e) {
   DES_ecb_encrypt((DES_cblock*)&e,
                   (DES_cblock*)&e,&ks,DES_DECRYPT);
   return e.x;}
T7 ADD7(T7 a,T7 b) {return E7(D7(a)+D7(b));}
T7 MUL7(T7 a,T7 b) {return E7(D7(a)*D7(b));}
BOOL LT7(T7 a,T7 b) {return D7(a)<D7(b);}
```

The disadvantage here is that you can't perform arithmetic operations on values encrypted by DES directly. This means that before each arithmetic operation you need to decrypt the operands, and afterwards you must re-encrypt the result. The overhead will be quite formidable. Also, you'll need to store the key somewhere in the program. For this particular implementation of DES, you also need to call DES_set_key_unchecked(&key,&ks) to create the internal key from the key material before you can perform any cryptographic operations. Obviously, this is going to affect the stealthiness of the representation.

You may not be able to compute with DES-encrypted values, but in some very specific cases you don't need to go outside the encrypted domain. Here, for example, we've defined a representation that only supports the *not-equal* comparison of encrypted values:

```
typedef struct {int x; int y;} T8;
T8 E8(T8 e) {
   DES_ecb_encrypt((DES_cblock*)&e,
                   (DES_cblock*)&e,&ks,DES_ENCRYPT);
   return e;}
```

```
T8 D8(T8 e) {
    DES_ecb_encrypt((DES_cblock*)&e,
                    (DES_cblock*)&e,&ks,DES_DECRYPT);
    return e;}
BOOL NE8(T8 a,T8 b) {return memcmp(&a,&b,sizeof(T8))!=0;}
```

This is enough to allow you to construct simple counted loops without having to step outside the encrypted domain:

```
for(i=0;i<5;i++)
    printf("HERE\n");
```
⇨
```
T8 v = E8(E8(E8(E8((T8){42,42})))); 
while (NE8(v,(T8){42,42})) {
    printf("HERE\n");
    v = D8(v);
}
```

The code in light gray can be computed at obfuscation time.

The RSA cryptosystem is *homomorphic* in multiplication. This means that to multiply two values that have been encrypted with RSA, you just multiply the encrypted values; there's no need to decrypt them first. Or, more formally, $E(x \cdot y) = E(x) \cdot E(y)$. RSA is defined by these equations, where M is the cleartext message and C the cryptotext:

$$C = M^e \bmod n$$
$$M = C^d \bmod p$$
$$n = pq$$
$$ed = 1 \bmod (p-1)(q-1)$$

e is known as the *public modulus*, d is the *private modulus*, and p and q are primes. It's easy to see that RSA is homomorphic in multiplication:

$$\left(M_1^e \bmod n\right) \cdot \left(M_2^e \bmod n\right) = \left(M_1^e \cdot M_2^e\right) \bmod n = (M_1 \cdot M_2)^e \bmod n.$$

Here's an example where the modulus M is 33, the public exponent is 3, and the private exponent is 7:

```
typedef int T9;
#define M 33
T9 E9(int e) {return (((e*e)%M)*e)%M;}
int D9(T9 e) {int t=(((e*e)%M)*e)%M; return (((t*t)%M)*e)%M;}
```

```
T9 ADD9(T9 a,T9 b) {return E9((D9(a)+D9(b)));}
T9 MUL9(T9 a,T9 b) {return (a*b)%M;}
BOOL LT9(T9 a,T9 b) {return D9(a)<D9(b);}
```

You can only represent numbers smaller than the modulus.

Notice that you still have to do addition by first de-obfuscating the operands. But in certain situations, addition can be converted to multiplication! For example, it's easy to transform simple counted for-loops to use multiplication rather than addition:

```
for(i=1;i<6;i++)
    printf("HERE\n");
```

```
for(i=E9(1);i!=E9(32);i=MUL9(i,E9(2)))
    printf("HERE\n");
```

Using RSA, this has the advantage that you never have to de-obfuscate the loop variable, unless, of course, its value is used inside the loop.

Problem 4.12   Can you think of a way to obfuscate floating-point variables without sacrificing accuracy and without causing too severe a performance degradation?

4.5.2 Encoding Booleans

Boolean variables are particularly easy targets for obfuscation since their value range is known, and is small. Unfortunately, while boolean *values* occur frequently in programs as conditions in loops and if-statements, long-lived boolean *variables* are much less common. As in the previous section, here are C functions that define an encoder EA() that converts from traditional C boolean values (0 and 1) to an encoded type TA, a decoder DA() that converts from TA back to 0 and 1, and functions corresponding to C's AND (&&) and OR (||) operations:

```
typedef int TA;
TA EA(BOOL e) {return  e;}
BOOL DA(TA e) {return e;}
BOOL ORA(TA a, TA b) {return DA(a)||DA(b);}
TA ORVA(TA a, TA b) {return EA(DA(a)||DA(b));}
BOOL ANDA(TA a, TA b) {return DA(a)&&DA(b);}
TA ANDVA(TA a, TA b) {return EA(DA(a)&&DA(b));}
```

Boolean expressions are used in two ways: to control the flow in control flow statements and to compute values that are stored in boolean variables. We'll use OR and AND in control flow statements, and ORV and ANDV when an expression is used in an assignment statement. Here's an example:

```
#define TRUE 1
#define FALSE 0
typedef int BOOL;

BOOL a = TRUE;
BOOL b = FALSE;
if (a && b) ...
else if (a || b) ...
else ...
BOOL c = (a || b) && 1;
BOOL d = (a && b) || 0;
```

⇨

```
TA a = EA(TRUE);
TA b = EA(FALSE);
if (ANDA(a,b)) ...
else if (ORA(a,b)) ...
else ...
TA c = ANDVA(ORVA(a,b),EA(TRUE));
TA d = ORVA(ANDVA(a,b),EA(FALSE));
```

You can use the same techniques we're showing you in this section for encoding boolean values to encode any enumerable type with a small range.

4.5.2.1 Algorithm $OBFBDKMRV_{bool}$ [28]: Multiple Values

Since there are so few boolean values, you can use multiple values to encode true and multiple values to encode false. In this example, any integers divisible by 2 represent true, and any integers divisible by 3 represent false:

```
typedef int TC;
TC EC(BOOL e) {return (e)?2*(3*(rand()%10000)+rand()%2+1):
                        3*(2*(rand()%10000)+1);}
BOOL DC(TC e) {return ((e%2)==0)?TRUE:FALSE;}
BOOL ORC(TC a, TC b) {return (a*b)%2==0;}
TC ORVC(TC a, TC b) {return EC(((a*b)%2==0));}
BOOL ANDC(TC a, TC b) {return gcd(a,b)%2==0;}
TC ANDVC(TC a, TC b) {return EC((gcd(a,b)%2==0));}
```

The call EC(TRUE) generates an integer without any factors of 3 and exactly one factor of 2, while EC(FALSE) generates an integer without any factors of 2 and exactly one factor of 3.

4.5.2.2 Algorithm *OBFCTJ*_{bool}: Splitting Booleans

Algorithm OBFCTJ$_{bool}$ [87,88,91] splits a boolean variable v into two parts, p and q. Here, we've also made p and q booleans, but other representations are of course possible:

v	p	q
T	F	F
F	F	T
F	T	F
T	T	T

Notice that there are two representations of true ($p = F, q = F$ and $p = T, q = T$) and two of false ($p = F, q = T$ and $p = T, q = F$)! This means that in different parts of the program you can have different definitions for true and false.

For maximum confusion, you should put p and q in different parts of the program, but for simplicity, let's put them together into one structure here:

```
typedef struct {int p; int q;} TD;

TD trues[]  = {(TD){0,0},(TD){1,1}};
TD falses[] = {(TD){0,1},(TD){1,0}};

TD ED(BOOL e) {return (e==TRUE)?trues[(rand()%2)]:falses[(rand()%2)];}
BOOL DD(TD e) {return (e.p==e.q)?TRUE:FALSE;}
```

ED(TRUE) randomly picks one of the true values. There are many possible ways for DD to convert back from the obfuscated to the original representation. Here, we've simply chosen to check if $p = q$. Other possibilities would be a table lookup, or to check that $2p + q \in \{0, 3\}$, or $p \otimes q = 1$, and so on. The fact that there are so many ways to perform the different boolean operations is what makes this representation so attractive: You can use different checks on the same variables in different parts of the code. The && and || operations are no different. Here, we've used a table lookup for && and an arithmetic expression for ||:

```
TD and[]    = {(TD){0,0}, // {0,0} && {0,0} = T && T = T
               (TD){1,0}, // {0,0} && {0,1} = T && F = F
               (TD){0,1}, // {0,0} && {1,0} = T && F = F
               (TD){1,1}, // {0,0} && {1,1} = T && T = T
               (TD){1,0}, // {0,1} && {0,0} = F && T = F
               (TD){1,0}, // {0,1} && {0,1} = F && F = F
               (TD){0,1}, // {0,1} && {1,0} = F && F = F
               (TD){0,1}, // {0,1} && {1,1} = F && T = F
               (TD){0,1}, // {1,0} && {0,0} = F && T = F
               (TD){1,0}, // {1,0} && {0,1} = F && F = F
               (TD){1,0}, // {1,0} && {1,0} = F && F = F
               (TD){0,1}, // {1,0} && {1,1} = F && T = F
               (TD){0,0}, // {1,1} && {0,0} = T && T = T
               (TD){1,0}, // {1,1} && {0,1} = T && F = F
               (TD){0,1}, // {1,1} && {1,0} = T && F = F
               (TD){1,1}  // {1,1} && {1,1} = T && T = T
            };
BOOL ORD(TD a, TD b) {return ((a.p==a.q)+(b.p==b.q))!=0;}
TD ORVD(TD a, TD b) {return ED(ORD(a,b));}
TD ANDVD(TD a, TD b) {return  and[8*a.p+4*a.q+2*b.p+b.q];}
BOOL ANDD(TD a, TD b) {return DD(ANDVD(a,b));}
```

In this example, we've generated the lookup tables at obfuscation time, but generating them at runtime would make the construction more resilient against static analysis attacks.

Problem 4.13 Can you think of a way to obfuscate booleans by representing them as floating point numbers and without getting into accuracy problems?

4.5.3 Encoding Literal Data

Literal data plays an important role in many programs. Most common are literal integers and strings, but initialized arrays are also not unusual. Literal data often carries much semantic information: An attacker who can identify a string such as, `"Please enter your password:"` or a highly random 1024-bit bitstring (probably a cryptographic key!) has already learned a lot about the program. There are many simple tricks for hiding such data: You can break up a key into many small pieces and spread the pieces over the program [325], you can xor a string with a known constant value, and so on. As much as possible, you'll want to avoid ever reconstituting the literal in cleartext during the execution. Sometimes it's unavoidable, such as when passing the data to a library routine. For example, you probably have to decode an encoded string before passing it to printf. In this particular case, depending on the encoding, it may be possible to print the encoded string character by character rather than first decoding all of it.

An alternative to encoding a literal as a literal in a different form is to convert it to *code* that generates the decoded value at runtime. As an example, let's encode the strings "MIMI" and "MILA" in a finite state transducer known as a *Mealy machine* [247]. This machine takes a bitstring and a state transition table as input and generates a string as output. In our case, we let Mealy(0100_2) produce "MIMI" and Mealy(0110_2) produce "MILA".

Below are the state transition graph and the corresponding next and out tables:

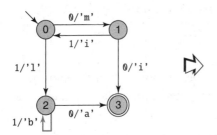

```
int next[][2] = {{1,2},
                 {3,0},
                 {3,2}};
char out[][2] = {{'m','l'},
                 {'i','i'},
                 {'a','b'}};
```

The notation $s_0 \xrightarrow{i/o} s_1$ means that if you're in state s_0 and see input i, you transfer to state s_1 and produce an o as output. The transfer is encoded by the next array (next[*state*][*input*]=*next state*) and the output is encoded by the out array (out[*state*][*input*]=*output*).

Notice the dark gray edge in the state transition graph above. It doesn't actually contribute to the two strings we want to encode, but it makes the machine produce a bogus string, Mealy(01110_2)="MILBA".

There are numerous ways to implement the Mealy machine. The most straightforward is to directly interpret the next and out tables:

```
char* mealy(int v) {
    char* str=(char*)malloc(10);
    int state=0,len=0;
    while (state!=3) {
        int input = 1&v; v >>= 1;
        str[len++]=out[state][input];
        state = next[state][input];
    }
    str[len]='\0';
    return str;
}
```

You can also hardcode the next and out tables as a switch-based interpreter:

```
char* mealy(int v) {
    char* str=(char*)malloc(10);
    int state=0,len=0;
    while (1) {
        int input = 1&v; v >>= 1;
        switch (state) {
            case 0: state=(input==0)?1:2;
                    str[len++]=(input==0)?'m':'l'; break;
            case 1: state=(input==0)?3:0;
                    str[len++]='i'; break;
            case 2: state=(input==0)?3:2;
                    str[len++]=(input==0)?'a':'b'; break;
            case 3: str[len]='\0'; return str;
        }
    }
}
```

Problem 4.14 In the example above, the finite state transducer only supports producing the string. For other operations, you have to generate and operate on the cleartext representation. Can you extend the Mealy machine framework to also support string concatenation, indexing, and other common string operations? Can your design handle destructive updates by modifying the machine on the fly?

• • •

Problem 4.15 The Mealy machine is very simple and probably easy to pattern match on. Can you come up with a method that automatically generates a large number of different implementations?

4.5.4 Encoding Arrays

Array obfuscations fall into two categories. First, you can reorder the elements of the array, which breaks the linear ordering that an adversary will expect. Second, you can restructure the array (breaking it up into pieces, merging it with other unrelated arrays, or changing its dimensionality) to hide from the adversary the structure that the programmer originally intended.

4.5.4.1 Algorithm *OBFZCW*: Array Permutation The easiest way to reorder the elements of an array A into a new array B is to provide a second permutation array P so that A[i] = B[P[i]]:

This may look suspiciously unstealthy, but this construction is, in fact, quite common in high-performance code.

The array obfuscation transformations are all defined by a function E(a, i) that takes the transformed array a and an index i as input and returns the address of the i:th element as output. The code of these transformations would typically be inlined, but we give them as separate functions here for clarity. Here's the code for permutation through an array:

```
int P[] = {7,5,1,3,8,9,0,2,4,6};

int* E(int a[],int p[],int i){
    return &(a[p[i]]);
}


*(E(B,P,1)) = 10;
int i,sum=0;
for(i=0;i<10;i++)
    sum += *(E(B,P,i));
```

```
A[1] = 10;
int i,sum=0;
for(i=0;i<10;i++)
    sum += A[i];
```

Any function that uniquely maps the index range onto itself (i.e., an isomorphism) will do as a permutation function. Algorithm OBFZCW [384] uses *homomorphic* function $f(i) = (i \cdot m)$ mod n, where n is the length of the array and m is an integer so that m and n are relatively prime. Here's an example where we've set $n = 10$ and $m = 3$:

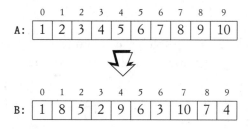

And here's the corresponding code:

```
int* E(int a[], int i){
    return &(a[i*3%10]);
}


int B[10];


*(E5(B,1)) = 10;
int i,j,sum=0;
for(i=0;i<10;i++)
    sum += *(E(B,i));
}
```

```
A[1] = 10;
int i,sum=0;
for(i=0;i<10;i++)
    sum += A[i];
```

4.5.4.2 Algorithm OBFCTJ_array: Array Restructuring Like other data types, arrays can be split up into pieces and the pieces can be scattered throughout the program. Also, the elements from several arrays of the same element type can be interleaved and merged into one array. Additionally, since arrays come in multiple dimensions, an n-dimensional array can be flattened into an array of $n - 1$ dimensions or folded into one with $n+1$ dimensions. Algorithm OBFCTJ$_{\text{array}}$ [87,88,91,117] provides such transformations.

The *array splitting* transformation splits an array A of length n into two arrays, B_0 and B_1 of lengths m_0 and m_1, respectively. Formally [117], you need a function *select* that determines the array into which each element should go, and two functions, p_0 and p_1, which give the location of each element in the new arrays:

$$select \quad : \quad [0\ldots n) \rightarrow [0, 1]$$
$$p_0 \quad : \quad [0\ldots n) \rightarrow [0, m_0)$$
$$p_1 \quad : \quad [0\ldots n) \rightarrow [0, m_1)$$

Then you get the following mapping between elements of A and elements of B_0 and B_1:

$$A[i] = B_{select(i)}[p_{select(i)}(i)]$$

Here's an example where we split array A into two arrays B and C so that the even-indexed elements go in B and the odd-indexed go in C:

Any other appropriate split function is, of course, possible. Here's what this transformation would look like in code:

```
int A[] = {1,2,3,4,5,
           6,7,8,9,10};
A[1] = 10;
int i,sum=0;
for(i=0;i<10;i++)
    sum += A[i];
```

```
int B[] = {1,3,5,7,9};
int C[] = {2,4,6,8,10};
int* E(int a1[],int a2[],int i){
    if ((i%2)==0) return &(a1[i/2]);
    else          return &(a2[i/2]);
}
*(E(B,C,1)) = 10;
int i,sum=0;
for(i=0;i<10;i++)
    sum += *(E(B,C,i));
```

The *array merging* operation is the inverse of splitting; it takes two arrays of compatible type and merges the elements into one array:

In this simple example, the merging function puts the elements from the A array at even indices and the elements from B at odd indices:

```
int A[] = {1,3,5,7,9};
int B[] = {2,4,6,8,10};
int i,sum=0;
A[1]=0;
for(i=0;i<5;i++)
   sum += A[i]*B[i];
```

```
int* E(int a[],int i,int part){
    return &(a[(i*2+part)]);
}
int C[] = {1,2,3,4,5,6,7,8,9,10};
int i,sum=0;
*(E(C2,1,0)) = 0;
for(i=0;i<5;i++)
    sum += (*E(C2,i,0))*(*E(C2,i,1));
```

If the arrays are of unknown length at compile time, or not of the same length, more complicated merging functions will be necessary.

A multi-dimensional array can be *flattened*, i.e., turned into a lower-dimensional array:

This is, of course, what compilers do when they translate multi-dimensional array operations to primitives that operate on a flat memory structure. Here's an example that turns a two-dimensional array into a one-dimensional array:

```
int A4[][5] = {{1,2,3,4,5},
                {6,7,8,9,10}};
A[0][1] = 10;
int i,j,sum=0;
for(i=0;i<2;i++)
   for(j=0;j<5;j++)
      sum += A[i][j];
}
```

```
int* E(int a[], int i1, int i2){
   return &(a[i1*5+i2]);
}
int B[10]  = {1,2,3,4,5,6,7,8,9,10};
*(E(B4,0,1)) = 10;
int i,j,sum=0;
for(i=0;i<2;i++)
   for(j=0;j<5;j++)
      sum += *(E(B4,i,j));
}
```

The *array folding* transformation is the inverse of flattening; it turns a k-dimensional array into a $k+$ one-dimensional array:

In this example, we turn a one-dimensional array into a two-dimensional one:

```
int A[] = {1,2,3,4,5,
           6,7,8,9,10};
A[1] = 10;
int i,sum=0;
for(i=0;i<10;i++)
   sum += A[i];
```

```
int* E(int a[][5], int i){
   return &(a[i/5][i%5]);
}
int B[][5] = {{1,2,3,4,5},
              {6,7,8,9,10}};
*(E(B,1)) = 10;
int i,sum=0;
for(i=0;i<10;i++)
   sum += *(E(B,i));
```

4.6 Breaking Abstractions

Abstractions play an important role in programming. Some abstractions are given to you (the instruction set architecture of the machine you're working on, the system call interface of the operating system, the classes in the Java library you link in with your program), and others you create yourself in the programs you write. The way you break your program into packages, modules, classes, and methods provides plenty of clues to an attacker. For example, two methods that are declared in the same class are probably related, and a class is presumably a specialization of its superclass. In this section, you'll see ways to break or hide these assumptions. First, Algorithm OBFWC$_{sig}$ modifies functions to make sure that their signatures don't give away any information. Next, you'll see how Algorithm OBFCTJ$_{class}$ splits and merges classes to hide the inheritance relationships. Algorithm OBFDMRVSL takes this one step further by destroying the *entire* class hierarchy in a Java program and encoding it as ordinary data. Algorithm OBFAJV, finally, adds a layer of interpretation in order to destroy the most basic of assumptions of a computing system, the immutability of the instruction set architecture.

4.6.1 Algorithm *OBFWC$_{sig}$*: Merging Function Signatures

The signature of a function gives away much of its semantics. At the very least, you can probably assume that two functions `foo` and `bar` with these signatures

```
int foo(int, int){...}
void bar(Window,String){...}
```

will have very different semantics. There are various ways of reducing the amount of information present in the signature. In Algorithm OBFWC$_{sig}$ [360], Chenxi Wang suggests making functions look as similar as possible by modifying them so that they all have the *same* signature. In practice, this is too expensive (if one function in the program has twenty arguments, you have to make *every* function in the program have at least twenty arguments!), and so it makes sense to merge them into a few equivalence classes.

We won't give an exact algorithm here, because the details will vary considerably from one language to another. The calling conventions can be very subtle [29], and you have to be careful to not introduce bugs in your transformation. The C standard, for example, allows function arguments to be evaluated in an arbitrary order, whereas the Java standard requires strict left-to-right evaluation. Regardless, if you decide to merge two function signatures by reordering their argument lists, you have to ensure that the evaluation of actual arguments is done in exactly the same order as in the original code, at least when argument evaluation can have side effects. Otherwise, in the case of Java, you would violate the standard, or in the case of C, you might tickle a platform-dependent bug in the code! For example, a C compiler is free to evaluate the arguments to `foo(i,++i)` in either order, but for the compiler the programmer is using, if this potential bug has never been triggered, your obfuscator probably shouldn't either.

In Java, a simple way to merge signatures is to make every method have the signature `Object foo(Object[])`. This is expensive, though, since it requires every argument of a primitive type to be boxed prior to the call and unboxed on entry to the method. In addition, an array has to be allocated for the parameters. An alternative is to make two or more methods have the same signature by a) converting every reference type to type `Object`, and b) inserting bogus arguments. Chenxi suggests a similar strategy for C, converting all large arguments (arrays and structs) to `void*` and inserting appropriate casts inside the method. Note, however, that if you apply this idea to typed distribution formats like Java bytecode, the type casts will be visible in the code and can hence be used to derive informative method signatures.

To see how this works in practice, have a look at this simple example:

```
typedef struct{int waldo;} thud_t;
void foo(int i, int j){}
void bar(int i, float f, int j, int k){}
void baz(char* s, thud_t t){
    int x = t.waldo;}
void fred(char* s, char* t){}
void quux(int i){}
void qux(char* s, int i, int j){}

int main() {
    int i;
    thud_t corge;
    foo(1,2);
    bar(3,4.2,8,9);
    baz("dude",corge);
    fred("yo","da");
    for(i=0;i<10000000;i++) qux("luke",1,2);
    quux(5);
}
```

The foo, bar, and quux functions are pretty similar, so it makes sense to modify them so that they all have the same signature, void (int, float, int, int). Similarly, baz and fred are also much alike, so let's modify them to both have the signature void (char*, void*). After merging, you get the following program:

```
typedef struct{int waldo;} thud_t;

void foo(int i, float bogus1, int j, int bogus2){}
void bar(int i, float f, int j, int k){}
void quux(int i, float bogus1, int bogus2, int bogus3){}
void baz(char* s, void* t){
    int x = ((thud_t*)t)->waldo;}
void fred(char* s, void* t){}
void qux(char* s, int i, int j){}

int main() {
    int i,bogus1,bogus2;
    float bogus3;
    thud_t corge,corge_cp;
    foo(1,bogus3,2,bogus1);
    bar(3,4.2,8,9);
    memcpy(&corge_cp,&corge,sizeof(corge));
    baz("dude",&corge_cp);
    fred("yo","da");
    for(i=0;i<10000000;i++) qux("luke",1,2);
    quux(5,bogus3,bogus1,bogus2);
}
```

Notice that we never touched qux. It's executed within a tight loop, and adding extra parameters would have been too costly. Note also that since C passes structs by value, we had to make a local copy of corge, which we then passed by reference to baz. Here, we've added bogus variables to pass as extra arguments, but in practice you would prefer random variables already available in the environment.

4.6.2 Algorithm OBF*CTJ*$_{class}$: Splitting and Merging Classes

In typical class-based object-oriented languages like Java, C#, or Eiffel, a class consists of instance variables (data fields), virtual methods (functions invoked indirectly through an object), and constructors (methods called on object creation to initialize instance variables). Classes can inherit from each other, meaning they include the features from the class (or classes) they extend. Thus, the classes in a program form an inheritance tree, or if the language supports multiple inheritance, a DAG. Algorithm OBFCTJ$_{class}$ [87,88,91,271,331] provides three ways to obfuscate this hierarchy, namely, by splitting a class into two classes, merging two classes into one class, and inserting bogus classes into the hierarchy.

To obfuscate a class, you need three primitive operations, MOVEUP, INSERT-EMPTY, and DELETEEMPTY. With these primitives, you can synthesize the *class merge* and the *class split* operations. The MOVEUP primitive takes a declared name in one class (such as a field, a method, or a constructor) and moves it up into the parent class. The INSERT-EMPTY primitive inserts a new empty class into the class hierarchy. The DELETE-EMPTY primitive, finally, removes an empty class. The details of these operations will depend on the language (does it have multiple inheritance like C++, does it support renaming of fields like Eiffel, does it have interfaces like Java?), so we will only discuss a simple language here: Java without interfaces.

Have a look at the four classes in the class hierarchy on the left:

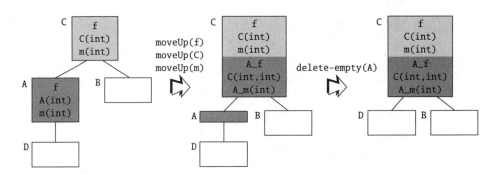

Suppose you want to merge class A into C. Given our primitives, you want to first execute MOVEUP(F), MOVEUP(M), MOVEUP(A), and then DELETE-EMPTY(A). You cannot simply move the declarations up to C, however, because their names (and signatures, in the case of the method and constructor) clash with declarations already in C. We'll get to the details in a minute, but you can see a few things in the right-hand side of the figure above: A's field f is simply renamed A_f, A's constructor is renamed C and is given an extra argument to distinguish it from the one already in C, and A's method m is renamed A_m. Because of method overriding, however, this is not enough. A method that did a=new A(); a.m() before the merge would do a=new C(); a.m() afterwards, and would wind up invoking the wrong method! Similarly, what should happen to a method that wants to distinguish an instance of A from an instance of C by using a runtime type test such as instanceof?

Class splitting is, unsurprisingly, the inverse of merging. In the example below, class A is split by first giving it an empty superclass D and then moving field f and constructor A (which gets renamed D) into it:

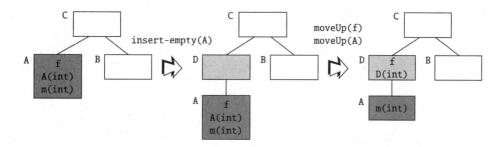

Unfortunately, you can't just move any old declaration up. Moving f is not a problem, since it will be available to any method or constructor in the subclass that uses it. Moving up any method or constructor, however, requires you to also move the declaration of any name that *it* uses, directly or indirectly. The MOVEUP() primitive takes care of this.

In Algorithm 4.6►282, you can see the definitions of the MOVEUP primitive for fields, methods, and constructors. Listing 4.3►283 gives an example where a class A (dark gray) is merged into its parent class C (light gray). To handle virtual method calls and runtime type checks, objects of type C and A are given an instance variable kind that is initialized to the name of the class by each constructor. Other less obvious representations are, of course, more desirable. Maintaining complete semantic equivalence between the original and obfuscated code is tricky; notice how the type cast turns into a complicated if-statement that checks the kind field, and if the variable is not of the right type, is forced to explicitly throw an exception.

4.6.3 Algorithm OBFDMRVSL: Destroying High-Level Structures

The *Self-Protecting Mobile Agents* (SMPA) project from *Network Associates Laboratories* was funded by DARPA to build an automated obfuscator that would protect mobile agents from attacks by untrusted hosts. It may be the most thorough study of obfuscation to date, at least of those that are known in the public literature, in that they built both an obfuscator and an automatic de-obfuscator. It's also the most depressing study to date, in that they found that it was *easier* to build the

---

Algorithm 4.6 Definition of the MOVEUP primitives used in Algorithm OBFCTJ$_{\text{class}}$ to split and merge classes.

MOVEUP(FIELD f):

1. Give f a unique name f'.
2. Rename any use of f to f'.
3. Move f' to the parent class.

MOVEUP(METHOD m):

1. Give m a unique name m'.

2. Rename any use of m to m'.

3. Move m' to the parent class P.

4. If P has a method $P.m$ with the same name and signature as m', rewrite $P.m$ as

   ```
   method P.m (...) {
       if (kind=="P")
           P.m's original code;
       else
           m'(...);
   }
   ```

5. Move up any declaration on which m depends.

MOVEUP(CONSTRUCTOR C):

1. Add dummy formal parameters to C until no constructor in the parent class P has the same signature.

2. Add dummy actual arguments to any calls to the constructor to match the new formals.

3. Add a field kind (if not already present) to P. Add kind="P" to all of P's constructors and kind=C to C.

4. Rename C to P and move it into P.

5. Replace any runtime typechecks with checks on kind.

6. Move up any declaration on which C depends.

---

de-obfuscator than the obfuscator and, on top of that, the de-obfuscator ran *faster* than the obfuscator! Unfortunately, to prevent malicious use, neither tool was ever released in the public domain.

The basic idea of the OBFDMRVSL [28,103] obfuscation algorithm is to remove as much of the high-level structures from Java's typed bytecode as possible. In the JVM, classes, fields, methods, and exceptions are all typed, and the types give the attacker useful clues as to what part of the program does what. Similarly, the strongly typed nature of the bytecode, and the fact that code and data can't be mixed, means that an adversary can easily reconstitute control structures.

If you were to write a compiler from Java to machine code, you would have to translate all the high-level features (classes, method dispatch, exception handling,

```
class C {
    int f;
    public C(int x){
        f=x;
    }
    int m(int x){
        return (f+=x);
    }
}

class A extends C {
    int f;
    public A(int x){
        super(x);
        f=x+1;
    }
    public int m(int x){
        return (f-=x);
    }
}

class B extends C {
    public B(int x){
        super(x);
    }
}

class D extends A {
    public D(int x){
        super(x);
    }
}
```

```
class C {
    public String kind;

    int f;
    public C(){}
    public C(int x){
        f=x;
        kind="C";
    }
    int m(int x){
        if (kind.equals("C"))
            return (f+=x);
        else
            return A_m(x);
    }
    int A_f;
    public C(int x, int dummy){
        this(x);
        kind="A";
        A_f=x+1;
    }
    int A_m(int x){
        return (A_f-=x);
    }
}

class D extends C {
    public D(int x){
        super(x,42);
    }
}

class B extends C {
    public B(int x){
        super(x);
    }
}
```

```
C c = new C(0);
A a = new A(0);
a = (A)c;
```

```
C c = new C(0);
C a = new C(0,42);

if (!((c instanceof D) ||
    (c.kind.equals("A"))))
    throw new ClassCastException("C");
a = c;
```

Figure 4.3 Example of merging a class A with its parent class C. The top of the figure shows the transformations on the class hierarchy. The bottom part of the figure shows transformations on instantiations and type checks using these classes.

dynamic memory allocation and deallocation, and so on) into the low-level operations supported by the hardware and operating system. This is, essentially, what the
SPMA tool does while staying within the Java bytecode domain. In other words,
both the original and obfuscated programs consist of Java class files, but in the obfuscated program there are no classes in the constant pool (every class is represented
by a unique integer), virtual method dispatch is done through explicit virtual tables
rather than the Java bytecode **invokevirtual** instruction, all memory is in the form of
a flat array (which includes the method call stacks), exception handling does not use
Java's built-in mechanism, and so on. In addition to these transformations, SPMA
also performs traditional data obfuscations.

Have a look at Figure 4.4▶285, where we've sketched how SPMA transforms a
program. The original program contains two methods, P and Q. Their control flow
graphs are merged and flattened using chenxification. Whenever possible, methods
from the standard library are merged the same way. Since the JVM limits the size of
a method, the obfuscated program will have several methods containing the basic
blocks from the original program. In Figure 4.4▶285, the basic blocks from P, Q, main,
and Hashtable.put are all merged into two methods, m1 and m2.

Java expects some methods to never change name or signature. For example,
the program has to have a method named main (where execution starts), and it
has to have exactly one argument, an array of strings. Therefore, in the obfuscated
program, main becomes a stub that jumps to the appropriate flattened method.
Similarly, to handle GUI events, you have to implement methods with a particular
name and signature (such as mousePressed(MouseEvent e)), and these, too, have
to be converted to stubs. In other words, even though the entire program has been
flattened into just a few huge static methods, the obfuscated code will still contain
remnants of the original one, with hints to the adversary as to where particular parts
of the execution originate.

4.6.3.1 An Example To remove the high-level structures from the Java bytecode,
SPMA flattens control flow (to make it difficult to reconstitute source-level control
structures), turns typed data into (almost) untyped data, merges methods (to remove
procedural abstraction), replaces classes with unique integers, implements method
dispatch through its own virtual method tables, makes use of its own method call
stack, and implements its own version of common classes from the Java library (to
avoid leaving hints from unobfuscatable library calls). In addition to synthesizing
high-level structures from low-level primitives, SPMA does some simple transformations on data, such as you saw in Section 4.5▶258. Since the SPMA tools were
never released in the public domain, we can't know the exact design decisions, so

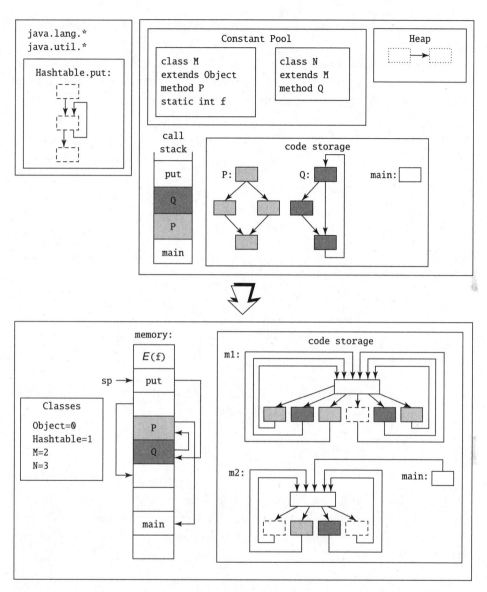

Figure 4.4 Example of a program obfuscated with the SPMA tool. On top is the original program. It consists of two classes, M and N, where M contains a method P and a static integer variable f, and N contains a method Q. Below that is the obfuscated program, where all methods have been merged into two chenxified methods, m1 and m2, and all data (method call stacks, heap, static data) has been merged into an array memory.

the example here is based on what can be gleaned from the published reports and from conjecture.

Have a look at the simple Java program below. It consists of two classes, A and B, B inheriting from A, and a main method that creates an instance of B and makes a virtual method call through this object to B's method n:

```java
class A {
   int i;
   int m() {return i;}
   void n(int i) {}
}
class B extends A {
   String s;
   public B(int i, String s) {
     this.i=i; this.s=s;
   }
   void n(int v) {
      int x = v*m();
      System.out.println(s+x);
   }
   public static void main(String[] args) {
      B b = new B(6,"42");
      b.n(7);
   }
}
```

Every data object in the original program is represented by a Memory object in the obfuscated program. Memory has one array for each primitive type and an array M of type Memory that allows objects to refer to each other in order to facilitate building arbitrary object graphs:

```java
class Memory {
      public int[] I;
      public Object[] L;
      public long[] J;
      public float[] F;
      public double[] D;
      public Memory[] M;
}
```

Every piece of data in the obfuscated program is fashioned out of Memory objects. This includes virtual method tables, method call stacks, and class instances. You could get rid of even more type information by representing memory as an array of raw bytes, but the performance hit would be considerable, and it's not clear how much more would be gained since the JVM's *instructions* are typed anyway and hence reveal information about the types of memory regions.

Before execution can begin, you need to create virtual method tables for every class. Class A's table consists of two numbers, 2 and 3. These refer to the case labels of the initial blocks of A's method m and method n, respectively, in the switch statement that implements the flattened methods. Since B inherits m from A, its virtual table entry for m also refers to case label 2:

```
public class DAnna {
    static Memory[] mem = new Memory[10];
    static int mc = -1;
    static Memory SP;

    static { // create memory and virtual tables
        for(int i=0;i<mem.length;i++)
            mem[i]=new Memory();
        mem[++mc].I=new int[]{2,3};              // {A.m,A.n}
        mem[++mc].I=new int[]{2,5};              // {B.m,A.n}
    }
```

A virtual table's index into the memory array (0 for A and 1 for B) also serves as the unique identifier for that class. A statement such as if (x instanceof A)... can then translate into if ((x.vtab==0)||(x.vtab==1)) ... . Any of the standard compiler tricks for $O(1)$ time type tests [114,376] could of course also be used.

Our program is small, so we can get away with only one chenxified method, m1, which is invoked directly from the stub main:

```
        static void m1() {
            mem[++mc].M=new Memory[2];
            SP=mem[mc]; // allocate main's AR

            int PC=0;
            while(true) {
                switch (PC) {
```

```
        ...                    // other blocks here
      case 1: {                // main ends here
        SP=SP.M[0];            // Deallocate n's AR
        return;                // return from main
      }
    }
  }
}
public static void main(String args[]) {
  m1();                        // stub call to m1()
}
```

SP is the method call stack pointer. Activations records (ARs) are just instances of Memory linked together on the M field.

The first thing main does is to create a new instance of B. This involves first allocating it (in our case, getting a new Memory object, creating storage for the block's fields i and s, and filling in the new object's virtual table pointer), and then invoking B's constructor to initialize the fields:

```
case 0 : {                         // main's 1st basic block
  Memory b=mem[++mc];              // Allocate new object
  b.I=new int[1];                  // space for "i"
  b.L=new Object[1];               // space for "s"
  b.M=new Memory[]{mem[1]};        // b's virtual table pointer
  SP.M[1]=b;                       // b=new B(6,"42")
  mem[++mc].M=new Memory[]{SP,b};// AR for B's constructor
  SP=mem[mc];
  SP.I=new int[]{6,6};             // RA=6
  SP.L=new ObfStr[]{new ObfStr(new char[]{'4','2'})};
  PC=4; break;                     // Call B's constructor
}
```

In this example, we haven't used any of the techniques you saw in Section 4.3.3 ▶229 for hiding the flow between blocks. Therefore, it's easy to see here that the constructor starts at case label 4. We set the return address (RA) to 6, meaning that after the constructor returns, we should continue execution at case block 6, main's second basic block.

The constructor gets the pointer to the new object (passed to it as `this`) and stores the argument values into the object fields:

```
case 4: {                          // body of B's constructor
   PC=SP.I[0];                     // get return address
   Memory this_=(Memory)SP.M[1];   // get this pointer
   this_.I[0]=SP.I[1];             // this.i=i
   this_.L[0]=(ObfStr)SP.L[0];     // this.s=s
   break;                          // return to main
}
```

After the constructor has finished executing, it returns to main's second basic block. To synthesize the call to `b.n(7)`, you must first look up which method to call (depending on `b`'s type this could be either `A`'s `n` or `B`'s `n`), and you do this by following the pointer to the virtual table from `b`:

```
case 6: {                          // main's call to b.n(7);
   SP=SP.M[0];                     // Dealloc constructor's AR
   Memory b=SP.M[1];               // main's local b
   mem[++mc].M=new Memory[]{SP,b}; // Alloc AR for n
   SP=mem[mc];
   SP.I=new int[]{1,7,0};          // {RA,7,space for n's x}
   SP.L=new Object[2];             // n's Evaluation stack
   PC=b.M[0].I[1];                 // virtual address of b.n;
   break;                          // call b.n
}
```

In our example, `b` points to a `B` object, so it's `B`'s `n` that you need to call, and looking at `B`'s virtual method table, you see that `n` starts at case label 5. There, we perform another virtual method call to `m`, again linking together activation records:

```
case 5: {                          // body of B.n
   Memory this_=SP.M[1];           // get this pointer
   mem[++mc].M=new Memory[]{SP,this_};
   SP=mem[mc];                     // AR for m
   SP.I=new int[]{7};              // RA=7
   PC=this_.M[0].I[0];             // this.m's virtual address
   break;                          // call B's m()
}
```

Method m just returns the value of the instance variable v, which you access by following the this pointer:

```
case 2: {                    // body of A's m
   PC=SP.I[0];               // return address
   Memory this_=SP.M[1];     // get this pointer
                             // <<< memory dump here >>>
   SP.I=new int[]{this_.I[0]}; // return this.i
   break;                    // return to n
}
```

Now we're as deep as we will go in the call chain of this simple example, so it's illustrative to examine what memory looks like. Here's the memory data structure right before the call to A.m() returns:

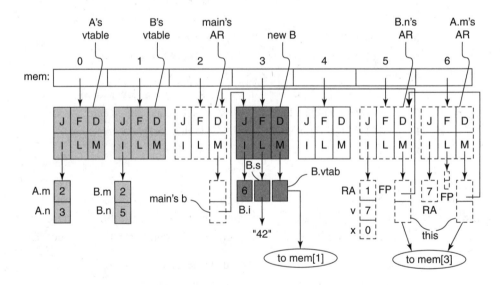

Blocks in light gray are virtual tables, in dark gray are activation records (AR), in dashed are class instances, and the block in white is garbage, left over from the call to B's constructor. There is clearly more information available in this structure than there would be in a raw array of bytes, but clearly less than in the original program.

Finally, here's n's second basic block, to which you return after the call to m:

```
case 7: {                           // n's 2nd basic block
   int rm=SP.I[0];                  // rm is m's return value
   SP=SP.M[0];                      // deallocate AR
   Memory this_=SP.M[1];            // get this pointer
   PC=SP.I[0];                      // get return address
   int v=SP.I[1];
   SP.I[2]=rm*v;                    // x=rm*v
   ObfStr s=((ObfStr)this_.L[0]); //
   ObfStr vs=new ObfStr(SP.I[2]); // vs=new String(x)
   System.out.println((new ObfStr(s)).append(vs).toJavaString());
   break;                          // return to main
}
```

There are a couple of things to notice here. First, we have left the evaluation of rm*v as is. We could have translated it into operations on our own evaluation stack rather than using Java's built-in stack, at considerable loss of performance. In fact, if you look at the memory dump above, you can see that we linked in such a stack of objects, although we never used it. The second thing to notice is that the string field s is actually not represented as a Java String but as an instance of our own ObfStr class. This is a complete reimplementation of java.lang.String. Normally, ObfStr would be treated the same as the user classes and its methods would be flattened and mixed in with the user methods; here we've cheated, though, and just call ObfStr's methods directly. While replacing common Java library classes with your own implementations removes a lot of information from the program, it's hard to remove *all* information. Whenever you call a remaining library method that needs a java.lang.String object, for example, you need to convert your obfuscated representation back to a String. This is what happens above when the program calls System.out.println.

4.6.3.2 Evaluation As you've seen, it's possible to remove much of the high-level information from a Java program, but it's hard to remove *all* the information. Algorithm OBFDMRVSL replaces a throw new Exception() with an ordinary jump to the basic block that handles it. However, exceptions that the Java environment throws implicitly, such as a divide by zero or a null pointer dereference, still must be handled the Java way. Similarly, you've seen how stubs are necessary for any methods that the

Java virtual machine expects to have a particular name and signature. Furthermore, any obfuscated object (such as a string or an integer that has been encoded using any of the techniques in Section 4.5 ▶ 258) needs to be converted to the original Java type before being passed to a library method. Any such remnants of the original program can provide valuable clues to an attacker.

The authors report that the code generated by their obfuscator was about 10 times larger and 4 to 20 times slower than the original. What's even more depressing is that reversing the transformations was easy; in fact, de-obfuscation was *easier* than obfuscation! We let the authors describe the design of their de-obfuscator themselves [103, pp. 23–24]:

> We developed a "de-obfuscator" (actually more of an analysis assistant) for our obfuscation tool. It worked by searching for patterns in the input program and running selected parts of the program. It was largely successful, in that it was able to determine method entry points, the structure of the class hierarchy, which methods were constructors, etc. . . .
>
> The de-obfuscator runs the <clinit> (static initialization, run when a Java class is loaded) of the program to retrieve the virtual tables and jump tables, . . .
>
> The control flow leaving each block was determined by pattern matching on the DAG representation of the basic block. Since our obfuscator produces basic blocks that use data-driven jumps, there is a calculation in each obfuscated basic block that returns the block to jump to. Our obfuscator output [sic] only a fixed number of formats for this calculation, so the de-obfuscator can match against those formats.
>
> After simplifying the control flow leaving each basic block, the de-obfuscator used the virtual tables (read from running the initializer) to determine which basic blocks were method entry points. Since no Java method (in the original program) can jump to code in other methods, this allowed complete determination of method composition. The virtual tables also associated methods with classes. Certain facts about the class hierarchy could also be determined from the virtual tables, such as superclass and interfaces.

In conclusion, the authors note that removing high-level information from a Java program and obfuscating data provides no extra security, and it comes at a high cost of implementation:

> Obfuscators are hard to implement.... the security gained is likely to be
> nonexistent to marginal.... Our obfuscation tool took over 2,000 hours
> to develop, for no to very marginal security.

4.6.4 Algorithm *OBFAJV*: Modifying Instruction Encodings

The lowest-level abstraction on a machine that an attacker is likely to care about
is the instruction set architecture. An attacker who learns about your program
by disassembling it, or single-stepping through it under a debugger, relies on his
understanding of this abstraction. In particular, he will have to know the instructions
the machine architecture supports, its addressing modes, and its register sets. He,
or the tools he's using, will also have to know how these are encoded, i.e., which bit
patterns correspond to which opcodes, addressing modes, and registers. It's hard
to break this abstraction if you want your program to run directly on the hardware.
But if you're willing to add a level of interpretation, you can construct whatever
instruction set architecture you want!

This is the basic idea of Algorithm OBFAJV [10]. The goal of this algorithm is
to produce diverse (and therefore more tamper-resistant) programs by generating a
unique interpreter and a unique instruction set for every distributed copy. Algorithm
OBFAJV does this by breaking the instruction encoding abstraction. The goal is for
every program to encode instructions differently, and for this encoding to change
at runtime. Thus, as the attacker is stepping through the program, learning about
which bit patterns correspond to which instruction semantics, he will find that the
encoding changes as he chooses different execution paths.

Have a look at this tiny example program, where the instruction PUSHC *c* pushes
the 3-bit constant *c*, ADD adds the two top elements on the stack, PRINT prints and
pops the top element on the stack, and EXIT stops execution:

```
        PUSHC 2
        PUSHC 5
        ADD
        PRINT
        SWAP  0
        PUSHC 2
        PUSHC 5
        ADD
        PRINT
        EXIT
```

The program thus prints 7 twice. SWAP *n* is a meta-instruction that says that "from here on, the instruction set changes." SWAP's parameter *n* is a reference to a node in the *instruction decoding tree*:

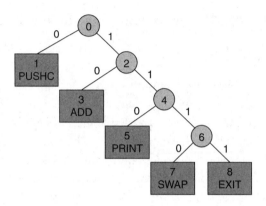

Each node in the tree has a number. Internal nodes (light gray) point to left and right subtrees, and leaves (dark gray) contain references to the code that implements the opcode semantics. Say that you see the bits $\langle 0, 0, 1, 1, 1, 1, 0 \rangle$ in the instruction stream. To decode, you'd go left from the root (since the first bit is a 0), find yourself at node 1, which is a leaf, and you know that you should execute the PUSHC instruction. PUSHC takes a 3-bit integer argument, so you extract the next three bits, $\langle 0, 1, 1 \rangle$, and push 3 on the stack. The remaining bits are $\langle 1, 1, 0 \rangle$. You start at the root of the tree again, go right (first bit is a 1) to node 2, go right (another 1) to node 4, go left (a 0), and find that the next instruction is PRINT. PRINT pops the top argument off the stack (the 3 that you just pushed) and prints it.

To diversify, or obfuscate, your program, all you have to do is to generate a decoding tree and to translate each instruction from the original program into the new instruction encoding. Notice that even if you start out with a language that has a fixed-length instruction set (such as a RISC machine), the resulting encoding is variable length.

Now it's reasonable to assume that after stepping through the program for a while, the attacker will learn that 0 is PUSHC, 1,1,0 is PRINT, and so on. For this reason, Algorithm OBFAJV adds the SWAP instruction, which changes the instruction encoding on the fly at runtime! Here, we've made SWAP *n* very simple; it just swaps the children of node *n*. In Algorithm OBFAJV, there are instructions that can make any modifications to the decoding tree. Here's what the tree looks like after SWAP 0 has been executed:

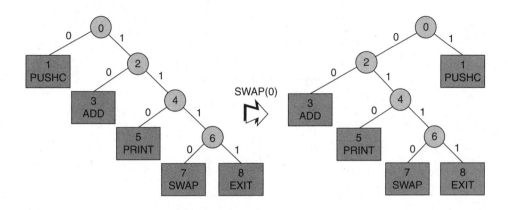

Here, now, is the complete encoding of the simple example program we started with, bit by bit:

```
PUSHC       2       PUSHC       5       ADD      PRINT
 0,    0,   1,   0,     0,   1,   0,   1,   1,   0,   1,   1,   0,

       SWAP                0
 1,    1,   1,   0,     0,   0,   0,

PUSHC       2       PUSHC       5       ADD      PRINT       EXIT
 1,    0,   1,   0,     1,   1,   0,   1,   0,   0,   0,   1,   0,   0,   1,   1,   1
```

Notice how the operator encoding is different after the SWAP instruction has executed! Before the swap, ADD is ⟨1, 0⟩; after the swap it's ⟨0, 0⟩.

Implementing the execution engine isn't hard. Here's the definition of the decoding tree nodes:

```
class Node{}
class Internal extends Node{
    public Node left,right;
    public Internal(Node left, Node right) {
        this.left = left; this.right=right;
    }
    public void swap() {
        Node tmp = left; left=right; right=tmp;
    }
}
```

```
class Leaf extends Node {
    public int operator;
    public Leaf(int operator) {
        this.operator=operator;
    }
}
```

And here's how you build the original decoding tree:

```
static Node[] tree = new Node[9];
static {
    tree[1]=new Leaf(0);     // PUSHC
    tree[3]=new Leaf(1);     // ADD
    tree[5]=new Leaf(2);     // PRINT
    tree[7]=new Leaf(3);     // SWAP
    tree[8]=new Leaf(4);     // EXIT
    tree[6]=new Internal(tree[7],tree[8]);
    tree[4]=new Internal(tree[5],tree[6]);
    tree[2]=new Internal(tree[3],tree[4]);
    tree[0]=new Internal(tree[1],tree[2]);
}
```

The program is just an array of bits, and the program counter is an index into this array:

```
static int prog[]={0,0,1,0,0,1,0,1,1,0,1,1,0,
                   1,1,1,0,0,0,0,
                   1,0,1,0,1,1,0,1,0,0,0,1,0,0,1,1,1};
static int pc = 0;
```

You need a function decode() that reads one bit at a time from the program array and walks the decoding tree until a leaf is found, and a function operand() that decodes a 3-bit integer from the program array:

```
static int decode() {
    Node t = tree[0];
    while (t instanceof Internal)
        t = (prog[pc++]==0)?((Internal)t).left:((Internal)t).right;
```

```
        return ((Leaf)t).operator;
    }
    static int operand() {
        return 4*prog[pc++]+2*prog[pc++]+prog[pc++];
    }
```

Finally, here's the interpreter itself, which calls the decode() and operand() functions to decode the instruction stream and swap() to modify the decoding tree:

```
static void interpret() {
    int stack[] = new int[10]; int sp = -1;
    while (true) {
        switch (decode()) {
            case 0 : stack[++sp]=operand(); break;          // PUSHC
            case 1 : stack[sp-1]+=stack[sp]; sp--; break;   // ADD
            case 2 : System.out.println(stack[sp--]); break; // PRINT
            case 3 : ((Internal)tree[operand()]).swap(); break; // SWAP
            case 4 : return;                                // EXIT
        }
    }
}
```

By itself, this transformation doesn't hold up to a dynamic attack. Once the adversary has found the interpret() function, he can ignore that the instruction encodings change every so often and just concentrate on which case of the switch statement gets executed! For this reason, Algorithm OBFAJV makes use of several other diversification techniques. To make sure that the instruction semantics are different from one copy of the program to the next (i.e., that every interpret() function looks different), Algorithm OBFAJV merges several instructions into new ones with unique and unknown (to the attacker) semantics (Proebsting's superoperators [292]). Furthermore, rather than representing the interpreted program as a static array of bits, as we did above, they break it up into basic blocks and move these blocks around in memory by storing them in a self-adjusting binary search tree.

As you can imagine, the main drawback of this algorithm, and any other algorithm [35,193,254] that adds a level of interpretation and obfuscation to the instruction set architecture, is that it incurs a significant runtime overhead. The authors of Algorithm OBFAJV report slowdown factors of between 50 and 3,500.

4.7 Discussion

Obfuscating transformations have many uses. One of the first applications was to generate a large number of diverse versions of the same program. The idea is to make every installation of the program unique and thereby making it harder for an adversary to construct automated attack scripts that work everywhere. In Chapter 8 (Software Watermarking), you'll see a related application: To prevent *collusive attacks* (where several differently marked programs are compared to find the location of a watermark), you apply different sets of obfuscations to every distributed copy of the program, thereby making them all different and harder to compare. A second application is to use obfuscation to make a program so convoluted that it becomes difficult to find and reverse engineer a secret algorithm. A third reason to obfuscate is to hide secret data, such as cryptographic keys. Finally, obfuscation can be used by the bad guys. For example, before making copies of your watermarked program, a software pirate can obfuscate it to make it difficult for you to extract the mark.

Let's have a look back at Section 2.2▸86 to see which defense primitives the different algorithms you've seen in this chapter make use of:

split/merge: Many obfuscation algorithms are based on splitting and merging. You can use splitting to break a language construct into smaller pieces and then protect each piece individually. You can use merging to sow confusion by combining unrelated constructs.

Algorithm OBFCTJ$_{bool}$, for example, splits up a boolean variable into two pieces that can then be stored in different parts of the program.

Splitting and merging often go together. Algorithm OBFCF$_{inoutline}$ splits a function into smaller parts that can then be merged with other, unrelated, functions. Similarly, Algorithm OBFCTJ$_{class}$ splits classes into smaller ones as well as merges unrelated classes. Algorithm OBFCTJ$_{array}$ splits arrays into pieces that can be scattered over the program, or merges unrelated arrays.

Several authors have suggested protecting a function by splitting its control flow graph into basic blocks and control flow edges and then hiding or protecting each part separately. Ge et al. [42,135], for example, store the control flow edges in a heavily obfuscated separate process.

mimic: The **mimic** primitive is closely related to *stealth*. Whenever you insert new code or transform existing code, you want to make sure that it fits in with the rest of the code in the program, i.e., that it mimics some aspect (or all aspects) of the existing code. You can also use the **mimic** primitive to make unrelated program pieces all look the same. Algorithm OBFWC$_{sig}$, for example, adds confusion by forcing all functions to have the same signature.

map: You can use the **map** primitive to systematically replace one construct with another. Algorithm OBFTP, for example, replaces identifiers with meaningless ones. Algorithms OBFCF$_{interp}$ and OBFAJV both add a layer of interpretation. This is really just a mapping from the original instruction set to a new, constructed instruction set.

    Algorithm OBFWHKD protects the basic blocks by reordering them and the control flow edges by hiding them in a jump table, also an instance of the **map** primitive.

duplicate: The **duplicate** primitive can make copies of an object to force the adversary to consider a large number of objects in the program while searching for the real secret. Algorithm OBFCTJ$_{bogus}$ does this by hiding the real control flow behind inserted bogus control flow, and Algorithm OBFCF$_{copy}$ similarly makes copies of functions.

indirect: As you've seen, adding a level of indirection is a common obfuscation technique. Algorithm OBFLDK replaces direct branches with jumps through a branch function, and Algorithm OBFCTJ$_{pointer}$ creates opaque predicates based on the difficulty of pointer analysis.

    Algorithm OBFWHKD$_{alias}$ adds a level of indirection to protect the entries in the chenxification jump table from being discovered.

reorder: Algorithm OBFCF$_{reorder}$ reorders code and data, and Algorithm OBFZCW permutes the elements of an array.

Obfuscation Theory

5

Let's reiterate what you hope to achieve when you create an obfuscated program. You would like to give a user an executable program but prevent him from understanding some part of its construction. For example, you may want to prevent the user from extracting secret keys you have embedded in the program, replacing the keys, understanding the algorithms, extracting specific functionality out of the program, or adding some functionality to the program.

In the previous chapter, you saw a large number of obfuscation techniques. We argued that these obfuscating transformations are useful, saying that the confusion they add to the program increases the complexity of analyzing and understanding it, using the static and dynamic program analysis techniques from Chapter 3. The premise of that chapter was that an attacker has a limited type and number of tools available to him. In our discussions, it was sufficient to show that an obfuscation technique increased the complexity of a program to a point where the attacker's tools are either too slow, too imprecise, or simply unable to compute the reverse transformation.

For example, consider the Perl program shown in Listing 5.1 ▶303. At first glance, this appears to be a grotesque ASCII art kitten rather than a legitimate Perl program, let alone one that does something useful. For instance, it does not appear to have any alphanumerics. However, a more close examination begins to reveal the tricks the author used. For example, once you note that Perl variable names can use non-alphanumerics and begin with sigils ($, @, and &), the kitten begins to resolve merely into a series of assignments to weirdly named variables. The author uses

logical and and or operations to construct alphanumerics out of strings that contain
only non-alphanumeric characters. Finally, in the shaded section, he uses Perl's
magic quote characters to call Perl again to decrypt the rest of the program and
then eval it.[1]

Problem 5.1   Hidden inside the obfuscated program show in Listing 5.1▸303 is the
name of the pirate cat on the cover of this book. Can you work out what his name is?

This is an example of increasing the size of a program to hide its functionality.
If you assume an attacker is not able to perform accurate string analysis to recognize
the string being built, then this may be an effective obfuscation technique.

Unfortunately, in reality you cannot restrict attackers to a particular set of tools
or type of attack for very long. In the above example, an attacker may simply run
the program and, using a debugger, step through the code until he arrives at the
eval instruction. He can then replace it with a print statement to determine what
the original program looked like. In other examples you saw in Section 4.3.4▸235,
we used opaque predicates and code duplication to increase the size of programs.
An attacker can use a weakness in the way we generate the opaque predicates to
distinguish them from the predicates that occur naturally in the program.

Simply padding out a program with bogus code that's really no more than nops
doesn't hinder the attacker very long. To be useful, the increased complexity must be
difficult to reverse, and this requirement is not well captured by how difficult it is to
perform a particular static or dynamic program analysis. The metrics we have been
using fail to capture how long it will take for an attacker to decipher an obfuscated
program, or indeed what it means to have deciphered an obfuscated program.

What you would really like to be able to do is prevent attackers from reversing
your obfuscation, irrespective of what tools they have. In order to determine the theoretical limits of obfuscation, you need much more rigorous models for obfuscation
and more stringent criteria for assessing the success of an obfuscation technique.
Here, you will discover a surprising finding: Whether obfuscation is feasible or not
will change depending on the formalization you choose.

For example, under one model suggested by Barak et al. [34], we require that
an obfuscated application does not leak *any* information to an attacker except what
is deducible from the program output. Under this model, Barak et al. showed
that obfuscation of general programs (and indeed of even large classes of simpler
programs) is impossible.

---

1. A program to obfuscate your own Perl programs in this style is available from this book's Web site.

Listing 5.1 Hello World program written in Perl. The code can be de-obfuscated by replacing the magic quotes (') in the shaded section with a `print` statement.

```
                                                              $=
                                                              $';
             =                                                ||$.
             $;                                               ;$_=
             |$|                                              (^@(%
             '*$                                              ~;#~~;
             _+&~                                             #~~;#~
             #~~;                                             ;#~~;#~
             ~;#~~                                            #~~;#~~;
             ~;#~~;                                           ;#~~;#~;
             #~~;#~~                                          #~~;#~~;#~
             #~~;#~~;                                         ;#~~;#~~;#~
             ~;#~~;#~~                                        ;#~~;#~~;#~
             ~;#~~;#~~               ;#~~;#~~;#~~             ;#~~;#~~;#~
             ~;#~~;#~~;       #~~;#~~;#~~;#~~;#~~;#~~;   #~~;#~~;#~~;
             #~~;#~~;#~~;#~~;#~~;#~~;#~~;#~~;#~~;#~~;#~~;#~~;#~~;#~
             ~;#~~;#~~;#~~;#@-__~~;#~~@-;;;#,.;_,./|,.););~~,./
             .);;;);;,../@,./.);;;,.*+,.;_,./|);#~~/.~~@-~~@-;
             .*+,.;_);;.~~@-,.;#);~~,./.,.;#,.-(,.;.,.;;~~@-,.*
             +);;;;@-__~~;#~~;#~~;#~~;#~~;#~~;#~~;#~~;#~~;#~
             ~;#~~;#~~;#~~;#~~;#~~;#~~;#~~;#~~;#~~;#~~;#~~;#~
             ~;#~~;#~~;#~~;#~~;#~~;#~~;#~~;#~~;#~~;#~~;#~~;#~~;
             #~~;#~~;#~~;#~~;#~~;#~~;#~~;#~~;#~~;#~~;#~~;#~~;#~~;
             #~~;#~~;#~~;#~~;#~~;#~~;#~~;#~~;#~~;#@-__@-__);@-);~~,.*+,
             ./|);;;~~@-~~~~;;/.,./@,.;.);();~~@-);;;,.(),.;.~~@-;.@-,.*+)
             ;~~,./.);;;,.;.~~@-;;-(,.*+);;;);;;,.;.,./|;./@,./|~~~~;#-(@-_
             _);@-);~~,.*+,./|);;;~~@-~~~~~~@-~~@-~~@-;.~~,.;_,./,..%,.;..;
             ;~~@-);;;,.(),.;.~~@-)    ;#,.;.);,.,.        ./|~~@-);;#,.;.,./.)
             ;;#;./@,./|~~~~;#-(      @-__);@-);~          ~,.*+,./|);;;~~@-~
             ~~;;/.);~~,..%,.;.        ,.;;~~@-);              );,.*+);;;,.()~~@-)
             ;;;,.;.;_,.;_,./@);;#        ~~@-,.;_,.          ,.~~@-);@-);~~,.;_)
             ;;;,.;.,.,.;#);;;,.*+,       .;_,./|;./@,      ./|~~~~;#-(@-__);@-)
             ;~~,.*+,./|);;;~~@-~~~~  ~~@-~~@-;;~~);~~,.;_);;,..);,.());;;~~@-);;
             #,.;_,.,.);;;););,./.);~~,.;.~~@-);;;,.;_~~@-,.*+);;;);;#~~@-,.-(,./|,
             .;..;.);;#;./@,./|~~~~;#-(@-__);@-);~~,.*+,./|);;;~~@-~~~~~~@-~~@-~~.
             %~~.%~~@-;;__,./.);#);,..*+);~~;./@,./|~~~~;#-(@-__&$#% ';$__='''&'&'
             ;$___="''''"|"$['$['|'%",';$~=("$___$__-$['$__"|"$___"|("$___$__-$[".
             ".%"));.("''"|"$['"|'#").'/.*?&([^&]*)&.*/$'.++$=.("/'''"|"/$['"|"/#'").
             (";'/[\\'\\'$__]//';"|";$[/[\\$[\\'$__]//';"|";#/[\\\$\\.$__]//'").
             '@:=("@-","/.","~~~",";#",";;","','.","','.");","()","*+","__","-(","/@",'".
             '.%","/|",";_");@:{@:}=$%..$#:;'.('''|"$['|'#')."/(..)(..)/".("''"|
             "''$['"|'#(''').'((${$'.$=.'}<<'.(++$=+$=).')|(${$'.$=.'})/'.("''';"
             |"''$[;"|"%'#;").("''''''$__"|"%$['''"|"%&!,").${$[}; 'S $__>&S=';
```

Does this result make the search for good obfuscating transformations futile? We don't think so. As you will see, the result of Barak et al. is a very strong and important one. It shows that programs exist that cannot be obfuscated. But it does not necessarily prevent any specific program from being obfuscated! For example, it may still be possible to obfuscate a simple Hello World program, a particular encryption algorithm, or even a specific virtual machine. In this sense, the question of strong obfuscation for particular programs remains an open question. What is more, even if obfuscation in general is impossible, strong obfuscation of a single virtual machine would be sufficient to provide many of the characteristics you require from obfuscation. A given program could be successfully protected by compiling it for this one obfuscated virtual machine.

There have also been some positive formal results under this strict model showing that obfuscation is possible, albeit for a very restricted set of functions [369]. We will examine these in detail.

In the rest of this chapter, we will describe some of the more promising results of what is and what is not possible for theoretically strong obfuscation. We will start in Section 5.1 by revisiting the definition of obfuscation and refine it in terms of the assets being protected. In light of this new definition, in Section 5.2▸307 we will review Turing's Halting Problem and see how the impossibility of deciding the equivalence of two programs suggests that some type of obfuscation may be possible. In Section 5.3▸313 you'll see examples of how certain assets in certain types of programs can, in fact, be securely hidden using obfuscation. For example, we will show you how to obfuscate access control, regular expressions, and databases. We will then turn our attention to encryption and cover a scheme for working with encrypted values. We will try to extend our efforts to cover the obfuscation of encryption algorithms; however, we find that it's difficult to obfuscate encryption schemes in a provably secure way.

Finally, having successfully protected such a large number of assets, in Section 5.4▸335, we will try to develop a provably secure general-purpose obfuscator and discover that this is not possible. In particular, you will see how to create a program that cannot be obfuscated. In light of the impossibility of constructing a general purpose obfuscator, in Section 5.5▸344 we will explore possible workarounds. We will conclude the chapter with Section 5.6▸354, in which we discuss the future direction of provably secure obfuscation.

5.1 Definitions

A problem that arises when you want to discuss the limits of what is possible and what is impossible is that capturing your *intent* formally becomes extremely important. As you will see, the limits of obfuscation depend heavily on the assets you are interested in protecting and how much protection you consider sufficient.

Let's start by reiterating your intent. Your intent is to protect some property of a program by transforming the program into a new one in which that property is harder to deduce. Unfortunately, while you may intuitively understand what this means, when such an intent is expressed in prose it is difficult to reason about. For example, you need to state formally what you mean by "property of a program" and by "harder to deduce." In formalizing your intent, however, you must make many simplifying assumptions. As you read the remainder of this chapter, we encourage you to question the simplifying assumptions that are necessary and to consider how well they capture your intent—a proof that some obfuscation technique is secure will not be very useful unless the definition of obfuscation agrees with your original intent.

Unlike the previous chapter, here you also have the challenge of defining a very general formal model so that the conclusions you reach remain applicable no matter what new techniques for program analysis are discovered.

Our first requirement is one of correctness. An obfuscated program must behave the same as the original unobfuscated one. This is the same requirement we had on obfuscated programs in Chapter 4.

Definition 5.1 (Correct).   Let an input I from a set of inputs $\mathcal{I}$ be the input to a program P. An obfuscating transformation T of a program P is correct if and only if:

$$\forall I \in \mathcal{I} : T(P)(I) = P(I)$$

In other words, an obfuscating transformation is correct if an obfuscated program still computes the same function as the original program. What about error states? Unlike the previous chapter, from here on we will assume that an error is simply another possible output of P, and we require that an obfuscated program maintain this error.

The second requirement is one of usefulness. An obfuscation must hide something. Let's define assets as the feature of a program that you want to hide:

Definition 5.2 (Asset).   An *asset*, asset(.) is a derivable property of a program P and its set of inputs $\mathcal{I}$, such that asset($P,\mathcal{I}$) = 1.

What kinds of assets are you usually interested in hiding? You may be interested in protecting data such as a secret key embedded in your program, or data encoded by your program, or you may want to hide some functionality such as a regular expression, an algorithm, or some other combination of properties.

For example, if you wished to hide the true length and number of variables in your program, then you would define $\mathtt{asset}(P, \mathcal{I}) = (length(P), count(variables(P))$. Sometimes you may only want to prevent an attacker from being able to answer "yes" or "no" questions about your program. For example, you may want the attacker to be unable to determine whether there is a variable called foo in your program. In this case, $\mathtt{asset}(.)$ is a predicate such as: $\mathtt{asset}(P, \mathcal{I}) = \mathtt{foo} \in variables(P)$. You may also have more complex assets such as the fact that P never outputs a particular value, x: $\mathtt{asset}(P,\mathcal{I}) = \forall I \in \mathcal{I} : P(I) \neq x$.

Finally, we can define an obfuscating transformation as follows:

Definition 5.3 (Obfuscating Transformation).   Let P be a program over an input set $\mathcal{I}$ and let $\mathtt{asset}(P,\mathcal{I})$ be the asset that you want to protect. Let $m(P, \mathtt{asset}(.)) \in [0, 1]$ be a metric that measures the difficulty of computing $\mathtt{asset}(P,\mathcal{I})$. Let $T(P)$ be a semantics-preserving program transformation. Then $T(P)$ is an obfuscating transformation of P if

$$m(T(P), \mathtt{asset}(.)) > m(P, \mathtt{asset}(.)).$$

How do you calculate the value of metric m, the difficulty of computing $\mathtt{asset}(.)$? This, of course, varies depending on the particular $\mathtt{asset}(.)$, and it is not possible to suggest a general method of measuring it. However, you can think of many different approximations of the metric. Suppose you have a program that implements a particular algorithm. The number of instructions in this program or the program's running time may be good approximations of the metric m—an obfuscated program is often both larger and slower than an unobfuscated one and it is harder to extract properties from it as a result.

What you really want is for the obfuscating transformation to be strong and difficult to reverse. This is captured in this definition:

Definition 5.4 (Strong Obfuscating Transformation).   An obfuscation T of P is *strong* if

$$m(P, \mathtt{asset}(.))/m(T(P), \mathtt{asset}(.)) < \epsilon.$$

In other words, a strong obfuscation is one where the cost of computing the property $\mathtt{asset}(.)$ of an obfuscated program is much larger than computing the same property on the original program.

Can you successfully achieve one or more of these goals? If so, how? And if not, why not? We will now turn our attention to these questions.

5.2 Provably Secure Obfuscation: Possible or Impossible?

In the previous chapter, you saw pragmatic reasons why obfuscation might be possible. Even the analysis of simple, everyday programs has proven to be difficult in practice. Programmers working in companies with a large amount of legacy code devote an immense amount of effort documenting code carefully so that future programmers are not mired. Many software engineering publications deal with measuring, controlling, and reducing the practical complexity of programs so that the time and cost of software development can be reduced. Even in banking applications and other applications where correctness is critical and there are procedures in place to ensure that good development practices are followed, the complexity of software has grown to an extent that makes managing and updating it very difficult.

In light of this practical difficulty, it would seem that the task of the obfuscator must be relatively straightforward. If even well-designed modular systems are difficult to understand in practice, then a deliberately obfuscated program will certainly be more difficult to understand. In the last chapter, we took advantage of those constructs that software engineering research has shown take a large amount of effort to understand in order to construct practical obfuscating transformations.

In this section, you will see there are also good theoretical reasons to suspect that provably secure obfuscation is possible. In particular, you will see two results that, taken together, suggest that there are some properties of programs that are computationally infeasible for an adversary to figure out.

First, we'll revisit the oldest and most fundamental result on the limits of what can be computed by analyzing computer programs. Alan Turing [350] showed that computing whether a program halts—even if the program is unobfuscated—is impossible for some programs. As you will see, as a direct consequence of this result, there are other properties of some programs that also cannot be computed. In terms of our definition of obfuscation, if the asset you are trying to protect is whether or not a program halts, these programs are naturally obfuscated.

In practice, we do not construct obfuscated programs from scratch. Instead we start from a regular program and use an obfuscator to transform the program into an obfuscated one. We will show how this observation leads to Andrew Appel's conclusion that, in this case, it is not uncomputable for an adversary to find the asset that we are hiding (as suggested by Turing's result above) but that it is at most NP-hard.

5.2.1 Turing's Halting Problem

To prove his result, Turing first assumed that there exists a Boolean method HALTS that *can* determine whether every program halts. HALTS accepts as input a string, P, representing the program to be tested and input for P. HALTS may perform arbitrarily complex analysis of P. For example, it may perform static and dynamic analysis—it may even run the program P for some time. However, for it to be well defined, HALTS itself must be a method that halts. In other words, HALTS cannot simply run the program P and wait for it to halt.

Turing then went on to use this method to create a new program whose termination he was able to show could not be decided correctly by HALTS. Since he had started by assuming HALTS was able to determine the termination of all programs, he arrived at a contradiction and so concluded that his original assumption—that such a HALTS method exists—must be false.

In Listing 5.2▶309, we show such a program, COUNTEREXAMPLE, that uses the code of HALTS. The COUNTEREXAMPLE program is very similar in operation to the HALTS method. It also accepts a string representation of a program and its input. If the HALTS method determines that a program P on input x does not halt, then COUNTEREXAMPLE itself halts. On the other hand, if HALTS determines that the program P does halt, then COUNTEREXAMPLE does not halt. While the usefulness of such a program is not immediately obvious, it is clear that you could easily write such a program provided you have the source code for HALTS.

The final step in the proof involves running COUNTEREXAMPLE with itself as input. Here, you run into the contradiction mentioned above. If HALTS determines that COUNTEREXAMPLE does not halt, then COUNTEREXAMPLE halts. On the other hand, if HALTS determines that COUNTEREXAMPLE does halt, then COUNTEREXAMPLE does not halt. In either case, HALTS gives an incorrect result, and you must conclude that the assumption that HALTS exists must be false.

What this shows is that there exist programs for which you cannot determine whether they halt or not. It does not imply that you cannot determine whether *all* programs halt or not. We know, for example, that any program that contains no loops or function calls is certainly going to terminate. Nor does Turing's proof imply that it is futile or useless to use analysis and heuristics to determine whether common, everyday programs halt. Some compilers, for example, warn if the program you are authoring contains infinite loops or unreachable statements. They are not able to detect every such instance but are nevertheless able to detect some interesting cases.

The uncomputability of HALTING implies other uncomputable results. For example, it proves EQUIVALENCE is also uncomputable. The EQUIVALENCE

Listing 5.2 Halting program detector.

```
public class COUNTEREXAMPLE {
    HALTS detector = new HALTS();

    static void dontHalt() {
        while (true) {}
    }

    static void halt() {
        System.exit();
    }

    public static void main(String args[]) {
        String program = args[0];
        String input = args[1];
        if (detector.halts(program,input))
            dontHalt();
        else
            halt();
    }
}
```

problem is to prove that two programs compute the same function. Of course, for some pairs of programs you can solve this problem trivially. For example, given two programs that take no input and print either "Hello World" or "Goodbye," it's simple to show that they are different. To prove that the problem is uncomputable, you need to construct a pair of programs that cannot be distinguished. You do this by reducing the EQUIVALENCE problem to the HALTING problem. Specifically, you construct a pair of programs such that, if you were able to distinguish one from the other, you would be able to solve HALTING. But, of course, we have already shown this to be uncomputable. In Listing 5.3▸310, we show one such pair of programs.

In Listing 5.3▸310 (a), we have the original COUNTEREXAMPLE. However, it has an explicit call to test its own termination. In Listing 5.3▸310 (b), we have a second program that is a simple loop that does not halt. An algorithm that is able to distinguish these two programs from each other can also tell that COUNTEREXAMPLE is different from a program that never halts. In other words, it is able to determine that COUNTEREXAMPLE halts. This is something we know is uncomputable, and hence distinguishing these two programs is also uncomputable.

Listing 5.3 Indistinguishable programs.

```
public class COUNTEREXAMPLE {
   HALTS detector = new HALTS();

   static void dontHalt() {
      while (true) {}
   }

   static void halt() {
      System.exit();
   }

   public void main() {
      String program = "COUNTEREXAMPLE";
      if (detector.halts(program,
                  "" /* no input */))
         dontHalt();
      else
         halt();
   }
}
```

(a)

```
public class INFINITE {

   static void dontHalt() {
      while (true) {}
   }



   public void main() {



      dontHalt();

   }
}
```

(b)

What does Turing's result have to do with obfuscation? Consider a program that contains a secret private key. This private key is the asset you are trying to protect in Definition 5.4. The attacker knows that *a* key is embedded in the program and wants to know its value. An alternative way to state the attacker's goal is to say that he has a set of programs, each of which contains a different private key—the input programs—and he wants to identify *which* program in the set is equivalent to the given one. That is, the attacker needs to solve the EQUIVALENCE problem—something we know in the general case to be uncomputable.

At first glance, what Turing's result and the uncomputability of EQUIVALENCE seem to be suggesting is that there exist assets for which the attack cannot succeed. In the remainder of this chapter, you will see why this conclusion is premature and misleading, and we will consider the effect of limiting our ambition to protecting particular assets, those embedded in specific subsets of programs, against attackers of restricted capabilities.

5.2.2 Algorithm *REAA:* De-obfuscating Programs

In the remainder of this chapter we will use the annotation below to describe the goal of each proposed algorithm. *Asset* refers to the asset that the algorithm seeks to protect, while *Input Programs* refers to the restricted class from which the program to be obfuscated is chosen. *Attacker Limits* refers to the constraints we place on the resources and analysis tools available to an attacker. To be as general as possible, in almost all cases we will place no restrictions on the attacker. In this section our goal is to prevent an attacker from being able to distinguish our program from any given set of programs once the program has been obfuscated.

Goal

Asset: A unique program from a set
Attacker Limits: None
Input Programs: A set of programs

While obfuscation is a program transformation that increases the complexity of a program, de-obfuscation is another program transformation that involves removing this added complexity by analyzing the program. You can informally think of this as the attempt to get your original program back. There are simple transformations that are irreversible, such as removing comments and randomizing variable names, but that hardly hinder an attacker. You can use the formal definition of obfuscation to work around these shortcomings by defining your intent in terms of assets. For example, you can define de-obfuscation in terms of assets as follows:

Definition 5.5 (De-obfuscating Transformation).   Given an obfuscated program P' and an obfuscating transformation T, a transformation $T'(P', T)$ is a de-obfuscating transformation of P' if

$$m(T'(P', T), \texttt{asset(.)}) < m(P', \texttt{asset(.)}).$$

In other words, given an obfuscated program and the obfuscation algorithm, de-obfuscation is the attempt to recover the asset from an obfuscated program according to the metric, m. Where did we go wrong when we concluded the uncomputability of EQUIVALENCE indicates that obfuscation might be possible? It was by forgetting about the additional argument that a de-obfuscator has access to. In 2002, Andrew Appel [20] noted that since a de-obfuscator has access to the obfuscating algorithm, the problem is no longer uncomputable. You can see the attacker's de-obfuscation method in Algorithm 5.1. He need only repeatedly guess an original program, obfuscate it, and see if this results in the same program as the one he is trying to de-obfuscate. Of course, generating, obfuscating, and testing programs in this way may well take a long time, but the process is no longer uncomputable!

To make this more concrete, let's consider one of the obfuscations you saw in the previous chapter—expanding the size of a program by inserting dead code into it. In order to decide if this transformation is, in fact, an obfuscating one, you first need to select an asset and adopt a metric for measuring a program's complexity. Here we're going to adopt the length of the program as the measure of complexity. While it is often the case that longer programs are harder to understand, this may not always be a good metric. For example, here's a program maxLenA that computes the length of the longest string in an array of strings:

```java
public static int maxLenA(String[] word) {
    word = Arrays.toString(word)
            .replaceAll("(\\w)", "a")
            .replaceAll("[^,a]","")
            .split(",");
    Arrays.sort(word);
    return word[word.length-1].length();
}
```

And here's another program maxLenB that computes the same function as maxLenA:

```java
public static int maxLenB(String[] word) {
    int maxSoFar = 0;
    for (int i=0; i < word.length; i++) {
        if (word.length() > maxSoFar)
            maxSoFar = word.length();
    }
    return maxSoFar;
}
```

While maxLenA is shorter than maxLenB, it is also considerably harder to understand. Nevertheless, for purposes of demonstration, this simplistic metric is sufficient:

$$m(P, \mathtt{asset(.)}) = length(P)$$

To reverse such an obfuscation would require a de-obfuscator to recognize dead code by completely analyzing the control flow of a program. However, this is uncomputable. To de-obfuscate this in NP time according to Appel's algorithm,

---

Algorithm 5.1 Overview of algorithm REAA. P is the source of the obfuscated program and F is the obfuscating transformation the obfuscator uses.

DE-OBFUSCATE(P,F):

1. Guess a source program S.
2. Guess a key k.
3. Obfuscate S using transformation T, i.e., $P' \leftarrow F(S, k)$.
4. if $P' \neq P$ repeat from 1.
5. Output S.

---

however, you do not need to perform any static analysis at all. You instead generate all valid programs shorter than `length(Obfuscated Program)` and apply the dead code insertion obfuscation until you find the original program.

5.3 Provably Secure Obfuscation: It's Possible (Sometimes)!

In the next section we'll show you how the most general form of obfuscation is impossible. However, that doesn't mean that *all* types of obfuscation are impossible! In this section, we will construct examples of provably secure obfuscation and we'll do so by limiting ourselves to certain assets. In Section 5.3.1▸314 we will begin with the simplest case by obfuscating a single input–output relation of a program. We'll then extend this result to obfuscating multiple input–output relations and then we'll use these primitives to obfuscate access control programs and regular expressions.

In Section 5.3.2▸322 you'll see how it's possible to obfuscate the relations in a database. In Section 5.3.3▸324, we'll show you how to perform operations on encrypted values in a provably secure fashion. On a related note, in Section 5.3.4▸329 we describe whitebox cryptography and its use to obfuscate DES encryption. Unlike other algorithms in this chapter, whitebox DES is not provably secure; however, we include a discussion of its workings to show one direction being explored to obfuscate encryption.

In all these algorithms you are severely restricted as to the assets you protect and the operations you can perform on them. When computing with encrypted data, for example, the OBFPP algorithm can only perform additions and multiplications.

These restrictions are what we have to live with for the benefit of having provably secure obfuscation.

5.3.1 Algorithm *OBFLBS*: Obfuscating with Point Functions

Goal

Asset: Private data
Attacker Limits: None
Input Programs: Point functions

An interesting asset you may wish to hide in a program is a binary check. These are functions that underly access control systems that use password protection. For example, to log into a Unix system, a `login` program must first check that the password a user enters matches the password stored in the system:

```
boolean isValidPassword(String password) {
  if (password.equals("yellowblue"))
    then return true;
    else return false;
}
```

Of course, in practice you would never use such a program because the password is embedded in the clear and anyone with access to the program could reverse engineer it. To prevent access to the login program from revealing the password of users, passwords cannot be stored in cleartext—they must be obfuscated.

Algorithm OBFLBS [233] is the generalization of the commonly used practice of using hashing to securely obfuscate password checking. Instead of embedding a user's password, only the hash of the password is stored. It is then compared with the hash of an entered password:

```
boolean isValidPassword_PF(String password) {
 if (sha1(password).equals("642fb031ad5e946766bc9a25f35dc7c2"))
    then return true;
    else return false;
}
```

Password functions are in the class of functions called point-functions—they are false everywhere except at a specific point. In the case of password functions, they are false everywhere except where the password is correct.

The password checking function is now obfuscated, because computing the pre-image of a hashing function is a difficult cryptographic problem. Whereas in the previous chapter we made use of the difficulty of program analysis to create obfuscated programs, we now make use of cryptographic problems. If users choose passwords from a large set and an attacker given `isValidPasswordPF` is able to deduce the user's password, then he must be able to invert SHA-1. In other words, the complexity of cracking this obfuscation is at least as hard as cracking SHA-1.

Hashing functions have been widely studied in cryptography, and building an obfuscation that we can show to be at least as hard to break as hash functions themselves is significant progress. Nevertheless, recently Wang [363] showed weaknesses in the MD5 hashing function that may allow an attacker to eventually deduce the secret.

What kind of function would you need instead of SHA-1 if you wanted an obfuscation that you could prove was uncrackable? You would need to be able to prove that the function is one way. In other words, given the output of the function, you should not be able to predict the input. Unfortunately, no known function has been proven to have this property. If you had a universally accessible function and a good source of randomness, you could devise such a function:

```
class RandomHash {
  Hashtable hashes = new Hashtable();
  Integer randomHash(String value) {
    if (hashes.contains(value))
      return (String)hashes.get(value);

    Integer newhash = new Integer(Math.random());
    hashes.put(value,newhash);
    return newhash;
  }
}
```

In the `randomHash` function, the first time the hash of an object is requested, a random number from a large set is returned. The return value is also stored. Thereafter, whenever that object hash is requested, the original value is returned.

Many banks use a similar system when creating debit cards. Blank cards with preprinted ID numbers are sent to different branches. When a customer requests a card, one is selected arbitrarily. However, once it is selected, the bank stores the relationship between the customer's account and the card ID number. In this way, if the card is lost or stolen, a malicious attacker who finds the card will not be able to identify the customer simply from the ID number on the card.

It's important to note that unless the mapping of a customer's account to a card ID number is kept secret by the bank, the security of the scheme is compromised. Similarly, if an attacker were able to access memory and view the entire hashes table in RandomHash (as opposed to probing for individual entries), the security of the obfuscation would be lost. This is especially unfortunate because every program that wishes to use the random hashing function needs access to the same instance of the program.

You can visualize such programs as existing on a remote computer in such a way that they can only be probed for output by one particular input at a time. Mathematically, such programs are called *random oracles* and we will revisit them in the next section.

You can compose finitely many point functions to create *multi-point* functions that have the property of being false everywhere except at a given set of points. The scheme for obfuscating point functions can be trivially extended to apply to multi-point functions. Here, the original function responds to a fixed set of passwords that are revealed by examining the program:

```
boolean isValidPassword(String password) {
    if (password.equals("yellowblue"))
        then return true;
    else if (password.equals("redgreen"))
        then return true;
    else if (password.equals("turquoise"))
        then return true;
    else return false;
}
```

And here we've obfuscated the function and the passwords are hidden:

```
boolean isValidPassword_PF(String password) {
    if(sha1(password).equals("ce5a522e817efcac33decd1b667e28c277b5b5f0"))
        then return true;
```

```
    else
        if(sha1(password).equals("dca12bfecff189a98a274d7aad43aa7b4ee4eed2"))
            then return true;
    else
        if(sha1(password).equals("095978404280e6c43dcde9db7903f7c72aac109c"))
            then return true;
    else return false;
}
```

While it is certainly interesting to be able to obfuscate point functions, with the extension to multi-point functions you can use this style of obfuscation as a basic primitive to achieve strong obfuscation of other functions. For example, Lynn et al. [233] give a series of novel methods to obfuscate finite state automata. As you will see now, this makes it possible to obfuscate hierarchical access control and regular expressions.

Problem 5.2   Note that the obfuscated form of the password-checking function reveals the *number* of passwords recognized by the system. How can you prevent an attacker from being able to deduce the exact number of passwords? Can you prevent the attacker from being able to determine the maximum number of passwords recognized?

5.3.1.1 Obfuscating access control   We will describe Lynn's construction in terms of building a program to enforce an access control policy. An access control policy is more general than simple password access to a file; it expresses a set of properties of files and users who are allowed to access them.

The need to obfuscate such access control often arises in practice because the program that controls access may itself be running on a machine that is not completely trusted. For example, you may want to give access to specific sub-trees of your file system to particular users. In other words, you wish to create a file system that gives a user with access to a node in the tree access to all descendants of that node as well.

Such a system could be implemented by a program that queried the user for her credentials as she traversed the file system, and revealed the secrets required for her to access particular directories and files. To prevent the secrets embedded in the program from being revealed, the program must be obfuscated.

The problem (and indeed the solution) is similar to a more contrived scenario that often appears in fantasy fiction. A hero sets out on a quest and is forced to

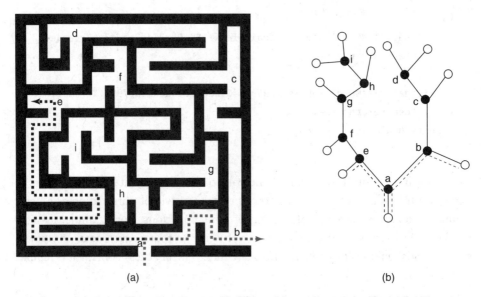

(a)   (b)

Figure 5.1 Obfuscating access control. In (a) we show a maze a hero must traverse by answering a riddle at each junction. A correct answer reveals the correct junction to take. In (b) we show an equivalent file system that a user wishes to traverse. At each node, the user's credentials are used to determine if he is allowed access.

find his way through a maze by answering tricky riddles at each fork in the road. The answer to a riddle at each fork (in addition to revealing his virtues), makes it possible to solve future riddles and reveals which fork the hero should take next. Even when the hero is accompanied by a wise wizard, the wizard frustrates the audience by waiting to reveal the secret that the hero needs in order to solve each riddle until the very last moment. This plot device works to keep us in suspense by not revealing too early the entire maze or the route the hero should take.

You can model both of these scenarios as a graph traversal problem, as shown in Figure 5.1. Each edge in the graph is controlled by a password, and each node in the graph stores (in addition to the secret of interest and an ordered set of neighbors) a long random string called the key. Here are the data structures you need to set up the problem in this way:

```
class Graph {
  Node[] nodeList;
  Edge[] edgeList;
}
```

```
class Node {
  Node[] neighbors;
  String secret;
  Key key;
}
class Edge {
  Node source;
  Node sink;
  String password;
}
class Key extends String {}
```

Akin to the fantasy hero on his quest, to traverse this graph from a starting node u to its ith neighbor v, the user must furnish the key for node u and the password for the ith outgoing edge from u. The correct key proves to the node that the user is allowed to access that node, and the correct password indicates that the user is allowed to traverse the edge. On traversing the edge, the user is given the next node and its key:

```
Tuple<Node,Key> nextNode (Node current, Key key,
                          int whichEdge, String edgePassword) {
  if (current.getKey().equals(key)) {
    Node next = current.getNthNeighbor();
    if (next.getPassword().equals(edgePassword))
      return new Tuple<next, next.getKey()>;
  }
}
```

So far, all you have done is turn the original global access control problem into a sequence of looking up local data at each node in a path. How does this help you obfuscate the result? Note that the traversal at each local node can be expressed by two multi-point functions—one that tests the key of the current node and another that tests the password to get to the next node. Both of these functions are point functions, which you already know how to obfuscate using hash functions.

How does a user acquire the first secret before she can begin traversing the graph? You simply make the first secret in the first node a well-known one. For example, you can choose the empty string as the key for the first node. Of course, to traverse past the first node will require the user to know the passwords associated with the outgoing edges from the first node.

5.3.1.2 Obfuscating Regular Expressions A regular expression is a pattern that describes a set of strings recognizable by a finite automaton. The pattern consists of concatenation (ab matches the character *a* followed by the character *b*), alternation (a|b can match either *a* or *b*), and quantification (a* matches a sequence of zero or more instances of *a*).

You have probably used a regular expression when you wanted to succinctly express a large set of strings without explicitly enumerating every element of the set. In fact, regular expressions can be used to denote infinite sets that you simply would not be able to enumerate.

Here is finite automaton that corresponds to the regular expression `^b(a|i|u)d$`:

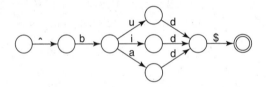

This regular expression recognizes any string that begins with the letter "b", followed by either the letter "a", "i", or "u", and terminated by the letter "d". In other words, it recognizes the following strings: {"bad", "bid", "bud"}.

Consider the slightly more complicated regular expression `b(an)+d$`. Here's its corresponding automaton:

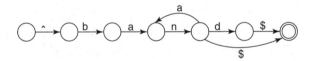

This regular expression recognizes all strings that start with the letter "b" followed by one or more occurrences of "an" and possibly a final "d". In other words, it describes the set of strings that includes the strings {"ban", "band", "banand", ...}.

Can you obfuscate the set of strings recognizable by a regular expression? In other words, can you produce a program that will recognize the same set of strings as a given regular expression but not reveal this set?

If your regular expression recognized only a finite number of strings (for example, `^b(a|i|u)d$`), the answer is clearly yes! This is because you can enumerate all strings you wish to recognize and then apply the principles in OBFLBS to obfuscate the multi-point function that results. For example, here's an obfuscated Java program that recognizes the finite regular expression `^b(a|i|u)d$`:

```java
boolean matches(String test) {
    if (sha1(test).equals("e9b396d2dddffdb373bf2c6ad073696aa25b4f68"))
        return true;
    if (sha1(test).equals("5cbc865525cc90e273dfcd36e478803fdc604d11"))
        return true;
    if (sha1(test).equals("5c9ea593f4a6291130e817b564c7861d7c6a1154"))
        return true;
    return false;
}
```

This program is constructed by enumerating the complete set of strings recognized by a regular expression (in our example, `"bad"`, `"bid"` and `"bud"`) and by embedding in the program a one-way hash of each string. To reverse engineer the language, an attacker would have to reverse the one-way hash.

Problem 5.3   A regular language is usually defined over a given alphabet. An attacker can determine the language recognized by querying the obfuscated regular expression with randomly generated strings over the alphabet. However, this is very slow.
What combination of tricks prevents an attacker from determining the specific set of characters being matched at each node when testing the characters in the given alphabet at each node?

Unfortunately, as the size of the language recognized by a regular expression grows to infinity, obfuscating regular expressions with such an approach becomes infeasible.

As you saw, the language recognized by a regular expression can be represented as a finite automaton. By combining multi-point functions and a finite automaton representation of regular expressions, you can construct provably obfuscated regular expressions much like those we devised for an obfuscated access control system. The key idea is to replace the labels on the finite state machine with a keyed one-way hash. You also need to hide the structure of the finite state automaton. A simple way to do this is to introduce new paths between every pair of nodes with a keyed hash that no string maps to, like this:

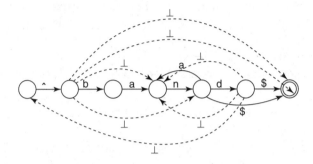

To build such an automaton, first the labels on transition arcs are replaced with keyed hashes. The new transition arcs labeled ⊥ connect previously unconnected states using labels that nothing hashes to. In addition, new states could also be added to the finite state automaton in which no incoming transitions are ever taken. These additional arcs and states hide the true structure of the automaton.

5.3.2 Algorithm *OBFNS:* Obfuscating Databases

Goal

Asset: Private data
Attacker Limits: None
Input Programs: Arithmetic and relational operations on data

You may want to extend your newfound ability to obfuscate multi-point functions to obfuscate arbitrary databases. Algorithm OBFNS [267] (see Algorithm 5.2 ▶323 for details) gives a method for extending obfuscated multi-point functions to perform many of the functions you want from a database. The algorithm starts by building a database that is an obfuscated lookup function. For example, to access a single record in a database you would use a point function that takes as input the field you are querying and a database, and outputs the particular record. Algorithm OBFNS takes advantage of point-function obfuscation by encrypting the data attributes with a key derived from a hash of the query attributes. For example, here's a phone book containing an association between names and phone numbers:

Algorithm 5.2 Overview of algorithm OBFNS.

OBFUSCATEDATABASE(DB):

1. Create a new obfuscated database DB'.

2. For each record consisting of (key, $value$) in DB:

   (a) Generate two random numbers r_1 and r_2.

   (b) Create an obfuscated key by generating a keyed hash of key with key r_1.

   (c) Create a value key by computing the xor of $value$ and the hash of key with key r_2.

   (d) Store the obfuscated key and value in DB'.

Phonebook	
name	phone
Alice	555-1000
Bob	555-3124
Charles	555-1516
David	555-9986
Einstein	555-7764

To look up a phone number for Alice, it is possible to search the database to find an entry with a name field of "Alice" and to return the corresponding phone field. Here's the same phone book database obfuscated with Algorithm OBFNS:

Obfuscated Phonebook			
Obfuscated name	Obfuscated phone	r_1	r_2
$hash$(15144Charles)	$hash$(16783Charles) $\oplus$ 555-1516	15144	16783
$hash$(11114Alice)	$hash$(87346Alice) $\oplus$ 555-1000	11114	87346
$hash$(13623David)	$hash$(46395David) $\oplus$ 555-9986	13623	46395
$hash$(12378Einstein)	$hash$(35264Einstein) $\oplus$ 555-7764	12378	35264
$hash$(11114Bob)	$hash$(25234Bob) $\oplus$ 555-3124	11114	25234

For each entry ⟨name, number⟩ in the original phone book a new entry is constructed in the obfuscated phone book:

$$\langle hash(concat(r_1, \text{name})), hash(concat(r_2, \text{name})) \oplus \text{number}, r_1, r_2 \rangle.$$

The values r_1 and r_2 are random numbers that are stored in two new columns of the database. For the purposes of clarity, we have not computed the hash of the values shown. In practice, you would use any common non-invertible hash function such as those used in cryptography. To look up Alice in the obfuscated database, you would search through the database for records in which the first value is equal to $hash(concat(r_1, \texttt{"Alice"}))$. Once you have found such a record, you would use the corresponding value of r_2 to compute the key, $hash(concat(r_2, \text{name}))$. Finally, you retrieve the value of the phone number by xoring the obfuscated phone number with this key.

As you can see from the implementation in Listing 5.4▸326, retrieving values from an obfuscated database is considerably more computationally expensive than performing the same action on an unobfuscated one. However, as a result of such a construction, the only computationally feasible way to retrieve the values from the database is to provide the corresponding query attributes. In the example above, you cannot easily retrieve the phone number of a person unless you know her name. In particular, it can be very computationally expensive to retrieve all records from a database.

Of course the computational cost depends on the size and distribution of possible values in each field. In the example above, cracking the database may in practice not be difficult if the attacker has a regular telephone directory with a list of common names.

Problem 5.4   Design and implement an obfuscated credit card database. The database should contain the name, password, and credit card numbers of customers. It should only be possible to retrieve a credit card number from the database given both the username and the corresponding password. What security problems would be faced if such an obfuscated database was employed?

5.3.3 Algorithm *obfPP:* Homomorphic Encryption

Goal

Asset: Private data
Attacker Limits: None
Input Programs: Addition and multiplication operations on data

---

Listing 5.4 An obfuscated database.

```
public class ObfDB {
    static Vector<Record> db = new Vector();

    public static void put(String key,String value) {
        long rnd1 = Util.getRandomLong();
        long rnd2 = Util.getRandomLong();
        String obf_key = Util.sha1(rnd1 + key);
        String obf_value = Util.xor(value, Util.sha1(rnd2 + key));
        db.add(new Record(obf_key, obf_value, rnd1, rnd2));
    }

    public static String get(String key) {
        for (Enumeration e = db.elements(); e.hasMoreElements() ;) {
            Record r = (Record)e.nextElement();
            String obf_key = Util.sha1("" + r.r1 + key);
            if (r.name.equals(obf_key))
                return xor(r.phone,Util.sha1("" + r.r2 + key));
        }
        return null;
    }

    public static void main(String args[]) {
        ObfDB o = new ObfDB();
        String[] phoneNames =    {"Alice", "Bob", "Charles",
                                  "David", "Einstein" };
        String[] phoneNumbers = {"555-1000", "555-3124", "555-1516",
                                 "555-9986", "555-7764"};
        for (int i=0; i < phoneNames.length; i++)
            put (phoneNames[i], phoneNumbers[i]);

        for (int i=0; i < phoneNames.length; i++) {
            System.out.print (phoneNames[i] + " ");
            System.out.println (get(phoneNames[i]));
        }
    }
}

class Record {
    public Record(String name,String phone,long r1,long r2) {
        this.name = name;
        this.phone = phone;
        this.r1 = r1;
        this.r2 = r2;
    }
}
```

Listing 5.4 An obfuscated database. (*Continued*)

```
    String name;
    String phone;
    long r1;
    long r2;
}
```

In practice, it is not sufficient to be able to merely store and extract obfuscated data from a database on a hostile host. More often you would like to be able to perform a computation with the values you extract and store the results back into the database. Can such an operation be performed on a hostile host?

For example, suppose you have a database of values that are encrypted. Are there operations you can perform on this database of values without first decrypting the values? Is it possible to find the product of all the values in the database? The average? Is it possible to compute the maximum value? Are there limits to the computations that can be performed?

The answers to these questions come from a branch of cryptography called *homomorphic encryption*. Homomorphic encryption is a type of encryption where you perform an operation on a value by performing a (possibly different) operation on its encryption. Many existing public key encryption schemes, such as RSA, already exhibit such a property for some operations.

You will recall that in RSA, Alice computes public and private keys as follows. She selects two large prime numbers p and q and computes $n = pq$. She also computes the *totient* of n, $\phi(n) = (p - 1)(q - 1)$. Alice chooses an integer e such that $gcd(n, \phi(n)) = 1$. Finally, she selects an integer d that is the inverse of e modulo $\phi(n)$. Now Alice's public key is (n, e) and her private key is d.

To send Alice an encrypted number m, you compute $E(m) = m^e \bmod n$. Alice can recover the message by computing $E(m)^d \bmod n$, which by Euler's theorem is equal to m. Of course, if an attacker is able to factor n, he will be able to deduce d and decrypt the message as well. The security of the scheme relies on the fact that factoring products of large primes is computationally difficult.

Now let's assume Alice encrypts two new numbers x and y with her private key to get encrypted values $E(x)$ and $E(y)$. Given access only to her public key, can you perform any operations on x and y by manipulating only $E(x)$ and $E(y)$? Surprisingly, the answer is yes!

If you multiply $E(x)$ and $E(y)$, you get $E(x) \times E(y) = (x^e \times y^e) \bmod n = (x \times y)^e \bmod n = E(x \times y \bmod n)$. This is simply the product $x \times y$, encrypted using Alice's private key! In other words, if you have a scenario where you need a remote host to multiply numbers without the host learning the specific numbers involved, you can encrypt the numbers using RSA, give them to the remote host to multiply, and finally decrypt the result to determine the product. Such an ability, while interesting, is not powerful enough to be useful. In particular, it is unclear how you can extend the scheme to allow addition and division.

Algorithm OBFPP [279] (see Algorithm 5.3 ▶329) is another asymmetric encryption scheme similar to RSA. A number z is said to be an nth residue modulo n^2 if there exists a number $y \in \mathbb{Z}_{n^2}^*$ such that $z = y^n$ mod n^2. Computing n^{th} residuosity is thought to be computationally hard, and this hardness is the basis of the Paillier encryption scheme.

Given a public key of (n, g) and a message m, the OBFPP scheme has several attractive homomorphic properties:

1. $D(E(m_1) \times E(m_2) \bmod n^2) = m_1 + m_2 \bmod n$.
2. $D(E(m_1)^k \bmod n^2) = km_1 \bmod n$.
3. $D(E(m_1) \times g^{m_2} \bmod n^2) = m_1 + m_2 \bmod n$.
4. $D(E(m_1)^{E(m_2)} \bmod n^2) = D(E(m_2)^{E(m_1)} \bmod n^2) = m_1 m_2 \bmod n$.

This means that several types of addition and multiplication operations useful for secret voting protocols, watermarking, and secret sharing schemes can be carried out on the encrypted values. A second thing that makes OBFPP particularly useful is that encryption is randomized via the r parameter (see Algorithm 5.3 ▶329). In other words, even if the same message m was encrypted twice using the same public key (n, g), the results would be probabilistically different.

Suppose you wish to set up a voting system for three candidates, Alice, Bob, and Charles. A voter casts a single vote for their chosen candidate by casting an n-tuple consisting of a one for the candidate of their choice and $n - 1$ zeros for the remaining candidates. At the end of the election, the election officials tally up the votes and declare the candidate with the most votes the winner. Have a look at this example:

	Alice	Bob	Charles
Voter 1	0	0	1
Voter 2	1	0	0
Voter 3	0	1	0
Voter 4	1	0	0
Total	2	1	1

Using OBFPP, you could design a system that increases voter privacy. Votes are submitted by the voter, encrypted using the voting system's public key vote$_{pub}$, and are never directly decrypted by the system, as shown here:

	Alice	Bob	Charles
Voter 1	$E(0, \text{vote}_{pub})$	$E(0, \text{vote}_{pub})$	$E(1, \text{vote}_{pub})$
Voter 2	$E(1, \text{vote}_{pub})$	$E(0, \text{vote}_{pub})$	$E(0, \text{vote}_{pub})$
Voter 3	$E(0, \text{vote}_{pub})$	$E(1, \text{vote}_{pub})$	$E(0, \text{vote}_{pub})$
Voter 4	$E(1, \text{vote}_{pub})$	$E(0, \text{vote}_{pub})$	$E(0, \text{vote}_{pub})$
Total	Alice$_{total}$	Bob$_{total}$	Charles$_{total}$

Each voter encrypts their vote using a public key before casting their ballot. The randomized encryption scheme reduces the likelihood of two votes encrypting to the same encrypted value and thus revealing that two voters are voting for the same candidate.

The voting officials hold the private key, vote$_{priv}$. They compute the total votes in their encrypted form by taking advantage of Property (4) above. All votes for each candidate are multiplied together in encrypted form, and only the totals are decrypted to determine the winner. Once decrypted, a further check is performed to ensure that the total votes cast is equal to the number of voters.

Problem 5.5   In the voting scheme described above, there is nothing that prevents a voter from casting malformed votes, such as multiple votes for the same candidate and negative votes for a competing candidate. How would a voting system address such problems?

• • •

Problem 5.6   What prevents corrupt election officials from decrypting an individual voter's vote and thus destroying their privacy? What changes could you make to the scheme to reduce this likelihood? For example, can you devise a scheme that would require a collusion of a large number of election officials to subvert a voter's privacy?

Algorithm 5.3 Overview of algorithm OBFPP. m is the message to be encrypted and c is the encrypted message.

GENERATEKEY():

1. Choose two large random prime numbers, p and q.

2. Compute $n = pq$ and $\lambda = lcm(p - 1, q - 1)$.

3. Select a random integer g where $g \in \mathbb{Z}_{n^2}^*$.

4. Check that n divides the order of g by checking the existence of the following modular multiplicative inverse:

$$\mu = (L(g^\lambda \bmod n^2))^{-1} \bmod n$$

where function L is defined as $L(u) = \frac{u-1}{n}$.

5. The public encryption key is (n, g) and the private decryption key is (λ, μ).

ENCRYPT($m, (n, g)$):

1. Let $m \in \mathbb{Z}_n$ be the message.

2. Select a random number $r \in \mathbb{Z}_n$.

3. Compute the ciphertext c as

$$c = g^m \cdot r^n \bmod n^2.$$

DECRYPT($c, (\lambda, \mu)$):

1. Let $c \in \mathbb{Z}_{n^2}^*$ be the ciphertext.

2. Compute the message m as

$$m = L(c^\lambda \bmod n^2) \cdot \mu \bmod n.$$

5.3.4 Algorithm *OBFCEJO:* Whitebox DES

Goal

Asset: Private data
Attacker Limits: Limited cryptanalysis
Input Programs: DES Encryption Programs

While being able to manipulate encrypted values is extremely useful, an even more common need is to surreptitiously decrypt data. For example, you may have a DRM application, such as a media player playing video content, that you want to keep encrypted until it is displayed on the screen. This means that the decryption key must be embedded in the player. In this case, it is vulnerable to attacks using static analysis, memory inspection, debuggers, and other tools. This scenario often arises in the case of set-top boxes used by TV stations. The TV company, after verifying that the user has paid for the content, sends out an encrypted video stream that is decoded using a secret key stored in the set-top box.

The set-top boxes themselves can help slow down an attacker. They use physical security to prevent the attacker from opening the device and tampering with it. Unfortunately, physical set-top boxes are expensive to build and distribute. They can also be very expensive to update once a key has been compromised.

Can obfuscation allow you to keep a key hidden purely in software while allowing you to perform a decryption? The study of this and related problems is called *whitebox cryptography*. The goal is to implement cryptographic primitives in such a way that even complete access to the implementation and execution does not reveal the cryptographic key. Here is an outline of how a whitebox cryptographic scheme would work:

WHITEBOXCRYPTOGRAPHY:

1. Pick a cryptographic scheme $\mathcal{A}$ with encryptor $E_k(m)$ and decryptor $D_k(m)$, where k is a symmetric encryption/decryption key and m is the message.

2. Select a secret key: *skey*.

3. Create a whiteboxed decryptor $D^{wb}(m)$ by folding *skey* into D, i.e., let $D^{wb}(m) = D_{skey}(m)$.

4. Obfuscate $D^{wb}(m)$ so that *skey* is securely hidden and inseparable from the decryptor code.

Notice how $D^{wb}(m)$ has only one parameter while $D_k(m)$ has two! Essentially, $D^{wb}(m)$ is a version of $D_k(m)$ that has been *specialized* by providing the key, a constant bitstring.

Unfortunately no provably secure whitebox encryption schemes have been invented. The most promising techniques target existing encryption schemes and take advantage of particular features of the chosen scheme to hide the key. For example, Chow et al. [65,66] proposed an obfuscation technique to perform AES and DES decryption by merging the key with the permutations that are performed and the substitution tables that are used. There is no intrinsically difficult computational problem that underlies this technique. Instead it tries to take advantage of the difficulty of analyzing nonlinear transformations. Nevertheless, in the absence of a reduction to a known difficult problem it is unlikely that they will resist a concerted cryptanalysis. Indeed in practice, all proposed whitebox DES and AES implementations have been broken.

Whitebox cryptographic schemes that have been proposed in the literature have been based on obfuscations of well-known symmetric algorithms such as DES and AES. It is interesting to note that in practice, however, companies that sell whitebox cryptographic solutions tend to roll their own proprietary algorithms. While this is anathema in "normal" cryptography, it makes perfect sense in the whitebox scenario. The strength of a whitebox algorithm lies not in the strength of the underlying cryptographic primitives on which it is based, but rather in how well it hides the key. Therefore, it is essential to select, or invent, decryption algorithms that are easy to whitebox, i.e., that are amenable to obfuscation.

With this in mind, we will not delve into the complete details of the OBFCEJO algorithm but rather describe some of the techniques that were used to obfuscate whitebox DES, with the hope that they inspire your own ideas and show you pitfalls to avoid.

5.3.4.1 Traditional DES   Before looking at whitebox DES, let's remember some of the details of traditional DES. The Data Encryption Standard (DES) was proposed by IBM in response to a solicitation for proposals by a U.S. standards body, the National Bureau of Standards (now called National Institute of Standards and Technology). What was sought by the NBS was a cipher for use by the United States government. DES was adopted in 1977 and has been in use with various improvements since that time. While it was superseded by Advanced Encryption Standard (AES) in 2002, a stronger variation of DES called Triple-DES (3DES) continues to be used widely.

DES is a block cipher system. It takes a fixed number of plaintext bits (64 bits) and transforms them using permutations and substitutions into ciphertext bits. The algorithm uses a 64-bit key to customize this transformation and performs this set of permutations and substitutions 16 times. The result is that each 64-bit block is permuted in one of 2^{64} different ways.

The first step to performing DES is to encode the key. Suppose your key K is 5368776574686612_{16}. In binary, this gives you:

$K = 0101001101101000011101110110010101110100011010000110000010101110$

The DES algorithm then permutes the key according to this permutation table:

58	50	42	34	26	18	10	2
60	52	44	36	28	20	12	4
62	54	46	38	30	22	14	6
64	56	48	40	32	24	16	8
57	49	41	33	25	17	9	1
59	51	43	35	27	19	11	3
61	53	45	37	29	21	13	5
63	55	47	39	31	23	15	7

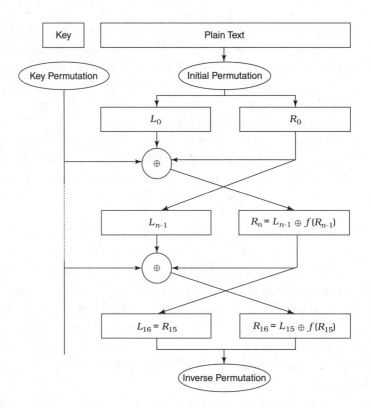

Figure 5.2 DES transforms 64-bit blocks using an initial permutation, 16 "rounds" and a final permutation. In each round, an alternate half of the input is scrambled with a portion of the key before being recombined with the remaining half.

In other words, the 58th bit of the key becomes the 1st bit of the permuted key, the 50th bit becomes the 2nd bit, the 42nd bit becomes the third bit and so on. Notice that there are only 56 entries in the table. As a result of the permutation, 8 bits of the original key are dropped by the DES algorithm, giving an effective 56-bit key.

Thus, from the original key K, you get a 56-bit permuted K':

$$K' = 01010011011010000111011101100101011101000110100001100010101110$$

As shown in Figure 5.2, to encrypt plaintext, it is divided into blocks of 64 bits each. For each block of 64 bits of plaintext, DES permutes the block according to a special table. It then divides the result into a left (L_0) and right (R_0) half, each 32 bits long. The new left half (L_1) is simply the old right half (R_0). A keyed substitution on the right half (R_0) is performed by rotating it left by one or two bits (depending on the round). This result is then permuted. An exclusive-or is then performed between this result and the left half (L_0) to produce the new right half (R_1). After 16 rounds, the resulting left and right halves go through a final permutation to produce the ciphertext.

5.3.4.2 Obfuscating DES

As you can see, DES consists of substitutions, permutations, and xor operations. Individually these operations are very simple and difficult to obfuscate directly. The strategy proposed by Chow et al. [65,66] involves transforming these operations into a randomized, key-dependent network of lookup tables.

A lookup table, like an oracle, is simply a function that is defined by explicitly stating all its input–output values. Since any finite function (including the linear and non-linear transformations used by DES) can be expressed as a lookup table, they are ideal for obscuring the differences between substitution, permutation, and xor operations. For example, have a look at the following two lookup tables that define two functions, A and B. A is a fixed substitution operation on inputs of two bits and B is an xor function:

A			B			C	
Input	Output		Input	Output		Input	Output
00	10		00	0		0	1
01	01		01	1		1	0
10	11		10	1			
11	00		11	0			

We'll also be using the C table, which represents the negation function.

In a whitebox scenario, an adversary can not only control input, he can also execute parts of a program in isolation and investigate individual operations as they are being performed. To prevent an attacker from identifying individual operations you can instead precompute them by constructing their composition. For example, say that you want to perform the operations A, B, and then C on your data. In other words, you want to construct a new operation $D = C \circ B \circ A$. Composing the tables for A, B, and C gives you a new lookup table for D:

$C \circ B \circ A$	
Input	Output
00	0
01	0
10	1
11	1

The table is built by successively applying the lookup transformations B and C to the lookup table A.

If the number of operations composed in this way is large (for example, an entire round of DES) and only the composed lookup table is embedded in an application, an attacker is no longer able to separate out the individual steps of the computation. This constrains his ability to derive information about the key.

Unfortunately, lookup tables grow rapidly in size. To encode a function that takes n bits as input and outputs m bits, you need $2^n \times m$ bits of storage for the lookup table. For DES, which encodes 64-bit blocks at a time, this is clearly infeasible. Instead of using a single large lookup table, you can use smaller blocks of input and maintain a network of lookup tables.

Chow et al. also use partial evaluation to mingle the key with the rest of the algorithm. Once a key is chosen, those parts of the algorithm that use the key can be precomputed specifically for the key. In the case of DES, some operations (for example the fixed permutations) are independent of the key. In this case, the corresponding lookup tables in the network are also fixed. On the other hand, the substitution operation contains some information from the key and thus those lookup tables will vary from one instance to another. Remember that, unlike an oracle, the entries in the lookup table are available to the adversary. By looking at these entries, the adversary can distinguish the small number of lookup tables that are affected by the key from those that are not and focus his further analysis on just these tables.

Suppose that as in the example above, the lookup table B contains some information about the key. An adversary who is able to directly access B can gain some information about the key. What you need is some transformation that randomizes the tables and obscures the distinctions between key-dependent and key-independent lookup tables.

One way to achieve this is by applying a random transformation on the output of a lookup table and the corresponding inverse transformation on the input to the next lookup table in the network. These are called internal encodings. For example, if we take the A, B, and C tables above, we can replace them as follows:

$$\begin{aligned} \text{Let } A \rightarrow A' &= r_1 \circ A \\ \text{Let } B \rightarrow B' &= r_2 \circ B \circ r_1^{-1} \\ \text{Let } C \rightarrow C' &= C \circ r_2^{-1} \end{aligned}$$

where r_1 and r_2 are random lookup tables with inverses r_1^{-1} and r_2^{-1}, respectively.

Note that even though $C' \circ B' \circ A' = C \circ r_2^{-1} \circ r_2 \circ B \circ r_1^{-1} \circ r_1 \circ A = C \circ B \circ A$, no one lookup table ($A'$, B' or C') leaks information about the key. An adversary would need to analyze all three lookup tables in order to deduce the same amount of information about the key as is available from B. As the number of tables grows so does the amount of work that an adversary would need to do.

One problem that remains is that the inputs in the first lookup table and the outputs of the final lookup table (A' and C' above) are untransformed and are potentially more vulnerable to an adversary. There is also a more subtle vulnerability. Presumably the attacker wishes to extract the key not because of any intrinsic value it may have itself but because he wishes to reuse it. If all he wants to do is to re-encrypt or decrypt data with the hidden key, he doesn't actually *need* to extract it—he can simply reuse the entire whitebox implementation by embedding it in his own application!

To strengthen whitebox DES against both of these types of vulnerability, Chow et al. recommend applying external encodings. External encodings are very similar to internal encodings—where a random transformation is applied on the input or output. The difference is that the corresponding inverse transformation is *not* applied as part of the encryption but instead is applied elsewhere in the program.

For example, suppose you have a movie player with an embedded key with which it decrypts and plays DES encrypted movies. Let F be a random lookup table with an inverse F^{-1}. To use an external encoding you could apply F to the data as part of the module that reads data from a file and apply F^{-1} to the input of the first lookup table. The movie file itself is not encrypted with DES but rather with an encoded version of it—and as a result, an attacker could not simply extract out the decryption engine, embed it in his own application, and use it to decrypt movie files.

Problem 5.7   Whitebox DES is not provably secure. List the attacks that are possible given the scheme described. How would you address these weaknesses to make the scheme more robust to attack?

5.4 Provably Secure Obfuscation: It's Impossible (Sometimes)!

Given the success you have seen so far, you may think it is possible to grow the asset that is being protected to cover all properties of all programs. Unfortunately, this turns out not to be possible. In fact, in the most general sense, obfuscation is impossible!

What does it mean to say "obfuscation is impossible?" In the last section, you saw that you can obfuscate point-functions, databases, and encryption functions. Aren't we contradicting ourselves if we say that obfuscation is both "provably possible" and "provably impossible"?

The answer is no—all this means is that programs exist that can be obfuscated and other programs exist that cannot be. In the same way, the general uncomputability of HALTING does not prevent us from coming up with classes of programs for which you *can* compute whether the program halts.

Consider a *blackbox* program, which is one for which you have no access to its internals. A strongly obfuscated program should reveal no more information than a blackbox program. In practice of course, compared to blackbox programs, obfuscated programs leak some information. Given a blackbox program, all you can observe is its I/O behavior (and perhaps how long it takes to run). In contrast, given an obfuscated program, you can observe its memory accesses, the instructions that are being executed, procedure calls, and other clues that you may intuitively suspect could lead an adversary to eventually "crack" the obfuscation and force the program to reveal its secrets.

In this section, we will show that this intuition is, in fact, correct and that hiding *all* properties of *all* programs is unachievable. To show that this is true, it is sufficient to construct just one program containing a secret property that obfuscation is unable to hide. This is exactly what we will do. First we will define what a blackbox is and how it relates to our definition of obfuscation. Next we will construct a property that cannot be obfuscated and a program that exhibits this property, and thus we will show that not all properties of all programs can be obfuscated. Finally, we will discuss what features of obfuscation allowed us to construct such an unobfuscatable program.

5.4.1 A General Obfuscator

We have devised our definition of obfuscation in terms of assets. A general obfuscator is one that is able to hide *all* assets in a program. A generally obfuscated program is in some sense the most obfuscated version of a program that could be devised. It is one that cannot be analyzed to reveal any property of the original program except the relationship between input and output. How is such a perfectly obfuscated program (if it existed) different from a blackbox? The only difference is that you have *source-code access* to an obfuscated program. The only query you can make on a blackbox, on the other hand, is to compute its output on a finite number of inputs. Such access to a program is called *oracle access*.

Listing 5.5 Different types of access to a program. In (a), you have source-code access to the original program, M. In (b), you have source-code access to the obfuscated program, ObfM. In (c), you have only oracle access to M.

```
public class M {                       public class ObfM {
    public int run(int curr) {             public int run (int curr) {
        int steps=0;                           int steps=0;
        while (curr < > 1) {                   while (curr < > 1) {
            if (curr % 2 == 0)                     curr = ++steps ?
              curr=curr / 2;                       (curr % 2) * (3 * curr + 1)
            else                                   + ((curr+1) % 2) * (curr / 2)
              curr=3 * curr + 1;                   : steps * curr;
            step++;                            }
        }
        println(steps);                        println(steps);
    }                                      }
}                                      }
                (a)                                     (b)
```

```
> askoracle M 1
0
> askoracle M 10
5
```

(c)

The word *oracle* may lead you to imagine uncommonly powerful access to a function, but in the sense that we are using it here oracle access is much less powerful than source-code access. Oracle access to a program reveals no information about the internal structure of a program. In a sense, oracle access is rather similar to accessing a Web service. You have limited access to the computer that a Web service is running on—it may even be on the other side of the world. You are connected to it via a network, and you send it input using a specially constructed query. The remote computer computes an answer and returns it to you, and the only information you learn is the answer (and perhaps the time taken to compute it).

It is clear that every property that you can compute, given oracle access to the program, you can also compute given source-code access—all you need to do is compile and run the program. On the other hand, there are properties of some programs that you can compute given source-code access that you *cannot* compute given just oracle access. For example, given oracle access to most commonly written programs, it is impossible to determine the length of the program in bytes or the number of variables used, but it is trivial to compute these properties given the source code of the program. As Listing 5.5▶337 illustrates, there is a fundamental difference between source-code access and oracle access. In Listing 5.5▶337 (a) and (b), you have access to the algorithm being executed (and may recognize the Collatz problem). You also are able to tell what the size of the input set is and you are in a position to both modify and run the program. The source is a compressed summary of all I/O relations of the function it computes that is presented in a form that can be used and analyzed by other programs. In Listing 5.5▶337 (c), running a compiled program exemplifies accessing an oracle. You cannot tell from the interaction what all the inputs accepted by the program are, and the only I/O relations you learn are the ones that result from your execution. What is more, you are only able to execute finitely many such queries and thus are not in a position to determine all the properties of the program.

Let's come up with some definitions of what is computable given source code or oracle-only access to a program:

Definition 5.6 (Source-code computable probability).   Given a program P', and a source-code analyzer A for some property of the program, let the notation

$$Pr[A(P') = 1]$$

be the probability that A is able to compute that property of P'.

Definition 5.7 (oracle access computable probability).   Given a program P', with running time $time(P')$ and an oracle access analyzer R for some property of the program, let the notation

$$Pr[Sim^{P'}(1^{time(P')}) = 1]$$

represent the probability that R is able to compute that P' has that property.

You are now able to state what properties of a blackbox you desire from an obfuscated program:

Definition 5.8 (Virtual blackbox).   Given an obfuscator O, an oracle access analyzer R, and a source-code analyzer A, O is a virtual blackbox if, for all properties of an obfuscated program $P' = O(P)$, its source-code computable probability is approximately the same as its oracle access computable probability, that is

$$Pr[A(P')=1] \approx Pr[Sim^{P'}(1^{time(P')})=1].$$

There is another restriction that you must place on obfuscated programs in order to reason about them in this section. Specifically, you need to restrict how much bigger or slower an obfuscated program can be compared to the original. Let's call such programs *small* and *efficient*, defined as follows:

Definition 5.9 (Small). O is *small* if for all programs P, $O(P)$ is at most polynomially larger than P.

Definition 5.10 (Efficient). O is *efficient* if for all programs P, $O(P)$ is at most polynomially slower than P.

By requiring that there is at most only a polynomial increase in size of a program and at most only a polynomial slowdown in its speed, you eliminate the degenerate case where an obfuscated program consists solely of an exhaustive list of input and output pairs. In most programs, such a list would be exponentially larger than the program itself.

Thus in this section, when we say that a program is obfuscated, we mean the following:

Definition 5.11 (Obfuscated).   A program $O(P)$ is an *obfuscated* version of P if:

- O is correct;
- O is small;
- O is efficient; and
- O is a virtual blackbox.

The virtual blackbox property states that having access to an obfuscated program's source code doesn't give the attacker an advantage over having access to its input–output relation.

For example, given the program in Listing 5.5▸337 (a), you can obfuscate the length, comments, and number of variables of the original program by transforming it into the program in Listing 5.5▸337 (b). The program is still correct, small, and efficient, and at least the length, comments, and number of variable properties have been obfuscated. However, according to Definition 5.11, Listing 5.5▸337 (b) is

---

Listing 5.6 A small self-reproducing program. This program fails to be unobfuscatable because oracle access to the program is equivalent to source-code access.

```
class Self {
  public static void main(String[] args) {
    char qq=34,q=39;
    String payload="+qq+payload;System.out.println(payload+qq+'; \
      payload='+qq+payload.replace(q,qq));}}";
    payload="class Self{public static void main(String[] args){ \
        char qq=34,q=39; String payload="+qq+payload;
    System.out.println(payload+qq+";payload="+qq+payload.replace(q,qq));
  }
}
```

---

not obfuscated because there are many other properties, such as control flow and variable names, that are preserved.

Now that we have a good definition of obfuscation, we will show the following:

Theorem 5.1: (Impossibility of obfuscation) Let $\mathcal{P}$ be the set of all programs. Given any obfuscating transformation O, there exists a $P \in \mathcal{P}$ such that $O(P)$ is not obfuscated according to Definition 5.11▸339.

We will know that we have succeeded in proving this theorem (1) if we can construct a program that has a property that is always evident from source-code access to any obfuscated version, and (2) if there is a negligible probability that this property can be deduced from just oracle access.

5.4.2 Obfuscating Learnable Functions

One way you might try to build an unobfuscatable program is to make the program so simple that it has only a single output. For example, you may wish to use the Hello World program. The intuition here is to build programs that are so trivial that they simply contain no structure rich enough to obfuscate.

The problem with this function is that its triviality, ironically, makes it *simpler* to obfuscate, given the definition. Simple functions are learnable with just a small number of oracle queries—in the case of Hello World, a table of input–output pairs consisting of a single entry mapping an input of the empty string to the output Hello World. As a result, all differences between oracle access and source-code access disappear. In other words, simple learnable programs like Hello World can be trivially rewritten as a single lookup table that is at most polynomially larger than the original. This lookup table reveals no more than oracle access to the program does and thus is a valid obfuscation of the program. What you instead require is a property that has a negligible likelihood of being revealed by oracle access.

One idea that you may want to try is using the self-reproducing program shown in Listing 5.6▶340. The idea here is that no matter how much an obfuscator obfuscates this program, when the program is run, it will still produce the original unobfuscated source code as output. This is guaranteed by the correctness requirement of an obfuscator. You may think that you have succeeded, because now that you have the original program, you can use it to compute any properties you like.

Unfortunately, your self-reproducing program is not a suitable candidate either, because it lacks the virtual blackbox property. Oracle access to a self-reproducing program reveals the entire source and thus is equivalent to source-code access!

5.4.3 Proving that Obfuscation Is Impossible

	Goal
Asset: All properties of a program	
Attacker Limits: None	
Input Programs: All possible programs	

You need your program to reveal its secret only when you have information that is available to any obfuscated version of a program but that is unavailable with just blackbox access. As we discussed earlier, the crucial difference between an obfuscated program and a blackbox program is that you have the source code for an obfuscated program. The source code is something that can be passed to another program and manipulated. You have no such access to a blackbox program—all you can do is query it. You cannot pass it to other programs or look inside it. Barak et al. rely on this difference by making their candidate counterexample crucially rely on its own source code:

This unobfuscatable program is very similar to the self-reproducing program in Listing 5.6▶340. However, instead of printing out its own source, it tries to *recognize* its own source. Listing 5.7▶342 shows a candidate counterexample, `Secret`. This program operates in two modes: *point mode* and *spy mode*. In point mode, the program behaves exactly like the point functions you saw in Section 5.3.1▶314. If the input to the program in point mode is the secret key value, the program prints out 1; otherwise, it prints out 0. In spy mode, the program takes as input a program—let's call it `Candidate`, and tests if `Candidate` behaves like `Secret`. If it does, `Secret` prints

Listing 5.7 An unobfuscatable program containing a secret S.

```java
public class Secret {
    final int POINT_MODE = 0;
    final int SPY_MODE = 1;
    final int S = 8544;

    public int pointFunction(int x) {
        if (x == S)
            return 1;
        else
            return 0;
    }

    public boolean behavesLikeMe(Program p) {
        int testPoint = S;
        int tests = 1000;
        boolean result = true;
        do {
            int result = p.run(testPoint);
            if (result != pointFunction(testPoint))
                return false;
            else if (result == Program.RAN_TOO_LONG)
                return false;
            int testPoint = (int)Math.random(Integer.MAXINT);
            test--;
        } until (test == 0);
        return result;
    }

    public void main(String args[]) {
        int mode  = getMode(args);
        Program p = getProgram(args);
        int input = getInput(args);
        switch (mode) {
        case POINT_MODE:
            System.out.println(pointFunction(input));
        case SPY_MODE:
            if (behavesLikeMe(p))
                System.out.println("The secret is "+S);
            else
                System.out.println("No secret for you.");
        }
    }
}
```

out the secret. As with point functions, oracle access to Secret gives you only a small probability of guessing the key.

You may wonder how Secret can test if Candidate behaves like itself, given that earlier in this chapter you saw that EQUIVALENCE is uncomputable. Fortunately, Secret can determine with a high degree of probability that Candidate is the same program by testing it at the secret input and a large number of other random points. If the programs Secret and Candidate agree at these points, there is a high degree of probability that they compute the same function. Furthermore, since the running time of Secret is known to Secret, and by our definition of obfuscation, any obfuscated program is *at most* polynomially slower than the original program, behaves-LikeMe can terminate any candidate that runs too long and will correctly return false.

To summarize, you now have a program, Secret, that when passed itself as input in spy mode, will output the secret. That is, if you have source-code access to Secret, no matter how obfuscated, you will be able to learn the secret. However, when an attacker is given only oracle access to Secret (in other words, when the attacker is unable to look at the source code of Secret, or to pass it as input to another program), he cannot learn much about the secret.

This contradicts the blackbox property of the definition of obfuscation and thus proves that the program Secret cannot be obfuscated according to Definition 5.11▶339. Since we constructed Secret without reference to any particular obfuscation algorithm, the existence of Secret proves Theorem 5.1▶340.

5.4.4 Discussion

One of the most interesting aspects of the proof of impossibility of obfuscation is to understand why the attacker is not able to use the oracle to get the information that source-code access would give him. Remember that if you *are* able to deduce the secret simply from oracle access to Secret, then according to Definition 5.11▶339 the program was indeed obfuscated and Theorem 5.1▶340 (Impossibility of Obfuscation) does not hold.

Why can't an attacker write a program that behaves like Secret? From our discussion of point functions, you already know that it is infeasible for an attacker to exhaustively test the oracle for the secret, and unlikely for an attacker to guess the secret. But why can't the attacker write a program that has access to the oracle? The program could simply relay all its input to the oracle and output the oracle's response. Since it is a program and not an oracle, it could now be passed to other programs, and if it was passed to Secret in spy mode, it would successfully trick Secret into revealing the secret S.

An attacker cannot do this because the candidate program he generates cannot be one that itself uses oracles. Specifically, an oracle is not allowed make a call to itself. This may seem like a trick—and it is a trick, but one that is necessary to make the unobfuscatable program possible. However, it is not an especially unusual one. In an earlier section, when we explored Turing's proof of HALTING, we insisted that COUNTEREXAMPLE was entirely self-contained—it was not allowed to make calls to other programs. In fact, if we relaxed the definition to allow such calls, Turing's proof of uncomputability would no longer hold. The same is true for the unobfuscatable program.

In software engineering terms, if an oracle is like a remote Web service, then prohibiting a program from using an oracle amounts to preventing (or detecting) a candidate program's attempt to communicate over the network. If Secret detects such an attempt, it can refuse to reveal its secret.

There is one other interesting observation we can make about the means by which Theorem 5.1▶340 (Impossibility of Obfuscation) was proven. First, no static analysis of the Candidate was required—it was cracked by taking advantage of the fact that Candidate is trying to leak its secret. How similar are the programs you usually want to obfuscate to Candidate? What does the unobfuscatable program imply about programs that do not attempt to conspire against the obfuscator? Finally, you now have proof that there exist programs that can be obfuscated and others that cannot be. Which class do useful programs belong to? Can we tweak the definition of obfuscation so that all useful programs are obfuscatable?

5.5 Provably Secure Obfuscation: Can It Be Saved?

You may wonder why we are so keen on *provable* obfuscation. After all, if the obfuscation techniques we have introduced so far are already sufficiently powerful in making reverse engineering of programs prohibitively expensive, is this not enough? Was this not what we had argued for earlier? In other words, what additional advantage does provable obfuscation give us that makes it worth pursuing?

General provable obfuscation, if it existed, would allow us to solve many important problems in cryptography. For example, in voting protocols you need to count the number of votes cast while maintaining the anonymity of the individual ballots. The OBFPP scheme we described is a specific example of the more general technique of *homomorphic encryption*. Homomorphic encryption schemes can help protect the privacy of a vote. However, if the only operations possible on an encrypted vote are addition and multiplication, the number of additional checks possible are limited. For example, the lack of support for relational testing prevents voting schemes based on OBFPP from being able to test the validity of each vote cast.

It may certainly be possible to come up with an encryption scheme that supports a particular set of operations, but it is time-consuming to create and test each new encryption system. Moreover, encryption schemes that support other functions, such as division, have also been difficult to develop. However, if a provably secure obfuscation scheme were developed, these problems would vanish. To see that, have a look at this program:

```
long homomorphicEncryption(long x,long y) {
    long privateKey = 0x1234...1234;
    long decryptX = decrypt(privateKey,x);
    long decryptY = decrypt(privateKey,y);
    long result = f(decryptX, decryptY);
    return encrypt(privateKey,result);
}
```

If we had provably secure obfuscation a program such as this one could be obfuscated and used as the homomorphic operator. The program uses an embedded private key to decrypt both of its arguments, applies an arbitrary operation, f, on them, and then uses the embedded private key to re-encrypt and return the result. The program itself is obfuscated, and the security of the obfuscation would guarantee the secrecy of the key.

Another use of provably secure obfuscation could be to develop new types of public key encryption schemes. In fact, with a provably secure obfuscator, you would be in a position to turn any private key encryption scheme into a public key encryption scheme. Given the difficulty of developing good public key encryption techniques, this would be hugely advantageous. To develop a new public key encryption scheme, you would embed your private key in a program like this:

```
long publicEncrypt(long x) {
    long privateKey = 0x1234...1234;
    return privateEncrypt(privateKey,x);
}
```

You would then obfuscate this program and release it as your public key. To encrypt a message to send to you, anyone could run the program with the message as argument. To decrypt the message, you would use your private key and decryption routine. The security of the obfuscation would ensure that your embedded private key would remain secure.

5.5.1 Overcoming Impossibility

Given the value of provable obfuscation and the proof that the general case is unsolvable, what future directions are possible and promising? The proof suggests that there exist programs that cannot be obfuscated. However, it does not suggest that any specific program is not obfuscatable. One promising possibility is to find a way to restrict the class of programs you are interested in obfuscating so as to exclude Secret.

For example, you have already seen that point functions can indeed be obfuscated. What would be the most useful program one could try to obfuscate? It would be a program capable of providing the most general functionality while remaining outside the domain of the proof. For example, you could choose to obfuscate a particular limited virtual machine. There is nothing directly in the proof you saw that suggests this is impossible. Once you have such an obfuscated virtual machine, your task is "simply" to deliver to this virtual machine the program you wish to execute in a form that it can execute that is nevertheless resilient to analysis. However, since the output of this virtual machine would be usable by an attacker, it is likely that the original impossibility proof could be adapted to show that the obfuscation of even particular virtual machines is impossible.

A more promising approach is to find an alternate definition of obfuscation that remains useful but prevents Theorem 5.1▶340 (Impossibility of Obfuscation) from being applicable. In the remainder of this section, we will explore both these directions for rescuing provable obfuscation. In Section 5.5.2 you will see *secure multiparty computation* which splits a program up and executes each piece by a separate party in such a way that no one party gains complete access to the asset you are trying to protect. In Section 5.5.3▶349 we will explore another approach that transforms an obfuscated program in such a way that it encrypts the output before returning it.

Both of these transformations turn the non-interactive definition of obfuscation into an interactive one that requires a server and a client to be present in order to execute an obfuscated program.

5.5.2 Definitions Revisited: Make Obfuscation Interactive

The definitions of obfuscation you saw in Section 5.1▶304 implied that once a program P has been obfuscated, it executes without further interaction with a server. Defined in this way, general provably secure obfuscation is impossible.

However, if you allow an obfuscated program to distribute its computation so some of it is not accessible to an attacker, this amounts to providing a blackbox to an obfuscated program where it can securely perform computation and store data. This is rather like *remote tamperproofing*, which you will learn more about in Section 7.5▶453. Of course it is then trivially possible for an obfuscated program to move *all* of its computation to the blackbox and be completely secure.

The interesting and open problem is what is the smallest amount of data and computation that needs to be performed by a blackbox in order to allow general purpose obfuscators to exist. The solution to this problem may come from an area called secure multi-party computation (SMC). The aim of SMC is to enable clients to carry out a distributed computation on private data without leaking this data to an adversary.

For obfuscation, the interesting special case is where the number of parties involved is two—the party who wishes to provide the securely obfuscated program and the party who wishes to run it. In this case, the asset to be protected is the private information on which the two parties perform the distributed computation—the obfuscator provides the asset and relies on SMC to ensure that the adversary is able to run the program without gaining access to this asset.

5.5.2.1 Cheapskate Problem   Let us look at an example using SMC. Suppose you and your friends wish to work out the average amount of pocket money you have, but you do not wish to tell anyone how much pocket money you have. Can you come up with a protocol that allows you to compute the average without revealing your allowance? In fact, you can! Have a look at this figure:

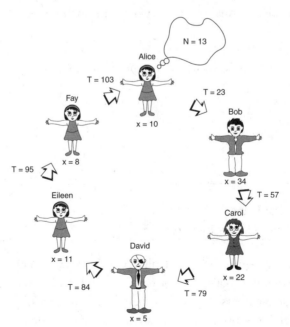

The algorithm starts by making all the participants stand around in a circle. The first person, Alice, begins by thinking of a random number N, adds her allowance x, and whispers the sum to Bob. Bob takes that number, adds his own allowance to it and whispers it to the next person in the circle, Carol. She, in turn, adds her own allowance, and so on. When the total finally returns to Alice, she substracts the random number N that she began with and announces the total to the group. Every member of the group can then divide the total by the number of people in the group and know the average allowance.

It is instructive to briefly examine how this protocol works. No one member at any time has sufficient information to decode the "running total." What attacks are possible in this scenario? What would happen if two people in the group were to collude? For example, if Bob and David colluded by sharing their totals, they could compute Carol's allowance. If the two colluding parties are separated by a larger number of people, they may not be able to tell what each person between them had as an allowance, but they would be able to have a much more accurate approximation of their total income than can be determined from the average.

A second attack that is possible is that any participant could lie about their income. While it is always the case in multiple-party computations that a participant can lie about his input, in this problem it is particularly advantageous for a participant to lie. If he is the only party to lie, at the end of the round he would be able to calculate the true total while every other person in the circle would have an incorrect value.

Can we do better than this? Can these problems be resolved? Can the protocol be extended to calculate functions other than the average?

5.5.2.2 Millionaire Problem

	Goal
Asset: Private data	
Attacker Limits: None	
Input Programs: All possible programs	

Suppose you and a friend wish to calculate which of the two of you is the richer but you do not want to reveal this information to each other. One way of managing this would be for each person to reveal their wealth to a trusted third party, who in turn would tell you who is richer. In such a scheme, no one friend would have an advantage, nor would they be able to gain much information about the other person's wealth—unless the trusted third party was compromised!

A secure multi-party computation allows you to perform these and other more complex types of computations without using a trusted third party. For example, suppose Alice and Bob are the two millionaires. Yao [379a] shows how they could work out which one of them is richer as follows:

1. Let Alice's wealth, a, and Bob's wealth, b, be integers between 0 and 5 million.

2. Bob picks a random N-bit integer, x, encrypts it using Alice's public key, $C = E_{Alice_{pub}}(x)$, and sends Alice $C - b + 1$.

3. Alice uses the her private key to generate $\langle Y_1, Y_2, Y_3 \cdots Y_5 \rangle$ such that $Y_n = D_{Alice_{priv}}(C - b + n)$. She can do this even though she does not know b because Bob sent her $C - b + 1$.

4. Alice generates a random prime p of length $N/2$-bits.

5. Alice computes $\langle Z_1, Z_2, Z_3 \cdots Z_5 \rangle$ such that $Z_n = Y_n \bmod p$.

6. Alice transmits p to Bob and sends him 5 numbers $\langle Q_1, Q_2, \ldots, Q_5 \rangle$ where $Q_n = Z_n$ if $n < a$ else $Q_n = Z_n + 1$.

7. Bob computes $x \bmod p$ and compares it to the bth number that Alice sent him. If they are equal then Alice is richer, else Bob is richer.

Problem 5.8   What weaknesses in this protocol might be used to compromise its integrity? Can you devise another protocol that is resistant to these problems?

While this solution is specific for the millionaire problem, it can be generalized to a two-party SMC problem as follows. Let Alice have an input $x = \langle x_1, \ldots, x_s \rangle$ and Bob have an input $y = \langle y_1, \ldots, y_r \rangle$. They wish to compute a publicly known function $f(x, y)$ without revealing information about their inputs that cannot be inferred from the output of the entire computation. Surprisingly, cryptographers have devised general protocols that are capable of computing arbitrary functions f between two or more parties.

5.5.3   Definition Revisited: Make Obfuscation Non-Semantics Preserving

Earlier in this chapter, we considered a definition of obfuscation based on indistinguishability and equivalence. According to that definition, a program P is obfuscated if an attacker is unable to distinguish it from every other program P' without running it. Alternatively, you could define obfuscation as the ability to compute some function (rather than merely a predicate) over the original program. While these are good candidates for the definition of obfuscation, they are all *stronger* than Definition 5.11►339 and thus are still susceptible to the uncomputability of obfuscation.

For a weaker definition of obfuscation, you need a definition that does not rely on oracles but rather on I/O access to the program itself. For example, you could define a virtual blackbox as follows:

Definition 5.12 (Virtual blackbox (Alternate)).   Given an obfuscated program P', an oracle-access analyzer R, and a source-code analyzer A, P' is a virtual blackbox if for each property of the program, the probability of computing that property given I/O access to P is approximately the same as the source-code computable probability of P'.

Under this definition, Theorem 5.1►340 does not apply, since it *is* possible to construct a Candidate program that is able to fool Secret into revealing S using nothing more than I/O access.

Another possibility is to remove the requirement that an obfuscated function maintain correctness—that the obfuscating transformation be semantics-preserving. At first sight, this may appear to be the least desirable axiom to lose—after all, your entire intent in using obfuscation is to protect a specific program, presumably because you are interested in the output of this program.

To prove that the program Secret could not be obfuscated, we did not analyze it but rather created an input—a program called Candidate—that had the same input–output behavior and thus would trick Secret into revealing S.

If the obfuscation algorithm was allowed to change the output of the program—for example by preventing the output of the program from leaking information to the attacker, then creating a program like Candidate would not be possible. For example, we can prevent the program from producing any information (which is not very useful) or by encrypting or obscuring the output.

Such a transformed program would not be useful in the same way that obfuscated programs are. In particular, to avoid the problems that Candidate runs into, extracting useful information from the output of such a transformed program cannot happen on the client. However, such transformations are ideal for remote execution.

Algorithm 5.4 Executing a remote procedure call between a server and a client.

SERVER RPE_SEND(P, I):

1. Encode P and I into P' and I', respectively, such that they are suitable for transmission over the network for the given client.

2. Send (P', I') to the client and wait for a response O.

3. Decode O to retrieve $P(I)$.

CLIENT RPE_RECEIVE(P', I'):

1. Decode P' and I' into P'' and I'', respectively.

2. Execute P'' with input I'', i.e., let $O \leftarrow P''(I'')$.

3. Encode the result O and send it back to the server.

5.5.3.1 Remote Procedure Call

A Remote Procedure Call (RPC) mechanism is a technique for implementing a client-server model of distributed computing. It allows a server to cause a subroutine on a remote machine to be executed and the result of the execution returned to the client. To execute an RPC, a server constructs a message containing the name of a specific procedure and serialized parameters and sends it to the client. The client deserializes the parameters, executes the requested procedure, serializes the result, and returns it to the server.

RPC mechanisms are useful in cases where the set of behaviors you may want from a remote service is small and as a result can be created as stored procedures on a remote server. It has the advantage that the computation is done at a remote location that an attacker is unable to debug or distort. If there is a computation that you wish to keep secret from an attacker, you could store it remotely on a server and provide access to it only via an RPC call.

For example, decrypting a message using a fixed key is ideally suited for RPC. The limitation of RPC is the need to have identified ahead of time the set of procedures you will require (and the keys you will use). What you really need is something Herzberg et al. [161] call *remote program execution* (RPE). We show an RPE protocol in Algorithm 5.4. It works similarly to a remote procedure call, except that, in addition to encoding a program for transmission, it encodes the program for execution on the target platform. The way to think about this is as an RPC where the target procedure is in fact a virtual machine. The argument to that remote procedure is a program encoded for that virtual machine and its return value is the output of the program.

Here's what this would look like:

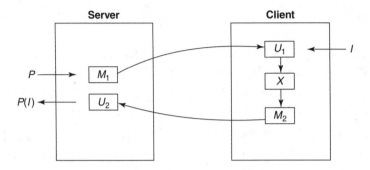

Here, the server uses transformer M_1 to encode program P for transmission and sends it to the client. The client uses transformer U_1 to decode the message and the virtual machine X executes P with input I. The client encodes the output using another encoder M_2 and sends it to the server where it gets decoded using transformer U_2.

At first glance you have not really gained anything. While it is true that the actual computation is happening on a protected server via the RPC, the fact that you need to encode the entire program for the virtual machine on the server means an attacker can intercept that program and statically analyze it to extract its assets.

Moreover, in real-world programs, the portions of a program that you want to protect are large and computationally expensive. Calls to the section of code you want to protect are deeply interwoven with the rest of the program. Moving these sections of the program to a remote server, irrespective of how it is encoded, would result in an unacceptable slowdown in the execution of your program.

What you would ideally like is to reverse the roles of server and client. You need the majority of the computation to be carried out on the client and to make the output of that computation be incomprehensible to the end user at the client. Then the client could request the server to perform the small amount of computation required to decrypt the output. Not only does this scheme not require extensive computation on the server, but encrypting the output has the advantage of side-stepping the impossibility-of-obfuscation result.

5.5.3.2 Whitebox Remote Program Execution Herzberg et al. [161] have suggested the construction by which remote program execution can be used to achieve this model of provably secure obfuscated execution. In their model, the server takes a program P and instead of merely encoding it for transmission, encodes and encrypts it for a particular virtual machine running on the client.

The client is an obfuscated program that consists of three parts: a decryption routine with an embedded key, a virtual machine, and an re-encryption routine with another embedded key. Here's what that would look like:

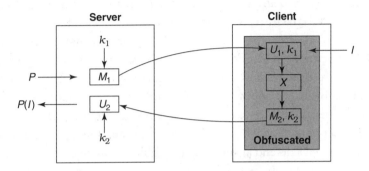

The server encodes a program P for transmission by transformer M_1 by encrypting it with a key k_1. The server sends the resulting package to the client, which first decodes it using the transformer U_1, which has k_1 embedded in it. The client then executes P using the virtual machine X with input I. The client encrypts the result using another encoder, M_2, which has key k_2 embedded within it. The client encrypts the result and returns it to the server where transformer U_2 decrypts and returns it to the end user. U_1, X, and M_2 on the client need to be obfuscated together in order to make them inseparable. The means to do so remains an open problem.

There are a couple of features worth noting in this proposal. First, decryption and encryption keys are built into the client. As such, they are vulnerable to a reverse-engineering attack. Of course, you already know how some types of encryption and decryption can be carried out using Algorithm OBFCEJO, for example. Unfortunately, this is not sufficient, because if an attacker can separate the individual steps, he can gain access to the decrypted program in memory. Instead, a method of obfuscation that makes the three steps shown inseparable is required.

Second, the security of the construction relies on the encrypted output not leaking any information. If any information leaks to an attacker, he will be able to construct a `Candidate` that communicates via that leaky channel and thus construct a program that is unobfuscatable. One example of such a channel is execution time. For example, suppose an attacker devises a program `Candidate`$_\infty$ that executes indefinitely when given a specific input I. No matter how this program was obfuscated before being passed to the client, when executed and given input I, it would be recognizable as the attacker's program. To close this channel, the virtual machine must only execute a given program for a fixed amount of time before returning its output.

The first limitation of secure multi-party computation is speed. The gain in privacy is attained with a large data overhead, and many of the protocols are extremely slow. As a result, only very simple arithmetic and relational computations are practical. Second, many secure multi-party computation algorithms are only resilient to passive attacks from malicious participants. This means, for example, that the protocol gives correct results only if the participants follow the protocol correctly. Some proposed algorithms require all participants to act honestly, while others work correctly if a majority of the participants are honest. For example, in the Cheapskate Problem, any one of the friends is able to secretly influence the total that is computed. They are able to derive information from the computed average while preventing other participants from doing so. As a result, they gain an unfair advantage. Other protocols defend against this possibility by allowing members to detect this type of fraud and stop the computation before their information has leaked.

To address these difficulties, many secure multi-party protocols are devised not to perform arbitrary computations but rather highly specific ones using optimized and efficient primitives. Nevertheless, secure multi-party computation can be used to build secure protocols for auctions, voting, private information retrieval, and other types of sensitive distributed computations, and in essence can allow you to build a slow, Turing complete, virtual machine.

5.6 Discussion

In this chapter you saw recent work on the theory and limits of obfuscation. We showed how fundamental problems in computer science such as the halting problem and the equivalence problem provide bounds on what kind of obfuscation is possible. You saw examples of provably secure obfuscation of point-functions used to obfuscate access control and regular expressions and the construction of an obfuscated database.

We also discussed encryption algorithms and how to perform some operations on encrypted values using properties of the underlying encryption scheme. We were not able to extend this scheme to securely hide the encryption or decryption itself. However, we showed you the whitebox approaches that currently are being used to try to securely obfuscate cryptographic algorithms like DES.

All of these examples were building up to the famous Theorem 5.1 ▸340, which states that, under a very strict definition of obfuscation, obfuscation is impossible, or, more precisely, programs exist that cannot be obfuscated.

You have also seen how contrived the counterexample required to prove this impossibility result was. This does not mean the theorem is inconsequential or unimportant. It helps us identify where the core difficulty in carrying out obfuscation lies.

Using this understanding, we were able to explore two workarounds for provable obfuscation that are applicable to a smaller class of programs: secure multi-party computation, where security is gained by distributing the computation among more parties, and whitebox remote procedure calls.

Whether or not obfuscation is possible appears to depend strongly on how you define obfuscation, the properties you want to protect, and the class of programs you are considering. There are many open questions in each of these workarounds. For example, are there interesting commonly used applications that cannot be executed using this design for obfuscated execution? To avoid the tyranny of the impossibility of obfuscation, you need to prevent the program you are obfuscating from being able to signal a single bit of information to a potential attacker. As a result, your encoded program on the client must be difficult to distinguish from any other encoded program in the class you are interested in. This is true for its execution time, memory usage, and any other factor that could be used by the program as a side channel. As you grow the class of programs you would like your obfuscator to obfuscate, it becomes increasingly difficult to prevent a program from being able to send such a signal.

Dynamic Obfuscation 6

The static obfuscation algorithms we showed you in Chapter 4 (Code Obfuscation) transform the code prior to execution. In this chapter, we'll show you *dynamic* algorithms that transform the program *at runtime*. In theory, you could turn any static algorithm into a dynamic one simply by including the obfuscator with the executable and transforming the code as it runs! In practice, however, obfuscators are large and slow programs, and for stealthiness and performance reasons we need small and quick runtime transformers.

When an attacker looks at statically obfuscated code, he sees a mess, but every time he runs the code, for example, under a debugger, he sees *the same* mess. Running the code multiple times, with different input data, he may be able to figure out what code is real and what is bogus. Dynamic obfuscation tries to counter this by making the code and the resulting execution path change as the program runs. Some algorithms are "semi-dynamic"—they perform a small, constant number of transformations (often one) at runtime—but many are *continuous*, making sure the code is in constant flux.

The first non-trivial dynamic obfuscation algorithm was published by Aucsmith [26] in 1996. Intel eventually spun off a company to implement and commercialize this algorithm for DRM applications. We will discuss this algorithm in detail in Section 6.2.2▶366.

Fred Cohen [76] suggests two dynamic obfuscation strategies. The first he calls *build-and-execute*. The idea is to generate code for a routine at runtime and then jump to it. The second idea is *self-modification*. Have a look at this version of the modular exponentiation routine:

```
int modexp(int y, int x[], int w, int n, int mode) {

    int R, L, k = 0, s = 1, t;

    char* p=&&begin;  while (p<(char*)&&end) *p++ ^= 99;

    if (mode==1) return 0;

    while (k < w) {

        begin:

        if (x[k] == 1)

            R = (s*y) % n;

        else

            R = s;

        s = R*R % n;

        L = R;

        end:

        k++;

    }

    p=&&begin; while (p  (char*)&&end) *p++ ^= 99;

    return L;

}

int main() {

    makeCodeWritable(...);

    modexp(0, NULL, 0, 0, 1);

    ...

    modexp(..., ..., ..., ..., 0);

}
```

The idea is for the code in dark gray to be xored with a key (99) until it needs to be executed, at which time it gets "decrypted," executed, and re-encrypted. The dashed code would normally execute at obfuscation time. When it gets called, it sets up the initial configuration by "encrypting" the dark gray code by xoring it with 99 and then returning. Every subsequent time the modexp routine gets called, the light gray code first decrypts the dark gray code and executes it, and then the dotted code re-encrypts it.

"Encrypting" binaries this way is an often reinvented protection technique, but ultimately an ineffectual one: In order to be executed, the code must, at some point in time, appear in cleartext! (See, however, Section 6.3.2▶392 for an algorithm that combines encryption and code mobility.) It's therefore always possible to run the program inside an emulator that prints out every executed instruction:

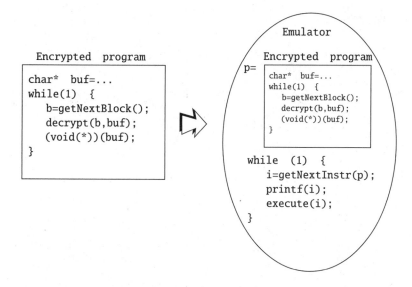

The instruction trace can later be analyzed (re-rolling loops, removing decrypt-and-jump artifacts, and so on) and the original code recovered.

In Section 6.1▶360, we give initial definitions. In Section 6.2▶362, we explore algorithms that make use of self-modifying code to keep the program in constant flux. In Section 6.3▶383, we look at a special case of self-modification, namely, the use of encryption as the runtime code transformer. In Section 6.4▶398, we conclude the chapter.

6.1 Definitions

A dynamic obfuscator typically runs in two phases. The first phase, at compile-time, transforms the program to an initial configuration and then adds a runtime code transformer. During the second phase, at runtime, the execution of the program code is interspersed with calls to this transformer. As a consequence, a dynamic obfuscator turns a "normal" program into a self-modifying one.

We can illustrate this using our defense model from Section 2.2▸86. Let program P have a function f that you want to protect. f has one basic block b. Let I be the initial and T the runtime transformers, respectively. At compile-time, you transform f (using the **map** primitive) with I:

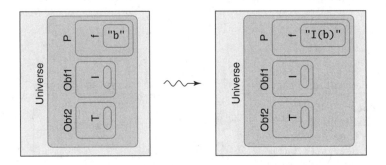

You then **merge** in T with P, since you will be using T as the runtime obfuscator:

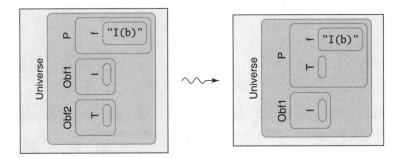

The resulting program is what you distribute to your customers. At runtime (or program startup time), f is transformed using T:

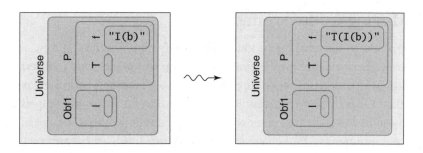

Finally, the **dynamic** primitive models that T can be applied multiple times:

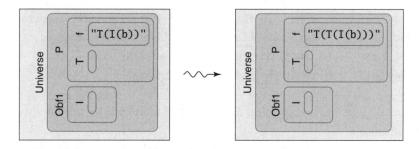

Different algorithms will schedule the transformations differently. Some will apply T once at startup or right before f is called; others will apply T continuously throughout the execution. It would, of course, be possible for T(I(f)), T(T(I(f))),T(T(T(I(f)))), . . . , to form an infinite sequence of syntactically different functions, but current algorithms cycle through a small number of configurations. For example, if I encrypts f, T could decrypt once at startup, leaving f in cleartext. Alternatively, T could decrypt f right before it gets called and re-encrypt after f returns. In this case, f cycles through only two states, ciphertext and cleartext, so that when control reaches f it must be in the cleartext state.

More formally, we get the following definition:

Definition 6.1 (Dynamic Obfuscation).   Let $O = (I, T, p)$ be a *dynamic obfuscation system* consisting of program-to-program transformations I and T. Let p be the *period* of T. Let $P = \langle f_0, f_1, \ldots, f_{n-1} \rangle$ be a program comprising n components to be obfuscated. Then $P_0 = \langle T, I(f_0), I(f_1), \ldots, I(f_{n-1}) \rangle$ is an initial obfuscated version of P. At runtime, for $i \geq 1$, $P_i = \langle T, T^i(I(f_0)), T^i(I(f_1)), \ldots, T^i(I(f_{n-1})) \rangle$ is a sequence of obfuscated configurations of P. $T^i(f)$ represents i applications of T to f. Since p is the period of T, $P_i = P_{i \bmod p}$.

6.2 Moving Code Around

All algorithms in this chapter produce self-modifying programs. At best, this will have serious performance implications; at worst, it will require you to insert highly unstealthy instructions to make sure that the newly modified code gets executed rather than the code that is currently in caches and in the instruction pipeline. On the x86 architecture, the processor will do the right thing without any specific help from the programmer. On the PowerPC architecture, however, before you jump to a modified code segment, you have to issue the following four instructions (r0 is a register containing the address of the modified instruction):

```
dcbst 0,r0      // make sure the data cache line is written to memory
sync            // make sure that the last instruction completed
icbi 0,r0       // invalidate the instruction cache line
isync           // clear the instruction pipeline
```

These instructions are highly unusual in normal code and will serve as an easy target for an adversary.

An additional issue is that the code pages you modify must be both writable and executable. Depending on your operating system, this will be more or less easy, and stealthy, to arrange. On Linux, for example, you need to use the mprotect system call to set the write bit for any page you intend to modify. See Listing 6.1▸363.

The algorithms in this section "move code around" to make it difficult to analyze. Algorithm OBFKMNM is the most straightforward of them all: It overwrites an instruction with a bogus one and then replaces the bogus instruction with the original before it gets executed. As you will see, it's not hard to attack using a debugger or emulator. Algorithm OBFAG$_{swap}$ divides a function into chunks and, as execution proceeds, cyclically swaps cells with each other. Algorithm OBFMAMDSB, finally, arranges the code so that several functions are merged so that they "share" the same location. At runtime, the location is patched to contain the function that needs to execute next, in essence making functions move in and out of the same location.

6.2.1 Algorithm *OBFKMNM*: Replacing Instructions

The first algorithm we're going to show you, Algorithm OBFKMNM [189–191], simply replaces instructions with bogus ones. At some point in the execution, before the bogus instruction is about to execute, update code restores the instruction back

Listing 6.1 C functions and types used in the examples in this book. `make-CodeWritable` and `allocExecutablePages` make code pages writable and allocate pages that can contain executable code, respectively. They are Linux-specific.

```c
#include <sys/mman.h>
#include <unistd.h>

typedef unsigned int uint32;
typedef char* caddr_t;
typedef uint32* waddr_t;

void makeCodeWritable(char* first, char* last) {
    char* firstpage = first - ((int)first % getpagesize());
    char* lastpage = last - ((int)last % getpagesize());
    int pages = (lastpage-firstpage)/getpagesize()+1;
    if (mprotect(firstpage,pages*getpagesize(),
                  PROT_READ|PROT_EXEC|PROT_WRITE)==-1)
        perror("mprotect");
}

char* allocExecutablePages(int pages) {
    template = (char*) valloc(getpagesize()*pages);
    if (mprotect(template,getpagesize(),PROT_READ|PROT_EXEC|PROT_WRITE)==-1)
        perror("mprotect");
}
```

to the original. At some point after the instruction has executed, a second piece of code again replaces the real instruction with a bogus one. The idea is to create a small window of time when the code is actually correct. Only during that small window can an adversary take a snapshot of the code.

Have a look at Listing 6.2 ▸ 364, where we give a simple example of a DRM media player. The statements in dashes would normally be performed at obfuscation time. They save the first byte of the instruction sequence that makes up the call to `printf` and then overwrite that byte with 0. At runtime, the code in light gray restores the byte and, after `printf` has finished executing, the dark gray code sets it back to 0 again. A real implementation would be done at the assembly or binary code levels and would more likely replace an instruction by a similar, but wrong, one rather than just overwriting it with an obviously bogus value.

An obvious attack on this algorithm is to run the program under emulation, monitoring any writes into the instruction stream. In most programs, these are

---

Listing 6.2 Algorithm OBFKMNM example.

```
int player_main (int argc, char *argv[]) {
   char orig = (*(caddr_t)&&target);
   (*(caddr_t)&&target) = 0;

   int digital_media[] = {10,102};
   int len = 2;
   int player_key = 0xbabeca75;
   int user_key = 0xca7ca115;
   int key = user_key ^ player_key;

   int i;
   for(i=0;i <len;i++) {
      (*(caddr_t)&&target) = orig;

      int decrypted = digital_media[i] ^ key;
      float decoded = (float)decrypted;
      target:
      printf("%f\n",decoded);
      (*(caddr_t)&&target) = 0;
   }
}

int main (int argc, char *argv[]) {
   makeCodeWritable(...);
   player_main(argc,argv);
}
```

---

unusual (jitting interpreters would be an exception) and likely to signal that something fishy is going on. Even using a simple debugger would be possible. Here, an attacker calls mprotect to set the code region to readable and executable, but not writable:

```
(gdb) call (int)mprotect(0x2000,0x3000,5)
(gdb) cont
Program received signal EXC_BAD_ACCESS, Could not access memory.
Reason: KERN_PROTECTION_FAILURE at address: 0x00002934
0x000028c0 in player_main (argc=1, argv=0xbffff31c) at kanzaki.c:30
30             (*(caddr_t)&&target) = orig;
(gdb) x/i $pc
0x28c0 <player_main+220>:       stb     r0,0(r2)
(gdb) print (char)$r0
$7 = -64
(gdb) print/x (int)$r2
$10 = 0x2934
```

When the program tries to write into the code stream, the operating system throws an exception. Then, the attacker examines the instruction at address 0x28c0 that caused the trap and finds that it tries to store the value in register r0 (−64) into the address stored in register r2 (0x2934). Now, all he has to do is replace the instruction at address 0x28c0, which does the modification, with a nop and the byte at address 0x2934 with −64, and he's done!

Problem 6.1 In a real implementation of OBFKMNM, there may be hundreds or thousands of updates to the code segment, and it would be infeasible for an attacker to remove each one of them by hand. Write an attack script that automates the process.

Algorithm 6.1▸366 gives an overview of the obfuscation. The idea is to find three points *A*, *B*, and *C* in the control flow graph, like this:

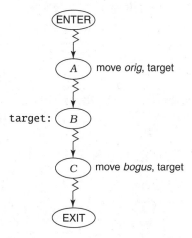

At *A*, you insert an instruction that overwrites the target instruction with its original value *orig*, restoring the routine to an executable state. At *C*, you likewise insert an instruction that overwrites the target with the bogus value. You have to choose *A*, *B*, and *C* such that every path to *B* flows through *A* and every path from *B* flows through *C*.

As you saw, this algorithm is susceptible to dynamic attacks. But what about static attacks? If an adversary can statically determine that an instruction modifies the text segment, and *which* location it modifies, then patching the executable to rid it of the self-modification isn't hard. To make things a bit more difficult for the adversary, you can compute the address of the target instruction using an opaque

---

Algorithm 6.1 Overview of algorithm OBFKMNM. P is the function to be obfuscated.

OBFUSCATE(P):

1. Select three points A, B, and C in P, such that:

    (a) A strictly dominates B,

    (b) C strictly post-dominates B, and

    (c) any path from B to A passes through C.

2. Let *orig* be the instruction at B.

3. Select an instruction *bogus* of the same length as *orig*.

4. Replace *orig* at B with *bogus*.

5. At point A, insert the instruction move *orig*, $v^{=B}$, where v is an opaque expression that evaluates to the address of point B.

6. Similarly, at point C, insert the instruction move *bogus*, $v^{=B}$.

---

expression. Ideally, the expression is hard enough to analyze that the adversary can't determine whether the move modifies the data or the text segment.

6.2.2 *OBFAG$_{swap}$*: Self-Modifying State Machine

Algorithm OBFAG$_{swap}$ [26,27] is the first known example of a serious attempt at software protection. In 1996 it was published in the academic literature by David Aucsmith and filed as a U.S. patent assigned to Intel. Later, Intel spun off *Convera*, a company to explore the algorithm for DRM applications.

Aucsmith's paper and patent incorporate three ideas worth exploring. First, the algorithm keeps the program in constant flux by splitting it up in pieces and cyclically moving these pieces around, xoring them with each other. This means that an adversary who tries to examine a protected program under a debugger will find that only some pieces of the program are in cleartext, and that the program exhibits a very unusual address trace. We call this part of the algorithm OBFAG$_{swap}$, and we will show you this aspect of the algorithm in this section. Second, the algorithm uses simple encryption to add a layer of protection that keeps even fewer pieces of the program in the clear. We call this part of the algorithm OBFAG$_{crypt}$, and we'll talk about it in the section on program encryption (Section 6.3.2▶392). Finally, the algorithm builds up a network of protected routines, each one checking one or more of the others, in such a way that to be successful an adversary must disable several checkers at once. We will explore this idea in the tamperproofing chapter when we discuss Algorithm TPCA (Section 7.2.1▸414).

To get the basic flavor of this algorithm, consider the following function f that has been split into six pieces, which we'll call cells:

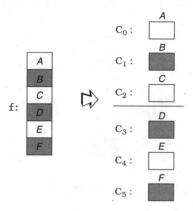

The cells are divided into two regions in memory, upper and lower. Execution proceeds in rounds, such that during each round every cell in upper memory is xored with a cell in lower memory. Each time, a new cell becomes in the clear and execution jumps there. During even rounds, the cells in upper memory are xored into the cells in lower memory; during odd rounds, lower cells are xored into upper memory cells. After a certain number of rounds, the function returns to its initial configuration. This is important, because it means that every time a function is called, its code is in the same, initial, state.

M_0 is the initial, obfuscated configuration of the function:

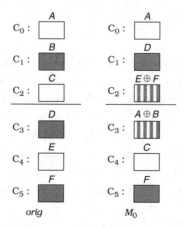

The top cell, the light gray C_0, is in cleartext—this is where execution will start. Cells 1, 4, and 5 are also in the clear, but some of them are not in the same location as in the unobfuscated code. C_2 and C_3, however, are *not* in cleartext; they are the xored version of two cells. This is why they are striped in the example above, to indicate they are a mixture of the two cells of the corresponding shading. Keep in mind that because of the nature of the xor operation, if you xor a "striped dark gray–medium gray" cell with a cleartext dark gray cell, you get the cleartext dark gray cell! Or, in general:

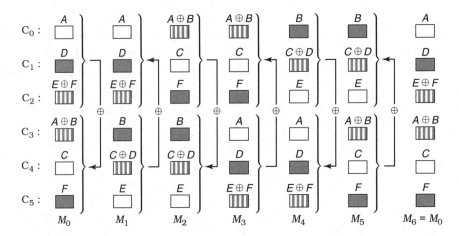

Have a look at this example execution of the function above:

$$C_0: \quad A \quad\Big| \quad A \quad\Big| \quad A \oplus B \Big) \quad A \oplus B \quad\Big| \quad B \quad\Big| \quad B \quad\Big| \quad A$$

When the function is called, execution starts at the cleartext cell 0, C_0. When C_0 has finished executing, *every cell in upper memory is xored with every cell in lower memory*, leading to configuration M_1. In this case, C_0 is xored into C_3, C_1 is xored into C_4, and C_2 is xored into C_5, but a different schedule is, of course, possible. Execution next jumps to C_3, and after it has finished executing, the cells in lower memory are xored into the corresponding cells in upper memory: C_3 into C_0, C_4 into C_1, C_5 into C_2. Cell C_1 is now in the clear, and execution continues there. Notice that after six rounds you're back to where you started, i.e., configuration M_6

is the same as M_0. As a consequence, every time you call this function it starts off in the same, initial configuration.

The reason this algorithm works is because you can use xor to swap two variables A and B:

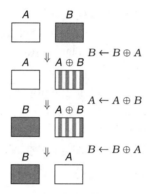

Since it takes three applications of xor to swap two cells, six applications will bring the cells back to their original state.

What should your attack model be for this algorithm? Well, the problem that this and many similar algorithms has is that one piece of code, the entry point, always has to be in cleartext. You have to start executing somewhere! It's easy to imagine an adversary crafting an attack where he sets a breakpoint at the entry point, runs the program until the breakpoint hits, dumps the cleartext code, sets a new breakpoint at the next cleartext cell, executes, dumps code, and so on.

Problem 6.2   Can you craft an attack script for your favorite debugger that iteratively unwinds code obfuscated with OBFAG$_{\text{swap}}$?

6.2.2.1 Building the State Machine   Algorithm 6.2▸370 gives an overview of Aucsmith's technique. The algorithm takes the function P to be obfuscated as input, along with the number of pieces n it should be split into. The output is n cells, where each cell C_c consists of three pieces:

IV_c
f = my space $\oplus$ other space
jump *next*

Algorithm 6.2 Overview of algorithm $\text{OBFAG}_{\text{swap}}$. n is the number of pieces into which P will be split.

$\text{OBFUSCATE}(P, n)$:

1. Split P into n pieces $P_0, \dots, P_{n-1}$.

2. Let $C_0, \dots, C_{n-1}$ be the memory cells in which the pieces will reside at runtime. The C_i:s are of equal size, large enough to fit the largest piece P_j.

3. Cells are, conceptually, divided into two spaces, *upper* ($C_0, \dots, C_{n/2-1}$) and *lower* ($C_{n/2}, \dots, C_{n-1}$). Each cell in the upper space partners with a cell in the lower space. Select a partner function $PF(c)$ that maps a cell number to the cell number of its partner, such as $PF(c) = c \oplus K$, for some constant K.

4. Let $IV_0, \dots, IV_{n-1}$ be the initial values of cells $C_0, \dots, C_{n-1}$, respectively.

5. Initialize a set of equations $E_1 = \{C_0 = IV_0, \dots, C_{n-1} = IV_{n-1}\}$ that expresses the current state of the memory cells as a function of their initial values.

6. Initialize a set of equations $E_2 = \{\}$ that expresses how a piece P_i can be recovered in cleartext from the initial values $IV_0, \dots, IV_{n-1}$.

7. Initialize a table *next* $= \langle P_0 =?, \dots, P_{n-1} =? \rangle$ that maps each subprogram P_i to the cell it should jump to in order to execute P_{i+1}.

8. For $p \in [0 \dots n - 1]$ do the following:

    (a) Select a cell C_c to hold piece P_p in cleartext.

    (b) Consult E_1 to find the current contents V of C_c. Update E_2 such that $E_2 = \{\dots, P_p = V, \dots\}$. Using Gaussian elimination, try to invert E_2 (i.e., find values for all the IV_i:s). If there is no solution, select another cell for P_p.

    (c) Update *next* $= \langle \dots, P_{p-1} = C_c, \dots \rangle$.

    (d) For even (odd) p:s, simulate a mutation where every cell C_i in upper (lower) space is xored with its partner cell $C_{PF(i)}$ in lower (upper) space. Update E_1 to reflect the new situation: $E_1 = \{\dots, C_{PF(i)} = C_{PF(i)} \oplus C_i\}$.

9. Using Gaussian elimination, find values for all the IV_i:s.

10. Construct and return each cell $C_c = (IV_c, f = \text{my space} \oplus \text{other space}, \text{jump } next(c))$, where f is the mutation function.

IV_c is the *initial value* of cell C_c, its value when the function is first called. f is the *mutation function*, the function that xors this cell with its partner cell in the other memory region. *next*, finally, is the number of the cell at which execution should continue after this one.

To construct these cells, the algorithm makes use of three data structures: two sets of equations E_1 and E_2, and a table *next*. E_1 expresses the current state of the memory cells as a function of their initial values. E_2 expresses how you can recover a piece P_i of the original program P from the initial values $IV_0, \ldots, IV_{n-1}$. The algorithm constructs the cells by "simulating" how they will be executed during runtime, updating E_1 and E_2 with each round. At the end of each round, the currently executing cell will issue a jump to the next cell. As you're constructing the cells, you'll fill in a table *next* that maps each cell to the cell it should jump to.

Let's continue with the example above (it's adapted from an example in Aucsmith and Graunke [27]), where a program P is split into $n = 6$ subprograms $P_0, \ldots, P_5$, which reside in 6 cells $C_0, \ldots, C_5$. P is straight-line code, so the subprograms will execute in the order $P_0, P_1, \ldots, P_5$. In the initial configuration in the simulation, each cell C_i contains its initial value IV_i:

The goal of the algorithm is to construct these initial values $IV_0, \ldots, IV_5$ and the schedule that determines which cell should be xored with which other cell. Initially, C_0 is in cleartext (shown in light gray); this is where execution will start. From this, you can draw the conclusion that the initial value in cell 0 should be P_0. You enter this fact into E_2.

In this example, we'll assume a very simple mutation function: During even rounds, each cell i in upper memory is xored with cell $i + 3$ in lower memory, and during odd rounds, cell i in lower memory is xored with $i - 3$.

During mutation round 1, you xor all the cells in upper memory with their partner cells in lower memory:

	$\underline{E_1}$	$\underline{E_2}$	$\underline{next}$
IV_0	$C_0 = IV_0$	$IV_0 \quad = P_0$	$C_0 \rightarrow C_3$
IV_1	$C_1 = IV_1$	$IV_0 \oplus IV_3 = P_1$	$C_1 \rightarrow ?$
IV_2	$C_2 = IV_2$		$C_2 \rightarrow ?$
$IV_0 \oplus IV_3$	$C_3 = IV_0 \oplus IV_3$		$C_3 \rightarrow ?$
$IV_1 \oplus IV_4$	$C_4 = IV_1 \oplus IV_4$		$C_4 \rightarrow ?$
$IV_2 \oplus IV_5$	$C_5 = IV_2 \oplus IV_5$		$C_5 \rightarrow ?$

Here, you've updated E_1 so that it contains the current values of each cell at this point in the simulation. You've also picked C_3 as the cell where execution should continue and updated *next* accordingly. Now, if C_3 is the next cell that will execute, then it must contain P_1, because that's the next piece of your program that should execute. In other words, $P_1 = C_3$ and $C_3 = IV_0 \oplus IV_3$, which is the reason you've updated E_2 to contain $P_1 = IV_0 \oplus IV_3$.

What does all this mean? Well, what it means is that when, during execution, you get to mutation round 2, cell C_3 will contain the cleartext value of program piece P_1. Furthermore, you constructed the value in C_3 by xoring the initial value in cell C_0 (P_0) into C_3. And *that* means that IV_3, the initial value in cell 3, must have been $P_0 \oplus P_1$. All this you can work out by Gaussian elimination of E_1 and E_2!

OK, on to round 2. After executing C_3, you xor all the cells in lower memory with their parter cells in upper memory:

	$\underline{E_1}$	$\underline{E_2}$	$\underline{next}$
IV_3	$C_0 = IV_3$	$IV_0 \quad = P_0$	$C_0 \rightarrow C_3$
IV_4	$C_1 = IV_4$	$IV_0 \oplus IV_3 = P_1$	$C_1 \rightarrow ?$
IV_5	$C_2 = IV_5$	$IV_4 \quad = P_2$	$C_2 \rightarrow ?$
$IV_0 \oplus IV_3$	$C_3 = IV_0 \oplus IV_3$		$C_3 \rightarrow C_1$
$IV_1 \oplus IV_4$	$C_4 = IV_1 \oplus IV_4$		$C_4 \rightarrow ?$
$IV_2 \oplus IV_5$	$C_5 = IV_2 \oplus IV_5$		$C_5 \rightarrow ?$

Let's pick C_1 as the cell to execute the next piece of your program, P_2. This means that IV_4 (what was initially in cell C_4 but which now has moved up to cell C_1!) must contain P_2. You add this fact as an equation in E_2.

At the end of mutation round 3, upper memory gets xored with lower memory, and you pick C_4 to contain P_3 in cleartext:

	$\underline{E_1}$	$\underline{E_2}$	$\underline{next}$
IV_3	$C_0 = IV_3$	$IV_0 = P_0$	$C_0 \to C_3$
IV_4	$C_1 = IV_4$	$IV_0 \oplus IV_3 = P_1$	$C_1 \to C_4$
IV_5	$C_2 = IV_5$	$IV_4 = P_2$	$C_2 \to ?$
IV_0	$C_3 = IV_0$	$IV_1 = P_3$	$C_3 \to C_1$
IV_1	$C_4 = IV_1$		$C_4 \to ?$
IV_2	$C_5 = IV_2$		$C_5 \to ?$

At runtime, after executing the code in cell C_4, in mutation round 4, lower memory gets xored with upper memory. You pick C_2 to contain P_4 in cleartext:

	$\underline{E_1}$	$\underline{E_2}$	$\underline{next}$
$IV_0 \oplus IV_3$	$C_0 = IV_0 \oplus IV_3$	$IV_0 = P_0$	$C_0 \to C_3$
$IV_1 \oplus IV_4$	$C_1 = IV_1 \oplus IV_4$	$IV_0 \oplus IV_3 = P_1$	$C_1 \to C_4$
$IV_2 \oplus IV_5$	$C_2 = IV_2 \oplus IV_5$	$IV_4 = P_2$	$C_2 \to ?$
IV_0	$C_3 = IV_0$	$IV_1 = P_3$	$C_3 \to C_1$
IV_1	$C_4 = IV_1$	$IV_2 \oplus IV_5 = P_4$	$C_4 \to C_2$
IV_2	$C_5 = IV_2$		$C_5 \to ?$

Since, at this point, C_2 contains $IV_2 \oplus IV_5$, you add the equation $IV_2 \oplus IV_5 = P_4$ to E_2. Now it's entirely possible that as you add equations to E_2 it becomes non-invertible, i.e., there's no way to solve it for initial values $IV_0, \dots, IV_5$. In that case, you'll need to backtrack and pick another cell to contain the next cleartext subprogram.

In mutation 5, you pick C_5 to contain the final subprogram, P_5:

	$\underline{E_1}$	$\underline{E_2}$	$\underline{next}$
$IV_0 \oplus IV_3$	$C_0 = IV_0 \oplus IV_3$	$IV_0 = P_0$	$C_0 \rightarrow C_3$
$IV_1 \oplus IV_4$	$C_1 = IV_1 \oplus IV_4$	$IV_0 \oplus IV_3 = P_1$	$C_1 \rightarrow C_4$
$IV_2 \oplus IV_5$	$C_2 = IV_2 \oplus IV_5$	$IV_4 = P_2$	$C_2 \rightarrow C_5$
IV_3	$C_3 = IV_3$	$IV_1 = P_3$	$C_3 \rightarrow C_1$
IV_4	$C_4 = IV_4$	$IV_2 \oplus IV_5 = P_4$	$C_4 \rightarrow C_2$
IV_5	$C_5 = IV_5$	$IV_5 = P_5$	$C_5 \rightarrow RET$

After the final xor operation, when the upper cells are xored with lower memory, we're back to the initial state, and the function is ready to be called again:

	$\underline{E_1}$
IV_0	$C_0 = IV_0$
IV_1	$C_1 = IV_1$
IV_2	$C_2 = IV_2$
IV_3	$C_3 = IV_3$
IV_4	$C_4 = IV_4$
IV_5	$C_5 = IV_5$

The purpose of this exercise was one thing—to construct the set of equations E_2! Now you can invert E_2 a final time to determine the initial values for the cells:

$$
\begin{cases}
\quad\quad\underline{E_2} \\
IV_0 \quad\quad = P_0 \\
IV_0 \oplus IV_3 = P_1 \\
IV_4 \quad\quad = P_2 \\
IV_1 \quad\quad = P_3 \\
IV_2 \oplus IV_5 = P_4 \\
IV_5 \quad\quad = P_5
\end{cases}
\implies
\begin{aligned}
IV_0 &= P_0 \\
IV_1 &= P_3 \\
IV_2 &= P_4 \oplus P_5 \\
IV_3 &= P_0 \oplus P_1 \\
IV_4 &= P_2 \\
IV_5 &= P_5
\end{aligned}
$$

Putting all this together, you get your final cells:

C_0	C_1	C_2	C_3	C_4	C_5
P_0	P_3	$P_4 \oplus P_5$	$P_0 \oplus P_1$	P_2	P_5
partner=C_3	partner=C_4	partner=C_5	partner=C_0	partner=C_1	partner=C_2
jump C_3	jump C_4	jump C_5	jump C_1	jump C_2	jump EXIT

6.2.2.2 Example Execution   To illustrate what happens during execution, let's assume you have a very simple program consisting of the binary values $P = \langle 000, 001, 010, 011, 100, 101 \rangle$. Break P up into six pieces and use the equations above to solve for initial values:

$$
\begin{cases}
P_0 & = & 000 \\
P_1 & = & 001 \\
P_2 & = & 010 \\
P_3 & = & 011 \\
P_4 & = & 100 \\
P_5 & = & 101
\end{cases}
\quad\Rightarrow\quad
\begin{cases}
IV_0 & = & P_0 & = & 000 \\
IV_1 & = & P_3 & = & 011 \\
IV_2 & = & P_4 \oplus P_5 & = & 001 \\
IV_3 & = & P_0 \oplus P_1 & = & 001 \\
IV_4 & = & P_2 & = & 010 \\
IV_5 & = & P_5 & = & 101
\end{cases}
$$

Here's the initial state M_0 and each of the mutation rounds M_1 through M_6:

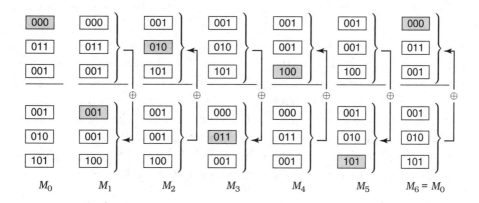

Note how during each round a new cell (in light gray) becomes cleartext, resulting in your executing the original program piece by piece: 000, 001, 010, 011, 100, 101. Also, after the last round, you've returned the program to its initial configuration.

6.2.2.3 Coding the Example   Normally, you will code an algorithm like this using a binary code editor that allows you to manipulate the program at the binary level. That doesn't lend itself well to explanation, however, so we've coded up a simple example here in gcc C. The mutation schedule is exactly the same as in the example we worked out above, except this time our source program is actual C code, consisting of 6 `printf` statements:

```
printf("SPGM0\n");
printf("SPGM1\n");
printf("SPGM2\n");
printf("SPGM3\n");
printf("SPGM4\n");
printf("SPGM5\n");
```

$$
\begin{cases}
P_0 & = & \texttt{printf("SPGM0\n")} \\
P_1 & = & \texttt{printf("SPGM1\n")} \\
P_2 & = & \texttt{printf("SPGM2\n")} \\
P_3 & = & \texttt{printf("SPGM3\n")} \\
P_4 & = & \texttt{printf("SPGM4\n")} \\
P_5 & = & \texttt{printf("SPGM5\n")}
\end{cases}
$$

Listing 6.3▸377 contains some auxiliary definitions we're going to need. The `xor(from,to,len)` function xors the cell starting at the address `from` into the cell starting at address `to`. The function `swap(from,to,len)` swaps two cells starting at `from` and `to`. The function `xor2(from,key,to,cellcount,cellsize)` also xors in a cryptographic key; we will use this function when we extend OBFAG$_{\text{swap}}$ to also use encryption in Section 6.3.2▸392.

Listing 6.4▸378 contains the actual obfuscated function `P`. The dashed section of code should be executed at obfuscation time—it uses `xor` and `swap` to set up the initial configuration. `ALIGN` is a macro that makes sure that every cell is the same size. The construct `&&label` is a gcc extension to C called *labels-as-values*. It takes the address of a local label that can be stored in a variable. We use this construct here to make the jump array `next`. One of the main headaches when coding this type of program at the source-code level is that the compiler may be too clever and start moving code around in unpredictable ways. For this reason, we've added the dummy array `a` of cell addresses—this tricks the compiler and prevents it from optimizing code between cells. This code should run fine on the x86 architecture, but on other machines you will have to add code to flush caches after each call to `swap` and `xor`. Notice how the main program calls `P()` *twice* (in light gray); after the first call has ended, the body of `P` is back to its initial state, ready for the second call.

6.2.3   OBF*MAMDSB*: Dynamic Code Merging

The goal of the algorithms in this chapter is to keep a program in constant flux in order to make sure that every time the adversary looks at the code, it's different in some way. Algorithm OBFMAMDSB [235] accomplishes this by letting two or

---

Listing 6.3 Auxiliary routines used in Algorithms OBFAG$_{swap}$ and OBFAG$_{crypt}$.

```c
void xor(caddr_t from, caddr_t to, int len) {
   int i;
   for(i=0;i<len;i++) {
      *to ^= *from; from++; to++;
   }
}

void swap(caddr_t from, caddr_t to, int len) {
   int i;
   for(i=0;i<len;i++) {
      char t = *from; *from = *to; *to = t;
      from++; to++;
   }
}

void xor2(caddr_t from,char key[],caddr_t to,int cellcount,int cellsize) {
   int i,c;
   for(c=0;c<cellcount;c++) {
      for(i=0;i<cellsize;i++) {
         if (from != NULL) {
            *to ^= *from;
            from++;
         }
         if (key != NULL)
            *to ^= key[c];
         to++;
      }
   }
}

#define CELLSIZE 64
#define ALIGN asm volatile (".align 64\n");
```

---

more functions *share* the same location in memory. A region of memory (which we'll call a *template*) is set up containing some of the code-bytes from the functions, more specifically, the ones they all have in common. Before a particular function is executed, an *edit script* is used to patch the template with the necessary code-bytes to create a complete version of that function. When another function assigned to the same template is about to be executed, the process repeats, this time with a different edit script.

Listing 6.4 Algorithm OBFAG$_{swap}$. This example continues in Listing 6.11 ▶ 397, where cells are also continuously encrypted and decrypted.

```
void P() {
    static int firsttime=1;
    if (firsttime) {
        xor(&&cell5,&&cell2,CELLSIZE);
        xor(&&cell0,&&cell3,CELLSIZE);
        swap(&&cell1,&&cell4,CELLSIZE);
        firsttime = 0;
    }

    char* a[] = {&&align0,&&align1,&&align2,...,&&align5};
    char* next[] ={&&cell0,&&cell1,&&cell2,&&cell3,&&cell4,&&cell5};
    goto *next[0];

    align0: ALIGN
    cell0:  printf("SPGM0\n");
            xor(&&cell0,&&cell3,3*CELLSIZE);
            goto *next[3];
    align1: ALIGN
    cell1:  printf("SPGM2\n");
            xor(&&cell0,&&cell3,3*CELLSIZE);
            goto *next[4];
    align2: ALIGN
    cell2:  printf("SPGM4\n");
            xor(&&cell0,&&cell3,3*CELLSIZE);
            goto *next[5];
    align3: ALIGN
    cell3:  printf("SPGM1\n");
            xor(&&cell3,&&cell0,3*CELLSIZE);
            goto *next[1];
    align4: ALIGN
    cell4:  printf("SPGM3\n");
            xor(&&cell3,&&cell0,3*CELLSIZE);
            goto *next[2];
    align5: ALIGN
    cell5:  printf("SPGM5\n");
            xor(&&cell3,&&cell0,3*CELLSIZE);
}
int main (int argc, char *argv[]) {
    makeCodeWritable(...);
    P(); P();
}
```

To illustrate this, suppose you want to obfuscate a program that contains two functions, f_1 and f_2. They have the following code-bytes:

$$f_1 \qquad f_2$$

0	10
1	5
2	6
3	20
4	99

0	10
1	9
2	3
3	20

At obfuscation time, Algorithm OBFMAMDSB would replace f_1 and f_2 with the template T and two edit scripts e_1 and e_2:

$$T$$

0	10
1	?
2	?
3	20
4	99

$$e_1 = [1 \rightarrow 5, 2 \rightarrow 6]$$
$$e_2 = [1 \rightarrow 9, 2 \rightarrow 3]$$

The template contains those code-bytes that f_1 and f_2 have in common. In the locations where f_1 and f_2 differ (indicated above by question marks), you can put whatever you want—the more confusing for an attacker the better.

At runtime, the first time the program wants to execute f_1 it must first patch T using e_1, replacing the code-byte at offset 1 with 5 and the code-byte at offset 2 with 6. If there's a subsequent call to f_1 (without an intervening call to f_2), you can dispense with the editing and jump directly to T. When the program calls f_2, on the other hand, it must first modify T using the edit script e_2. In this way, the T memory region will constantly change, first containing an incomplete function and then alternating between containing the code-bytes for f_1 and f_2.

Algorithm 6.3▶380 contains an overview of this technique. The first step is to decide which functions should be in the same *cluster*, i.e., which should reside in the same template at runtime. If your code looks like this

```
main() {
    while(1) {
        f₁();
        f₂();
    }
}
```

Algorithm 6.3 Overview of Algorithm OBFMAMDSB. P is the program to be obfuscated, $f_1, f_2, \ldots$ are the functions in P, G is its call graph, and D is profiling data collected over representative runs.

OBFUSCATE(P, G, D):

1. Create a set
   $C = \{\ldots, \{f_i, f_j, \ldots\}, \ldots\}$ where each element is a set of the functions that should belong to the same cluster: $C \leftarrow \text{CLUSTER}(P, G, D)$.

2. For each cluster c_k in C do the following:

   (a) Create a template T_k containing the intersection of the code-bytes of the functions in c_k.

   (b) For each function f_i in c_k create an edit script e_i such that applying e_i to the code-bytes of T_k creates the code-bytes of f_i.

3. Return a new program consisting of the main program from P, the templates T_k, the edit scripts e_i, and a code edit routine patch(T_k, e_i).

CLUSTER(P, G, D):

1. Put each function in its own cluster, i.e., $C \leftarrow \{\{f_1\}, \{f_2\}, \ldots\}$.

2. Use the profiling data D to choose the two cheapest clusters c_i and c_j to merge. Merging them will minimize the number of function edits. $c_i \cup c_j$ must not contain two functions that can be active at the same time: i.e., there must be no path between them in the call graph.

3. $C \leftarrow C - \{c_i, c_j\} \cup \{c_i \cup c_j\}$.

4. Repeat from 2 until the required level of obfuscation has been reached, the maximum overhead has been exceeded, or no more merges are possible.

5. Return C.

---

it would be unwise to put f_1 and f_2 in the same cluster, since much time would be spent editing the template as control goes back and forth between the two functions. Profiling data collected from representative runs can help you make the best cluster assignment. No two functions on the same call chain can be in the same cluster, since that would require them to both reside in cleartext in the template at the same time, which of course isn't possible.

Have a look at Listing 6.5 ▸381 for a simple example. The unobfuscated program looks like this:

```
int val = 0;
void f1(int* v) {*v=99;}
void f2(int* v) {*v=42;}
int main (int argc, char *argv[]) {
    f1(&val);
    f2(&val);
}
```

Listing 6.5 Example of Algorithm OBFMAMDSB. Listing 6.6▶382 gives the `diff` and `patch` routines.

```
EDIT script1[200], script2[200];
char* template;
int template_len, script_len = 0;
typedef void(*FUN)(int*);
int val, state = 0;

void f1_stub() {
   if (state != 1) {
      patch(script1,script_len,template);
      state = 1;
   }
   ((FUN)template)(&val);
}

void f2_stub() {
   if (state != 2) {
      patch(script2,script_len,template);
      state = 2;
   }
   ((FUN)template)(&val);
}

int my_main (int argc, char *argv[]) {
   f1_stub();
   f2_stub();
}

void f1(int* v) {*v=99;}
void f2(int* v) {*v=42;}

int main (int argc, char *argv[]) {
   makeCodeWritable(...);
   template = allocExecutablePages(...);
   diff((caddr_t)f1,f1SIZE,(caddr_t)f2,f2SIZE,
        script1,script2,
        &script_len,template, &template_len);
   memset(f1,0,f1SIZE);  memset(f2,0,f2SIZE);
   my_main(argc,argv);
}
```

Listing 6.6 Algorithm OBFMAMDSB routines for creating a script and patching a template using that script.

```
typedef unsigned int uint32;
typedef char* addr_t;
typedef struct {uint32 offset; char value;} EDIT;

void diff (addr_t prof1, int len1, addr_t prof2, int len2,
           EDIT script1[], EDIT script2[],  int *script_len,
           char template[], int *template_len) {
   int i, s=0;
   *template_len = (len1>len2)?len1:len2;
   for(i=0; i<*template_len; i++) {
       if       (i >= len1)         template[i] = *prof2;
       else if (i >= len2)         template[i] = *prof1;
       else if (*prof1 == *prof2) template[i] = *prof1;
       else {
          template[i] = 0;
          script1[s].offset = script2[s].offset = i;
          script1[s].value = *prof1;
          script2[s].value = *prof2; s++;
       }
       prof1++; prof2++;
   }
   *script_len = s;
}

void patch (EDIT script[], int script_len, char template[]) {
   int i,t;
   for(i=0; i<script_len; i++)
      template[script[i].offset] = script[i].value;
}
```

In a real implementation, the dashed code in main would run at obfuscation time, using the diff routine (Listing 6.6) to construct the template and two edit scripts script1 and script2. In this simple example, we instead construct the template at runtime and simulate removing the original functions from the code by zeroing them out using memset. For each function call, you construct a stub that uses the patch routine to edit the template and then executes an indirect jump to it. We can use a state variable to bypass the patch in the cases when the template is already in the right state.

Madou et al.'s [235] implementation does away with the extra (unstealthy) state variable by overwriting the stubs with the appropriate code whenever there's a state change. The paper also shows how to create edit scripts that are compact and minimize edit costs.

This algorithm has a simple trade-off between performance and level of protection. The more frequently the templates change (i.e., the more often they have to be edited from containing one function to containing another), the harder the code is to understand and the slower it will be. Madou et al. give some performance numbers: With an average of 3.6 functions per template, the average slowdown for the SPEC benchmarks was 17.7%, with a maximum slowdown of almost a factor of 2.

A major problem with this algorithm is that the patch routine and the edit scripts are left in the clear. It should therefore not be hard for an adversary to analyze the obfuscated program statically and recover the original program by running each call that it finds to $patch(T_k, e_i)$. Madou et al. propose to, essentially, keep the scripts in encrypted form and decrypt them at runtime. This prevents a static attack (assuming the cryptographic key can be effectively hidden), but it still doesn't stop a dynamic attack where the adversary intercepts and saves any code that becomes in the clear after a call to patch.

Problem 6.3 Dynamic obfuscation is difficult to implement. Typical systems work by manipulating programs post-compilation, i.e., at the binary code level. Could you develop a system similar to the examples you've seen in this chapter that instead allows dynamic transformations to be written at the source-code level? The main problem is tricking the compiler into generating truly position-independent code so that functions, and parts of functions, can be moved around freely. Consider building your tool on top of a C source transformation system such as CIL [272].

6.3 Encryption

There have been any number of proposals for using encryption to protect software: "We use encryption to protect the confidentiality of data with great success," so the argument goes, "so, surely this means encrypting a program to protect the intellectual content *it* contains will work well too." The basic idea is simple: Encrypt the program at obfuscation time, store the key in the executable (or force the user to enter it every time the program is run), and decrypt and execute at runtime.

Unfortunately, by and large, software protection by encryption turns out to be just a really bad idea. It affords little protection, it can have a huge performance overhead, and in spite of being such a simple idea, there are serious implementation issues.

Many descriptions of code encryption algorithms put much emphasis on which cryptographic algorithm to use, what the proper key length should be, and so on. However, the "security" that these algorithms affords is never contingent on the strength of the underlying algorithm but on more mundane issues such as where in the executable you store the key. In fact, the use of the term "encryption" for what these algorithms do is really stretching the terminology. Cryptographic systems assume that the key is secret, but in code encryption systems it is merely "hidden"— both the decryptor and the key must reside in the executable itself.

In many ways, the problem with code encryption is similar to the problem you face in a DRM system. There, too, you use encryption, but to protect media, not code. And there, too, you need to ship the key with the item you're trying to protect. And for the same reasons, the cryptographic system you use in a DRM system is much less important than the techniques you use to hide the key and the cryptographic primitives themselves.

There are basically two straightforward attacks against code-hiding systems:

1. Since the key is embedded in the executable—find the key!
2. Since the code must be decrypted in order to execute it—capture it when it is in cleartext!

In practice, therefore, you should think of code encryption more like "temporary code hiding," a way to ensure that code is in cleartext for as short a period of time as possible. For this reason, there is no need to make implementations any more complicated than necessary: Xoring the code with a random "key string" is every bit as "secure" as encrypting it with Triple DES, and quite a bit faster. Also, while in the cryptographic world using well known and trusted algorithms such as DES and RSA is standard practice, in the code encryption world this is a bad idea. These algorithms have easy-to-recognize signatures, both in their code (fixed number of rounds, use of unusual instructions such as xor) and in their dynamic behavior.

If you do want to build a protection-through-encryption system, you have to make a number of engineering decisions:

bulk/on demand: Do you decrypt the entire program at once at program load time or do you decrypt on demand, as code is needed for execution?

fine/coarse granularity: Do you decrypt small pieces (say, a basic block) at a time (inefficient but ensures that only a small piece of code is ever in cleartext), or do you decrypt at the function or module level?

key-as-data/key-as-code: Do you store the key as data values in the program, or do you derive the key from code?

keep-in-the-clear/re-encrypt: Do you keep the decrypted code decrypted, or do you re-encrypt each piece of code as it is no longer needed, making sure that as little code as possible is ever in cleartext?

Regardless of the choices you make, whether in the end it's worth the trouble is still highly dubious.

We're going to show you two algorithms in this section. OBFCKSP is a straightforward medium-grained (function-level), on-demand, key-as-code, re-encrypting algorithm. Algorithm OBFAG$_{crypt}$ is an extension to OBFAG$_{swap}$ from Section 6.2.2▶366 that xors the code cells with a key stream as they are moved back and forth between the upper and lower memory regions. Later in the book (Section 7.2.4▶431) you will see how the Skype VoIP client is protected using a bulk, coarse, key-as-data, keep-in-the-clear encryption scheme.

6.3.1 *OBFCKSP:* Code as Key Material

The goal of code encryption is to keep as little code as possible in the clear at any point in time during execution. At one extreme, you can decrypt the next instruction, execute it, re-encrypt it, decrypt the next instruction, execute, and so on. This way, only one instruction is ever in the clear, but as a result, the performance overhead will be huge. At the other extreme, you can decrypt the entire program once, prior to the start of execution, and leave it in cleartext. This will have little impact on execution time but will make it easy for the adversary to capture the decrypted code.

Algorithm OBFCKSP [54] takes an intermediate approach and decrypts one function at a time. When the program starts up, it's all encrypted—all except for the main function, which is in the clear. Before you jump to a function, you first decrypt it, and when the function returns to the caller, you re-encrypt it. However, if that was all that you did, all the functions on the current call chain (from main to the current function) would be in the clear. For this reason, the first thing a function must do when it's called is to encrypt the function that called it, and before it returns, it must decrypt it again. You can think of this as walking around a house where every door is always kept locked—you unlock one door at a time, walk through, and re-lock it behind you. This way, Algorithm OBFCKSP makes sure that at any one point in time, two functions at most will be in the clear.

Two questions remain, however. First, what should you use as the encryption key? You could just store the key as data, of course, but this has some serious problems. Cryptographic keys are much more "random" than ordinary data, and this makes them easy to spot [325]. For this reason, Algorithm OBFCKSP uses the *code* of one function as the key to encrypt/decrypt another function. The second problem is deciding the cryptographic system to be used. This turns out to be easy: *It doesn't really matter*! Unlike "normal" cryptographic applications, the key isn't truly secret; instead, it's hidden somewhere in the program. Therefore, the normal assumptions of cryptography don't apply. Instead, *all* the security this and other code encryption algorithms afford you is a function of how well the key is hidden. Using RSA over DES will not gain any measurable improvement in security, since if you have access to the key both will be equally easy to "break"! This is similar to the situation in DRM, where it doesn't matter much which algorithm you use to encrypt the media, since all the security rests with how well you can hide and protect the key in the media player. You can therefore go ahead and use the simplest (and fastest) cryptographic algorithm you can think of.

Algorithm 6.4▸387 gives an overview of OBFCKSP. There are three cases to consider, depending on whether the call graph is a tree, DAG, or a circular graph. In the simplest case, illustrated by the small DRM example in Listings 6.7▸388, 6.8▸389, and 6.9▸390, the call graph is tree-shaped:

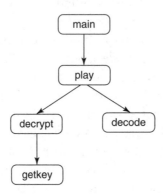

Before and after every procedure call, you insert calls to a guard function that decrypts/re-encrypts the callee, using a hash of the cleartext of the caller as key. These calls are in light gray in Listings 6.8▸389 and 6.9▸390. On entrance and exit of the callee, you encrypt/decrypt the caller using a hash of the cleartext of the callee as key. These calls are in dark gray. The code in dashed produces the obfuscated program, where every function is encrypted with the hash of the cleartext of its caller

---

Algorithm 6.4 Overview of algorithm OBFCKSP. P is the program to be obfuscated; G its call graph.

OBFUSCATE(P, G):

1. For every function call $f \to g$ for which there is no other call $h \to g$, decrypt g before jumping to it and re-encrypt g after returning from the call:

$$f() \ \{$$
$$\quad decrypt\ g\ using\ \mathsf{hash}(f)\ as\ key$$
$$\quad g();$$
$$\quad encrypt\ g\ using\ \mathsf{hash}(f)\ as\ key$$
$$\}$$
$$g()\ \{\ldots\}$$

   Modify P by encrypting g with the hash of the cleartext of f as the key.

2. For every set of function calls $f_1 \to h_1 \to g$, $f_2 \to h_2 \to g$, $\ldots$ insert code to decrypt/encrypt g in all f_i:s using a combination of the hashes of the encrypted $h_1, h_2, \ldots$ as key:

$$f_i()\ \{$$
$$\quad decrypt\ g\ using\ \mathsf{hash}(h_1) \oplus \mathsf{hash}(h_2) \oplus \ldots\ as\ key$$
$$\quad decrypt\ h_i\ using\ \mathsf{hash}(f_i)\ as\ key$$
$$\quad h_i();$$
$$\quad encrypt\ h_i\ using\ \mathsf{hash}(f_i)\ as\ key$$
$$\quad encrypt\ g\ using\ \mathsf{hash}(h_1) \oplus \mathsf{hash}(h_2) \oplus \ldots\ as\ key$$
$$\}$$
$$h_i()\ \{g();\}$$
$$g()\ \{\ldots\}$$

   Modify P by encrypting g with the hash of the ciphertexts of $h_1, h_2, \ldots$ as key.

3. For every function g, insert code to encrypt g's caller on entry and to re-encrypt it when g returns, using the hash of the cleartext of g as the key:

$$g()\ \{$$
$$\quad encrypt\ g's\ caller\ using\ \mathsf{hash}(g)\ as\ key$$
$$\quad \ldots$$
$$\quad decrypt\ g's\ caller\ using\ \mathsf{hash}(g)\ as\ key$$
$$\}$$

4. Add the functions in Listing 6.7 ▶388 and a hash function from Section 7.2.2 ▶418 to P.

Listing 6.7 Encryption/decryption guards used in Algorithm OBFCKSP. hash1 is defined in Section 7.2.2▶418.

```
void crypto (waddr_t proc,uint32 key,int words) {
   int i;
   for(i=1; i<words; i++) {
      *proc ^= key;
      proc++;
   }
}

void guard (waddr_t proc,int proc_words,
             waddr_t key_proc,int key_words) {
   uint32 key = hash1(key_proc,key_words);
   crypto(proc,key,proc_words);
}

void guard2 (waddr_t proc,int proc_words,
              waddr_t key_proc1,int key_words1,
              waddr_t key_proc2,int key_words2) {
   uint32 key1 = hash1(key_proc1,key_words1);
   uint32 key2 = hash1(key_proc2,key_words2);
   uint32 key  = key1 ^ key2;
   crypto(proc,key,proc_words);
}
```

as key. In a real system, the dashed code wouldn't be shipped with the program but would be executed at protection time, after which the encrypted code would be written to file.

So what if the call graph is shaped like a DAG, like this?

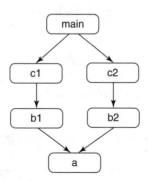

Listing 6.8 Example of Algorithm OBFCKSP. Encryption/decryption functions are shown in Listing 6.7▶388. The code continues in Listing 6.9▶390.

```
int player_main (int argc, char *argv[]) {
   int user_key = 0xca7ca115;
   int digital_media[] = {10,102};
   guard((waddr_t)play,playSIZE,(waddr_t)player_main,player_mainSIZE);
   play(user_key,digital_media,2);
   guard((waddr_t)play,playSIZE,(waddr_t)player_main,player_mainSIZE);
}
int getkey(int user_key) {
   guard((waddr_t)decrypt,decryptSIZE,(waddr_t)getkey,getkeySIZE);
   int player_key = 0xbabeca75;
   int v = user_key ^ player_key;
   guard((waddr_t)decrypt,decryptSIZE,(waddr_t)getkey,getkeySIZE);
   return v;
}
int decrypt(int user_key, int media) {
   guard((waddr_t)play,playSIZE,(waddr_t)decrypt,decryptSIZE);
   guard((waddr_t)getkey,getkeySIZE,(waddr_t)decrypt,decryptSIZE);
   int key = getkey(user_key);
   guard((waddr_t)getkey,getkeySIZE,(waddr_t)decrypt,decryptSIZE);
   int v = media ^ key;
   guard((waddr_t)play,playSIZE,(waddr_t)decrypt,decryptSIZE);
   return v;
}
```

The problem is determining what key to use to decrypt a. Normally, you'd use the cleartext of the caller as key, but now there are two callers, and hence two possible keys! Algorithm OBFCKSP solves this by moving the decryption of a from the direct callers (b1 and b2) to the callers' callers (c1 and c2) and using a combination of the *ciphertexts* of b1 and b2 as key. Listing 6.10▶391 illustrates this case. The decryption/encryption code is in light gray. Additional code, in dark gray, is necessary since the actual caller of a can no longer be determined statically.

The final case to consider is when the program is recursive, i.e., when the call graph contains cycles:

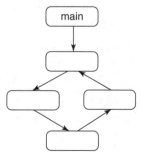

Listing 6.9 Continued from Listing 6.8▸389.

```
float decode (int digital) {
    guard((waddr_t)play,playSIZE,(waddr_t)decode,decodeSIZE);
    float v = (float)digital;
    guard((waddr_t)play,playSIZE,(waddr_t)decode,decodeSIZE);
    return v;
}
void play(int user_key, int digital_media[], int len) {
    int i;
    guard((waddr_t)player_main,player_mainSIZE,(waddr_t)play,playSIZE);
    for(i=0;i<len;i++) {
        guard((waddr_t)decrypt,decryptSIZE,(waddr_t)play,playSIZE);
        int digital = decrypt(user_key,digital_media[i]);
        guard((waddr_t)decrypt,decryptSIZE,(waddr_t)play,playSIZE);

        guard((waddr_t)decode,decodeSIZE,(waddr_t)play,playSIZE);
        printf("%f\n",decode(digital));
        guard((waddr_t)decode,decodeSIZE,(waddr_t)play,playSIZE);
    }
    guard((waddr_t)player_main,player_mainSIZE,(waddr_t)play,playSIZE);
}
int main (int argc, char *argv[]) {
    makewritable();
    guard((waddr_t)getkey,getkeySIZE,(waddr_t)decrypt,decryptSIZE);
    guard((waddr_t)decode,decodeSIZE,(waddr_t)play,playSIZE);
    guard((waddr_t)decrypt,decryptSIZE,(waddr_t)play,playSIZE);
    guard((waddr_t)play,playSIZE,(waddr_t)player_main,player_mainSIZE);
    player_main(argc,argv);
}
```

The simplest solution is to keep the entire cycle in cleartext, i.e., decrypt it as it is entered and re-encrypt it when the cycle is exited. For programs that contain many mutually recursive functions (such as recursive-descent parsers), this would lead to much of the program being in cleartext for the duration of the execution.

Cappaert et al. [54] report on the performance overhead for some small programs. Execution speed was 2.7 to 91 times slower than the original program. When inlining the guard code (a reasonable thing to do since leaving the guard in cleartext makes it an obvious target of attack), one of their programs was 2.8 times larger and ran 1,379 times slower than the original.

Problem 6.4 In practice, this algorithm is complicated by indirect function calls and especially multi-threading. If two threads can execute the same function simultaneously, they will have to coordinate (using appropriate locking) which does the decryption and which does the encryption. Work out the details and measure the additional performance overhead!

Listing 6.10 Dealing with multiple paths to the same function in Algorithm OBFCKSP. Encryption/decryption functions are shown in Listing 6.7 ▸388.

```
int my_main (int argc, char *argv[]) {
    guard((waddr_t)c1,c1SIZE,(waddr_t)my_main,my_mainSIZE);
    c1();
    guard((waddr_t)c1,c1SIZE,(waddr_t)my_main,my_mainSIZE);
    guard((waddr_t)c2,c2SIZE,(waddr_t)my_main,my_mainSIZE);
    c2();
    guard((waddr_t)c2,c2SIZE,(waddr_t)my_main,my_mainSIZE);
}
void c1() {
    guard2((waddr_t)a,aSIZE,(waddr_t)b1,b1SIZE,(waddr_t)b2,b2SIZE);
    guard((waddr_t)b1,b1SIZE,(waddr_t)c1,c1SIZE);
    b1();
    guard((waddr_t)b1,b1SIZE,(waddr_t)c1,c1SIZE);
    guard2((waddr_t)a,aSIZE,(waddr_t)b1,b1SIZE,(waddr_t)b2,b2SIZE);
}
void c2() {
    guard2((waddr_t)a,aSIZE,(waddr_t)b1,b1SIZE,(waddr_t)b2,b2SIZE);
    guard((waddr_t)b2,b2SIZE,(waddr_t)c2,c2SIZE);
    b2();
    guard((waddr_t)b2,b2SIZE,(waddr_t)c2,c2SIZE);
    guard2((waddr_t)a,aSIZE,(waddr_t)b1,b1SIZE,(waddr_t)b2,b2SIZE);
}
waddr_t caller;
uint32 callerSize;
void b1() {
    caller = (waddr_t)b1;
    callerSize = b1SIZE;
    a();
}
void b2() {
    caller = (waddr_t)b2;
    {callerSize = b2SIZE;
    a();
}
void a() {
    guard(caller,callerSize,(waddr_t)a,aSIZE);
    ...
    guard(caller,callerSize,(waddr_t)a,aSIZE);
}
int main (int argc, char *argv[]) {
    makeCodeWritable(...);
    guard((waddr_t)b1,b1SIZE,(waddr_t)c1,c1SIZE);
    guard((waddr_t)b2,b2SIZE,(waddr_t)c2,c2SIZE);
    guard((waddr_t)c1,c1SIZE,(waddr_t)my_main,my_mainSIZE);
    guard((waddr_t)c2,c2SIZE,(waddr_t)my_main,my_mainSIZE);
    guard2((waddr_t)a,aSIZE,(waddr_t)b1,b1SIZE,(waddr_t)b2,b2SIZE);
    my_main(argc,argv);
}
```

6.3.2 *OBFAG_{crypt}*: Combining Self-Modification and Encryption

In Section 6.2.2►366, you saw how Algorithm OBFAG_{swap} splits a function up into pieces (called *cells*) that are continuously moved around during execution. More specifically, the cells are separated into two memory regions, upper and lower, and during each round, the cells of one region are xored into the cells of the other. As a result, at each point in time some cells will be in cleartext while others will be scrambled. Ideally, only the cell currently being executed should be in the clear, but unfortunately, this isn't the case with OBFAG_{swap}. In this section, you will see how this algorithm can be extended (to Algorithm OBFAG_{crypt} [26,27]) by xoring in a secret key string to make more of the cells unreadable.

6.3.2.1 An Example Let's continue with the example from Section 6.2.2►366. There, we started out with a function broken up into six cells:

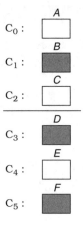

Then, in alternate rounds, we would xor the cells in upper memory with those in lower, or those in the lower region with those in the upper. This time, we're also going to xor in a cryptographic key. In the graphical examples, we'll represent the key as a box with wavy lines. Here are some examples of the type of operations we will be performing:

In the first operation, a cleartext cell is xored with a key to make an encrypted cell. In the second, an encrypted cell is xored with a key to make it a cleartext cell. In the third, a cell that consists of two cells (white and gray) xored together with a key becomes a cleartext striped cell by xoring it with a cleartext white cell and the key.

Have a look at this example:

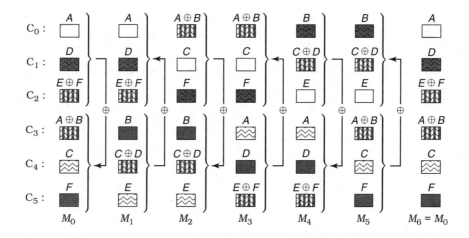

M_0 is the initial configuration, what the function looks like after it's been obfuscated but before execution starts. C_0 (in light gray) is in cleartext since this is where execution will start. All the other cells are xored with a key string, and in some cases, with another cell. Different cells have been encrypted with different keys. After C_0 has finished executing, all the cells in upper memory are xored into their respective partner cells in lower memory *and* with a key, each cell with a different one. This gives you the configuration in M_1. We have fixed the schedule in such a way that execution should continue in C_3. For C_3 to become cleartext, we've therefore fixed the keys so that the following will happen:

$$A \oplus A \oplus B \oplus key = B$$

In other words, the key that C_3 was originally encrypted with is the same one that it is now xored with. The final round, M_6, yields a configuration identical to the initial one, M_0. This means that the process is ready to start over the next time the function is called.

6.3.2.2 Deriving the Keystream We're not going to give a formal algorithm for constructing the keystream, but we will work through an example to give you the basic idea of how it's done. You're going to need two keystreams, which we'll call KG = $\langle KG_0, KG_1, \ldots \rangle$ and KS = $\langle KS_0, KS_1, \ldots \rangle$. KG contains the values the cells will be xored with initially, so it will contain one key per cell. In this example, we're going to restrict the keys to three values, {k, b, 0}. KS is a keystream from which you will extract keys during execution. Every time the n cells of the upper half of memory get xored with the n cells of lower memory, you're also going to xor in n elements from KS.

Let's set KG=$\langle 0, k, b, k, b, 0 \rangle$. This gives you this initial configuration, M_0:

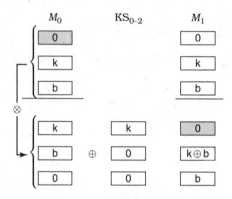

We're only showing the key values that get xored in. C_1 actually contains $k \oplus IV_1$ (IV_1 is the initial value of C_1) that we worked out in OBFAG$_{\text{swap}}$. Since C_0 must be in cleartext, KG_0 *had to* be 0. C_5 also must be in cleartext because it must be in the clear during M_6, and so you set KG_5 to 0 also. The rest of KG you can choose freely. After C_0 has finished executing, the upper region gets xored with the bottom one *and* with the first three elements of the KS keystream, KS_{0-2}. Your schedule tells you that C_3 must now be in the clear, and since it was originally xored with k, you must again xor with k to get the cleartext cell back. The rest of KG you can choose freely, so you set $KS_{0-2} = \langle k, 0, 0 \rangle$.

After round M_1 is finished executing, you xor low memory into high memory, along with $KS_{3-5} = \langle k, b, 0 \rangle$. Why did we choose these keys? Well, you know that C_1 must now become cleartext and that it will be computed as $C_1 \leftarrow C_5 \oplus C_1 \oplus KS_4$. This gives you the little equation

$$(k \oplus b) \oplus k \oplus KS_4 = 0$$

which you can easily solve with $KS_4 = b$. The rest of KS_{3-5} you can choose freely:

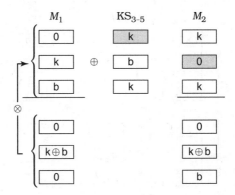

For the next round, you derive that $KS_{6-8} = \langle b, k \oplus b, k \rangle$:

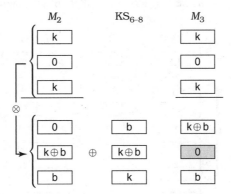

And for the next round, you get $KS_{9-11} = \langle k, k, k \oplus b \rangle$:

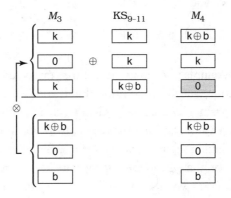

And for the next round, $KS_{12-14} = \langle k, k \oplus b, k \rangle$:

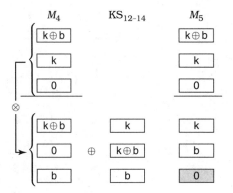

Computing the key for the final round involves more restrictions, since configuration M_6 must be the same as M_0. Setting $KS_{15-17} = \langle b, b, b \rangle$ gives you the required result:

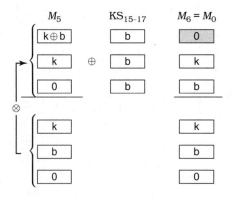

The final keystream you've derived is

$$KS = \langle k, 0, 0, k, b, k, b, k \oplus b, k, k, k, k \oplus b, k, k \oplus b, b, b, b, b \rangle.$$

6.3.2.3 Coding the Example   You only need three minor changes to the code in Listing 6.4▸378 to account for the encryption. First, you need to add the KG and KS keystreams to the program. Here, we've hardcoded them as literal arrays. This is, of course, highly suspicious and easy for an adversary to locate, although we could have done a bit better by making them character strings. Better still would be to have a pseudo-random function that, given the appropriate key as input, will generate the required keystream. Second, you have to replace the xor function with another one, xor2 from Listing 6.11▸397, which also xors in the appropriate key. Finally, you have

Listing 6.11 Example of Algorithm OBFAG_{crypt}, combining self-modification with encryption. This code extends that of Listing 6.4▶378.

```
static char KG [] = {0,'k','b','k','b',0};
static char KS[][3] ={{'k',0,0},{'k','b','k'},{'b','k'^'b','k'},
        {'k','k','k'^'b'},{'k','k'^'b','b'},{'b','b','b'}};
void P() {
    static int firsttime=1;
    if (firsttime) {
        xor2(&&cell5,NULL,&&cell2,1,CELLSIZE);
        xor2(&&cell0,NULL,&&cell3,1,CELLSIZE);
        swap(&&cell1,&&cell4,CELLSIZE);
        xor2(NULL,KG,&&cell0,6,CELLSIZE);
        firsttime = 0;
    }
    char* a[] = {&&align0,&&align1,&&align2,:::,&&align5};
    char* next[] ={&&cell0,&&cell1,&&cell2,&&cell3,&&cell4,&&cell5};
    goto *next[0];

    align0: ALIGN
    cell0:  printf("SPGM0\n");
            xor2(&&cell0,KS[0],&&cell3,3,CELLSIZE);
            goto *next[3];
    align1: ALIGN
    cell1:  printf("SPGM2\n");
            xor2(&&cell0,KS[2],&&cell3,3,CELLSIZE);
            goto *next[4];
    align2: ALIGN
    cell2:  printf("SPGM4\n");
            xor2(&&cell0,KS[4],&&cell3,3,CELLSIZE);
            goto *next[5];
    align3: ALIGN
    cell3:  printf("SPGM1\n");
            xor2(&&cell3,KS[1],&&cell0,3,CELLSIZE);
            goto *next[1];
    align4: ALIGN
    cell4:  printf("SPGM3\n");
            xor2(&&cell3,KS[3],&&cell0,3,CELLSIZE);
            goto *next[2];
    align5: ALIGN
    cell5:  printf("SPGM5\n");
            xor2(&&cell3,KS[5],&&cell0,3,CELLSIZE);
            return
}
```

to initialize the cells with the KG keystream. We show the new code in Listing 6.11▶397. The code that, in a real implementation, would be executed at obfuscation time has been marked dashed.

6.4 Discussion

All the algorithms in this chapter share one characteristic: They modify the code segment of the program at runtime. This has three immediate consequences:

1. It makes the program harder to analyze statically.
2. It has the potential of making the program *much* slower.
3. It can make the protection routines less stealthy.

Static analysis becomes hard because the code segment is now treated both as code *and* as data, and any modifications to the code have to be tracked by the analyzer. In Section 3.1.1▶119, you saw the kinds of contortions Algorithm REAMB had to go through to build a control flow graph that, more or less accurately, reflects the changes a self-modifying program goes through.

   The significant overhead of these algorithms results from the very features that make modern processors so efficient at being "confused" by self-modifying code. At the very least, whenever the code segment changes, the instruction pipeline must be flushed, the contents of data caches must be written to memory, and instruction caches must be invalidated.

   Stealth suffers for several reasons. First, few real programs use self-modifying code. As you've seen, a simple attack is to write-protect the code segment and see where the operating system throws an exception. Second, a consequence of the high overhead of these algorithms is that it may not be possible to protect an entire program. Instead, you may have to confine the obfuscation to those routines that contain security-sensitive code. As a result, most of your program will execute "normally" while a small part will write into its own code segment. It won't require much thought for the adversary to decide which part of your program to examine first. Finally, many of the algorithms you've seen in this chapter make extensive use of xor operations. With the exception of cryptographic routines and low-level graphics primitives, xors are unusual in real code.

   Referring back to the model in Section 2.2▶86, what types of operations do the algorithms in this chapter perform? First, since they all continuously modify the code at runtime, they must all make use of the **dynamic** primitive. In addition to

dynamic, Algorithm OBFAG$_{\text{crypt}}$ uses the **reorder** primitive to move cells between upper and lower memory regions. In addition to *that*, Algorithm OBFAG$_{\text{swap}}$ uses **map** to xor a keystream with the encrypted cells to recover the cleartext code. Algorithm OBFCKSP also uses **map** to decrypt/encrypt functions. Algorithm OBFMAMDSB takes two functions, f_1 and f_2, and splits them up into two edit scripts e_1 and e_2 and a template t, such that **merge**$(t, e_1) = f_1$ and **merge**$(t, e_2) = f_2$.

Software Tamperproofing

7

To tamperproof a program is to ensure that it "executes as intended," even in the presence of an adversary who tries to disrupt, monitor, or change the execution. Note that this is different from obfuscation, where the intent is to make it difficult for the attacker to *understand* the program. In practice, the boundary between tamperproofing and obfuscation is a blurry one: A program that is harder to understand because it's been obfuscated ought also be more difficult to modify! For example, an attacker who can't find the decrypt() function in a DRM media player because it's been thoroughly obfuscated also won't be able to modify it or even monitor it by setting a breakpoint on it.

The dynamic obfuscation algorithms in Chapter 6 (Dynamic Obfuscation), in particular, have often been used to prevent tampering. In this book, we take the view that a pure tamperproofing algorithm not only makes tampering difficult but is also able to *detect* when tampering has occurred and to *respond* to the attack by in some way punishing the user. In practice, tamperproofing is always combined with obfuscation:

1. If you both obfuscate and tamperproof your code, an attacker who, in spite of the tamperproofing, is able to extract the code still has to de-obfuscate it in order to understand it;

2. Code that you insert to test for tampering or effect a response to tampering must be obfuscated in order to prevent the attacker from easily discovering it.

Watermarking and tamperproofing are also related. In fact, if perfect tamperproofing were available, watermarking would be easy: Just watermark with any trivial algorithm, tamperproof, and by definition the attacker will not be able to destroy the mark! It's precisely because we don't have perfect tamperproofing that we need to worry about watermarking stealth: We have to assume that an attacker who can find a watermark will also be able to modify the program to destroy the mark.

The prototypical tamperproofing scenario is preventing an adversary from removing license-checking code from your program. So ideally, if the adversary is able to change your code on the left to the code on the right, the program would stop working for him:

```
if (license_expired()) {
    printf("pay me!");
    abort();
}
```

⇨

```
if (false) {
    printf("pay me!");
    abort();
}
```

One way of thinking about this is to note that the program consists of two pieces of semantics: the piece that both you and the adversary want to maintain (because it constitutes the core functionality of the program) and the piece that *you* want to maintain but that the adversary wants to remove or alter (the license check). Clearly, maintaining the core semantics and removing the checking semantics are both important to the adversary. If not, it would be easy for him to destroy the tamperproofing code: Simply destroy the program in its entirety! The adversary may also want to *add* code to the program in order to make it perform a function that you have left out, such as the print function in an evaluation copy of a program.

There are many kinds of invariants that *you* may want to maintain but that your *user* may want to violate. For example, a free PDF reader might let you fill in a form and print it but not save it for later use. This is supposed to act as an incentive for buying the premium product with more functionality. However, from the user's point of view it's also an incentive for hacking the code to add this "missing feature." Other products don't allow you to print, games don't provide you with an infinite supply of ammunition, evaluation copies stop working after a certain period of time, VoIP clients charge you money to make phone calls, DRM media players and TV set-top boxes charge you to watch movies or listen to music, and so on. In all these scenarios, someone's revenue stream is depending on their program executing exactly as *they* intended it to, and an adversary's revenue stream (or debit stream) depends on modifying the semantics of the program to execute the way *they* want it to.

While not technically a case of modifying the program, observing its execution to steal algorithms, cryptographic keys, or any other proprietary code or data from the program secrets is sometimes also considered a form of tampering. For example, a common application of tamperproofing is to protect cleartext data or the cryptographic keys themselves in a digital rights management system. If an attacker can insert new code (shown here shaded) in the media player, he will be able to catch and save the decrypted media:

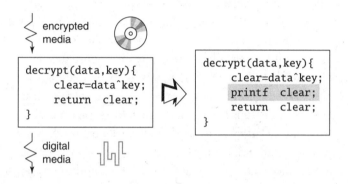

Observing the player under a debugger can achieve the same result without actually modifying the code:

```
> gdb player
(gdb) break decrypt.c:3
commands
    printf "%x\n",clear
    continue
end
```

Here, we've set a breakpoint on the decrypt function such that, whenever we enter it, the cleartext media gets printed and execution continues.

Technically, an attacker typically modifies the program with the intent to force it to choose a different execution path than the programmer intended. He can achieve this by:

1. Removing code from and/or inserting new code into the *executable file* prior to execution;

2. Removing code from and/or inserting new code into the *running program*;

3. Affecting the runtime behavior of the program through external agents such as emulators, debuggers, or a hostile operating system.

A protected program can try to detect that it's running under emulation, on a modified operating system, or inside a debugger, but this turns out to be hard to do reliably. For example, how can you detect that a user has turned back the system clock so as not to trigger your "license-expired" check? We will show a few popular techniques, but in practice, tamperproofing algorithms tend to focus on making sure that the program's static code and data haven't been changed, even if this certainly isn't enough to ensure it's running properly.

Conceptually, a tamperproofing system performs two tasks. First, it monitors the program (to see if its code or data have been modified), and the execution environment (to see if this is hostile in any way). Second, once it has determined that tampering has occurred or is likely to occur, a response mechanism takes over and retaliates in a suitable manner. This can range from making the program exit gracefully to punishing the user by destroying his home directory. In simple systems, detection and response are tightly integrated, such as if (emulated()) abort(), but this makes it easy for an attacker to work backwards from the point of response to the point of detection and modify the program to bypass the tamperproofing code. It's therefore important to separate the checking and the response functions as widely as possible, both spatially (they should be far away from each other in the executable) and temporally (they should be far away from each other in the execution trace).

Typical software tamperproofing approaches rely on self-checking code, self-modifying code, or adding a layer of interpretation. In general, these techniques are not suitable for type-safe distribution formats like Java bytecode—in Java it's simply not possible to stealthily examine your own code or generate and execute code on the fly. In this chapter, therefore, you will mostly see algorithms that protect binary executables.

Some algorithms are based on the idea of *splitting* the program into two pieces, allowing most of the program to run without performance penalty in the clear (open to user tampering) and the remainder to run slower, but highly protected. The protected part could be run on a remote trusted machine, in a tamper-resistant hardware module such as a smartcard, or in a separate thread whose code has been heavily obfuscated.

This chapter is organized as follows. In Section 7.1▶405, we give essential definitions. In Section 7.2▶412, we present algorithms based on the idea of *introspection*, i.e., tamperproofed programs that monitor their own code to detect modifications. In Section 7.3▶440, we discuss various kinds of response mechanisms. In Section 7.4▶444, we cover so-called *oblivious hashing* algorithms that examine the *state* of the program for signs of tampering. In Section 7.5▶453, we discuss *remote tamperproofing*, i.e., how we can determine that a program running on a remote machine has not been tampered with. In Section 7.6▶464, we summarize the chapter.

7.1 Definitions

An adversary's goal is to force your program P to perform some action it wasn't intended to, such as playing a media file without the proper key or executing even though a license has expired. The most obvious way to reach this goal is to modify P's executable file prior to execution. But this is not the *only* way. The adversary could corrupt any of the stages needed to load and execute P, and this could potentially force P to execute in an unanticipated way. For example, he could force a modified operating system to be loaded; he could modify any file on the file system, including the dynamic linker; he could replace the real dynamic libraries with his own; he could run P under emulation; or he could attach a debugger and modify P's code or data on the fly.

Your goal, on the other hand, is to thwart such attacks. In other words, you want to make sure that P's executable file itself is healthy (hasn't been modified) and that the environment in which it runs (hardware, operating system, and so on) isn't hostile in any way. More specifically, you want to ensure that P is running on unadulterated hardware and operating systems; that it is not running under emulation; that the right dynamic libraries have been loaded; that P's code itself hasn't been modified; and that no external entity such as a debugger is modifying P's registers, stack, heap, environment variables, or input data.

In the following definition, we make use of two predicates, $I_d(P, E)$ and $I_a(P, E)$, which respectively describe the integrity of the application (what the defender would like to maintain) and what constitutes a successful attack (what the attacker would like to accomplish):

Definition 7.1 (Tampering and Tamperproofing). Let $I_d(P, E)$ and $I_a(P, E)$ be predicates over a program P and the environment E in which it executes. P is successfully tamperproofed if, throughout the execution of P, $I_d(P, E)$ holds. It is successfully attacked if, at some point during the execution of P, $I_a(P, E) \land \text{not } I_d(P, E)$, holds and this is not detectable by P.

For example, in a cracking scenario, I_a could be, "P executes like a legally purchased version of Microsoft Word," and I_d could be, "The attacker has entered a legal license code, and neither the OS nor the code of P have been modified." In a DRM scenario, I_a could be, "P is able to print out the private key," and I_d could be,

"The protected media cannot be played unless a valid user key has been entered ∧ private keys remain private."

Conceptually, two functions, CHECK and RESPOND, are responsible for the tamperproofing. CHECK monitors the health of the system by testing a set of invariants and returning true if nothing suspicious is found. RESPOND queries CHECK to see if P is running as expected, and if it's not, issues a *tamper response*, such as terminating the program.

7.1.1 Checking for Tampering

CHECK can test any number of invariants, but these are the most common ones:

code checking: Check that P's code hashes to a known value:

```
if (hash(P's code) != 0xca7ca115)
    return false;
```

result checking: Instead of checking that the code is correct, CHECK can test that the *result* of a computation is correct. For example, it is easy to check that a sorting routine hasn't been modified by testing that its output is correct:

```
quickSort(A,n);
for (i=0;i<(n-1);i++)
    if (A[i]>A[i+1])
        return false;
```

Checking the validity of a computed result is often computationally cheaper than performing the computation itself. For example, while sorting takes $O(n \log n)$ time, checking that the output of a sort routine is in sorted order can be done in almost linear time. Result checking was pioneered by Manuel Blum [43] and has been used in commercial packages such as LEDA [145].

environment checking: The hardest thing for a program to check is the validity of its execution environment. Typical checks include, "Am I being run under emulation?", "Is there a debugger attached to my process?", and, "Is the operating system at the proper patch level?" While it might be possible to ask the operating system these questions, it's hard to know whether the answers can be trusted or if we're being lied to! The actual methods used for environment checking are highly system-specific [166].

As an example, let's consider how a Linux process would detect that it's attached to a debugger. As it turns out, a process on Linux can be traced only once. This means that a simple way to check if you're being traced is to try to trace yourself:

```
#include <stdio.h>
#include <sys/ptrace.h>
int main() {
    if (ptrace(PTRACE_TRACEME))
        printf("I'm being traced!\n");
}
```

If the test fails, you can assume you've been attached to a debugger:

```
> gcc -g -o traced traced.c
> traced
> gdb traced
(gdb) run
I'm being traced!
```

Another popular way of detecting a debugging attack is to measure the time, absolute or wall clock, of a piece of code that should take much longer to execute in a debugger than when executed normally. In the light gray code in the example in Listing 7.1 ▸ 408, a divide-by-zero exception is thrown that the gdb debugger takes twice as long to handle as non-debugged code.

Here's the output when first run normally and then under a debugger:

```
> gcc -o cycles cycles.c
> cycles
elapsed 31528: Not debugged!
> gdb cycles
(gdb) handle SIGFPE noprint nostop
(gdb) run
elapsed 79272: Debugged!
```

Listing 7.1 Code to detect if a Linux process is running under a debugger or not. The code in light gray throws a divide-by-zero exception. The x86 `rdtsc` instruction returns the current instruction count, and the `cpuid` instruction flushes the instruction pipeline to ensure proper timing results.

```
#include <stdio.h>
#include <stdint.h>
#include <signal.h>
#include <unistd.h>
#include <setjmp.h>

jmp_buf env;

void handler(int signal) {
    longjmp(env,1);
}

int main() {
    signal(SIGFPE, handler);
    uint32_t start,stop;
    int x = 0;
    if (setjmp(env) == 0) {
        asm volatile (
            "cpuid\n"
            "rdtsc\n" : "=a" (start)
        );
        x = x/x;
    } else {
        asm volatile (
            "cpuid\n"
            "rdtsc\n" : "=a" (stop)
        );
        uint32_t elapsed = stop - start;
        if (elapsed > 40000)
            printf("elapsed %i: Debugged!\n",elapsed);
        else
            printf("elapsed %i: Not debugged!\n",elapsed);
    }
}
```

The bound on the instruction count will have to be adjusted depending on the architecture and the debugger on which the program is run.

Depending on our needs, CHECK may be more or less *precise*, i.e., it could detect tampering close in time to when the tampering occurred, or not. A really imprecise detector is *unsafe*, in that it may fail to detect tampering until after the tampered program is able to cause permanent damage. Consider this timeline of the execution of a program P:

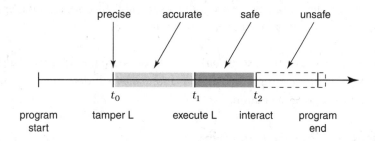

At some time t_0, a location L·in P is modified by the attacker. The timeline doesn't show it, but this could either be prior to execution (if P's executable file is modified), during program start-up (if the loader is doing the modification), or during execution (if an attached debugger is doing the modification). At some later time t_1, the program reaches location L and the modified code gets executed. At time t_2, the first "interaction event" after t_0 occurs, i.e., this is the first time that the modified P has the chance to cause permanent damage by writing to a file, play protected content, send secret data back over the Internet, and so on.

A *precise* checker detects the attack "immediately" after the modification has taken place, perhaps within a window of a few instructions. With a precise detector, you're able to immediately punish a user who is experimenting by making random changes just to see "what happens." An *accurate* checker detects at some later time, but before t_1, which allows it to prevent the modified code from ever being executed, for example, by patching L. A *safe* detector waits until after the modified code has been executed, but before the first interaction event. At that point, the program is in an unintended and indeterminate state, but the detector knows this and can prevent any permanent damage by terminating the program. Finally, an *unsafe* detector waits until after the interaction event at t_2 or even until after program termination (postmortem detection) to detect tampering. At this point, permanent damage may have been inflicted, and the only remaining course of action may be to report the violation.

Definition 7.2 (Detector precision).   Let t_0 be the time tampering occurs, t_1 the time the tampered code gets first executed, and t_2 the time of the first interaction event following the tampering. A *precise* detector detects tampering at time t_0, an *accurate* during (t_0, t_1), a *safe* detector during $[t_1, t_2)$, and an *unsafe* detector during $[t_2 \dots)$.

Some tamperproofing systems will run CHECK only once on start-up. Such *static* systems catch modifications to the program's executable file, but not tampering that happens at runtime, for which a *dynamic* detector is necessary:

Definition 7.3 (Detector execution). A tamper-detector is *static* if detection happens only once at program load time and *dynamic* if detection is continuous throughout program execution.

7.1.2 Responding to Tampering

RESPOND executes a predetermined response to a detected attempt at tampering. Here are some possible responses:

terminate: Terminate the program. Some time should pass between detection and termination to prevent the attacker from easily finding the location of the detection code.

restore: Restore the program to its correct state by patching the tampered code and resetting any corrupted data structures.

degrade results: Deliberately return incorrect results. The results could deteriorate slowly over time to avoid alerting the attacker that he's been found out.

degrade performance: Degrade the performance of the program, for example, by running slower or consuming more memory.

report attack: Report the attack, for example, by "phoning home" if an Internet connection is available.

punish: Punish the attacker by destroying the program or objects in its environment. For example, if the *DisplayEater* program detects that you're trying to use a pirated serial number, it will delete your home directory [126]. More spectacularly, the computer itself could be destroyed by repeatedly flashing the bootloader flash memory.

7.1.3 System Design

There are many possible locations within a computing system for CHECK and RESPOND. Most obviously, you could integrate them directly in the binary code of your program:

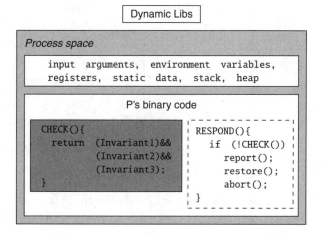

CHECK can check invariants over the binary code itself, over the static and dynamic data of the process, or over the environment (hardware and operating system) in which the program is running. We call this kind of organization a *self-checking* system. Note that in this design it's possible (and desirable!) for one of CHECK's invariants to be a check on the integrity of its own code and RESPOND's code. Without such a check, the adversary will start his attack by disabling CHECK or RESPOND, leaving himself free to further tamper with the program itself.

It's also possible for CHECK and RESPOND to run from within the hardware, the operating system, the dynamic loader, or a separate process.

Definition 7.4 (Integration). A tamperproofing system is *self-checking/self-responding* if the checker/responder is integrated within P itself. It is *external-checking/external-responding* if it runs in a different process from P but on the same computing system as P, and it is *remote-checking/remote-responding* if it is running on a different computing system than P.

A tamperproofing system can be self-checking but remote-responding, and so on.

Remotely checking the health of a program is an important subproblem known as *remote tamperproofing*. Here, you've put self-checkers in your program on the user's site:

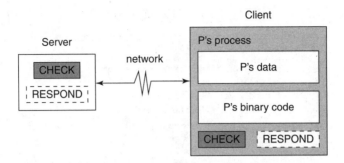

In addition, checkers running on your own server site check for tampering by monitoring the communication pattern for anomalies. You'll read more about remote tamperproofing in Section 7.5▶453.

7.2 Introspection

We will devote the remainder of the chapter to describing tamperproofing algorithms from the literature. In this section, we will talk about two algorithms that use *introspection*. This essentially means the program is augmented to compute a hash over a code region to compare to an expected value. While this is a straightforward idea, as always, the devil is in the details.

Introspection algorithms insert code like this into the instruction stream:[1]

```
· · · · · · · · ·
start  =  start_address;
end    =  end_address;
h = 0;
while (start < end) {
    h = h ⊕ *start;
    start++;
}
if (h != expected_value)
    abort();
goto *h;
· · · · · · · · ·
```

---

1. We will call these functions *hash functions*. Some authors prefer the term *checksumming*, and others prefer *testing*. The term *guard* is sometimes used to collectively refer to the hash function and the response code.

The light gray part (the initialization) sets up the code region that is to be checked. The dark gray part (the loop) computes a hash value over the region using some operation ⊕. The light gray and dark gray parts together form the CHECK function, while the dashed and dotted parts show two possible RESPONDers. The dashed responder simply terminates the program if the loop computes the wrong value (i.e., if the code region has been tampered with). The dotted responder instead uses the value computed by the loop to jump to the next program location. If the code region has been tampered with, the program will jump to the wrong location and eventually malfunction. This idea is used in the tamperproofing of the Skype client, which you'll learn more about in Section 7.2.4▶431. There are many possible variants of this idea. You could use the hash value as part of an arithmetic computation, for example, causing the program to eventually produce the wrong output, or you could use it in an address computation, eventually causing a segmentation fault.

Prototypical attacks on an introspective tamperproofing systems are based on pattern matching. They run in two steps:

1. Find the location of the checker and/or responder, either by

    (a) searching for suspicious patterns in the static code itself, or by

    (b) searching for suspicious patterns in the dynamic execution.

2. Disable the response code, either by

    (a) replacing the if-statement by if (0) ... , or by

    (b) pre-computing the hash value and substituting it into the response code.

Static pattern matching could, for example, target the initialization section. If the loop bounds are completely unobfuscated, it should be easy for the adversary to look for two code segment addresses followed by a test:

```
start = 0xbabebabe;
end   = 0xca75ca75;
while (start < end) {
```

A dynamic pattern matcher could look for data reads into the code segment, which will be unusual in typical programs. Depending on the nature of the tamper response, disabling means ensuring that the test on the hash value never succeeds or that the jump goes to the correct location, regardless of what value the loop actually computes:

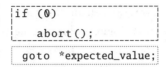

```
if (0)
    abort();
goto *expected_value;
```

In this section, we'll show you two algorithms that make these types of attacks harder. The idea is to have multiple checkers and for checkers to check each other so that it's never enough to just disable one of them—you have to disable many or all of them. The TPCA algorithm builds up a network of checkers and responders so that checkers check each other and responders repair code that has been tampered with. Algorithm TPHMST refines this further by hiding the *expected_value* hash which, because of its randomness, is an easy pattern-matching target.

Another strategy to make pattern-matching attacks harder is to use a library of a large number of hash functions and to be able to obfuscate these thoroughly. We discuss this in Section 7.2.2▶418.

In Section 7.2.4▶431, we'll show you the heroic effort the Skype engineers went through to protect their clients and protocol from attack (in part, using introspection), and the equally heroic effort two security researchers went through (in part, using pattern matching) to crack the protection.

As it turns out, pattern matching is not the only possible attack against introspection algorithms. We will conclude the section by showing you algorithm REWOS, which is a generic and very clever attack that with one simple hack to the operating system disables *all* introspection-based algorithms! We'll also show you Algorithm TPGCK, which uses self-modifying code to counter this attack.

7.2.1 Algorithm *TPCA*: Checker Network

The TPCA [24,59] algorithm was invented by two Purdue University researchers, Hoi Chang and Mikhail Atallah. The algorithm was subsequently patented and with assistance from Purdue a start-up, Arxan, was spun off. The basic insight is that it's not enough for checkers to check just the code: they must check each other as well! If checkers are not checked, they are just too easy to remove. The algorithm builds up a network of code regions, where a region can be a block of user code, a checker, or a responder. Checkers compute a hash over one or more regions and compare it to the expected value. Responders in this algorithm are typically *repairers*, and if the checker has discovered that a region has been tampered with, a responder will replace the tampered region with a copy stored elsewhere. Multiple checkers can

---

Algorithm 7.1 Overview of algorithm TPCA. P is the program to be protected, in a form that makes control explicit, such as a control flow graph or a call graph. G is a directed *guard graph* describing the relationship between code regions, checkers, and responders.

TAMPERPROOF(P, G):

1. Let P's nodes be $n_0, n_1, \ldots$, representing code regions.

2. Let G's nodes be $n_0, n_1, \ldots$ (representing code regions), $c_0, c_1, \ldots$ (checkers), and $r_0, r_1, \ldots$ (responders). G has a edge $c_i \xrightarrow{c} n_j$ if c_i checks region n_j and an edge $r_i \xrightarrow{r} n_j$ if r_i repairs region n_j.

3. Insert the responders in P so that they dominate the region they check.

4. Insert the checkers in P so that at least one checker dominates every corresponding responder.

5. Connect checkers to responders by inserting variables, as necessary.

---

check the same region, and multiple responders can repair a tampered region. A nice consequence of this design is that you can achieve arbitrary levels of protection (at a concomitant increase in size and decrease in performance) by adding more checkers and responders and more complex relationships between them.

Have a look at the example in Listing 7.2▶416, a program that implements a simple DRM system. For simplicity, we've made code regions identical to functions, but in general this isn't necessary. A region could comprise multiple functions or parts of functions, and regions could be overlapping. We've inserted the checkers (in dark gray) and responders (light gray) so that they *dominate* the call to the function they check and repair. This way, you'll know that when a function gets executed it will be correct. For example, consider the `decrypt` function in Listing 7.2▶416. Before making the call to `getkey`, `decrypt` computes a hash of `getkey`'s code, and if it doesn't match (i.e., `getkey` has been tampered with), it repairs `getkey` by replacing it with a stored copy (`getkeyCOPY`).

Algorithm 7.1 gives an overview of the technique. To tamperproof a program, you need two graphs. P is the program's control flow graph (if you want to protect individual basic blocks) or a call graph (if you're content protecting one function at a time). A second graph G, the *guard graph*, shows the relationship between regions to be protected and the checkers and responders that check them. Corresponding to the example in Listing 7.2▶416, here is P (left) and G (right):

Listing 7.2 DRM player tamperproofed with algorithm TPCA.

```
#define getkeyHASH 0xce1d400a
#define getkeySIZE 14
uint32 getkeyCOPY[] = {0x83e58955,0x72b820ec,0xc7080486,...};
#define decryptHASH 0x3764e45c
#define decryptSIZE 16
uint32 decryptCOPY[] = {0x83e58955,0xaeb820ec,0xc7080486,...};
#define playHASH 0x4f4205a5
#define playSIZE 29
uint32 playCOPY[] = {0x83e58955,0xedb828ec,0xc7080486,...};

uint32 decryptVal;

int main (int argc, char *argv[]) {
   {uint32 playVal = hash((waddr_t)play,playSIZE);
   int user_key = 0xca7ca115;
   {decryptVal = hash((waddr_t)decrypt,decryptSIZE);
   int digital_media[] = {10,102};
   if (playVal != playHASH)
      {memcpy((waddr_t)play,playCOPY,playSIZE*sizeof(uint32));
   play(user_key,digital_media,2);
}

int getkey(in0 user_key) {
   {decryptVal = hash((waddr_t)decrypt,decryptSIZE);
   int player_key = 0xbabeca75;
   return user_key ^ player_key;
}

int decrypt(int user_key, int media) {
   {uint32 getkeyVal = hash((waddr_t)getkey,getkeySIZE);
   if (getkeyVal != getkeyHASH)
      {memcpy((waddr_t)getkey,getkeyCOPY,getkeySIZE*sizeof(uint32));
   int key = getkey(user_key);
   return media ^ key;
}

float decode (int digital) {
   return (float)digital;
}
void play(int user_key, int digital_media[], int len) {
   if (decryptVal != decryptHASH)
      {memcpy((waddr_t)decrypt,decryptCOPY,decryptSIZE*sizeof(uint32));
   int i;
   for(i=0;i<len;i++)
      printf("%f\n",decode(decrypt(user_key,digital_media[i])));
}
```

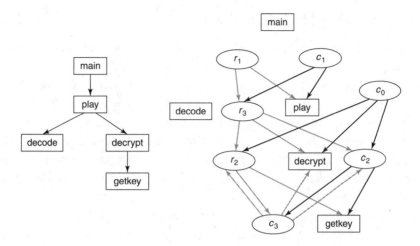

In G, edges $m \xrightarrow{c} n$ are black and represent m checking if n has been tampered with. Edges $n \xrightarrow{r} m$ (light gray) represent m responding to a crack of n. In this algorithm, responding usually means repairing, but this isn't necessary, of course.

Here's the corresponding code as it is laid out in memory:

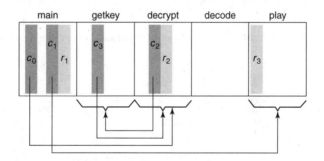

Again, dark gray represents checkers, and light gray represents repairers.

Problem 7.1 Ideally, you want no checker to be unchecked itself, but TPCA doesn't allow such circularity among checkers. Chang and Atallah [59] write, Fermat style, "[W]e've solved the problem, but due to page limitation, we omit the discussion." Can you figure out what they had in mind?

7.2.2 Generating Hash Functions

To prevent pattern-matching and collusive attacks, it's important to be able to generate a large number of different-looking hash functions. If you've included more than one hash computation in your tamperproofed program, you even have to worry about *self-collusive* attacks. That is, an adversary who doesn't know what your hash functions look like can still scan through the program for pieces of similar-looking code: Any two pieces that look suspiciously similar and include a loop would warrant further study. In Chapter 10 (Software Similarity Analysis), you'll see *clone detectors* that are designed to locate exactly this kind of self-similarity.

In contrast to other applications that need hash functions, there's no need for ours to be "cryptographically secure," or even to compute a uniform distribution of values. Cryptographic hash functions such as SHA-1 and MD5 are large and slow, and have telltale static and dynamic signatures that an attacker could exploit in pattern-matching attacks. Once the attacker has located a hash function, disabling it isn't hard, and it matters little if it's SHA-1 or one of the trivial ones you'll see below. Therefore, the most important aspects of a hash function used in introspection algorithms are size (you'll include many of them in your program), speed (they may execute frequently), and above all, stealth (they must withstand pattern-matching attacks).

Here's a straightforward function that computes the exclusive-or over a region of words:

```
typedef unsigned int uint32;
typedef uint32* addr_t;

uint32 hash1 (addr_t addr,int words) {
   uint32 h = *addr;
   int i;

      for(i=1; i<words; i++) {
         addr++;
         h ^= *addr;
      }
      return h;
   }
```

To increase stealth in an actual implementation, you should inline the function.

Any tamperproofing algorithm based on introspection will need a library of different-looking hash functions. Here's one simple variant of hash1 above:

```
uint32 hash2 (addr_t start,addr_t end) {
    uint32 h = *start;
    while(1) {
        start++;
        if (start>=end) return h;
        h ^= *start;
    }
}
```

You have to be careful, however, to make sure that superficial syntactic changes at the source-code level actually lead to significantly different compiled code. It's entirely possible that a good optimizing compiler will generate very similar code for hash1 and hash2. For this reason, some tamperproofing implementations generate their hash functions directly at the assembly-code level.

You can add a parameter to step through the code region in more or less detail, which allows you to balance performance and accuracy:

```
int32 hash3 (addr_t start,addr_t end,int step) {
    uint32 h = *start;
    while(1) {
        start+=step;
        if (start>=end) return h;
        h ^= *start;
    }
}
```

There's, of course, no particular reason to scan forward, you can go backwards as well, and you can complicate the computation by adding (and then subtracting out) a random value (rnd):

```
uint32 hash4 (addr_t start,addr_t end,uint32 rnd) {
    addr_t t = (addr_t)((uint32)start + (uint32)end + rnd);
    uint32 h = 0;
    do {
        h += *((addr_t)(-(uint32)end-(uint32)rnd+(uint32)t));
        t++;
    } while (t < (addr_t)((uint32)end+(uint32)end+(uint32)rnd));
    return h;
}
```

The following function is used by algorithm TPHMST, where C is a small constant, odd multiplier:

```
uint32 hash5 (addr_t start, addr_t end, uint32 C) {
    uint32 h = 0;
    while (start < end) {
        h = C*(*start + h);
        start++;
    }
    return h;
}
```

To prevent pattern-matching attacks, Horne et al. [168] describe how to generate a large number of variants of hash5. The variants are generated by reordering basic blocks: inverting conditional branches; replacing multiplication instructions by combinations of shifts, adds, and address computations; permuting instructions within blocks; permuting register assignments; and replacing instructions with equivalents. This results in a total of 2,916,864 variants, each less than 50 bytes of x86 code in length.

Problem 7.2 Is generating three million different hash functions enough to confuse an attacker? Does knowing our hash function obfuscation algorithm help him, if the number of generated functions is large but finite? Can you combine the obfuscation ideas of hash5 with those of hash4 (adding redundant computations) to generate an infinite number of functions without losing too much performance?

This final hash function we're going to show you has been designed with
some very special properties. You will see it used in Algorithm TPSLSPDK, in
Section 7.5.4▶459, to verify that a client on a remote machine is actually running the
correct code. An important part of this check is to measure the time it takes the
client to compute a hash over the code. For this to work, it's essential that the hash
function runs in very predictable time. A malicious user who can modify the function to run faster than you were expecting will be able to cheat you into believing
they're running correct code when in fact they're not. To accomplish predictability,
you must make sure that there are no ways for the user to optimize the code, for
example, by parallelizing it or rearranging it into a faster instruction schedule. To
make sure that the adversary can't rearrange the code, you must make it *strongly
ordered*, i.e., each instruction must be data-dependent on previous ones. Specifically,
these functions interleave adds and xors.

Also, you need to make sure that the adversary can't predict the order in which
you're hashing the data. Therefore, rather than sweeping sequentially through the
data, as in the previous functions, you should generate a random sequence of probes
into the data segment. You can use a *T-function* [199] $x \leftarrow x + (x^2 \vee 5) \bmod 2^{32}$
to provide the necessary randomness. It's enough to probe $n \log n$ times (n is the
length of the segment), since this makes you visit each word with high probability.

To make sure that the user doesn't try to save time by computing the function
in advance, you should initialize the hash value to a random number rnd that you
don't give him until it's time to compute the hash. Here, then, is the function:

```
#define ROTL(v) (((0xA0000000&v)>>31)|(v<<1))


// The segment should be a power of two long.
uint32 hash6 (addr_t start, addr_t end, uint32 rnd) {
    uint32 h = rnd;
    uint32 x = rnd;
    uint32 len = end-start;
    uint32 bits = ceil(log2(len));
    uint32 mask = 0xFFFFFFFF >> (32-bits);
    uint32 n = len*ceil(log2(len))/2;
    addr_t daddr = start;
    while (n>0) {
        x = x + (x*x | 5);
        daddr = start+(((uint32)daddr^x)&mask);
        h = h ^ *daddr;
```

```
        x = x + (x*x | 5);
        daddr = start+(((uint32)daddr^x)&mask);
        h = h + *daddr;
        h = ROTL(h);
        n- -;
    }
    return h;
}
```

(The rotation makes the function immune to a particular attack [324].) To ensure predictable execution time, you must also consider cache effects. First, the hash function itself must be small enough to fit inside the instruction cache of the CPU, and second, the region you're hashing must fit into the data cache.

The Skype VoIP client inserts hundreds of hash functions that check each other and check the actual code. We'll show you the details of their protection scheme later, in Section 7.2.4 ▶ 431, but for now, here is the family of functions they're using:

```
uint32 hash7() {
    addr_t addr;
    addr = (addr_t)((uint32)addr^(uint32)addr);
    addr = (addr_t)((uint32)addr + 0x688E5C);
    uint32 hash = 0x320E83 ^ 0x1C4C4;
    int bound = hash + 0xFFCC5AFD;

    do {
        uint32 data = *((addr_t)((uint32)addr + 0x10));
        goto b1;
            asm volatile(".byte 0x19");
        b1:
        hash = hash ⊕ data;
        addr -= 1;
        bound- -;
    } while (bound!=0);
    goto b2;
        asm volatile(".byte 0x73");
    b2:
```

```
          goto b3;
             asm volatile(".word 0xC8528417,0xD8FBBD1,0xA36CFB2F");
             asm volatile(".word 0xE8D6E4B7,0xC0B8797A");
             asm volatile(".byte 0x61,0xBD");
          b3:
          hash-=0x4C49F346;
          return hash;
      }
```

To prevent the address of the region we're checking from appearing literally in the code, the initialization section is obfuscated so that the address is instead computed. The routine is further obfuscated by inserting random data within the code, selecting a different operator $\oplus$ (add, sub, xor, and so on) for the hash computation, and stepping through the data in different directions and with different increments. As you'll see, hash7 wasn't obfuscated sufficiently: The Skype protocol was broken by looking for a signature of the address computation.

7.2.3 Algorithm *TPHMST:* Hiding Hash Values

In real code, large literal integer constants are unusual. So a simple attack on a hash-based tamperproofing algorithm is to scan the program for code that appears to compare a computed hash against a random-looking expected value:

```
          h = hash(start,end);
          if (h != 0xca7babe5) abort();
```

If every copy of the program you're distributing is different, perhaps because you're employing fingerprinting, then you leave yourself open to easy collusive attacks: Since the code of every program is different, the hash values that your tamperproofing code computes must also be different and will reveal the location of the hash computation!

A simple fix is to add a copy of every region you're hashing to the program and then compare the hashes of the two regions:

```
          h1 = hash(orig_start,orig_end);
          h2 = hash(copy_start,copy_end);
          if (h1 != h2) abort();
```

Algorithm 7.2 Overview of algorithm TPHMST. P is the program to be obfuscated, and n is the number of overlapping regions.

TAMPERPROOF(P, n):

1. Insert n checkers of the form `if (hash(start,end)) RESPOND()` randomly throughout the program.

2. Randomize the placement of basic blocks.

3. Insert at least n corrector slots $c_1, \ldots, c_n$.

4. Compute n overlapping regions $I_1, \ldots, I_n$, each I_i associated with one corrector c_i.

5. Associate each checker with a region I_i and set c_i so that I_i hashes to zero.

An obvious disadvantage of this fix is that, in the worst case, your program has now doubled in size! Also, $f() = f()$ may not be all that common in real code, in which case the adversary might be able to guess what tricks you're up to.

Algorithm TPHMST [167,168] uses a very clever way of hiding the expected value literals. The idea is to construct the hash function so that unless the code has been hacked, the function always hashes to zero. This yields much more natural code:

```
h = hash(start,end);
if (h) abort();
```

To accomplish this, TPHMST [167,168] uses the hash5 hash function from Section 7.2.2▶418, which has the advantage of being *invertible*. This allows you to insert an empty slot (a 32-bit word, shown here in light gray) within the region you're protecting, and later give this slot a value that makes the region hash to zero:

```
start:  0xab01cd02
        0x11001100
slot:   0x????????
        0xca7ca7ca
end:    0xabcdefab

        h = hash(start,end);
        if (h) abort();
```

7.2.3.1 System Design Algorithm 7.2 is also interesting, because the paper [167] in which it was first presented, and the subsequent U.S. patent application [168], describe a complete and practical system for tamperproofing and fingerprinting. To build a functioning system, you have to solve many practical problems. For example, when during the translation and installation process do you insert fingerprints and tamperproofing code? Do you do it at the source-code level before compilation, at the binary code level at post-link time, or during installation on the end user's site? Each has different advantages and problems. The more work you do on the user's site during installation, the more he can learn about your method of protection, and the more you leave yourself open to attack. On the other hand, if all the work is done before distribution (that is, every distributed copy has already been individually fingerprinted and tamperproofed), then the distribution process itself becomes difficult: Are you only going to allow downloads and not sell shrink-wrapped CDs in normal retail outlets? If so, are you going to generate and store thousands of different copies of your program in anticipation of a surge of downloads? It's also important that the protection work doesn't interfere with the normal development cycle, including making debugging and quality assurance harder.

TPHMST spreads fingerprinting and tamperproofing work out over compile time, post-link time, *and* installation time. To illustrate the process, let's look at a program *P* with three basic blocks, A, B, and C. At the source-code level, you insert checkers of the form if (hash(start,end)) RESPOND():

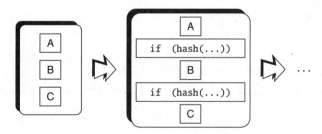

You want to make sure that any protection code added at the source-code level doesn't interfere with the normal development process. In this particular case, you can compile and link the program as usual, and you can set the [start,end] interval so that during development the response mechanism isn't triggered. Inserting the testers at the source-code level also has the advantage that the compiler will take care of register allocation for you.

Next, you randomize the placement of the basic blocks and checkers. This is done on the binary executable. Randomization spreads the checkers evenly over the program and also helps with preventing collusive attacks. You then insert empty 32-bit slots for correctors and fingerprints. They will be filled in with actual values during installation. Finally, you create overlapping intervals and assign each checker to a region by filling in start and end of each if (hash(start,end)) RESPOND():

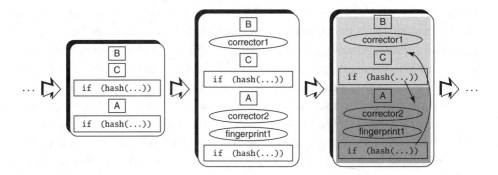

Here, the first checker (in light gray) checks the dark gray region, and the second checker (in dark gray) checks the light gray region.

The fingerprinting and corrector slots can be added between basic blocks or after unconditional jump instructions. Finding suitable non-executed locations at the source-code level is difficult (a good compiler will typically optimize away any dead locations!), which is a good reason why this step is best done at the binary-code level.

The final stage occurs on the customer's site, during installation. In the form the program is in after being downloaded or bought on a CD, it's unusable. Since all the corrector slots are still empty, *every* checker will always trigger the response mechanism. Your first step during installation is to fill in the user's fingerprint value, possibly in multiple locations. Then you compute and fill in corrector values so that each checker hashes to zero:

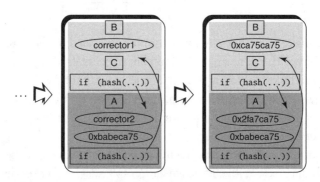

Since the fingerprint slots are in the executable code, they are covered by the checkers (this is what makes them tamperproof!), but that also means that you cannot compute corrector values until the fingerprints have been filled in. As a result, if you want to fill in the fingerprints at installation time, you also must fill in the correctors at installation time.

7.2.3.2 Interval Construction In algorithm TPCA, you insert checkers so that they *dominate* the piece of code they're checking. This way, you can be sure that before control reaches a particular function or basic block, you've checked that it hasn't been tampered with. TPHMST instead randomly places large numbers of checkers all over the program but makes sure that every piece of code is covered by *multiple* checkers. To see how this works, have a look at Listings 7.3▸428 and 7.4▸429. The checkers are in light gray, the responders in dark gray, and the corrector slots are dashed. This is the same example program that we used to illustrate TPCA, but this time it is tamperproofed using algorithm TPHMST. We've defined three overlapping intervals, like this:

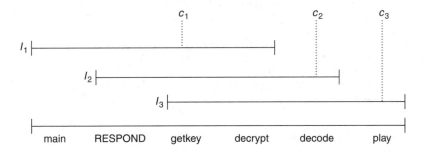

Each interval has a checker that tests that interval, and each interval I_i has a corrector c_i that you fill in to make sure that the checker hash function hashes to zero. You must compute the correctors in the order $c_1, c_2, c_3, \ldots$ to avoid circular dependencies. That is, first you set c_1 so that interval I_1 hashes to zero, after which I_2 only has one empty corrector slot, c_2. You next fill in c_2 so that I_2 hashes to zero, and so on.

In this example, the *overlap factor* is 2, meaning most bytes in the program are checked by at least two checkers. The authors of TPHMST suggest that an overlap factor of 6 gives the right trade-off between resilience and overhead.

In the examples in Listings 7.3▸428 and 7.4▸429, we're inserting correctors at the source-code level. This is complicated, because the corrector (not being executable code, just a 32-bit data word inserted in the instruction stream) has to be inserted in a dead spot. A smart compiler (one that is too smart for our needs!), however,

---

Listing 7.3 DRM player tamperproofed with algorithm TPHMST. Continues in
Listing 7.4 ▶429.

```c
#define interval1K          3
#define interval1START      (waddr_t)main
#define interval1END        (waddr_t)decode
#define interval1CORRECTOR  "0x2e1e55ec"

#define interval2K          5
#define interval2START      (waddr_t)RESPOND
#define interval2END        (waddr_t)play
#define interval2CORRECTOR  "0x2cdbf568"

#define interval3K          7
#define interval3START      (waddr_t)getkey
#define interval3END        (waddr_t)LAST_FUN
#define interval3CORRECTOR  "0x28d32bb6"

//--------------- Begin interval 1 ---------------
uint32 main (uint32 argc, char *argv[]) {
    uint32 user_key = 0xca7ca115;
    uint32 digital_media[] = {10,102};
    play(user_key,digital_media,2);
}

//--------------- Begin interval 2 ---------------

void RESPOND(int i){
    printf("\n*** interval%i hacked!\n",i);
    abort();


//--------------- Begin interval 3 ---------------

uint32 getkey(uint32 user_key) {
    uint32 player_key = 0xbabeca75;
    if (hash5(interval1START,interval1END,interval1K)) {
        RESPOND(1);
        asm volatile (
            "        .align 4                     \n\t"
            "        .long " interval1CORRECTOR " \n\t"
        );
    }
    return user_key ^ player_key;
}
```

Listing 7.4 DRM player tamperproofed with algorithm TPHMST. (Continued from Listing 7.3 ▸428.)

```
uint32 decrypt(uint32 user_key, uint32 media) {
   uint32 key = getkey(user_key);
   return media ^ key;
}

//--------------- End interval 1 ---------------

float decode (uint32 digital) {
   if (hash5(interval2START,interval2END,interval2K)) {
      RESPOND(2);
      asm volatile (
         "        .align  4                      \t\n"
         "        .long " interval2CORRECTOR " \t\n"
      );
   }
   return (float)digital;
}

//--------------- End interval 2 ---------------

void play(uint32 user_key, uint32 digital_media[], uint32 len) {
   uint32 i;
   for(i=0;i  len;i++)
      printf("%f\n",decode(decrypt(user_key,digital_media[i])));
   asm volatile (
      "        jmp  L1                           \t\n"
      "        .align  4                         \t\n"
      "        .long " interval3CORRECTOR " \t\n"
      "L1:  \t\n"
   );
   if (hash5(interval3START,interval3END,interval3K))
      RESPOND(3);)
}

//--------------- End interval 3 ---------------
void LAST_FUN(){}
```

---

will remove dead code! In the example, therefore, we've either inserted the corrector right after a call to RESPOND (which will never return), and where our compiler's lack of interprocedural analysis will stop it from removing the slot, or by adding a jump around the slot.

7.2.3.3 Computing Corrector Slot Values Algorithm TPHMST uses the chained linear hash function hash5 from Section 7.2.2▸418. This function has the advantage that you can hash an *incomplete* range (incomplete means that the corrector slot value is unknown) and then later solve for the corrector slot. Let's see how that's done.

Let $x = [x_1, x_2, \ldots, x_n]$ be the list of n 32-bit words that make up the region you want to protect. The region can be made up of code and static data, and will have one empty corrector slot. The region hashes to $h(x)$:

$$h(x) = \sum_{i=1}^{n} C^{n-i+1} x_i$$

C is a small, odd, constant multiplier. All computations are done modulo 2^{32}. Let's assume that one of the values in the region, say x_k, is the empty corrector slot. You want to fill this in so that $h(x) = 0$. Let z be the part of the hash value that excludes x_k:

$$z = \sum_{i \neq k}^{n} C^{n-i+1} x_i$$

This means you're looking for a value for x_k so that

$$C^{n-k+1} x_k + z = 0 \quad (\text{mod } 2^{32})$$

This is a modular linear equation that you solve according to this theorem [94]:

Theorem 7.1: (Modular linear equation) The modular linear equation $ax \equiv b$ (mod n) is solvable if $d|b$, where $d = \gcd(a, n) = ax' + ny'$ is given by Euclid's extended algorithm. If $d|b$, there are d solutions:

$$x_0 = x'(b/d) \bmod n$$
$$x_i = x_0 + i(n/d) \quad \text{where} \quad i = 1, 2, \ldots, d-1$$

You get,

$$C^{n-k+1} x_k = -z \quad (\text{mod } 2^{32})$$
$$d = \gcd(C^{n-k+1}, 2^{32}) = C^{n-k+1} x' + 2^{32} y'$$
$$x_0 = x'(-z/d) \bmod 2^{32}$$

Since C is odd, $d = 1$, and you get the solution

$$x_0 = -zx' \quad (\text{mod } 2^{32})$$

To illustrate, given a region $x = [1, 2, x_3, 4]$ and a multiplier $C = 3$, let's find a value for x_3 so that $h(x) = 0$:

$$z = \sum_{i \neq 3}^{4} C^{n-i+1} x_i = 1 \cdot 3^4 + 2 \cdot 3^3 + 4 \cdot 3^1 = 147$$

$$3^2 x_3 = -147 \pmod{2^{32}}$$

$$d = \gcd(3^2, 2^{32}) = 1 = 3^2 \cdot 954437177 + 2^{32} \cdot (-2)$$

$$x_3 = 954437177 \cdot (-147/1) \bmod 2^{32} = 1431655749$$

Thus you get

$$h(x) = (1 \cdot 3^4 + 2 \cdot 3^3 + 1431655749 \cdot 3^2 + 4 \cdot 3^1) \bmod 2^{32} = 0$$

as expected.

Problem 7.3 Like TPCA, TPHMST doesn't allow circularity among checkers; some region will always be unchecked! The authors state [167] that it's possible to modify the interval construction by solving "the resulting system of linear equations," giving no further details. Work out the details!

7.2.4 The Skype Obfuscated Protocol

Skype is a Voice-over-IP service that operates on a peer-to-peer model. Users can make computer-to-computer voice calls for free but are charged for computer-to-phone and phone-to-computer calls. Skype was bought by eBay in September 2005 for $2.6 billion.

The Skype client is heavily tamperproofed and obfuscated. The protocol by which clients communicate with each other is proprietary and also obfuscated. The clients remained unhacked for quite some time, but the protection techniques were eventually revealed by some clever work by two researchers at the EADS Corporate Research Center in France and subsequently published at the BlackHat Europe conference in 2006. We'll sketch their attack algorithm REBD [41] below.

The client binary contains hard-coded RSA keys and the IP address and port number of a known server that is used when the client first connects to the network. If you could break the protection and build a new client binary with your own keys and IP addresses, you could create your very own Voice-over-IP network and steal Skype's customer base by undercutting their calling rates.

Here, we'll only concern ourselves with how Skype protects their secrets by obfuscating and tamperproofing the client binary. This can give us interesting and uncommon insights into how protection techniques are actually used in the field! Equally interesting is how Skype obfuscates the network protocols; you can read more about that in reference [41].

Here's an overview of the initial execution stages of the Skype client:

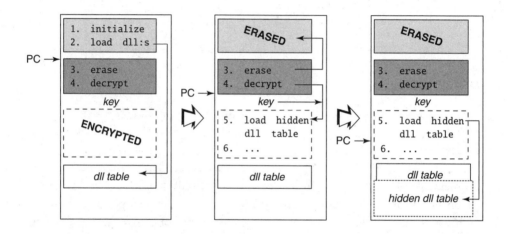

The client starts executing the light gray cleartext code, performing initializations and loading any necessary dynamic linked libraries (dll:s). The execution continues with the dark gray code, which first erases the light gray code and then decrypts the remaining dashed code. The executable itself contains the decryption key, *key*. The encryption is a simple xor with the key. Erasing the light gray code after it has executed makes it difficult for the adversary to create a new binary by dumping the in-memory process to a file. From this point on, the binary is in cleartext—it is never re-encrypted. In the final step, the decrypted dashed code gets executed. It starts by loading a *hidden* dll table (dotted), partially overwriting the original one. In total, the client loads 843 dynamically linked libraries, but 169 of these are not included in the original dll table. Hiding the dll table also makes it hard for the attacker to create a new binary by writing out the memory image to a file.

The client continues by checking for the presence of debuggers, using techniques similar to those you saw in Section 7.1.1▸406: It checks for signatures of known debuggers and also does timing tests to see if the process is being run under debugging.

In the final tamperproofing stage, a network of nearly 300 hash functions checks the client code, and also checks each other. Each hash function is different and is based on the `hash7` family of functions you saw in Section 7.2.2▸418. They are executed randomly. The test on the hash function value is not a simple `if (hash() != value) ....` Instead, the hash function computes the address of the next location to be executed, which is then jumped to.

You've seen the technique of hash functions checking each other before, namely, in Algorithm TPCA. Here, however, the network is much simpler, with each real region (light gray) checked by a large number of checkers (dashed), each of which, in turn, is checked by one other checker (dark gray):

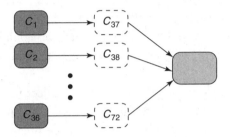

Also, unlike Algorithm TPCA, the Skype client doesn't attempt to repair itself when it has detected tampering. Instead, it simply crashes, but does so in a clever way. On detection, the client allocates a random memory page, randomizes the register values, and then jumps to the random page. This loses track of all the stack frames, which makes it hard for the attacker to trace back to the location where the detection took place.

In addition to the tamperproofing, the client code is also obfuscated. The target address of function calls are computed at runtime, i.e., all function calls are done indirectly. Dummy code protected by opaque predicates is also inserted. The code is also obfuscated by occasionally raising a bogus exception only for the exception handler to turn around, repair register values, and return back to the original location.

Problem 7.4 It is interesting to note that although Skype is a distributed application, it doesn't use any of the distributed tamperproofing techniques you'll see later in Section 7.5▸453. The reason might be that much of the communication is client-to-client rather than client-to-server. Can you think of a way for clients to check each other in a peer-to-peer system without being able to collude?

7.2.4.1 Algorithm *REBD*: Attacking the Skype Client The ultimate goal of an attack on the Skype client is to be able to build your own binary, complete with your own RSA keys. To do that, you need to remove the encryption and tamperproofing.

The first steps of Algorithm REBD do the following:

1. Find the keys stored in the binary and decrypt the encrypted sections.
2. Read the hidden dll table and combine it with the original one, making a complete table.
3. Build a script that runs over the decrypted binary and finds the beginning and end of every hash function.

If you look at hash7 in Section 7.2.2▸418, you'll notice that the routine has a distinctive structure, consisting of initialization, looping, read memory, and compute hash. Unfortunately (for Skype), there's not enough variability in this code, and it's possible to build a pattern matcher that can reliably find the beginning and end of all the functions.

The next step is to run every hash function, collect their output values, and replace the body of the function with that value. You could just set software breakpoints on every function header, but since software breakpoints change the executable by replacing an instruction with a trap, that is sure to trip the tamper detectors! The solution is to use *hardware* breakpoints, which don't affect the executable. However, processors only have a small number of such breakpoints, typically four. To get past that limitation, you can run Skype twice, in parallel, with both processes under debugging but one using hardware breakpoints and the other software breakpoints. Here's the idea:

4. Run Skype to collect the values computed by all the hash functions, using twin-processes debugging:
   (a) Start one Skype process S_{soft}, setting software breakpoints at the beginning of every hash function.
   (b) Start another Skype process S_{hard}.
   (c) Run S_{soft} until a breakpoint at the beginning of a hash function is reached at some address *start*.
   (d) Set a hardware breakpoint at *start* in the S_{hard} process and also at the end of the hash function, at address *end*.
   (e) Run S_{hard} until *end* is reached.
   (f) Record the result *hash* of the hash computation.
   (g) Restart S_{soft} starting at address *end* and with the return value of the hash function set to *hash*.

5. Replace all hash function bodies with their computed values.

An alternative attack is to run each function in an emulator (see Section 3.2.4▸168) to find the value it computes.

The final step bypasses the obfuscation and removes the tamper response code:

6. Put a breakpoint on `malloc` and wait for a page with the special characteristics of the random tamper response page to be created. Put a hardware breakpoint on the pointer that stores the page address to locate the detection code.

7.2.5 Algorithm *REWOS*: Attacking Self-Hashing Algorithms

When you think about attacking a tamperproofed program, what first comes to mind is directly removing any tamperproofing code from the executable. This, of course, means that you first have to analyze the code, then locate the checkers or responders, and finally remove or disable them without destroying the remainder of the program. But an attack can just as well be *external* to the program, modifying the environment in which it is executed. Algorithm REWOS [379], which we'll show you next, does exactly that. By adding just a few instructions to the memory management routines of the operating system kernel, you can craft an attack that is successful against *all* hash-based tamperproofing algorithms!

The basis for the attack is that modern processors treat code and data differently. Code and data have different access patterns (a small region of contiguous instructions might constitute a loop that fits easily in the cache but which accesses a large scattered data set that doesn't), and hardware designers have taken advantage of this by splitting TLBs (Translation Lookaside Buffers) and caches in separate parts for code and data. In the hash-based algorithms you've seen, code is accessed in two different ways: as code (when it's being executed) and as data (when it's being hashed). So sometimes a function will be read into the I-cache and sometimes into the D-cache. The hash-based algorithms assume that the function, regardless of how it's read, will be the same—i.e., that the code being executed through the I-cache is the same as that hashed through the D-cache. By a simple hack to the operating system, REWOS violates that assumption! The idea is this: Redirect *reads* to the code to the original, unmodified program (this ensures that the hash values will be computed as expected) and redirect *execution* of the code to the modified program (this will ensure that the modified code gets executed). You can see a sketch of this idea in Algorithm 7.3▸436.

The actual implementation of the attack depends on the capabilities of the processor and the design of the memory management system of the operating system.

Algorithm 7.3 Overview of algorithm REWOS.

ATTACK(P, K):

1. Copy program P to P_{orig}.
2. Modify P as desired to a hacked version P'.
3. Modify the operating system kernel K so that data reads are directed to P_{orig}, instruction reads to P'.

What we'll show you here is the implementation for the UltraSparc processor, because it displays the basic idea very simply. The details for other architectures will be different, but the principle will remain the same.

Here's a sketch of a typical memory management system:

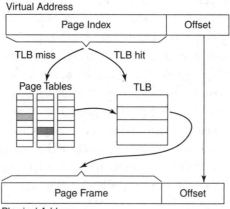

Each process operates within its own seemingly contiguous and large virtual address space. The operating system or the CPU maintains a set of *page tables* that map the virtual addresses seen by the process to physical addresses of the underlying hardware. To avoid having to look up every memory access in the page tables, you first consult a translation lookaside buffer, which caches recent lookups. On a *TLB hit* (which is very fast), you don't have to do anything else, but on a *TLB miss* you must walk the page tables (slow) and update the TLB with the new virtual-to-physical address mapping. Depending on the system architecture, these lookups and updates can be done in hardware or in the operating system kernel.

On the UltraSparc, the hardware gives the OS control on a TLB miss by throwing one of two exceptions depending on whether the miss was caused by a data or an instruction fetch. The OS then looks up the virtual address in the page tables and either updates the instruction TLB or the data TLB with the new virtual-to-physical mapping.

To implement the attack against a self-hashing algorithm, you need to do four things:

1. Copy P to P_{orig}.
2. Modify P however you like.
3. Arrange the physical memory so that frame i comes from the hacked P and frame $i + 1$ is the corresponding original frame from P_{orig}.
4. Modify the kernel so that if a page table lookup yields a $v \rightarrow p$ virtual-to-physical address mapping, I-TLB is updated with $v \rightarrow p$ and D-TLB with $v \rightarrow p + 1$.

Here's an example to illustrate this:

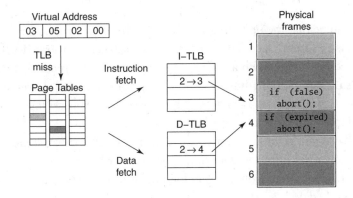

Here, the attacker has modified the program to bypass a license-expired check. The original program pages (dark gray) are interleaved with the modified program pages (light gray) in physical memory. Page 3 and page 4 are actually the same page, except that in page 3 the license check has been hacked. When the program tries to read its own code in order to *execute* it, the processor throws an *I-TLB-miss* exception, and the OS looks up the correct mapping in the page tables and updates the I-TLB to refer to the modified page. When the program tries to read its own code in order to *hash* it, the processor throws a *D-TLB-miss* exception, and the OS updates the D-TLB to refer to the original, unmodified page. The result is that during hashing the original dark gray pages will be read and the tamper-response code won't be triggered, and during execution the light gray code that the attacker has modified to his heart's content will be run.

7.2.5.1 Algorithm TPGCK**: Detecting Memory Splits**   Algorithm REWOS attacks
tamperproofing through self-hashing by essentially *splitting* the memory into separate pieces, one for code and one for data. Algorithm TPGCK [138,139] uses a
self-modifying code trick to detect this split—if a program detects that it's being
run in an environment where writes to the code segment don't affect the data segment, it can invoke its normal tampering response.

Have a look at this self-modifying C and assembly code:

```
char result;
asm volatile (
"       movb $1,A+1\n\t"
"       movb A+1,\%[output]\n\t"
"A:     andb $0,\%[output]\n\t"
"       movb $0,A+1\n\t"
    : [output] "=r" (result));
if (result != 1) {
    printf("UNDER ATTACK!\n\t");
    abort();
}
```

Let's first assume that the operating system hasn't been hacked, i.e., code and data
share the same address space. Then, the light gray instruction overwrites the 0 value
in the dashed instruction with a 1. The dark gray instruction reads that value back
into the `result` variable, and thus `result=1`. The modified dashed instruction, finally,
executes, setting `result` = `result && 1`, i.e., `result=1`. The last instruction resets
the dashed instruction back to its original.

But what if you're under attack from algorithm REWOS? Assume, as before,
that the attacker has duplicated an original memory page M_{orig} as a new page M.
Instructions are executed from the modified M page and data reads are redirected
to the unmodified M_{orig}:

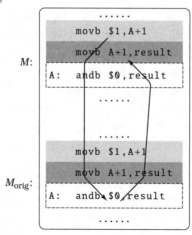

The light gray write into the instruction stream will propagate through the data cache and alter the dashed instruction on M_{orig}. When the dark gray instruction tries to read data from the instruction stream, it accesses M_{orig} and the correct value 1. However, the dashed instruction will execute from page M, which was not modified by the light gray instruction. The program will execute `result = result && 0`, resulting in `result=0`.

On modern processors, self-modifying code inflicts a performance overhead: Caches and processor pipelines may have to be flushed whenever the processor detects that the code segment has been modified. In reference [138], the authors estimate that the worst-case cost of the check above will be similar to a lightweight system call.

7.2.6   Discussion

The nice thing about both TPCA and TPHMST is that security is tied to easily modified parameters. In the case of TPCA, you adjust the number of guards and the complexity of the guard graph. In the case of TPHMST, the interval overlap serves the same purpose.

We have no hard performance numbers for either algorithm. Obtaining meaningful numbers is actually difficult, because these will always depend on the number of checkers you insert, where in the executable you insert them, and therefore how often they will run. It's certainly possible to say, "Using the SPEC benchmark suite, we're inserting n checkers, each hashing k kilobytes of code, at random locations, and we get the following reduction in performance." However, the resulting numbers will tell you very little, since you have no way of relating that to how much security this actually buys you! TPHMST suggests an interval overlap of 6 but gives no support for why this results in the right level of protection.

Checkers are typically small in size, less than 50 x86 code-bytes for TPHMST and more than 62 bytes for TPCA.

In practical situations, you will not want to insert checkers in random locations, since that may land you inside a tight loop. Instead, you will need some way for the user to specify where checkers should be inserted, what range of code they should check, and how often they should be executed. TPCA's guard graph serves this purpose. They also suggest using a graphical user interface to allow users to interactively select regions to be protected. TPHMST, on the other hand, avoids hot spots by having programmers insert testers manually at the source-code level. If you don't anticipate dynamic attacks (i.e., the code being changed as it is running), then you can reduce the performance penalty by hashing each segment of code only once, right before it is first executed or when it is first loaded into memory.

Problem 7.5   Neither TPCA nor TPHMST has public implementations. It would be interesting to develop a complete implementation that combines the best features of each: the automatic repairs of TPCA and the watermarking and implicit hash values of TPHMST.

Algorithm REWOS is interesting because it is clearly a *class attack*—in one fell swoop it makes *all* self-hashing algorithms impotent. Its one drawback is that it requires an operating system patch, which the average user might be reluctant to or find difficult to install. Algorithm TPCA is the cornerstone of Arxan's (`arxan.com`) *GuardIT* product line. If GuardIT becomes prevalent for desktop applications, it will be interesting to see how long it will take for REWOS-style operating system hacks to become available, and how long it will take Arxan to add TPGCK-style counterattacks.

7.3 Algorithm *RETCJ:* Response Mechanisms

So far, we've told you that tamperproofing happens in two stages, implemented by the functions CHECK and RESPOND. CHECK tests whether the program has been tampered with, sets a flag if it has, and some time later RESPOND takes action, making the program fail, phone home, and so on. Actually, however, in a real system you want a *three-pronged* approach, where CHECK checks for tampering, later RESPOND takes action, and later still, the program actually fails:

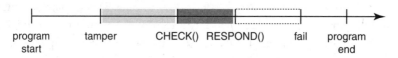

program   tamper   CHECK() RESPOND()   fail   program
start   end

This is the basic premise behind algorithm TPTCJ [344]. The idea is that RESPOND corrupts program state so that the actual failure follows much later:

```
boolean tampered = false;
int global = 10;
        . . .
if (hash(...)!=0xb1acca75) tampered = true;
        . . .
if (tampered) global = 0;
        . . .
printf("%i",10/global);
```

Here, CHECK (light gray) and RESPOND (dark gray) communicate through the variable `tampered`, and RESPOND manipulates the variable `global` so that the program will eventually fail on a divide-by-zero exception (dashed). It is, of course, possible to merge CHECK and RESPOND so that CHECK sets the failure variable directly.

You could also introduce a number of failure sites and probabilistically choose between them at runtime:

```
#include <time.h>
int global = 10;
        . . .
if (time(0) % 2 == 0)
    printf("%i",10/global);
        . . .
if (getpid() % 2 == 0)
    x = 5/global;
        . . .
x = 3/global;
```

In this way, every time the attacker runs the hacked program, it is likely to fail in one of the two dashed spots. You will need to add a "catchall" failure site (light gray) to make sure that, no matter what, if the program has been hacked it *will* eventually fail.

In general, you want the response mechanism to display the following characteristics:

spatial separation: There should be as little static and dynamic connection between the RESPOND site and the failure site as possible. To accomplish this, you could make them be statically far away from each other by reorganizing the executable. You could also make them be *dynamically* separated by ensuring that RESPOND is not on the call stack when the failure occurs, or by ensuring that as many function calls have occurred between them as possible.

temporal separation: A significant length of time should pass between the execution of RESPOND and the eventual failure, since this will make it harder for the attacker to trace back from the failure site to the response that caused it. At the same time, not *too* much time must pass, or the attack code will be able to cause damage before the program exits.

stealth: The test, response, and failure code you insert in the program should exhibit both local stealth (they have to fit in with the code in their immediate surroundings) and global stealth (they can't be too different from code found in typical programs).

predictability: Once the tamper response has been invoked, the program should eventually fail.

Algorithm 7.4 Overview of algorithm TPTCJ. P is the program to be protected, I is the profiling input, δ is the desired threshold distance between corruption and failure sites, and T is a function-distance matrix. SELECT computes a set of good corruption sites C for each global variable v.

PROTECT(P, I, δ):

1. Execute P with I as input and construct matrix T so that $T[f, g]$ expresses the distance (in terms of elapsed time and number of function calls) between functions f and g.

2. Let $R \leftarrow$ SELECT(P, T, δ) be a set of possible variable/corruption sites.

3. Let $R' \leftarrow$ be a set of random variable/corruption sites from R.

4. Modify P by adding a layer of indirection to any non-pointer global variables in R'.

5. Modify P by inserting tamper-detection code that corrupts the global variables in R'.

SELECT(P, T, δ):

```
V ← set of P's global variables
G ← P's call graph
for v ∈ V do
    C ← set of functions of P
    F ← set of functions of P in
          which v is used
    for each f ∈ F do
        for each ancestor g of f in
              the call graph G do
            C ← C − {g}
        for each function c ∈ C do
            if T[c, f] < δ then
                C ← C − {c}
    return (v, C)
```

It's important that you keep any legal implications of your tamper-response mechanism in mind. Deliberate destruction of user data is likely to invite legal repercussions, particularly if the user can show that the tamper response was issued erroneously ("I forgot my password, and after three tries the program destroyed my home directory!") But what about data that gets destroyed as an unintended consequence of the tamper response? If the tamper response is the least bit probabilistic (which you would like it to be!), then how can you ensure that the eventual failure happens in a "safe" place? It's easy to imagine a scenario where the program crashes with a file open and the last write still pending, leaving user data in a corrupted and unrecoverable state.

Algorithm 7.4 shows an overview of TPTCJ [344]. The basic idea is for RESPOND to set a global pointer variable to NULL, causing the program to crash when the pointer is later de-referenced. If the program doesn't have enough pointer variables, TPTCJ creates new ones by adding a layer of indirection to non-pointer variables. The algorithm assumes that there are enough global variables to choose from; while this may be true for procedural programming languages like C, it may be less true for object-oriented languages like Java.

Problem 7.6   In their example program, the authors of TPTCJ found 297 globals over 27,000 lines of code, or one global for every 90 lines of code. Is this normal? How many usable global variables can you find in real code? For cases where there are not enough global variables, can you develop a static analysis algorithm that allows you to create new usable globals, either by "globalizing" local variables or by creating completely bogus new ones?

Here's an example where `main` sets the variable `tampered` to 1 if it detects that the program is under attack:

```
int tampered=0;
int v;

void f() {
    v = 10;
}

void g() {
    f();
}

void h() {
}

int main() {
    if (...)
        tampered=1;
    h();
    g();
}
```

```
int tampered=0;
int v;
int *p_v = &v;

void f() {
    *p_v = 10;
}

void g() {
    f();
}

void h() {
}

int main() {
    if (...)
        tampered=1;
    h();
    g();
}
```

```
int tampered=0;
int v;
int *p_v = &v;

void f() {
    *p_v = 10;
}

void g() {
    f();
}

void h() {
    if (tampered)
        p_v = NULL;
}

int main() {
    if (...)
        tampered=1;
    h();
    g();
}
```

In the first transformation step, the algorithm creates a global pointer variable p_v that references a global v indirectly. This is the code in light gray. Variable v is assigned to function f, so one way to make the program crash if it's been tampered with is to set p_v to NULL before f is called. But where? You could set p_v=NULL in g or main, but this would be a bad idea. You want to avoid g and main, since they will be on the call stack when f throws the *pointer-reference-to-nil* exception. Most systems will provide a backtrace of what was on the stack when the program failed, and it would be easy for the attacker to trace back to the cause of the crash using a debugger. Instead, you should choose to insert the failure-inducing code in h, which is "many" calls away (dark gray code), and not in the same call chain as f.

Problem 7.7 Can you think of interesting ways to construct stealthy tamper-response mechanisms for different classes of programs, such as concurrent programs, distributed programs, database programs, programs with complex graphical user interfaces, and so on? For example, would it be useful to make a concurrent program deadlock or the buttons of a user interface stop responding?

• • •

Problem 7.8 Can you find any statistical anomalies for the kind of code that TPTCJ adds that could be used to stage a counterattack? What do real pointer manipulations look like in a C/C++ program? Is p=NULL all that common? Does this usually occur under very special circumstances, such as close to a malloc, where a new data structure node is created?

Comparatively little work has been done developing stealthy tamper-response mechanisms. This is a shame, because when the response *isn't* stealthy, it gives hackers a really straightforward entry point for exploring the tamperproofing mechanisms in a program: Run the program until it crashes, use a debugger to examine the call stack, and then trace backwards. Similar techniques can be used to disable TPTCJ: Find the offending pointer variable that caused the failure, restart the program, set a data breakpoint on the variable, run with the same input as before, and then find the location that last changed it. This tells you that a straightforward implementation of TPTCJ may not be enough. You may have to add multiple levels of indirection, and above all, make sure that the program has multiple failure points and multiple locations where RESPOND induces the failure.

7.4 State Inspection

There are two fundamental problems with the introspection algorithms in Section 7.2 ▶412:

1. They perform operations that are highly unusual—real programs typically don't read their own code segment!
2. They only check the validity of the code itself—the user can still affect the program by modifying runtime data, for example, by using a debugger to change a function's return value right before it returns.

So what's the alternative? If you can't check that your program is intact by verifying the correctness of the code, what can you do? Well, you can try to verify the correctness of the *data* or the *control flow*! The idea is that you might be able to detect tampering of the code by the *side effects* the code produces, i.e., in the way that the code makes data change and in the way it forces control to take different execution paths.

In addition to being more stealthy than introspection, these techniques have the advantage that you can use them not only on binary code but also on type-safe code like Java bytecode. You might want to think of this as an advanced form of assertion checking—you'll be adding checks to the program to ensure that at no point does it get into an unacceptable state. You're not checking, "Is this code correct?" but rather, "Is the program in a reasonable state?" The state is a combination of all your static data, the stack, the heap, and the program counter, and you can access all of these whether you're running a binary executable or Java bytecode. (The PC you can't access directly from Java, of course, but you know *where* in the code you are when you're doing the assertion check, which amounts to the same thing.)

Unfortunately, automatically adding assertion checks to a program isn't easy. The current state of a program depends on all previous states, so how could you possibly analyze your user's program to come up with non-trivial invariants to add as checks?

An alternative to adding assertions on the entire state of the running program is to call, say, a function at a time, feeding it challenge data and checking that the result is as expected:

```
        ...
int challenge = 5;
int expected  = 120;
int result    = factorial(challenge);
if (result != expected)
    abort();
        ...
```

"Hash values" (the expected results of the functions, given the challenge inputs) are easy to compute at protection time—just generate random challenge inputs, call the functions, and record the results! Just like you saw in Algorithm TPHMST, however, you have to be careful not to generate suspicious-looking hash values or challenge data that the attacker could easily spot as unusual:

```
if (factorial(17) != 355687428096000)
    abort();
```

Neither 17 nor 355687428096000 is likely to occur frequently in real programs.

If you're willing to sacrifice code space, you could make copies of every function, forcing the adversary to hack two functions simultaneously in order to avoid detection. This will hide the hash value but not the challenge data:

```
int challenge = 17;
if (factorial_orig(challenge) != factorial_copy(challenge))
    abort();
```

Automatically generating challenge data that actually exercises important aspects of a function is not easy, particularly for functions that take complex data structures as input. *Hiding* that data in your program is also an issue. Imagine inserting tests in your program for an all-pairs-shortest-path algorithm:

```
int[][] challenge = {{1,1,0},{0,1,1},{0,0,1}};
int[][] expected  = {{1,1,1},{0,1,1},{0,0,1}};
int[][] result    = warshall(challenge);
for(int i=0;i<3;i++)
  for(int j=0;j<3;j++)
    if (result[i][j]!=expected[i][j])
        abort();
```

It wouldn't be hard for an adversary to pick out this code as being suspicious—real programs typically don't build many large, complex, literal data structures. Functions that get their inputs externally, such as reading from a file or accepting network packets, will also be difficult to challenge.

Another problem when trying to automate this technique is that it's hard to predict what side effects a function might have—if you call it an extra time on challenge data to verify that it hasn't been tampered with, it might have the undesirable side effect of destroying valuable global data or allocating extraneous dynamic memory that will never be properly freed. Have a look at this class:

```
class Widget {
    String thing;
    static List all = new List();
    public Widget(String thing) {
        this.thing = thing;
        all.add(thing);
    }
}
```

If you make many challenges to this class without realizing that it keeps track of every instance ever created, you might get into nasty memory problems. To avoid (some of) these problems, you could challenge functions only at certain times during execution, such as at start-up time, when changes to global state are less likely to have ill effects. Of course, this gives the adversary more opportunities to attack your code.

Finally, what should you do about functions that have non-deterministic behavior? If you're lucky, you'll at least discover this at protection time, by running the function multiple times on the same challenge input and realizing it doesn't always generate the same output. But then what? You can always rely on programmer code annotations, but as programs evolve these are notoriously difficult to maintain.

In the remainder of this section, you will see two *oblivious hashing* algorithms. They're called *oblivious* because the intent is that the adversary should be unaware that his code is being checked. The first algorithm, TPCVCPSJ, inserts hash computations at the source-code level (although there's no reason why it couldn't be done at lower levels). The hash is computed based on the values of variables and the outcome of control flow predicates. The second algorithm, TPJJV, very cleverly hashes binary instructions without actually reading the code!

7.4.1 Algorithm *TPCVCPSJ*: Oblivious Hash Functions

To verify that a program is executing correctly, you could, conceptually at least, collect the entire execution trace, compress it, and compare it to the expected trace. For example, in Section 3.2.3►163 you saw how Algorithm RELJ compresses a trace into a context-free grammar. In practice, even these compressed traces are too large for our purposes, and as is always the case when you add protection code to a program, you also have to worry about stealth. Algorithm TPCVCPSJ [61,178] computes a *hash* over the execution trace by inserting instructions that monitor changes to variables and control flow. You can balance the level of protection against the amount of overhead by varying the number of hash computations that you insert.

At the source-code level, you can imagine defining a global hash variable and a macro UPDATE(h,v), which uses some combination of arithmetic and logical operations to include a value v into the hash:

```
int hash;
#define UPDATE(h,v) (h+=v)
```

You'd then transform assignment statements like this:[2]

---

2. The expression $(e_1, e_2, \ldots, e_n)$ uses C's comma operator to evaluate the e_is in order and then returns the value of e_n.

```
int tmp;
x = (tmp=expr,UPDATE(hash,tmp),tmp)
```

x = *expr* ⟹

To hash the outcome of a conditional expression, you'd perform this transformation:

if (*expr*) ... ⟹

```
int tmp;
if (tmp=expr,UPDATE(hash,tmp),tmp) ...
```

Have a look at this example, an extract from a DRM system:

```
int play (int user_key, int player_key,
          int digital_media[], int len) {
    int i=0;
    while(i<len) {
        printf("%f\n",(float)(user_key^player_key^
                              digital_media[i]));
        i++;
    }
}
```

The procedure unlocks an encrypted media file by decrypting it with a user and a player key. To protect play, you first modify it to compute a hash value using the transformations above to insert calls to the UPDATE macro:

```
int play (int user_key, int player_key,
          int digital_media[], int len) {
    int i=0;
    int t;
    while(t=i<len,UPDATE(hash,t),t) {
        printf("%f\n",(float)(t=user_key,UPDATE(hash,t),
                              t^player_key^digital_media[i]));
        i=(t=i+1,UPDATE(hash,t),t);
    }
}
```

You then generate some challenge input for play, run it on that input, and record the result. At some appropriate places in the program, you then insert a challenge call and check the result against the expected hash value:

```
int player_main (int argc, char *argv[]) {
    ...
    int user_key = 0xca7ca115;
    int player_key = 0xbabeca75;
    int digital_media[] = {10,102};
    hash = 0;
    play(user_key, player_key, digital_media, 2);
    if (hash != -1795603921) {
        printf("HACKED!");
        abort();
    }
    ...
}
```

Regardless of whether you call play as part of the regular computation or as a challenge, the hash is still computed, so there will be a general slowdown, depending on how many hash computations you add.

Global variables are quite uncommon, so to avoid inserting code that is too unstealthy you can pass the hash variable as an extra argument to the function:

```
int player_main (int argc, char *argv[]) {
    int hash = 0;
    play(user_key, player_key, digital_media, 2, &hash);
    ...
}


int play (int user_key, int player_key,
          int digital_media[], int len, int* hash) {
    ...
}
```

Also for stealth reasons, you should vary the operators used in the hash computation to match those found in the function you're protecting. This is easy to do by providing a collection of UPDATE macros:

```
#define UPDATE1(h,v) (h+=v)
#define UPDATE2(h,v) (h^=v)
#define UPDATE3(h,v) (h-=v)
```

A serious issue is what to do with functions that have side effects. You could always add an extra parameter to functions that access a global variable and pass a reference to the global variables along to all calls. This assumes you can do an accurate static analysis to determine which functions need access to which global variables (either to use themselves or to pass along to functions *they* call that may need them), and this becomes difficult in the presence of function pointers, for example.

An even worse problem is functions that are non-deterministic because they depend on the time of day, network traffic, thread scheduling, and so on. You could try to statically detect such locations in the code, you could rely on code annotations provided by the programmer, or you could try to run the program a few times on the same data and find locations where the computed hash varies. None of these solutions is particularly attractive. Static analysis of non-deterministic programs is likely to be hard and produce overly conservative results, programmer annotations are notoriously unreliable, and dynamic analysis is unlikely to catch all non-deterministic locations in the program.

7.4.2 Algorithm *TPJJV*: Overlapping Instructions

The x86 architecture has some interesting properties that allow you to play cute tricks unavailable on a RISC architecture. In particular, the x86 uses a variable-length instruction encoding (instructions can be anywhere from one to fifteen bytes long) and has no alignment requirements for instructions (an instruction can start at any address). This allows you to have one instruction *inside* another, or one instruction *overlapping* another, and to share instructions between two blocks of code. Overlapping two blocks in itself adds a level of tamperproofing, since modifying one instruction will affect both pieces of code.

Algorithm TPJJV [178,179] takes the tamperproofing to another level by overlapping basic blocks of x86 instructions so that when one block executes, as a side effect it also computes a hash over the second block. The hash value can then be compared to the expected value, much as you've seen in previous algorithms. The real advantage of this technique is that (unlike Algorithms TPHMST and TPCA) the hash is computed *without* explicitly reading the code. This makes the algorithm invulnerable to memory-splitting attacks like REWOS.

Here are two basic blocks with entry points B_0 and B_1:

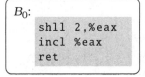
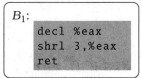

The easiest way to merge them is to interleave the instructions and insert jumps to maintain semantics:

B_0:
```
shll 2,%eax
jmp   I₁
```

B_1:
```
decl %eax
jmp   I₂
```

I_1:
```
incl %eax
jmp   I₃
```

I_2:
```
shrl 3,%eax
```

I_3:
```
ret
```

The merged block has two entry points, B_0 and B_1. This merging by itself doesn't accomplish much. What you really want is for the two blocks to also *share instruction bytes*. To accomplish this, you replace the jump instructions with bogus instructions that take a (large) immediate value as one of its operands. This operand will *mask* out the instruction from the other basic block by including the instruction in its immediate operand. Look here:

B_0:
```
shll 2,%eax
xorl %ecx,next 4 bytes  // used to be jmp  I₁
```

B_1:
```
decl %eax
jmp   I₂
nop
incl %eax
...
```

What happened? Well, we replaced the jump from B_0's first instruction to its second with an `xorl` instruction. This instruction takes a four-byte immediate operand, the

first byte of which will be the `decl %eax` instruction, the second and third byte
will be `jmp` I_2, and the fourth will be a `nop` that we had to add as padding. What
does this mean? Well, at runtime when you jump to B_1, you will execute the `decl`
instruction just as before and then jump to B_1's second instruction, also as before. In
other words, the B_1 block will execute unchanged. When you jump to B_0, however,
things are a little different. You start by executing the `shll` instruction as before,
and then proceed to execute the new `xorl` instruction, which has embedded in its
immediate operand the four bytes from `decl;jmp;nop`! After the `xorl`, you go straight
to B_0's second instruction, `incl`. If you had properly initialized register `%ecx`, the
`xorl` instruction would compute a hash over the instructions from block B_1. You
could test this value later, and if it's incorrect execute the appropriate response.

Let's look at this example in more detail. Here are the two blocks again, but
this time we give the x86 code bytes explicitly:

```
B0
↓
shll $2,%eax  incl %eax  ret            B1
                                        ↓
C1  E0  02    40         C3             decl %eax  shrl $3,%eax  ret
0   1   2     3          4
                                        48         C1  E8  03    C3
                                        0          1   2   3     4
```

Each block has three instructions, which translates into five code bytes each. We've
given the offset of each code byte below the byte and indicated the start of execution
for each block with an arrow.

After merging the two blocks and inserting hashing and padding instructions,
you get the following seventeen code bytes:

```
B0
↓
shll $2,%eax   xorl $90E98148,%ecx    incl %eax   addl $9003E8C1,%ecx     ret

C1  E0  02  81  F1   48    81  E9  90    40    81  C1  C1  E8   03    90   C3
0   1   2   3   4    5     6   7   8      9     10  11  12  13   14    15   16

            decl %eax    subl $C1814090,%ecx    shrl $3,%eax  nop  ret
            ↑
            B1
```

On top of the bytes, we indicate what instructions we execute when we start at offset
0 in order to execute block B_0. Below the code bytes, we show what gets executed
when you start at offset 5 in order to execute block B_1. In either case, as you execute
one block, you also compute a hash over the other block into register `%ecx`. If the
adversary were to change the byte at offset 9, for example, changing the `incl %eax`

instruction to something else, this will be caught when you execute B_1 and use the
`subl` instruction to compute the hash.

One problem with this algorithm is that it's hard to predict its precision. When
will you actually detect tampering? In our example, you won't detect any tampering
of B_0 until you execute B_1 and when that occurs will, of course, depend on the flow
of control.

Whether this algorithm as *state inspection* or *introspection* is debatable. Since
you're hashing instructions, this makes the algorithm closer in flavor to TPHMST and
TPCA, but on the other hand when you're actually computing the hash you're working on runtime values (or, at least, runtime immediate operands of instructions)!
Classification aside, this is a clever use of the x86's architectural (mis-)features.

The overhead depends on the level of overlap. Jacob et al. [178] (from where
the example above has been adapted) report that the protected binary can be up to
three times slower than the original.

7.5 Remote Tamperproofing

Remote tamperproofing is an important special case of tamperproofing. In this scenario, the program you want to protect (which we'll call C) runs remotely on the
adversary's untrusted site (the *client* site) but is in constant communication with
a trusted program S on your (*server*) site. In addition to providing services to the
client, the server wants to detect and respond to any tampering of C:

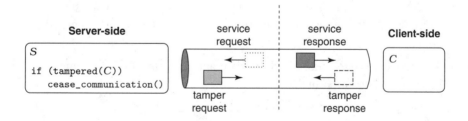

As in typical client-server scenarios, the client sends *request-for-service* packets (dotted) over the network to the server, which returns *service-response* packets (dark
gray). In a computer game, for example, the client may tell the server, "I just entered dungeon 372!" to which the server responds with a list of the nearby monsters.
The server may also ask the client for information about the state it's in (or deduce
that state from the service-request messages it receives) in order to detect if C is
under attack.

There are many applications that fit neatly into this model. In networked computer games, for example, the game server provides continuous information to the player clients about their surroundings. Players will often try to hack the clients to gain an unfair advantage over other players, for example, by being able to see parts of a map (which, for performance reasons, is being held locally) that they're not supposed to see.

7.5.1 Distributed Check and Respond

Just like in single-processor tamperproofing, in the client-server scenario you need two functions, CHECK and RESPOND. As you've seen, responding to tampering can take many forms, including reporting violations back to you. In the client-server scenario, response is even simpler: Just terminate communication! The assumption here is that the server is providing a service without which the client can't make progress, and this means that refusing to provide that service is the ultimate punishment.

Unfortunately, while responding is easy, the CHECK function is harder to implement. The reason is that you have no direct access to C's code—it's running on a remote site! For example, while it's certainly possible for you to ask the client to send you a hash of C's code to verify he hasn't tampered with it, there's nothing stopping him from lying about the hash value!

There are four classes of attacks:

1. The attacker can reverse engineer and modify C's code.
2. The attacker can modify the running environment of C, for example, by running it under debugging or emulation, or under a modified operating system.
3. The attacker can execute multiple simultaneous instances of C, some of which might have been modified.
4. The attacker can intercept and replace network messages.

7.5.2 Solution Strategies

Many solutions to the remote tamperproofing problem are variants of various levels of "sharing" the C code and data between the server and the client. At one extreme, all of the C code and data resides on and is executed by the server. This is sometimes known as *software as a service*. Whenever the client wants to make progress, it has to contact the server, passing along any data it wants the server to process, and wait for the server to return computed results. This kind of server-side execution can lead to an unacceptably high compute load for the server and unacceptably high latency for the client. On the other hand, since all the sensitive code resides server-side, there is no risk of the client tampering with it. At the other extreme, the client runs all its own code and does all the work. This requires the server to share all its data with the client, which can be bandwidth-intensive. Since all computation is done client-side, it's more difficult for the server to guarantee that the client has not tampered with the code. Most systems will settle on an intermediate level solution: Some computation is done server-side, some client-side, and this balances computation, network traffic, and tamper-detection between the two. In Section 7.5.3 we'll show you Algorithm TPZG, which automatically splits the computation of a sequential program over the client and the server. It was originally designed to protect against piracy, but subsequent development [57] has extended this idea to the remote tamperproofing scenario.

A second idea is to extend the introspection algorithms of Section 7.2▶412 to the client-server scenario. The idea is for the server to ask the client to compute a hash over its code and compare it to the expected value. However, this isn't enough, since there's nothing stopping the client from lying about the hash! Algorithm TPSLSPDK(Section 7.5.4▶459) solves this problem by measuring the time it took for the client to compute the hash, making sure that it didn't have time to tamper with the code.

Finally, Algorithm TPCNS (Section 7.5.5▶462) extends the idea of dynamic obfuscation from Chapter 6 to the client-server scenario. The idea is for the server to force the client to accept newly obfuscated versions of its code, ideally at such a quick pace that it can't manage to keep up its reverse engineering efforts.

7.5.3 Algorithm *TPZG:* Slicing Functions

Algorithm TPZG [382] was developed to prevent piracy. The idea is to slice the program into an open part that resides on the client and a hidden part that resides on the server. Extra communication is added so that the client can access those parts of the code that reside on the server. Assuming that this extra communication doesn't leak too much information, it should be difficult for the adversary to reconstitute the hidden parts. This prevents piracy (if the adversary can't get access to all the code, he can't copy it!) but also prevents tampering with the part of the code that is hidden on the server.

There are three main obstacles that make this idea impractical. First, being tied to a server works well when you're connected to a network but less well when you're on an airplane. This is a problem for piracy prevention, but not for remote tamperproofing, where the assumption is that you *are* always connected. The second

---

Algorithm 7.5 Overview of algorithm TPZG. f is a function selected for splitting, and v is a local variable in f.

PROTECT(f, v):

1. Compute a forward slice of f, starting with the statements that define v.

2. Determine which variables should be completely hidden (i.e., should reside only on the server) and which should be partially hidden (i.e., should reside both on the client and the server).

3. Examine each statement in the slice and split it between the client function Of and the server function Hf$_i$.

4. If x is a partially hidden variable, then

   - translate $x \leftarrow rhs$ to $x \leftarrow rhs$; Hf$_i(x)$ where Hf$_i(x)$ updates x on the server.

   - translate

     $$lhs \leftarrow \ldots x \ldots$$

   to

     $$x \leftarrow \text{Hf}_i();$$
     $$lhs \leftarrow \ldots x \ldots$$

   where Hf$_i(x)$ gets the current value of x from the server.

---

problem is *latency*. Networked applications are carefully designed to tolerate high latency—functions where high latency is unacceptable are kept on the client side, and the remaining functions can be kept on the server. If you move additional functions to the server side, latency may become intolerable. The final problem is *bandwidth*. If the client keeps large data structures and some of the operations on these structures are moved to the server, there may not be enough bandwidth to move the data back and forth.

Algorithm TPZG bypasses the network latency and bandwidth problems by only considering scalar data (functions on arrays and linked structures are kept on the client) and restricting the client and server to both run on the same local area network.

Algorithm 7.5 sketches how to split a function f into one part, Of, which runs on the client, and several parts, Hf$_i$, which run on the server and which the client accesses through remote procedure calls.

Let's look at a simple example to illustrate the algorithm. Below left is the original function f that runs client-side. You've determined that you want to hide variable a on the server. You start by computing a forward slice on a (see Section 3.1.5 ▶ 141). We show this in light gray to the right:

```
static int f(int x, int y) {
   int a = 4*x + y;

   int c;
   if (y < 5)
      c = a*x+4;
   else
      c = 2*x+4;

   int sum = 0;
   for(int i=a;i<10;i++)
      sum += i;

   return x*(sum+c);
}
```

```
static int f(int x, int y) {
   int a = 4*x + y;

   int c;
   if (y < 5)
      c = a*x+4;
   else
      c = 2*x+4;

   int sum = 0;
   for(int i=a;i<10;i++)
      sum += i;

   return x*(sum+c);
}
```

You want to protect all the light gray code, so you put it server-side in the six functions Hf1 ... Hf6:

```
static int Ha = 5;
static int Hc = 0;
static int Hsum = 0;

static void Hf1(int x, int y) {
   Ha=4*x+y;
}
static boolean Hf2(int y, int x) {
   if (y < 5) {
      Hc = Ha*x + 4;
      return true;
   } else
      return false;
}
```

```
static void Hf3(int c) {
   Hc = c;
}
static void Hf4(int sum) {
   Hsum = sum;
}
static void Hf5() {
   for(int i=Ha;i<10;i++)
      Hsum += i;
}
static int Hf6() {
   return Hsum+Hc;
}
```

Finally, you rewrite f to 0f, the new function that will run client-side:

```
static int f(int x, int y) {
   int a = 4*x + y;

   int c;
   if (y < 5)
      c = a*x+4;
   else
      c = 2*x+4;

   int sum = 0;
   for(int i=a;i<10;i++)
      sum += i;

   return x*(sum+c);
}
```

⇨

```
static int 0f(int x, int y) {
   Hf1(x,y);



   int c;
   if (!Hf2(y,x)) {
      c = 2*x+4; Hf3(c);
   }



   int sum = 0; Hf4(sum);
   Hf5();



   return x*Hf6();
}
```

The client accesses the hidden functions by making remote procedure calls to the server. The variable c is *partially hidden*. This means that, for performance reasons, it resides both on the client and the server, and the code that updates it is split between the two.

Zhang and Gupta [382] report runtime overhead from 3% to 58%, but as always, this depends on the amount of protection that is added, in this case, how much of the program is hidden on the server and the amount of extra communication overhead this introduces. Zhang and Gupta's measurements were done over a local area network. In many scenarios, it is more likely that the server and client are farther away on the network and the extra latency that is introduced may well make this method too slow, or at the very least, will significantly reduce the size of the slice that can remain hidden. Here's a rough measurement of packet turnaround times, as reported by tracepath, starting at york.cs.arizona.edu:

target site	# hops	ms
rorohiko.cs.arizona.edu	1	0.2
cse.asu.edu	10	5
www.stanford.edu	12	25
www.usp.ac.fj	12	153
www.eltech.ru	23	201
www.tsinghua.edu.cn	19	209

Going to `www.stanford.edu` from `york.cs.arizona.edu` is 125 times slower than staying within the local area network, even though Stanford is geographically in the state next to Arizona.

7.5.4 Algorithm *TPSLSPDK:* Measuring Remote Hardware

If you find yourself in a *very* restricted environment, it should be possible to *measure* aspects of the untrusted client to verify that it is running the correct software. This is the premise behind Algorithm TPSLSPDK [322–324], known as the *Pioneer* system. After the Pioneer protocol has run, the server can be sure that

1. a particular executable E on the client hasn't been modified,

2. the client has executed E, and

3. E was not tampered with during execution.

To get these guarantees, you have to assume a system configuration with some very limiting properties:

1. The server knows the exact hardware configuration of the client, including CPU model, clock speed, memory latency, and memory size. The client only has one CPU.

2. The communication latency between the server and the client is known, for example, as a result of their being on the same LAN segment of the network.

3. The network is configured so that during verification the client is unable to communicate with any system other than the server.

4. The executable the server wants the client to run should not need to invoke any other software on the client, and it can execute at the highest processor privilege level with interrupts turned off.

Given these restrictions, the server can ask the client to compute a hash over its own code and return the value to the server. The hash function is carefully constructed so that if the client tries to cheat, he will either return the wrong hash value or the hash computation will take longer than expected to compute. This explains the very strict requirements above: If the server doesn't know the client's computational power and the speed of communication, it can't estimate what is a reasonable time in which to compute the hash, and if the client isn't prevented from arbitrary network activity, it could farm out the hash computation to a faster machine. A successful cheat by the client means that he is able to return the correct hash value within the expected time while at the same time running tampered code.

7.5.4.1 Applications In spite of such a restricted scenario, there are potential applications. For example, say that you want to check a small device such as a cell phone, PDA, or smartcard for viruses. You could plug it in directly to your computer over a dedicated wire and use the Pioneer protocol to verify that the phone is running uncompromised code. Similarly, if you're a network administrator, you could configure the routers on your LAN so that the machine you want to check for malware cannot communicate with any other machine during the verification process. Or say you're an inspector of voting machines. You could unplug a machine from its network connection, connect it to your laptop, and then use Pioneer to check that the machine is running the correct certified code.

In all these cases, it is reasonable to assume that you have perfect knowledge of the computing power of the client—you just have to make sure that your communication with it has predictable latency and that there is no way for it to communicate with other systems. Given that, Pioneer guarantees that the desired executable is loaded into memory and executed, and that there is no rogue code on the client that can interfere with the execution.

7.5.4.2 The Pioneer Protocol Have a look at this overview of the Pioneer protocol (numbers indicate the order of events):

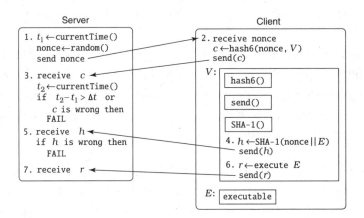

On the client-side is the executable E, which the server wants the client to run untampered. At the heart of the system is the verifier V, which the client will use to prove its trustworthiness to the server. V includes the three functions hash6(), send(), and

SHA-1(). The send() function is used for data transfer with the server, hash6() we defined in Section 7.2.2▶418, and SHA-1() is a cryptographic hash function.

In the first steps of the protocol, the client must convince the server that none of the functions in V has been tampered with. The client can then use these functions to send the server a SHA-1 hash over E. If the hash matches, the server can be sure that E has not been tampered with. The final step is for the client to run E and return the result to the server.

To convince the server that he hasn't tampered with V, the client sends him a hash (computed by hash6()) over the verifier code. Notice that hash6() computes the hash over itself, thus verifying itself! The server then compares the hash against the expected value.

There are several potential problems here. First, the client could pre-compute the hash value, tamper with the code, and when challenged, send the server the value it expects. The protocol, therefore, starts with the server creating a *nonce* (a random value) and sending it to the client. The client is forced to use the nonce to initialize hash6(), and this makes it impossible for him to cheat by pre-computing the hash value.

The second problem is that the client can cheat by executing extra instructions. To prevent this, the server measures the time it takes for the client to compute the hash over V. This leads to a third problem: The client could run an optimized version of hash6() that allows him to slip in extra instructions and still return the hash value within the expected time! For this reason, hash6() has been designed to be *time optimal*, i.e., there should be no way to speed it up by reordering instructions, replacing one instruction with another, and so on.

In step 3 of the protocol, the server verifies that the client has computed the expected hash value over V within the expected amount of time. In steps 4 and 5, the client computes a SHA-1 hash of the executable E and the server compares it against the expected value. Again, the client has to factor in a nonce to prevent precomputation. At this point, the server knows that E hasn't been tampered with. In steps 6 and 7, finally, the client runs E and transfers its return value to the server.

You must also make sure that no other process is running on the system until after V and E have finished executing. To accomplish this, you must require V and E to run at the highest CPU privilege level with all maskable interrupts disabled. We don't show it in the protocol sketch above, but the hash computation in step 2 also includes processor state in order to assure the server that the V and E run unperturbed. During step 2, you therefore install new handlers for all non-maskable interrupts and exceptions.

Problem 7.9 This algorithm extends the code-hashing idea to the remote tamperproofing scenario. Can you do the same for the *oblivious* hashing idea from
Section 7.4▶444?

7.5.5 *TPCNS*: Continuous Replacement

The final idea to prevent tampering of remotely executing code that we're going
to show you we call *remote tamperproofing by continuous replacement*. The basic idea is to make the client code difficult to analyze by keeping it in constant
flux, i.e., by continuously obfuscating the client code. Ideally, the adversary will
find that the client code is changing so quickly that before he has managed to
analyze and modify the current version, the server has generated a new one. Algorithm TPCNS [83] presents this high-level overview of a continuous replacement
system:

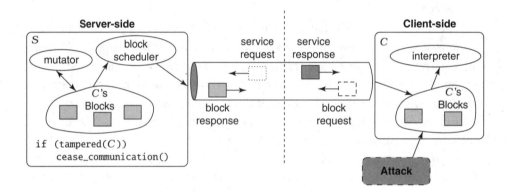

In this design, both the server and the client maintain a representation of the *C* code
(the code run by the client) in what we'll call a *bag of blocks*. The client executes
out of its bag by selecting a block to run, jumping to it, selecting the next block,
and so on. The server, on the other hand, has a *mutator* process that continuously
modifies its bag of blocks and shares any modified blocks with the client. Sharing
can happen if the client asks the server for a block it doesn't have (at any one point
in time, the client might hold only a subset of all the code blocks), sending a *request-
block* packet (in dashed) to the server, and getting a new block (in light gray) in
return. The server may also *push* blocks onto the client. A *block scheduler* process
on the server determines which blocks to return or push to the client and at what
time.

The level of tamperproofing you achieve through this setup is determined by

1. the rate at which the server generates mutated blocks and pushes them onto the client, and
2. the rate at which the adversary can analyze the client code by monitoring the continuously changing bag of blocks.

To reduce network traffic, you want to keep the block replacement rate as low as possible. At the same time, you want to make the rate high enough to be sure the client doesn't have enough time to analyze the program between updates!

The obfuscating block transformations should have the following properties:

- The server must be able to apply the transformations over and over again, creating an infinite stream of differently obfuscated blocks.
- It should be more resource-consuming for the client to analyze new blocks than for the server to generate them.
- The client shouldn't be able to simply ignore new blocks pushed to it.

The last point is important. An adversary can simply monitor the bag of blocks, and once it has received all of C's code, just take a snapshot of the bag and analyze it off-line.

Several of the obfuscating transformations you saw in Chapter 4 (Code Obfuscation) can be applied multiple times. A simple implementation of TPCNS could, for example, have only two transformations, one that splits a block in two and another that merges two blocks together. Together these two transformations would generate an infinite sequence of different blocks.

Unfortunately, such transformations won't stop the adversary from ignoring new blocks sent to it and simply executing old blocks it has already seen, analyzed, and tampered with. To prevent such attacks, TPCNS requires the server to support a third type of transformation, *interface obfuscation*. The idea is to continuously modify the remote procedure call (RPC) interfaces by which the server provides services to the client. The server can transform these RPCs by, for example, renaming them, reordering their arguments, adding bogus arguments, changing argument types, and splitting and merging calls. An adversary who chooses to ignore block updates will eventually execute an old block that issues an expired RPC. This will alert the server that the client is under attack.

The main advantage of continuous replacement tamperproofing is that you have several knobs that you can tweak to balance the level of protection versus performance degradation:

1. You can increase the rate of block push (the server telling the client to invalidate an old block and replace it with a new one) in order to increase the amount of analysis work the client has to do, at the cost of increased network traffic.

2. You can make blocks more or less obfuscated using any of the algorithms in Chapter 4 (Code Obfuscation), with more obfuscation leading to longer analysis times but worse client performance.

There's no known implementation of the continuous replacement idea. We therefore don't yet know the push rate and level of obfuscation necessary to ward off attacks. It seems reasonable to believe, however, that "reasonable" replacement and obfuscation rates would be enough to defend the client against manual attacks, i.e., attacks where the adversary analyzes the client code by executing it interactively under a debugger. Whether it's enough to protect the client against automated attacks (where the adversary attaches a static analysis tool to the client in order to analyze new blocks automatically as they appear in the block bag) is an entirely different question.

7.6 Discussion

Tamperproofing addresses the *trustworthiness* of a piece of code and the environment in which it executes. As the producer of a program, you want to include certain restrictions on how it's used—maybe it can't be executed after a certain period of time—and you include code in the program to check that the conditions of use are met. If a user changes the program in any way, you can no longer trust it, since these usage checks may have been disabled. To trust a program, you have to be sure that absolutely nothing about it has changed: code can be neither removed nor added. If, for example, you have *removed* pieces of the program—to distribute a partially functional trial version, for example—you want to be sure that no one adds the missing pieces back in.

We've shown you five basic methods for making a program difficult to tamper with:

1. You can add code to the program that checks that the original bits have not been changed (Algorithms TPCA and TPHMST, and for remote tamperproofing, TPSLSPDK);

2. You can add code to the program to check that it's not running in a hostile environment (Algorithm TPGCK);

3. You can check that the program's runtime data structures are always in acceptable states and that the control flow follows reasonable paths (Algorithms TPCVCPSJ and TPJJV);

4. You can split the program into two pieces, where one piece is protected from the attacker by running it remotely or on tamper-resistant hardware (Algorithm TPZG).

5. You can use the obfuscation algorithms from Chapter 4 (Code Obfuscation) and Chapter 6 (Dynamic Obfuscation) to make the program harder to understand and hence tamper with (Algorithm TPCNS uses this for remote tamperproofing).

In practice, these algorithms are often combined. For example, we normally don't think of obfuscation as a tamperproofing technique in its own right, since it lacks the ability to execute a *response* when an attack has been discovered. However, obfuscation plays an important role in making tamperproofing code more stealthy. You saw this in Section 7.2.2▶418, where we obfuscated the hash functions used in introspection algorithms in order to make them less susceptible to pattern matching attacks. Introspection algorithms like TPCA and TPHMST are also commonly augmented with code to check if the program is running under a debugger or emulator.

In Section 2.2.10▶110, we presented the **detect-respond** defense model primitive. In the model, an object is protected by monitoring a desirable invariant and executing a response if the check fails. Algorithms TPCA, TPHMST, TPSLSPDK, TPCVCPSJ, and TPJJV all fit in this primitive. For TPCA and TPHMST, the invariant is a simple hash of the code, whereas for TPCVCPSJ and TPJJV, the invariant is the hash of runtime data values.

The TPZG algorithm first applies the **split** primitive, breaking up the application into two parts and making one part inaccessible to the attacker. Since the hidden part is protected by running it on a remote server or on tamperproof hardware, the attacker can't tamper with it at all. TPZG can combine splitting with tamperproofing by monitoring the communication between the two parts of the program, reporting any suspicious exchanges as possible tampering.

Problem 7.10   None of the algorithms in this chapter has public implementations, so it would be interesting to develop working systems that could be compared for efficiency and resilience to attack.

Software Watermarking

In the last few chapters, we have shown you techniques you can use to prevent an attacker from deciphering the inner workings of your program or from modifying it. But what happens if these lines of defenses fail? In this chapter, we will discuss *software watermarking*—a technique for embedding a unique identifier into the executable of a program. A watermark is much like a *copyright notice*; it asserts that you claim certain rights to the program. Just like the copyright notice in this book won't prevent you from making photocopies for all your friends,[1] the presence of this unique identifier in your program won't prevent an attacker from reverse engineering it or pirating it. However, if the identifier continues to exist in every pirated copy, then it will allow us to show that the program the attacker claims to be his is actually ours. *Software fingerprinting* is similar to watermarking, but here, every copy you sell will have a different unique mark in it, one per customer. If you happen on an illegally redistributed copy of your program, you will be able to trace it back to the original owner and take legal action.

This chapter is organized as follows. In Section 8.1▶468, we will introduce watermarking by looking at its history, some simple algorithms for marking media objects, and the ways in which watermarking an object can help you protect it as intellectual property. In Section 8.2▶478, we will show you some simple examples of how software can be watermarked and give formal definitions needed for the rest of

---

1. Don't. Every paragraph in this book has been surreptitiously watermarked using algorithms from Section 8.1.4▶475. We swear.

the chapter. In Sections 8.4▸486, 8.5▸494, and 8.6▸498, we describe static watermarking algorithms, that is, watermarks that are embedded in the executable itself. In Chapter 9 (Dynamic Watermarking), you will see a different class of algorithms that embed the watermark in the dynamic behavior of the program. In Section 8.8▸522, we look at *steganographic* embeddings, i.e., ways to secretly embed a long message into a program as a means of covert communication. In Sections 8.9▸526 and 8.10▸533, we discuss algorithmic techniques needed to implement many software watermarking algorithms. In Section 8.11▸537, finally, we summarize.

8.1 History and Applications

The art of *media watermarking* may have first been practiced in the West in the late thirteenth century, when discerning Italian customers and merchants in the town of Fabriano could examine paper for embossed watermarks. This was apparently a reliable means of identifying the paper mill at which it was produced, and perhaps even the artisan who smoothed the paper with a "calendar" stone [217]. Over the next seven hundred years, watermarking found many more applications. These include making currency difficult to forge and allowing artists to secretly but deliberately sign their paintings, and more esoteric uses such as identifying pirates of logarithm tables and astronomical data [358]. Since the 1990s there has been considerable interest in using *digital watermarks* as a protective measure for digital imagery. Since then, many algorithms targeting all kinds of media objects have appeared. Now, there are algorithms to protect video, images, music, DNA, network traffic, three-dimensional meshes, natural language, shredded documents, radio and television communication, and so on. In 1996, the idea of embedding identifiers was first applied to software, namely, algorithm WMDM (patented by Microsoft [104]), which we will discuss further in Section 8.4.1▸488.

8.1.1 Applications

Assume for a moment that you have algorithms available to embed an identifier (a string or an integer, typically) into a media object. That is, you have a function *embed*(M, k, w) that embeds the watermark w into the audio/video/image object M, using the secret key k, and a function *extract*(M_w, k), which extracts w from the marked object M_w using the same secret key. In the next few sections, we will show you how this can actually be done, but for now let's concentrate on how you could *use* such marks to protect your rights [97] to an object. Although we'll be considering media objects here, the same ideas apply to software [266], which will be our focus in the rest of the chapter. We use the images in Figure 8.1▸469 to illustrate the different kinds of applications of watermarking.

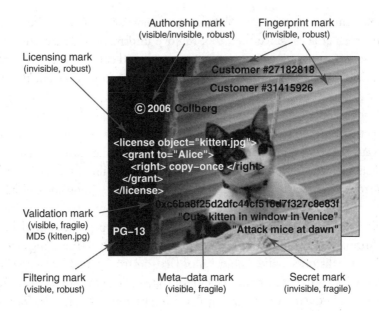

Figure 8.1 Examples of watermark applications.

8.1.1.1 Visible vs. Invisible Marks Depending on what aspect of your rights you're trying to protect, you will want the embedded mark to be *visible* or *invisible*. A visible mark is sometimes exactly that—conspicuously displayed on the media object for anyone to see—and thereby acting as a deterrent against misuse. The copyright notice displayed on the inside cover of this book is an example. But we'll take a broader view here and define a visible mark as one that the end user *could be able to view*, whether it is directly visible or not. The watermark that you can see when you hold a bank note up to the light is an example. An invisible mark, then, is one that can only be extracted using a secret not available to the end user.

8.1.1.2 Robust vs. Fragile Marks In addition to the visibility of a mark, we will also classify it as being *robust* or *fragile*. A robust mark is difficult to modify, either accidentally (for example, by converting an image or audio clip between the digital and analog domains) or deliberately (by actively launching an attack to destroy the mark). A fragile mark could be easily destroyed by transformations to the cover object. A further distinction is sometimes made between a robust mark that survives common signal processing operations and a *tamper-resistant* one that also survives hostile attacks.

Common lossy compression schemes (such as jpeg and mpeg) remove information from the media object that we wouldn't be able to perceive anyway, and a robust mark must withstand this. Shrinking an image or cropping pieces from it are also dangerous attacks, since they, too, remove information. There are also many signal-processing operations (resampling, contrast and color adjustment, dithering, recompression) that can destroy the mark. Finally, you cannot assume that the media will stay in the same form, and so the mark has to remain, even if an image gets printed, photocopied, and rescanned; an mp3-file gets played through speakers; or a video gets transfered from PAL to NTSC. As you will see later in this chapter, in the software watermarking domain you also have to make sure the mark survives format conversions (compiling source to binary, decompiling, translating from one language to another) and distortive transformations (obfuscation and optimization).

In media watermarking, the robustness of an algorithm is typically evaluated by attacking a marked object with a collection of transformations. Benchmark programs such as Stirmark [282] (which is used to evaluate image watermarking algorithms) are designed to distort a marked object enough to destroy embedded marks but to be subtle enough to not diminish the value of the object. You can similarly evaluate the robustness of a software watermarking algorithm by subjecting it to the obfuscating transformations from Chapter 4.

8.1.1.3 Authorship Marks

The most obvious application of watermarking is to embed an identification of the copyright owner in the cover object. This is called an *authorship mark*. If you want the mark to act as a deterrent to would-be thieves, you'll want it to be visible. However, you also want to prevent an attacker from removing the mark (you'll want it to be robust) and for that reason many authorship marks are made invisible.

Digimarc's MyPictureMark tool can embed both visible and invisible marks in your images. The visible marks act as a deterrent, and the invisible ones allow a special web-spider to search for images on the Web with embedded marks. *Playboy* uses this tool to track illegal uses of pictures downloaded from its Web site.

8.1.1.4 Fingerprint Marks

A second application is to *serialize* the cover object, i.e., to embed a different mark in every distributed copy. This is often called *fingerprinting*. While the authorship mark identifies the copyright owner, the fingerprint uniquely identifies the purchaser of the object. If you should find a copy of your content where you don't expect it to be (such as downloadable from a Web site, on a pirated DVD, and so on), you can extract the mark and trace the content back to the person who originally purchased it. A famous example is the case of the actor Carmine Caridi, who gave away copies of Academy Award screening tapes, unaware that they had been marked with his name [181].[2] This idea can also be applied to programs, where it is common for a company to distribute beta copies of its software to collaborating companies in order to allow them to check for compatibility issues. If a collaborator leaks their fingerprinted beta copy into the public domain, you can extract the name of the culprit from the copy and take legal action.

In 1997 [198], it was discovered that for over twenty years Japanese advertisers had paid for TV ads that were never actually run. *Broadcast monitoring* is another application of fingerprinting that can be used to combat this practice. The idea is to fingerprint a piece of music with the radio station that purchased it for airplay and then to monitor all stations to count the number of times each song is played. This ensures that only those stations that bought the rights can play the song and allows you to collect accurate royalties. The same technique can be used to count the number of times TV stations run ads in order to ensure that the customer gets the number of broadcasts they paid for.

8.1.1.5 Licensing Marks   A *licensing mark* encodes, invisibly and robustly, the way the cover object can be used by the end user. It can be as simple as the date after which a downloaded review copy of a program cannot be executed, or it can be complex business rules that describe the ways in which a digital movie can be read, copied, played, resold, and so on. Any system that processes the marked object (such as by playing the video or executing the program) will have to extract these rules and abide by them.

Licensing marks are an integral part of any DRM system. The usage rules could be stored as meta-data (in file headers, for example), but using watermarking ensures that the data remains, even after transformations on the object such as translation from one video format to another or one programming language to another.

8.1.1.6 Meta-Data Marks   *Meta-data marks* are visible and (possibly) fragile marks that embed data that the end user might find useful. An image could encode a caption, for example, or the shutter speed and aperture of the shot.

8.1.1.7 Validation Marks   A *validation mark* is used by the end user to verify that the marked object is authentic and hasn't been altered or falsified. For example, you may want to detect if a crime scene photo has been doctored by moving, say, a gun from one person's hand to another. A common technique is to compute a digest of an object and embed it in the object itself as a watermark. A digest is

---

2. Caridi was later expelled from the Academy of Motion Picture Arts and Sciences.

a cryptographic hash such as computed by MD5 or SHA-1. The user can verify that the object hasn't been changed by comparing a digest of the photo to the one embedded in the photo. Java signed applets similarly embed a digest of the code in the distributed jar-file. Validation marks need to be fragile (even a miniscule change to the document should change the embedded mark) and visible (since the user needs to be able to see it to use it for validation).

8.1.1.8 Filtering Marks A *filtering* or *classification mark* carries classification codes to allow media players to filter out any inappropriate (pornographic or otherwise objectionable) material. The mark needs to be robust so that your fifteen-year-old son can't easily remove it and visible so that media players can read it.

8.1.1.9 Secret Marks A *secret mark* is used for covert communication, i.e., to let two parties communicate without anyone noticing. This is also known as *steganography*, and you will see more of this in Section 8.8▶522. The requirements of steganography are different from those of watermarking and fingerprinting in that robustness matters not at all, but invisibility is vitally important. Steganography appeared on the public's radar screen when *USA Today* [195] claimed that:

> Hidden in the X-rated pictures on several pornographic Web sites and the posted comments on sports chat rooms may lie the encrypted blueprints of the next terrorist attack against the United States or its allies.

These ideas resurfaced after the September 11, 2001, attacks [206], but subsequent studies failed to find any evidence of steganographic content on the Internet [294].

8.1.1.10 Inadvertent Authorship Marks An *inadvertent authorship mark*, or *birthmark*, appears naturally in the cover object without your having to insert it explicitly. They are therefore not really watermarks. For example, the markings of the kitten in Figure 8.1▶469 could be seen as its birthmarks, and they allow you to distinguish him from all other cats. You'll read more about birthmarks in Chapter 10 (Software Similarity Analysis).

8.1.2 Embedding a Mark in Audio

Before we show you how to embed a mark in a program, let's have a look at some media watermarking algorithms. A common theme in media watermarking is that in all digital media objects there is some "extra space" that can be used to embed data. This space is the result of the limits of human perception. Our auditory system is limited in frequency range and in the dynamic changes we can perceive, the human eye can only detect a certain range of colors, and so on. Lossy compression schemes such as jpeg make use of this, "throwing away" parts of an image that a human wouldn't be able to perceive anyway. In watermarking, instead of throwing away the extra space, you can use it to embed data. We're going illustrate this by looking at a few media watermarking algorithms [37,98], starting with those that target audio.

Problem 8.1 As you read the rest of this chapter, keep these media-marking algorithms in the back of your head. Can you think of ways to reuse these ideas to mark software? It would seem that software and natural-language algorithms would have much in common, since natural and programming languages share many features.

A popular way of marking audio such as mp3-files is *echo hiding*. The idea is to embed echoes that are short enough to be imperceptible to the human ear. Here, we've added a really short echo to represent a 0-bit, a longer one to represent a 1-bit:

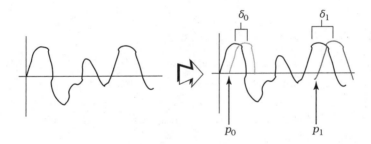

But how do you know *where* in the audio file to insert the mark? And how do you find the mark again? A common method is to use a pseudo-random number generator initialized by a secret key *key* to trace out the sequence of locations $p_0, p_1, \ldots$ in the file where the echoes should be embedded. To extract the watermark, you use the same secret key to visit the same locations.

It is likely that there are some parts of a piece of music that you shouldn't alter, and so the embedder needs to avoid them. For example, an artificial echo during a very quiet section of a performance is likely to be noticeable. The same is true of watermarking images: It's probably not a good idea to make wholesale changes to a uniformly blue sky. When marking software, you face similar problems, such as the need to stay away from hot spots and from parts of the code where the particular watermarking code you embed would be unstealthy.

A popular media watermarking technique is *Least Significant Bit* (LSB) encoding. By definition, the LSB of an audio sample or pixel value is the one that contributes least to your perception and so should be possible to alter without adversely affecting quality. For example, to embed a message in a piece of music, you could subtly alter samples:

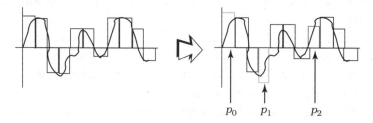

As usual, a pseudo-random number generator initialized by a secret key can trace the locations in which to embed a mark. Without access to the key, it is difficult for an adversary to extract the mark. *Destroying* the mark, on the other hand, is not so hard: Simply randomly replace the least significant bit of every sample with a randomly chosen 0 or 1!

8.1.3 Embedding a Mark in an Image

Patchwork [37] is a simple image watermarking algorithm that embeds a single bit by manipulating the brightness of pixels. In this algorithm, you use a pseudo-random number sequence to trace out pairs (A, B) of pixels. During embedding, you increase the brightness of A by a small amount, and decrease B by the same small amount. Here's an exaggerated example:

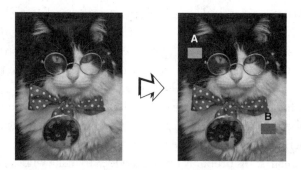

What's so clever about this scheme is that the average brightness of the image hasn't changed! This means that it is hard for the adversary to detect that the image has

---

Algorithm 8.1 Sketch of the Patchwork image watermarking algorithm.

EMBED(P, *key*):	RECOGNIZE(P, *key*):
1. Init_RND(*key*); $\delta \leftarrow 5$.	1. Init_RND(*key*); $S \leftarrow 0$.
2. $i \leftarrow$ RND(); $j \leftarrow$ RND().	2. $i \leftarrow$ RND(); $j \leftarrow$ RND().
3. Adjust the brightness of pixels a_i and b_j: $a_i \leftarrow a_i + \delta$; $b_j \leftarrow b_j - \delta$.	3. $S \leftarrow S + (a_i - b_j)$.
	4. repeat from 2 $\approx$ 10,000 times.
4. Repeat from 2 $\approx$ 10,000 times.	5. if $S \gg 0 \Rightarrow$ output "marked!"

---

been marked. To extract the mark, you visit the same sequences of pairs of pixels (A, B) and sum up the differences of their brightness. For a completely random sequence of pixels, you'd expect this sum to be zero. If it's much greater than 0, you've detected that the image has been marked. Algorithm 8.1 has a sketch of the technique.

We classify watermarking recognizers as *blind* or *informed*. To extract a blind mark, you need only the marked object and the secret key, whereas to extract an informed mark, you need extra information, typically the original, unwatermarked object. So far, the algorithms you've seen have had blind recognizers.

8.1.4 Embedding a Mark in Natural-Language Text

In *natural-language watermarking* you embed a message in, for example, an English language text. The algorithms you choose for embedding will naturally depend on the actual representation of the text. There are three basic representations that can be marked:

- The text itself with formatting (spaces and line breaks) intact, such as an ASCII text representation; or
- Free-flowing text, i.e., the sequence of letters, words, sentences, and paragraphs that make up the text, without regard for formatting; or
- An *image* of the text (such as a PostScript or PDF representation).

In a PDF document, say, marking is very similar to marking audio or images. You embed data in alterations that are too minor to be perceptible by humans. For example, you can encode a 0-bit or a 1-bit by subtly changing the spacing between words or lines:

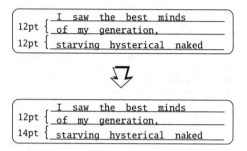

In a plain text file with formatting, you can encode the mark in white space so that one space means a 0-bit and two spaces mean a 1-bit:

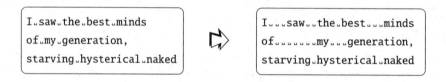

A very popular way of watermarking free-flowing text is to replace words with synonyms. If you assume that the words {*nude, unclothed, undressed, naked*} are equivalent, i.e., wherever one occurs the others could be used equally well then you can embed two bits of watermark whenever one of them occurs in a sentence:

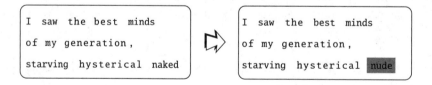

There are many similar techniques, for example, based on inserting spelling or punctuation errors.

More interestingly, you can encode a mark in the syntactic structure of an English text. The idea is to devise a watermark extraction function that computes a bit from a sentence, and then, by means of syntactic transformations, modify the sentence until it embeds the *right* bit (your watermark bit). Say, for example, that you want to embed a 1-bit in the sentence below left. However, your watermark extraction function returns a 0-bit. You then apply the *cleft sentence* syntactic transformation in the hope that the extractor function will now return 1:

```
I saw the best minds
of my generation,
starving hysterical naked
```

```
It was the best minds
of my generation that I saw,
starving hysterical naked
```

If that doesn't work, you can continue trying other transforms such as *passivization*, or even combinations of transforms.

Atallah et al. [25] implemented and expanded on this scheme. Their algorithm has three main ideas. First, since a single sentence is too small to embed an entire watermark, you chunk up the watermark in pieces and embed one piece per sentence. Many software watermarking algorithms that you will see do the same thing. Second, you will need a function that computes a sequence of bits, one per syntax-tree node, for a sentence. Modifying the structure of the sentence will modify these bits, which then, hopefully, will embed a piece of the watermark. Some software watermarking algorithms (such as WMSHKQ) use a similar iterative process to embed a mark. Third, you will need a special *marker* sentence that precedes every watermark-bearing sentence and that points out *where* in the modified syntax tree the watermark chunk is embedded. Algorithm 8.2 ▶ 478 has a sketch of the watermark embedder and recognizer.

The scheme can be extended to work not just at the syntactic but also at the *semantic* level [23]. For example, information given in one sentence can be copied or moved into another sentence, information that is repeated multiple times in a paragraph can be removed, or information can be replaced with equivalent information:

```
I saw the best minds
of my generation,
starving hysterical naked
```

```
I saw the best minds of my
generation. They were starving
hysterical naked. None, baby,
none were smarter than them. Nor
more lacking in supply of essential
nutrients or in more need of
adequate clothing. Baby.
```

Algorithm 8.2 Sketch of the natural-language watermarking algorithm of Atallah et al. [25]. The input document $\langle s_1, s_2 \ldots \rangle$ consists of English language sentences.

EMBED($\langle s_1, s_2 \ldots \rangle$, W, *key*):

1. Let $T = \langle T_1, T_2 \ldots \rangle$ be a list of the syntax trees of sentences $\langle s_1, s_2 \ldots \rangle$.

2. Let $B_i = \langle \ldots 0, 1 \ldots \rangle$ be a sequence of bits, one per tree node, computed from tree T_i and *key*.

3. Let T' be the trees from T sorted on their B_i values.

4. Pick the first tree from T' (let it be T_{i-1}) to be a *marker* sentence.

5. Apply transformations to tree T_i until the next chunk of bits from watermark W is embedded at position p within the tree's B_i.

6. Apply transformations to the marker T_{i-1} until position p is embedded within it.

7. Remove T_{i-1} and T_i from T' and repeat from 4 until all of W is embedded.

RECOGNIZE($\langle s_1, s_2 \ldots \rangle$, *key*):

1. Define T, T', and B_i, as in the EMBED algorithm.

2. Assume the first tree in T' (T_{i-1}) is a marker sentence and let p be the position embedded within its B_{i-1}.

3. Extract the next chunk of bits of watermark W from position p within T_i's B_i.

4. Remove T_{i-1} and T_i from T' and repeat from 2 until all of W is extracted.

The idea is to keep trying different semantic transformations, including combinations of transformations, until each sentence embeds the required bits.

8.2 Watermarking Software

To understand how you could watermark a program, let's start by considering some simple means of embedding an identifier in a program. The simplest and perhaps most obvious way is to place a copyright notice comment in the source files or to include the notice in the set of files you distribute with your program. But these sort of identifiers are trivial for an attacker to remove. In fact, comments are automatically stripped out by a compiler during compilation. For an embedding technique to be useful, it must be resilient to such simple attacks. For this purpose, a watermark must be an integral part of the program. For example, you could embed the watermark as string constants included in the source of a program:

```
public class Fibonacci {
   String copyright = "Copyright © Doris";
   public int fibonacci (int n) {
     if (n <= 2)
       return 1;
     else
       return fib(n - 1) + fib(n - 2);
   }
}
```

Such an embedding is called a *static watermark*. Static watermarks take a program *P* and a watermark *w* and produce a watermarked program *P'*. These types of embeddings typically permute the original code or they insert new but non-functional code. In either case, to extract a static watermark, a static recognizer analyzes the code directly:

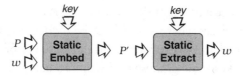

As usual, embedding and extracting the watermark can be done at the source level, on architecture-neutral bytecode, or on binary code, and just as we saw for media watermarking algorithms, embedding and recognition make use of a secret key.

In a sense, copyright notices already serve as a static watermark in some existing programs. Try extracting some from your favorite executable:[3]

```
bash> strings /usr/bin/netscape | grep Copyright
Copyright (C) 1995, Thomas G. Lane
Copyright (C) 1998 Netscape Communications Corporation.
bash>
```

---

3. But first check that you're not violating the software license, the DMCA, or any local laws.

Are such static strings embedded in a program sufficient to watermark a program? How can he remove such static marks? Clearly, an attacker can simply search for strings that appear to contain copyright information. If these strings are not used anywhere else in the program, removing them is a simple matter. In order to make your mark resilient to these sorts of attacks, you can use the opaque predicates from Chapter 4 to make it appear that the watermark string is actually being used. Now the attacker cannot mechanically remove all copyright strings with the same level of confidence:

```
public class Fibonacci {
  public int fibonacci (int n) {
    String copyright = "Copyright © Doris";
    if (P^F)
      n = length (copyright);
    if (n <= 2)
      return 1;
    else
      return fib(n — 1) + fib(n — 2);
  }
```

In the remainder of the chapter, we will examine more sophisticated techniques for encoding and embedding a software watermark. As you can probably imagine, a program has many places where a signal can be hidden, such as in the choice of variable names, the order of instructions, and the structure of a program's control flow graph. What makes some of these places more suitable than others?

Problem 8.2   Which comes first, watermarking or obfuscation? If you were trying to protect your program, would you watermark it before or after obfuscation? Does it make a difference? If so, what are the advantages and disadvantages of each order?

8.3 Definitions

A software watermarking or fingerprinting system is comprised of three functions:

$$embed(P, w, key) \rightarrow P_w$$
$$extract(P_w, key) \rightarrow w$$
$$recognize(P_w, key, w) \rightarrow [0.0, 1.0]$$

The *embed* function takes a program P as input and transforms it into P_w by embedding the mark w. Since you must assume that the attacker knows the marking algorithm you're using, there needs to be some other secret that *you* have but the attacker doesn't; if there wasn't, he'd be able to extract the mark as easily as you can! That secret is the *key*. The key used by *embed* is also used by the *extract* function to retrieve w from P_w. Exactly how the key is used is up to the algorithm, but typically it traces out the location(s) where the watermark is embedded. The embedding must preserve program semantics, i.e., P and P_w must have the same input/output behavior. The *recognize* function takes the watermark w as input and returns how confident we are that P_w contains w. These and the other definitions in this section are taken from reference [90].

There are many possible variations of these definitions. For example, in a *non-blind* watermarking system, the *extract* and *recognize* functions take an additional argument, the unwatermarked program:

$$extract_{\text{nb}}(P, P_w, key) \rightarrow w$$
$$recognize_{\text{nb}}(P, P_w, key, w) \rightarrow [0.0, 1.0]$$

In certain situations, recognition might be easier or more reliable in a non-blind system than in a blind one. For example, an algorithm could compare P_w with P to help get a fix on the location of w.

The job of the attacker is to discover the functions *detect* and *attack*:

$$detect(P_w) \rightarrow [0.0, 1.0]$$
$$attack(P_w) \rightarrow P'_w$$

The *detect* function models the attacker's ability to figure out whether a program is in fact watermarked or not. The *detect* function is really the attacker's version of your *recognize* function, where he doesn't have access to the key. The *attack* function models the attacker's ability to disturb P_w in such a way that you will no longer be able to reliably extract w from it. A perfectly accurate *detect* function doesn't have *false negatives* (i.e., it never says P_w isn't watermarked when in fact it is):

$$\forall P, w : detect(embed(P, w)) \geq 0.5$$

Nor does it have *false positives* (i.e., it never says that P is watermarked when in fact it isn't):

$$\forall X : detect(X) < 0.5 \Rightarrow \forall S, P, w : embed_S(P, W) \neq X$$

$$recognize(P_w, w) \rightarrow \begin{cases} P_w \text{ is watermarked with } w! & (\textit{true positive}) \\ P_w \text{ is not watermarked with } w! & (\textit{false negative}) \end{cases}$$

$$recognize(P, w) \rightarrow \begin{cases} P \text{ is watermarked with } w! & (\textit{false positive}) \\ P \text{ is not watermarked with } w! & (\textit{true negative}) \end{cases}$$

Figure 8.2 The results that the *recognize* function can return for a watermarked program P_w and an unwatermarked program P.

8.3.1 Watermark Credibility

The terms *true/false positive/negative* occur frequently in the literature, so we'll spend some time explaining them in detail. In this context, *true/false* expresses whether your recognizer returns a correct result or not, and *positive/negative* represents whether that result is, "Yes, watermarked!" or "No, not watermarked!" Have a look at Figure 8.2, where we've summarized the four possible results that the *recognize* function can return.

When given a watermarked program P_w as input, the *recognize* function could say that P_w is in fact watermarked, and we call this a *true positive*. Or it could say that P_w *isn't* watermarked when in fact it is—a *false negative*. Often, *recognize* isn't perfect (it will sometimes produce false negatives, i.e., say that P_w isn't watermarked), and so we want it to have a *false negative rate* as low as possible. False negatives can occur because the recognizer is broken or because your adversary has modified P_w to prevent you from extracting the mark.

When given an *un-watermarked* program P as input, a good *recognize* function should tell us that P isn't watermarked, a *true negative*. But it could wrongly say that P *is* watermarked, a *false positive*. It's very important that your recognizer has a low *false positive rate*. If it doesn't, if there's a high risk that for many un-watermarked programs (or programs watermarked with your competitor's mark) the recognizer will say that it contains your mark, then it will be hard for you to argue in court that it is a credible recognizer. Your adversary will just argue that, sure, your watermark occurs in the program on his hard disk, but your recognizer is so unreliable that you can use it to extract just about any mark from any program!

The *credibility* of a watermarking algorithm is a measure of how strongly it proves authorship. In this book, we will define credibility of a watermark recognizer as having a *low false positive rate*. We can illustrate credibility with this figure:

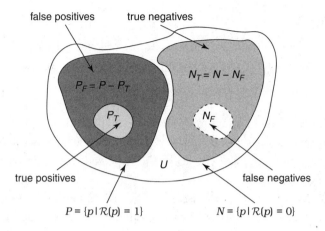

$$P = \{p \mid \mathcal{R}(p) = 1\} \qquad N = \{p \mid \mathcal{R}(p) = 0\}$$

Here, U is the universe of programs, P is the set of positives (the set of programs for which the recognizer $\mathcal{R}$ returns 1), and N is the set of negatives (the set of programs for which the recognizer returns 0). P_F is the set of false positives. A recognizer with high credibility should have a low value for

$$\frac{|P_F|}{|U|}.$$

Thus, in an ideal scenario with a perfect recognizer that has neither false positives nor false negatives, the dark gray area and the dashed area above are both empty.

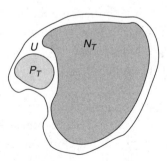

In this situation, the recognizer will return true only for programs that have actually been watermarked, and false for programs that have not.

8.3.2 Attacks

Let's look at the possible attack scenarios. In the following, let's assume that Doris marks a program P with w using key key, and then sells P_w to Axel:

$$P_w = embed(P, w, key)$$

In a *brute-force* attack, Axel simply generates all possible keys and finds the correct one by applying Doris' public *recognize* function. If he knows something about Doris' key distribution, he can cut down the expected search time by generating the more likely keys first.

Before Axel can resell P_w, he must ensure that the fingerprint has been rendered useless, or else Doris will be able to prove that her intellectual property rights have been violated.

In an *additive attack*, Axel adds his own watermark w' to Doris' already watermarked program P_w:

$$recognize(attack(P_w), key, w') > 0.5$$
$$recognize(attack(P_w), key, w) > 0.5$$

Since both marks are now present in P_w, this will sow confusion when Doris takes Axel to court—he can argue that her mark is bogus, or at least that his mark predates hers!

If Axel can figure out where in P_w w is hidden, he can try to *crop* it out. After the attack, Doris can no longer recognize the mark (because it is no longer there!):

$$recognize(attack(P_w), key, w) < 0.5$$

This is called a *subtractive attack*. Obviously, Axel's attack must be semantics-preserving. To be more precise, after he has cropped out the watermark, the attacked program must still be intact enough that it has some value to him. For example, if, after the attack, the mark is indeed gone but the program has become prone to random crashes, his customers probably won't be happy buying his pirated wares, regardless of his cut-rate pricing.

In a *distortive attack*, Axel applies semantics-preserving transformations uniformly over the program. His hope is that the transformations will scramble the program, and the mark it contains, so that Doris can no longer extract the mark:

$$extract(attack(P_w), key) \not\rightarrow w$$

The advantage of a distortive over a subtractive attack is that there is no need to know the exact location of the mark—the adversary applies transformations over the entire program, so that regardless of where the mark is located, it will be affected. Of course, the disadvantage is that many distortive transformations will degrade the program, either making it larger or slower. So Axel has to come up with a set of transformations that are highly likely to sufficiently distort the mark but that will leave the program fast enough and small enough to still be of value to him and his customers.

In image, audio, and video watermarking, distortive attacks are very common and can be quite devastating. The reason is that there are many transformations that change the digital object quite substantially (and hence are likely to destroy the mark) but cannot be perceived by humans [18,283].

Craver [100] describes several so-called *protocol attacks*. For example, say that Doris takes Axel to court for intellectual property infringement and shows the judge that she can extract her mark w from P_w using her key k:

$$recognize(P_w, k, w) > 0.5$$

Axel can counter by producing his own bogus key k' and mark w' that he "extracts" from P_w:

$$recognize(P_w, k', w') > 0.5$$

Since *recognize* is a public function, he can spend as much time as he needs to come up with this (k', w')-pair.

Or Axel can tell the judge that it is Doris who is not playing by the rules of the protocol, and that *he* is the one who has the "correct" recognition function, *recognize'*. It is easy enough for him to come up with a function that extracts his bogus mark w' using a key k' from P_w:

$$recognize'(P_w, k', w') > 0.5$$

Protocol attacks have to be countered legally rather than technically. For example, Doris' lawyer could call an expert witness to examine Axel's embedder, recognizer, and extractor, and Axel would have to explain how they work. The witness could expose, for example, if Axel's *recognize'* function is designed to always return ``Axel's program!`` for any program it's applied to.

8.3.3 Watermarking vs. Fingerprinting

In a watermarking scenario, copies of the program that you distribute are identical and all contain the same mark in the same place. In a fingerprinting scenario, on the other hand, every copy you're distributing contains a different mark. In other

---

Algorithm 8.3 Convert between an integer V and a permutation of $\langle 0, 1, \ldots,$ $len - 1\rangle$. len should be at least n, where $V <= n!$. Adapted from reference [202].

```
int2perm(V, len):                    perm2int(perm, len):

perm = ⟨0, 1, 2, ... , len − 1⟩         V=0
for(r = 2; r <= len; r++)               f = 0
    swap perm[r-1] perm[V % r]          for(r = len; r >= 2; r--)
    V = V / r                               for(s = 0; s < r; s++)
return perm                                     if(perm[s] == r - 1)
                                                    f = s;
                                                    break;
                                            swap perm[r − 1] perm[f]
                                            V = f + r *V
                                        return V
```

---

words, each user gets his own unique version of the program, and as a result, you can trace an illegal copy back to whoever bought it first. The problem with this scenario is that you leave yourself open to *collusive attacks*: The attacker can buy several differently marked programs and find the location of the marks through the programs' differences. We model this as $detect(\overline{P_w})$ and $attack(\overline{P_w})$, where $\overline{P_w}$ is the set of programs that the attacker has access to.

8.4 Watermarking by Permutation

In his book *Disappearing Cryptography* [367], Peter Wayner shows how you can embed a secret message in any ordered list, such as a shopping list, a top-10 list, and so on.[4] In this section, we're going to show you that the same idea can be used to embed a watermark in any list of programming language constructs that can be reordered, renumbered, or renamed.

The fundamental insight is that you can easily convert between an integer and a permutation. Algorithm 8.3 gives the details. To embed the watermark 6, you compute int2perm(6) = $\langle 2, 3, 1, 0\rangle$, find some part of your program that has four "items" that can be reordered without changing the meaning of the program, perform the reordering, and you're done. There are plenty of such "items" in most programs.

---

4. On Peter Wayner's site, `http://www.wayner.org/books/discrypt2/sorted.php`, you can experiment with embedding a message in an arbitrary list in this way.

In many languages, for example, the order of declarations is *free*. This means that functions or variable declarations can be reordered to embed a mark. In the example in Listing 1.6▶39, we showed that the case-labels in a switch-statement may be reordered to embed a mark. You can even reorder assignment statements within a function, as long as there are no dependencies between them. For example, because of the data dependencies in the example below (see Section 3.1.3▶132), statements A and B can be reordered but B and C cannot, and neither can C and D:

$$
\begin{aligned}
&\texttt{A: X = 5;} \\
&\texttt{B: Y = 8;} \\
&\texttt{C: X = X + Y;} \\
&\texttt{D: Y = 9;}
\end{aligned}
$$

Recognition isn't as straightforward. To extract the permutation from the watermarked program, you need to know what each item's order was in the *original* program. Say, for example, that you used the permutation int2perm(4) = ⟨1, 0, 2⟩ to reorder the three original statements to the left, yielding the marked program on the right:

$$
\begin{aligned}
s_0 &: \texttt{Z = 5;} \\
s_1 &: \texttt{Y = 8;} \\
s_2 &: \texttt{X = 9;}
\end{aligned}
\qquad\Rightarrow\qquad
\begin{aligned}
s_1 &: \texttt{Y = 8;} \\
s_0 &: \texttt{Z = 5;} \\
s_2 &: \texttt{X = 9;}
\end{aligned}
$$

Unfortunately, during recognition there's no way of knowing that Y=8 was originally the second statement, and so there's no way of recovering the permutation! There are two ways of solving this problem. The first is to make the recognizer *non-blind*, i.e., to give it access to both the original and the watermarked program. The second is to put the program in a *canonical form* prior to marking. Here, we first sort the statements lexicographically and then apply the permutation:

$$
\begin{aligned}
&\texttt{Z = 5;} \\
&\texttt{Y = 8;} \\
&\texttt{X = 9;}
\end{aligned}
\qquad\Rightarrow\qquad
\begin{aligned}
s_0 &: \texttt{X = 9;} \\
s_1 &: \texttt{Y = 8;} \\
s_2 &: \texttt{Z = 5;}
\end{aligned}
\qquad\Rightarrow\qquad
\begin{aligned}
s_1 &: \texttt{Y = 8;} \\
s_0 &: \texttt{X = 9;} \\
s_2 &: \texttt{Z = 5;}
\end{aligned}
$$

To extract the permutation, you compare the location of each statement with its location in the lexicographically sorted order.

8.4.1 Algorithm WMDM: Reordering Basic Blocks

The first actual algorithm we're going to show you, WMDM [104,156,263], appears in a patent from 1996 issued to Microsoft [104]. As published, it's actually just *half* of an algorithm: It shows how to embed a fingerprint in a program but says nothing of how to extract it again. Myles et al. [263] and Hattanda and Ichikawa [156] later presented more detailed implementations.

A typical compiler will translate each function in a program into a control flow graph. These graphs are manipulated by the code optimizer and code generator to improve code quality. The final step of compilation is to *linearize* [5] the graph to find the order in which the basic blocks should be placed in the executable file. Algorithm 8.4 embeds the watermark by reordering the basic block placement. Figure 8.3 shows an example.

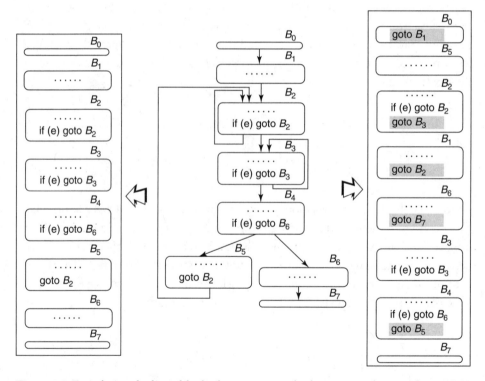

Figure 8.3 Reordering the basic block placement to embed a watermark using the WMDM algorithm. In the center is the original control flow graph, to the left is the "standard" linearization generated by a typical compiler, and to the right is the linearized graph after reordering. Extra goto statements that had to be inserted to maintain semantics are shown in light gray. Adapted from reference [104].

Algorithm 8.4 Overview of algorithm WMDM. Embedding and recognition can be repeated for some or all functions in the program. Long watermarks can be split over several functions. If the recognizer is non-blind, it needs the original, unwatermarked program as input.

EMBED(P, W):

1. Select a function f from P and build its CFG G.

2. Canonicalize G by

   (a) optimizing away any unnecessary branches and by

   (b) making any identical basic blocks different (insert redundant instructions, renumber registers, reorder independent instructions, etc.).

3. Let perm=int2perm(W).

4. If length(perm) is greater than the number of basic blocks, abort.

5. Linearize G into $B = \langle b_1, b_2, \ldots \rangle$.

6. Reorder B according to perm, inserting branches where the fall-through case has changed.

RECOGNIZE($P[$, $P_{\text{orig}}]$):

1. Select a function f from P with linearization $B = \langle b_1, b_2, \ldots \rangle$ and build its CFG G.

2. Find a CFG G' corresponding to G, prior to watermark embedding:

   Blind: Let G' be a canonical version of G, optimizing away any unnecessary branches.

   Non-blind: Find a function f' with CFG G' in P_{orig} such that G and (after canonicalization) G' have the same basic blocks.

3. Linearize G' into $B' = \langle b'_1, b'_2, \ldots \rangle$ using the same algorithm as during embedding.

4. Extract the permutation perm by identifying identical blocks in B and B' and output perm2int(perm).

There are two wrinkles with this method. First, the basic block reordering will sometimes cause fall-through cases to change, and this means that extra branches may need to be inserted to maintain the correct semantics. We've marked these branches in light gray in the example in Figure 8.3▶488. A second problem is that the same function may contain several basic blocks that are identical. If you can't tell one block from another, the recognizer can no longer recover the permutation! To prevent this situation, the embedder can either simply ignore functions with identical basic blocks, or it can insert bogus code (such as nops) until all blocks are unique.

All algorithms based on reordering, regardless of whether they reorder basic blocks, function declarations, statements, and so on, display similar advantages and disadvantages. First, they are really easy to defeat: The attacker simply has to reorder every "reorderable" list of items in the program himself! Second, reordering typically suffers very minor overhead, both for the defender and the attacker. Hattanda and Ichikawa report performance overhead of 0%–11% for three standard high-performance computing benchmarks, and Myles et al. show negligible slowdown for a set of Java benchmarks. WMDM does require us to insert a few extra branches, but except for highly performance-critical kernels, this is unlikely to cause much of a problem. Third, the data rate depends on the number of reorderable items, and this will be highly dependent on what kind of items you're reordering and on the application itself. If you have m items to reorder you can encode

$$\log_2(m!) \approx \log_2(\sqrt{2\pi m}(m/e)^m) = \mathcal{O}(m \log m)$$

watermarking bits. Hattanda and Ichikawa report a watermark data rate of roughly 2% of code size. Stealth is also an issue for these algorithms. The code generated from WMDM will look weird: No self-respecting compiler would generate such convoluted linearizations! Similarly, algorithms that embed the mark by reordering declarations will be unstealthy, since programmers don't order declarations randomly, and compilers typically lay out variables and functions in the order in which they occur in the source code.[5]

8.4.2 Renumbering

Closely related to reordering is *renumbering*. If a language has m identical items $R = \{R_0, R_1, \ldots, R_{m-1}\}$, you can embed a mark by providing a function $f : R \to R$ that replaces every use of R_i with $f(R_i)$.

The most obvious source of interchangeable objects in a program is the register file. To simplify, let's assume that the function you want to mark uses every register $\{R_0, \ldots, R_{m-1}\}$. Start by normalizing the function by renumbering the registers so that the first register being assigned to is R_0, the second is R_1, and so on:

```
R2 = 1;            R0 = 1;
R0 = R2 + 5;       R1 = R0 + 5;
R0 = R0 * 2;       R1 = R1 * 2;
R1 = R0 * R2;      R2 = R1 * R0;
```

5. Some compiler optimizations do reorder functions and variables within the executable in order to improve locality [284]. To be effective, these algorithms usually work on the entire executable rather than on individual modules, and they are therefore less commonly used in practice.

Next, convert your watermark into a permutation. Let's make the watermark be 4 and the permutation int2perm(4) = $\langle 1, 0, 2 \rangle$. Then apply the register renumbering permutation $\Pi = \langle \pi(R_0) = R_1, \pi(R_1) = R_0, \pi(R_2) = R_2 \rangle$ to the normalized code:

$$
\begin{array}{l}
R_0 = 1; \\
R_1 = R_0 + 5; \\
R_1 = R_1 * 2; \\
R_2 = R_1 * R_0;
\end{array}
\qquad \Rightarrow \qquad
\begin{array}{l}
R_1 = 1; \\
R_0 = R_1 + 5; \\
R_0 = R_0 * 2; \\
R_2 = R_0 * R_1;
\end{array}
$$

To extract the permutation, you just have to consider the first definition of every register in the function.

Watermarking by renumbering registers in this way is just as weak as reordering basic blocks. To destroy the mark, you simply renumber the registers randomly. If your compiler's register allocator doesn't select registers uniformly (and I bet it doesn't), then stealth will suffer also.

8.4.3 Algorithm WMQP: Improving Credibility

A problem with reordering and renumbering algorithms is weak credibility. Since any order could represent a potential watermark, you get a high false positive rate. One simple way to lower the false positive rate (and thereby increase credibility of the mark) is to increase the length of the watermark—the longer the mark is, the less likely it is to occur in a program by chance. Naturally, you prefer shorter marks in order to avoid growing the executable. In their implementation of WMDM, Myles et al. pre- and post-pended the watermark with a magic number, effectively making the mark both longer and less likely to occur by chance. An alternative is to select watermarks from a sparse space: In Section 8.9.3 ▶531, you will see how to turn a 32-bit watermark into a 48-bit sparse code.

The next algorithm we're going to show you, WMQP [263,297], selects the register assignment in a way that gives a credible watermark. The origin of this algorithm is a series of papers by Qu et al. [210,297–299,377] dealing with the watermarking of hardware designs. They suggest that the algorithm can also be applied to software, which Myles [260,261] did. The general idea is that for any approximation algorithm, there are many solutions that are equally good, or at least "good enough" for the application. By adding extra constraints to a problem, where these constraints represent the watermark you want to embed, you get a solution that contains the mark.

To illustrate this idea, we're going to consider the NP-complete Graph Coloring problem. Graph coloring is often used in compilers to do register allocation. Have a look at this little example program:

```
B = B + A
C = C + A
D = D + A
```

We say that two variables *interfere* if they are live at the same time. This means they both can't be assigned to the same register at the same time. To represent this information, you create an *interference graph*, where the nodes are the variables of the program and there's an edge between two nodes if the corresponding variables interfere. For the example above, variable A has to reside in different registers than B, C, and D, resulting in this interference graph:

A compiler would build such a graph to decide which variable should reside in which register. To find an acceptable register assignment, the compiler would next color the graph so that two nodes connected by an edge don't have the same color. The colors represent registers, so this is the same as saying, "Assign any two variables alive at the same time to different registers." Assuming there are two registers, you get the following coloring, where we've used light gray for register R_0 and dark gray for R_1:

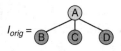

Given this coloring, the compiler can assign variable A to register R_0 and B, C, D to R_1 and then generate this machine code for the program:

load R_0,A

load R_1,B
add R_1, R_1, R_0
store B, R_1

```
load R₁,C
add R₁, R₁, R₀
store C, R₁


load R₁,D
add R₁, R₁, R₀
store D, R₁
```

Now, to embed the watermark you add fake dependencies to the graph, forcing a different coloring. For example, let's add an edge between C and D, giving you this new interference graph:

$I_W =$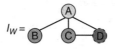

This graph needs to be colored differently, since C and D cannot reside in the same register anymore. We use dashed for register R_2. The new code looks like this:

```
load R₀,A


load R₁,B
add R₁, R₁, R₀
store B, R₁


load R₁,C
add R₁, R₁, R₀
store C, R₁


load R₂,D
add R₂, R₂, R₀
store D, R₂
```

Algorithm 8.5▸494 gives an overview of the idea.

As a watermarking algorithm for software, WMQP isn't very interesting. Just like other renumbering and reordering embeddings, it's easy for your adversary to use randomization to destroy the mark. What's more interesting is how it allows for a clean definition of credibility. Since you're adding constraints to the original

---

Algorithm 8.5 Overview of WMQP.

EMBED(F, W):

1. Build the control flow graph G for the function F.

2. Perform a liveness analysis on G.

3. Build the interference graph I.

4. Perform a register allocation.

5. Embed W by adding fake interferences to the interference graph.

6. Perform a new register allocation and update the code.

RECOGNIZE(F):

1. Build the control flow graph G for the function F.

2. Perform a liveness analysis on G.

3. Build the interference graph I_W to get the watermark coloring.

4. Perform a register allocation.

5. Build the interference graph I_{orig} to get the original coloring.

6. Compare I_{orig} and I_W to recover bits of the watermark.

---

interference graph I_{orig} to make the watermark graph I_W, I_W must have *fewer* solutions than I_{orig}. Also, every solution to I_W must also be a solution to I_{orig}:

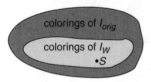

$$\text{credibility} = \frac{|\text{solutions to } I_W|}{|\text{solutions to } I_{orig}|}$$

The more constraints you add, the fewer solutions you'll get. If the difference between the number of solutions to I_W and I_{orig} is large, the odds that a particular solution S appears in the program by chance become low enough that it can be used as credible evidence in a court of law.

Another reason why this algorithm isn't of practical interest is that for architectures with small register files, the extra constraints you add may cause a performance hit. Coloring a graph with many constraints may require the compiler to insert *spill code* (extra instructions to store and restore the value of a register into memory) to free up registers.

8.5 Tamperproofing Watermarks

If we had perfect tamperproofing, watermarking would be easy! Just pick whatever embedding algorithm has the highest data rate or credibility, embed your mark, tamperproof the program, and you're done! Since no one can, by definition, modify the program, the recognizer will have no problem extracting the mark. Unfortunately, there are a few problems with this idea: Unbreakable software tamperproofing doesn't exist, the watermark recognizer might be confused by the changes the tamperproofer makes to the program, and tamperproofing will typically have a performance hit on the program. An alternative to tamperproofing a watermarked program is to use an *error-detecting* or *error-correcting* mark, one for which you can either detect that it has been tampered with, or which can withstand some (usually small) degree of tampering.

In Chapter 7 (Software Tamperproofing), you saw general algorithms for tamperproofing. Here, we're going to show you one watermarking algorithm that has been designed specifically with tamperproofing in mind.

8.5.1 Algorithm *WMMC:* Embedding Media Watermarks

In a patent from 1996, Moskowitz and Cooperman presented Algorithm WMMC [255], which includes two interesting insights. The first observation is that because these days many programs contain media objects (images, video, audio), and we already know how to watermark them, a simple way to watermark a program is to find a media object stored in the code and watermark *it*. If the program doesn't contain a media object, you can easily add a bogus one. Here's an example:[6]

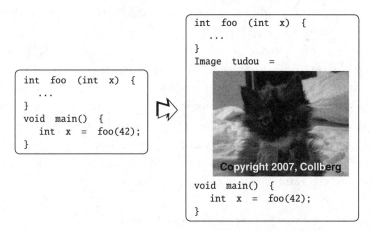

Unfortunately, there are many ways to disturb the mark in an image. Peticolas' Stirmark [282] tool, for example, contains a collection of transforms known to make most image watermarks un-extractable without introducing visible distortions. So a simple attack is to apply Stirmark to all the images in a program, obliterating any watermarks. The second clever insight of the WMMC algorithm is to protect the

---

6. No kittens were harmed in the making of this book.

mark by encoding an "essential" part of the program into the image! To invoke that piece of code, you first have to extract it and then jump to it:

```
Code  decode  (Image  m)  {
   ...
}
Image  tudou  =

   int  foo  (int  x)  {
      ...
   }

   Copyright 2007, Collberg

void  main()  {
   Code  c  =  decode(tudou);
   int  x  =  c.execute(42)
}
```

Here we've taken function foo and embedded it into the image. Every call to foo has to be replaced by a decode and an indirect jump. What's so neat about this idea is that any attack to the image (such as running Stirmark on it) is likely to modify the embedded code as well, and this is very likely to cause the program to crash.

As clever as this algorithm is, it has serious stealth issues. Very few programs extract code from an image and then jump to it! If you can't hide that this is going on, you leave yourself open to a simple attack: Your adversary will locate the point where the code is extracted, capture it, add it to the program, modify every call to go directly to the new code, and then destroy the watermark in the image using Stirmark.

In type-safe languages like Java, there will typically be one easily identifiable function that loads new code into a running program. Your adversary only has to search through the program for a call to this function in order to find an easy target for attack. In Java, you have to add a special class loader to the program that will extract the new class and load it into the executing program:

```
class ImageLoader extends java.lang.ClassLoader {
   public java.lang.Class findClass(String name) {
      java.awt.image.BufferedImage bi = javax.imageio.ImageIO.read(
         ClassLoader.getSystemResourceAsStream("tudou.png"));
         byte[] b = extractClassFromImage(bi);
         return defineClass(name,b,0,b.length);
   }
}
```

This type of code doesn't occur frequently in normal programs and should be easy for an adversary to identify.

You might think that in untyped binary machine code the situation would be different, but there are surprising similarities. Consider the following C program:

```
#include <stdio.h>
int foo (int x) {
    return 6*x;
}
int main (int argc, char *argv[]) {
    printf("%i\n",foo(7));
}
```

We compiled `foo` to x86 machine code and inserted it inside an array `TUDOU` that simulates an "image": first the picture itself (the first 8 bytes), then `foo` (16 bytes), and then a copyright notice (the final 9 bytes). We used `memcpy` to simulate extracting `foo` into an area `FOO`, and then converted the call to `foo` to a jump into this area:

```
#include <string.h>

char TUDOU[] =
    {'T', 'U', 'D', 'O', 'U','!',  '!', '!',
     0125,0211,0345,0213,0125,0010,0211,0320,
     0001,0300,0001,0320,0001,0300,0135,0303,
     'C', 'O', 'P', 'Y', 'R', 'I', 'G', 'H','T'};

int main (int argc, char *argv[]) {
    char* FOO = allocExecutablePages(...);
    memcpy(FOO,TUDOU+8,16);
    printf("%i\n",((int(*)(int))(FOO))(7));
}
```

Just like in the Java case, we had to add some extra system code. In Linux, data pages are non-executable by default, so we had to call `mprotect` in `allocExecutablePages` (Listing 6.1 ▸363) in order to remap the code page. Again, this type of code is unusual in real programs. The indirect call to the decoded `foo`, on the other hand, actually doesn't look that strange. Here's the original call to the static `foo` (left) and the indirect call of the decoded `foo` (right):

```
call    0x8048464 <foo>
```

```
mov     0xfffffff8(%ebp),%eax
call    *%eax
```

Indirect calls like these are common in object-oriented languages, where they are the result of translating virtual method invocations.

Problem 8.3   Implement a machine-code version of WMMC for the architecture/ operating system of your choice. Pay particular attention to stealth—how many easy-to-identify attack targets can you eliminate?

Problem 8.4   WMMC states that an "essential" piece of the software should be embedded. Can you give a formal definition of "essential?" How easy is it to identify such pieces? Do all/most programs have them? Do essential pieces of real programs also take up a large fraction of the execution time? If so, does that make them unsuitable for embedding?

8.6 Improving Resilience

Improving the resilience of watermarks turns out to be difficult. As you saw in Chapter 4, code is so fluid and so susceptible to transformation that there seems to be an infinite number of ways of moving code around, splitting and merging pieces of code, adding redundant code, and so on. Given this situation, constructing a watermark that will remain intact after an adversary attacks it with extensive code transformations seems an impossible task. In the next chapter, you will see several algorithms where the recognition procedure is *dynamic*, i.e., the watermark is revealed only when the program executes, and only for a special input sequence that takes the place of the watermark key. These watermarks definitely seem more resilient to attacks than the static ones we've showed you so far, but they achieve this at the cost of being more cumbersome to use. Algorithm WMSHKQ, which you will see in this section, makes a valiant attempt at improving resilience while keeping the recognition procedure static. The idea is to modify some *statistic* property of the program, in this case, the frequencies of instruction patterns.

8.6.1 Algorithm *WMSHKQ*: Statistical Watermarking

Algorithm WMSHKQ [85,147,336] embeds a watermark by changing the statistical properties of the program. The technique is modeled on a method of watermarking media known as *spread spectrum*. The basic idea is to identify a set of statistical measures $m_1, \ldots, m_n$, compute a vector $c = \langle c_1, \ldots, c_n \rangle$, where c_i is the frequency of measure m_i in the cover program P, and then iteratively modify the program until c is "different enough" from the original to embed the watermark. Algorithm 8.6▶499 gives a more detailed description.

Algorithm 8.6 Overview of algorithm WMSHKQ. On success, EMBED returns a pair (P, w) of the watermarked program and the chosen watermark vector w. $0 < \sigma < 1$ is the detection threshold. The code book $\mathcal{B}$ is a set of n code transformers where each τ_i increases the occurrence of the code group *group* by replacing the instructions in *pat* with those in *rep*: $\mathcal{B} = \left\{ \begin{array}{l} \tau_1 : \ (group, pat) \Rightarrow rep \\ \tau_2 : \ (group, pat) \Rightarrow rep \\ \cdots \qquad\qquad \cdots \end{array} \right\}$

EMBED($P, \mathcal{B}$):

1. Choose an n-coordinate vector $w = \langle w_1, \ldots, w_n \rangle$ whose coefficients are randomly distributed.

2. $c \leftarrow$ EXTRACTVECTOR($P, \mathcal{B}$).

3. Let $d = c + w$ be the desired instruction group frequencies after watermarking.

4. If $c \geq d$, then return (P, w) or else repeat:

   (a) Select an instruction group i whose frequency needs to be increased, i.e., $c_i < d_i$.

   (b) Select a transformation

   $$\tau : (i, pat) \Rightarrow rep$$

   from the code book that will increase the frequency of group i and transform P accordingly.

   (c) $c \leftarrow$ EXTRACTVECTOR($P, \mathcal{B}$).

EXTRACTVECTOR($P, \mathcal{B}$):

1. For each group $group_i$ in $\mathcal{B}$, count the frequency c_i of the group in the code, and form the vector $c = \langle c_1, \ldots, c_n \rangle$.

2. Return c.

RECOGNIZE($P, P_{\text{orig}}, \mathcal{B}, w, \sigma$):

1. $c \leftarrow$ EXTRACTVECTOR($P, \mathcal{B}$).

2. $d \leftarrow$ EXTRACTVECTOR ($P_{\text{orig}}, \mathcal{B}$).

3. Compute a similarity measure $Q \leftarrow sim(d - c, w)$ between $d - c$ and w.

4. If $Q > \sigma$ then return marked or else return unmarked.

8.6.1.1 Embedding There's nothing stopping you from choosing any statistical measure you want as the basis for the algorithm, but the security of the algorithm relies on there being enough measures (n has to be large), and so it's natural to let each m_i be the frequency of a particular group of instructions in the program. Also, there should already be a high occurrence of the m_i:s in the program, since increasing the frequency of an instruction group that occurs infrequently would be highly unstealthy. The algorithm keeps a codebook of transforms $\tau : (G, P) \Rightarrow R$ that increase the number of occurrences of instruction group G, given a code pattern R, by replacing P with R.

Problem 8.5 Can you think of statistical measures other than instruction groups in which to embed the mark?

There are a couple of different ways to increase the frequency of an instruction group G. The most obvious one is to add a copy of G in such a way that it is never executed. It could, for example, be protected by an opaque predicate: $\mathtt{if}\,(P^F)\,G$. In languages with overloading (such as Java, Ada, and C++), you can alternatively add an entire new function with a formal parameter list that ensures that it can never be called. In this transformation, the frequency + is increased by adding an overloaded function P(int x) that will never be called:

$$
\tau : \left(\ +,\ \boxed{\begin{array}{l} \texttt{void P() \{} \\ \quad \cdots \quad + \quad \cdots \\ \texttt{\}} \end{array}}\ \right) \ \Rightarrow \ \boxed{\begin{array}{l} \texttt{void P() \{} \\ \quad \cdots \quad + \quad \cdots \\ \texttt{\}} \\ \texttt{void P(int x) \{} \\ \quad \cdots \quad + \quad \cdots \\ \texttt{\}} \end{array}}
$$

In languages with inheritance, you can similarly find the first definition of a virtual method P in a class C in the class hierarchy and add a new method with the same name and signature in a superclass of C. Since the type system will ensure that P can never be called, you can add whatever code you want to it. Here, E.P() will never be called:

$$
\tau: \left(+,\;
\begin{array}{l}
\texttt{class E \{}\cdots\texttt{\}} \\
\texttt{class C extends E \{} \\
\quad\texttt{void P() \{} \\
\qquad\texttt{...} \\
\quad\texttt{\}} \\
\texttt{\}}
\end{array}
\right)
\Rightarrow
\begin{array}{l}
\texttt{class E \{} \\
\quad\texttt{void P() \{} \\
\qquad\texttt{...} + \texttt{...} \\
\quad\texttt{\}} \\
\texttt{\}} \\
\texttt{class C extends E \{} \\
\quad\texttt{void P() \{} \\
\qquad\texttt{...} \\
\quad\texttt{\}}
\end{array}
$$

A second method is to replace a section of code with a different but semantically equivalent one that contains the instruction group G. For example, if you need to increase the number of divisions in the program, you can use this simple transform, using the arithmetic identity "0 divided with anything is still 0":

$$
\tau: \left(\; /,\; \boxed{\texttt{X = 0}}\;\right) \Rightarrow
\begin{array}{c}
\text{Let } Y \text{ be an available variable } \neq 0 \\
\boxed{\texttt{X = 0/Y}}
\end{array}
$$

The final method is to insert a piece of code that is not semantically neutral (i.e., it has an effect on the behavior of the program). Before any use of an affected variable, you have to add "fix-up" code that restores semantic neutrality. Here's a transformation where we increase the number of additions by two first by subtracting one from a variable and then by adding the one back in before using the affected variable:

$$
\tau: \left(\; +,\; \boxed{\texttt{... X ...}}\;\right) \Rightarrow
\begin{array}{l}
\alpha \text{ has no use of } \texttt{X} \\
\texttt{X = X + (-1)} \\
\quad\vdots \\
\quad\texttt{.}\alpha \\
\texttt{X = X + 1} \\
\quad\vdots \\
\texttt{... X ...}
\end{array}
$$

Above, we pretended that the transformations are done at the source-code level rather than the compiled-code level. This hides the fact that the transformations typically insert instructions other than the ones we want to increase. For example, here's a transformation on stack code that replaces an `inc` instruction to increase the occurrence of the `push_const;add` instruction group:

$$\tau : \left(\boxed{\begin{array}{l} \texttt{push\_const} \\ \texttt{add} \end{array}} , \boxed{\texttt{inc X}} \right) \leadsto \boxed{\begin{array}{l} \texttt{load X} \\ \texttt{push\_const 1} \\ \texttt{add} \\ \texttt{store} \end{array}}$$

The problem is that by applying this transformation you've now also increased the number of loads and stores, the number of `load; push_const` groups, and the number of `add; store` groups, and maybe this is not what you wanted to do—maybe you're now *farther* away from the vector of metrics you're looking for than you were before! The consequence is that your watermark embedder will have to employ a heuristic to search its way to a version of the program with the right instruction group distribution. For example, you could simply try the transformation and if it gets you closer to a solution accept it, if not undo it and try another one. There's no guarantee that this procedure will terminate, which means that at some point you may have to give up and report embedding failure.

8.6.1.2 Recognition Recognition is mostly straightforward. WMSHKQ is an *informed* watermarking algorithm, so the input to the recognizer includes the original cover program P_{orig}, the watermark vector w that was generated by the embedder, and a confidence variable σ. Cox [98, page 408] defines the following correlation coefficient:

$$sim(d, w) = \frac{\sum_{i=1}^{n} \bar{d}_i \bar{w}_i}{\sqrt{\sum_{i=1}^{n} \bar{d}_i^2} \sqrt{\sum_{i=1}^{n} \bar{w}_i^2}}$$

where $\bar{x}$ is the result of subtracting out the mean from x:

$$\bar{x}_i = x_i - \frac{1}{n} \sum_{i=1}^{n} x_i$$

The confidence variable σ could be set, for example, to 0.6, but this needs to be experimentally verified.

Listing 8.1 Original Java bytecode GCD method (on the left) and corresponding code watermarked with WMSHKQ (on the right).

```
                                    static int gcd(int x,int y)
                                    loop:
                                        iload_0      // while (x%y!=0){
                                        iload_1
                                        irem
                                        ifeq return
                                        iload_0      //    int t=x-(x/y)*y
                                        iload_0
                                        iload_1
                                        idiv
                                        iload_1
                                        imul
                                        isub
                                        istore_2
                                        iload_1      //    if (y==0)
                                        ifne opaque
                                        iload_2
                                        iconst_5     //        t=t-5
                                        isub
                                        istore_2
                                    opaque:
static int gcd(int x,int y)             bipush 100   //    t=100-(t+1)
loop:                                   iload_2
    iload_0      // while (x%y!=0){     iconst_1
    iload_1                             iadd
    irem                               isub
    ifeq return                        istore_2
    iload_0      //    int t=x%y        iload_1      //        x=y
    iload_1                             istore_0
    irem                               bipush 100   //    t=100-(t+1)
    istore_2                           iload_2
    iload_1      //        x=y          iconst_1
    istore_0                            iadd
    iload_2                             isub
    istore_1     //        y=t          istore_2
    goto loop    // }                   iload_2      //        y=t
return:                                 istore_1
    iload_1      // return y            goto loop    // }
    ireturn                         return:
                                        iload_1
                                        ireturn
```

Have a look at the example in Listing 8.1, where we watermark a GCD method using a code book of three rules:

- Replace x%y with x-(x/y)*x (in light gray),

- Insert never-executed code protected by an opaque predicate (dark gray), and

- Insert x=*const*-(x+1) followed by fixup code x=*const*-(x+1) (in dashed and dotted boxes).

All three rules increase the frequency of the `isub;istore` instruction group. Note that in addition to the four new copies of `isub;istore`, we had to insert a multitude of other instructions.

8.6.1.3 Discussion A serious problem with WMSHKQ is that it's difficult to come up with a large set of transformations that:

1. Are small (say, on the order of four instructions),
2. Affect instruction groups that occur frequently in common programs, and
3. Are not trivially undoable.

The transformations proposed in the three known implementations of this algorithm (Stern et al. [336] for x86, Collberg et al. [85] and Hachez [147] for Java bytecode; only the Collberg implementation is publicly available) all seem to be undoable by trivial obfuscations or by a competent optimizer. Hachez, for example, suggests a register-renumbering scheme for marking Java programs, a transformation that is obviously trivial to undo—a decompile-recompile is likely to do it. The result is that any inherent robustness of the algorithm is canceled out by the lack of robustness of the transformations.

   Other problems with the algorithm are that it is informed and has a low bit-rate. As described here, we embed a single bit in the program, *watermarked* or *not watermarked*. Hachez [147] suggests to separate the program into k collections of functions of size $\frac{1}{k}$, and mark each set individually. That begs the question of how to reliably recover the sets. Hachez uses a hash of "the maximum stack size, the number of exceptions, the size of the code, and the size of the local variables table, ... " to identify each function, all properties that are easy for an attacker to modify.

Problem 8.6 Can you think of a way to increase the resilience of WMSHKQ by adding some simple tamperproofing? Since there's a multitude of small transformations done all over the program, this may mean that you will have to add multiple small tamperproofing code all over the program! Does your tamperproofing code reduce the stealthiness by indicating which parts of the code embed the watermark?

8.7 Improving Stealth

There are essentially three approaches to making introduced watermarking code more stealthy. You can:

1. Make the introduced code look more like original code, or
2. Make original code look more like the introduced code, or
3. Make all code, original and introduced, look like some third type of code.

In this section, we'll show you three algorithms that attempt to improve stealth. The first one, WMMIMIT [251–253], makes a copy of an existing function and makes small changes to it in order to embed the mark. Since the function originates in the cover program, presumably it looks like the type of code the programmer typically writes. The second algorithm, WMVVS [79,80,354,355], creates a function that embeds the watermark from scratch. It then adds a uniform mess of branches all over the program to make it appear as if the watermark belongs to the cover program. In other words, it turns the entire program into something that is definitely unstealthy, unusual, and suspicious-looking, but at least the cover program *and* the watermark function will look equally funky. Algorithm WMCC [95,96] tries to be both statically and dynamically stealthy: It only inserts integer additions and multiplications (very common operators), and the inserted code executes in tandem with the code of the cover program. Unfortunately, as you will see, the integer constants that it inserts and the integer values that it computes at runtime are both highly unusual and thus prime targets for attack.

8.7.1 Algorithm WM*MIMIT:* Mapping Instructions

Algorithm WMMIMIT [251–253] is a very simple watermarking algorithm, where embedding a mark is done in three steps:

1. Add an unrelated dummy function D to the program.
2. Modify D's opcodes and literal arguments to embed the mark.
3. Add a bogus call if (P^F) $D()$, protected by an opaque predicate, to tie D to the cover program.

For example, in Java bytecode you can embed three bits of watermark for any binary integer arithmetic instruction that you find, replacing the instruction with an instruction that has the same signature. Here's an example translation table:

$$000 \rightarrow \texttt{iadd}, \quad 001 \rightarrow \texttt{isub}, \quad 010 \rightarrow \texttt{imul}, \quad 011 \rightarrow \texttt{idiv},$$
$$100 \rightarrow \texttt{irem}, \quad 101 \rightarrow \texttt{ior}, \quad 110 \rightarrow \texttt{iand}, \quad 111 \rightarrow \texttt{ixor}$$

Similarly, you can replace any immediate operands by pieces of the watermark value.

Introducing some random outside function into the program really isn't a good idea, since it might look vastly different from the rest of the code. An obvious improvement (suggested by Myles et al. [263]) is to instead embed the mark in a copy of a function already *in* the program. This should greatly increase stealth.

Even with this improvement, the resulting code is still likely to be unstealthy: In real code, not all arithmetic instructions occur with the same frequency (additions are much more common than divisions, for example), and some immediate operands (think $-1, 0, 1, 2$) are much more common than others.

8.7.2 Algorithm WMVVS: Watermarks in CFGs

In a paper from 2001 [355] and a subsequent patent [354] assigned to Microsoft, Venkatesan et al. describe a technique that is equal parts watermarking and obfuscation. The problem they attack is hiding a *sparse cut* between the original program and the added watermark code. Say, for example, that you added a single bogus function $f()$ containing the watermark code to the program, but you never called it anywhere. Since it's reasonable to assume that most functions in a program are actually called at least once, $f()$ would be easy to find and remove. To prevent this, you could, like in the previous algorithm, add a single bogus call if (P^F) $f()$ to confuse the attacker. However, if typical functions in the program get called more than once, then again, the watermark would be easy to find! The attacker could build the call graph for the program and examine any functions that appear to be called from only a few places. He'd be looking for a sparse cut in the graph, a set of edges that, when removed, will separate the graph into two pieces with as few edges broken as possible. There are many such algorithms.

The solution is to bind the watermark function to the rest of the program as tightly as possible so that it appears to be just as "important" as the original functions. In WMVVS [79,80,354,355], this is done by adding bogus control flow edges between the original code and watermark code. In fact, the algorithm adds bogus control flow edges between *every* piece of code in the program! The ultimate goal is to make the resulting program a uniform mess of branches so that the adversary has no way of separating "essential" parts of the program that get called everywhere from less essential, less well-connected parts, such as watermark code. This technique can, of

---

Algorithm 8.7 Overview of WMVVS.

EMBED(P, W, k):

1. Split W into k smaller values, $\{w_0, \ldots, w_{k-1}\}$. For example, use the partial sum-splitting algorithm in Algorithm 8.8 ▶512.

2. Encode each value w_i into a graph G_i. For example, use the RPG graphs in Section 8.10.5 ▶536.

3. Convert each graph G_i into a CFG C_i. This means generating executable code for each basic block such that the C_i:s can be executed with predictable behavior.

4. Merge the C_i:s into P by inserting function calls.

5. Add additional (never-executed) calls between functions, protected by opaque predicates. Continue adding control flow edges until there are no weakly connected parts of the program.

6. Mark each basic block in P to indicate whether it is part of the watermark or not.

RECOGNIZE(P, t):

1. Identify the marked nodes in P.

2. Any function f_i that has more than $t\%$ nodes marked is considered as a possible watermark function.

3. Construct the CFG C_i for function f_i and decode the graph into watermark value w_i.

4. Combine $\{w_0, \ldots, w_{k-1}\}$ into the watermark value W.

---

course, be used not just to protect a watermark but to tie *any* piece of code tightly to the rest of the program. For example, you could use it to make it hard to remove license checking code.

Although we suspect Microsoft has an internal implementation of WMVVS,[7] the paper gives no implementation details. Here, we'll describe a Java implementation by Collberg et al. Algorithm 8.7 gives an overview of the technique. The difference between an implementation for a binary machine code and one for a typed bytecode is essentially that the latter has severe restrictions on what kind of branches can be added. In binary machine code, there's nothing stopping us from jumping from any place in the code to any other place, including jumping into the middle of a function body. In Java, jumps to a method can only go to its entry

---

7. We once asked them to give us a copy "so we can break it," but never got a response, affirmative or negative.

point, and branches *within* a method are restricted by what the Java verifier can analyze.

Problem 8.7   It would be interesting to examine some Microsoft programs to look for evidence that WMVVS is being used in practice. Before attempting this, consult a (good) lawyer to make sure you are not violating the DMCA or any other pertinent laws in your jurisdiction.

8.7.2.1 Embedding   The WMVVS embedding routine has four main stages:

1. Encode the watermark integer W as a graph G.
2. Turn G into a control flow graph C.
3. Add C to the original program P.
4. Tie C to P by adding bogus control flow edges.

Real functions in real programs are typically small. A preliminary step is therefore to break up any large watermark integer into a set of smaller numbers $\{w_0, \ldots, w_{k-1}\}$, each of which can then be encoded into reasonably sized functions.

The goal of the embedding is to produce, from each watermark piece w_i, a function f_i that encodes that piece. We've already seen two ways of doing this: WMDM permutes the linearization of the function's basic blocks, and WMMIMIT selects new arithmetic instructions. Here, we're going to use a different idea, namely, to convert w_i into a control flow graph whose *structure* embeds the graph. Embedding watermarks as graphs is an idea you will see again in the next chapter on dynamic watermarking, in Section 9.1▶546. In Section 8.10▶533, you will see several different kinds of graph encodings. We call the functions that convert between graphs and watermark integers *graph codecs*. The RPG graphs of Section 8.10.5▶536 are particularly well suited for this algorithm.

If you care about the stealth of the watermark function, you have to consider the structure of the CFG very carefully. In addition to being a *legal* CFG, you want it to be a *likely* CFG. This means that the following conditions must hold:

1. The basic blocks should have out-degree of one or two, since that's what the translation of normal control structures like if- and while- statements result in.

Only switch-statements generate basic blocks with higher out-degree, and
they're unusual in real code.

2. The CFG should be *reducible* (see Section 4.3.4►235), since programs built
   from properly nested control structures (if, while, exit, continue, and so on)
   result in reducible CFGs.

3. The CFG should be "shallow," since in real code few functions have deeply
   nested control structures.

If you embed your mark in the structure of a CFG, there is one attack, the *edge-flip*
attack, that is so trivial that it's essential that the CFGs protect against it: To disrupt
the watermark, your adversary could simply run through the entire program and
randomly flip the jump case and the fall-through case of all conditional branches!
Like this:

With only a small performance hit,[8] the adversary has now completely obliterated
the mark. So you need to add one more condition:

4. The CFG should be resistant to edge flips.

Of the graph families of Section 8.10►533, the reducible permutation graphs (RPGs,
Section 8.10.5►536) are the best fit: They have a maximum outdegree of 2, are
reducible and shallow, and are resistant to edge flips.

Let's watermark a simple program with the watermark $W = 1024$. This number
is too large to encode as a single function—it would be huge and easy to find.
Instead, let's use the partial sum-splitting algorithm in Algorithm 8.9►524 to turn W
into the set of smaller integers $\bar{w} = \{4, 2, 2, 2, 2\}$. We then turn each integer into an
RPG. Here's the one that encodes the number 4:

---

8. A smart compiler might arrange the code so that the fall-through case is the most common case,
improving locality.

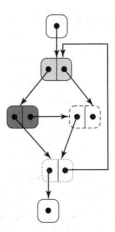

The next step is to convert this graph into a CFG by populating each basic block with executable code. Here's method m4 that corresponds to the graph above:

```
public static int bogus;
public static int m4(int i) {
    i = i & 0x7BFF;
    bogus += 2;
    i -= i >> 2;
    do {
        i = i >> 3;
        label: {
            if (++bogus <= 0) {
                i = i | 0x1000;
                if ((bogus += 6) == 0)
                    break label;
            }
            ++bogus;
            i = i * 88 >>> 1;
        }
        i = i | 0x4;
    } while((bogus += 6)<0);
    bogus += 2;
    return i;
}
```

Algorithm 8.8 Overview of algorithm WMASB. P is the original program, W the message to be embedded, $\mathcal{B}$ the codebook used for embedding through instruction selection, and $\mathcal{M}$ a statistical model of real code.

BUILDCODEBOOK(*maxlen*):

1. Let $\mathcal{B}$ be an empty codebook.

2. Let I be a set of common short instruction sequences for the architecture.

3. Pick an instruction sequence $S = \langle o_1, o_2 \ldots \rangle \leftarrow \langle n_1, n_2 \ldots \rangle \leftarrow \langle i_1, i_2 \ldots \rangle$ from I, where $\langle n_1, n_2 \ldots \rangle$ is a list of instructions, $\langle i_1, i_2 \ldots \rangle$ a list of their inputs (registers, immediate operands, and flags), and $\langle o_1, o_2 \ldots \rangle$ is a list of their outputs.

4. Randomly generate an instruction sequence $Q = \langle o_1', o_2' \ldots \rangle \leftarrow \langle n_1', n_2' \ldots \rangle \leftarrow \langle i_1', i_2' \ldots \rangle$ where $\langle n_1', n_2' \ldots \rangle$ is no longer than *maxlen*, only contains integer instructions, does not contain any control flow instructions, and where all immediate operands are chosen from a small set of common values, such as $\{-1, 0, 1, 31\}$.

5. Execute S and Q for all possible input values. If they return the same outputs for all the same inputs, add $S = Q$ to $\mathcal{B}$.

6. Repeat from 3.

EMBED(P, W, $\mathcal{B}$, $\mathcal{M}$, *key*):

1. $W' = W$ encrypted with *key*.

2. Let P' be a canonicalized version of P. Sort block chains within procedures, then procedures within modules, and finally modules within the program. Order the instructions in each block in a standard order. Replace each instruction with the first alternative from the codebook $\mathcal{B}$.

3. *Code layout:* Embed bits from W' by reordering code segments within the executable. To avoid long, unstealthy jumps, first reorder basic block chains within procedures, then procedures within modules, and finally modules within the program.

4. *Instruction scheduling:* For each basic block b in the program, build the dependency graph and generate all valid instruction schedules (orderings). Embed bits from W' by picking one of the schedules. Avoid generating bad schedules. Use the statistical model $\mathcal{M}$ to find the appropriate frequency by which to generate different schedules for blocks with the same dependency graphs.

Algorithm 8.8 Overview of algorithm WMASB. P is the original program, W the message to be embedded, B the codebook used for embedding through instruction selection, and M a statistical model of real code. (*Continued*)

---

5. *Instruction selection:* Embed bits from W by replacing instructions from P' with equivalent ones from the code book B. Use M to match instruction frequencies of real programs.

6. In the first instructions of the program, embed information necessary for the recognizer to locate basic blocks it could not find by itself.

RECOGNIZE(P, B, *key*)

1. Discover basic blocks using information stored in the first instructions of P.

2. As in the EMBED algorithm, let P' be a canonicalized version of P.

3. Recover bits W from the code layout, instruction scheduling, and instruction selection by comparing P and P'.

4. Return W decrypted with *key*.

The code for each basic block has the same shading as the corresponding graph node. We would have to add four additional methods m0,m1,m2,m3 corresponding to the remaining watermark pieces. They would all have the same structure (since every piece corresponds to the watermark 2), but the basic blocks could be made completely different to foil pattern matching attacks.

Problem 8.8 Even though RPG graphs were designed to mimic the CFGs of real functions, clearly they don't. Examine RPGs and random CFGs from real programs, and analyze why this is the case. Can you find a different class of graphs that maintains the benefits of RPGs but that are closer to real CFGs? Consider, for example, *series-parallel graphs* [187].

It's a good idea to make sure that the watermark functions can actually execute, and that they will execute predictably and efficiently. This will make it much easier to embed calls to them. In this case, m4(x) has been designed to always return a non-negative integer, regardless of what argument is passed to it. This way, you can use it as an opaque predicate! It's also important that you ensure that the control flow can't be optimized away. Method m4 uses a global variable bogus in the guards of all control flow statements. An adversary or compiler would need to do some serious inter-procedural static analysis to determine that m4 or any of its internal flow could be safely removed.

The main contribution of WMVVS is the way the algorithm ties the watermark code to the surrounding program. The idea is to add bogus control flow between not only the real code and the watermark code, but different parts of the original program as well. As long as you make sure that the watermark functions have no bad side effects or cannot get into an infinite mutual recursion, you can insert calls to them just about anywhere. Calls to the original functions in the program will need to be protected by false opaque predicates unless you can determine that they are side effect free.

In Listing 8.2▶514 is an example with two of the five watermark methods, m3 and m4, one original method P, and the main method. Notice how some of the calls to the watermark methods have been used as opaque predicates. For example, since m3(x) is designed to always return a non-negative integer, the expression m3(9)>=0 is opaquely true and won't affect the while-loop in which it occurs.

Problem 8.9   Algorithm WMMIMIT embeds the mark by modifying arithmetic instructions of a function already in the program. This may lead to more stealthy watermark functions than building the CFG from scratch, as suggested here. Is it possible to combine these two ideas? Can you modify a CFG or combine several CFGs already in the program to embed the mark?

Problem 8.10   Exception-handling code can result in very convoluted control flow graphs. Can you think of a way to encode RPG watermark graphs using exception handlers? Is the result more or less stealthy than using normal control constructs?

8.7.2.2 Recognition   To extract the watermark, you must somehow be able to detect which basic blocks in the program belong to the watermark CFG and which belong to the cover program. WMVVS does this by *marking* the basic blocks. One way to

Listing 8.2 Example of how WMVVS ties pieces of a program closer together. Calls to watermark functions are in light gray, and calls to original functions are in dark gray.

```
public void P(boolean S) {
    if (S)
        System.out.println("YES");
    else
        System.out.println("NO");
}

public void main (String args[]) {
    for (int i=1; i<args.length; i++) {
        if (args[0].equals(args[i])) {
            P(true);
            if (m4(3)<0)
                P(false);
            return;
        }
    }
    m3(-1);
    P(false);
}


public int bogus;
public int m4(int i) {
    i = i & 0x7BFF;
    bogus += 2;
    i -= i >> 2;
    do {
        if (i<-6)
            P(bogus<i);
        i = i >> 3;
        label: {
            if (++bogus <= 0) {
                i = i | 0x1000;
                m3(0);
                if ((bogus+=6)==0)
                    break label;
            }
            ++bogus;
            i = i * 88 >>> 1;
        }
        i = i | 0x4;
    } while ((((bogus += 6)<0)
          && (m3(9)>=0))
    bogus += 2;
    return i;
}

public int m3(int i) {
    i = i ^ i >> 0x1F;
    i = i / 4 * 3;
    do {
        i -= i >> 3;
        if((bogus += 11) <= 0)
            break;
        i = i / 5 * 4;
        if (i<0)
            P(false);
    } while( i < 0 );
    i = i / 7 * 6;
    ++bogus;
    bogus += 2;
    return i;
}
```

think of this is that there's a watermark recognizer function isMarked(b) that works on basic blocks and that returns 0 for regular blocks and 1 for blocks belonging to a watermark graph. Many of the algorithms in this chapter for watermarking programs can be simplified to marking straight-line code. For example, you could reorder the instructions so that if they're in lexicographic order, isMarked(b) returns 0, else 1. Or you could add extra bogus instructions, such as int $A = 0; \ldots A \leftarrow A +$ const, varying the value of const until the last bit of a message digest (such as SHA_1) of the basic block produces the correct mark value.

Problem 8.11 Thoroughly investigate different methods for basic-block marking. Are some more resilient to attack than others? What about performance overhead? Stealth? Would dynamic techniques (i.e., executing the program or parts of it—we will look at this idea in detail in the next chapter) be helpful at all?

Once you've identified which basic blocks belong to a watermark graph, recognition becomes straightforward. You start by computing the mark value for each basic block in the program and assume that any function that has more than t% blocks marked (for some suitable value of t, such as 60) is a watermark function. This provides a measure of tamper-resistance: You will be able to recover the mark as long as the attacker is only able to modify a small number of basic blocks. You then construct CFGs for the watermark functions, decode each one into an integer watermark piece, and combine the pieces into the complete watermark value.

8.7.2.3 Discussion We just wrote, "You will be able to recover the mark as long as the attacker is only able to modify a small number of basic blocks." However, there really is no compelling reason why the attacker, if he can destroy the mark in one node, wouldn't be able to destroy them in most every node. Basic-block marking is the Achilles' heel of the algorithm: We really know of no secure method of marking blocks, particularly since we have to assume that the adversary is aware of the marking method we're using. If we did know how to securely mark the straight-line code of a basic block, then surely we would know how to mark more complex programs. And if we did, then the watermarking problem would already be solved!

Collberg et al. [80] report that for watermarks up to 150 bits, program size increased from 40% to 75%. For the CaffeinMark benchmarks, they measured a slowdown from 0% to 36%. The size increase and the performance hit will depend on a number of factors, in particular, the block-marking algorithm used and the number of bogus edges added between methods.

Stealth, as always, is tricky. First, the structure of the control flow graph has to mimic that of real methods. The RPG graphs were specifically designed to look like real control flow graphs: they're both skinny and reducible. Still, only 2 of 3,236 methods in the SpecJVM benchmarking suite have CFGs that are RPGs! Furthermore, the basic blocks themselves must also, even though artificially generated, look normal. In the implementation that Collberg et al. report on, the basic blocks of the generated watermarking methods consist of 20% arithmetic instructions compared to only 1% for normal Java methods. In other words, an implementation has to be extremely careful in how watermark methods are generated or they will be trivial for an attacker to locate.

Problem 8.12 Since there's no publicly available binary code implementation of WMVVS to experiment with, implement one yourself! It would be particularly interesting to embed the watermark code *inside* an already existing function rather than having each CFG be in its own function, as is the case in the implementation we described here. Does this make a difference for the strength of the algorithm?

8.7.3 Algorithm WMCC: Abstract Interpretation

Cousot and Cousot's watermarking algorithm WMCC [95,96] is based on a form of static analysis known as *abstract interpretation*. We explained the basic idea of this analysis technique in Section 3.1.6▶143. The watermarking algorithm was first presented in POPL'04 [95] and subsequently patented. The patent is assigned to the French *Thales group*, the ninth-largest defense contractor in the world.

Problem 8.13 Acquire a Thales *Starstreak Close Air Defense Missile* on the black market, disassemble it, and examine the software for traces of watermarking. (Prior to attempting this, be sure to consult a lawyer and an explosives expert.)

The idea is to embed the watermark in such a way that you can perform a very special static analysis to extract it. As usual, we must suppose that the particular analysis is well known to the attacker, so there must also be a special secret (the watermark key) that is known to us, but not to the attacker, and without which the analysis won't return the watermark. The algorithm given in POPL'04 is based on a constant propagation data flow analysis, but you can imagine using other problems as the basis for an abstract interpretation watermarking algorithm.

Let's start with a simple example to illustrate the basic idea. Throughout this section, we're going to assume that you're embedding the watermark value $W =$ 21349 using the secret key key = 30001. The watermarking code you're going to embed in the cover program comes in two parts, an initialization of a new integer variable (in light gray) and an update of that variable (in dark gray), which should go inside a loop. In the simplest case, it could look something like this:

```
int f = -158657;
for(...)

     . . .

f = 81351;

     . . .
```

To extract the mark, you perform a constant propagation static analysis, *reducing all computations modulo the secret key*. In this simple example, for every point • in the program, you start with an empty set of possible values for variable f:

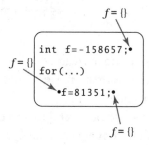

After two rounds of data flow analysis (visiting statements in top-down order), you find that f has the same constant value at every point in the function, the watermark value 21349:

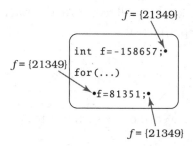

Without knowing the secret key, it would not be easy to extract the mark.

8.7.3.1 Embedding To embed the watermark, you must first look through the cover program for an appropriate function containing a loop and merge in the watermark code. Here, we've found a function that computes a factorial:

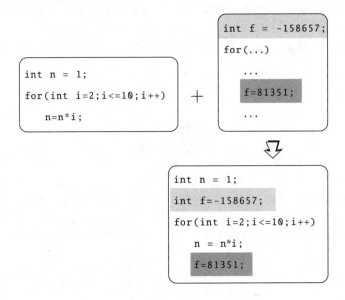

Obviously, the code above is too unstealthy, so you need to obfuscate it. Unfortunately, you can't use all the transformations we learned about in Chapter 4—many of them would so mess up the code that the static analysis would no longer be able to extract the mark! So you need to be careful to find a set of transformations that are strong enough to make the watermark code stealthy but subtle enough that they won't disturb the watermark extraction algorithm. The Cousots suggest replacing f=*const* inside the loop with f=P(f), where $P(x)$ is a polynomial. The reason is that the abstract interpretation constant propagation analysis won't be confused by the additions and multiplications that make up the polynomial. Of course, you need to pick $P(x)$ so that $P(x)$ (mod *key*) still reduces to the watermark value. Let's choose $P(x)$ as a second-degree polynomial

$$P(x) = a \cdot x^2 + b \cdot x + c$$

where you want to pick the coefficients such that the polynomial evaluates to the watermark:

$$W = a \cdot W^2 + b \cdot W + c \quad (\text{mod } key)$$

Next, pick small constants for *a* and *b*, and solve for *c*:

$$a = 4$$
$$b = 1566$$
$$c = W - a \cdot W^2 + b \cdot W \quad (\bmod\ key)$$
$$c = 21349 - (1566 * 21349 + 4 * 21349 * 21349) \quad (\bmod\ 30001) = 21494$$

This gives you this obfuscated code from which, as before, the static analysis will be able to figure out that f is constant:

```
int n = 1;
int f=-158657;
for(int i=2;i<=10;i++)
    n=n*i;
    f=81351;
```

⇨

```
int n = 1;
int f=-158657;
for(int i=2;i<=10;i++)
    n=n*i;
    f=f*(4*f+1556)+21494;
```

Finally, computing the entire polynomial in one place is a bad idea, so it's a good idea to break it up into smaller pieces and spread the parts throughout the loop. Here's the final result:

```
int n = 1;
int f=-158657;
for(i=2;i<=10;i++)
    int g=f*4;
    g=g+1566;
    n=n*i;
    g=g*f;
    f=g+21494;
```

The Cousots also suggest breaking up the initialization part f=-158657 into a polynomial evaluation, for example, f = 1*(1-111353)-47305, but this is too easily defeated to be a valuable obfuscation.

8.7.3.2 Recognition To recognize the watermark, you run a constant propagation data flow analysis, reducing all computations modulo *key*. Any variable that turns out to be constant under this analysis is a candidate watermark value. Here's the example again, where after a few rounds of data flow analysis, you find that f is constant in the function (and hence a candidate for a watermark) whereas n isn't.

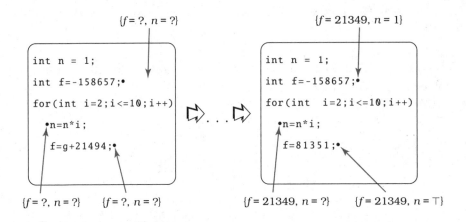

$\top$ represents an unknown (non-constant) value.

The Cousots note that this algorithm is especially well suited to languages such as Java, where programs are distributed in a typed bytecode. The reason is that to recognize the watermark, you need to be able to reverse engineer the program with enough precision that you can run a data flow analysis over it. Specifically, you need to be able to build a control flow graph for every function, and this is trivial for typed bytecodes. On the other hand, it would be relatively easy for an adversary to thwart recognition of a watermark embedded in a binary code—he simply has to insert enough weird, bogus, indirect branches to prevent you from being able to build an accurate control flow graph. You saw an example of this kind of transformation in Algorithm OBFLDK, in Section 4.3.5▶239.

8.7.3.3 Discussion The algorithm makes a good attempt at being statically stealthy: It introduces only fairly uncomplicated integer expressions containing only constants, additions, and multiplications. It seems quite reasonable that most programs will contain loops that already manipulate integers in a similar way and in which the watermark code can be inserted. Unfortunately, the code contains telltale signs that can give away the location of the code. Most importantly, the constants that the algorithm inserts are highly unusual. In a collection of Java programs we studied [82], we found that 63% of all literal integers are 0, powers of two, or powers of two plus/minus one, and most constants are small: 93% are less than 1,000. To increase stealth, it would be possible to break up large constants into combinations of smaller, more common ones. The adversary could, unfortunately, use simple constant propagation data flow analysis to recombine them again. An alternative strategy for increasing stealth is to sprinkle large integer decoys all over the program to get the attacker's attention away from the ones used in the watermark code.

One important advantage of this algorithm is that the inserted watermark code is actually executed. Many software watermarking algorithms suggest inserting bogus code protected by an opaque predicate, but this leads to obvious targets of attacks: Run the program a few times with representative input data and examine any never-executed locations closely for potential watermarking code. However, even if the code WMCC inserts is actually executed, and thus not open to this type of attack, the sequence of *values* that the code computes in the loop are seemingly random-looking: In the example above, the f variable takes on the values -158657, 1657077990, 1029506174, 937449950, -1076691106, ... In other words, while the operations the watermarking code executes are common, the *values* they compute may not be. You can imagine running a program and monitoring the values of any integer variable, flagging as suspicious any locations within loops where a variable takes on very large values or non-monotonically increasing/decreasing values. This presupposes that such progressions are, in fact, unusual in real executing programs, but we're not aware of any study that confirms this. The closest is a study by Zhang et al. [383], who note that for the SPEC benchmarks, "Not only do a mere ten values occur in at least 50% of memory locations, on an average nearly 50% of accesses involve just ten distinct values."

Problem 8.14   As presented here, WMCC relies on a constant propagation data flow analysis to extract the mark. Can you think of another static analysis problem that would also work? Is one analysis better than another?

Problem 8.15   The Cousots implemented WMCC but never released the code. Build your own implementation and evaluate the actual data rate, static and dynamic stealth, and resilience to attack.

8.8 Steganographic Embeddings

The goal of watermarking an object is to embed a (usually fairly short) identifier that uniquely identifies the object and that is as difficult to locate and destroy as possible. The assumption is always that an adversary knows that the object is marked and with which algorithm it is marked; he just doesn't know the secret key needed to extract the mark. The adversary is *active*; he can modify the marked object to try to make it impossible for you to extract your mark. So simply speaking, when you watermark an object, you care about the data rate of the algorithm, the stealth of the embedding, and how resilient the mark is to modification.

While the techniques used for watermark embedding can also be used for *steganographic embedding*, the goals are different. The goal of a steganographic embedding is to covertly send a message between two parties. The attacker is monitoring communication—at the first sign of a possible hidden message between you and your co-conspirator, he can take action, such as cutting off communication or alerting authorities. The assumption is, again, that he knows about the embedding algorithm, but he *doesn't* know which objects are marked and which are not. Also, he is *passive*, he doesn't try to modify objects to destroy any embedded data. Rather, he is satisfied if he can reliably detect which objects contain hidden messages and which don't. For this reason, you only care about data rate and stealth (you want to send as large a message as possible, and you don't want to be found out), not resilience to modification.

Two systems have been built to steganographically embed messages in x86 binaries: Stilo [12,13] (Algorithm WMASB, available from http://trappist.elis.ugent. be/~banckaer/stilo.html) and Hydan [119] (http://www.crazyboy.com/hydan). They are interesting because they make a concerted effort to embed as much data as possible while at the same time trying to ensure that the embedding is as stealthy as possible. Of course, they don't worry about resilience at all, and so the resulting embeddings are easy to destroy should you want to, but that's always the assumption in steganography. Both algorithms are similar to Algorithm WMSHKQ, from earlier, in this chapter, in that they embed data by selecting between equivalent instructions. They also use instruction reordering similarly to Algorithm WMDM. In fact, the whole idea here is to look for *every* possible place in the executable where a choice can be made and to embed a bit by choosing one of them! In this section, we will look at Algorithm WMASB in detail, particularly its careful balance between embedding rate and stealth.

8.8.1 Algorithm *wMASB:* The Compiler as Embedder

Algorithm 8.8▶511 gives an overview of WMASB [12]. The basic idea is for the message embedder to "play compiler." Whenever it has a choice about which code to generate or the order in which to generate it, it picks the choice that embeds the next few bits from the message *W*. There are, essentially, four sources of ambiguity that you can take advantage of: code layout (ordering of chains of basic blocks), instruction scheduling (order of instructions within basic blocks), register allocation (which registers to use for each instruction), and instruction selection (which of equivalent instructions to use to implement a particular operation). The x86 has a small register file, with little opportunity for choice, so WMASB ignores register allocation.

8.8.1.1 Embedding Before embedding can start, you must put the program in a canonical form. This will be the starting point for the recognizer. For example, to embed the value *k* in function ordering, the embedder first sorts all the functions within a module and then picks the *k*:th permutation. The recognizer extracts *k* by first sorting the functions and then comparing the sorted order with the actual order found in the module. Similarly, you should put all instructions within a basic block in a standard order and pick an instruction ordering from all possible alternatives.

Before you can embed data in the instruction selection, you need a codebook $\mathcal{B}$ that, for common instruction sequences, lists all alternatives with the same semantics. Given $\mathcal{B}$, you can embed the value *k* by selecting the *k*:th alternative. We saw this already in WMSHKQ, but in that algorithm the codebook was built manually. Algorithm WMASB, on the other hand, builds an exhaustive codebook using *superoptimization* [142,184,244]. To find an instruction sequence with the same semantics as a given sequence *S*, the algorithm generates every possible sequence *Q* and then executes *S* and *Q* on all possible inputs to make sure they are equivalent. Obviously, this is time-consuming, so you have to make restrictions on *Q*: Only very short sequences (on the order of four instructions) can be checked, you only allow a small number of fixed immediate operands, and so on. Algorithm 8.8▶511 gives the details.

Given the codebook, it's now easy to consider each instruction of the program (or short sequences of instructions) and replace it with an equivalent. To embed the value *k*, you simply choose the *k*:th equivalent instruction. The authors report that for the x86 they find many equivalents. For example, for the statement EAX=(EAX/2), they found 3,078 different encodings of three instructions. The problem, however, is that many of these equivalents are unstealthy, in that they would not occur in normal programs, and hence cannot be used. Also, Algorithm 8.8▶511 embeds a random

---

Algorithm 8.9 Splitting an integer V into n pieces, and combining P pieces back into the original value, using the partial sums-splitting algorithm.

```
split(V, n):

int totalBits = number of bits(V);
if (totalBits == 0) totalBits++;
int[] P = new int[n];
int l = totalBits/(n − 1);
if (totalBits % (n-1) != 0)
    l++;
int shift = 0;
for (int i = 1; i<n; i++)
    int mask = (1<<l)-1;
    P[i] = (V>>>shift) & mask;
    shift += l;
int sum = l-1;
P[0] = sum;
for (int i=1; i<n; i++)
    P[i] = sum = sum+P[i];
return P;
```

```
combine(P, n):

sort(P);
int l = P[0]+1;
int V = 0;
for (int i = 1; i < n; i++)
    int part = P[i] - P[i-1];
    V += (part<<((i-1)*l));
return V;
```

---

bitstring, and thus you'd be likely to pick equivalent instruction encodings from the codebook with equal probability. This would be unstealthy, since some instruction sequences are much more common than others. So the algorithm needs to pick instructions in a biased way, using a statistical model $\mathcal{M}$ that describes the distribution of code patterns in real programs.

You can also embed data by reordering instructions within basic blocks. Of course, you can't swap two instructions, if one depends on the other, so you first need to build a data dependency graph (see Section 3.1.3 ▶ 132) from which you generate all the possible schedules (instruction orderings), picking the k:th ordering to embed the value k. Here, too, you need to be careful about stealth. A really suboptimal schedule would be suspicious, because no compiler would be likely to generate it. Also, it is probably unusual for two basic blocks in a program to have identical dependency graphs but different schedules, since it would imply that the compiler was using a non-deterministic instruction scheduling algorithm! The model $\mathcal{M}$ must include information about just how common this situation is.

You could, if you wished, reorder all the basic block chains, putting them, essentially, in random places in the executable. The data rate would be impressive, but it would be highly unstealthy. Compilers lay out code to take advantage of locality. Two basic blocks will execute more efficiently if they reside on the same cache line, two functions calling each other will be faster if they reside on the same page, and so on.

For this reason, algorithm WMASB reorders basic block chains within procedures, then procedures within modules, and finally modules within the program.

8.8.1.2 Recognition   For many watermarking algorithms that target binary code, recognition is much harder than embedding. The reason is that you have much less information available during recognition than during embedding. This figure illustrates what a typical compile/link/watermark-chain might look like in a Unix environment:

Here, two modules x.c and y.c are compiled with the C compiler **cc**, linked together with the **ld** linker, and watermarked with a tool **wm**. The resulting executable a_1.out is stripped of all symbolic information, and the result, a_2.out, is shipped to users. *Extracting* the watermark (or, in our present scenario, the steganographic message) is done on this stripped binary executable. Whether the missing symbols will cause trouble for the recognizer or not depends on how much structure it needs to recover in order to be able to extract the mark.

Like many other algorithms, WMASB needs to reconstruct the program's control flow graph. This means being able to accurately find the beginning and end of every basic block. Some basic blocks will be easy for the recognizer to find by itself, but some are likely to be lost by an inadequate static analysis. A clever contribution by WMASB is to embed whatever extra information the recognizer will need to adequately identify basic blocks *in the first few instructions of the program*. This, of course, will sacrifice some embedding space, but it is necessary for accurate recognition.

8.8.1.3 Discussion   In their experiments, the authors of WMASB achieve an encoding rate of $\frac{1}{27}$ *before* being careful to generate stealthy code. With stealthy code, the encoding rate goes down to $\frac{1}{89}$. In other words, for every 89 codebytes, you can embed one byte of steganographic message.

Because of its large instruction set, on the x86 there's plenty of opportunity to embed data in instruction selection. Unfortunately, it turns out that little data can be embedded *stealthily* in this way—real code just doesn't use many unusual instruction sequences. Furthermore, the WMASB implementation only takes single instruction frequencies into account. This would make it possible for an adversary to consider frequencies of digraphs or trigraphs (sequences of two or three instructions) in order to find evidence of unusual instruction sequences.

Instruction scheduling and code layout fare much better. Instruction scheduling does well because there's a great deal of variation of schedules from one executable to the next. It's therefore possible to use many schedules for embedding without sacrificing stealth. Code layout does well because it's determined largely by source code, which the adversary doesn't have access to.

In total, roughly 58% of the encoding space comes from code layout, 25% from instruction scheduling, and 17% from instruction selection. This is an interesting result, since of these three techniques, code layout is the easiest to implement, and (because of the need to build a code book) instruction selection is the hardest! It also shows how important it is to carefully study real code to determine what is, and what is not, stealthy in the real world.

Problem 8.16   We discussed some studies of real code in Section 3.4.1▶191, but there clearly is a need for more data. Ultimately, what is needed is a model that would allow us to ask, "How unstealthy would it be to add code segment C to function F in program P written in language L?"

Problem 8.17   Can you use Wayner's mimic functions [365,366] to generate random but real-looking source or binary code embedding a steganographic message?

8.9 Splitting Watermark Integers

All watermarking algorithms can benefit from splitting the mark up into pieces. There can be several reasons:

- Several smaller pieces may be easier to hide in a stealthy way than one large piece.

- Some algorithms have a data rate that is limited by, for example, the size of functions. You can split up a large mark into smaller ones that can be more easily embedded.

- To improve resilience to attack, you can embed a set of *redundant* pieces in such a way that it is only necessary to recover a subset to get the original watermark back.

In this section, we will look at two algorithms for splitting an integer watermark. The first is a simple one based on partial sums that breaks up a large mark into an unordered set of smaller ones. The second algorithm makes use of the Chinese Remainder Theorem to break up the mark into a set of redundant pieces for which you only need to recover a small subset. Finally, we're going to look at a simple algorithm for creating *sparse codes* that helps to increase the credibility of a watermark.

8.9.1 Splitting a Large Mark into Small Pieces

The Partial Sum Splitter in Algorithm 8.9▶524 splits a watermark value v into a multiset S of k integers, $k \geq 2$. Each piece is smaller than v, allowing you to embed many small marks rather than one big one. This algorithm has no built-in error correction: To recover the mark, you'd better find the exact set of pieces. There is, however, no ordering between the pieces, so there's no need to find them in order. This is helpful for algorithms like WMVVS, which embed the watermark in functions. Functions are trivial for an adversary to reorder in a module, so it's important to not have to rely on the ordering of pieces.

This is how you can split a watermark value v into a multiset $\bar{s} = \{s_0, s_1, ..., s_{k-1}\}$ of k pieces:

1. Compute the minimum exponent l such that v can be represented using $k - 1$ digits of base 2^l. We're going to use one element of $\bar{s}$, s_0, to hold l, which gives us $k - 1$ pieces in which to encode the actual value.

2. Split v into $k - 1$ digits $\bar{v} = \langle v_0, v_1, \ldots, v_{k-2} \rangle$ such that $0 \leq v_j < 2^l$ and $v = \sum_{j=0}^{k-2} 2^{jl} v_j$.

3. Let $s_0 = l - 1$ and $s_i = s_{i-1} + v_{i-1}$.

To illustrate, let's split the watermark value $v = 31415926$ into $k = 10$ pieces. Since $\sum_{i=0}^{8} 3 \cdot 4^i < v < \sum_{i=0}^{8} 7 \cdot 8^i$, the minimum radix is 8, which gives you $l = 3$. This produces a list $\bar{v} = \langle 6, 6, 1, 7, 5, 6, 7, 6, 1 \rangle$ and finally the multiset $\bar{s} = \{2, 8, 14, 15, 22, 27, 33, 40, 46, 47\}$.

Recovering v from $\bar{s} = \{s_0, s_1, ..., s_{k-1}\}$ proceeds in the reverse:

1. Let $k = |\bar{s}|$. Sort $\bar{s}$ so that $s_0 \leq s_1 \leq \cdots \leq s_{k-1}$.

2. Set $l = s_0 + 1$.

3. For each $0 \leq j \leq k - 2$, set $v_j = s_{j+1} - s_j$.

4. $v = \sum_{j=0}^{k-2} 2^{jl} v_j$.

Working from the same example as before, $\bar{s} = \{2, 8, 14, 15, 22, 27, 33, 40, 46, 47\}$, we get $k = 10$ and $l = s_0 + 1 = 3$. $v_0 = s_1 - s_0 = 6$, $v_1 = s_2 - s_1 = 6$, and so on, giving

$\bar{v} = \langle 6, 6, 1, 7, 5, 6, 7, 6, 1 \rangle$, as before. Finally,

$$v = 2^{0 \cdot 3} \cdot 6 + 2^{1 \cdot 3} \cdot 6 + 2^{2 \cdot 3} \cdot 1 + 2^{3 \cdot 3} \cdot 7 + 2^{4 \cdot 3} \cdot 5 + 2^{5 \cdot 3} \cdot 6$$
$$+ 2^{6 \cdot 3} \cdot 7 + 2^{7 \cdot 3} \cdot 62^{8 \cdot 3} \cdot 1 = 31415926$$

8.9.2 Redundant Watermark Pieces

You would like to generate a redundant set of pieces of the watermark and let the adversary destroy *some* of them. As long as you can recover enough pieces, you should be able to reconstruct the original watermark. The algorithm [78] we present here is based on the General Chinese Remainder Theorem [202,276]:

Theorem 8.1: (General Chinese Remainder) Let $k \geq 2$, $m_1, \ldots, m_k \geq 2$, and $b_1, \ldots, b_k \in \mathcal{Z}$. The system of equations

$$\begin{cases} x \equiv b_1 \bmod m_1 \\ \quad \cdots \\ x \equiv b_k \bmod m_k \end{cases}$$

has solutions in $\mathcal{Z}$ if and only if $b_i \equiv b_j \bmod gcd(m_i, m_j)$ for all $1 \leq i, j \leq k$. If the system of equations has solutions in $\mathcal{Z}$, then it has a unique solution in $\mathcal{Z}_{lcm(m_1, \ldots, m_k)}$.

The algorithm splits the watermark W into a large number of *unordered* pieces. Each piece is an integer representation of $W \equiv x \bmod p_i p_j$, and together the pieces form a system of equations whose solution is the watermark W. Algorithm 8.10▸529 shows how to split W.

This algorithm takes an extra argument *key*, which we use to run each watermark piece through a block cipher. This makes every piece 64-bits in length and "random-looking." This prevents an adversary from guessing one of the small prime integers $p_1, \ldots, p_r$ that the algorithm relies on in order to destroy the corresponding piece.

Here's an example of how to split the watermark number 17 into 3 pieces:

1. You start by picking three numbers that are pairwise relatively prime. You choose $p_1 = 2$, $p_2 = 3$, $p_3 = 5$.

2. Next, you split $W = 17$ into a system of three equations:

$$\begin{cases} 17 \equiv 5 \bmod p_1 p_2 \\ 17 \equiv 7 \bmod p_1 p_3 \\ 17 \equiv 2 \bmod p_2 p_3 \end{cases}$$

Algorithm 8.10 Splitting an integer W into a redundant set of pieces, and combining the pieces back into the original value, using Chinese remaindering.

SPLIT(W, *key*):

(a) Pick r pairwise relatively prime integers $p_1, \ldots, p_r$ such that $W < \prod_{k=1}^{r} p_k$.

(b) Split W into $\frac{r(r-1)}{2}$ pieces, each piece of the form $W \equiv x_k \bmod p_{i_k} p_{j_k}$, where $0 \leq x_k < p_{i_k} p_{j_k}$, and then turn each $W \equiv x_k \bmod p_{i_k} p_{j_k}$ into an integer by an enumeration scheme:

```
sum ← 0
for i ← [0 ... r − 1]
    for j ← [i + 1 ... r]
        v_k ← W mod p_i p_j + sum
        // W ≡ v_k mod p_i p_j
        sum ← sum + p_i p_j
```

This gives us $\frac{r(r-1)}{2}$ integers v_k.

(c) Put each piece through a block cipher: $w_k = E_{key}(v_k)$. This step will make sure that every piece is the same length (e.g., 64 bits) with "random" bit patterns.

COMBINE($\{w_1, \ldots, w_k\}$, *key*):

(a) Decipher the w_is using the same block cipher as was used during splitting, such that $v_k = D_{key}(w_k)$.

(b) Invert the enumeration scheme to turn each v_k into a statement of the form $W \equiv x_k \bmod p_{i_k} p_{j_k}$:

```
for i ← [0 ... r − 1]
    for j ← [i + 1 ... r]
        if v_k ≥ p_i p_j
            v_k ← v_k − p_i p_j
        else
            return "W ≡ v_k mod p_i p_j"
```

(c) Solve [129] the resulting system of equations for W.

---

3. The enumeration scheme turns these equations into three integers 5, 13, 18:

$$5 \bmod p_1 p_2 \Rightarrow 5 \qquad\qquad\qquad = 5$$
$$7 \bmod p_1 p_3 \Rightarrow p_1 p_2 + 7 \qquad\quad = 13$$
$$2 \bmod p_2 p_3 \Rightarrow p_1 p_2 + p_1 p_3 + 2 = 18$$

4. To make this example manageable, let's use $E(x) = x \text{ xor } 11111_2$ as a very simple "block cipher." This gets you three 5-bit bit-strings to embed in the

program:

$$w_1 = E(5) = 11010_2$$
$$w_2 = E(13) = 10010_2$$
$$w_3 = E(18) = 01101_2$$

Assume for the moment that during recognition you are "magically" able to extract exactly those k bit-strings $w_1, w_2, \ldots, w_k$ that you embedded in the program. Then, merging them together to get the watermark back is straightforward, as you can see in Algorithm 8.10 ▶ 529.

Here's an example showing how you combine the three watermark pieces $v_1 = 11010_2$, $v_2 = 10010_2$, $v_3 = 01101_2$:

1. First, start by decrypting each piece using $D(x) = x$ xor 11111_2 as your block-cipher decryptor. This gets you back the three integers 5, 13, and 18:

$$D(11010_2) = 5$$
$$D(10010_2) = 13$$
$$D(01101_2) = 18$$

2. Then, invert the enumeration scheme and recreate the system of equations:

$$5 \Rightarrow W \equiv 5 \bmod p_1 p_2$$
$$13 = p_1 p_2 + 7 \Rightarrow W \equiv 7 \bmod p_1 p_3$$
$$18 = p_1 p_2 + p_1 p_3 + 2 \Rightarrow W \equiv 2 \bmod p_2 p_3$$

3. Finally, solve for W. The General Chinese Remainder Theorem tells you a solution must exist, since

$$5 \equiv 7 \bmod gcd(2 \cdot 3, 2 \cdot 5)$$
$$5 \equiv 2 \bmod gcd(2 \cdot 3, 3 \cdot 5)$$
$$7 \equiv 2 \bmod gcd(2 \cdot 5, 3 \cdot 5)$$

This gets you the original watermark $W = 17$ back.

The interesting thing to notice here is that you actually don't need all three equations to combine the mark. In general, W can be reconstructed uniquely from any subset of equations provided that each modulus from $p_1, \ldots, p_r$ is represented at least once. This means that you just need $\lceil \frac{r}{2} \rceil$ pieces to reconstruct the mark. So in our example, even if one of the three pieces was lost during recognition, you'd still be able to recover W!

8.9.2.1 Filtering Out Bogus Pieces   In some algorithms, such as WMCCDKHLS$_{paths}$ in Section 9.3 ▶583, during the recognition phase you will be faced with an enormous number of potential watermark pieces. Most of the pieces will have nothing to do with the mark: Some may occur randomly as a by-product of recognition, and some may be the result of an attack that has destroyed a real watermark piece. Algorithm 8.11 ▶532 shows a two-phase filtering step to extract those pieces that could make up a consistent set of congruence equations.

Here's an example (taken from reference [78]) to make this a little bit clearer. Say that after the first filtering step you're left with this set of equations:

$$\begin{cases} W \equiv 5 \bmod p_1 p_2 \\ W \equiv 7 \bmod p_1 p_3 \\ W \equiv 1 \bmod p_2 p_3 \\ W \equiv 0 \bmod p_1 p_2 \end{cases}$$

The first two equations are recovered original equations, the third one has been slightly damaged in transfer (the 1 used to be a 2) either maliciously or through an error during recognition, and the fourth has nothing to do with the watermark at all.

The idea is to build a graph G where each equation is a vertex and there's an edge between two vertices if the corresponding equations are inconsistent. Here's G for the equations above:

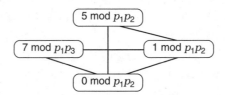

For example, there's an edge between $W \equiv 5 \bmod p_1 p_2$ and $W \equiv 0 \bmod p_1 p_2$ because W can't simultaneously be 5 and 0 mod $2 \cdot 3$! The algorithm proceeds by removing nodes from the graph until a consistent set of equations is found. In this case, you're left with $W \equiv 5 \bmod p_1 p_2$ and $W \equiv 7 \bmod p_1 p_3$, which are consistent according to the Chinese Remainder Theorem.

8.9.3 Sparse Codes for Increased Credibility

The credibility of a watermark is a measure of how believable it is. If your recognizer finds a watermark in a program, how confident are you that it is, in fact, your watermark and not the result of a spurious signal or an attack? If you cannot be confident, then a watermark is not a good indicator of ownership—a pirate will argue that your watermark ended up in his program by chance.

Algorithm 8.11 Filtering out unwanted watermark pieces. From reference [78].

$\text{FILTER}(\langle W \equiv x \bmod p_1 p_2, \dots \rangle)$:

1. In the first step, take a vote on the most popular value for $W \bmod p_i$, for each
   i. If the highest vote getter is twice as popular as the second highest, remove
   any congruence $W \equiv x_k \bmod p_i p_j$ that contradicts this:

   ```
   for  p ∈ p₁,p₂,...,pᵣ  do
       for  each  W ≡ xₖ mod pᵢpⱼ  do
           if  p = pᵢ  or  p = pⱼ  then
               vote[xₖ mod p]++


       if highest_count(vote) >2*next_highest_count(vote) then
           max  ←  most popular  W mod p
           for  each  W ≡ xₖ mod pᵢpⱼ  do
               if  (p = pᵢ  or  p = pⱼ)  and  (max ≠ xₖ mod p)  then
                   remove  W ≡ xₖ mod pᵢpⱼ
   ```

2. From the remaining congruences, build two graphs G and H. The nodes of
   these graphs are the congruences themselves. Given two congruences c_1 and c_2

   $$c_1 : W \equiv x \bmod p_1 p_2$$
   $$c_2 : W \equiv y \bmod q_1 q_2$$

   there's an edge between c_1 and c_2 in G if they are inconsistent, i.e., if
   $((p_1 = q_1 \land p_2 = q_2) \lor (p_1 = q_2 \land p_2 = q_1)) \land x \neq y$ or if the p_is and q_is agree
   on exactly one prime, i.e., if
   $((p_1 = q_1 \lor p_1 = q_2) \land (x \bmod p_1) \neq (y \bmod p_1)) \lor ((p_2 = q_1 \lor p_2 = q_2) \land (x \bmod p_2) \neq (y \bmod p_2))$. There's an edge between c_1 and c_2 in H if
   they are consistent, because the p_is and q_is *agree* on exactly one prime, i.e., if
   $((p_1 = q_1 \lor p_1 = q_2) \land (x \bmod p_1) = (y \bmod p_1)) \lor ((p_2 = q_1 \lor p_2 = q_2) \land (x \bmod p_2) = (y \bmod p_2))$.

3. Execute the following algorithm to repeatedly remove the congruence from H
   that agrees with the most number of other congruences and that we therefore
   consider a true statement, and add it to a set U of consistent equations

   ```
   U ← ∅
   while  G ≠ ∅  do
       v ←  a node  in  H  with  max  degree,  such  that  v ∉ U
       S ←  G's neighbors
       G ← G − S
       H ← H − S
       U ← U ∪ {v}
   return  U
   ```

Algorithm 8.12 Armoring the watermark to make it more credible.

ARMORWATERMARK(W):

1. Select a watermark bit string W of size N bits, where N is a multiple of 16. A typical value would be $N = 32$.

2. Select a random seed S, which is used to initialize a random number generator. This seed is kept secret and used during recognition.

3. Build a random code table K_{code} that maps from 16 bits to 64 bits. This table consists of all 2^{16} key strings. Each key string maps to a unique random 64-bit value string.

4. Divide the watermark W into blocks of 16-bit pieces and encode each piece, replacing it with the corresponding value in the lookup table. The resulting bit string $W_{armored}$ is an armored bit string of length $N_{armored} = N \times \frac{64}{16}$.

5. Embed $W_{armored}$ into the program.

How can you improve the credibility of your watermark? One possibility is to pick your watermark from a sparse space, for example, from a random code table [265]. Suppose your watermark is a 32-bit number. You start by building a table of 2^{16} 48-bit random strings. Then you encode your watermark by looking up each 16-bit half of the watermark in this table and embedding the corresponding 64-bit random string. Algorithm 8.12 gives the details.

The sparseness of this code gives it a strong error-detection property, which in turn reduces the chance of a false positive watermark: If a string is chosen uniformly at random from the set $\{0, 1\}^{64}$, the probability of this string is in the code table and thus a legal codeword is only $\frac{2^{16}}{2^{64}} = 2^{-48}$.

8.10 Graph Codecs

Graphs are common in programs—think control flow graphs, heap graphs, register interference graphs. Some watermarking algorithms (WMVVS,WMCT) take advantage of this by encoding the mark in the structure of a graph and then embedding the graph into the program.

A *graph codec* [79] consists of the two functions *encode* and *decode*:

$$encode_C(n) \rightarrow G$$
$$decode_C(G) \rightarrow n$$

The *encode* function turns a number n into a graph G, and *decode* turns G back into the number. A codec works on a particular graph family, C. In the most trivial of codecs, *encode*(n) simply generates a singly linked list G of length n, and *decode*(G) traverses the list and returns its length. This graph family has a horrible bitrate, and in this section we're going to show you how you can do better.

8.10.1 Oriented Parent-Pointer Tree

The first interesting codec works on the *oriented parent-pointer tree* family. The codec idea is based on a branch of graph theory known as *graphical enumerations* [152], which is concerned with counting and listing all the members of a graph family. Here's an enumeration of the members of the oriented parent-pointer tree family with seven nodes, ordered in "largest subtree first" order (see Knuth [202, Section 2.3.4.4] for an algorithm):

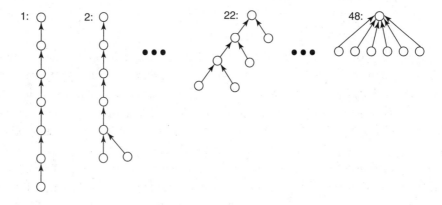

There are 48 elements in the enumeration, which means you can embed the numbers 1 through 48: *encode*(n) simply returns the nth tree G in the enumeration, and *decode*(G) looks up G in the enumeration and returns its index. This graph family is so simple that this can be done efficiently (i.e., in polynomial time), but for more complex graph families you run into the graph-isomorphism problem.

8.10.2 Radix Graphs

When it comes to bitrate, the best we know of is the *radix graph* family. The idea is very simple. First make a circular linked list of length k. We'll call this the *spine* of the graph. Then add an extra pointer field representing a base-k digit to each node. The actual representation should be key-dependent, but one example could be where a self-pointer represents the digit 0, a pointer to the next node in the chain represents a 1, a pointer to the node after that represents a 2, and so on. For example, the radix-6 expansion of the watermark number 4,453 is $0 \cdot 6^5 + 3 \cdot 6^4 + 2 \cdot 6^3 + 3 \cdot 6^2 + 4 \cdot 6^1 + 1 \cdot 6^0$, and the corresponding radix graph looks like this:

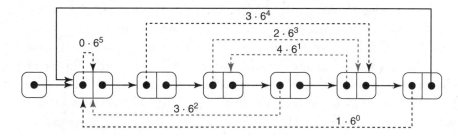

The spine is in black, and the extra edges representing radix-k digits are dashed.

8.10.3 Permutation Graphs

A *permutation graph* uses the same basic singly linked circular structure as the radix graphs. The difference is that the k extra pointers encode a permutation of the integers $[0, 1, \cdots, k-1]$ rather than a radix-k expansion. To create a permutation graph, you simply convert your watermark number into a permutation π (as in Algorithm 8.3 ▶486), create a circular list of the length of the permutation, and then encode the permutation by setting node i's extra pointer to point to $\pi(i)$. For example, from the permutation $\pi = \langle 9, 6, 5, 2, 3, 4, 0, 1, 7, 8 \rangle$, you construct this graph:

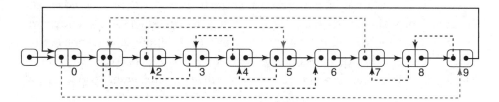

Because you have a higher degree of freedom when setting the pointers in a radix graph than in a permutation graph, radix graphs have a slightly better bitrate. But what's interesting from the point of resilience to attack is that permutation graphs have an error-detecting capability that you don't get from radix graphs: If an adversary changes any one of the non-spine pointers, you'd find out! If he's smart enough to change two pointers, well, you'd never know. You may think that this is a very minor improvement over radix graphs—and you'd be right—but it does show that selecting one graph family over another can make a difference.

8.10.4 Planted Plane Cubic Trees

A particularly interesting graph family is *planted plane cubic tree* (PPCT) graphs. They are binary trees where every interior node (except the root) has two children. They derive their name from the fact that in the underlying (undirected) version of the graph, every node (except the root and the leaves) has exactly three incident edges. PPCTs are easy to enumerate using a Catalan recurrence [141,152]. You can make them more resilient to modification by a) marking each leaf with a self-pointer, and b) creating an outer cycle from the root to itself through all the leaves:

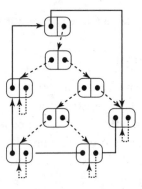

The outer cycle is shown in black, self-pointers are dotted, and tree edges are dashed.

PPCTs have several interesting error-correcting properties: Single edge- and node-deletions can be detected and corrected, as can single edge- and node-insertions, and the graphs are resilient to edge flips. Multiple simultaneous errors can, however, neither be detected nor corrected. The added error resistance of PPCTs, of course, comes at a cost: a lower bitrate than the other graphs in our arsenal.

8.10.5 Reducible Permutation Graphs

Reducible permutation graphs (RPGs) [79,80] are members of a graph family that was developed specifically for use with the WMVVS algorithm (Section 8.7.2 ▶506). They are resistant to edge flips. Here's an example:

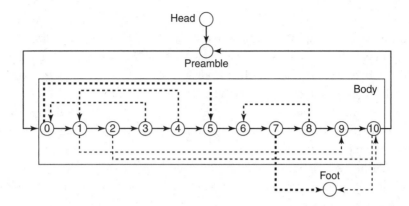

What's particularly interesting about RPGs is that they're *reducible flow graphs*. In other words, they resemble control flow graphs constructed from structured control constructs such as if, while, repeat, and so on. This means that, at least in theory if not in practice, they are stealthy when encoded as CFGs and embedded among real code.

Like CFGs, RPGs have a unique entry node (the *head*) and a unique exit node (the *foot*). The *body* encodes a permutation that's its own inverse. The *preamble* contains zero or more nodes from which all later nodes can be reached.

8.11 Discussion

By now, you should know that there are five problems you need to solve in order to design a new software watermarking algorithm:

1. You need a *language structure* into which the mark should be encoded. For example, WMDM and WMVVS use control flow graphs, and in the next chapter you will see that WMNT uses threads, WMCT uses a dynamically built graph structure, and WMCCDKHLS$_{paths}$ embeds the mark in the control flow of the program by adding extra branches.

2. You need a way to *encode* the watermark number into this kind of structure, and to *decode* the structure back into the number. WMDM turns the watermark number first into a permutation and then uses this permutation to reorder the basic blocks of the CFG. WMCT and WMVVS use the methods you saw in the previous section to encode a number into the topology of a graph.

3. You need to *trace* out appropriate locations at which to embed the watermark structure. Static algorithms may use the secret key to find embedding locations. In function-based algorithms like WMDM, you may just go ahead and embed the mark in every function. The dynamic watermarking algorithms you'll see in the next chapter often use a special run of the program to find locations that are visited for a secret input sequence, and then analyze this trace for good embedding locations. Some algorithms will use profiling to stay away from hot spots.

   During watermark extraction, you need a way to *locate* the structure in which the watermark was encoded among all the other structures of the same kind in the program. For example, to find the watermark CFG, Algorithm WMVVS marks its basic blocks.

4. You need to be able to *embed* the watermark at the appropriate location and tie it to the surrounding code. This is sometimes a trivial operation, but for some algorithms (WMVVS and WMNT, for example) it requires additional work, for example, to tie the watermark code tightly to the rest of the program. During watermark *extraction*, you tease out the structure that was embedded from the surrounding code.

5. Finally, you need an *attack model*, a description of the power, tools, knowledge, and methods the adversary has at his disposal. And you need ways to *protect* the watermark so that it can be extracted after these attacks, or at least you need to be able to show that a successful attack would render the program too slow or too large to be of any use to the attacker. For example, the different graph codecs in Section 8.10▶533 allow WMVVS to provide a trade-off between bitrate and resilience to attack. Also, WMVVS covers the program with a uniform layer of bogus branches to hide an otherwise weak cut between the watermark CFG and the rest of the program. WMASB builds a statistical model of real code in order to avoid embedding a steganographic message in unstealthy code.

So when you set out to design a new algorithm, you can think of it as having to fill in the five slots of this tuple:

⟨*language structure, encoder/decoder, tracer/locator, embedder/ extractor, attacker/protector*⟩

Many early descriptions of software watermarking algorithms stopped after filling in the first two or three slots. Today we know you need to do better. There are an infinite number of ways to introduce a number into a program, but just inventing a new embedding method is of little use. Unless you provide a believable attack model and means to protect the mark against these attacks, you have accomplished little.

8.11.1 Embedding Techniques

Let's look back at the defense model in Section 2.2 ▶ 86 and see which techniques are used in the algorithms we've showed you in this chapter:

- Several of the algorithms you've seen make use of the **reorder** primitive to embed the mark: WMDM reorders basic blocks; WMQP renames registers; WMASB reorders instructions within basic blocks, basic block chains within functions, functions within modules, and modules within programs; and WMSHKQ reorders instructions.

- WMASB and WMSHKQ embed a mark using the **map** primitive by replacing instruction sequences with equivalent ones.

- WMSHKQ uses the **duplicate** primitive to make copies of instruction sequences in order to increase their frequency.

- WMVVS uses the **split** primitive to break the watermark into smaller pieces. This helps avoid building huge and unstealthy functions. During recognition, **merge** puts the pieces back together again.

- WMMC uses the **detect-respond** primitive to tamperproof the watermark.

Problem 8.18 Can you think of language constructs that none of the algorithms you've seen so far use for embedding? Do they lend themselves to making algorithms that are superior in some way? As an example, would it be possible to embed a watermark in a language's exception handling mechanism?

8.11.2 Attack Models

The most interesting use of marking code is for fingerprinting, embedding unique customer identifiers in each distributed copy of a program. That, however, leaves us open to collusive attacks. Depending on the sophistication of the marking method, something as simple as a Unix diff on a disassembly of the program might be enough to reveal the location of the marking code. Fukushima and Sakurai [132] discuss this in an attempt at attacking WMMIMIT. As a countermeasure, they randomly reorder all the functions of the fingerprinted programs. This clearly isn't enough. An attacker would certainly sort the functions (based on, say, a combination of code length, arguments, instructions, stack depth, and so on) prior to doing the diff-ing.

Problem 8.19   Is there some advantage to embedding several marks, each using a different algorithm? Assume that the attacker knows your universe of embedding algorithms but not the actual subset you've applied. Can you then ensure that your multiple embeddings will cause little overhead while at the same time forcing the attacker to apply enough disrupting transformations that the de-watermarked program becomes too slow or large to be useful? Is there a "good" order in which to embed and recognize the mark so that they don't affect each other?

Problem 8.20   How would you go about watermarking a functional programming language such as Haskell? How about a logic language such as Prolog?

Problem 8.21   Which is best, embedding a mark in a performance-critical part of the program, or embedding it in code that is hardly ever executed? The answer may seem obvious, but it isn't. Embedding the mark inside a tight loop may cause the program to be too slow to be useful for us. On the other hand, if you embed the mark in pieces of the program that are seldom or never executed, such as initialization code or error handling code, that gives the attacker much more freedom in manipulating the code. Even distortive attacks that use the highest levels of obfuscation to disturb the mark (such as chenxification or adding a level or two of interpretation) are unlikely to have any adverse performance effects. Is there a good way to balance the embedder's need to stay away from hot spots with the need to make potential attacks expensive?

Dynamic Watermarking

In the last chapter, you saw several algorithms that introduce a unique watermark number directly into the executable of a program. All of the algorithms make use of one of two basic ideas: Either encode the identifier as a permutation of the original code, or insert it in new but non-functional code. Reordering can be applied to any list-like language construct, such as statements, lists of declarations, function arguments, or lists of switch-statement labels. New code can be inserted by making sure that either it is never executed or its execution has no effect. Regardless of the embedding method, the algorithms in Chapter 8 have one thing in common: The watermark recognizer extracts the mark by analyzing the code itself.

Both methods suffer from the same problem, namely, that the same types of semantics-preserving transformations that you use to insert the mark can be used by the attacker to seriously confuse the recognizer. If *you're* able to reorder your code to embed the watermark, you have to assume that *the attacker* can also reorder the code, destroying the mark or even embedding his own mark in the process! And if *you're* able to insert new code into the program to embed the mark, you have to assume there's nothing stopping *the adversary* from disrupting your recognizer by inserting his own code!

Now, you may object that "if only we had perfect tamperproofing techniques available, watermarking would be reduced to a trivial problem—just watermark the code using one of the simple algorithms from Chapter 8 and then protect it from ever being altered." And you're right, this does sound like a very attractive solution. Here's a simple example. To embed the watermark, we simply permute data-independent statements. To tamperproof the mark, add dependencies that prevent the statements from being reordered. In the example below, we've added calls to an opaque function that, regardless of its argument, always returns 0:

$$
\begin{array}{c}
\texttt{int A = 1;} \\
\texttt{int B = 2;} \\
\texttt{int C = 3;}
\end{array}
\quad \Longrightarrow \quad
\begin{array}{c}
\texttt{int C = 3 + } f^{=0}(0); \\
\texttt{int A = 1 + } f^{=0}(C); \\
\texttt{int B = 2 + } f^{=0}(A);
\end{array}
$$

To attack this mark by reordering the statements, the adversary needs to figure out that f is opaquely equal to 0, *and* that it is free of side effects. Other difficult static analysis problems (such as data-dependence analysis; see Section 3.1.3 ▶ 132) could also be used to create fake dependencies.

Even more interesting would be to explore combining a simple watermarking algorithm with the tamperproofing techniques you saw in Chapter 7 (Software Tamperproofing). Surprisingly, by and large, this hasn't been thoroughly investigated. An exception is Algorithm TPHMST, which simply adds 32-bit integers to the executable prior to tamperproofing it using introspective techniques. One potential problem with tamperproofing is that the transformations performed on the code to protect it might destroy the watermark itself. Many types of tamperproofing techniques are also difficult to apply to typed bytecode since they require introspection of the code.

Problem 9.1   Can you think of a way to combine a very simple static watermarking method (such as WMDM) and a tamperproofing method (such as TPCA)? Can you predict the overhead (or implement and empirically evaluate)? What are the possible attacks?

Any software protection algorithm that inserts new code may also run into stealthiness issues. If the new code doesn't fit in well with surrounding code, you may leave yourself open to simple pattern-matching attacks. In practice, this will often mean that an algorithm that inserts new code into a program can only be used on those programs that already contain code of the appropriate kind.

So are there any alternatives to these simple watermarking methods? Since code is so fluid, it seems that any algorithm that manipulates code at the *static* level is likely to produce marks that are easy to destroy. Several projects have attempted to embed the mark at the *semantic* level. In other words, to embed the mark, you add code to the program that changes its internal behavior, and to recognize the mark, you examine this behavior. Another way to think about this is to say that you introduce new code into the program that isn't the watermark itself but that *produces* the watermark as the program executes. Typically, you will have to run the program to extract the watermark, so these algorithms are known as *dynamic watermarking* algorithms. As always, you want the watermark recognizer to use a secret key, and in the case of dynamic watermarking, the key is a special input sequence $\mathcal{I}_1, \cdots, \mathcal{I}_k$ to the program P:

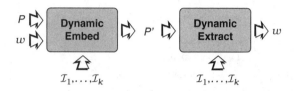

For example, to extract the watermark embedded into a word processing program, you would run it on a particular file with a particular sequence of actions, such as

$$\langle \texttt{spell check, enter text, change font,} \ldots \rangle.$$

At the end of this sequence, the watermark will have been constructed "somewhere in the program." We're deliberately vague about the exact nature of the mark: It could be program output, it could be a user-level data structure, it could be dynamically generated code, and so on. We're also vague about the nature of the recognizer. Its design will obviously depend on how the mark is represented, but a typical recognizer will examine the state of the program (threads, stacks, static and heap data, and registers) and extract the mark from it. A simple implementation would run the program under a powerful debugger, and when all the secret input has been entered, would have the debugger dump the entire state of the program to a file that can be further analyzed and the mark extracted.

This gives us the following definition:

Definition 9.1 (Dynamic Watermarking).   A watermarking algorithm is *dynamic* if its extractor is defined as

$$R(P_w, \langle I_0, I_1, \ldots \rangle) \rightarrow w,$$

where P_w is a program marked with w, $\langle I_0, I_1 \ldots \rangle$ is a valid input sequence to P_w, and in order to extract w, R executes P_w with $\langle I_0, I_1 \ldots \rangle$ as input.

Variations of this definition are, of course, possible, such as replacing "extractor" with "recognizer" in the obvious way. Note that the definition says nothing about the watermark embedder. There's nothing stopping you from having a static embedder with a dynamic extractor, but in practice the embedder often also executes the program in order to find suitable locations in which to embed the mark.

The main advantage of dynamic over static watermarking is that simple semantics-preserving transformations are less likely to affect the mark. For example, say that given the secret watermarking input sequence ⟨"hello", "world"⟩, your mark will be stored in a global variable called watermark:

```
int watermark=0;
...
if (read() == "hello")
    if (read() == "world")
        watermark=42;
...
```

An attacker might apply various transformations to the code in an attempt to destroy the mark:

```
int watermark=0;
int x = 3;
...
x = x*2;
if (read()=="hello")
    if (read() == "world")
        watermark= x*6+6 ;
...
```

A static recognizer looking for "watermark=<number>" in the program might get really confused by these changes to the code, since it's hard to anticipate all of the myriad variations that are possible. A dynamic recognizer, on the other hand, would simply run the code, look at the value of the watermark variable, and read out the mark. As long as the transformations don't affect the semantics of the program, at the end of the secret input sequence, watermark will still hold the value 42.

Of course, it's not as simple as that. You've already seen plenty of data-obfuscating transformations that are semantics-preserving but that could *still* destroy the mark in this example. For example, splitting the watermark variable into several pieces that are then scattered throughout the program would make recognition very difficult. So you still have to be careful when you choose the kind of state in which you store the mark. There are three considerations:

1. It should be difficult for the adversary to modify the state (because it would require extensive static analysis to get it right); or

2. Modifying the state would make the program too slow or too large to be useful; or

3. It should be easy to tamperproof the state.

For example, it might well be too costly for the adversary to split every integer variable in the entire program to ensure that he has successfully destroyed the mark. Also, if your language allows introspection, you could tamperproof the mark by inserting code that checks that the `watermark` variable is, in fact, an integer variable.

One of the main disadvantages of static watermarking is that to tamperproof the mark you need to inspect the code segment of the program, because this is where the mark is stored. For binary code, this is certainly possible, but it is potentially expensive and hard to do stealthily, since few programs read their own code segment. For typed bytecode, the situation is even worse, since you have to use easily identified routines from the language's standard library to read and check the code. The nice thing about dynamic watermarking systems is that there is no need to tamperproof the code itself: Instead, you can just inspect the variables (or other dynamic state) that hold the mark for tampering, and this is much easier to do stealthily than checking the code.

There are three problems with dynamic watermarking algorithms that make them unsuitable in some applications. The first problem is that, as of yet, there are no dynamic algorithms that can protect *parts* of programs. That is, you can only watermark entire applications, not individual modules and classes. That's because the program needs to be executed in order to recognize the mark, and you may not know how to execute individual classes. Second, dynamic watermarks have to be executed to be recognized, and this can make automatic recognition of programs (say, of programs downloaded off the Web) difficult. With a command-line program that only reads data from a file, this is not a problem, but automatically feeding a sequence of mouse clicks at precise intervals to a program with a complex graphical user interface is non-trivial. It can also be dangerous, unless the programs you are attempting to recognize are contained well within a sandbox. Finally, to ensure correct recognition, it is necessary to have complete control over the execution environment and to be sure that any non-determinism in the program won't affect the recognizer. If the watermark is built only when the input to the program includes a particular sequence of network packets, you have to make sure that during recognition these packets will be delivered at exactly the right times. Alternatively, you may choose the special input sequence to your program in such a way that non-determinism won't affect recognition. However, even this might be difficult to do, because some changes to the user interface may make your original method of user input impossible. For example, if your secret input was the mouse click on a drop-down list, and an attacker replaced the drop-down list with an input field, much of the functionality of the program may be retained but it will no longer be possible to cause your dynamic watermark to be expressed.

Dynamic watermarking systems have to be evaluated differently than static ones. First, there's both a dynamic and a static data rate. The static data rate measures how much extra code you insert in the program, while the dynamic rate measures how much extra data is generated at runtime. Similarly, you have to consider static as well as dynamic stealth. An algorithm is statically stealthy if the code you insert blends in with surrounding code, and it's dynamically stealthy if any data structures constructed at runtime fit in with the original data in the program. In practice, dynamic data rate and dynamic stealth are less of a problem than their static counterparts. Most programs today build huge data structures, and it's unlikely that any extra watermarking data would have a noticeable impact.

In the remainder of this chapter, we are going to take an in-depth look at four dynamic watermarking algorithms: WMCT, WMNT, WMCCDKHLS$_{paths}$, and WMCCDKHLS$_{bf}$. The WMCT algorithm encodes the watermark in a graph structure, WMNT encodes in the threading behavior, and the remainder encode in the branching behavior of programs. WMCT, WMNT, and WMCCDKHLS$_{paths}$ are all platform-independent, while WMCCDKHLS$_{bf}$ was designed specifically for native executables.

9.1 Algorithm *WMCT:* Exploiting Aliasing

The first dynamic watermarking algorithm, WMCT [86,90,280], was published in 1999. The underlying idea is similar to something you saw in Chapter 4 (Code Obfuscation): Since alias analysis is hard, construct a dynamic pointer-based structure that's difficult for the adversary to analyze or manipulate safely. In Section 4.4.1 ▶247, the graph we use to construct opaque invariants, which are useful for control flow obfuscations: "If pointers p and q into graph G are never aliased then …". In this section, you'll see how we can use the graph to encode a dynamic watermark.

Intuitively, this seems like a good idea, particularly for object-oriented programs. Dynamically linked structures are ubiquitous in object-oriented programs, so it's likely that adding another one won't stand out too much. You can make the graph as big as you want (keeping in mind that bigger implies less stealth, of course), so bitrate should be reasonable. And as long as you don't build the graph over and over again inside a tight loop, overhead should be negligible. That's the theory. In practice, you have to be very careful about how you construct the graph, where you insert it, how you protect it from being destroyed (accidentally during recognition or deliberately by semantics-preserving transformations), and how you avoid leaving very simple code signatures for the adversary to search for.

9.1.1 A Simple Example

But before delving deeper into the algorithm, let's look at a simple example. We'll start with a Java program M that reads a list of numbers from the command line and prints YES if the first number occurs in the remaining ones. Here's the code and two example runs:

```
public class M {
    public void main (String args[]) {
        for (int i=1; i<args.length; i++) {
            if (args[0].equals(args[i])) {
                System.out.println("YES");
                return;
            }
        }
        System.out.println("NO");
    }
}
```

```
> java M 2 3 4 5 2
YES
> java M 2 3 4 5 3
NO
```

As always, it's never possible to hide *anything* in a program of this size, so you're going to have to suspend disbelief for a moment while you imagine that you're actually watermarking a million-line program, not an eleven-line one. With that in mind, let's see how you can embed the number "2" in this program.

The first thing you need to do is to construct a graph that encodes the number 2. In Section 8.10▶533, we described several graph encodings in detail. Here, we're using a radix encoding. The idea is to construct a circular linked list (dark gray nodes) that forms the spine of the graph and then add pointers (dashed) that encode the digits of a base-2 expansion of the number 2, $1 \cdot 2^1 + 0 \cdot 2^0$:

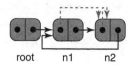

root   n1   n2

The next thing to do is to pick a special input sequence that triggers the watermark graph to be built. In this artificial example, you don't have much to choose from, so let's pick ⟨''the first argument is 2''⟩ as your secret input. Now convert the graph to code that builds it, and finally, embed the code into the program so that it gets executed only when the first argument is 2. Here it is:

```
public class M {
    class WMNode {public Node spine, digit;}
    public static WMNode root;
    public void main (String args[]) {
        if (args[0].equals("2")) {
            WMNode n2 = new WMNode();
            n2.digit = n2;
            Node n1 = new WMNode();
            n2.spine = n1;
            n1.spine = n2;
            n1.digit = n2;
            root = new WMNode();
            root.spine = n1;
        }
        for (int i=1; i<args.length; i++) {
            if (args[0].equals(args[i])) {
                System.out.println("YES");
                return;
            }
        }
        System.out.println("NO");
    }
}
```

The code in dark gray builds the spine of the graph, the light gray code encodes the radix-k digits, and the dashed code defines the watermark node type. To extract the watermark, you run the program, making sure that 2 is the first argument. When you get to the end of the input, you examine the heap for a linked structure that could be the watermark graph, and finally, you decode the graph back to the watermark number. Nothing could be easier!

However, you will no doubt already have discovered several problems. First, the embedded watermark code isn't very stealthy at all! It consists of news and pointer assignments, while the rest of the code just works on strings. So at least in this environment, the algorithm doesn't produce very stealthy marks. This tells us that WMCT won't be useful in numerical programs or string manipulation programs but will fit in nicely in typical object-oriented programs that do lots of manipulation of dynamically allocated objects. Second, the global static variable root is necessary in order to hold on to the graph and prevent it from being garbage collected. Java programs contain few static globals, so this is a dead giveaway to an attacker. In languages like C++ without garbage collection (or like Modula-3, where you have a choice between a collected and a user-controlled heap), you won't have this problem. Third, to create the graph you need a node type with at least two outgoing edges. Here, we had to create one from scratch, which we called "`WMNode`"—we might just as well have written the attacker a note: "Look for the watermark here!"

9.1.2 Recognition Problems

And those are just a few of the problems with this algorithm! Others are discussed in this section. First, during watermark extraction, we said you should "examine the heap for a linked structure that could be the watermark graph"—how do you do that when there could be millions of objects on the heap?! The key insight is that once you've finished entering the secret input and the program is done consuming it (which in our case means it has stopped allocating any more objects as a result of the input), one of the last objects that was allocated ought to be the root node of the graph. The root is a special node from which all other nodes in the graph are reachable—having such a special node makes it easy to ensure parts of the graph aren't garbage collected. So there's no need to examine the entire heap; just start looking for the root of a potential watermark graph in reverse allocation order.

Of course, examining the heap for graph structures might be a difficult technical problem. In C, there's no runtime type information to tell you which words are pointers and which are integers. In fact, in general there's no way to tell where one heap object ends and the next one begins. So you may need to use a special implementation of `malloc` to give you more information to work with. In type-safe languages like Java and C#, things are a bit easier. In Java, the JVMTI framework (used to build debuggers and profilers, for example) allows you to run a program as a subprocess and examine its state during execution much as a debugger would. With JVMTI, you can iterate through the active threads of the program, getting to their static variables and stack data, and through them access all live heap objects. If you have access to your language implementation's runtime system, you can also modify it to time-stamp every allocated dynamic object; finding the root then is as simple as a linear scan over the live objects on the heap.

A second problem you must deal with is *where* in the program you should embed the code that builds the watermark graph. If you have a good understanding of your program, finding a suitable location by hand might not be that hard. Obviously, the location you choose had better depend on user input—it's no good if it gets executed every time the program executes independent of the input (for example, at the beginning of the program run before any input has been consumed). Ideally, it should be executed *only* for your one specific, secret, unlikely-to-occur-in-normal-use input. You do have to be careful that the location is executed deterministically for your chosen input. In other words, regardless of what else is going on during watermark recognition (what other programs are running, what the network traffic is like, what seed the random number generator has been initialized with, what time of day it is, and so on), your chosen secret input must always cause the watermark code to be executed. So avoid threads with race conditions or code like this:

```
int now = java.lang.System.currentTimeMillis();
java.util.Random rnd = new java.util.Random(now);
if (rnd.nextFloat() < 0.5) {
    ...
    root = new WMNode();
    ...
}
```

To make the embedding stealthy, you should also prefer locations that already manipulate objects over those that do numerical or string processing. Finally, it's prudent to stay away from hot spots. The watermark-building code may not be particularly slow (and, ideally, it should only execute for the special input), but you'll want to be extra careful that the code doesn't execute "by chance" and start to fill up the heap with watermark graphs.

Of course, you would like a tool that automatically embeds the marking code for you, rather than having to do it by hand yourself. We know of two implementations of WMCT, one in the SandMark tool [81] from the University of Arizona, and JavaWiz by Palsberg's group [280] at Purdue. JavaWiz is an unkeyed variant of the algorithm (i.e., it's not dependent on user input). It's therefore sufficient to embed the watermark on a path that will always be reached from the program entry point. In SandMark, the user has to annotate locations in the source that are suitable for watermark code, i.e., locations that are input dependent but deterministic for the special input. A tracing run produces the sequence of those locations that are hit on the special input sequence, and among those locations, the "best" (with respect to stealth, for example) subset is chosen. If you're not sure whether your code is deterministic or not—you may have some undetected race conditions, for example!—you can run the trace "enough" times to make sure that you get the same trace points for every run.

We'll spend the remainder of this section describing how to increase the bitrate, resilience to attack, and stealth of WMCT. Algorithm 9.1 ▸551 gives an overview of the

---

Algorithm 9.1 Overview of algorithm WMCT.

EMBED(P, W, I):

1. Choose a graph family F and construct a graph G from F whose topology encodes W. F is chosen as a trade-off between high bitrate and resilience. If high resilience is needed, cycle the graph.

2. Split G into $k \geq 1$ pieces $G_1, G_2, \ldots, G_k$. Choose k as a trade-off between stealth and bitrate. Encode each G_i into code C_i that builds it.

3. Locate points $p_1, p_2, \ldots p_k$ along the path that P takes on input I. Avoid hot spots, locations unstealthy for graph-building code, and locations with non-deterministic behavior.

4. Insert C_i at p_i. Trade higher stealth for lower bitrate by adding tamperproofing code to avoid weak cuts.

RECOGNIZE(P, I):

1. Run P with I as input.

2. At the end of the input, examine the heap for roots of possible watermark graphs G in reverse allocation order.

3. Uncycle and decode G into the watermark W.

---

embedding and recognition procedures. WMCT is interesting because it's the first watermarking algorithm based on the hardness of a static analysis problem (alias analysis), and the first one whose implementation is described in detail in the literature. We will spend significant time describing this algorithm because we think you'll find it interesting to see *just how hard* it is to get an implementation that is reasonably robust and leaves no room for very simple attacks.

9.1.3 Increasing Bitrate

Let's look at three basic ideas for increasing the amount of data you can embed using WMCT:

1. You can choose an efficient graph encoding from Section 8.10▸533,

2. You can be efficient in the kind of code you generate to build the graphs, or

3. You can spread the graph over the entire program, embedding small pieces in different places.

By itself, splitting a watermark graph into smaller pieces doesn't increase the bitrate. Instead, it increases stealth, smaller graphs being harder to find than larger ones, and this allows you to embed larger graphs without raising suspicion. There is, in fact, a strong correlation between bitrate and stealth. In one sense, WMCT has infinite embedding capability: There's nothing stopping you from embedding an arbitrarily large graph! But, of course, such a graph would stick out like a sore thumb in any but the largest of programs. So the real question you have to ask yourself is, "In a program of a particular size with a particular mix of instructions written in a particular programming style, what amount of graph-building code can we add without raising the suspicion of a human reader and without changing the local and global instruction mix to alert an automatic de-watermarking tool?" Since we don't have good models for either human or machine stealth, we can't answer this question conclusively.

There are actually two types of bitrate, one dynamic and one static. In most cases, you will just care about the static rate, which is the amount of graph-building code you have to insert in the program. The dynamic bitrate measures how much dynamic data is added to the heap. Usually this will be irrelevant, since you expect the watermark graph to be built only during recognition, and the heap typically has lots of data in it to begin with.

9.1.3.1 Choosing an Efficient Graph Encoding
A good start to increasing the bitrate is to choose a graph family from Section 8.10▶533 that generates the smallest graphs possible, for the largest possible watermarks. But this isn't enough. What you really want is a family of graphs from which you can generate as little *graph-building code* as possible for as large watermark numbers as possible.

To see this, consider the graph family of *oriented parent-pointer trees*. In these graphs, every node has only one pointer, which points to its parent. This is quite efficient! However, if you're in a garbage-collected environment like Java, you'll run into serious problems when implementing this family. Since there's nothing pointing to the leaves, the entire structure consists of non-live objects that will be recycled by the garbage collector! So you will also have to be sure to include extra pointers to all the leaf nodes. The extra leaf pointers will, of course, reduce the overall bitrate. You'll see an example of this shortly.

The *radix graph* family has a higher static bitrate than any other class we know of. You can see in Figure 9.1▶553 that the size of the Java bytecode needed to build the graph grows very modestly with the size of the watermark.

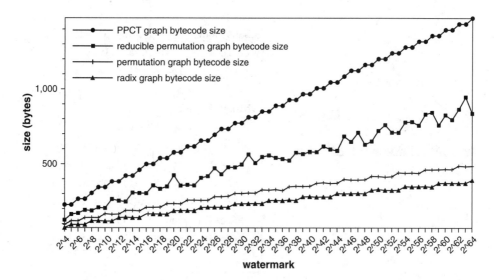

Figure 9.1 Sizes of the graph-building Java bytecode as a function of the size of the finger-print. This figure is taken from reference [90].

9.1.3.2 Generating Minimal Code

Once the graph codec from Section 8.10 ▶533 has constructed a watermark graph from your watermark integer, you have to generate code that builds this graph. You do a depth-first traversal of the graph starting at its root, and emit a n_k = new() for every node in reverse topological order. When you've generated code for nodes n_i and n_j, you can generate code for any edge between them, such as n_i.edge1 = n_j. Unlike graphs that you find in most math textbooks, the graphs we talk about in this chapter are *directed multigraphs* (you can have more than one edge between two nodes) with an ordering on a node's outgoing edges. In other words, you can have both edges $n \xrightarrow{\text{edge1}} m$ and $n \xrightarrow{\text{edge2}} m$, and there's a definite difference between them.

Depending on the graph family and your target language, you might be able to do better than such a straightforward code generation. If the same subgraph occurs many times in the graph, it might make sense to factor out that code into a subroutine. Some approaches to code compaction [112] have used similar ideas.

To see that code generation strategies matter, have a look at the light gray code segment below that builds the 48th tree in the parent-pointer tree encoding. To make sure that the graph is not garbage collected, we've had to add static pointers to every leaf:

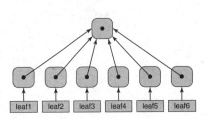

```
class Node {public Node parent;}
static Node leaf1,leaf2,leaf3,
            leaf4,leaf5,leaf6;
    ...
void buildGraph() {
  Node r = new Node();
  (leaf1 = new Node()).parent = r;
  (leaf2 = new Node()).parent = r;
  (leaf3 = new Node()).parent = r;
  (leaf4 = new Node()).parent = r;
  (leaf5 = new Node()).parent = r;
  (leaf6 = new Node()).parent = r;
}
```

The generated Java bytecode is 99 bytes, but if you're a bit more clever you can use an array instead and build the entire graph in a single loop, using only 48 codebytes:

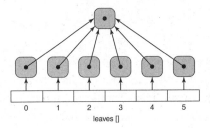

```
class Node {public Node parent;}
static Node[] leaves;
    ...
void buildGraph() {
  Node r = new Node();
  Node[] l = leaves = new Node[6];
  for(int i=0; i<6; i++)
    (l[i] = new Node()).parent = r;
}
```

Problem 9.2   Define a minimalist language made up of, say, news, pointer assignments, arrays, and while-loops. Construct an algorithm that takes a graph as input and generates minimal code that builds the graph in your language. To simplify, limit the problem to certain families of graphs.

9.1.3.3 Increasing Stealth and Bitrate by Graph Splitting   Small watermark numbers will be encoded into small graphs, and assuming that you can find a place in the code that already does some allocation and pointer manipulation, you can

probably embed the entire graph there without having to worry too much about stealth. But for large graphs, stealth *is* a concern. The watermark 2^{32} in a radix graph encoding has eleven nodes, resulting in a total of 113 bytecode instructions. This doesn't sound too bad for a 32-bit watermark, but what's troubling is that only nine different kinds of instructions are emitted (those corresponding to Java's `new()` and `p.field  =  q` statements), and this leaves a telltale signature that will be easy for an attacker to spot.

It makes sense to split up large watermark graphs into smaller pieces and spread them over the program. Here's an example where a four-node graph is built in two pieces of two nodes each:

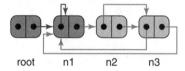

root   n1   n2   n3

The first component of the graph is in light gray and the second is in dark gray. Here's a program that first builds the light gray part, then the dark gray part, and then combines the two using the dashed code:

```
public static Node root;
public static Node n2;
public void main (String args[]) {
    if (args[0].equals("2")) {
        n2 = new Node();
        Node n3 = new Node();
        n2.digit = n3;
        n2.spine = n3;
    }
    for (int i=1;i<args.length;i++) {
        if (found(args[0], args, i)) {
            System.out.println("YES");
            return;
        }
    }
    System.out.println("NO");
}
```

```
public boolean found (
    String value,
    String args[],
    int i) {
    if (value.equals(args[i])) {
        if ((i == 4)&&(n2 != null)) {
            Node n1 = new Node();
            n1.digit = n1;
            n1.spine = n2;
            Node n3 = n2.spine;
            n3.spine = n1;
            n3.digit = n1;
            root = new Node();
            root.spine = n1;
        }
        return true;
    }
    return false;
}
```

The more pieces you break a graph into, the more code you have to generate to merge the pieces back together! So it's important that you choose a graph-splitting algorithm that minimizes the number of edges that cross the cut between components [216]. In Figure 9.2 ▶556, you can see how the size of the Java bytecode generated for a radix graph grows as you split it into two to five components.

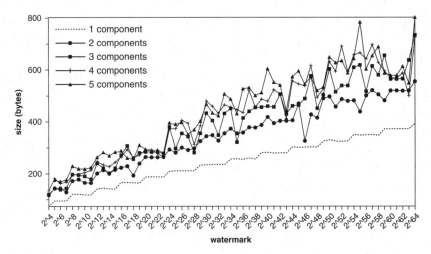

Figure 9.2 Size of Java bytecode for building a radix graph split into two or more components. This figure is taken from reference [90].

For the watermark 2^{32}, a single graph requires 236 codebytes, two components require 327, three require 348, four require 433, and five require 423 bytes.

When you split the graph, you have to keep the garbage-collection issue in mind. Each component should be a connected graph, and there should be a root node from which all nodes in a component are reachable. This is the case with the light gray component in the example above: n2 holds onto its root node, ensuring that it doesn't get collected prematurely. The final issue you need to consider is that on non-recognition runs, you may try to merge two graph components together even though one of them hasn't been built! This is the case, for example, if the light gray code hasn't executed by the time you reach the dark gray code: n2 will be null and without the dotted guard, you would get a null-pointer exception.

Problem 9.3 One problem with breaking the graph into small pieces is that you have to somehow connect them again. In the example above, we do this through the global variable n2. A different idea is to break the watermark *number* into smaller pieces, convert each piece into a graph, and then embed all the graphs in different parts of the program. During recognition, you have to extract each graph individually, convert it to a number, and merge these numbers back into the watermark. You could run several recognition runs, one for each subgraph, each with different secret input sequences, or you could produce all graphs on the same run. Which is the better strategy, breaking the watermark number or the watermark graph? Compare and contrast!

9.1.4 Increasing Resilience to Attack

Typical dynamic structures in real programs are simple: Lists are more common than trees, trees are more common than DAGs, sparse graphs with low out-degree are more common than dense graphs, and so on. To be stealthy, therefore, your watermark graph G should be as simple as possible. Also, you want G to be small (the graph encoding should have a high bitrate), and if you're in a garbage-collected environment, you want all nodes to be reachable through a single root node that you can hold onto in order to make sure that the entire structure won't be collected prematurely. Finally, you want G to be resilient to small perturbations. If the adversary is able to destroy a small piece of the graph (or there's a small error during watermark extraction), you still want to be able to extract the mark. In other words, you want the graph to have error-correcting properties.

9.1.4.1 Protecting against Edge Flips   With the exception of oriented parent-pointer trees, the graphs in Section 8.10▶533 are all multigraphs with an ordering on the outgoing edges. This makes them vulnerable to a very simple attack: Simply reorder the edges! We call this attack an *edge flip*. In a typed language like Java bytecode, this is ridiculously simple: Just rename the fields representing the graph edges. If there are only two fields in the node object, this won't present too much of a problem for the watermark recognizer: Just try both orderings. But the number of orders to try grows exponentially with the number of pointer fields in the nodes, so an adversary can (at some additional space cost) add bogus fields to slow down the recognizer.

Some languages have *introspective* capabilities. Java's reflection mechanism, for example, allows a running program to examine itself, including its classes, the fields those classes have, the types of those fields, and so on. You can use this to tamperproof your watermark node class to make sure that a class' fields have not been reordered and that additional fields have not been added to confuse you:

```
class Node {public Node spine, digit;}
Node n1 = new Node();
...
java.lang.reflect.Field[] F = Node.class.getFields();
if (!((F.length == 2) &&
    (F[0].getName().equals("spine")) &&
    (F[1].getName().equals("digit")) &&
    (F[0].getType() == Node.class) &&
    (F[1].getType() == Node.class)))
  java.lang.System.exit(42);
```

Unfortunately, reflection is rarely used in real programs, so this type of tamperproofing is highly unstealthy.

Problem 9.4   C doesn't have reflection capabilities, but can you think of a similar way to protect a graph in a weakly typed language?

Instead, what you really want is a graph family where edge flips don't matter. The oriented parent-pointer tree is such a family, since they only have one outgoing edge in the first place! Unfortunately, they don't have any other good error-correcting properties, as any other minor change to the graph will make the recognizer return a completely different watermark number, and there's no way for you to even detect that an attack has occurred. A more interesting graph family is *planted plane cubic tree* (Section 8.10.4▶536) graphs, which are resilient to edge flips and some other small perturbations.

The reducible permutation graphs that we presented in Section 8.10.5▶536 can, of course, be used to build dynamic graphs as well as the CFG watermarks they were used for in the WMVVS algorithm. They maintain the same strong properties, including resistance to edge flips.

9.1.4.2 Protecting Against Node Splitting   A particularly nasty attack is *node splitting*. The idea is very simple: The attacker replaces every dynamic object you allocate with two, where the first one points to the second. The attacker will have to add extra code everywhere in the code where the split object is referenced to ensure that the transformation is semantics-preserving. In a typed code, this transformation is easy and requires no expensive analysis. Here's an example attack:

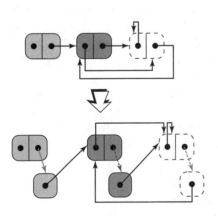

```
class Bogus {public Bogus L;}
class Node extends Bogus {
    public Node R;}
    ...
Node n1A = new Node();
Bogus n1B = new Bogus();
n1A.L = n1B;
Node n2A = new Node();
Bogus n2B = new Bogus();
n2A.L = n2B;
Node n3A = new Node();
Bogus n3B = new Bogus();
n3A.L = n3B;
n1B.L = n2A;  n2A.R = n3A;
n2B.L = n3A;  n3A.R = n3A;
n3B.L = n2A;
```

You should keep in mind that we're assuming the attacker doesn't know where your watermark code is embedded. If he did, you've already lost! So under that assumption, the best he can do is to apply the distortive transformation uniformly over all the code in the program, splitting *every* object type and adding an extra level of indirection to *every* pointer de-reference. In many programs, this would lead to significant slowdown and extra memory consumption.

To protect yourself from the node-splitting attack, you can replace each node in the watermark graphs with a *k*-cycle, and each edge with an *m*-path. Any node split will fall on a cycle or path and will disappear during watermark extraction as you shrink cycles and paths back into nodes and edges. Unfortunately, as can be expected, you get a huge decrease in bitrate and stealthiness. The Java bytecode for this example is 408 bytes compared to 54 bytes for the uncycled graph:

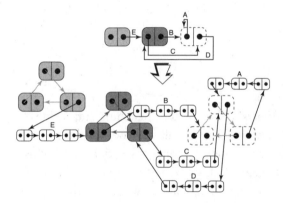

```
node n0 = new Node();
...

n0.R = n4;     n1.L = n7;
n1.R = n14;    n10.L = n18;
n10.R = n13;   n11.L = n23;
n11.R = n6;    n12.L = n2;
n13.R = n3;    n14.R = n0;
n14.L = n5;    n15.R = n20;
n16.L = n5;    n17.L = n11;
n18.L = n22;   n19.R = n15;
n2.R = n19;    n2.L = n11;
n20.R = n14;   n21.L = n16;
n22.L = n17;   n23.L = n21;
n3.R = n10;    n4.R = n8;
n5.R = n1;     n6.R = n2;
n7.L = n9;     n8.R = n1;
n9.L = n12;    root = n3;
```

In Figure 9.3 ▶560, you can see that twice as much dynamic memory gets allocated as for an uncycled radix graph.

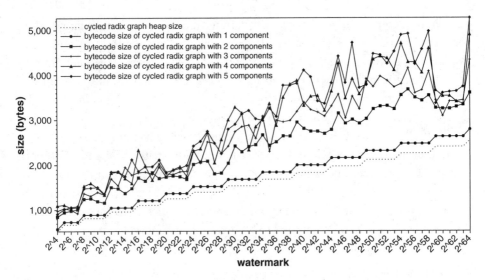

Figure 9.3 Bytecode sizes and runtime heap sizes for cycled radix graphs. This figure is taken from reference [90].

9.1.4.3 Protecting Against Alias Analysis

In a pattern-matching attack on your watermarked program, the attacker would analyze all the code in the program that builds some sort of linked structure, looking for any location that builds a structure from your graph library. In general, this requires him to do a *shape analysis* [137,311], which in turn requires a smart alias analysis. We talked about this in Section 3.1.4▶134.

How do you thwart such an attack? Well, you can look at what types of code current alias analysis algorithms find most difficult to analyze: They typically break down for code that builds very deeply recursive structures (no problem there, with your convoluted graphs!) and for code with destructive updates. That is, alias analysis algorithms do very well for constructive code, which just *builds* a linked structure, but poorly for code that both builds and *changes* structures. So to throw off your attacker, you can insert exactly this type of code along the path the program takes on the secret input. Here's an example where the watermark graph gets built in two steps:

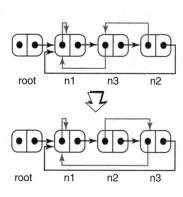

```
Node n3 = new Node();
Node n2 = new Node();
n3.spine = n2; n2.digit = n3;
Node n1 = new Node();
n1.digit = n1; n1.spine = n3;
n3.digit = n1; n2.spine = n1;
root = new Node();
root.spine = n1;
...
Node tmp = root.spine.spine;
root.spine.spine = tmp.spine;
tmp.spine.spine = tmp;
tmp.spine = tmp.digit;
```

First, the dark gray code builds an erroneous watermark graph, and then in the second step, it gets fixed up by the light gray code into the correct graph. Of course, there are endless opportunities for creating, destroying, modifying, and fixing up the graph. The more changes to the graph you make on the way, the harder it will be for the attacker to analyze the code, but the bitrate will go down (you're adding more code!) and the overall stealth may also suffer.

9.1.5 Increasing Stealth

When deciding how to go about attacking a system, an adversary will always choose the path of least resistance. You may think that "the right" way to attack WMCT is to build a state-of-the-art pointer analyzer, but since this would amount to actual hard work, a smart hacker will look for a cheaper way in. This is why the *stealth* of the introduced code is so important. If the attacker can find the root of the graph stored in a global variable, or realize that your graph is made up of nodes called WMNode, or note that a section of code that builds a linked structure is not attached to the rest of the program, his work is more than halfway done. Our stealthiness goal has to be to force the attacker to analyze, by hand or by advanced static analysis, every line of the program. If a very quick and simple scan of the code allows him to conclude that the watermark cannot possibly be in, say, 90% of the code, then you have lost. With this in mind, let's consider a few of the obvious stealth problems with the code we've generated so far.

9.1.5.1 Avoiding Global Variables First, you've seen that having to store the root of the graph in a global variable is a dead giveaway. Object-oriented programs, in particular, have few globals, and it's easy to scan the code for where they are being assigned to. Two solutions come to mind to alleviate this problem: You can litter the program with bogus global variables, or you can pass the root of the graph in formal method parameters. Here's an example where we've split the graph into two components. Normally, you'd have to store a pointer to node n2 in a global variable so that the light gray component will be accessible when it's merged with the dark gray component, but instead you can pass n2 in a formal parameter:

```
public static void main (
   String args[]) {
   Node n2 = null;
   if (args[0].equals("2")) {
      n2 = new Node();
      Node n3 = new Node();
      n2.digit = n3;
      n2.spine = n3;
   }
   for (int i=1; i<args.length; i++) {
      if (found(args[0],args,i,n2)) {
         System.out.println("YES");
         return;
      }
   }
   System.out.println("NO");
}
```

```
public static boolean found (
   String value, String args[],
   int i, Node n2) {
   if (value.equals(args[i])) {
      if ((i==4)&&(n2!=null) {
         Node n1 = new Node();
         n1.digit = n1;
         n1.spine = n2;
         n2.spine.spine = n1;
         n2.spine.digit = n1;
         Node root = new Node();
         root.spine = n1;
      }
      return true;
   }
   return false;
}
```

In practice, of course, this is only possible if there's a direct runtime path between the two graph-building sites. If, on the other hand, the two components are built by two different threads, some other means of communication has to be used. The SandMark [81] tool uses a tracing run to determine suitable locations for embedding. During the trace, they also build an accurate call graph that allows them to pick locations between which there are direct communication paths using only formal parameters.

9.1.5.2 Avoiding Unstealthy Node Classes One serious problem of WMCT is that it requires a Java class (or C struct, or Pascal record, and so on) to represent the nodes of the graph. If there are only a few such data structures in the program, it will be an easy task for the attacker to examine them to see which ones are being used to create suspicious linked structures.

In the Java library, there are a few (on the order of twenty) classes that you can reuse for graph nodes. If none of these classes is used in the original program, their presence may raise suspicion, of course. Also, you should try to reuse any classes that are already in your program, extending them as necessary to get the right number of pointers:

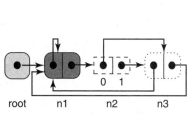

```
class Person {public Object spouse;}
class Node extends Person {
    public Object digit;}
    ...
Node n1 = new Node();
n1.digit = n1;
java.awt.Event n3 =
    new java.awt.Event(n1,0,n1);
Object n2[] = {n3,n3};
n1.spouse = n2;
root = new Person();
root.spouse = n1;
```

root   n1   n2   n3

One nice aspect of the parent-pointer family of graphs (Section 8.10.1▶534) is that each node only requires one pointer. So you could hijack any type of data structure with one pointer in each node, such as a person object pointing to its parent, a singly linked list node object, and so on. All the other graph families you've seen require two pointers out of each node, and these types of nodes are much less likely to occur naturally in real programs.

9.1.5.3 Avoiding Weak Cuts   An important contribution of algorithm WMVVS (Section 8.7.2▶506) is the insistence on the importance of avoiding *weak cuts*. The intuition is that if a piece of code is not strongly connected to the rest of the program, it is suspicious. So far, the graph-building code you've generated hasn't been connected at all to the host program, which is suspicious indeed! In WMVVS, the authors solve the problem by adding a large number of bogus branches between every part of the program. If you do this with a high degree of uniformity, then the watermark code will be as tightly bound to the rest of the program as every other piece of code. The disadvantage is that you need to introduce many opaque predicates. It is also difficult to apply to typed bytecode, since you cannot directly jump from one method into the middle of another method, and the type system may prevent you from certain complex control flow within a method. This is true in Java, for example, where you have to be careful not to introduce control flow that violates the verifier rules.

A simpler idea [345,346] is to give the appearance that some value computed from your graph is actually used by the surrounding code. Here's an example where we compute an opaque value $k^{=1}$ (k is always equal to 1) from the graph (in light gray) and use that to "modify" the value of n (dark gray). We've also introduced a more direct check on the graph that both ties it closer to the original code and adds some trivial tamperproofing (dashed):

```
public static void main (String args[]) {
    int n = args.length;
    if (args[0].equals("2")) {
        ...
        Node root = new Node(); root.spine = n1;
        Node n2 = new Node(); n1.spine = n2;
        n1.digit = n2; n2.spine = n1; n2.digit = n2;
        ...
        Node p = root.spine; int k = 0;
        while (p.spine != root.spine) {
            p = p.spine; k++;}
        n *= k;
    }
    for (int i=1; i<n; i++) {
        if (args[0].equals(args[i]) &&
            ((root==null)||(root.spine!=root.spine.spine))) {
            System.out.println("YES"); return;
        }
    }
    System.out.println("NO");
}
```

Problem 9.5 How common are weak cuts in real programs? Write a tool to do the necessary analysis and apply it to a randomly chosen set of programs downloaded from the Web. Start with a rigorous definition of *weak cut*.

9.1.6 Discussion

Using WMCT to embed a 20-bit watermark with the radix graph encoding only requires 141 bytes of Java bytecode. But as you've seen, this is only a part of the story. Once you've cycled the graph, added code to tie it to the rest of the program, added tamperproofing code, and so on, the increase in code size will be much more substantial. As a result, of course, the authors' claim for the stealth of the algorithm

("Real OO programs have lots of news and pointer assignments in them, so if you add more of that, how bad can it get?") is no longer so obviously valid.

Any performance overhead due to this algorithm should be minimal. The graph-building code is executed only for the special input, and so the only source of overhead is executing the guards that determine if you're on the special path or not.

The chief advantage of the algorithm is that the watermark resides in the data-space of the program rather than in the code space, as you saw for the static algorithms in the last chapter. This gives you a much higher degree of freedom in designing stealthy tamperproofing techniques. Checking that a variable has a particular value is much more common in real programs than checking that a piece of code hasn't been modified!

Unless you have a *very* careful implementation of this algorithm, it's reasonable to believe that the most simple and therefore serious attacks will look for telltale code signatures. If you can't hide that a particular node type has multiple outgoing pointers, the first thing an attacker will do is scan the code for allocations of such nodes. And unless your graph is very small or you're able to spread the graph-building code over a large area, the attacker will certainly scan for multiple news within the same method.

This algorithm, and its implementation, gives valuable insight into the difficulty of software watermarking in general. As this section has shown, it is difficult to get high stealth, resilience, and bitrate all at the same time. Also, you've seen that not all watermarking algorithms will be appropriate for all programs—WMCT should work well for object oriented programs that do much dynamic allocation. It should be much less appropriate for mostly numeric programs.

Problem 9.6   Implement WMCT in a weakly typed language such as C or C++. What makes embedding and recognition easier and harder than in a typed language implementation? Which attacks become easier and harder? What tricks can you play with the type system to improve resilience to attack?

9.2   Algorithm *WMNT*: Exploiting Parallelism

The adversary's goal is to analyze and understand enough of your program to be able to apply a transformation that makes your watermark unrecognizable, while otherwise maintaining semantics. *Your* goal is to make this analysis as hard as possible. In the previous section, you learned how to make de-watermarking difficult by basing the algorithm on a known hard static analysis problem, pointer analysis.

In Algorithm WMNT [264,265], watermark resilience is instead based on the difficulty of analyzing multi-threaded programs. The idea is to embed new threads into single-threaded portions of your program so that when given the right input, the dynamic behavior of the threads is distinctive and encodes the watermark.

How can you control the dynamic behavior of threads and make them distinctive? You could introduce code that explicitly starts and stops threads to exhibit a distinctive pattern, but such code would be very unstealthy. Most programs do not often attempt to start and stop threads explicitly. Even in languages like Java where multi-threading is an integral part of the language, starting and stopping threads is rare and even discouraged. We can do better using *locks*, a device commonly used in multi-threaded programs.

Locks control access to variables and sections of code. In an unsynchronized multi-threaded program, two or more threads may try to read or write to the same area of memory or try to use resources simultaneously. This results in a *race condition*, a situation in which two or more threads or processes are reading or writing some shared data and where the final result depends on the timing and scheduling of the threads.

A *mutual exclusion* object (usually called a *mutex*) is a type of lock typically used by different threads to share resources in a controlled manner and get around the problem of race conditions. It allows only one thread to execute a piece of code at a time. A mutex has two states, *locked* and *unlocked*. Threads adopt a convention where before a thread uses a shared resource, it locks the corresponding mutex. Other threads attempting to lock a locked mutex will block and wait until the original thread unlocks it. Once the mutex is unlocked, the queued threads contend to acquire the lock on the mutex. Which thread gets to run is decided by priority, order of execution, or by some other algorithm. The nature of multi-threaded execution, and the number of factors that can affect the timing of thread execution, means that which thread acquires the lock is difficult to predict and appears to be largely random [277].

How does WMNT use locks to embed a watermark? Let's start by trying to influence which threads execute which blocks merely by manipulating the nesting of locks.

Suppose you have the trivial `run` method shown in Listing 9.1▶567 (a). This method simply calls two methods, `blockA` and `blockB`. To build a watermark that relies on threading behavior, you need more threads of execution. Let's introduce two threads to execute these blocks. You can see this in Listing 9.1▶567 (b). You have to introduce additional monitors and predicates to ensure that the program remains semantically equivalent to the original. You also have to introduce a call to

Listing 9.1 Three semantically equivalent programs illustrating how Algorithm
WMNT controls thread behavior. In (a), a single thread executes blockA and blockB
sequentially. In (b), blockA and blockB get executed sequentially by either thread
t0 or t1. In (d), blockA and blockB get executed sequentially, but the same thread
executes both blocks. Can you fill in the missing block with a program that causes
different threads to execute blockA and blockB sequentially?

```
                                      boolean doneA = false;
                                      boolean doneB = false;
                                      Mutex mutex2 = new Mutex();
                                      Mutex mutex1 = new Mutex();
public void run () {                  public void run () {
                                        Thread t0 = new Thread () {
                                          public void run () {
                                            lock mutex1;
                                              if ( !doneA ) {
    blockA();                                  blockA(); doneA = true;
                                              }
                                            unlock mutex1;
                                            lock mutex2;
                                              if ( !doneB ) {
    blockB();                                   blockB(); doneB = true;
                                              }
                                            unlock mutex2;
                                          }
                                        };
                                        Thread t1 = new Thread ( t0 );
                                        t1.start(); t0.start();
                                        t1.join();  t0.join();
}                                     }

            (a)                                   (b)


                                      boolean doneA = false;
                                      boolean doneB = false;
                                      Mutex mutex2 = new Mutex();
                                      Mutex mutex1 = new Mutex();
                                      public void run () {
                                        Thread t0 = new Thread () {
                                          public void run () {
                                            lock mutex1
                                              if ( !doneA ) {
                                                blockA(); doneA = true;
                                              }
             ?                                lock mutex2;
                                            unlock mutex1;
                                              if ( !doneB ) {
                                                blockB(); doneB = true;
                                              }
                                            unlock mutex2;
                                        } };
                                        Thread t1 = new Thread ( t0 );
                                        t1.start(); t0.start();
                                        t1.join();  t0.join();
                                      }

            (c)                                   (d)
```

join(), which forces the main thread to block until the child threads t1 and t2 have completed executing.

Notice that this new program has four possible combinations in which threads t1 and t2 can execute the functions blockA and blockB. First, either thread t1 or t2 will win the contention for mutex1, and the winning thread executes the function blockA. Second, once mutex1 has been released, both threads will contend for mutex2, and the winning thread gets to execute blockB. So you get the following four possible execution orders:

1	2	3	4
t1: blockA	t1: blockA	t2: blockA	t2: blockA
t1: blockB	t2: blockB	t1: blockB	t2: blockB

This is the way in which monitors are usually used, but it turns out that this isn't particularly useful to us.

Now have a look at the light gray code in Listing 9.1▸567 (d), where we've switched the order in which you lock and release the monitors. This code is almost identical to (b) and is in fact semantically equivalent—they both execute blockA and blockB sequentially. Now, however, whichever thread wins the first contention and then locks on mutex1 is the *only* thread that tries to lock mutex2. The losing thread is still waiting on mutex1, so the winning thread is guaranteed to win again! This means that whichever thread executes blockA also executes blockB. Since there are only two threads, there are now only two possible paths:

1	2
t1: blockA	t2: blockA
t1: blockB	t2: blockB

The two snippets are very similar, differing only in the order of lock operations. If you had a snippet of code (c) that caused different threads to execute different blocks, you would be able to distinguish the behavior of (b) from (d) at runtime solely by watching their execution. You could use this distinction in behavior to dynamically decode a bit of the watermark. Of course, you would still have the problem that the snippets are *statically* different, but later you'll will see how to overcome this problem.

Problem 9.7 Write the missing code snippet in Listing 9.1▸567 (c) that uses only lock and unlock calls to guarantee two different threads will execute blockA and `blockB`. Are two threads sufficient to encode a bit in this way? What problems arise when using only two threads?

To make Algorithm WMNT useful, there are several hurdles to overcome. First, it turns out that using two threads as in the examples above is not enough to robustly recognize a watermark—how can you tell which thread is which? In the next section, we'll show you the widget that WMNT uses to encode a single bit of the watermark using three blocks. The idea is that if all three blocks are run by different threads, a 0-bit is encoded, but if two blocks are run by the same thread, a 1-bit is encoded.

The second problem is how to find suitable embedding locations. We solve this, as in WMCT, by running the program with the special key input sequence under tracing. From the trace we pick out blocks that can be run in separate threads, thereby embedding the mark.

The third problem is stealth. In a simple implementation of WMNT, the watermark widgets that embed a 0-bit are, unfortunately, statically different from those that embed a 1! In Section 9.2.4▶579, you'll see how to overcome these problems using opaque predicates.

9.2.1 Embedding Watermarking Widgets

To embed a thread-based watermark, you need a widget that uses locking to encode a single watermark bit. The widget executes an existing block in the program using three threads. Locks will ensure that the original semantics of the program are maintained. Let's adopt the convention that if the same thread executes the three blocks of the widget, it encodes a 0-bit and if the same thread executes the first and third blocks, and a different thread executes the second block, it encodes a 1-bit. We've illustrated this in Figure 9.4▶570.

There are several features that you would like these widgets to have. They must be difficult to distinguish from each other, and they should incorporate some part of the original program. This way, even if the adversary identifies the watermarking code, he cannot simply rip it out of the program. Listing 9.2▶571 shows the two widgets that encode a 0-bit and a 1-bit, respectively. To embed a watermarking bit w into a basic block B, you do the following:

1. Divide B into three sequential pieces: A, B, and C;

2. Replace B with the appropriate widget;

3. Replace `pieceA`, `pieceB`, and `pieceC` (in dotted) in the widget with A, B, and C, respectively.

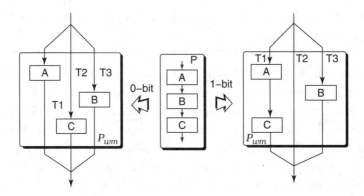

Figure 9.4 Overview of how different threads execute each of the pieces in a 0-bit and 1-bit watermarking widget in WMNT.

The widgets will execute the pieces sequentially. Figures 9.5 ▸572 and 9.6 ▸573 show the runtime behavior of the widgets for a 0-bit widget and a 1-bit widget, respectively.

Have a look at the code for the 0-bit widget in Listing 9.2 ▸571 (a). Notice how the three new threads contend for `mutex0` and how the winner proceeds to execute the first predicate. This causes `pieceA` to be executed by the winner, while the other threads wait. The winning thread then executes `pieceA` and sets `doneA` to be true. It can do this confident that none of the other threads will attempt to read the value of `doneA` until it releases `mutex0`. Similarly, the winning thread is guaranteed to acquire a lock on `mutex1`.

As you follow the rest of the execution of the program, notice that the two widgets differ from each other only on the three monitor instructions, highlighted in dark gray, and the predicate, highlighted in light gray. These differences are responsible for the different thread behavior that encodes the watermark bit. While any thread can win the contention for `mutex0`, the order of the remaining lock and unlock calls are forced. The two static differences between our widgets are responsible for the different thread behavior. You can dynamically detect and decode these differences as a watermark.

Now that you can embed a single bit watermark, we can give an algorithm for embedding your watermark bit string using these widgets (see Algorithm 9.2 ▸574). For the watermark bit string to be recognized correctly, the widgets that correspond to bits in the watermark must be executed in the correct order. To ensure this, you collect a trace of your program run using the secret key input and select a subsequence of blocks from the trace in which to embed your widgets.

Listing 9.2 Watermarking widgets for Algorithm WMNT. Snippet (a) encodes a 0-bit and (b) a 1-bit watermark. The pieces highlighted in dotted are replaced with code from the original program. The differences between the two widgets are highlighted in light gray and dark gray.

```
boolean doneA=false;              boolean doneA=false;
boolean doneB=false;              boolean doneB=false;
boolean doneC=false;              boolean doneC=false;
boolean doneD=false;              boolean doneD=false;

Object mutex0 = new Object();     Object mutex0 = new Object();
Object mutex1 = new Object();     Object mutex1 = new Object();
Object mutex2 = new Object();     Object mutex2 = new Object();

monitorenter ( mutex0 );          monitorenter ( mutex0 );
if ( !doneA ) {                   if ( !doneA ) {
  pieceA;                           pieceA;
  doneA = true;                     doneA = true;
  monitorenter ( mutex1 );          monitorenter ( mutex1 );
  monitorexit ( mutex0 );           monitorexit ( mutex0 );
  monitorenter ( mutex_orig );      monitorenter ( mutex_orig );
  monitorexit ( mutex_orig );       monitorexit ( mutex_orig );
}                                 }
if ( !doneB ) {                   if ( !doneB ) {
  pieceB;                           pieceB;
  doneB = true;                     doneB = true;
  monitorexit ( mutex0 );           monitorexit ( mutex0 );
  monitorenter ( mutex1 );          monitorenter ( mutex1 );
}                                 }
if (((doneC || doneD))) {         if (( (!doneC) )) {
  doneC = !doneC;                   doneC = !doneC;
  if ( doneD )                      if ( doneD )
    monitorexit ( mutex1 );           monitorexit ( mutex1 );
  else {                            else {
doneD = !doneD;                   doneD = !doneD;
    monitorenter ( mutex2 );          monitorenter ( mutex2 );
    monitorexit     ( mutex2 );       monitorexit     ( mutex0 );
    monitorexit     ( mutex1 );       monitorexit     ( mutex2 );
}                                 }
} else {                          } else {
  pieceC;                           pieceC;
  doneC = !doneC;                   doneC = !doneC;
  monitorexit ( mutex0 );           monitorexit ( mutex1 );
}                                 }
             (a)                               (b)
```

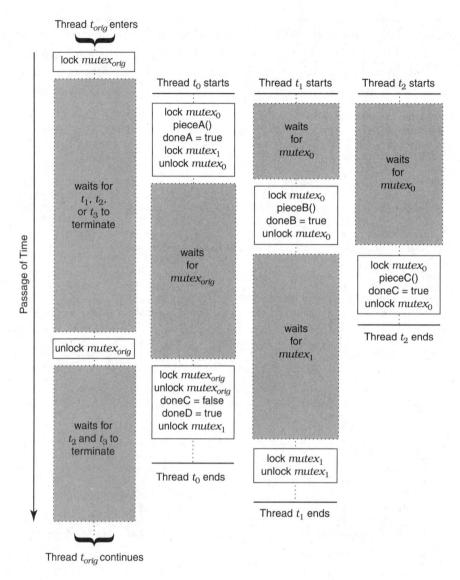

Figure 9.5 The dynamic behavior of watermarking code that embeds a 0 bit. Different threads execute pieceA, pieceB, and pieceC. Note that all lock acquisitions and releases are well paired and no dead locks occur.

The trace of the program P with the key input I selects a path through the program. From this trace you choose r blocks, where r is the number of bits in your watermark bit-string, and for every chosen block you embed the watermarking widget that corresponds to each bit. When you attempt to do this, you will find that

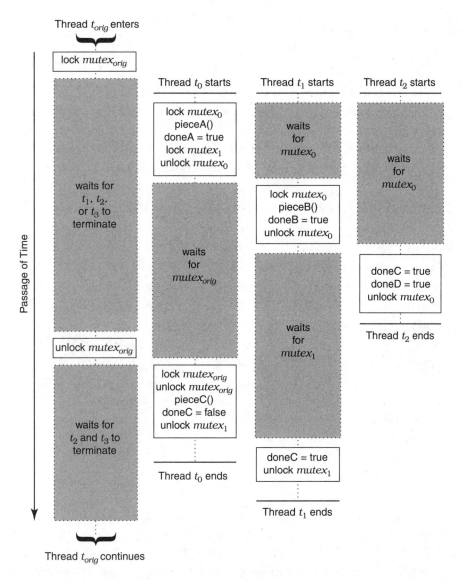

Figure 9.6 The dynamic behavior of watermarking code that embeds a 1 bit. The same threads execute pieceA and pieceC, and a different thread executes pieceB. Note that all lock acquisitions and releases are well paired and no deadlocks occur.

if you select blocks that occur more than once in a trace, watermark bits that you embed early may conflict with watermark bits that you try to embed later. To avoid this situation, you should simply avoid selecting basic blocks that occur multiple times in a trace.

Algorithm 9.2 Overview of Algorithm WMNT.

EMBED(P,W,I):

1. Let t be a trace of P run with the secret input I. The trace contains a list of every basic block executed and the ID of the thread that executes it.
2. Encode W as a bit string $w_1, w_2, \cdots, w_r$.
3. Select r blocks in t and divide each into three pieces, pieceA$_r$, pieceB$_r$, and pieceC$_r$.
4. For each w_i, if w_i is 0, replace the basic block with the code in Listing 9.2▶571 (a) else replace the basic block with the code in Listing 9.2▶571 (b).

RECOGNIZE(P,I):

1. Annotate every `lock` call in the program so that when executed, it stores a tuple (LOCK, obj$_i$, T_i), where obj$_i$ is the object being locked and T_i is the ID of the thread that executes the call.
2. Annotate every `unlock` call in the program so that when executed, it stores a tuple (UNLOCK, obj$_i$, T_i), where obj$_i$ is the object being unlocked and T_i is the ID of the thread that executes the call.
3. Execute the program P with key input I, retaining a record of its trace $D = [(op_1, obj_1, T_1), (op_2, obj_2, T_2), \dots]$ where op$_i$ is either "LOCK" or "UNLOCK".
4. Decode the watermark from D, searching for the patterns in Table 9.1▶578 and recognizing a 0 bit or 1 bit, respectively.

Problem 9.8   If you had a choice of programming language in which to implement WMNT, which language features would you look for that would make it especially suitable? What aspects of the language would make the technique harder to implement? What language features would make an implementation less stealthy?

9.2.2 Embedding Example

To illustrate the embedding process, let's watermark the program N shown in Listing 9.3▶575. We want to embed the number 2, which we'll represent as the bit string 10_2 in this program. Let's pick $\langle 1, 3, 1, 4, 1 \rangle$ as our secret key input, which will cause the watermark to be expressed.

Listing 9.3 A single-threaded example program N used to illustrate Algorithm WMNT.

```
public class N {

  public static String nth ( int i ) {
    String nth = "";
    if ( i == 2 )
      nth_B1: nth = "nd";
    else if ( i == 3 )
      nth_B2: nth = "rd";
    else
      nth_B3: nth = "th";
    nth_B4: return i + nth;
  }

  public static void main (String args[]) {
    for (int i=1; i<args.length; i++) {
      if (args[0].equals(args[i])) {
          String nth;
          main_B1: nth = nth ( i );
                   System.out.println("YES");
                   System.out.println( args[0] + " is " + nth );
        return;
      }
    }
    main_B2: System.out.println("NO");
  }
}
```

Now you can start the process of watermarking. The first thing you will need to know is which basic blocks get executed when we run the program with the secret input. So you collect a trace in which you record the basic blocks as they get executed, and the ID of the thread that executes it. Keep in mind that in a single-threaded program, basic blocks may not always be executed in the same order even when given the same input. For example, a program may depend on the current time, random numbers, or the timing of the network or hard-disk, or other unpredictable values. In a multi-threaded program, this problem is greatly exaggerated. Any two threads in a program may interleave in an exponentially large number of ways. You can minimize the effect by recording the ID of the thread that is executing a block. In many well-written programs free of race conditions, the order of basic blocks that are executed by a single thread is, in fact, deterministic. In a typical real-life program, there will be a large number of basic blocks in the trace. From this trace, you will select *n* basic blocks in which to embed the *n*-bit watermark.

In our example program N in Listing 9.3▶575, there is only a single thread of execution. Before you can start the embedding, you need to perform a control flow analysis and determine the basic blocks in the program. In Listing 9.3▶575, we've identified the blocks with labels. You then execute the program with the secret input ⟨1, 3, 1, 4, 1⟩, which gets you the following trace:

```
> java N 1 3 1 4 1
YES
```

#	Block ID	Thread ID
1	main.B1	thread_1
2	nth.B3	thread_1
3	nth.B4	thread_1

On a non-watermark-expressing input sequence, you would get a different basic block trace:

```
> java N 2 3 4 5 3
NO
```

#	Block ID	Thread ID
1	main_B2	thread_1

From the trace, you choose blocks in which to embed your watermark bit string 10_2. Let's choose blocks main.B1 and nth.B3. Block main.B1 consists of three statements, and you can divide it easily into three pieces, each consisting of a single statement. Block nth.B3 has only a single statement. To break it into three pieces, you can either leave two of them empty or you can first add two bogus statements. For simplicity, let's keep two of the pieces of nth.B3 empty.

You now remove from the program the block that occurs first in the trace, main.B1, and replace it with a 1-bit widget. Within this widget, you replace occurrences of pieceA, pieceB, and pieceC with the three statements from main.B1, respectively:

```
pieceA   ⇒   nth = nth(i)
pieceB   ⇒   System.out.println(''YES'')
pieceC   ⇒   System.out.println(args[0]+'' is ''+nth)
```

Similarly, you replace the second block in the trace, nth.B3, with a 0-bit widget. Within the widget you replace pieceA with nth=''th'' and leave pieceB and pieceC empty.

Now, when the program is run it will execute and produce output identical to the original. In addition, when it is run with your secret input, the 1-bit widget will be executed followed by the 0-bit widget. In the next section, you will see how to recognize the watermark that is expressed as a result of the embedding.

9.2.3 Recognition

To recognize the mark, you start by collecting a trace of the threading behavior of the program when executing with the secret key input. The presence of the watermark should be evident in the threading behavior of the program, but how do you extract this from the trace? You could search through the trace and find those instances where the same thread executed consecutive basic blocks. Each instance would be decoded as a 0-bit of the watermark. However, you have to keep in mind that such sequences may occur very often in a program irrespective of whether it carries your watermark. Also, an attacker could easily split basic blocks using dummy `if`-statements, and this would lead to spurious bits being inserted into the watermark.

One way of working around this problem is to try to recognize and filter out the spurious signals. We will show an example of how to do this when we discuss WMCCDKHLS$_{paths}$, later in this chapter. In this section, we will use an alternate solution. Have a look at Table 9.1▶578, which gives the lock and unlock calls produced by our watermarking widgets. Notice that the patterns of these calls are different from each other. To identify our watermark bits, you can scan through our trace, searching for these patterns of lock and unlock calls.

You need the trace to include information about the threading behavior of the program. You annotate every occurrence of the `lock` and `unlock` instructions so that it records the object being locked or unlocked and the thread ID, T_i, which executes the call. You then execute the program with your secret input I and collect the resulting trace.

Some of these `lock` and `unlock` calls are from the embedding of the encoded watermark, while others are from the original program. However, you cannot guarantee that the thread IDs you see will be the same as they were when you watermarked the program. An attacker may have renamed some of these threads. Indeed, even the operating system may choose to allocate thread IDs differently. What you *can* search for, however, is the pattern of calls that have to be preserved. For this reason, we do not explicitly name the threads we are searching for in Table 9.1▶578, calling them T_W - T_Z instead.

There are different ways you could search through the trace for these patterns. For example, you could use a regular expression to search for the start of a watermark widget by searching for three lock calls on three different monitors. The full regular expression would find the complete pattern shown in Table 9.1▶578. A regular expression is built for each set of four thread IDs that are found in the

Table 9.1 The dynamic pattern of lock and unlock calls made by 0-bit and 1-bit encoding widgets in Algorithm WMNT.

	0-bit widget			1-bit widget	
Call	Mutex	Thread ID	Call	Mutex	Thread ID
lock	`mutex_w`	T_W	lock	`mutex_w`	T_W
lock	`mutex_x`	T_X	lock	`mutex_x`	T_X
lock	`mutex_y`	T_X	lock	`mutex_y`	T_X
unlock	`mutex_x`	T_X	unlock	`mutex_x`	T_X
lock	`mutex_x`	T_Y	lock	`mutex_x`	T_Y
unlock	`mutex_x`	T_Y	unlock	`mutex_x`	T_Y
lock	`mutex_x`	T_Z	lock	`mutex_x`	T_Z
unlock	`mutex_x`	T_Z	lock	`mutex_z`	T_Z
unlock	`mutex_w`	T_W	unlock	`mutex_x`	T_Z
lock	`mutex_w`	T_X	unlock	`mutex_z`	T_Z
unlock	`mutex_w`	T_X	unlock	`mutex_w`	T_W
lock	`mutex_z`	T_X	lock	`mutex_w`	T_X
unlock	`mutex_z`	T_X	unlock	`mutex_w`	T_X
unlock	`mutex_y`	T_X	unlock	`mutex_y`	T_X
lock	`mutex_y`	T_Y	lock	`mutex_y`	T_Y
unlock	`mutex_y`	T_Y	unlock	`mutex_y`	T_Y

trace. If one of these regular expressions successfully recognizes a substring in the trace, that substring is decoded as the corresponding bit. You continue to decode consecutive bits in the trace until all watermark bits have been identified.

At this point, you may wonder how to deal with the situation where more than one watermark string is found. Certainly the watermarker may know the string that she embedded in the program and check that it occurs in the set of watermarks that are found. However, the credibility of a recognizer that outputs a large set of "potential" watermarks may be called into question. Using the sparse code tables we showed you in Section 8.9.3 ▶531 to encode the mark can solve this problem.

There is an additional benefit of using the sparse code tables—it helps prevent an attacker from inserting random bits into the watermark using his own lock and unlock calls. At first glance, it may seem that an attacker can introduce as many lock and unlock calls as needed until your recognition fails. However, this is not really the case. The attacker has to lock and unlock some monitor that he knows is not being used—otherwise he runs the risk of causing deadlock! For example, if he tries to introduce a new lock on mutex$_{\text{orig}}$ anywhere inside a widget, the widget will no longer function correctly. Alternatively, he can attempt to lock a newly created mutex, which he can guarantee is unlocked in the hope of obscuring the recognition. However, in order for the recognizer to report some decoding of an armored watermark as correct, it must also occur in your random code table. This is highly unlikely to occur by chance and is difficult for an attacker to force.

9.2.4 Avoiding Pattern-Matching Attacks

If you compare the two widgets in Listing 9.2 ▶ 571 closely, you can see that there are detectable differences between the widgets that embed a 0 bit and a 1 bit. An attacker can use these differences to statically distinguish between them. In this section, we will show how to use opaque predicates to eliminate these apparent differences between the two watermarking widgets. If your library of opaque predicates is such that the opaquely true and opaquely false predicates resemble each other, then an attacker would not be able to use pattern-matching attacks to statically read, eliminate, or modify the watermarks. Also, for reasons of stealth, it must not be obvious to the attacker which predicates are opaque (and need to be attacked) and which predicates are real (and must be maintained for program correctness). In other words, you need the predicates to appear similar to predicates that already appear in your program. If the original program contains some pointer manipulation, it makes sense to use the algorithm from Section 4.4.3 ▶ 251, which creates opaque predicates from a combination of threading and aliasing effects.

You can use the opaque predicates to eliminate the static differences between the 0-bit and 1-bit watermark widgets. In Listing 9.2 ▶ 571, we've marked the differences between the widgets in dark gray and light gray. They occur in the predicate and in the choice of monitors that are unlocked.

Let's eliminate the statically analyzable difference between the monitors first. To do this, replace the monitorexit calls using the following construction:

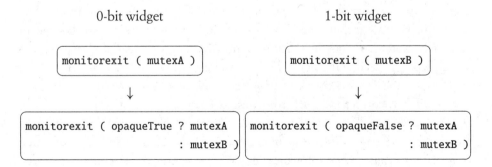

The attacker can't distinguish between these constructions without deciphering the opaque predicates. Similarly, you can take advantage of opaque predicates to erase the differences between the two predicates, as follows:

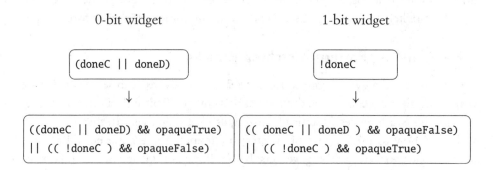

0-bit widget   1-bit widget

```
(doneC || doneD)
```

```
!doneC
```

↓   ↓

```
((doneC || doneD) && opaqueTrue)
|| (( !doneC ) && opaqueFalse)
```

```
(( doneC || doneD ) && opaqueFalse)
|| (( !doneC ) && opaqueTrue)
```

With these changes, the watermarking widgets are now statically indistinguishable from each other and more resistant to pattern-matching attacks.

9.2.5 Tamperproofing Widgets

Now that we have addressed the problem of distinguishing 0-bit widgets from 1-bit widgets, let us put ourselves back in the place of an attacker. How would he likely attempt to remove a WMNT watermark? One obvious way is to locate all the thread-based watermarking widgets in a program and just remove them. After all, the widgets are quite distinctive, and you could pattern match on them, identifying the three original pieces of executable code within them, and replace the widget with a concatenation of these three pieces.

To defend against such an attack, you have to make the widgets harder to locate. With WMCT watermarks, we did this by making the watermarking code look like the rest of the program. We chose to use linked graph data structures to encode the watermark in a program that already contains linked graph data structures. For Algorithm WMNT, we will use a different technique. Instead of making the watermark look like the rest of the program, we will add a large amount of tamperproofing code that looks like the watermark! While the tamperproofing widgets will look like watermarking widgets, the pieces of executable code they will contain will be incorrect. We will further design the locks such that the incorrect code never gets executed. This means that if an attacker tries to turn everything that looks like a watermark widget into straight code, he will also turn these tamperproofing widgets into straight code. However, now the semantic errors contained in the program will get executed.

Algorithm 9.3▸581 shows how to embed these widgets in a program. The tamperproofing widgets themselves, shown in Listing 9.4▸582, are statically similar to a watermarking widget. The number of tamperproofing blocks is chosen by the user.

Algorithm 9.3 Embedding tamperproofing widgets in Algorithm WMNT.

EMBEDTAMPERPROOFWIDGETS(t, N_{tamper}):

1. Select N_{tamper} blocks from the trace t. N_{tamper} is a user-configured number of tamperproofing widgets that will be inserted into the trace. The tamperproofing widgets will be inserted following each selected block.

2. For every selected basic block:

   - Generate three new basic blocks of stealthy but incorrect code called `pieceA`, `pieceB`, and `pieceC`.

   - Create a new copy of the code shown in Listing 9.4▸582 with the newly generated `pieceA`, `pieceB`, and `pieceC`.

   - Append the new widget following the selected basic block.

A large number of tamperproofing blocks makes it harder for an attacker to find the true watermark widgets. However, they also slow down the program considerably.

Finally, you need to generate incorrect code to embed in the tamperproofing widgets. For example, you could assign random values to live variables, use an appropriate basic block from elsewhere in the method, or execute code that has user observable side effects.

Notice how similar the tamperproofing widget is to the watermarking widgets. We have used the opaque predicate trick from the previous section to ensure that there are no statically detectable differences between watermarking and tamperproofing widgets that would make it possible for an attacker to distinguish between them.

9.2.6 Discussion

As you saw in Listing 9.2▸571, embedding a WMNT watermark entails the addition of a large amount of code. Every 16 bits of watermark requires 18 kilobytes of Java bytecode. In addition, WMNT needs to add a large number of tamperproofing widgets to distract an attacker. Each of these tamperproofing widgets is also 18 kilobytes in size. They further require the use of opaque predicates. The implementation of opaque predicate that the authors use has an overhead of an additional class of 884 bytes. This class can be instantiated and reused by all opaque predicates in a program. Each use of an opaque predicates requires 108 bytes. All in all, this algorithm considerably bloats the size of an application.

Listing 9.4 Tamperproofing code for Algorithm WMNT that embeds neither a 0 bit nor a 1 bit. The `pieceA`, `pieceB`, and `pieceC` slots will be replaced by never-executed incorrect code.

```
boolean doneA = opaqueTrue;
boolean doneB = opaqueTrue;
boolean doneC = opaqueFalse;
boolean doneD = opaqueFalse;
Object mutex0 = new Object ();
Object mutex1 = new Object ();
Object mutex2 = new Object();
monitorenter ( mutex0 );
if ( !doneA ) {
  pieceA;   doneA = !doneA;
  monitorenter ( mutex1 );
  monitorexit ( mutex0 );
  monitorenter ( mutex_orig );
  monitorexit ( mutex_orig );
}
if ( !doneB ) {
  pieceB;   doneB = !doneB;
  monitorexit ( mutex0 );
  monitorenter ( mutex1 );
}
if ( ( ( doneC || doneD ) && opaqueFalse  ) ||
      ( (     ! doneC     ) && opaqueTrue  ) ||
      opaqueTrue ) {
  doneC = !doneC;
  if ( doneD )
    monitorexit ( opaqueTrue ? mutex0 : mutex1 );
  else {
    doneD = !doneD;
    monitorenter ( mutex2 );
    monitorexit  ( opaqueTrue  ? mutex0 : mutex2 );
    monitorexit  ( opaqueFalse ? mutex1 : mutex2 );
  }
} else {
  pieceC;   doneC = !doneC;
  monitorexit ( mutex1 );
}
```

The large number of threads in each of these widgets has another unfortunate effect: It can significantly increase the performance cost of creating new threads. WMNT also relies heavily on increasing the potential thread-contention in a program. In older versions of Sun's JVM, prior to version 1.5, this introduces a significant and measurable slowdown in a program. This makes WMNT a poor choice for applications where speed is critical.

The key advantage of WMNT is that the analysis required by multi-threaded applications is significant, minimizing the number of tools available to an attacker. What is more, the algorithm addresses the stealth problem we identified in WMCT. Instead of trying to make the watermark stealthy, WMNT increases the number of other components in the program that appear similar to the watermark but behave differently. This shifts the security of the scheme from the inability to distinguish the watermark from the rest of the program to the inability to distinguish the watermark from tamperproofing code.

The major disadvantage of this scheme is that it aims to be secure only against static analysis. Against an attacker who has the ability to execute the program, WMNT may fail very easily. In particular, the tamperproofing and watermarking widgets can easily be distinguished from the rest of the program. On a given input that results in the execution of these widgets, it's easy for an attacker to tell whether the pieces embedded within the program are executed or not, and thus he can distinguish tamperproofing widgets and watermarking widgets quickly.

Problem 9.9   Implement WMNT in a language (such as Erlang) designed to handle thousands of simultaneous threads. Is the overhead different than for a Java-based implementation?

9.3 Algorithm *WMCCDKHLS*~paths~: Expanding Execution Paths

The language structure in which WMCCDKHLS~paths~ [78] encodes the watermark is *forward branches*. The thinking is that there are lots of if-statements in a program, so adding a few more couldn't hurt. Encoding can be relatively straightforward. For example, to embed a bit, you could just add an extra bogus branch to the program. On the special input, the branch should be taken for a 1 bit and fall through for a 0 bit (however, see below why this simple scheme is a bad idea!). The attack model is that the adversary can disrupt the watermark by adding branches to the program himself, since if *you* can, you have to assume that so can he! Algorithm 9.4 uses the error-correcting watermark-splitting algorithm of Section 8.9.2▸528 to protect the watermark. The idea is to split the mark into many redundant pieces that are spread throughout the program, and during recognition, to use the error-correcting code to ensure that only a subset of the pieces is necessary to recover the mark.

Algorithm 9.4 Overview of algorithm WMCCDKHLS$_{\text{paths}}$. P is the original program, P_w is the watermarked program, W is the watermark, and I is the secret input sequence.

EMBED(P, W, I):

1. Let t be a trace of P run with the secret input I. The trace contains a list of every basic block executed and current values of available variables at block entry points.

2. Split W into a redundant unordered set of integer pieces $w_1, w_2, \cdots, w_r$ using the splitting algorithm from Section 8.9.2 ▸528.

3. Turn each w_i into code with a branching pattern that will trace out the bits of w_i. WMCCDKHLS$_{\text{paths}}$ uses either a linear sequence of if-statements or a loop. Using information from the trace, insert the new code at locations encountered on input I.

RECOGNIZE(P_w, I):

1. Let t be a trace of P_w run with the secret input I. The trace contains a list of every basic block executed.

2. Generate a bit sequence from the branching behavior of the trace, and using a sliding window technique, split it into pieces $w_1, w_2, \cdots$.

3. For long traces, there will be a large number of w_i:s. Filter out the ones that are unlikely to be part of the watermark. Combine the remaining w_i:s into the watermark W.

9.3.1 Encoding and Embedding

As usual, let's start by looking at an example. The following program counts the number of times its first command-line argument occurs among the remaining arguments:

```
int R = 0;
int a = parseInt(args[0]);
int i = 1;
while (B1:i < args.length) {
    B2:int b = parseInt(args[i]);
    if (B3:a==b) B4: R++;
    B5:i++;
}
B6:println(R);
```

```
> java M 4 3 1 2 4 6 4 5
2
> java M 4 3 1 2 8 6 9
0
```

Table 9.2 Trace of the original program for algorithm WMCCDKHLS~paths~. The input is 4 3 1 2 4 6 4 5. A $\Rightarrow$ indicates that this is the first time a branch is taken. We've omitted variables a (which doesn't change) and R (which we don't care about).

#	Loc	i	b	Branch	bit	#	Loc	i	b	Branch	bit
0	B1	1		B1→B2	⇒B2	16	B5	4	4		
1	B2	1				17	B1	5		B1→B2	0
2	B3	1	3	B3→B5	⇒B5	18	B2	5			
3	B5	1	3			19	B3	5	6	B3→B5	0
4	B1	2		B1→B2	0	20	B5	5	6		
5	B2	2				21	B1	6		B1→B2	0
6	B3	2	1	B3→B5	0	22	B2	6			
7	B5	2	1			23	B3	6	4	B3→B4	1
8	B1	3		B1→B2	0	24	B4	6	4		
9	B2	3				25	B5	6	4		
10	B3	3	2	B3→B5	0	26	B1	7		B1→B2	0
11	B5	3	2			27	B2	7			
12	B1	4		B1→B2	0	28	B3	7	5	B3→B5	0
13	B2	4				29	B5	7	5		
14	B3	4	4	B3→B4	1	30	B1	8		B1→B6	1
15	B4	4	4			31	B6	8			

We've added labels (in light gray) in order to be able to refer to locations within the code. In Table 9.2, you can see what happens when you trace the program with this input sequence. We've listed the basic blocks in the order they get executed, and the changing values of variables i and b. We will use traces like this during embedding (to find places where we can insert new branches to encode the mark) and during recognition (to extract the branching patterns that encode the mark).

An important step of the algorithm is to extract a bit string from the conditional forward branches that get executed for the special input. We ignore all backwards branches, since these indicate loops, and the adversary could easily confuse us by loop unrolling and other loop transformations. There are numerous ways of extracting a bit sequence from the executing branches, but you have to be careful not to leave yourself open to trivial attacks. Say, for example, that you do the obvious thing and write down a 0 every time a branch is taken and a 1 when it's not. To destroy your mark, the adversary can simply invert the branch condition, changing some of your if (P) T else E into if $(!P)$ E else T! There is an alternative encoding that gets around this attack: Record the outcome of the branch the first time it was executed and compute a bit from subsequent executions, a 0 bit if it goes the same way as the first time, a 1 bit otherwise. For example, consider the trace in Table 9.2▶585. When you take the branch from B1 (trace point #0) the first time, you don't generate a bit but simply record that you jumped to block B2. For the subsequent six times that you do the test at B1 (trace points #4,8,12,17,21,26), you also jump to B2, which generates six 0 bits. The seventh time, at trace point 30, you instead jump to B6, which therefore generates a 1 bit. The full trace generates the bit sequence 0000010001001.

To embed a watermark simply requires you to add new branches to the program that don't change its behavior but add the watermark bits to the trace when the program is run with the special input. WMCCDKHLS$_{paths}$ has two ways of encoding the watermark bits, as a sequence of if-statements (one per bit of watermark) and as a loop.

Let's say you want to embed the watermark 10010_2 at location B4 in the example program. At B4, there are the three available interesting user variables a, b, and i that you can potentially reuse to encode your bits. You look at the trace in Table 9.2▶585 and notice that the first time execution passes B4 (trace point #15), a=b=i=4, and the second time (trace point #24), a=b=4,i=6. Perfect! Now all you have to do to embed 10010_2 is to insert these branches:

```
int u = 0;
if (A0:i==b) A1:u++;
if (A2:a==b) A3:u++;
if (A4:a==b) A5:u++;
if (A6:i==b) A7:u++;
if (A8:a==b) A9:u++;
if (P^F) live_var += u;
```

How does this work? The first time you reach A0, i==b and you branch to A1. You don't generate a watermark bit at this point but instead record the fact that A0 was followed by A1. You record the same information for the remainder of the if-statements: A2 is followed by A3, A4 by A5, and so on. The next time you execute these statements, you write down a 0 bit if the branch goes to the same location as the first time, and write down a 1 bit otherwise. At A0, the branch fails (since i=6,b=4) and you branch to A2. Since the first time you branched to A1, you write down a 1 bit. At A2, you generate a 0 bit, since a=b and you branch to A3, just as the first time.

To make sure that a simple static analysis won't decide that these statements are dead code, it's a good idea to bind the generated code to the rest of the program. In this example, we simply added the statement if (P^F) live_var += u where an opaque statement makes it appear as if the variable u is actually being used.

Since the trace gives you exact knowledge of variable values at every point during the recognition run, it's easy to generate arbitrarily complex conditions to confuse a pattern-matching attack. If you need to generate a true statement and the trace tells you that a=4, then you could generate a>0, a&1==0, a!=3, and so on. And once you have several true statements available, you can join them together with a conjunction (&&) to make other true statements. Note that this is different (and easier) than generating opaque predicates that have to be true for a range of input conditions.

Problem 9.10   Depending on the behavior of the original trace, it might be possible to hijack bit strings generated by the unwatermarked program. If, for example, you want to insert 0110110 and the original trace already has 011011, you just have to add one extra branch. How feasible is this? Assuming that your watermark pieces are 64-bit blocks with random distribution of bits, do a preliminary study of the behavior of some real programs to see if they exhibit the required behavior.

You can also encode the watermark as a loop. Let's say you want to insert the five watermark bits 11010_2. During the loop, it will be most convenient to shift out the bits from the right, so first reorder the bits so that the least significant bit becomes the most significant, i.e., 01011_2. Then add a priming 0 bit to the least significant position, which gets you $010110_2 = 16_{16}$. You insert this value into a loop like this:

```
int u = 0;
long bits = 0x16;
for(int k=0; k<6; k++,bits>>=1)
    if ((bitsA&1)==1) A1:u++; else A2:;
if (P^F) live_var+=u;
```

The loop will consider the bits in the order $\langle 0, 1, 1, 0, 1, 0 \rangle$. The first time around the loop, the priming 0 bit is tested; the test fails; and you branch to block A2. The next iteration, you shift out a 1 from the bits variable, and the branch goes to block A1. Since this is different from the priming block, you write down a 1 bit. The next iteration also goes to A1, and so you write down another 1 bit. During the next iteration, however, the test fails, and you branch to A2, the same block as the priming block, and so you write down a 0 bit.

Problem 9.11   Can you think of additional code-generation strategies? If there are only a small number of possible ways to generate the branching sequences, what will the consequences be for the stealthiness of the algorithm?

Now that you have these two embedding techniques available, let's return to our example. Here's what it looks like after it's been watermarked with the three watermark pieces 11010_2 (code in light gray), 10010_2 (dark gray), and 01101_2 (dashed).

```
int u = 0;
long bitsA = 0x16;
for(int k=0; k<6; k++,bitsA>>=1)
    if (B10:(bitsA\&1)==1) B11:u++; else B12:;

int R = 0;
int a = parseInt(args[0]);
int i = 1;
while (B1:i<args.length) {
    B2:int b = parseInt(args[i]);
    if (B3: a==b) {
        B4:R++;
        if (B20:i==b) B21:u++;
        if (B22:a==b) B23:u++;
        if (B24:a==b) B25:u++;
        if (B26:i==b) B27:u++;
        if (B28:a==b) B29:u++;
        B30:
    }
    B5:i++;
}
long bitsB = 0x2c;
for(int k=0; k<6; k++,bitsB>>=1)
    if (B40:(bitsB\&1)==1) B41: u++; else B42:;
B6:println(R);
```

During watermark recognition, you run the program with the special input, and you get a new, longer trace (Table 9.3 ▸589). The result is a new, longer, generated bit sequence where the new watermark pieces have been inserted among the original bits:

0000010001001

⇓

11010 0000010001 10010 001 01101

Table 9.3 Trace of the watermarked program for algorithm WMCCDKHLS$_{paths}$.

#	Loc	i	b	Branch	bit	#	Loc	i	b	Branch	bit
0	B10			B10→B12	⇒B12	38	B30	4	4		
1	B12					39	B5	5	4		
2	B10			B10→B11	1	40	B1	5		B1→B2	0
3	B11					41	B2	5			
4	B10			B10→B11	1	42	B3	5	6	B3→B5	0
5	B11					43	B5	6	6		
6	B10			B10→B12	0	44	B1	6		B1→B2	0
7	B12					45	B2	6			
8	B10			B10→B11	1	46	B3	6	4	B3→B4	1
9	B11					47	B4	6	4		
10	B10			B10→B12	0	48	B20	6	4	B20→B22	1
11	B12					49	B22	6	4	B22→B23	0
12	B1	1		B1→B2	⇒B2	50	B23	6	4		
13	B2	1				51	B24	6	4	B24→B25	0
14	B3	1	3	B3→B5	⇒B5	52	B25	6	4		
15	B5	2	3			53	B26	6	4	B26→B28	1
16	B1	2		B1→B2	0	54	B28	6	4	B28→B29	0
17	B2	2				55	B29	6	4		
18	B3	2	1	B3→B5	0	56	B30	6	4		
19	B5	3	1			57	B5	7	4		
20	B1	3		B1→B2	0	58	B1	7		B1→B2	0
21	B2	3				59	B2	7			
22	B3	3	2	B3→B5	0	60	B3	7	5	B3→B5	0
23	B5	4	2			61	B5	8	5		
24	B1	4		B1→B2	0	62	B1	8		B1→B40	1
25	B2	4				63	B40	8		B40→B42	⇒B42
26	B3	4	4	B3→B4	1	64	B42	8			
27	B4	4	4			65	B40	8		B40→B42	0
28	B20	4	4	B20→B21	⇒B21	66	B42	8			
29	B21	4	4			67	B40	8		B40→B41	1
30	B22	4	4	B22→B23	⇒B23	68	B41	8			
31	B23	4	4			69	B40	8		B40→B41	1
32	B24	4	4	B24→B25	⇒B25	70	B41	8			
33	B25	4	4			71	B40	8		B40→B42	0
34	B26	4	4	B26→B27	⇒B27	72	B42	8			
35	B27	4	4			73	B40	8		B40→B41	1
36	B28	4	4	B28→B29	⇒B29	74	B41	8			
37	B29	4	4			75	B6	8			

The question now, of course, is how do you find these pieces? They certainly won't be shaded for you! One possibility is to insert "framing bits" at the beginning and end of each piece. Similar techniques are used in digital signal processing to indicate the beginning and end of transmission frames. Algorithm WMCCDKHLS$_{\text{paths}}$ uses a different technique: Each watermark piece is expanded to a 64-bit block with randomness properties that lets you, with a high degree of probability, tell a watermark piece from a naturally occurring bit pattern. You can read more about this idea in Section 8.9.2▶528.

Before turning to recognition, there is one more issue to consider in the example above, one that you have probably already noticed—the dark gray code got inserted inside a loop! To avoid potential hot spots, you can profile the program prior to embedding. In the authors' SandMark implementation [78] of WMCCDKHLS$_{\text{paths}}$, they simply use the trace itself to approximate a more accurate profile.

9.3.2 Recognition

In the WMCCDKHLS$_{\text{paths}}$ attack model, the adversary can add branches to the program to disrupt the recognizer. Under this model, the advantage you have over the attacker is that you only need to add watermark branches in a few spots, but the attacker needs to add them uniformly over the entire program to be sure he's destroyed your mark. This is assuming, of course, that the mark is stealthy enough that he can't pinpoint its location—an assumption that may not hold for this algorithm. But more about that later.

So we're assuming that the adversary can lightly sprinkle bogus branches over the program to disrupt our mark, but he can't insert them *en masse* in every possible location. It's because of this assumption that we generate a large number of redundant watermark pieces and let the adversary destroy *some* of them. As long as you can recover enough pieces, you can reconstruct the original watermark.

To start the recognition process, you run the program with the special input and collect a trace, much as you did during the embedding phase. The result is a long string of bits, one bit per branch encountered during the run. Next, you slide a window over the string and extract every contiguous 64-bit substring. Obviously, this can be an enormous set of pieces! Most of the pieces will have nothing to do with the mark. WMCCDKHLS$_{\text{paths}}$ uses the algorithm in Section 8.9.2▶528 to split and recombine the mark. It is designed for exactly this situation, having a *filtering step* (Algorithm 8.11▶532) that disposes of pieces that could not contribute to the mark.

9.3.3 Discussion

Earlier in this chapter, we discussed one of the main drawbacks of dynamic watermarking methods, namely, the risk that the recognizer will be affected by small changes to the execution environment such as packet delivery times in the network and the initialization of random number generators. For example, one of the variables in our trace might hold the process ID or the current time, and if we use that variable to build a watermark piece, that piece may never be recognized. One of the advantages this algorithm has over other dynamic algorithms is that, because of the redundancy of the inserted watermark pieces, we're potentially more resilient against these types of events. You can think of these decoding failures as simply another type of attack, except the adversary isn't evil, just non-deterministic!

A real Achilles' heel of the algorithm seems to be stealth, which is rather surprising. After all, the algorithm just inserts if-statements—and programs have plenty of those!—and it even reuses the program's original variables in the branch condition. The problem is that we only have two kinds of watermark structures: a loop construction, which is unusual in its bit manipulation, and a linear sequence of 64(!) if-statements, again highly unusual in real programs. For the algorithm to be truly useful, stealth must be improved. Ideally, to prevent pattern-matching attacks, you need to be able to generate an "infinite" number of different watermark code patterns, and it seems unlikely that for this algorithm doing so will be possible. Alternatively, some obfuscation method might be developed that would confuse a pattern-matching attack.

The cost of watermark embedding (in terms of added code) depends on the number of watermark pieces you insert, which is dependent of course, on the level of resilience to attack you want. In the authors' Java implementation, there's a fixed 5% program-size increase plus 25 bytes of Java bytecode for each watermark piece. How this affects performance depends entirely on how successful the watermark embedder is at staying away from hot spots. The cost to the attacker is the number of branches *he* has to insert in order to be sure he destroys enough watermark pieces, and how much these slow down the program. This, again, depends on the ability of the attacker to stay away from inner loops, and how cheaply he can make the opaque predicates he needs in his branch conditions. He can't make the conditions *too* simple or we will simply ignore them during watermark recognition! In the authors' experiment, a 512-bit watermark could be destroyed by increasing the number of branches in the program by 150%, and this resulted in a 50% slowdown. Obviously, this will be different from one program to the next, depending on the program's performance characteristics.

Problem 9.12   Can you come up with an *informed* version of WMCCDKHLS$_{\text{paths}}$?
Would it make sense to run the original and watermarked programs in parallel on
the same input, and extract the watermark from the differences in their branch
sequences?

9.4 Algorithm WM*CCDKHLS*$_{\text{bf}}$: Tamperproofing Execution Paths

Have a look back at the control flow obfuscation Algorithm OBFLDK that we presented in Section 4.3.5▸239. The idea is to route unconditional branches through a
special function, called a *branch function*, so that it's difficult for an observer to figure out their actual target. In this example, an unconditional jump to b is converted
into a call to the branch function `bf`:

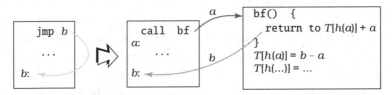

When `bf` is entered, it will have its return address a on the stack. At obfuscation
time, a was inserted into a minimal perfect hash table T and mapped to $b - a$. To
effect a jump to b, all that that branch function has to do is to add $b - a$ to its return
address, issue the return instruction, and control will continue at address b!

The branch function implements a mapping $\{a_1 \rightarrow b_1, a_2 \rightarrow b_2, \ldots, a_n \rightarrow b_n\}$
of unconditional branches from address a_i to address b_i. The idea of Algorithm
WMCCDKHLS$_{\text{bf}}$ [78] is to extend this mapping to also encode a watermark. Specifically, to add the i:th bit w_i of the watermark, you extend the mapping with one
$a_i \rightarrow b_i$, representing a branch from a_i to b_i. If $w_i = 1$, then $a_i \rightarrow b_i$ represents a
forward jump ($a_i < b_i$), and if $w_i = 0$, $a_i \rightarrow b_i$ represents a backwards jump
($a_i > b_i$).

Unlike other algorithms you've seen, WMCCDKHLS$_{\text{bf}}$ doesn't try to protect
the watermark by making it stealthy or error-correcting. It instead relies on the
tamperproofing features inherent in the branch function to stop the adversary from
making *any* changes to the binary. By definition, if the adversary can't modify the
binary, he can't impede the recognizer's ability to find the watermark! Thus, this
algorithm's resilience to attack is directly tied to Algorithm OBFLDK's resilience to
attack. And as you saw in Algorithm REMASB (Section 4.3.6▸242), there *are* attacks
against branch functions.

9.4.1 Embedding

Algorithm 9.5▸594 gives a sketch of the embedding and recognition procedures. The embedding starts by finding some location `begin` at which there's an unconditional jump to a location `end`. Then, to embed a k-bit watermark, you *split* this jump into a sequence of $k + 1$ unconditional jumps:

$$\langle \text{begin} \rightarrow a_1, a_1 \rightarrow a_2, a_2 \rightarrow a_3, \ldots a_k \rightarrow \text{end} \rangle$$

The forward or backward direction of each jump embeds one bit of the watermark.

Here's an example to illustrate the embedding procedure. Below left is a region of code with an unconditional jump from `begin` to `end`. We've also found three locations a_1, a_2, a_3 that directly follow an unconditional jump. These "holes" in the instruction sequence (shown in light gray) are ideal locations in which to insert our bogus branches—control can never fall through to them! To the right is the transformed code after we've inserted a 3-bit watermark:

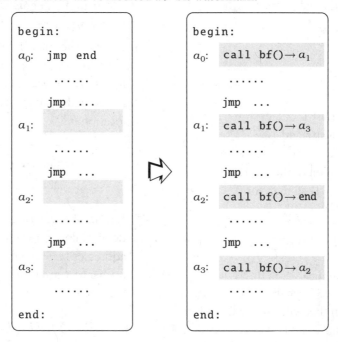

The watermark is embedded by replacing the holes with bogus calls to the branch function. Here, the `call bf()` $\rightarrow \alpha$ notation means a call to the branch function `bf` that actually effects an unconditional jump to location α. The first call is inserted at location `begin`, also called a_0 here, and jumps forward to location a_1. From a_1 we jump forward again to a_3, then backward to a_2, and finally, forward again to

---

Algorithm 9.5 Overview of algorithm $\text{WMCCDKHLS}_{\text{bf}}$. P is the original program, P_w is the watermarked program, and $W = \langle w_0, w_1, \ldots, w_{k-1} \rangle$ is a k-bit watermark.

EMBED(P, W):

1. Find an unconditional branch from location begin to location end:

   ```
   begin: jmp end
          ......
     end:
   ```

2. Find k locations $\{a_1, \ldots, a_k\}$, each of which immediately follows an unconditional jump:

   ```
          jmp  ...
    a_i:
   ```

3. Create a list L of length $k + 2$. Let $L[0] = $ begin and $L[k + 1] = $ end. Let the remaining entries be a permutation of the addresses $\{a_1, \ldots, a_k\}$ so that, for $0 \leq i < k$,

   $$L[i] < L[i + 1] \quad \text{if} \quad w_i = 1$$
   $$L[i] > L[i + 1] \quad \text{if} \quad w_i = 0$$

4. For each $0 \leq i \leq k$, insert at location $L[i]$ a call to the branch function that will cause a branch to location $L[i + 1]$.

   ```
          jmp  ...
   L[i]: call bf() → L[i+1]
   ```

Recognize(P_w):

1. Find locations begin and end that bracket the watermark.

2. Trace P_w from when control reaches begin until it reaches end to obtain a sequence of code addresses $T = \langle l_0, l_1, l_2, \ldots \rangle$.

3. Find the branch function bf by looking for function calls in the trace T that don't return to the instruction immediately following the call.

4. Analyze the trace T to find pairs of addresses (a_i, b_i) where, at location a_i, a branch function call is made that returns to location b_i:

   ```
   a_i:  call bf() → b_i
   ```

5. Extract the watermark by determining, for each pair of addresses (a_i, b_i), whether they form a forward or a backward branch:

   $$a_i < b_i \quad \Rightarrow \quad w_i = 1$$
   $$a_i > b_i \quad \Rightarrow \quad w_i = 0$$

---

location end. This means that the transformation is semantics-preserving—the code may be jumping around a lot at runtime, but actually all you're doing is branching unconditionally from begin to end!

At runtime, the sequence of addresses that the branch function actually will jump to is $\langle a_0, a_1, a_3, a_2, \text{end} \rangle$. By looking at whether branches go forward or backward it's easy to see from the sequence that the 3-bit watermark w that you embedded is $\langle 1, 1, 0 \rangle$:

$$a_0 < a_1 \quad \Rightarrow \quad w_0 = 1$$
$$a_1 < a_3 \quad \Rightarrow \quad w_1 = 1$$
$$a_3 > a_2 \quad \Rightarrow \quad w_2 = 0$$

9.4.2 Recognition

Watermark recognition is straightforward, as always, as long as the program hasn't been attacked! In that case, you can supply the begin and end locations directly to the recognizer and trace all branches from begin to end. In the case of the example above, you'd get a trace that looks like this:

```
begin :  call   bf,
   bf :  ret    a₁,
   a₁ :  call   bf,
   bf :  ret    a₃,
   a₃ :  call   bf,
   bf :  ret    a₂,
   a₂ :  call   bf,
   bf :  ret    end
```

Here, a_1 : call bf means that at address a_1, a call was made to the function at address bf, and bf : ret a_2 means that at address bf, a return jump was made to address a_2. Looking at the trace, you can easily identify the branch function: It's the function that gets called multiple times but never returns to the instruction immediately following the call! Once you've identified the branch function, you can again analyze the trace and extract the pairs of addresses (*from*, *to*), where *from* is the location of the call to the branch function and *to* is the address to which it returns. From our example, you'd get the list of pairs $\langle (\text{begin}, a_1), (a_1, a_3), (a_3, a_2), (a_2, \text{end}) \rangle$, and by looking at the direction of the branches it's easy to extract the mark.

The problem occurs when there's been an attack on P_w. There will be many calls to the branch function from all over the program, and unless you know where begin and end are, how are you going to know which calls to the branch function represent the watermark? This is why it's so important for Algorithm WMCCDKHLS~bf~ that

P_w is thoroughly tamperproofed: Any minuscule change to the binary can throw off the recognizer.

9.4.3 Tamperproofing the Branches

Any attack on the executable that moves code around or inserts new code will cause addresses to change. Unless the attacker is clever enough to update the branch function table accordingly, as soon as the branch function is called, control will continue at the wrong address, causing the program to crash.

This simple form of tamperproofing doesn't help if the adversary completely removes the branch function from the executable! As you saw in Section 4.3.6▶242, branch functions are very dynamically unstealthy. This makes it easy to recover the branch function table and replace each `call bf()` → α with an unconditional jump to α.

One way around this attack is to extend the branch function to have side effects. In this example, we start out with a situation where the branch function call at address `begin` dominates an unconditional branch (shown in dark gray):

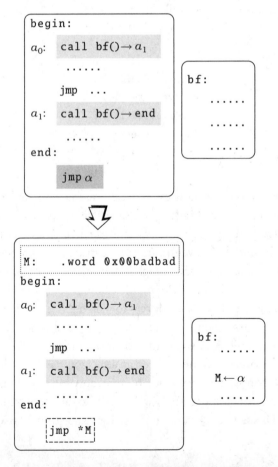

In the original code, the dark gray branch goes directly to some address α, but in the transformed dashed branch, we instead jump indirectly via a memory location M. Originally, M contains a bogus address, but once bf has been called, M gets updated to α. If an attacker replaces the calls to bf at a_0 and a_1 with unconditional branches that he has extracted from the branch function table, M never gets updated with the right address and the dashed branch will go to the wrong location.

For more thorough tamperproofing, M can be updated much more cleverly than this, of course. Rather than giving M its correct value as soon as bf gets called the first time, it could be updated incrementally over several calls to bf. In the example above, there are two calls being made to bf before control reaches the dashed jump. Each of these calls could update some subset of M's bits, ensuring that all the calls to bf in the code must be left intact.

9.4.4 Discussion

In Section 7.2.3 ▶ 423, you saw for the first time a watermarking algorithm that uses tamperproofing to protect the mark. The watermarking algorithm that Algorithm TPHMST uses is completely trivial: It just inserts 32-bit watermarking words in random places in the executable! By itself, that is neither a resilient nor a stealthy marking algorithm. But given the tamperproofing of TPHMST, you might not care! As long as the adversary is unable to modify the executable, the watermarks will remain intact. Algorithm WMCCDKHLSbf uses a similar strategy. The main feature isn't so much how the mark is embedded but how the branch function makes the executable harder to tamper with.

The main attack against WMCCDKHLSbf is an attack against its stealth. Branch functions are highly dynamically unstealthy, which for this algorithm is both an advantage and a disadvantage. It's an advantage because the watermark recognition procedure needs to find the branch function in order to extract the watermark! On the other hand, it's also a disadvantage because the unstealthiness makes it easy for an adversary to find the function. You saw examples of such an attack in Algorithm REMASB (Section 4.3.6 ▶ 242).

A nice aspect of WMCCDKHLSbf is that it has a very modest effect on performance. The authors [78] report an increase in program size ranging from 5% to 16% when watermarking programs from the SPEC benchmark suite with 128-, 256-, and 512-bit watermarks. The algorithm seems to be insensitive to the watermark size: The average increase in program size was 10.8% for 128-bit marks and 11.4% for 512-bit marks. The runtime slowdown was negligible, partially because the implementation is careful to stay away from hot spots.

Problem 9.13   Unlike the other algorithms in this chapter, WMCCDKHLS$_{bf}$ doesn't use any special input to derive the location of the watermark. In fact, the authors' implementation requires the user to supply the addresses `begin` and `end` manually. They state: "We expect to augment the implementation in the near future to use a framing scheme that would allow these addresses to be identified automatically." Can you help the authors to work out the details?

9.5 Discussion

You've encountered several new ideas in this chapter. Most obviously, embedding the watermark in the dynamic state of the program rather than in the static text of the program is interesting. You'll see the same idea reappear when we discuss birthmarking algorithms in Chapter 10 (Software Similarity Analysis).

Compared to static watermarks, dynamic marks are easier to tamperproof and harder for the attacker to destroy. But as you've seen, the idea is not without its complications:

- Dynamic watermarking algorithms make it difficult to watermark individual modules and classes, since these don't execute independently;
- Non-determinism can cause watermark recognition to fail;
- Programs with little input will be hard to mark, since you need many input-dependent places in the program in which to insert a mark;
- It is harder to automate the recognition of dynamic watermarks than static watermarks;
- It can be hard to ensure that a watermark is truly dynamic and cannot be easily detected or decoded statically.

Let's look again at the defense model in Section 2.2▸86 and see which techniques are used in the algorithms you saw in this chapter. Obviously, by their nature, all the algorithms use the **dynamic** primitive, but in addition they combine several other defense ideas:

- WMCT exploits the difficulty of alias analysis (the **indirect** primitive) by encoding the watermark as a graph structure. WMNT exploits the difficulty of analyzing multi-threaded programs by encoding the watermark in the order in which threads get executed (the **reorder** primitive).

- WMCT relies heavily on stealth (i.e., the **mimic** primitive) to protect the mark: By building dynamic structures, it mimics the behavior of many object-oriented programs. Similarly, WMCCDKHLS$_{paths}$ adds branches that are ubiquitous in real programs.

- WMCT and WMCCDKHLS$_{paths}$ both **split** the watermark into pieces and **merge** them back together again during recognition. In the case of WMCT, each piece is smaller than the original mark, increasing stealth and bitrate. All of the pieces need to be found during recognition. WMCCDKHLS$_{paths}$, on the other hand, increases resilience to attack by splitting the watermark into a *redundant* set of pieces (the **duplicate** primitive), only some of which must be recovered.

- The WMCT algorithm increases resilience to attack by continuously modifying the watermark graph structures at runtime. This is another use of the **dynamic** primitive.

- WMNT protects the watermark by adding a large number of watermark decoys, looking very similar to real watermark pieces (the **mimic** and **duplicate** primitives). If the attacker tries to manipulate any code that looks like a watermark, he may inadvertently cause the incorrect code contained in the decoys to execute, an instance of the **detect-respond** primitive.

It should come as no surprise that these ideas can be combined. For example, the credibility of the watermarks in algorithms WMCT and WMVVS could be improved by picking the watermark number from a sparse table (as suggested in WMNT) and then encoding this number as a graph. Algorithm WMCCDKHLS$_{paths}$ splits the watermark into a set of redundant pieces, and, of course, this idea can be applied in the other algorithms as well.

None of the algorithms presented here explicitly considers collusive attacks. It could well be that dynamically fingerprinted programs are easier to attack than statically fingerprinted ones. Two programs that have been differently fingerprinted using a dynamic algorithm differ in two ways: statically (since they embed different marks, the code that builds these marks must be different) and dynamically (for the special input sequences, the two programs will execute differently).

In the previous chapter, we mentioned that if we had perfect tamperproofing available, watermarking would be a solved problem: Simply mark using the most trivial algorithm and then protect the resulting program from being manipulated in any way. Of course, tamperproofing the code requires us to read it, and this, as we've noted, is hard to do stealthily for binary code and impossible to do stealthily for typed bytecode. Dynamic watermarking bypasses this problem by embedding the mark in runtime data structures rather than in static code. This is an improvement over static algorithms, since it means that the tamperproofing code just needs to read data (which the program does anyway), not instructions.

WMNT and WMCCDKHLS$_{paths}$ can both have a significant negative effect on performance: WMNT adds many threads to the program, and WMCCDKHLS$_{paths}$ adds many extra branches. Generally speaking, the other algorithms in this chapter can be implemented with little extra overhead.

Problem 9.14 Leaving all other considerations aside, what's the least amount of code you can imagine inserting into a program to embed a dynamic watermark? Can you hijack the code that's already in the program to do some of the work? What type of program would be best suited to this?

• • •

Problem 9.15 Look at the list of protection mechanisms we described in Section 2.2▶86 that have not been used to build watermarks. Can you think of ways that they can be used to watermark software?

• • •

Problem 9.16 Can you think of a way to use a dynamic technique to protect individual modules or classes of a program?

• • •

Problem 9.17 In modern multi-core processors, there may be many spare cycles available. Would any of the algorithms in this chapter be able to make use of these to reduce overhead? Can you think of other algorithms that could?

Software Similarity Analysis

10

So far, the algorithms you've seen, whether for obfuscation, tamperproofing, or watermarking, have had one thing in common: They've all been based on code transformations. That is, they take an unprotected program as input, apply one or more transformations on the code, and produce a more protected program as output. You can see this view of intellectual property protection reflected in the defense model in Section 2.2►86: Each of the protection primitives takes an unprotected universe as input and produces as output one in which a precious object is better protected than before.

In this chapter, you'll see a very different view of intellectual property protection. Rather than hardening your program to make it more resistant to attack, we're going to assume that it's been released into the wild completely unprotected. There could be many reasons for this. Maybe your program was performance-critical and you couldn't afford the additional overhead that obfuscation, tamperproofing, and watermarking incur. Maybe the program is legacy code and has been in the field long before the techniques in this book were invented. Or maybe the adversary was able to strip out the protection code you *did* add, but you'd still like to assert your intellectual property rights.

The techniques in this chapter are *property*-based rather than transformation-based. That is, the fundamental question we're interested in is: *Do programs A and B share some property that would indicate that they also share a common origin?* A prototypical attack scenario is *code lifting*, i.e., where the adversary copies an important library from your program and incorporates it into his own code. This is a serious threat in the computer gaming industry, where libraries for graphics, physics, scripting, and so on are commonly supplied by third-party vendors, and these vendors' revenue is entirely tied to the licensing fees they can extract from the manufacturers of the games.

In this chapter, we'll examine four intellectual property protection scenarios: *software birthmarking*, *software forensics*, *plagiarism detection*, and *clone detection*. In all four, the essential operation is determining how *similar* two programs (or pieces of programs) are to each other or whether one program is *contained* (partially or in full) within another. In *software forensics*, you want to determine who wrote a particular program. The idea is to compare it against a corpus of programs by possible authors and see whose programming style is most similar. In *plagiarism detection*, you want to determine if a student has copied a program (in whole or in part) by comparing it to programs from other students in the class. *Software birthmarking* is similar to plagiarism detection in that you want to determine if two programs share the same origin. The difference is that birthmark detection algorithms typically compare programs at the binary rather than the source-code level and usually assume there is a much more active and potent adversary. *Clone detection* is a branch of software engineering that locates similar pieces of code that are the result of *copy-paste-modify* programming. This isn't an intellectual property protection problem, per se, but we discuss it here since the algorithms developed for clone detection could be adapted for the other scenarios.

Some algorithms for identifying similarities in two programs work directly on the source or binary code. More common, however, is to first convert to a more convenient representation, such as trees or graphs, and then compare *them*. For this reason, we've divided this chapter into sections for *k-gram-based analysis* (Section 10.3▶616), *API-based analysis* (Section 10.4▶625), *tree-based analysis* (Section 10.5▶631), *graph-based analysis* (Section 10.6▶635), and *metrics-based analysis* (Section 10.7▶644). However, we'll start by examining the different applications of software similarity analysis (Section 10.1) and different possible definitions of similarity (Section 10.2▶611). We'll conclude with a discussion in Section 10.8▶652.

10.1 Applications

Let's start by looking at a few different intellectual property protection scenarios that are all based on being able to compare two or more programs for similarity or containment. To give you a general idea of how tools for clone detection, forensic analysis, plagiarism detection, and birthmarking work, we'll give very high-level algorithm sketches. In subsequent sections, you'll see more detailed algorithms based on different program representations.

10.1.1 Clone Detection

After a program has gone through several development cycles, it tends to contain many instances of duplicated code. Often the duplicates are the result of a *copy-paste-modify*-style of programming: A programmer finds an existing code segment that's almost, but not quite, what he's looking for, simply makes a copy of it, specializes the code as necessary, and adds the copy to the program. A better strategy would be to abstract the code segment into its own function and replace both the original and the copy with appropriately parameterized calls, but this requires both time and a deeper understanding of the original code. Copy-paste-modify is both simpler and faster, at least in the short run. In the long run, however, it becomes a maintenance headache, since a bug in the original code will need to be fixed in all the clones.

Clone detection is the process of locating similar pieces of code in a program. The detection phase is followed by an abstraction phase, where clones are extracted out into functions and replaced with calls to these functions. Here, the clone detector found that function f3 is a clone of f1:

In the abstraction phase, the clone detection tool created a new version P′ of P with f1 and f3 removed and replaced by f(r). f(r) is a version of f1 where the parameter r represents the differences to f3. For such replacement to make sense, f1 and f3 have to be similar enough that creating f(r) is easy and that this parameterized version appears "natural" to programmers who have to continue maintaining the code. Algorithm 10.1▸604 shows a high-level sketch of a clone detector.

Clone detectors are a software maintenance tool, and as such work on improving the program's source code. Some work on the source directly, but most first transform it into a higher-level representation (*rep* in Algorithm 10.1▸604), such as a token sequence, an abstract syntax tree, or a program dependence graph.

Unlike the scenarios you'll see next, in the clone detection scenario you don't expect programmers to be malicious. They don't deliberately try to hide that they've copied a piece of code; it just becomes naturally "obfuscated" as the result of the

---

Algorithm 10.1 Sketch of algorithm for clone detection and abstraction. P is a program, *threshold* is the minimum similarity between two segments of code to consider them clones, and *minsize* is the minimum size of a code segment to warrant abstraction.

DETECT(P, *threshold*, *minsize*):

1. Build a representation *rep* of P from which it is convenient to find clone pairs. Collect code pairs that are sufficiently similar and sufficiently large to warrant their own abstraction:

   ```
   res ← ∅
   rep ← convenient representation of P
   for every pair of code segments f, g ∈ rep, f ≠ g do
       if similarity(f, g) > threshold &&
                size(f) ≥ minsize && size(g) ≥ minsize then
          res ← res ∪ ⟨f, g⟩
   ```

2. Break out the code pairs found in the previous step into their own function and replace them with parameterized calls to this function:

   ```
   for every pair of code segments ⟨f, g⟩ ∈ res do
       h(r) ← a parameterized version of f and g
       P ← P ∪ h(r)
       replace f with a call to h(r₁) and g with a call to h(r₂)
   ```

3. Return *res*, P.

---

specialization process. To make the copied code fit in with its new environment, it's common for the programmer to rename variables and to replace literals with new values. More unusual are major structural changes such as removing or adding statements.

This book is about protecting the intellectual property contained in programs. We therefore don't have any particular interest in clone detection per se, since cloning code is a case of the programmer "stealing" from himself or from his teammates, not from another party! However, as you will see, the techniques developed for clone detection are similar to those used to detect malicious copying of code, and it's reasonable to believe that the two communities could learn from each other.

Also, in Section 7.2.4▶431 you saw how the Skype binary was protected by adding several hundred hash functions. This protection was ultimately defeated through the realization that all the hash functions were similar, and once one had been found, locating the others was easy. This attack was done by hand, but it would be interesting to investigate whether a clone detector would have been able to find the functions by looking for self-similarity within the binary.

10.1.2 Software Forensics

Software forensics is concerned with determining *who* wrote a particular piece of code. One useful application is to trace a piece of malware back to its author. For example, after you realize an intrusion has taken place, you look through your system and find the remnants of the intruder's attack code. If you could determine who wrote the code, you would not only help in tracking down the culprit but also aid by providing evidence useful in future prosecution.

   This use of software authorship analysis is similar to how handwriting analysis is already used in law enforcement to trace the author of a document. It is also similar to authorship analysis of literary works. There are well-known disputes of authorship that go back hundreds of years, such as those involving *The Federalist Papers* and the works commonly attributed to Shakespeare that have been been studied with modern statistical techniques [121,256].

   Handwriting analysis extracts features such as how the writer dots his i's and compresses or expands his text. Literary analysis extracts features such as word usage, punctuation, and sentence length that may be unique to an author's style. In software forensics, you similarly extract features from a program that you believe will be unique to a programmer's coding style. More specifically, in order to determine the likely author of a program P, you need to start out with a universe U of possible authors and samples of their writing. The result of the analysis is a list of the authors in decreasing likelihood that they are the programmer who wrote the code:

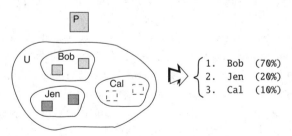

In this example, you start out with a universe of three programmers, Bob, Jen, and Cal, and two samples each of code they've written. You extract features from each of those samples and from the program P whose authorship is under dispute. After comparing the features, you determine with a medium degree of probability that Bob is the author of P, and with a high degree of probability that Jen and Cal are not.

If software authorship analysis is to be truly useful, two propositions must be true. First, there must be aspects of a programmer's coding style that set him apart from other programmers. Second, this style must be consistent between programs written by the same author, even when those programs come from different domains. The first proposition is still debated; we have yet to converge on a "right" set of characteristics that distinguish programmers from each other. The second proposition is easier to accept. Over time, we collect programming habits: how we indent our code, how we choose variable names, how large we allow our functions and modules to grow, and which algorithms and data structures we prefer for common tasks (quicksort vs. mergesort for sorting, hash tables vs. binary search trees for dictionaries, and so on). While an author's style may change over time as he becomes familiar with more programming paradigms, programming languages, and algorithms, it's not entirely unlikely that *some* of these characteristics will remain unchanged.

Algorithm 10.2 ▶ 607 shows a sketch of the three steps to authorship classification: Determine which coding features are good indicators of authorship, collect those features from sample code of suspected authors and from the program under dispute, and compare the feature sets for similarity.

Not all characteristics that you could possibly collect from a program will be useful in determining authorship. An important preprocessing step is therefore to examine a large corpus of programs to determine those features of programming style that are programmer-specific, i.e., that vary little from one program to another written by the same programmer but that show large variations between code written by different programmers.

The next step is to collect the set of characteristics (the author *profile*), for each author from the sample programs and from the one for which you want to determine authorship. For the identification result to be accurate, you need a significant sample set from each author. Depending on your particular situation, this may or may not be available.

Most of the work on software forensics has been on the analysis of source code. The reason is that many programmer-specific features (such as code layout and variable naming) are stripped away by the compilation process. This is unfortunate, since in some settings such as when analyzing a virus for hints on who might have written it, source code is not available.[1] This means that only those features of the program that remain intact after compilation can be used for analysis. They include choice of data structures, choice of compiler (different compilers will have different code-generation patterns), choice of programming language (a program using the

---

1. We've been told that the FBI can now determine malware authorship, but we're not aware of any published accounts of this fact.

Algorithm 10.2 Sketch of software forensics algorithm for author identification. A is a set of authors who might have written an unknown program P. For all authors $a \in A$, $U[a]$ is a set of sample programs written by a.

DETECT(A, U, P, *threshold*):

1. Using a large corpus of programs from different authors, determine the set of characteristics C that show a high degree of variability between authors but a low degree of variability within programs by the same author.

2. Collect sets of characteristics from the sample programs of each author, and from P:

> $sig \leftarrow \emptyset$
> for each author $a \in A$ and code sample set $s \in U[a]$ do
> $profile[a] \leftarrow$ characteristics C extracted from s
> $sig \leftarrow$ characteristics C extracted from P

3. Determine which authors' profiles share the most characteristics with P:

> for each author $a \in A$ do
> $sim \leftarrow$ similarity(sig, $profile[a]$)
>   if $sim > threshold$ then
> $res \leftarrow res \cup \langle a, sim \rangle$
> return res sorted on similarity

---

object-oriented features of C++ will leave telltale signs in the binary code that will distinguish it from a pure C program, Modula-2 programs will have array bound checks, while C programs won't, and so on), and preference for certain library and system calls when there are more than one possible choice.

In software forensics research, the attack model is typically a very weak one, namely, that the author of the code does not try to actively disguise its origins. It's reasonable to assume, however, that a prolific virus author would try his best to somehow vary his style enough that once he's been identified as the author of one virus, he cannot automatically be linked to others.[2] Manually altering one's programming style probably isn't practical, since programming is hard enough without having to consciously do things in a way that's unnatural. More convenient would be running the code through an obfuscator before releasing it into the wild.

---

2. This assumes, of course, that the malware writer is actually concerned about being caught! Many hackers are proud of their handiwork and happy to leave telltale fingerprints all over it.

In addition to authorship analysis, there are two other problems studied in software forensics [130]. *Software characterization* tries to draw conclusions, Sherlock Holmes style, about the psychological makeup and educational and cultural background of the author of a program based on aspects of his coding style:

```
┌─┐        ⎧  1.  Ph.D.-level
│P│  ⇨     ⎨  2.  Former Icon programmer
└─┘        ⎨  3.  Steeped in Microsoft style
           ⎩  4.  Tall, formative years in Texas, drives a Volvo,...
```

For example, in the analysis of the famous *Internet worm*, it appeared that its author (who turned out to be Robert T. Morris) had a penchant for linked lists. The reason, it's been conjectured, was that his first programming courses were taught in LISP [332]. *Software discrimination*, finally, tries to identify which pieces of a program were written by different authors (and, possibly, to identify who those authors are), again based on samples of their coding:

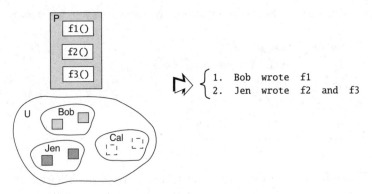

```
         ⇨   ⎧  1.  Bob wrote f1
             ⎩  2.  Jen wrote f2 and f3
```

10.1.3 Plagiarism Detection

Plagiarism of programming assignments appears to be common in computer science classes. The copying of assignments can take many forms. At one extreme end, a student just hands in a verbatim copy of his friend's program, merely changing the author line of the header comment.[3] At the other end of the spectrum, the student makes radical changes to the program to hide the origin of the code. Common operations include renaming of identifiers, reordering of functions, and rewriting of comments. There are intermediate forms of plagiarism between these two extremes,

---

3. As if this isn't cheeky enough, adding to the instructor's incredulity is the students' explanation: "Of course our programs look the same—there's only one way to solve this assignment!"

such as "borrowing" one or more difficult functions from a friend (or fishing them out of the trash can or nabbing them off the printer) while writing the bread-and-butter code from scratch.

In a plagiarism-detection scenario, you make pair-wise comparisons between all of the programs handed in by the students and order them from most to least similar:

$$
\begin{cases}
\langle \text{P1}, & \text{P2} \rangle = 70\% \\
\langle \text{P1}, & \text{P3} \rangle = 20\% \\
\langle \text{P2}, & \text{P3} \rangle = 10\%
\end{cases}
$$

Many systems give more comprehensive outputs, such as side-by-side comparisons of pairs of highly suspect programs, color-coded so that the instructor can confront the students with graphic "evidence" of their cheating.

While there are many kinds of rewrites the student could attempt in order to fool the plagiarism detector, he is still limited by the need for the code to look "reasonable." For this reason, running the code through a general-purpose obfuscator (such as you saw in Chapter 4) probably isn't a good idea, particularly if the instructor examines the code manually to grade on style. For example, the student may get away with renaming a variable `windowSize` to `sizeOfWindow` but would likely lose points if he named it `x93`. Similarly, replacing a while-loop with a for-loop is probably OK, but completely unrolling the loop would look too suspicious. Thus, for plagiarism detection, you can assume a weaker attacker than for software forensics but probably a stronger attacker than for clone detection.

Algorithm 10.3 shows a sketch of a typical plagiarism-detection algorithm. Elenbogen and Seliya [120] point out that this algorithm won't work if the student is

---

Algorithm 10.3 Overview of plagiarism-detection algorithm. U is the collection of programs submitted by students.

DETECT(U, *threshold*):

res ← ∅
for each pair of programs $f, g \in U$ do
    sim ← similarity(f, g)
    if *sim* > *threshold* then
        res ← *res* ∪ ⟨f, g, sim⟩
res ← *res* sorted on similarity
return *res*

Algorithm 10.4 Overview of birthmarking algorithm.

DETECT(P, Q, *threshold*):

$bm_P \leftarrow$ signal extracted from P
$bm_Q \leftarrow$ signal extracted from Q
if similarity(bm_P, bm_Q) > *threshold* then
   return "copy"
else
   return "not copy"

---

outsourcing his assignments to an unscrupulous third party. Such "programming mills" can be found on the Internet or simply by posting a note for "help with CS101" on a university bulletin board. Elenbogen and Seliya instead suggest to use a form of style analysis like you saw in the section on software forensics. The idea is to track the style of the student as it changes throughout the course of the semester. Presumably, the style will improve as he gets feedback from the instructor, but this can be controlled for by comparing his changing style with the similarly changing style of the rest of the students in the class. Assuming everyone gets the same feedback, their style should change at the same pace. There are a lot of assumptions here, and it's unclear whether it's possible to collect data that's believable enough that a student will fess up when confronted with it, let alone convince a plagiarism review board that the student needs to be reprimanded.

10.1.4 Birthmark Detection

Our primary interest in this chapter is in *birthmark detection*. Although birthmarking is also concerned with detecting similarities between programs, it differs in some respects from clone detection, software forensics, and plagiarism detection. First, birthmarks are primarily extracted from executable code, such as x86 binaries or Java bytecode, rather than from source code. Clone detection and plagiarism detection by definition work on source code, and most algorithms proposed for authorship analysis do too, although there's a real need for analysis of malware binaries. Second, birthmark detection assumes a much more active and competent adversary than what you've previously seen. Unlike clone detection and plagiarism detection, there's no need to keep the code pretty enough to remain fit for further human consumption. Therefore, the adversary is free to mangle the code in any way he can think of in order to thwart the birthmark detector.

    In the birthmarking scenario, the assumption is that the adversary goes through the following steps to lift code from some program P into his own program Q:

1. Copy one or more sections of code from P into Q.

2. Compile Q, as necessary, into binary code or bytecode.

3. Apply semantics-preserving transformations, such as obfuscation and optimization, to Q and distribute the resulting program.

Birthmark detection, then, becomes the process of extracting properties of code that are invariant to common semantics-preserving transformations:

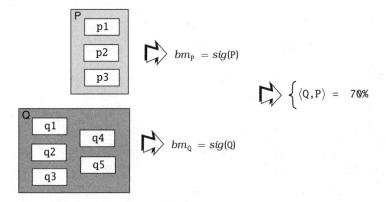

Here, we've extracted birthmarks from programs P and Q and determined that a large part of P has been included in Q.

Some birthmark detection algorithms assume that *all of* of P's code has been lifted into Q. That is, Q is simply a version of P that has been sufficiently obfuscated to make it possible for the adversary to argue that Q is an independently developed program whose behavior is identical to that of P. In a more common scenario, some central part of P is lifted into Q, maybe no more than a few functions or a few modules.

10.2 Definitions

The definition of birthmarking and attacks on birthmarks mirror those you saw for watermarking in Section 8.3 ▶ 480. The major difference is that unlike watermarking, birthmarking has no *embed* function. Also, all the functions in a birthmarking system are unkeyed. As a result, in a birthmarking system, the *extract* function extracts the birthmark b directly from a program p:

$$extract(p) \rightarrow b$$

A birthmarking system also needs a function *contains*:

$$contains(b_q, b_p) \rightarrow [0.0, 1.0]$$

It compares two birthmarks b_q and b_p extracted from programs q and p to determine if p is contained in q. Typically, we'll combine *embed* and *contains* into a function *detect*:

$$detect(q, p) = contains(extract(q), extract(p))$$

Finally, a function *attack* models the adversary's ability to transform a program, for example, using obfuscation, to prevent us from recognizing it:

$$attack(p) \rightarrow p'$$

A prototypical attack involves first cropping out a piece of our program p and then embedding it into another program. In a successful attack, the *detect* function is unable to determine that our original program has been incorporated, in part or in full, into the attacker's program:

$$detect(attack(p), p) < 0.5$$

Like watermarking algorithms, birthmarking algorithms can be static or dynamic. In the dynamic case, the *extract* function takes an extra argument, a specific input I:

$$extract(p, I) \rightarrow b$$

The birthmark is extracted from the dynamic state of the program as it is executed on input I, rather than from the code itself. Dynamic birthmarking algorithms detect the theft of an entire program, while a static algorithm can detect the lifting of individual modules.

A *credible* birthmarking algorithm has a low false positive rate. That is, there's a low probability that $detect(q, p) > 0.5$ if p and q are independently developed.

10.2.1 Similarity Measures

What does it mean for two pieces of code to be "similar"? Clearly, many definitions are possible. We could ask for semantic similarity, we could ask for textual source-code similarity, or we could ask for similarity under a particular set of code transformations.

The algorithms in this chapter extract "signals" from two or more programs and compare these signals for similarity. These signals take different forms. They can be sequences or sets of features that have been extracted, or they can be trees or graphs representing the structure of the programs. Regardless of what form these signals take, there must be some way to compare two of them to see how similar they are.

10.2.1.1 Sequence Similarity Since sequences are common structures in many areas (such as bioinformatics), the literature is rife with proposals for sequence-similarity measures. We'll just mention two of the most common ones here.

The similarity between two sequences of equal length can be defined as the fraction of elements that are the same. This is used in the birthmarking algorithms by Tamada et al. that you'll see in Section 10.4.1►626. This similarity measure is based on the definition of Hamming distance:

Definition 10.1 (Hamming distance and similarity). Let f be a function that computes a feature vector $f(d) = \langle d_1, \ldots, d_n \rangle$ from a document d. Let p and q be documents with feature vectors $f(p) = \langle p_1, \ldots, p_n \rangle$ and $f(q) = \langle q_1, \ldots, q_n \rangle$, respectively. Then the Hamming distance between p and q is defined as

$$distance(p, q) = |\{\forall 1 \leq i \leq n \bullet p_i \neq q_i\}|$$

and the similarity between p and q is defined as

$$similarity(p, q) = 1 - \frac{distance(p, q)}{n}$$

Another common metric is Levenshtein distance, also known as edit distance. This is a more suitable metric than Hamming distance when the two sequences are of unequal length. The idea is that the number of operations necessary to turn one string into another is a measure of how different they are:

Definition 10.2 (Levenshtein [Edit] distance and similarity). The edit distance $distance(p, q)$ between two sequences p and q is the minimum number of operations needed to transform p into q, using insertions, deletions, and substitutions. The similarity between p and q is defined as:

$$similarity(p, q) = 1 - \frac{distance(p, q)}{\max(|p|, |q|)}$$

For example, the Levenshtein distance between "whiten" and "kitten" is 3, since three operations are necessary and sufficient to turn one word into the other:

$$\text{whiten} \xrightarrow{\text{insert } \mathbf{t}} \text{whitten} \xrightarrow{\text{delete } \mathbf{h}} \text{witten} \xrightarrow{\text{substitute } \mathbf{k} \text{ for } \mathbf{w}} \text{kitten.}$$

(Three substitutions are also possible.) The two words have a similarity of 0.5:

$$similarity(\text{whiten, kitten}) = 1 - \frac{3}{6} = \frac{1}{2}.$$

10.2.1.2 Set Similarity   Broder [49] defines the *containment* and *similarity*[4] of two documents. You can use this similarity measure on the sets of k-grams that you'll see in Section 10.3 ▸ 616, for example. Here are the definitions:

> **Definition 10.3** (Similarity and containment).   The similarity *similarity*(p, q) between two documents p and q is defined as
>
> $$similarity(p, q) = \frac{|f(p) \cap f(q)|}{|f(p) \cup f(q)|}$$
>
> where $f(d)$ is a function that computes a set of features from a document d. Similarly, the *containment*(p, q) of p within q is defined as
>
> $$containment(p, q) = \frac{|f(p) \cap f(q)|}{|f(p)|}$$

To illustrate, consider these two sets:

$$
\begin{aligned}
p &= \{1, 3, 7, 8, 9, 11\} \\
q &= \{2, 7, 9, 11\}
\end{aligned}
$$

Their similarity is given by

$$similarity(p, q) = \frac{|\{1, 3, 7, 8, 9, 11\} \cap \{2, 7, 9, 11\}|}{|\{1, 3, 7, 8, 9, 11\} \cup \{2, 7, 9, 11\}|} = \frac{|\{7, 9, 11\}|}{|\{1, 2, 3, 7, 8, 9, 11\}|} = \frac{3}{7}$$

The fraction of p that's contained within q is given by

$$containment(p, q) = \frac{|\{1, 3, 7, 8, 9, 11\} \cap \{2, 7, 9, 11\}|}{|\{1, 3, 7, 8, 9, 11\}|} = \frac{|\{7, 9, 11\}|}{|\{1, 3, 7, 8, 9, 11\}|} = \frac{3}{6}$$

---

4. Broder uses the term *resemblance* instead of similarity.

and the fraction of q that's contained within p is given by

$$containment(q, p) = \frac{|\{2, 7, 9, 11\} \cap \{1, 3, 7, 8, 9, 11\}|}{|\{2, 7, 9, 11\}|} = \frac{|\{7, 9, 11\}|}{|\{2, 7, 9, 11\}|} = \frac{3}{4}$$

10.2.1.3 Graph Similarity A variety of graph similarity measures are possible. For example, you can adapt the edit distance metric for sequences to work on graphs: The distance between two graphs is the number of operations (insertions, deletions, and substitutions of nodes and edges) necessary to turn one graph into the other. Here, we're instead going to use a metric based on the size of the *maximal common subgraph* of the two graphs [50]:

Definition 10.4 (Common subgraphs). Let G, G_1, and G_2 be graphs. G is a *common subgraph* of G_1 and G_2 if there exists subgraph isomorphisms from G to G_1 and from G to G_2.

$\qquad$ G is the *maximal common subgraph* of two graphs G_1 and G_2 ($G = mcs(G_1, G_2)$) if G is a common subgraph of G_1 and G_2 and there exists no other common subgraph G' of G_1 and G_2 that has more nodes than G.

In this example, the shaded nodes induce a maximal common subgraph of G_1 and G_2 of four nodes:

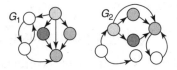

$\qquad$ The similarity and containment of two graphs is defined similarly to the other measures you've seen:

Definition 10.5 (Graph similarity and containment). Let $|G|$ be the number of nodes in G. The *similarity*(G_1, G_2) of G_1 and G_2 is defined as

$$similarity(G_1, G_2) = \frac{|mcs(G_1, G_2)|}{\max(|G_1|, |G_2|)}$$

The *containment*(G_1, G_2) of G_1 within G_2 is defined as

$$containment(G_1, G_2) = \frac{|mcs(G_1, G_2)|}{|G_1|}.$$

We say that G_1 is γ-isomorphic to G_2 if

$$containment(G_1, G_2) \geq \gamma, \gamma \in (0, 1].$$

For the graphs G_1 and G_2 above, you get

$$similarity(G_1, G_2) = \frac{4}{7} \text{ and } containment(G_1, G_2) = \frac{4}{6}.$$

10.3 *k*-gram-Based Analysis

With definitions out of the way, let's now look at actual algorithms! The remainder of the chapter is organized around different program representations. Some will be simpler than others, some will allow more powerful comparisons between programs, and some support more advanced attack scenarios. First we'll look a *k-gram hashes*.

Comparing sets of *k*-grams of two documents is a popular method of computing their similarity. This idea has been used for plagiarism detection of text documents and source code, for authorship analysis of code, and for birthmark detection of executable code. In this section, you'll see Algorithm ssSWA$_{\text{winnow}}$ [6,7,316], which is used in the MOSS source-code plagiarism detection system. MOSS is used extensively to catch cheating in programming assignments in computer science courses. Algorithm ssMC$_{\text{kgram}}$ also uses *k*-gram-based analyses, but for computing Java byte-code birthmarks.

10.3.1 *ssSWA$_{WINNOW}$:* Selecting *k*-gram Hashes

A *k*-gram is a contiguous length *k* substring of the original document. To illustrate the idea, consider the short document A consisting of the string yabbadabbadoo:

	0	1	2	3	4	5	6	7	8	9	10	11	12
A:	y	a	b	b	a	d	a	b	b	a	d	o	o

By sweeping a window of size 3 over A, you get the set of 3-grams for A:

A: yab abb bba bad ada dab abb bba bad ado doo

We'll also call these *shingles*. Here's a second document C consisting of the string doobeedoobeedoo:

	0	1	2	3	4	5	6	7	7	9	10	11	12	13	14
C:	d	o	o	b	e	e	d	o	o	b	e	e	d	o	o

Algorithm 10.5 Compute a set of *k*-gram hashes for a document *P*. *k* is the length of each shingle and *W* the size of the winnowing window.

---

kGRAM(*P*, *k*, *W*):

1. Let *N* be the length of *P*. Construct a list *shingles* consisting of $N - k + 1$ substrings of *P* by sweeping a size *k* window over *P*.

2. Construct a length $N - k + 1$ list *hashes* by computing a hash over each string in *shingles*.

3. Construct a length $|hashes| - W + 1$ list *windows* by sweeping a size *W* window over *hashes*.

4. Construct a set *selected* of hashes:

    selected ← ∅
    ```
    for each window w ∈ windows do
        min ← smallest rightmost hash in w
        if min wasn't already selected in the previous window then
    ```
            selected ← *selected* ∪ {*min*}

5. Return *selected*.

The shingles for this document are:

```
C:  doo  oob  obe  bee  eed  edo  doo  oob  obe  bee  eed  edo  doo
```

What are the similarities between A and C? Well, that's easy to see; just compare the sets of shingles! In this case, the only shingle that appears both in A and C is doo: It occurs once in A and three times in C. This could be a fluke, of course, but it could also be that we've just uncovered a case of plagiarism where doo was copied three times from A into C.

How well this will work in practice depends on if you can choose a good value for *k*. If, in the previous example, you'd have set *k* = 4, you wouldn't have seen *any* similarity between A and C:

```
A:  yabb  abba  bbad  bada  adab  dabb  abba  bbad  bado  adoo
C:  doob  oobe  obee  beed  eedo  edoo  doob  oobe  obee  beed  eedo  edoo
```

How you choose k depends on the type of document you're working on. In general, you need to choose k so that common idioms of the document type have lengths less than k. This will filter out incidental similarities such as the word *the* in English or *if* in source code.

The most interesting property of k-grams is that they're somewhat insensitive to permutations. Say that, in an effort to thwart you from detecting his attempts at plagiarism, the adversary reorders yabbadabbadoo into bbadooyabbada. From this obfuscated document, you now get this set of shingles:

```
A': bba bad ado doo ooy oya yab abb bba bad ada
```

Notice how the doo 3-gram still remains intact. This means that you'll compute the same rate of similarity with document C as before!

In practice, it will be too inefficient to compute and store all the shingles of a large document, or in the case of plagiarism detection, a large set of documents. Instead, the shingles are first hashed and then a small subset of them is kept for further analysis. If k is large, computing a hash from scratch for each shingle will be too expensive, so instead you use a "rolling hash function" that computes the hash of a shingle by extending the previous one [192]. For ease of exposition, in the examples in the remainder of this section we'll use the following function to compute hashes from shingles:

$$
hash(s) = \begin{cases}
\text{obe} \Rightarrow 15 & \text{abb} \Rightarrow 2 & \text{bee} \Rightarrow 16 \\
\text{bba} \Rightarrow 3 & \text{bad} \Rightarrow 4 & \text{yab} \Rightarrow 8 \\
\text{ydo} \Rightarrow 14 & \text{eed} \Rightarrow 17 & \text{byd} \Rightarrow 13 \\
\text{doo} \Rightarrow 1 & \text{ada} \Rightarrow 5 & \text{edo} \Rightarrow 18 \\
\text{ado} \Rightarrow 7 & \text{coo} \Rightarrow 10 & \text{dab} \Rightarrow 6 \\
\text{oob} \Rightarrow 11 & \text{oby} \Rightarrow 12 & \text{sco} \Rightarrow 9
\end{cases}
$$

Using this function, you can create a hash for each of the shingles in document A above:

```
A:   yab   abb   bba   bad   ada   dab   abb   bba   bad   ado   doo
    A0:8  A1:2  A2:3  A3:4  A4:5  A5:6  A6:2  A7:3  A8:4  A9:7  A10:1
```

The notation we use here is $D_P : V$, where D is the name of the document from whence the shingle came, P is the shingle's position within D, and V is its value.

There will be approximately the same number of hashes as there are tokens in the original document. It therefore becomes impractical to keep more than a small number of them. A common approach is to only keep those that are 0 mod p, for some p. This has the disadvantage of possible long gaps in a document from which no hash is selected. A better approach is to use a technique known as *winnowing*. The idea is to sweep a window of size W over the sequence of hashes and choose the smallest one from each window (in case of ties, choose the rightmost smallest). This ensures that there's no gap longer than $W + k - 1$ between two selected hashes. Here are the windows of size 4 for document A above, where we've marked the selected hashes in dark gray:

$$
\begin{array}{llll}
(A_0:8 & A_1:2 & A_2:3 & A_3:4) \\
(A_1:2 & A_2:3 & A_3:4 & A_4:5) \\
(A_2:3 & A_3:4 & A_4:5 & A_5:6) \\
(A_3:4 & A_4:5 & A_5:6 & A_6:2) \\
(A_4:5 & A_5:6 & A_6:2 & A_7:3) \\
(A_5:6 & A_6:2 & A_7:3 & A_8:4) \\
(A_6:2 & A_7:3 & A_8:4 & A_9:7) \\
(A_7:3 & A_8:4 & A_9:7 & A_{10}:1)
\end{array}
$$

The final set of hashes chosen from A then becomes $\{A_1:2, A_2:3, A_6:2, A_{10}:1\}$. Algorithm 10.5▸617 shows a sketch of how to construct the k-grams.

10.3.2 $ssSWA_{MOSS}$: Software Plagiarism Detection

In software plagiarism detection, you need to do pairwise comparison of n programs. For this reason, for large n and large programs, performance can be a problem. Algorithm $ssSWA_{MOSS}$ handles this by postponing the quadratic step for as long as possible. To see how this works, let's continue with our example. In addition to the A document yabbadabbadoo, which has the hashes $\{A_1:2, A_2:3, A_6:2, A_{10}:1\}$, let's add a B document scoobydoobydoo

	0	1	2	3	4	5	6	7	8	9	10	11	12	13
B:	s	c	o	o	b	y	d	o	o	b	y	d	o	o

with the hashes

$$\{B_0:9, B_1:10, B_2:11, B_6:1, B_7:11, B_{11}:1\}$$

and a C document doobeedoobeedoo

	0	1	2	3	4	5	6	7	8	9	10	11	12	13	14
C:	d	o	o	b	e	e	d	o	o	b	e	e	d	o	o

with the hashes

$$\{C_0:1,\ C_1:11,\ C_2:15,\ C_6:1,\ C_7:11,\ C_8:15,\ C_{12}:1\}$$

The second step in Algorithm 10.6▸621 is to build an *index* over all hashes of all the documents. The index maps each hash value to the set of document locations where they occur:

1:	$A_{10}:1,$	$B_6:1,$	$B_{11}:1,$	$C_0:1,$	$C_6:1,$	$C_{12}:1$
2:	$A_1:2,$	$A_6:2$				
3:	$A_2:3$					
9:	$B_0:9$					
10:	$B_1:10$					
11:	$B_2:11,$	$B_7:11,$	$C_1:11,$	$C_7:11$		
15:	$C_2:15,$	$C_8:15$				

The third step is to hash the documents again, this time using the index to construct, for every document, a list of matching hashes in the other documents:

A:	$B_6:1,$	$B_{11}:1,$	$C_6:1,$	$C_{12}:1,$	$C_0:1$	
B:	$A_{10}:1,$	$C_0:1,$	$C_6:1,$	$C_7:11,$	$C_1:11,$	$C_{12}:1$
C:	$A_{10}:1,$	$B_2:11,$	$B_7:11,$	$B_6:1,$	$B_{11}:1$	

Note that until now we've been able to avoid any quadratic behavior! The final step is, for each pair of documents, to traverse their lists of hashes and extract those they have in common. Here's the final result:

```
[A,B]:  B₆:1,   A₁₀:1,   B₁₁:1
[A,C]:  C₀:1,   C₆:1,   A₁₀:1,   C₁₂:1
[B,C]:  C₀:1,   C₆:1,   C₇:11,   C₁₂:1,   C₁:11,   B₂:11,   B₆:1,   B₇:11,   B₁₁:1
```

The document pairs with the longest lists of hashes are most likely to be instances of plagiarism. It's common to present the results graphically, with similarities color-coded to help convince the culprits of their guilt. In this side-by-side comparison between documents B and C, light gray represents hash value 1 and dark gray hash value 11:

Algorithm 10.6 Overview of the MOSS algorithm for plagiarism detection. *docs* is a list of documents. *k* is the shingle size, long enough for common idioms to have lengths shorter than *k*. *W* is the window size used in the winnowing algorithm.

DETECT(*docs*, *k*, *W*):

1. Canonicalize the documents by removing incidental differences.

2. Fingerprint all documents using Algorithm 10.5 ▸ 617. Build *index*, a map from hash values to the set of document positions at which they occur:

> *index* ← ∅
> **for each document** *d* ∈ *docs* **do**
>   *H* ← kGRAM(*d*, *k*, *W*)
>   **for each** *k*-gram hash *h* = d_p : *v* ∈ *H* **do**
>   *index*[*v*] ← *index*[*v*] ∪ {*h*}

3. Again, fingerprint all documents. Look up each fingerprint in the *index* and construct a list *matches*[*d*] for each document *d* of all matching fingerprints:

> **for each document** *d* ∈ *docs* **do**
>   *matches*[*d*] ← ∅
>   *H* ← kGRAM(*d*, *K*, *W*)
>   **for each** *h* = $d_{\_}$: *v* ∈ *H* **do**
>   **for each** *k*-gram hash *v* ↦ r_p : *v* ∈ *index*, *r* ≠ *d* **do**
>   *matches*[*d*] ← *matches*[*d*] ∪ {r_p : *v*}

4. For each pair of documents (d^1, d^2) construct *pairwise*[(d^1, d^2)], the set of *k*-grams shared by d^1 and d^2:

> **for each pair of documents** (d^1, d^2) ∈ *docs*, d^1 ≠ d^2 **do**
>   *pairwise*[(d^1, d^2)] ← ∅
>   **for each** *h* = d_p^2 : *v* ∈ *matches*[d^1] **and** *h* = d_p^1 : *v* ∈ *matches*[d^2] **do**
>   *pairwise*[(d^1, d^2)] ← *pairwise*[(d^1, d^2)] ∪ {*h*}

5. Sort the sets in *pairwise* by size and return the document pairs (d^1, d^2) with the most hashes in common.

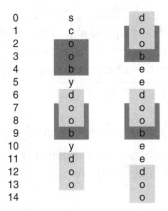

10.3.2.1 Example—Source Code To try to thwart detection, a software plagiarist might use simple transformations such as reordering functions, renaming variables, and reformatting the code. k-gram analysis itself takes care of coarse-grained reordering, but some preprocessing is necessary to handle variable renaming and reformatting. Algorithm 10.6▸621 takes care of this by a preprocessing step that canonicalizes the code. The details will depend on the nature of the input language, but for typical source code you might rename all variables to V, replace all integer literals with 9, and remove all unnecessary whitespace.

Let's look at an example with three different versions of the Fibonacci function. Document A is the original one. Document B was copied from A and obfuscated by reformatting, reordering expressions, and renaming identifiers. Document C was copied from B by replacing the if-statement with a conditional expression:

```
A:      int fib(int n) {
            if (n <= 1)
                return n;
            else
                return fib(n-1) + fib(n-2);
        }


B:      int fibonacci(int a) {
            if(1<a) return fibonacci(-2+a)+fibonacci(-1+a);
            else    return a;
        }


C:      int fibonacci(int a) {
            return (1<a)?fibonacci(-2+a)+fibonacci(-1+a):a;
        }
```

After canonicalization, the documents look like this:

```
A:      int V(int V){if(V<=9)return V;else return V(V-9)+V(V-9);}


B:      int V(int V){if(9<V)return V(-9+V)+V(-9+V);else return V;}


C:      C: int V(int V){return(9<V)?V(-9+V)+V(-9+V):V;}
```

With $k = 6$ and $W = 6$, you get a resemblance between A and B of 47%, between B and C of 46%, and A and C of 25%.

10.3.3 *ssMC_{kgram}*: *k*-gram Java Bytecode Birthmarks

Birthmark detection is different from plagiarism detection in several respects: You're working on executable code (binaries or bytecode) rather than source code, you assume a powerful obfuscating adversary rather than one concerned about keeping the code relatively pretty, and you want to compare two programs against each other rather than making pairwise comparisons between n programs.

$\text{ssMC}_{\text{kgram}}$ is a k-gram-based birthmarking algorithm that computes a mark over Java bytecode opcodes. The birthmark for a class is the set of all the opcode k-grams for the methods in the class. Order and frequency of the shingles are ignored. Ignoring the frequency means that common obfuscations such as duplicating blocks won't affect the birthmark.

Here's our Fibonacci example again, this time written in Java:

```java
class Fib1 {
   static int fib1(int n) {
      if (n <= 1)
         return n;
      else
         return fib1(n-1)+fib1(n-2);
   }
}


class Fibonacci3 {
   static int fibonacci3(int a) {
      if(1<a) return fibonacci3(-2+a)+fibonacci3(-1+a);
      else    return a;
   }
}
```

```
class Fibonacci4 {
  static int fibonacci4(int a) {
    return (1<a)?fibonacci4(-2+a)+fibonacci4(-1+a):a;
  }
}
```

For performance reasons, many instruction set architectures will have several instructions with close to identical semantics. Java bytecode, for example, has ten instructions that all push an integer constant: `iconst_1`, ... , `iconst_5`, `bipush`, `sipush`, `ldc`, `ldc_2`, and `iconst_m1`. An almost trivial obfuscation that would disrupt *k*-gram-based birthmarking algorithms is to replace instructions with similar ones. To counter that, a preprocessing step should canonicalize the opcodes by renaming them to generic ones. In the bytecode below, for example, all the integer push instructions are renamed `iPUSH`, all the integer load instructions `iLOAD`, and so on. Compiling the `Fib1` class above and canonicalizing the bytecodes yields this code:

```
aload_0              aLOAD
invokespecial        invokespecial
return               return
```

```
class Fib1 {
  Fib() {}
  static int fib1(int n) {
    if (n <= 1)
      return n;
    else
      return fib1(n-1)+fib1(n-2);
  }
}
```

```
iload_0              iLOAD
iconst_1             iPUSH
if_icmpgt            iIFCMP
iload_0              iLOAD
ireturn              iRETURN
iload_0              iLOAD
iconst_1             iPUSH
isub                 iSUB
invokestatic         invokestatic
iload_0              iLOAD
iconst_2             iPUSH
isub                 iSUB
invokestatic         invokestatic
iadd                 iADD
ireturn              iRETURN
```

The first three instructions come from the default constructor, and the remaining come from the `fib1` function itself. The bytecodes in mostly capital letters represent equivalence classes of canonicalized instructions.

Here's the hash table for the 3-gram shingles:

$$
hash(s) = \begin{cases}
\texttt{aLOAD,invokespecial,return} \Rightarrow 1 \\
\texttt{iLOAD,iPUSH,iIFCMP} \Rightarrow 2 \\
\texttt{iPUSH,iIFCMP,iLOAD} \Rightarrow 3 \\
\texttt{iIFCMP,iLOAD,iRETURN} \Rightarrow 4 \\
\texttt{iLOAD,iRETURN,iLOAD} \Rightarrow 5 \\
\texttt{iRETURN,iLOAD,iPUSH} \Rightarrow 6 \\
\texttt{iLOAD,iPUSH,iSUB} \Rightarrow 7 \\
\texttt{iPUSH,iSUB,invokestatic} \Rightarrow 8 \\
\texttt{iSUB,invokestatic,iLOAD} \Rightarrow 9 \\
\texttt{invokestatic,iLOAD,iPUSH} \Rightarrow 10 \\
\texttt{iSUB,invokestatic,iADD} \Rightarrow 11 \\
\texttt{invokestatic,iADD,iRETURN} \Rightarrow 12 \\
\texttt{iPUSH,iLOAD,iIFCMP} \Rightarrow 13
\end{cases}
$$

`iLOAD,iIFCMP,iPUSH`	$\Rightarrow 14$
`iIFCMP,iPUSH,iLOAD`	$\Rightarrow 15$
`iPUSH,iLOAD,iADD`	$\Rightarrow 16$
`iLOAD,iADD,invokestatic`	$\Rightarrow 17$
`iADD,invokestatic,iPUSH`	$\Rightarrow 18$
`invokestatic,iPUSH,iLOAD`	$\Rightarrow 19$
`iADD,invokestatic,iADD`	$\Rightarrow 20$
`iADD,iRETURN,iLOAD`	$\Rightarrow 21$
`iRETURN,iLOAD,iRETURN`	$\Rightarrow 22$
`invokestatic,iADD,GOTO`	$\Rightarrow 23$
`iADD,GOTO,iLOAD`	$\Rightarrow 24$
`GOTO,iLOAD,iRETURN`	$\Rightarrow 25$

Given this hash function, the three classes hash into these sets:

```
Fib1:        {1,  2,  3,  4,  5,  6,  7,  8,  9,  10, 11, 12}
Fibonacci3:  {1,  12, 13, 14, 15, 16, 17, 18, 19, 20, 12, 21, 22}
Fibonacci4:  {1,  13, 14, 15, 16, 17, 18, 19, 20, 23, 24, 25}
```

Notice how 1 occurs in all sets; it corresponds to the shingle from the default constructor. The containment measure is 17% for [Fib1,Fibonacci3], 8% for [Fib1, Fibonacci4], and 75% for [Fibonacci3,Fibonacci4].

10.4 API-Based Analysis

Application programs don't exist in a vacuum. Rather, they interact with the system on which they run through a set of standard library types and calls. On Unix, these are the system calls defined by the operating system (such as open, read, and write) or the standard libraries that provide higher-level abstractions on top of these (such as stdio and math).

What's interesting is that some of these library functions can be replaced by the programmer. For example, in Java, you don't have to use the standard java.util.Hashtable; you could replace it with your own implementation. Similarly, on Unix, you could replace all the functions in the math library with your own. You saw this in Algorithm OBFDMRVSL (Section 4.6.3 ▶281), which replaces common Java libraries with its own versions. This can be a useful obfuscation not only because it obscures the interface between the application code and the library, but because it makes the library code amenable to obfuscation as well.

What's even more interesting is that some standard library functions *cannot* be replaced. If you want to write something to a file (or a socket, a pipe, and so on) on Unix, you *have to* use the `write` system call or one of the library functions that call `write`. Similarly, in Java, if you want to open a window, you had better create an instance of `java.awt.Frame` or one of its subclasses.

There are several birthmarking algorithms that are based on this observation. The idea is that the way a program uses the standard libraries or system calls (we'll collectively call them APIs from now on) is not only unique to that program but also difficult for an adversary to forge.

As we already mentioned, not all APIs are created equal. To be really useful for birthmarking purposes, the use of an API needs to be difficult to obfuscate. That is, it needs to be

- *atomic* (i.e., a call can't be obfuscated by splitting it up in pieces),
- *state-full* (i.e., calls can't easily be added or removed, since this would affect the state of the system),
- *non-forgeable* (i.e., its use can't be replaced by the use of another API), and
- common in real code.

For example, on Unix, the `read` system call isn't a good candidate for an API birthmark, since it isn't atomic; a single call can be obfuscated by splitting it into two or more calls. The Unix `gettimeofday()` and `getpid()` system calls also aren't good candidates, since they are state-less; an adversary can disrupt the birthmark by sprinkling calls to these functions willy-nilly all over the program. The use of the standard `malloc` library can easily be forged by replacing it with another one. Finally, the `ioctl` (*i-o-control*) system call is atomic, non-forgeable, and state-full, but basing a birthmarking algorithm on the use of this call would not be very useful, since it occurs sparingly or not at all in most application programs.

10.4.1 *ssTNMM:* Object-Oriented Birthmarks

Tamada and co-authors have presented a collection of algorithms for collecting birthmarks from Java API types and method calls. $ssTNMM_{SMC}$ [343] computes the birthmark from the sequence of method calls within a class, $ssTNMM_{IS}$ computes the birthmark of a class from the inheritance path from the root class to the class, and $\textsc{ssTNMM}_{UC}$ computes the birthmark of a class from the types (other defined classes) it uses.

To illustrate these marks, we're going to use this simple Java program:

```
class Feline extends javax.swing.JFrame {
   public Feline (String title) {
      setTitle(title);
      setDefaultCloseOperation(javax.swing.JFrame.EXIT_ON_CLOSE);
      getContentPane().add(new javax.swing.JLabel(getLabel()),
                              java.awt.BorderLayout.CENTER);
      pack();
   }
   String getLabel() {
      return "k1773n".replaceAll("1","i").
            replaceAll("7","t").replaceAll("3","e");
   }
   public static void main(String[] args) {
      new Feline("Tudou").setVisible(true);
   }
}
```

All the birthmarks rely on the concept of a "well-known class." Well-known classes include those from the standard Java library and any class from projects that have become standard in the open-source community. Other, unknown classes are ignored.

The $\textsc{ssTNMM}_{IS}$ birthmark for a class C is the sequence of its super-classes, except for any that are not well known. For the `Feline` class above, you get the sequence of classes in light gray:

```
java.lang.Object
    extended by java.awt.Component
        extended by java.awt.Container
            extended by java.awt.Window
                extended by java.awt.Frame
                    extended by javax.swing.JFrame
                        extended by Feline
```

In this particular example, all the super-classes of `Feline` are well known. If, say, `java.awt.Window` would have been an unknown type, it would have been replaced by a wildcard * to indicate that it could be matched against any type. This handles the situation where an attacker replaces java.awt.Window with their own class.

The SSTNMM$_{SMC}$ birthmark for a class is computed by scanning top to bottom in the class file, and top to bottom over the bytecode for every method found, extracting those calls that go to methods in well-known classes. For Feline above, you get the methods in light gray:

```
javax.swing.JFrame
setTitle
setDefaultCloseOperation
getContentPane
getLabel
javax.swing.JLabel
java.awt.Container.add
pack
java.lang.String.replaceAll
java.lang.String.replaceAll
java.lang.String.replaceAll
Feline
setVisible
```

The intuition here is that replacing a method call from the standard library is hard for the attacker, because it may require rewriting a large chunk of code. This is sometimes, but certainly not always, true. For example, replacing the java.lang.Integer constructor with something else would be hard, since many other classes in the standard library rely on it and would also have to be rewritten. On the other hand, replacing java.lang.String.replaceAll with a different implementation is close to trivial, since that method is simple to implement and is known to have no side effects. This birthmark can also be disrupted by reordering method calls. Reordering calls within a method is non-trivial, since it requires you to know their data dependencies. Reordering all the methods within a class (and thereby reordering the calls they make) is trivial, however.

The SSTNMM$_{UC}$ birthmark of a class is the sorted sequence of well-known classes that occur as super-classes, interfaces, and in declarations of methods and variables. For the Feline class, you get the types in light gray:

```
Feline
java.awt.Container
java.lang.String
javax.swing.JFrame
javax.swing.JLabel
```

Disrupting this birthmark by removing a well-known class may be hard, but *adding* new types to the list is clearly trivial: Just create instances of well-known classes that have no dangerous side effects.

All the SSTNMM are sequences, so you can use any of the sequence similarity measures you saw in Section 10.2.1▶612. In their experiments, Tamada et al. used the measure in Definition 10.1▶613, which computes the similarity based on the number of identical element pairs.

10.4.2 *ssTONMM:* Dynamic Function Call Birthmarks

In Sections 6.3▶383 and 7.2.4▶431, you saw how programs can protect themselves by encrypting the executable and not decrypting themselves until they are run. This presents a problem for static birthmarking algorithms; two identical programs that have been encrypted with different keys will appear completely different! One way to deal with this is to capture the program once it's been decrypted and run the static birthmark over the cleartext code. Another way is to use a *dynamic* birthmark that computes a signal over the execution trace rather than the code itself.

The SSTONMM [341,342] algorithm computes the birthmark from a trace of the well-known library calls that are executed from a run of the program on a particular input. On Unix, the `ltrace` utility can be used to trace system and dynamic library calls. Have a look at this trivial C program:

```c
#include <stdio.h>
#include <time.h>
int main() {
    printf("%i\n%i\n",getpid(),clock());
}
```

For this program, the Unix command `ltrace  -S  main` generates this output (light gray are system calls and dark gray are dynamic library calls):

⟨ execve ,   brk ,   access ,   open ,   fstat64 ,
mmap2 ,   close ,   open ,   read ,   fstat64 ,
mmap2 ,   mmap2 ,   mmap2 ,   mmap2 ,   close ,
mmap2 ,   set_thread_area , mprotect , mprotect , munmap ,
__libc_start_main , clock ,   times ,   getpid ,   getpid ,
printf ,   fstat64 ,   mmap2 ,   write ,   exit_group ⟩

The first 21 calls are responsible for setting up the executable in memory and will be the same for all applications. You can see how the dynamic library function `getpid` calls the corresponding system call `getpid` and how the library function `clock` calls the system call `times`.

To compare two programs p and q, you run them on the same input, collect the traces of relevant API calls, and then compare the traces for similarity. You can compare the traces directly, of course, but that can be problematic if the attacker has reordered calls or inserted bogus ones. Another strategy is to compare the *frequency* of the different calls rather than their strict order. Here's a histogram of call frequencies we've constructed from the sequence of Unix system and dynamic library calls you just saw:

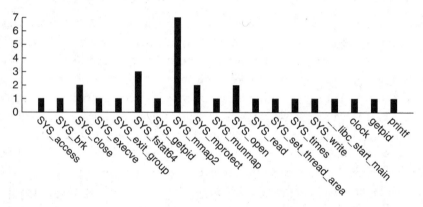

To compare two traces, you'd construct the histograms for both of them and compute their similarity by subtracting the frequencies. You'll see the same idea in Algorithm ssLM later in this chapter.

10.4.3 *ssSDL:* Dynamic *k*-gram API Birthmarks

ssSDL [317,318] combines several ideas you've seen already into one birthmarking algorithm:

1. Collect sequences of well-known API calls executed for a particular input,
2. Ignore calls that are so common they are unlikely to serve as good similarity indicators (for example, any calls to methods in Java's `java.lang.String` class), and
3. Construct the birthmark as a set of *k*-grams from the API call sequence.

The advantage of this algorithm is that the birthmark becomes substantially smaller than if you were to keep the entire trace. The actual size of the trace will depend on the value of k. For $k = 1$, for example, the birthmark will be just the set of API functions executed! For $k = 2$, the set will be larger (the pairs of executed API calls, and so on). The sets of k-grams from two programs p and q can be compared for similarity using Definition 10.3▶614, as before.

Schuler et al. [318] evaluated both the false positive rate of the algorithm and its resilience to attack. Comparing the traces of a set of six individually developed programs, all performing the same task, the similarity ranged from 9% to 26%. In other words, the algorithm showed a low false positive rate. In a second experiment, 11 differently obfuscated versions of 12 programs were constructed using two Java obfuscators (SandMark [2] and Zelix KlassMaster [3]). They had no effect on the extracted birthmarks. Neither of these obfuscators was specifically designed to destroy API-based algorithms, however, so it's debatable just how much this test says about the resilience of ssSDL.

ssSDL seems like an attractive dynamic API-based algorithm, since the size of the birthmark can be easily adjusted by setting the shingle and winnowing window size (K and W in Algorithm 10.5▶617).

10.5 Tree-Based Analysis

Programs in source form are naturally hierarchical, i.e., tree-structured. Nested statements in structured programming languages form trees, in languages without multiple inheritance classes form a tree, operators and operands in an expression form a tree, and so on. An abstract syntax tree (AST) is a convenient program representation when you want to manipulate code in a form that's very close to source. It maintains all the information that's in the source in a tree form, usually omitting formatting and comments. Note that an AST is different from a *parse tree*, which contains artifacts left over from the parsing process. The AST, on the other hand, as the name implies, *abstracts* away from any parsing process and only maintains the information that's in the original program. You saw an example of an AST in Section 3.3.2▶180, in Chapter 3, when you read about decompilation.

There aren't that many software similarity algorithms that use trees as their program representation. Here, you'll see only one algorithm, ssEFM, which finds clones in ASTs.

10.5.1 *ssEFM:* AST-Based Clone Detection

Let's assume you want to look for clones in this program:

```
(5 + (a + b)) * (7 + (c + 9))
```

You start by parsing it and building a corresponding AST S:

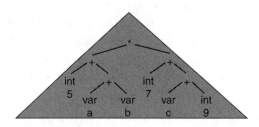

Let's first examine a very simple (and inefficient) approach to finding clones in an AST. After building the tree, you construct from it *all* possible *tree patterns*. A tree pattern is a subtree of S where one or more subtrees have been replaced with a wildcard. We'll call these wildcards *holes* and represent them using a question mark character (?). Here are some of the patterns for the AST above:

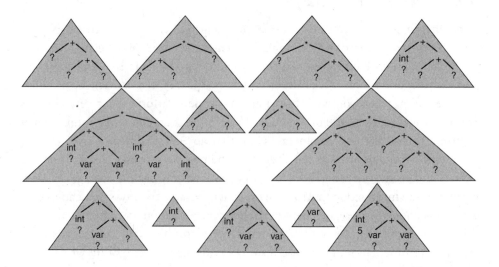

For clarity, in this section we'll shade the ASTs themselves in dark gray and the tree patterns in light gray.

So what's a clone in the context of an abstract syntax tree? It's simply a tree pattern for which there's more than one match in the AST! Look through the patterns above and compare them to S—which patterns would make a good clone?

In general, a tree pattern has the potential to be a good clone if it

1. Has a large number of nodes (you want clones that are as large as possible),
2. Occurs a large number of times in the AST (you want patterns that occur at least twice), and
3. Has few holes (a pattern with many holes will result in a clone with many parameters).

This pattern seems like it might make a good choice

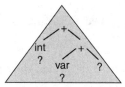

since it matches two large subtrees of S:

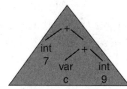 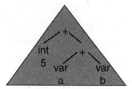

Once you have identified this pattern as a good clone, you extract it into its own function (or, in this case, macro) and replace all occurrences with a call:

```
#define CLONE(x,y,z) ((x)+((y)+(z)))
CLONE(5,a,b) * CLONE(7,c,9)
```

As long are you're willing to ignore performance, it's not hard to turn this basic idea into an algorithm. Start by building up a *clone table*, a mapping from each pattern to the location (or multiple locations) in S where it occurs. Here are a few of the entries in this table:

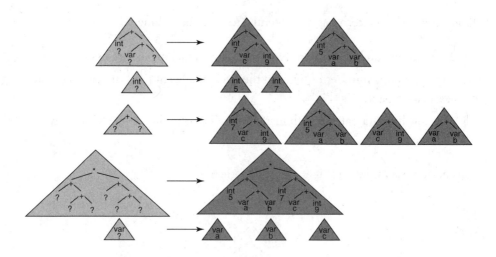

Now, all you have to do is sort the table so that the entries with the largest patterns, most number of occurrences, and the fewest number of holes appear first, and you're almost done! A human programmer can then scour the list from most likely to least likely clones and manually, or with some automatic help, choose the best candidates for clone extraction.

Unfortunately, this algorithm won't scale to large programs, since the AST will produce an exponential number of tree patterns. Algorithm ssEFM therefore resorts to heuristics, which iteratively *grow* larger tree patterns from smaller ones. The details are complicated, and we'll omit them here, and instead we'll leave you with an example to illustrate the basic idea behind the heuristic. Have a look at this entry in the clone table:

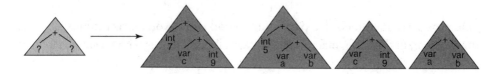

How would it be possible to grow the pattern larger so that it still matches as many of the occurrences as possible? One possibility is to specialize the pattern by filling in the left branch with var(?), forming a new pattern +(var(?),?), which would match two of the occurrences. Another possibility would be to specialize the pattern by filling in its right branch by +(?,?), forming +(?,+(?,?)). It's natural to settle on this pattern since it is larger, although it only matches two occurrences rather than four:

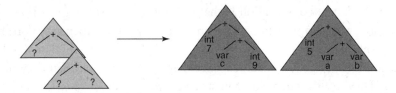

After two more steps of specialization, we arrive at the final pattern, which matches two occurrences in S:

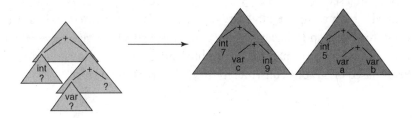

Using their Asta tool, Will Evans et al. [125a] report finding this clone 10 times across a set of Java classes:

```
for(int i=0; i<?₁; i++)
    if (?₂[i] != ?₃[i])
        return false;
```

In one of the occurrences, the third hole ($?_3$) was filled with a variable x, and in another occurrence with a field reference x.y. This shows that the strength of the algorithm is that it allows structural matching: Holes can accept *any* subtree, not just simple literals or variables, as in simpler algorithms.

10.6 Graph-Based Analysis

Programs are graph-like structures. Functions are naturally represented as control flow graphs, dependencies between statements within a function as dependence graphs, possible calls between functions as call graphs, inheritance relationships between classes as acyclic graphs, and so on. Given this, it makes sense to ask whether program similarity can be computed over graph representations of programs.

An unfortunate complication is that subgraph isomorphism is NP-complete, so straightforward graph comparisons are going to be too expensive. Fortunately, graphs computed from programs are not general graphs. Control flow graphs will not be arbitrarily large, for example, since they correspond to functions written by humans. They're also much closer in structure to a very restricted class of graphs known as *series-parallel graphs* [188] than to general graphs. Similarly, call graphs tend to be very sparse, since a function will call at most a handful of other functions. For such reasons, heuristics can be very effective in approximating subgraph isomorphism on graphs generated from programs.

Here, you'll see three similarity algorithms based on graphs. Algorithms SSKH and SSLCHY both compute similarity over program dependence graphs (PDGs), and do so for clone and plagiarism detection, respectively. SSMC$_{wpp}$, on the other hand, is a dynamic birthmarking algorithm and computes the similarity of two programs based on graphs constructed from their runtime traces.

10.6.1 *ssKH:* **PDG-Based Clone Detection**

In Section 3.1.3 ▸132, you learned about program dependence graphs, PDGs. The nodes of the graph are the statements of a function, and there's an edge $m \rightarrow n$ between two nodes m and n if n is data-dependent on m (m computes a value and n uses it) or n is control-dependent on m (m represents a predicate that determines whether n gets executed or not). PDGs have the nice property that semantics-preserving reordering of the statements of a function won't affect the graph. This makes them useful for clone detection, which we'll discuss here, and plagiarism detection, which you'll see in the next section.

The basic idea of algorithm SSKH [208] is to build a PDG for each function of the program and to compute two isomorphic subgraphs by slicing backward along dependency edges starting with every pair of *matching nodes*. Two nodes are matching if they have the same syntactic structure. Every reachable pair of matching nodes are added to the two slices until no more nodes can be added. You can see the details in Algorithm 10.7 ▸637.

Have a look at the (rather contrived) example below, where two very similar pieces of code have been intertwined within the same function:

Algorithm 10.7 Overview of Algorithm SSKH.

DETECTCLONES(P):

1. For each function $f_i \in P$ construct its program dependence graph G_i.

2. Assign nodes to equivalence classes based on their syntactic structure, ignoring variable names and literal values.

3. For each pair of nodes $m \in G_i$ and $n \in G_j$ that belong to the same equivalence class, find two subgraphs $S_i \subset G_i$ and $S_j \subset G_j$ such that m is a node in S_i, n is a node in S_j, and S_i and S_j are isomorphic:

    (a) Slice backward from m and n in lock-step, adding m's predecessor node to S_i and n's predecessor node to S_j only if they are in the same equivalence class;

    (b) If nodes m and n correspond to a predicate p in a statement if (p) ... or while (p) ... slice forward one step from m and n and add their control-dependence successors to S_i and S_j, respectively.

    (S_i, S_j) form a *clone pair*.

4. If one clone pair (S'_i, S'_j) is contained in another clone pair (S_i, S_j), i.e., $S'_i \subseteq S_i$ and $S'_j \subseteq S_j$, remove (S'_i, S'_j).

5. Transitively combine related clone pairs into larger clone groups.

6. Return the set of clone groups.

```
a₁: a = g(8);
b₁: b = z*3;
a₂: while(a<10)
    a₃: a = f(a);
b₂: while(b<20)
    b₃: b = f(b);
a₄: if (a==10) {
    a₅: printf("foo\n");
    a₆: x=x+2;
}
b₄: if (b==20) {
    b₅: printf("bar\n");
    b₆: y=y+2;
    b₇: printf("baz\n");
}
```

The algorithm starts by considering the two nodes a_4 and b_4. It finds that they're matching (they have the same syntactic structure), so the algorithm continues by considering their predecessors in the graph, a_3 and b_3. These match too, and so are added to the slice. Nodes a_1 and b_1 are also predecessors of a_4 and b_4, respectively, but they don't match and are not added to the slice. Next, the algorithm adds nodes a_2 and b_2 to the slice, since they match and are predecessors of a_3 and b_3, respectively. At this stage, the algorithm has identified the light gray and dark gray node sets as potential clones:

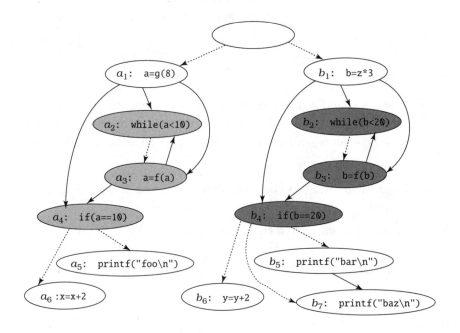

A human programmer who examined this code would probably identify a_5/b_5 and a_6/b_6 as also belonging to the clone. Unfortunately, slicing backward from a_5/b_5, for example, would never include a_6/b_6 in the clone, and slicing backward from a_6/b_6 would never include a_5/b_5! The reason is that there are no dependencies between these nodes. They are, however, control-dependent on the predicate in the if-statement a_4/b_4 that contains them. For this reason, whenever you see a predicate in an if-statement or while-statement, you slice *forward* one step from that node and add any matching nodes to the slice. This leads you to the final clone pair from which you can extract the clone code into a macro or function:

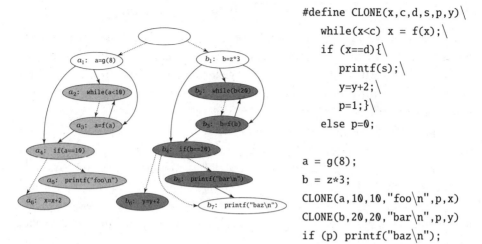

```
#define CLONE(x,c,d,s,p,y)\
    while(x<c) x = f(x);\
    if (x==d){\
        printf(s);\
        y=y+2;\
        p=1;}\
    else p=0;


a = g(8);
b = z*3;
CLONE(a,10,10,"foo\n",p,x)
CLONE(b,20,20,"bar\n",p,y)
if (p) printf("baz\n");
```

Notice that the clone returns a value 0 or 1 in the p variable. This is used to make sure that node b_7, which is not part of the clone, will be executed only for the second use of the clone.

What's particularly nice about this algorithm is that it handles clones where statements have been reordered, clones that are non-contiguous, and clones that have been intertwined with each other. Cases where variables have been renamed or literal constants have been given new values are also easily handled, since nodes are said to match only if they have the same syntactic structure.

Unfortunately, Komondoor and Horwitz [208] report depressing performance numbers. A 11,540-line C program takes 1 hour and 34 minutes to process. A further problem with the algorithm is that it produces many variants of the same clone (250 clone groups were found in a program of 11,060 lines of code) and these have to be examined manually to find the clones that are truly useful to extract.

Problem 10.1   Would it be possible to use non-graph-based analyses and still reap many of the same benefits of PDG-based analysis, but at a lower cost? For example, could a prepass over the code to canonicalize it followed by, say, a k-gram-based analysis work just as well in finding reordered or intertwined clones? The prepass could reorder independent statements in lexicographic order, rename variables by first use, turn all for-loops into while-loops, break complex statements into 3-address statements, and so on.

10.6.2 *ssLCHY:* PDG-Based Plagiarism Detection

Like Algorithm ssKH, Algorithm ssLCHY [232] uses PDGs, but does so for plagiarism detection rather than clone detection. The major differences between the two algorithms are that ssLCHY employs a general-purpose subgraph isomorphism algorithm rather than slicing, and in order to speed up processing, uses a preprocessing step to weed out unlikely plagiarism candidates.

Algorithm 10.8▸640 gives an overview of the method. The first problem you need to solve is what it should mean for one PDG to be considered a plagiarized version of another. Since you expect some manner of obfuscation of the code on part of the plagiarist, you can't require the two PDGs to be completely identical. You instead need to relax the requirement to say that the two PDGs should be γ-isomorphic in accordance with Definition 10.5▸615. Liu et al. set $\gamma = 0.9$, argue that "overhauling

---

Algorithm 10.8 Overview of Algorithm ssLCHY. P is the original program and Q the plagiarism suspect. K is the minimum number of nodes a PDG should have to be considered. γ is a relaxation parameter for the subgraph isomorphism test.

DETECT(P, Q, K, γ):

1. For each function $p_i \in P$ ($q_i \in Q$) construct its program dependence graph G_i (H_j).

2. Let R be the set of all pairs of graphs (G_i, H_j).

3. Filter out unlikely plagiarism candidates from R:

    (a) Remove from R any pair (G_i, H_j) such that G_i or H_j have fewer than K nodes.

    (b) Remove from R any pair (G_i, H_j) such that $|H_j| < \gamma |G_i|$.

    (c) Let $\mathcal{F}(g) = (u_1, \dots, u_k)$ be the frequencies of the k different node kinds in PDG g. Remove from R any pair (G_i, H_j) where $\mathcal{F}(G_i) \not\approx \mathcal{F}(H_j)$.

4. Do a pairwise comparison of the remaining pairs in R:

```
for each pair of graphs (Gᵢ, Hⱼ) ∈ R do
    if Hⱼ is not γ-isomorphic to Gᵢ then
        R ← R − {(Gᵢ, Hⱼ)}
```

5. Return R, the set of plagiarism candidates.

(without errors) 10% of a PDG of reasonable size is almost equivalent to rewriting the code."

The algorithm handles the second problem, performance, by using three filtering steps that together typically prune out $\frac{9}{10}$ of all program pairs from consideration. The first filter ignores any graph that has too few nodes to be interesting. The second filter removes (g, g') from consideration if $|g'| < \gamma|g|$, since this pair would never pass a γ-isomorphism test anyway. The final filter removes (g, g') from consideration if the frequency of their different node types is too different. For example, if g consists solely of function call nodes and g' consists solely of nodes representing arithmetic operations, it's unlikely they're related.

Algorithm ssLCHY was designed to be robust against common techniques plagiarists use to thwart detection. A PDG is not affected by transformations such as statement reordering, variable renaming, replacing while-loops with for-loops, or flipping the order of branches in if-statements. This doesn't mean, of course, that there aren't other transformations that affect the PDG! Since each PDG is built from a function, a plagiarist could use inter-procedural transformations such as inlining and outlining to alter the graph significantly. He could also add bogus dependencies between variables to introduce spurious edges in the PDGs. You saw an example of this obfuscation in Section 4.4.4 ▸ 253, where we added bogus variable dependencies in order to confuse a slicing tool.

Of course, in an academic setting, using such powerful transformations could well prove counterproductive: While they may prevent a student's plagiaristic activities from being detected, in the end they may make his program so ugly that he will no longer receive a passing grade!

10.6.3 $ssMC_{wpp}$: Dynamic Whole Program Birthmarks

To compare two programs for similarity, you could just run them in parallel and compare their execution traces. Not only is this inconvenient if the traces are long, but you might also get easily thrown off track if your adversary has made modifications to the program he has copied. What you'd like is to compress the two very long traces into more compact representations that capture the salient aspects of the traces, and then compare these representations. Algorithm $ssMC_{wpp}$ [260,262] uses Algorithm RELJ, which you saw in Section 3.2.4 ▸ 168, to compress traces into context-free grammars. These grammars can then be represented as directed acyclic graphs that form the actual birthmark.

Consider once more the modular exponentiation routine. Below is its control flow graph (the body of the main loop has been outlined into a function `foo()`), and the DAG grammar that results from executing the basic blocks in the order

$A, BCDF, BCDF, BCEF, BCEF, BCEF, BCEF, BCEF, BCEF, G:$

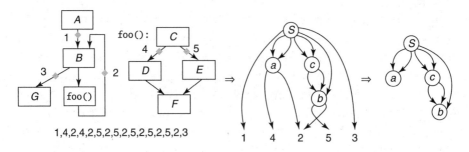

Algorithm SSMC_{wpp} throws away all terminal symbols and keeps the remainder of the DAG as the *whole program birthmark*. This is the rightmost graph above. The birthmark captures, in a reasonably compact representation, the program's repetitive execution pattern.

To compare an original program P and a suspected derivative Q, you run them both on the same input, collect their traces, construct context-free grammars from each trace, throw away the terminal symbols, build the DAGs, and use Definition 10.5▶615 to compute *containment*(P, Q). This gives you a measure of how much of P can be found within Q. In practice, Definition 10.5▶615 would be too expensive to compute exactly, since it relies on subgraph isomorphism, which is NP-hard even for directed acyclic graphs. Heuristics can be used to approximate the metric, however, since the DAGs produced from Algorithm RELJ are highly stylized: They are sparse, they have a unique start node with a very high out-degree, and the remaining nodes have a very low in- and out-degree. Ginger Myles describes a heuristic based on these properties in her Ph.D. thesis [260].

The attack model here is similar to what you've seen before, namely, the adversary applying semantics-preserving transformations to the code to try to thwart birthmark detection. In a sense, he's wrapping the original program P inside a layer of obfuscation to form a new program Q. At runtime, Q performs all the same actions as P, possibly in a different way from P, along with additional, bogus actions that P does not.

To evaluate the robustness of Algorithm SSMC_{wpp}, we must ask ourselves how different kinds of obfuscations affect the birthmark DAG. Let's have a look at a few examples. First, let's insert an opaque predicate protecting a completely bogus if-then-else construct comprising basic blocks $G, H, I,$ and J:

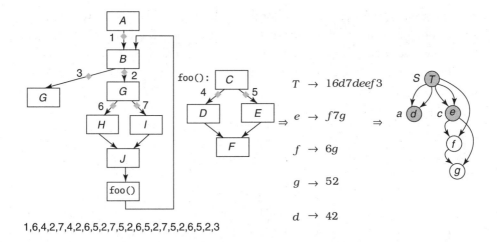

1,6,4,2,7,4,2,6,5,2,7,5,2,6,5,2,7,5,2,6,5,2,3

The pruned birthmarking graph is above right. In this section, we're identifying graphs by their root node labels, so this is graph T. The light gray nodes are those that are part of the maximal common subgraph of the original graph S and T, $mcs(S, T)$. Labels next to the nodes indicate the subgraph mapping to the nodes in S. Using the formulas for containment and similarity of graphs in Definition 10.5 ▶615, we get that $containment(S, T) = \frac{|mcs(S,T)|}{|S|} = \frac{3}{4}$ and $similarity(S, T) = \frac{|mcs(S,T)|}{\max(|S|,|T|)} = \frac{3}{5}$.

Adding a few bogus branches is a pretty benign control flow obfuscation. Let's instead see what happens when we chenxify the code:

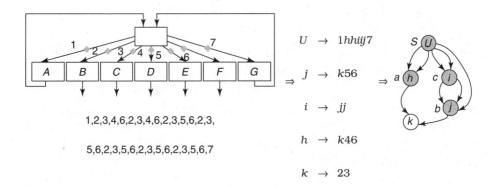

1,2,3,4,6,2,3,4,6,2,3,5,6,2,3,

5,6,2,3,5,6,2,3,5,6,2,3,5,6,7

Even though this obfuscation makes substantial changes to the static layout of the code, maybe surprisingly, the runtime execution pattern is left pretty much intact: $containment(S, T) = \frac{4}{4}$ and $similarity(S, T) == \frac{4}{5}$.

The grammars generated by Algorithm RELJ capture the repetitive pattern of an executing program. This means that any transformation that hides looping can be an effective attack. Splitting a loop in two is one such transformation, as is loop unrolling. Here's what happens when you perform a single unrolling of the loop in the example program:

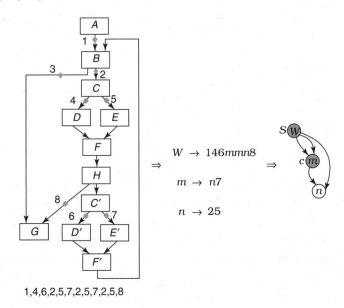

$$W \rightarrow 146mmn8$$

$$m \rightarrow n7$$

$$n \rightarrow 25$$

1,4,6,2,5,7,2,5,7,2,5,8

The nodes C', D', E', and F' are specialized copies of C, D, E, and F, respectively. Since this is a while-loop, you need to insert an extra test between each copy of the loop body. This is node H in the CFG above. Since there is much less repetition now, the resulting graph becomes smaller, and containment and similarity are significantly reduced: $containment(S, T) = \frac{2}{4}$ and $similarity(S, T) == \frac{2}{4}$.

It's unclear how this algorithm would perform on substantial traces of real programs. In [221], Jim Larus reports that in one of his test cases, an original 1598MB trace was compressed into a 6.6MB grammar. This may be impressive, but comparing two graphs with millions of nodes for similarity may still prove prohibitively expensive!

10.7 Metrics-Based Analysis

In Section 3.4.2▸193, in Chapter 3 (Program Analysis), we gave you a very brief overview of *software metrics*. You also saw them in Chapter 4 (Code Obfuscation), where it was suggested that they could be used to measure how poorly structured a program is after obfuscation. Conte et al. [92] define the concept like this: "Software metrics are used to characterize the essential features for software quantitatively, so that classification, comparison, and mathematical analysis can be applied." Here, we're going to revisit software metrics in the context of comparing code for similarity.

We'll show you two metrics-based algorithms. SSKK does clone detection by looking for pieces of code with similar metrics values. This is less precise than the algorithms you've seen previously, but it also has the potential for being a whole lot faster. SSLM does authorship analysis by comparing the metric values of samples of authors' code.

10.7.1 *ssKK:* **Metrics-Based Clone Detection**

The basic assumption behind software complexity metrics is that you can learn something about a program by counting various aspects of it. Algorithm SSKK [209] takes this one step further and makes the assumption that two pieces of a program that are similar (are potential clones) will also have similar metrics, and furthermore, that two pieces of code that are *not* clones will have different metrics.

The basic idea is simple. First, build the abstract syntax tree for the program. Second, in a bottom-up pass over the tree, compute a set of complexity metrics for each subtree. Finally, do a pairwise comparison of the metrics for each subtree. Constructs with similar metrics values are more likely to be clones.

To illustrate this, let's have a look at these two functions and their corresponding abstract syntax trees:

```
int foo () {                      int bar () {
    int a,g;                          int b,v,x;
    if (a==0)  {                      while (b==0) {
        g++;                              frob();
        baz();                            int v=x+1;
    };                                }
}                                 }
```

Attached to each node is a 4-tuple of metrics values:

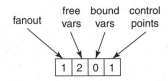

Fanout is the number of function calls made by the construct, *free vars* is the number of variables referenced in the construct but not declared in it, *bound vars* is the number of variables that are declared and referenced in the construct, and *control points* is the number of predicates used in control constructs. The counts are cumulative, meaning the metrics for a node n is the sum of those of n's children.

To see if foo and bar are potential clones, you simply compare their metrics' tuples for similarity, for example, using the Euclidean distance, $similarity(\bar{p}, \bar{q}) = \sqrt{\Sigma(p_i - q_i)^2}$. In our case, foo and bar are very close; they have a Euclidean distance of only 1 unit. Still, looking at the source, it seems pretty unlikely for them to be clones! The reason for this discrepancy is that the metrics we chose are not precise enough to distinguish between even pretty distinct pieces of code. There are hundreds of software metrics proposed in the literature, and it's possible that adding more of them into the mix could improve precision.

Regardless of the metrics chosen, it's likely that ssKK will be much less precise than the other algorithms you've seen that are based on more direct code comparisons. However, it's also likely to be much more efficient, since it requires a single pass over the code to compute the metrics, followed by simple pairwise comparisons of the metrics tuples. In spite of its imprecision it could, therefore, be useful as a quick-and-dirty preprocessing step to other algorithms to weed out parts of the program that can't possibly be clones.

10.7.2 *ssLM:* Metrics-Based Authorship Analysis

Authorship analysis is mostly done at the source-code level. Since as programmers we adopt certain formatting habits (how we indent our code, how we choose identifiers, how we format our comments, and so on), it's reasonable to believe that there might be enough clues in source code to tell the programs of different authors apart. Of course, it's not clear *which* features in source code are useful in order to discriminate between authors! It could well be that so many students have been steeped in the same programming style (for example, K&R [196] C) that many formatting features are no longer distinctive enough to successfully tell one author from another.

Krsul and Spafford [211] classify source-code metrics into three categories. *Programming layout metrics* include measures related to indentation, where brackets are placed, how comments are formatted, and so on. These metrics are not very robust—tools like pretty printers and structure editors will easily destroy them. *Programming style metrics* include metrics such as average variable length and internal structure of identifiers (Hungarian vs. camel-back notation, for example). Finally, *programming structure metrics* are related to the maturity, ability, and training of the programmer. They include average number of lines of code per function, preference for particular algorithms and data structures, and so on. We've listed the metrics that Krsul and Spafford used in their experiments in Tables 10.1▸649, 10.2▸650, and 10.3▸650.

10.7.2.1   Classification Using Histograms

Algorithm 10.9▸648 gives the four routines that SSLM [220] uses to map a program to the most likely author. HISTOGRAM (P, m) uses metric m to extract numeric data from program P, from which it then builds a normalized histogram. Table 10.4▸651 gives some examples where we've built histograms over metrics PRO1, PSM5, and STY1bg using training programs from three programmers, Alice, Bob, and Charlie. For example, Alice's histogram for the PRO1 metric was built from the values $\langle 20, 30, 30, 40, 40, 50 \rangle$. Because of the normalization, each histogram shows the "shape" of a particular programmer's behavior on a particular metric. The DISTANCE(M, P_1, P_2) routine in Algorithm 10.9▸648 compares two programs P_1 and P_2 for similarity over a set of metrics M by subtracting their corresponding histograms.

CLASSIFY(Q, A, M', P^t) finds the most likely author for an unknown program Q. It starts by computing the histograms over the metrics in M' for the training programs in P^t. It then computes the histograms for Q and returns the author whose histograms match the best.

10.7.2.2   Selecting the Right Metrics

Tables 10.1▸649, 10.2▸650, and 10.3▸650 list a total of fifty metrics. There are also many possible variants, such as computing the standard deviation of the average program line length metric PRO1. Some of these metrics will be relevant to distinguishing one programmer from another, and others will not be. How do you find the combination that gives the most precise results?

A simple strategy is to exhaustively enumerate all combinations of metrics and see which ones perform best on the evaluation data. This is what BESTMETRICS(A, M, P^t, P^e) in Algorithm 10.9▸648 does. It first trains histograms using the training programs P^t and then evaluates these histograms using the evaluation programs P^e. This is what we've done here:

Algorithm 10.9 Overview of the SSLM algorithm. A is a set of authors, P_a^t is training data (programs) for author $a \in A$, P_a^e is evaluation data (programs different from those in P_a^t) for a, M is a set of metrics, and Q is a program of unknown authorship.

HISTOGRAM(P, m):

1. Extract the sequence of numeric data $N = \langle x_0, x_1, \ldots \rangle$ corresponding to metric m from program P.

2. Construct the histogram $H = \langle (x_0, y_0), (x_1, y_1), \ldots \rangle$:

   (a) Let y_i be the number of occurrences of x_i in N.

   (b) Normalize the histogram by dividing each y-value by the sum of all the y-values.

   (c) Interpolate any missing intermediate values.

3. Return H.

DISTANCE(M, P_1, P_2):

```
S ← 0
for m ∈ M do
    h₁ ← HISTOGRAM(P₁, m)
    h₂ ← HISTOGRAM(P₂, m)
    for x ∈ range(m) do
        S ← S + |h₁(x) − h₂(x)|
return S
```

BESTMETRICS(A, M, P^t, P^e):

```
for all subsets M′ of M do
    winners[M′] ← 0
    for all authors a₁ ∈ A do
        min ← ∞
        winner ← nobody
        for all authors a₂ ∈ A do
            D ← DISTANCE(M′, Pᵉₐ₁, Pᵗₐ₂)
            if D < min then
                min ← D
                winner ← a₂
        if winner=a₁ then
            winners[M′] ← winners[M′]+1
W ← M′ with largest winners[M′]
return W
```

CLASSIFY($Q, A, M′, P^t$):

```
min ← ∞
winner ← nobody
for all authors a ∈ A do
    D ← DISTANCE(M′, Q, Pᵗₐ)
    if D < min then
        min ← D
        winner ← a
return winner
```

Table 10.1 Programming layout metrics. Adapted from reference [211].

Name	Description
STY1a	Indentation of C statements within surrounding blocks.
STY1b	Percentage of open curly brackets ({) that are alone in a line.
STY1c	Percentage of open curly brackets ({) that are the first character in a line.
STY1d	Percentage of open curly brackets ({) that are the last character in a line.
STY1e	Percentage of close curly brackets (}) that are alone in a line.
STY1f	Percentage of close curly brackets (}) that are the first character on a line.
STY1g	Percentage of close curly brackets (}) that are the last character in a line.
STY1h	Indentation of open curly brackets ({).
STY1i	Indentation of close curly brackets (}).
STY2	Indentation of statements starting with the `else` keyword.
STY3	In variable declarations, are variable names indented to a fixed column?
STY4	Separators (spaces, newlines, or none) between the function names and the parameter lists in function declarations.
STY5	Separators (spaces, newlines, or none) between the function return type and the function name in function declarations.
STY6a	Use of borders to highlight comments.
STY6b	Percentage of lines of code with inline comments.
STY6c	Ratio of lines of block style comments to lines of code.
STY7	Ratio of white lines to lines of code.

	Alice	Bob	Charlie
PRO1	Charlie, Alice, Bob	Bob, Charlie, Alice	Charlie, Alice, Bob
PSM5	Bob, Alice, Charlie	Alice, Bob, Charlie	Charlie, Bob, Alice
STY1bg	Charlie, Alice, Bob	Charlie, Alice, Bob	Alice, Charlie, Bob
PRO1,PSM5	Alice, Charlie, Bob	Bob, Alice, Charlie	Charlie, Alice, Bob
PRO1,STY1bg	Charlie, Alice, Bob	Bob, Charlie, Alice	Charlie, Alice, Bob
PSM5,STY1bg	Bob, Alice, Charlie	Alice, Bob, Charlie	Charlie, Alice, Bob
PRO1,PSM5,STY1bg	Alice, Charlie, Bob	Bob, Alice, Charlie	Charlie, Alice, Bob

We started with the training data turned into histograms in Table 10.4▸651. Then, for each combination of metrics and for each potential author, we classified the evaluation programs written by that author and noted the result. For example, the entry marked in dark gray is the result of classifying an evaluation program written by Alice using a combination of the PRO1 and STY1bg metrics. The result ranked Charlie as the most likely author, followed by Alice, and then Bob. In other words, PRO1 and STY1bg is probably not a good combination of metrics. We've marked all the tests that were successful, i.e., they ranked the actual author highest, in light gray.

Table 10.2 Programming style metrics. Adapted from reference [211].

Name	Description
PRO1	Mean program line length (characters per line).
PRO2a	Mean local variable name length.
PRO2b	Mean global variable name length.
PRO2c	Mean function name length.
PRO2d	Mean function parameter length.
PRO3a	Some identifiers use the underscore character.
PRO3b	Temporary variables are named XXX*nnn*, tmp*nnn*, or temp*nnn*.
PRO3c	Percentage of variable names that start with an uppercase letter.
PRO3d	Percentage of function names that start with an uppercase letter.
PRO4	Global variable count to mean local variable count ratio.
PRO5	Global variable count to lines of code ratio.
PRO6	Use of conditional compilation.
PRO7	Preference of either `while`, `for`, or do loops.
PRO8	Comments nearly an echo of the code?
PRO9	Standard or ANSI C format function parameter declaration.

Table 10.3 Programming structure metrics. Adapted from reference [211].

Name	Description
PSM1	Percentage of `int` function definitions.
PSM2	Percentage of `void` function definitions.
PSM3	Program uses a debugging symbol or keyword (`debug`, `dbg`).
PSM4	The assert macro is used.
PSM5	Lines of code per function.
PSM6	Variable count to lines of code ratio.
PSM7	Percentage of global variables that are declared static.
PSM8	The ratio of decision count to lines of code.
PSM9	Is the `goto` keyword used?
PSM10	Generic software complexity metrics, as found in Section 3.4.2 ► 193.
PSM11a	Are error results from `malloc`-related system calls ignored?
PSM11b	Are error results from I/O routines ignored?
PSM11c	Are error results from other system calls ignored?
PSM12	Does the programmer rely on the internal representation of data objects, such as the size and byte order of integers?
PSM13	Do functions have unexpected side effects?
PSM14	Do comments and code agree?
PSM15	Development phase metrics (compilers/editors/development styles used).
PSM16	Software quality metrics.

Table 10.4 Three metrics PRO1, PSM5, and STY1bg were extracted from training programs written by three programmers Alice, Bob, and Charlie. The histograms are normalized between 0.0 and 1.0. The histogram for the STY1bg metric shows the frequency of the different possible placements of brackets, i.e., the labels on the x-axis refer to metrics STY1b, STY1c, . . . , STY1g.

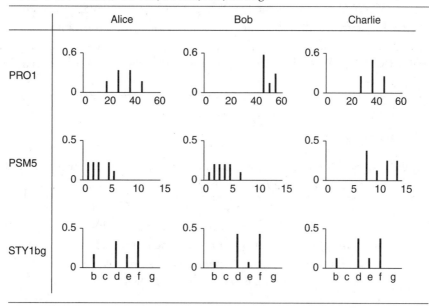

PRO1 and STY1bg is not a good combination, but STY1bg by itself is even worse, since it misclassifies *every* author's test data. The best combination seems to be PRO1 with PSM5, since it correctly classifies all test programs with the fewest number of metrics. You can get an intuition for the reason why by looking at Table 10.4. Notice how Bob's PRO1 is markedly different from those of Alice and Charlie. PRO1 isn't enough by itself to tell Alice's and Charlie's programs apart, though, since their profiles are very similar. PSM5, on the other hand, doesn't distinguish Alice from Bob but does distinguish the two of them from Charlie. Thus, it makes sense that PRO1 and PSM5 together would form a good combination.

In practice, exhaustively enumerating and testing all combinations of metrics won't scale. There are many well-known techniques that can be used to heuristically eliminate those metrics that don't contribute much to the classification. Krsul and Spafford [211] tried a number of techniques, including a statistical method known as *discriminant analysis*, a neural network-based classifier, and a Gaussian classifier. ssLM used a genetic algorithm-based classification method. Krsul and Spafford found that Gaussian likelihood classifiers and neural network classifiers gave very low error rates. The Gaussian classifier was able to correctly classify 100% of the programs used in the experiments. It identified the metrics PRO1 (mean program line length), PRO2a (mean local variable name length), PRO2c (mean function name length), PRO1S (standard deviation for program line length), PRO2bS (standard deviation for global variable name length), and STY1c (percentage of open curly brackets ({) that are the first character in a line) as the most significant.

Problem 10.2   Can you think of a way to use software metrics for birthmarking? For plagiarism detection?

10.8 Discussion

Many of the algorithms in this chapter fit into this general pattern, where P and Q are programs and $\mathcal{R}$ is a program representation:

```
rep_P ← convert P into representation R
rep_Q ← convert Q into representation R
for every piece p ∈ rep_P and q ∈ rep_Q do
    if similarity(p, q) > threshold then
        . . .
```

The algorithms differ in the problems they tackle (clone analysis, software forensics, birthmarking, and plagiarism analysis), of course, but they're similar in the kinds of trade-offs they have to make:

1. Should we use a simple or more powerful program representation?
2. Should we do similarity testing on a fine- or coarse-grained granularity?
3. Should we use a small but lossy or large but precise representation?
4. Should we use a precise but expensive or a heuristic but fast similarity testing algorithm?
5. Should we assume a powerful adversary who can make wholesale modifications to the program or one with limited abilities?

For example, on one extreme, you've seen algorithms that use program representations that are nothing more than lists or sets of extracted numerical metrics. These are simple to build and manipulate but more difficult to extract useful information from. On the other extreme, you've seen algorithms that work on complete program

Table 10.5 Summary of similarity analysis algorithms.

	Algorithm	**Representation**	**Static/Dynamic**
clone	SSKH	PDG	static
	SSKK	metrics	static
	SSEFM	sets of AST subtrees	static
forensics	SSLM	metrics	static
plagiarism	SSLCHY	PDG	static
	$SSSWA_{MOSS}$	sets of k-grams of source text	static
birthmarking	SSSDL	k-grams of API call sequences	dynamic
	$SSMC_{kgram}$	sets of k-grams of bytecodes	static
	$SSTNMM_{SMC}$	sequence of API calls	static
	$SSTNMM_{IS}$	sequence of classes	static
	$SSTNMM_{UC}$	sets of classes	static
	SSTONMM	frequencies of API calls	dynamic
	$SSMC_{wpp}$	graph	dynamic

dependence graphs. PDGs are powerful representations, since they naturally abstract away from the order between two independent statements. Of course, PDGs are more difficult to build and require more memory to store than simple sets of metrics.

In the future, it would be nice to see a more comprehensive approach to software similarity analysis. As you've seen in this chapter, clone analysis, software forensics, birthmarking, and plagiarism analysis have many points in common, and future research would certainly benefit from cross-fertilization. The summary in Table 10.5 might serve as inspiration for such future work.

Problem 10.3   Have a look at Table 10.5. Can you identify interesting holes in the available research that might serve as a starting point for interesting future work? For example, it seems like dynamic techniques haven't been tried on clone detection, authorship analysis, or plagiarism detection! Could there be a thesis topic lurking in there? And might there be some benefit to basing a plagiarism detector on sampling AST subtrees?

Hardware for Protecting Software

11

The focus of this book is on software-based techniques for software protection. The advantage of software-only approaches is exactly that—they require no special hardware to run. This means that your protected program should run everywhere, regardless of the capabilities your customer's hardware happens to have. The disadvantage is that the code is always available to the attacker to examine and modify. You can make it more difficult for him to do so, using the obfuscation and tamperproofing techniques from previous chapters, but the code *is* there ready to be attacked, and with the current state of the art, given an adversary with enough tenacity, defenses will eventually be breached.

There have been many attempts at enhancing software protection by adding some sort of hardware support. The basic idea is to add a physical module that you assume will resist observation, tampering, and copying by a malicious user. The module contains a secret—such as a serial number, a piece of code, or a cryptographic key—and the security of the program rests on keeping this secret. We call the secret and the hardware it's wrapped in the *root of trust*, and the fact that you're allowed to trust that it won't be subverted is what sets hardware approaches apart from software-only approaches.

Another way of looking at the difference between software-based and hardware-based systems is that hardware-based protection often has an easily identifiable point of failure: There's a single strongly guarded root of trust that, if subverted, will compromise your system, and everyone knows what that is. For example, in a

TPM-based system (Section 11.2►670), the root of trust is a secret key stored inside an integrated circuit. Everyone knows that the key is there and that shaving off the top of the packaging would likely reveal it. Software-based protection systems, on the other hand, tend to rely on several layers of weaker protection, all of which have to be penetrated to get at a secret, and it's much less clear where exactly the secret is, and how to get to it. This isn't exactly security-by-obscurity, or at least doesn't have to be. A company might well publish which obfuscation and tamperproofing transformations it's using, but not the *subset* they've applied to a particular program, the *order* in which they've applied them, or *where* in the code they've applied them. This is equivalent to revealing which crypto-system you use but keeping the key secret.

There's of course no reason why software- and hardware-based techniques can't co-exist, and in practice they often do. You might, for example, obfuscate and tamperproof your program before encrypting it for execution on a secure processor. If an adversary is able to somehow extract the secret key and decrypt the program, he still has to get past the software-based protection to get at the *real* secret. Similarly, you could fingerprint your program before writing it to a CD and protecting the CD from copying. If the disk copy protection fails and the program escapes into the wild, you might still be able to use the fingerprint to trace it back to the original customer.

In this chapter, we'll start by talking about disk and dongle protection (Section 11.1►657) against software and media piracy. By disk protection we mean distributing a program on a physical medium such as a CD or a floppy disk, and applying techniques that make copying the disk difficult. This idea has been applied both to software distributions (especially games) and media (audio CDs and video DVDs). Dongles are also used to protect a program from piracy. A dongle is a hardware token that you distribute along with your program that the customer attaches to an I/O port of their computer. The program occasionally calls a function on the dongle, and if it receives the wrong response, refuses to run. The premise is that it is much harder to clone the dongle than it is to make a copy of the program, so anyone in possession of the dongle is likely a legal purchaser of the program. Here, the root of trust is the function hidden inside the dongle. An adversary who can extract this function can completely bypass the protection by emulating the dongle in software.

In Section 11.2►670, we will show how a *trusted platform module* (TPM) can be used to boot a trusted environment in which your program can run without fear of being pirated, observed, or tampered with. A TPM is a small chip attached to the motherboard of a PC. Everyone who wants to communicate safely with that PC must trust the TPM not to be compromised. The TPM (or, more specifically, a secret key stored in it) and the BIOS stored in ROM on the motherboard together form the root of trust in this case. During the boot sequence, the TPM and the BIOS collaborate to *measure* the various software and firmware that together make up the PC. To measure, in this case, simply means to compute a cryptographically secure hash of a piece of code. To make sure that you're talking to a trustworthy computer (one that promises not to steal the secrets in your software or leak encrypted media content), you ask it to give you a list of all the software running on it, along with their hashes. This includes hashes of the bootloader, the OS kernel, any kernel modules, start-up scripts, and so on, and any piece of code on that computer that could possibly violate your trust in it. If those hashes correspond to well-known trusted software, you can allow the computer to run your software without fear of it being compromised. The IBM/Lenovo ThinkPad laptops have been shipping with a TPM chip for several years now, although there are no fully deployed systems that allow you to use them to measure trustworthiness.

In Section 11.3▶683, the root of trust is a processor that can execute encrypted programs. More precisely, it's the private half of a public key key-pair stored inside it. To distribute a program to a customer, you first encrypt it with his processor's public key. That way, the program is completely tied to his computer, no one else can execute it, and you've solved the piracy problem. This assumes, of course, that the key remains hidden, and that there are no *side-channel attacks*, i.e., clever ways to extract the cleartext of the program through means the designers didn't think of. In Section 11.4▶695, we'll show you some attacks like that. They include watching the bus between the CPU and memory, guessing and injecting encrypted instructions and watching how the CPU reacts, and causing faults in the CPU that will coax it to give up its secrets.

11.1 Anti-Piracy by Physical Distribution

In this section, we cover ways to protect software by means of *physical distribution*. There are two basic ideas: Either you protect the medium (CD, floppy disk, and so on) on which the software is distributed so that it's difficult to copy, or along with the software you also distribute a piece of hardware (a token, a dongle) without which the program cannot run.

These copy protection schemes have a long history, filled with lots of easily broken schemes! One of the problems is that users have expectations of what they should be allowed to do with software or media that they legally bought and own, and often the copy protection scheme gets in the way of letting them do that. The frustration they experience from an overly cumbersome copy protection scheme easily subverts any qualms they might have about the ethics of breaking it. For example, users get upset if they can't easily make backup copies of software or media they bought and to play/run it both on their laptop and their desktop computers. Similarly, they can't see why a DVD they legally bought on vacation in a foreign country won't play on their DVD player at home because of the region code protection. Also, they get annoyed when a program demands that the original distribution disk has to occupy the CD drive, or the dongle has to take up a port on their computer, preventing other uses. Finally, many disk protection schemes work by subverting format standards. This often means that disks won't play/run on all devices; you may find that the copy-protected CD you just bought will play on your home stereo but not in your car. There's an important lesson here: If you're going to use a copy protection scheme at all, you must not make it so inconvenient to users that they feel they have the right to break it.

11.1.1 Distribution Disk Protection

Back before online content distribution became ubiquitous, people actually bought software, music, and movies on hard media such as tape, floppy disks, CDs, and DVDs. Since it's easy to make copies of such media, piracy quickly became a problem. In response, music and software producers devised methods to prevent legally purchased products from being copied over to blank media. Many of these protection methods are based on one of these four ideas [144]:

1. Record using a format that doesn't conform to the medium specification in the hopes that this will confuse the reading hardware and copying software;
2. Insert errors in unimportant parts of the disk so that disk copying will fail;
3. Have the disk reader test some aspect of the original disk that will not carry over to a copy;
4. Encrypt the content.

11.1.1.1 Audio CD Protection To illustrate, let's start by looking at how copy-protected audio CDs work. The principle is simple. You want a consumer to be able to play his legally purchased CD in any "normal" audio CD player, including the player in his car, his Walkman, and so on. You *don't* want him to be able to play it on his computer, however, since if a software player can read the music off the disk to play it, the player can also store the music to a file, allowing the consumer to later burn it onto a CD-R or upload it to a file-sharing site.

There are many standardized formats for writing data onto the silvery 12cm optical disks we think of as CDs or DVDs [19,144,148]. Have a look at this (highly simplified) picture:

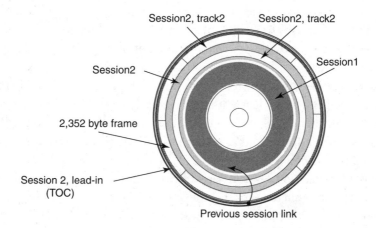

The data and audio on the CD are written in *sessions*. In the picture above, there are two sessions, in light gray and dark gray, respectively. Each session is made up of *tracks*. On an audio CD, each track corresponds to one song. Session 2 above has two tracks and hence two songs. Each track is made up of 2,352 byte *frames*, consisting of 2,048 bytes of data and various header and error correction information. Additionally, each session starts with a *lead-in* that contains the *table of contents* (TOC) and ends with a *lead-out* (not shown) that terminates the session. The sessions are linked together so that the lead-in of session n points to the beginning of session $n - 1$. Audio CDs typically only contain *one* session. If a CD player encounters a multi-session CD, it will simply ignore any session after the first one.

Audio CD protection methods work by abusing the CD standard. The trick is staying close enough to it so that hardware audio CD players will still be able to play the music but far away enough from it that computer CD drives will reject the CD. For example, the TOC entries can mismark the audio tracks as data or give the wrong track start times. Many audio CD players ignore the track types in the TOC. Also popular is adding extra sessions with missing or erroneous TOCs [148–150]. A widely publicized countermeasure [304] is to cover the extra sessions by writing on the CD surface with a felt-tip pen. This way computer CD drives will ignore the extra sessions and go straight for session 1 that contains the audio tracks.

11.1.1.2 CD-ROM Protection Software distributed on CDs uses a different standard, ISO9660 [175]. Many protection techniques that have been invented are still based on the same idea: Abuse the standard so that disk-copying software or CD burners will have problems with it [56, Chapter 4]. For example, ISO9660 restricts the name of the disk to be made up of the characters [A-Z0-9_], and a simple trick to trip up CD burners is to insert a blank in the name. Similarly, the TOCs could report the wrong sizes of files, or the total amount of data stored could appear to be larger than the physical media supports.

You can also insert frame errors on the disk in areas that don't contain real data. These areas won't be read when a program is executed off the disk, but disk-to-disk copiers will fail when trying to read them. For example, you can change the error correcting code in a frame so that hardware won't be able to correct for the error and give up on copying the disk.

In contrast to audio CDs, software distributions consist of executable content. This allows the program to check that the original CD is in the CD drive, refusing to run if it's not. This presupposes that it's possible to produce original CDs with *birthmarks*, traits that are unique to original CDs but that will not be reproduced by copying software and CD burners. The *CD-COPS* [56,304] (http://www.linkdata.com) system measures and verifies the angle between two sectors of the CD, something that will not be maintained in a burned copy. The algorithm goes something like this:

1. Add the following code to your program:

   ```
   int expected = prompt the user for the verification code written on the CD;
   verify that a CD is in the drive;
   Sector first = read the first sector on the CD;
   Sector last = read the last sector on the CD;
   int angle = compute the angle between first and last;
   if (angle != expected) abort();
   ```

2. Produce the gold master for your CD and send it to the plant to be manufactured.

3. Receive a shipment of CDs. They've all been produced from the same glass master and hence they're all identical.

4. Measure the angle between the first and the last sectors on one of the CDs and print it as the verification code on the cover of all CDs.

Each CD production run will produce different birthmarks and all are likely to be different from those of burned copies. To defeat the protection, the adversary needs to bypass the checks in the software.

11.1.1.3 Floppy Disk Protection   Preventing floppy discs from being copied was among the first software protection techniques. This is now just of historical interest. Many techniques were similar to the ones you saw above in that they abuse the published disk format specification or introduce defective sectors that would cause errors during reading. However, since floppies are writable, this lends itself to some specific techniques. For example, you could use a laser to burn off the magnetic layer at a very specific point on the floppy. The program would then try to write a byte to that spot and then read it back; if the same byte was read as was written, the floppy must be a copy [124].

In early microcomputer systems, the floppy would contain a copy of the operating system itself. In other words, the first thing the computer would do when a floppy was inserted would be to boot from the first few sections of the disk. Next, it would load and run the actual application. This would allow the software producer to replace the disk read routine with one that would use a nonstandard disk format (such as having different size sectors, different number of sectors, different sector numbering, and so on), making the disk unreadable with an unmodified OS [315].

11.1.1.4 DVD Movie Protection   No content protection scheme has caused as much controversy as the DVD *Content Scrambling System* (CSS). The encryption scheme used was a closely guarded secret only released to licensed player manufacturers. This made it impossible to build software players for open-source operating systems such as Linux. The system was eventually cracked [337], leading to lawsuits [348] and heated debate as to whether source code is covered under freedom of speech statutes [349].

The goal of the DVD decryption process is of course to unlock the encrypted media stored on the disk. To do this, you first need to derive a *disk key* K_d, which is the main secret needed to unlock the disk contents. The only (legal) way to get the disk key is to have one of the player keys licensed from the *DVD Copy Control Association* hidden within every DVD player. Once you have the disk key, you can derive a *title key* K_t, which is used to unlock a particular work on the disk. Finally, given K_t you can read a sector i on the disk, and along with a *sector key* sk_i, decode the media.

Stevenson [337] gives a complete cryptanalysis of the entire content scrambling system. Here, we'll restrict ourselves to discuss the salient aspects.

Each DVD movie disk contains a block of keys in a hidden area, and each licensed player likewise contains a set of keys hidden inside a chip (if it's a hardware player) or inside an obfuscated region of memory (if it's a software player):

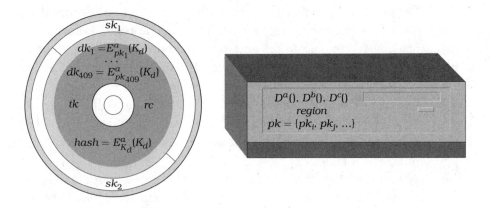

The player contains:

- A small set of secret *player keys* $pk = \{pk_i, pk_j, \dots\}$ that were assigned to it as part of the DVD CSS licensing process;
- A region code *region* used to restrict which region DVDs the player is allowed to play; and
- Three decryption functions $D^a_{key}()$, $D^b_{key}()$, and $D^c_{key}()$.

The DVD disk's hidden key-block consists of:

- 409 keys $dk_1, dk_2, \dots, dk_{409}$, which are the result of encrypting the disk key K_d with each of the 409 possible player keys:

$$
\begin{aligned}
dk_1 &= E^a_{pk_1}(K_d) \\
dk_2 &= E^a_{pk_2}(K_d) \\
&\cdots \\
dk_{409} &= E^a_{pk_{409}}(K_d)
\end{aligned}
$$

E^a_{key} is the encryption function corresponding to the D^a_{key} decryption function;
- A *title key tk* (there's actually one title key per work on the disk, but we show only one here);
- A region code *rc* that must match the player's region; and

- A value *hash* that is the disk key K_d encrypted with itself as key:

$$hash = E^a_{K_d}(K_d)$$

- One *sector key sk_1, sk_2, ...* per sector.

Suppose that the player has been assigned the 2nd key, pk_2. Then to play a particular DVD, it starts by deriving a disk key K_d by decrypting dk_2 using pk_2 as the key:

$$K_d \ \leftarrow \ D^a_{pk_2}(dk_2)$$

The player next checks that K_d is actually a valid key using the *hash* value stored on the disk:

$$K_d \ \overset{?}{=} \ D^a_{hash}(K_d)$$

If the test fails and there is more than one player key, you can continue and try the next one.

Given the disk key K_d and the title key *tk* of the work on the disk you want to watch, the player can derive a title key K_t:

$$K_t \leftarrow D^b_{K_d}(tk)$$

Finally, the player decrypts the data using the K_t key and the sector key sk_i stored with each sector *sector$_i$*:

$$data_i \leftarrow D^c_{K_t \oplus sk_i}(sector_i)$$

The encrypted player keys stored on a DVD (the dk_i:s) serve as a *white list* of trusted players. If, at some point, a player becomes compromised, future DVD releases can omit that player's key. As a result, that player will not be able to play any future content.

It's clear that the security of the entire system relies on the player keys remaining secret. The way that CSS was first cracked was, in fact, by reverse engineering a badly protected software player, *Xing* [348], and extracting its player keys.

As it turns out, due to cryptographic design flaws, there are other ways to attack CSS. First, the key-size is too small, 40 bits, due to export restrictions at the time. Second, only 25 of those bits are put to good use, making brute-force attacks trivial [337]. In fact, all player keys have since been recovered (http://www.free-dvd.

`org.lu/random-numbers.txt`). David Touretzky, in a feline metaphor we totally approve of, states in a declaration to the Superior Court of California [348]:

> At this point, there is nothing secret about DVD encryption. The cat has been long out of the bag. In fact, she's produced several litters of kittens.

Problem 11.1   We've left out several parts of the CSS system, for example, how the decryption functions work (they use *linear feedback shift registers*) and how a DVD drive and player authenticate each other. Although there are many public domain implementations available, none of them is particularly informative. Implement an *algorithm animation* of the entire process suitable for use in an educational setting.

11.1.1.5 High-Definition Movie Protection Blu-ray discs use an upgradable form of copy protection. The idea is to include in disk players a virtual machine that runs a program read from the Blu-ray disc. This program, rather than a program hardwired into the player, is responsible for implementing the rights protection. The program can ask the player what software and firmware versions it's running, what output devices are connected to it, and so on, and then decide what rights the user has to consume the media [203]. For example, a particular disc might contain a program that will let a user play the content if a compliant TV is connected to the player, but not if a media recorder is. Similarly, it can refuse to play the content on any known compromised players. There is always the possibility that the protection will be cracked and the content released in the wild, but since the security code resides on the disc itself, the idea is that it can be upgraded when the next title is released. Some security will always reside in the player, however. For example, it may be impossible to upgrade the security policies contained on the media disks to make up for a vulnerability in the virtual machine.

11.1.2 Dongles and Tokens

Dongles are hardware devices distributed with a program to prevent piracy. The idea is that while a program is only a bag of bits and hence easy to copy, copying a physical device is much harder and costlier. In order for the program to run, the dongle must be connected to the user's computer, and this allows the program to periodically query it to make sure that it's present and genuine.

Dongles have a long history [285]. The first devices were passive, nothing more than RS232 connectors with certain pins connected to each other, and filled with epoxy to hide the internals and protect them from tampering. The program would send an output signal on one pin and check that the same signal would appear at another pin. As adversaries became more adept at bypassing these simple schemes, the devices became more complex. Today, dongles are active devices with built-in processors, powered by the port to which they were connected, and sometimes backed up by a battery:

The program continually sends challenges to the dongle and stops running (or punishes the user in other ways, as we discussed in Section 7.3 ▶ 440) if it doesn't receive the expected response.

11.1.2.1 A Typical Dongle API   Listing 11.1 ▶ 666 shows a typical API for a dongle, based loosely on Aladdin's HASP technology [8,185]. The dongle has a small amount of internal memory that the application can access, a battery-backed internal real-time clock, an identifier unique to every dongle, a counter, a password, a pseudo-random number generator, and an encryption engine with a hardcoded key. The system time and the counter are used to set a bound on the number of times, or the length of time, the user can run the application. They are both initialized by the manufacturer. Every time the dongle is accessed the counter is decremented and when it reaches zero the dongle ceases to function. The API consists of a single function whose first argument determines the operation.

When the user starts up a protected program, the program connects with the dongle and passes it the pseudo-random number seed:

```
public class Main {
    static String password = "heyahaya";
    static final long timeout = 1281964454908L;
    static final long seed = 260124545;
    static java.util.Random rnd;
```

Listing 11.1 An API for a typical dongle.

```
class Dongle {
  private static long count = 3;
  private static long memory[]=new long[127];
  private static String password = "heyahaya";
  private static final long ID = 2376423;
  private static final long KEY = 0xab0ab012;
  private static java.util.Random rnd;

  public static final byte LOGIN = 0;
  public static final byte ISPRESENT = 1;
  public static final byte ENCODE = 2;
  public static final byte DECODE = 3;
  public static final byte READ = 4;
  public static final byte WRITE = 5;
  public static final byte GETID = 6;
  public static final byte GETTIME = 7;

  public static final long PRESENT = 0xca75ca75;

  static long call(byte operation, String pw, long arg1, long arg2) {
    if (!pw.equals(password) || (count<0)) return -1;
    switch (operation) {
      case LOGIN     : count--; rnd=new java.util.Random(arg1); return 0;
      case ISPRESENT : return PRESENT;
      case ENCODE    : return arg1^KEY;
      case DECODE    : return arg1^KEY;
      case READ      : return memory[(int)arg1];
      case WRITE     : memory[(int)arg1]=arg2; return 0;
      case GETID     : return ID;
      case GETTIME   : return System.currentTimeMillis();
      default        : return -1;
    }
  }
}
```

```
public static void main (String args[]) {
  Dongle.call(Dongle.LOGIN,password,seed,0);
  rnd = new java.util.Random(seed);
  if (Dongle.call(Dongle.GETTIME,password,0,0)>timeout)
    System.exit(-1);
  ...
  }
}
```

Both the dongle and the program have the same random number generator. They may be implemented differently (in the dongle perhaps as a *linear feedback shift register* [133], in the program as a software function), but given the same seed, they compute the same sequence of numbers. If the program is distributed as a trial version, the program can also query the dongle's internal real-time clock to see if the trial period has expired.

The ISPRESENT call of the API is the most fundamental—it simply lets the program check that the dongle is plugged in. To exhaust the resources of the attacker, you must add a *large number* of calls to the program, possibly in the thousands:

```
if (Dongle.call(Dongle.ISPRESENT,password,0,0)!=Dongle.PRESENT) {
   System.err.println("No dongle present"); System.exit(-1);}
...
long here = Dongle.call(Dongle.ISPRESENT,password,0,0);
...
boolean OK = here == Dongle.PRESENT;
...
if (!OK) System.exit(-1);
```

Ideally, you should obfuscate the challenge calls such that automatic removal becomes difficult. Just as you saw in Chapter 7 (Software Tamperproofing), it's essential to separate the code that detects tampering (in this case, the call in light gray that checks if the dongle is present) from the code (dark gray) that checks the result, and from the code (dashed) that takes action if tampering is detected.

You can also use the NEXT API call to get the next pseudo-random number from the dongle and compare it to the next one generated from the program's own generator:

```
if (rnd.nextLong()!=Dongle.call(Dongle.NEXT,password,0,0))
   System.exit(-1);
```

It's important to tie the dongle and the program as tightly together as possible. You can do this using the small amount of memory contained on the dongle, which you access using the READ and WRITE calls. For example, you can jump to a particular piece of code, depending on the value stored in the dongle memory, or even store a (small but essential) piece of code directly in the memory, decoding and jumping to it when needed. In either case, if the dongle isn't present, the program will cease to function:

```
Dongle.call(Dongle.WRITE,password,23,100);
...
switch ((int)Dongle.call(Dongle.READ,password,23,0)) {
   case 10:   secret1++; break;
   case 100:  System.out.println("REDHEAD");  break;
   default:   System.exit(-1);
}
```

In this example, the light gray code stores the value 100 at address 23 in the dongle memory. The dark gray code reads that memory address, and if it still holds the value 100, will next jump to the correct (dashed) code. If the dongle is no longer plugged in or has been tampered with, the program will instead jump to tamper-responding code.

The ENCODE and DECODE functions encrypt and decrypt a value using an internally stored key. You can encrypt an important piece of data and decrypt it only when needed.

```
static long secret = Dongle.call(Dongle.ENCODE,password,77,0);
...
secret = Dongle.call(Dongle.DECODE,password,secret,0);
secret = Dongle.call(Dongle.ENCODE,password,secret+1,0);
...
```

It used to be popular for dongles to contain proprietary encryption algorithms, but now standard ones, such as AES, are often used.

The GETID function returns an identifier unique to every dongle. It, too, can be used to encode data:

```
static long secret = 99 ^ Dongle.call(Dongle.GETID,password,0,0);
...
secret ^= Dongle.call(Dongle.GETID,password,0,0);
secret++;
secret ^= Dongle.call(Dongle.GETID,password,0,0);
...
```

To further confuse the attacker, you can sprinkle bogus calls to the dongle all over your code:

```
Dongle.call((byte)42,password,secret1,secret2);
```

Unfortunately, since the interface is well defined and likely well known to the attacker, it's probably not too difficult to mechanically remove such calls.

There is nothing stopping you from combining the tamperproofing techniques you read about in Chapter 7 with a hardware dongle. For example, you could hash the code and store the expected hash values in the dongle's memory.

11.1.2.2 Attacking Dongles

There are many problems with dongles. Since they are physical devices—these days, often implemented as a USB token or a smartcard—they contribute to the cost of distribution. If they contain a battery, it will eventually have to be replaced. If they are lost, the owner will have to request a new copy and, while waiting for one to arrive in the mail, won't be able to use a legally purchased program. For these reasons, dongles today are used only to protect very expensive programs.

On top of these logistic issues associated with protecting your program with a dongle, they also appear easy to attack [99]. A major reason is that it's difficult to obfuscate the interface to the dongle. As an application programmer, you need to have a well-defined API to work against, or else it will be onerous to add protection to your program. But if the interface is well documented for you as a defender, we have to assume it's well documented for the adversary as well! There are three basic methods of attack [99,286] against a dongle-protected program:

1. Reverse engineer the dongle itself, either duplicating it or disabling it by modifying the hardware.

2. Remove or disable the API calls in the application program.

3. Modify the dongle driver to call a software emulator that behaves just like the dongle rather than calling the dongle itself.

Direct attacks on the hardware are never done. The most popular attack instead targets the layer between the application program and the dongle itself. If the adversary can manage to build a software emulator of a particular dongle, then attacking *any* protected program becomes trivial: Just link in the emulator! The Web is full of freeware emulators [99] for various dongles, and there are companies that promise to make emulators on demand (`http://www.nodongle.com`):

> We can make Emulators for any protection type, Hasp4, HaspHL, Sentinel Super Pro, Aladdin Hardlock, . . . , any protection.
>
> Our emulators are 100% perfect, 100% guaranteed. 100% private, . . .
>
> Dongle Emulator is a software to allow your program to run without any key attached

>   We dont have fixed prices, our prices depends [sic] on protection, not
>   program price dependent, this will be very cheap if compared with program
>   price...
>
>   Send a email with some infos about your program, like name and pro-
>   tection, so we can give you a personalized answer.

The same kind of attacks that are used to disable protection in a tamperproofed
program can be used to remove calls to the dongle API. If the response code (such
as putting up a box saying "please insert the key") is in close proximity to the code
that checks if the key is indeed present, then simple debugging techniques can be
used to locate and bypass the check. Since the API is well known, it's also easy to
search through the code, even at the binary level, for telltale call signatures. For this
reason, it's often suggested that application programmers should refrain from using
the standard library calls provided by the dongle manufacturer and instead interact
with the dongle directly. That is, there's a need to obfuscate and tamperproof the
application's interaction with the dongle.

11.2 Authenticated Boot Using a Trusted
Platform Module

This book, of course, is all about how a program protects itself in the *untrusted
host scenario*. In other words, we're looking at situations where a program executes in an environment you don't trust, an environment that can potentially
examine (reverse engineer), modify (tamper), and copy (pirate) your program.
The techniques we've shown you have been entirely software-based, relying on
obfuscation (to make a program harder to examine), tamperproofing (to make
modification harder), and watermarking (to trace copying). What if, instead, you
could trust the execution environment? What if you could convince yourself that
a remote host runs hardware, operating system, and applications that are all benign and won't violate your intellectual property rights? This is the purpose of
authenticated (or *trusted) boot*: Before you agree to communicate with a system
(to allow it to buy a program from you, for example), you ask it to prove that it
won't do anything bad. This scenario is the same as in Section 7.5.4▶459, where the
TPSLSPDK algorithm measured the trustworthiness of remote hardware. That protocol, however, is software-only; now we're going to throw trusted hardware into
the mix.

Specifically, in this section, we're going to show you a system that makes use of
a *trusted platform module* (TPM) [30,47,47,123,143,243,339,340,372]. Some PCs

(such as IBM laptops) already have a TPM soldered onto the motherboard, and there are research systems built on top of them to provide trust. However, at present, we're aware of no actual deployed systems. The AEGIS [21,22] system from a group at the University of Pennsylvania seems to be the first published account of a trusted boot architecture. In this section, we're going to roughly follow the implementation put forth by a group at IBM [312,313].

So how does a system convince you that it's benign? Well, it uses a combination of *social trust* ("You should trust P because everyone else does"), *hardware trust* ("You should trust that the secrets stored in P are safe because we've wrapped them in plastic"), and *transitive trust* ("If you trust P and P trusts R, you really should trust R"). Let's start by looking at hardware and transitive trust, and leave social trust for later.

11.2.1 Trusted Boot

Let's consider a scenario where you want your program to run on Bob's computer. Your program contains a secret, however, so you encrypt it, and you tell Bob to boot a special operating system *eOS* that handles encrypted executables. But you don't want to hand over the program to eOS until Bob has convinced you that nothing could possibly go wrong—that there's no way he'll be able to extract the secret. So what *could* go wrong? Well, first, Bob could tell you he booted into the version of eOS you gave him, when in fact he first hacked it to leak the encryption keys. So you ask him to compute a cryptographic hash over the kernel and send it to you. If the hash matches that of the eOS you trust, you should be fine, assuming for a moment that Bob can't lie about the hash. Of course, the kernel was started by a bootloader, and Bob could have hacked *it* to modify the eOS image before loading it. So you ask Bob to send you a hash of the bootloader. Of course, the bootloader was started by the BIOS, and *it* could have been hacked! So Bob sends you a hash of *it*, but . . . . You see where this is going.

Anything that's running on Bob's computer could affect whether you should trust it or not. We mentioned the OS, the BIOS, and the bootloader, but other application programs, firmware [159] in connected devices, kernel modules, OS configuration files, and scripts could also do damage. The idea of a trusted boot is to *measure every* potentially hostile piece of code running on a computer and compare it against a library of *known good measurements*. When we say "measure" we really mean "compute a cryptographic hash of" and a "known good measurement" is just a hash of a program you trust. If Bob can convince you that his computer, from the ground up, only runs code you trust, then you should have no problem handing him (or selling him) a program to run.

Here's how trusted boot works, in a turtle-shell [246]:

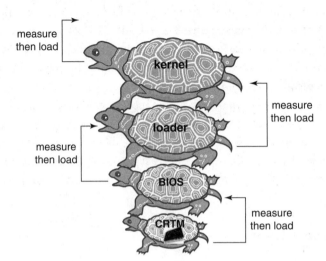

At the very bottom of the stack of turtles, are two things you need to trust implicitly: the *core root of trust for measurement* (CRTM) and the *tamperproof module*. The CRTM is a piece of code contained in the BIOS that measures itself and the BIOS before letting the BIOS execute. You have to trust the TPM, too, because this is where the measurements are stored.[1] The BIOS measures the bootloader, stores away the measurement (remember, this is nothing more complicated than a hash, such as a SHA-1, of the code), and then lets the bootloader execute. The bootloader measures the OS kernel, saves the result, and loads the OS. The OS needs to measure any kernel modules, configuration files, and so on, that it relies on, and store them in the TPM before it can let any applications run.

Notice how the turtles at the bottom are smaller than those on top. This is not accidental (although awfully cute)—we drew them this way to indicate two things. First, the size of the turtle is proportional to the size of the code: The CRTM is a part of the BIOS boot block and might need to fit in 512 bytes or so. The programs get bigger as we go up the stack. The TPM is also "small": It's not part of the CPU (at least not yet) but typically soldered onto the motherboard, and it's supposed to be cheap so that manufacturers won't hesitate to include it on their platforms. Second, the whole stack will easily topple over if either the CRTM or the TPM is compromised. The CRTM contains measurement code that can't be modified,

---

1. Actually, the storage within the TPM is limited, so only a summary of the measurements is stored there. More about that later.

and the TPM contains cryptographic keys (and a summary of the measurements themselves!) that must not be allowed to leak. So the CRTM contains the most critical code of the system and is also the smallest piece of code. It seems reasonable to believe that small programs that contain secrets are easier to attack than larger ones. Also, the TPM is supposed to be cheap but needs to be heavily tamperproofed in order not to leak any secrets. You already see we have some problems here, but more about that later.

There's a big difference between the *secure boot* of an operating system and an *authenticated boot*. During a secure booting process, you check that code is unadulterated *before* loading and activating it. This ensures that you only ever boot a system consisting of code that you trust. With an authenticated boot, there are no such guarantees. Bob can run whatever malicious code he wants on his system; the only thing he *cannot* do is lie about it! When you ask him, he will provide a list of software and hardware that comprise his system—it's then up to you to decide whether you trust such a system enough to want to continue communicating with it. It's the job of the TPM and the CRTM (and, as you'll see shortly, a trusted third party) to convince you that, indeed, you can assume that the measurements are real. But it's up to you to decide whether you think that the corresponding software is benign or not.

Problem 11.2   Redraw the figure above as a stack of kittens.

11.2.2 Taking Measurements

To make the authentication protocols concrete, we're going to model a computer system as a Java program. Have a look at the code in Listing 11.2▶675, which shows the measurement process in more detail. Each component of the computer system is represented as a static Java class. The computer is made up of a BIOS, a BootLoader, an OSKernel, and the TPM. When the user presses the power button, the Computer.POST() (*power on and self test*) function gets called, which immediately loads and runs the BIOS. The BIOS, in turn, initializes the TPM by calling its POST() function and then invokes the CRTM (contained inside the BIOS itself). The only thing the CRTM does is compute a SHA-1 hash over the BIOS. The BIOS next runs the BootLoader, but not before having computed a hash over its code. The BootLoader, in turn, measures and calls the OSKernel, which measures and calls, in our simple model, one particular Application.

We're deliberately ignoring important parts of a real system, such as option ROMs on the motherboard and firmware in connected devices, but these would

Listing 11.2 Java model of a computer with a TPM chip.

```
class Computer {
   public static void POST() {BIOS.run();}
   static class BIOS {
      static byte[] code = {...};
      public static byte[] savedBIOSHash;
      public static byte[] savedBootLoaderHash;
      public static byte[] savedOSKernelHash;
      static class CRTM {
         public static void run()  {
            BIOS.savedBIOSHash = TPM.SHA1(BIOS.code);
            TPM.extend(0,BIOS.savedBIOSHash);
         }
      }
      public static void run() {
         TPM.POST();
         BIOS.CRTM.run();
         savedBootLoaderHash = TPM.SHA1(BootLoader.code);
         TPM.extend(1,savedBootLoaderHash);
         BootLoader.run();
      }
   }
   static class BootLoader {
      public static byte[] code = {...};
      public static void run()  {
         BIOS.savedOSKernelHash = TPM.SHA1(OSKernel.code);
         TPM.extend(2,BIOS.savedOSKernelHash);
         OSKernel.run();
      }
   }
   static class OSKernel {
      public static byte[] code = {...};
      public static LinkedList[] SML;
      public static void run()  {
         SML = new LinkedList[TPM.NumberOfPCRs];
         for (int i=0; i<TPM.NumberOfPCRs; i++)
            SML[i] = new LinkedList();
         SML[0].addLast(BIOS.savedBIOSHash);
         SML[1].addLast(BIOS.savedBootLoaderHash);
         SML[2].addLast(BIOS.savedOSKernelHash);
         TPM.extend(10,TPM.SHA1(Application.code));
         SML[10].addLast(TPM.SHA1(Application.code));
         TPM.extend(10,TPM.SHA1(Application.input));
         SML[10].addLast(TPM.SHA1(Application.input));
         Application.run();
      }
   }
```

Listing 11.2 Java model of a computer with a TPM chip. (*Continued*)

```
                    static class Application {
                        public static byte[] code  = {...};
                        public static byte[] input = {...};
                        public static void run() {}
                    }
                    static class TPM { ... }
                }
```

---

be treated no differently than other software. *Any* code that can compromise the
trustworthiness of the system needs to be measured, and you need to measure it
before it starts running and has a chance to corrupt the system.

Notice how each measurement is stored in two places: on the TPM (using the
TPM.extend() call) and in the kernel in an array of lists, *stored measurement list* (SML).
When you challenge the computer to prove that it's benign, it will return this list so
that you can check that all the measurements correspond to programs you trust.

The reason that the SML is stored in the kernel and not on the TPM itself is that
it could potentially get very large; there might be several hundred pieces of code
that need to get measured, and their hashes couldn't all fit on the TPM. However, just
storing the hashes in the kernel isn't enough, since the kernel could be malicious and
lie about them! The TPM therefore stores a "summary" of the hashes—a "digest of the
digests"—in on-chip registers. There are 24 of these *platform configuration registers*
(PCR), and they're 20 bytes long, the size of a SHA-1 hash. To save a measurement
into the TPM, you call its extend() function:

```
    static class TPM {

        ...

        public static final int NumberOfPCRs = 24;
        private static byte[][] PCR;

        ...

        public static void extend (int i, byte[] add) {
            ubyte[] res = new byte[PCR[i].length + add.length];
            System.arraycopy(PCR[i], 0, res, 0, PCR[i].length);
            System.arraycopy(add, 0, res, PCR[i].length, add.length);
            return SHA1(res);
        }
    }
```

The extend(i,add) function doesn't just assign a new value to a PCR[i], but rather *extends* it by computing PCR[i] = SHA1(PCR[i] ‖ b). This way, each PCR[i] register becomes a combination of all hashes ever assigned to it. Furthermore, the construction preserves the order in which the measurements were added.

11.2.3 The TPM

Let's turn our attention to the TPM itself, since it's clearly at the heart of the system. For right now, you can think of it as having the following data and functions:

```
static class TPM {
    private static KeyPair EK;
    private static byte[][] PCR;
    private static byte[] ownerSecret;

    public static void extend (int i, byte[] b)
    public static Object[] quote(byte[] nonce)

    public static byte[] SHA1 (byte[] b)
    public static byte[] signRSA(Object data, PrivateKey key)
    public static KeyPair generateRSAKeyPair()
    public static byte[] RND(int size)

    public static void atManufacture()
    public static void takeOwnership(byte[] password)
    public static void POST()
}
```

A TPM goes through three important life events, which we represent by the three functions atManufacture(), takeOwnership(), and POST(). At manufacturing time, the TPM gets a unique identity, an RSA key pair called the *endorsement key* (EK). Once the TPM has been given an EK, no one can ever give it another one. When the owner takes possession of the computer, he invokes the takeOwnership function to initialize the TPM with a secret password. This prevents others from issuing sensitive commands to it. Finally, at start-up time, the POST function clears internal data to get ready for a new round of measurements. In particular, it zeros out the PCR registers. Here are the three life-event routines:

```
public static void atManufacture() {
  EK = generateRSAKeyPair();
}
public static void takeOwnership(byte[] password) {
  ownerSecret = password;
}
public static void POST() {
  PCR = new byte[NumberOfPCRs][];
  for(int i=0; i<NumberOfPCRs; i++) PCR[i] = new byte[20];
}
```

The TPM isn't built for bulk encryption but contains functionality for generating RSA keys, signing and encrypting with RSA, a (true) random-number generator, and a SHA-1 cryptographic hash function.

Some of the information in the TPM is volatile and some is stored in non-volatile memory. The EK, for example, will survive a power-off, but the PCRs will be reset.

11.2.4 The Challenge

OK, Axel's computer has successfully booted, and as a result, its TPM and the OS kernel are full of measurements—now what? Have a look at Listing 11.3 ▶678, which shows the Challenger, the code that you will run to query Axel's computer to determine if it's trustworthy enough for you to talk to him.

Here's an overview of the challenge protocol:

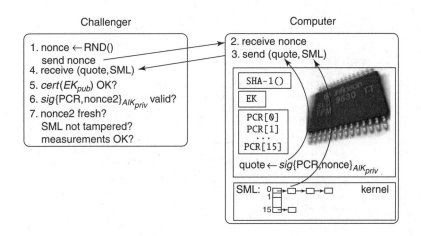

Listing 11.3 Challenging a remote system.

```
class Challenger {
    static byte[] BIOSHash = SHA1(BIOSCode);
    static byte[] bootLoaderHash = SHA1(bootLoaderCode);
    static byte[] OSKernelHash = SHA1(OSKernelCode);
    static byte[] ApplicationHash = SHA1(ApplicationCode);
    static byte[] ApplicationInputHash = SHA1(ApplicationInput);
    static byte[][] whiteList = {BIOSHash, bootLoaderHash, ...};

    static boolean untamperedSML(LinkedList[] SML, byte[][] PCR) {
        for (int i=0; i<PCR.length; i++) {
            byte[] res = new byte[20];
            ListIterator iter = SML[i].listIterator();
            while (iter.hasNext()) {
                byte[] b = (byte[]) iter.next();
                res = extend(i, res, b);
            }
            if (!java.util.Arrays.equals(PCR[i],res)) return false;
        }
        return true;
    }
    static boolean onWhitelist(byte[] b) {
        for(int i=0; i<whiteList.length; i++)
            if (java.util.Arrays.equals(whiteList[i],b)) return true;
        return false;
    }
    static boolean trustedCode(LinkedList[] SML) {
        for (int i=0; i<SML.length; i++) {
            ListIterator iter = SML[i].listIterator();
            while (iter.hasNext()) {
                byte[] b = (byte[]) iter.next();
                if (!onWhitelist(b)) return false;
            }
        }
        return true;
    }
    public static boolean challenge() {
        byte[] nonce = RND(20);
        Object[] response = Computer.report(nonce);
        byte[] nonce2 = ... // Unpack the response
        byte[][] PCR = ...
        byte[] sig = ...
        LinkedList[] SML = ...
        boolean OK = java.util.Arrays.equals(nonce,nonce2);
        OK &= verifyRSAsignature(new Object[]{nonce,PCR},
                AIK.getEKPublicKey(), sig);
        OK &= untamperedSML(SML,PCR);
        OK &= trustedCode(SML);
        return OK;
    }
}
```

To avoid a replay attack, start by creating a random value, a *nonce*, and send it in a challenge to Axel's computer. These are steps 1 and 2. His computer asks the TPM for a *quote*, i.e., the values of the PCRs, signed with a new key called the *attestation identity key* (*AIK*):

```
public static Object[] quote(byte[] nonce){
    AIK = generateRSAKeyPair();
    Object[] data = {nonce,PCR};
    byte[] sig = signRSA(data, AIK.getPrivate());
    return new Object[]{nonce,PCR,sig};
}
```

It then collects the stored measurement list SML from the kernel, packages it all up, and returns the package to you. These are steps 3 and 4. In step 5, you look up a certificate corresponding to the TPM's public key EK_{pub} and verify that the TPM belongs to a trusted computer. This could involve asking the certification authority that issued the certificate if it's on the revocation list, i.e., the list of known compromised TPMs. In step 6, you validate the signature on the package you received from Axel's computer. Since only the TPM knows the private key AIK_{priv} that the package was signed with—not even Axel knows it—only the TPM could have signed the package.

Then you have to check that the SML hasn't been tampered with. This is done by the untamperedSML() function in Listing 11.3 ▶678. It walks through the stored measurement lists, and just like the TPM did during the boot sequence, merges the values together by simulating the TPM's extend() function. If the aggregate measurements match those of the PCRs, you can be sure that the stored measurement list wasn't tampered with.

The final step is to check if the measurements actually correspond to code you trust. This is done using the trustedCode() function in Listing 11.3 ▶678. You can either check the measurements in the SML against a whitelist of code you trust or against a blacklist of code you don't. In either case, you (or some authority you trust) must keep a list of all trustworthy software, and as soon as a vulnerability is found, update this list.

11.2.5 Social Trust and Privacy Issues

In the challenge protocol, the remote computer's TPM manufactures a special RSA keypair, the *attestation identity key* (*AIK*), before engaging in the challenge protocol. For privacy reasons you don't want anyone to be able link multiple transactions

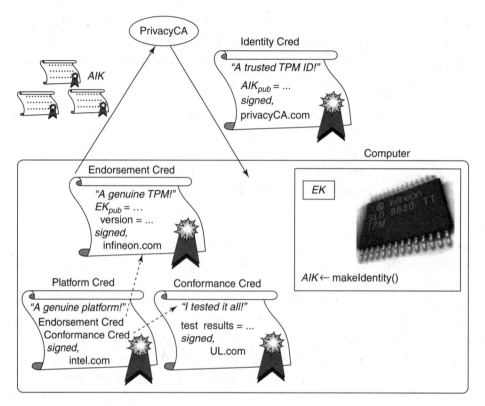

Figure 11.1 Protocol to manufacture an identity credential.

together. Therefore, no one must be able to find out that the *AIK* and the EK actually represent the same computer—no one, that is, except a a trusted third party called the *Privacy Certification Authority*, PrivacyCA. The PrivacyCA knows all the public keys EK_{pub} of all manufactured TPMs. The computer and the PrivacyCA engage in a protocol to manufacture an *identity credential* that the computer can use to prove that it's a compliant tamperproof platform without revealing exactly *who* it is.

Have a look at the protocol in Figure 11.1. The computer holds three credentials, the *endorsement credential*, the *platform credential*, and the *conformance credential*. The endorsement credential states that the TPM is genuine and that the EK_{pub} is the public part of the endorsement keypair that was squirted into it during manufacture. The endorsement credential is signed by the TPM manufacturer. The platform credential states that the TPM and the motherboard it's been soldered onto make up a trusted system. The manufacturer of the platform signs the credential. Finally, the conformance credential is signed by a testing lab and certifies that the platform has been tested by a third party and conforms to certain security properties.

To obtain an identity credential, the computer first asks the TPM to manufacture a new *AIK* key-pair. It then bundles up AIK_{pub} together with all the credentials and sends them off to the PrivacyCA. The PrivacyCA looks at the credentials and convinces itself that they belong to a genuine tamperproof platform. If so, it issues the identity credential and returns it to the computer. The protocol is highly technical and we omit the details [31] here.

The endorsement, platform, and conformance credentials are published in the form of digital certificates signed by companies willing to put their good name behind a guarantee that a particular computer can be trusted. This is a form of social trust—you don't trust the particular piece of hardware, per se, you trust that the companies that manufactured and tested it are trustworthy. In other words, you assume that they took great care in ensuring that no security flaws were allowed to creep in during the manufacturing process because, if they didn't, their brand name could be irreparably damaged.

Having to rely on a trusted third party such as the PrivacyCA is certainly limiting. First, the PrivacyCA will be involved in *every* transaction and hence needs to be highly available. Second, if its security is ever compromised and its transaction records made public, the identity of every TPM will be revealed. To avoid potential privacy breaches and the PrivacyCA becoming a performance bottleneck, a second verification protocol, *direct anonymous attestation* (DAA) [48,53], has been developed. This protocol avoids a trusted third party altogether.

Problem 11.3   Extend our Java model (you can get the code from our Web site) to implement the complete *make-identity* protocol. Add a simple algorithm animation to illustrate the protocol.

11.2.6 Applications and Controversies

Much has been written about the TPM chip and its potential applications, good and bad [15,310]. Some of the controversy stems from the distaste many have for digital rights management (and the chilling effect it might have on fair use of copyrighted material), some stems from privacy issues, and some simply arises because of technical doubts that authenticated boot has any hope of succeeding in the real world.

From a technical perspective, authenticated boot would seem to present an administrative nightmare. One problem is that you, as a challenger, must have a policy in place to decide what to do when you encounter an unknown hash value. It could be the result of a new version of a program you know, an entirely new program you've never heard of, or a known program whose security has been compromised. If you encounter a single unknown measurement value, do you completely distrust the remote system and refuse to talk to it further? On the one hand, if you're amazon.com and your policy is to not accept a purchase from any system that hasn't installed all the latest security patches, you might quickly find yourself out of business. On the other hand, if the remote computer has even a single altered file, its security could have been completely compromised.

In IBM's implementation of authenticated boot, their database of measurements for Redhat Fedora contains about 25,000 measurements. A typical SML contains 700 to 1,000 measurements. It would seem a herculean task to manually determine which measurements to trust and which not to. Instead, a typical strategy is to boot a "trusted system," i.e., one where all known security patches have been applied, and measure all modules, configuration files, and scripts, and store their hashes in a whitelist. Additionally, you can boot a system with known root-kits and trojans and store the hashes of infected files in a blacklist. Given all the different operating systems available, all of which come in myriad versions and configurations, even with a semi-automated system to collect measurements, keeping up-to-date white- and blacklists available would seem close to impossible. Add to that having to measure the firmware of every device that could potentially be plugged in, every application that could possibly run, and having to determine which combinations could possibly constitute a security threat, and it's hard to imagine that TPM-based security will ever become widespread.

Still, there has been much *speculation* about potential uses and abuses of the technology. The most obvious application is to help digital rights management media players to run untampered on PCs. Before you're allowed to buy and download a movie, the movie distributor would verify that only approved software and hardware is installed on your computer. So if you happen to have a copy of the *SoftICE* debugger (a mainstay in the hacker arsenal of tools) on your hard disk, are running a slightly out-of-date kernel, or your media player has been blacklisted, you're out of luck.

If your OS happens to be localized to a part of the world where the movie has yet to appear in theaters, the distributor may decide to refuse the download. Since the OS can't lie about any of the files on the hard disk, including any configuration files (the TPM guarantees that), it can't lie about where in the world it's running.

In other words, without having to use the tamperproofing techniques in Chapter 7 (Software Tamperproofing), you can build a media player that can't be tampered with. That is, you're guaranteed that the untampered player executable will be loaded properly—the TPM makes no guarantees as to what happens post load time. The player could, for example, contain a vulnerability that makes it behave improperly, and then all bets are off.

Software and media can be protected from piracy in similar ways. Microsoft would encrypt Office (or Disney would encrypt *Finding Nemo*) with a special *sealing* key *Seal*. When *Seal* is created by the TPM, it will be made to depend on the current values in the PCRs. That way, should you reboot with slightly different systems software (maybe you've hacked the OS to leak the decrypted Office binary), the PCRs will have changed, the *Seal* will be different, and hence you'll be unable to decrypt and run/view your legally purchased copy—until, of course, you reboot with the old OS version or are able to convince Microsoft/Disney that the new version you're running is actually benign and that they should issue you a new copy. *Seal* also depends on the TPM itself. This means that your friend who has a computer identical to yours (down to the last PCR value) will not be able to watch the copy of *Finding Nemo* issued to you.

Of course, the trust could extend both ways. Maybe you won't be willing to upload your credit card information to microsoft.com to buy the latest version of Office until you can verify that Microsoft's servers are running the latest versions of software you trust (Linux kernel 2.6.25-rc3, Apache Tomcat version 6.0.16, and so on) and there are proper safeguards in place not to leak your personal information. Somehow we doubt this scenario is likely to materialize.

11.3 Encrypted Execution

The academic literature and the patent databases are teeming with proposals for processors that execute encrypted programs. A patent [40] and paper [39] by Robert Best seem to have been the first, followed by Markus Kuhn's *TrustNo 1* processor [213], and more recently, Stanford's XOM project [45,228–230]. There are many others. The details differ among the different designs, of course, but the underlying principles remain the same. A typical design has these features:

1. The CPU is trusted and can neither be tampered with nor examined. Everything else is open to attack: An adversary is free to examine and tamper with off-chip memory, bus traffic, the operating system, connected devices, and so on.

2. Since RAM is too large to be manufactured on the same die as the CPU, data and code are stored encrypted off-chip. They're fetched and decrypted by the CPU as needed and kept in cleartext for as long as they're inside the CPU. Data is re-encrypted before being stored back to RAM.

3. The CPU is augmented with algorithms for (fast) symmetric and (slow) asymmetric encryption.

4. Each CPU contains the private part of a unique asymmetric key-pair.

The goal is to provide *privacy* (no one can examine the code and extract any secrets it contains), *integrity* (no one can execute tampered code), and *copy protection* (only code destined for a particular CPU is allowed to run).

To get an idea of how code encryption will provide all this, have a look at this figure:

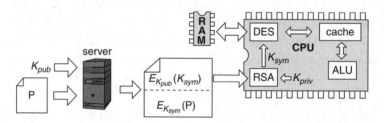

To buy a program P from the server, you start by handing it your public RSA key K_{pub}. The private part K_{priv} is stored safely inside your CPU—not even you can get to it. The server generates a symmetric key K_{sym} (a DES key, say), and encrypts P with it. We call K_{sym} the *session key*. It then encrypts the session key with K_{pub}. The server now creates a new executable file consisting of the encrypted code and a file header containing the encrypted session key, i.e., $[E_{K_{pub}}(K_{sym}) \| E_{K_{sym}}(P)]$. You download this file and give it to the operating system to execute. The operating system gives the CPU the encrypted session key, and the CPU decrypts it with its private key. With the session key in the clear, the CPU can now read the encrypted code, decrypt it, and execute it. The DES engine sits between external RAM and the cache so that every piece of code or data that gets read or written will first pass through it. In other words, external RAM is always encrypted, internal data and code is always in the clear, and the private key K_{priv} and the decrypted symmetric key K_{sym} never leave the CPU.

This design solves the privacy problem, since no code or data ever leaves the CPU unencrypted. It also solves the copy-protection problem, since each program is directly tied to the one CPU that's allowed to execute it through encryption with the CPU's private key. It *doesn't* yet solve the integrity problem, since there's nothing stopping an adversary from modifying or moving encrypted code around, but we'll get to that later. In Section 11.3.3 ▶ 690, you'll also see that privacy is, in fact, not guaranteed by this system, since memory bus traffic can leak revealing patterns of computation.

11.3.1 The XOM Architecture

As a representative example of this type of processor design, let's have a look at Stanford's XOM architecture. Although never implemented in silicon, the design is complete enough to have been simulated in software, and an operating system, *XOMOS*, was built to run on top of it.

In a multi-tasking operating system, several programs can execute at the same time, and each one may have different security requirements. In fact, since encrypted programs are slower than cleartext programs, a single program may want to switch between running in unencrypted mode for bread-and-butter code and encrypted mode for security-sensitive code. For this reason, the CPU supports *compartments*, which are logical containers that protect one process' code and data from being observed or modified by another process. Keep in mind that in the scenario we're working in here, the operating system is untrusted, which means that it must run in its own compartment. Even a severely subverted operating system won't be allowed to examine or manipulate another protected process!

A CPU will only support a small number of compartments. Let's assume 4, numbered 0 ... 3. Compartment 0 (the *null* compartment) is special—that's the insecure compartment where code runs unencrypted. There's a special ACTIVE register that holds the number of the currently executing compartment. Each compartment is associated with a session key, and a *session-key table* maintains the mapping between compartment ID and the corresponding session key.

Every cache line and every register is tagged with a compartment ID to mark which compartment code and data it belongs to. For efficiency reasons, code and data that's on-chip is kept in cleartext, but the tags ensure that only the owner of a datum can access it. Only on a cache flush do you have to encrypt data and write it out to RAM.

To illustrate, let's consider a very concrete situation where two programs *A* and *B* are running:

There are two compartments, 1 and 2, for programs A and B, respectively. Compartment 2 is the currently active one. The session-key table maps the compartment IDs to their corresponding session keys, A_{sym} and B_{sym}, respectively. You can see from their tags that registers r1 and r2 belong to compartment 2, register r3 to compartment 1. Register r0 is unprotected, which means that compartments 1 and 2 could use r0 for insecure communication. We've made the simplifying assumption here that a cache line can hold only one word, either code or data. The cache line corresponding to address 1 holds an instruction belonging to compartment 2, and address 3 holds a data value also belonging to 2. At address 2, there's an instruction that belongs to compartment 1.

All instructions and data values are in the clear on the CPU. You don't have to worry about outside forces, since we're assuming that the CPU can't be probed or tampered with, and *inside* the CPU, the tags will ensure that no information can be leaked between compartments. Specifically, the operating system (which runs in its own compartment) can't be manipulated to reveal any secrets of an encrypted application.

Off-chip, code and data are stored encrypted with the appropriate session key. Encryption is at the cache-line level, which means that compilers must arrange it so that code and data belonging to different compartments aren't stored on the same cache line. Let's continue with the example above:

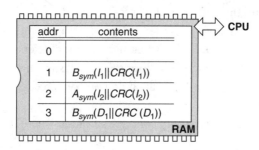

What happens when the CPU tries to load data value D_1 at address 3 into register r0? Well, it first looks in the cache but finds the cache line empty, so a cache miss is generated and $B_{sym}(D_1\|CRC(D_1))$ is read from address 3. The CPU looks up the key for the active compartment in the session-key table, finds B_{sym}, and uses it to decrypt the cache line. Because of the encryption, you can be pretty sure that the adversary hasn't been able to examine D_1, but you can't be sure that he hasn't *modified* it. He could have, for example, swapped it for another encrypted value from some other part of the code. For this reason, every cache line is *hashed*, and the hash is stored with the cache line. Now you can check that the hash matches, and if so, load D_1 into register r0 and set r0's tag to 2. If it *doesn't* match, you know the data has been tampered with and you throw an exception. Since the hash is stored encrypted, you can assume that the adversary can't modify it, and so there's no need to use a cryptographically secure hash function. A faster check, such as a *cyclic redundancy check* (CRC), will do.

11.3.1.1 ISA Modifications XOM requires us to make some changes to the instruction set architecture. First, you need secure load and store instructions:

secure_load *reg, addr*: On a cache miss, load the cache line at address *addr* and decrypt using the session key of the currently active process. If the hash doesn't validate, throw an exception. Store the decrypted value in *reg* and tag *reg* with the tag of the active process.

secure_store *reg, addr*: If *reg*'s tag is different from the active tag, throw an exception. Otherwise, store *reg*'s contents to the cache line corresponding to *addr* and set its tag to the tag of the currently active process. On a cache flush, compute a hash of the cache line and its virtual memory address, encrypt the cache line and the hash with the session key, and write to memory.

The reason for including the virtual address in the hash is so that an adversary can't copy encrypted code from one region of memory into another region.

You also need *insecure* load and store instructions, which function pretty much like loads and stores on a normal machine, except that they work on data in the null compartment:

load *reg, addr*: Load the value at address *addr* into register *reg* and set its tag to 0.

store *reg, addr*: If *reg* isn't tagged with 0, throw an exception. Otherwise, write it to address *addr*.

It's necessary to have some way of moving data between compartments. For example, you need to be able to move data owned by the operating system (that it has read from a device, say) into a user process. Two instructions take care of changing ownership tags:

move_to_null *reg*: If *reg*'s tag is different from the active tag, throw an exception. Otherwise, set *reg*'s tag to 0.

move_from_null *reg*: If *reg*'s tag is isn't 0, throw an exception. Otherwise, set *reg*'s tag to the tag of the currently active process.

Two processes executing in different compartments can now (insecurely) exchange data: The first process loads the data into a register and changes its tag to 0, and the second changes the tag from 0 to its own tag value.

The hardware needs special instructions to support interrupt handling. The problem is that on an interrupt, the operating system must be allowed to save away the registers of the executing process in order to be able to service the interrupt. But at the same time, the OS isn't trusted and so can't be allowed to *examine* the values in the registers! To solve this conundrum, you need to create three special registers (let's call them $0,$1,$2) in which the compartment can package up and encrypt a register value owned by another compartment without ever examining its value. You need two new instructions, save and restore:

save **reg addr**: Assume *reg*'s tag is T. Encrypt *reg* with the session key corresponding to T and store the result in register $0. Compute a hash *CRC* (*reg*||*reg_number*) of the register's value and the register's number and store it in register $1. Finally, store T in register $2 and write ($0,$1,$2) to *addr*.

restore **reg addr**: Read ($0,$1,$2) from *addr*. Use the tag in $2 to look up the session key and decrypt the data in register $0. If the hash in register $1 doesn't match the register contents and register number, throw an exception. Otherwise, store the decrypted value in *reg* and set the tag to that in $2.

Finally, you need two instructions to enter and exit protected mode:

enter **addr**: The encrypted session key is stored at address *addr*. If it's already been loaded into a slot in the session-key table, just set the ACTIVE register to the slot tag. Otherwise, load the key, decrypt it with the CPU's private key, store into an empty slot in the session-key table, and set the ACTIVE register. Start fetching and decrypting instructions.

exit: Set ACTIVE to 0. Stop decrypting instructions.

The exit instruction can be generated directly by user code or implicitly on an interrupt.

11.3.2 Preventing Replay Attacks

The restore instruction can be abused to launch a *replay attack*. The trick the adversary can play is to make the operating system reload the same registers several times. With some extra circuitry, we can prevent this. The idea is to use an extra key to encrypt the registers and on every interrupt invalidate the old key and generate a new one.

However, this doesn't help against an attack where the adversary replays old values from *memory*! Because the address of a memory location is included in the hash value stored with the datum, the adversary can't move memory around, but there's nothing stopping him from saving a value from a particular location and then later writing it back into the same location. Crafting a successful attack in this way requires considerable care and good fortune, but it's not impossible.

To protect against replay attacks, you must somehow check that a value you write into memory hasn't been changed the next time you read from the same location. A relatively efficient way of doing that is to keep a tree of cryptographically secure hashes (such as SHA-1) known as a Merkle tree [249]:

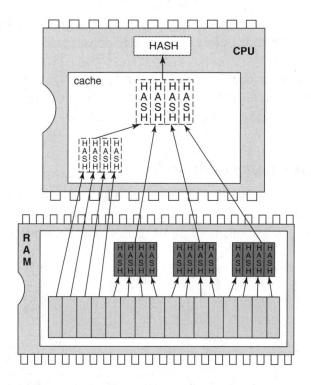

The leaves of the tree are chunks of memory (light gray) that you want to protect. Internal nodes are hashes of child nodes. The root of the tree is a hash stored protected on the CPU that hence can't be manipulated. When you write a value to memory, you have to update the hashes all the way up to the root. Similarly, when you read a value from memory, you have to read and verify the hashes, again from the leaf all the way up to the root. The root itself doesn't have to be checked, since it never leaves the CPU.

A reply attack won't work here. Even if the adversary changes a word in memory to its previous value, and to hide the attack changes the hash in the parent node with *its* previous value, and so on recursively up the tree, he *still* won't be able to change the root of the hash tree.

The problem with this approach is performance. The extra space cost is considerable: With a 4-way tree, $\frac{1}{4}$th of memory is taken up by hashes. The extra cost in memory bandwidth is even more disturbing. A perfectly balanced m-ary tree of memory of size N will require $\log_m(N)$ hash checks per read, which could equate to tens of reads of hashes whenever you read a value from memory. This is obviously unacceptable.

The solution [134] is to cache parts of the tree on chip in the L2 cache. Any value stored in the cache you can trust and read directly without having to walk up the tree and verify hash values. A write to a cached value likewise doesn't incur any hashing activity. Not until a cache line is evicted do you have to update its parent hash node.

With these and other optimizations, Gassend et al. [134] report a less than 20% performance hit across a set of nine benchmarks. This, of course, would be on top of the performance degradation of XOM itself.

11.3.3 Fixing a Leaky Address Bus

An adversary who's unable to directly examine an executable, perhaps because it's been encrypted, may still be able to extract information from it by examining its control flow execution pattern. Consider this example, which computes $R = y^x \bmod n$ [205]:

```
s[0] = 1;
for(k=0; k<w; k++) {
    if (x[k] == 1)
        R[k] = (s[k]*y) mod n;
    else
        R[k] = s[k];
    s[k+1] = R[k]*R[k] mod n
}
return R[w-1];
```

This *modular exponentiation* routine is commonly used in RSA and Diffie-Hellman public key algorithms, where x is the private key, w bits long. In the XOM architecture, code and data don't move, i.e., while every block of code is encrypted, it resides in the same location in memory throughout execution. So if your encrypted blocks are laid out like this in memory

000	100	200	300	400	500	600
$E_k(B_0)$	$E_k(B_1)$	$E_k(B_2)$	$E_k(B_3)$	$E_k(B_4)$	$E_k(B_5)$	$E_k(B_6)$

an adversary who is able to monitor the address bus while a secret message is being decrypted might see something like this:

$$\langle 000,$$

$$100, \quad 200, \quad 300, \quad 500,$$
$$100, \quad 200, \quad 300, \quad 500,$$
$$100, \quad 200, \quad 400, \quad 500,$$
$$100, \quad 200, \quad 300, \quad 500,$$
$$\cdots$$
$$100,$$
$$600\rangle$$

From this address trace, he can draw several conclusions. First, there's an obvious loop involving B_1 and B_5. Second, from B_2, control either goes to B_3 or B_4, and from B_3 and B_4 we always proceed to B_5. This is the telltale signature of an if-then-else statement. Given this information, the adversary can now completely reconstruct the control flow graph. He still has no clue what should go inside each block, of course, since each individual block is encrypted. However, if he's able to figure out that this is, in fact, the modular exponentiation routine of a public key cryptosystem, he can deduce the key simply by examining the trace! A branch $B_2 \rightarrow B_3$ indicates a 0 and a branch $B_2 \rightarrow B_4$ indicates a 1 (or possibly the opposite). Finding out that this routine is the modular exponentiation routine might not be that hard—the structure of the control flow graph makes for a pretty accurate fingerprint.

This is a form of a *side-channel attack*. Some variants use execution time [205] to distinguish between B_3 and B_4, while others use energy consumption. In both cases, the measurements can be rather noisy, but this can be offset by running multiple experiments. You'll see more of this in Section 11.4.4▸705.

Watching addresses go by on the address bus can also give the adversary noisy data. For example, if a routine is small enough to at least partially fit in on-chip caches, then some branches *will not* be exposed on the bus, and an adversary will not learn everything just by observing the address bus. The easiest way around this is for him to turn off caching altogether, for architectures that allow this.[2] If this attack isn't available, others are. He can, for example, interrupt the process frequently and coax the operating system to flush caches on a context switch.

So let's assume that all branches are exposed, i.e., if a branch is taken, it results in the target block being fetched from memory. As you saw from the example above, not only does this information leakage allow an observer to reconstruct the control flow graph, it can also allow him to learn about data values.

Several schemes [140,385,386] have been devised for preventing the address bus from leaking information. They share the same basic idea—blocks must be constantly permuted in memory—but differ in how they make this efficient. We'll show you a technique proposed by Zhuang et al. [385]. The idea is to include a *shuffle buffer* within the CPU that keeps a subset of the memory blocks. A block is simply a cache line. Whenever a block is needed from memory, it's swapped with a random block from the shuffle buffer. In other words, a block M is read from memory, a block S is selected randomly from the shuffle buffer, M replaces S in the buffer, and S is written back to M's location.

Here's an example. You start with the 7 blocks from our example program, all residing in memory. The CPU has a 3-slot shuffle buffer. First, three blocks are selected from memory and brought in to populate the shuffle buffer:

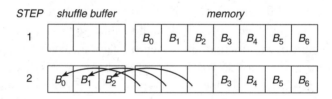

Next, B_4 is needed, so it's brought in from memory, replacing block B_1, which was selected randomly from the shuffle buffer, and B_1 is written back to memory, in B_4's place:

---

2. On the Intel x86, you set bit 30 of status register `CR0`, although this can't be done directly from user code.

Next, B_0 is swapped with B_6, B_4 with B_5, and, finally, as the program finishes executing, the blocks in the buffer are written back to memory:

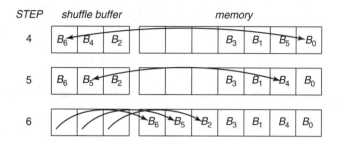

Here's a sketch of the architecture of the system, shown right after step 5 in the example trace you just saw:

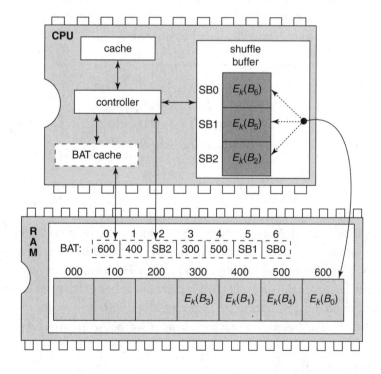

The *block address table* (BAT) keeps track of where blocks currently reside, either at an address in memory or at an index in the shuffle buffer. On a cache miss, the controller queries the BAT for the current location of the block. If the block is in the shuffle buffer already, it's returned to the cache. If, on the other hand, it's in memory, it's loaded and stored in both the cache and the shuffle buffer. Whatever block was evicted from the buffer gets written back to the location of the loaded block. An on-chip *BAT cache* reduces the latency of checking the BAT. This is essential, since every access request from the cache has to go through the BAT.

11.3.4 Fixing a Leaky Data Bus

Let's assume that your encrypted code blocks are laid out linearly in memory and that their encrypted values are 0000, 1000, and so on:

000	100	200	300	400	500	600
$E_k(B_0) =$ 0000	$E_k(B_1) =$ 1000	$E_k(B_2) =$ 2000	$E_k(B_3) =$ 3000	$E_k(B_4) =$ 4000	$E_k(B_5) =$ 5000	$E_k(B_6) =$ 6000

Then an adversary who has tired of watching the address bus (because he's noticed that blocks are being continuously relocated and he can learn nothing from their addresses) can take to watching the data bus instead:

$$\langle 0000,$$
$$1000, \quad 2000, \quad 3000, \quad 5000,$$
$$1000, \quad 2000, \quad 3000, \quad 5000,$$
$$1000, \quad 2000, \quad 4000, \quad 5000,$$
$$1000, \quad 2000, \quad 3000, \quad 5000,$$
$$\cdots$$
$$1000,$$
$$6000\rangle$$

As long as blocks have unique ciphertexts, watching the blocks go by on the data bus reveals as much as watching addresses go by on the address bus! Fortunately, it's not hard to defend against this attack: Whenever a block is written back at a new location, you have to make sure that it has a different ciphertext than when it was last read. This can be done by xoring the cleartext block with its new address prior to encrypting it. This technique is used, for example, by the *Arc3D* architecture [140].

11.3.5 Discussion

We don't hold out much hope that encrypted execution will become mainstream anytime soon. From the discussion above it should be clear that if you really want to protect your program, you have to make sure that you hide *everything* that's going on inside the CPU, and you have to protect *every* piece of code and data that gets stored off-chip. You cannot leak any information in the address stream or any information on the data bus, and you can't let the adversary change or replay a single bit in memory without your detecting it. An architecture that fulfills all these requirements is likely to be both complex and slow.

The original XOM architecture was evaluated under simulation. An operating system (XOMOS) was built (by modifying a standard operating system) to take advantage of the hardware. On top of XOMOS, two applications were run to evaluate performance. The actual performance numbers depend heavily on the coarseness of the protection: How much of the application runs in protected mode, and how frequently does it have to make a XOM transition? In the author's experiments [228], they saw mostly small performance hits ($\leq 6\%$ increase in processor cycles), but for one experiment, they saw a 129% hit. The other protection techniques you saw in this section for fixing replay attacks and leaks to the address and data bus will incur additional overhead on top of that for XOM itself.

System-on-a-chip designs would avoid many of the problems you saw in this section. If the CPU and RAM both reside in the same physical capsule, then there's no need to worry about anyone snooping on the bus—unless, of course, they decide to break the capsule open to peek inside . . . . This will be the topic of our next section!

11.4 Attacks on Tamperproof Devices

The very basic idea of the hardware designs we showed you in Section 11.2▸670 and Section 11.3▸683 is to provide a physical layer of protection between an attacker and secret code (often, cryptographic algorithms and protocols) and data (key material). The assumption is that this barrier won't be broken and that wrapping code and data inside silicon, plastic, or metal will make them impervious to observation and manipulation. If the assumption is violated, all bets are off.

In this section, we're going to show you how this physical barrier is implemented and how it can be bypassed. We're first going to look at a board-level attack against Microsoft's XBOX gaming console (Section 11.4.1▸696). Here, Microsoft's engineers assumed that "probing the high-speed busses would be too hard," and hence left them unencrypted. MIT grad student Andrew Huang was undeterred by this, and . . . tapped the busses! As a result, he recovered the cryptographic key that was the root of all security on the machine and opened the door to playing copied games, booting Linux, and running unapproved software on the XBOX. In Section 11.4.2▸697, we'll show you the popular Dallas Semiconductor DS50002FB microcontroller that encrypts all memory and bus traffic. Undeterred by this, then-German undergraduate student Markus Kuhn crafted a clever attack that tricks the processor into dumping all its encrypted memory (in cleartext!) on an output port. The idea is to feed guessed encrypted instructions to the chip and see how it reacts. Finally, we're going to show you a broad range of attacks against smartcards (Section 11.4.3 ▶ 701). Because of the economic incentive to break smartcard security (it can allow you free public transport, mobile phone calls, and pay-TV pornography), well-funded attackers have gone to great lengths to coax secrets out of cards, and card manufacturers have gone to great lengths to develop defenses against these attacks. Some attacks are *invasive* (they open up the card in order to probe or manipulate its internals) and some are *non-invasive* (they examine the card's behavior, such as its power consumption or execution time to deduce the stored key material).

11.4.1 Tapping the Bus—The Microsoft XBOX Hack

In 2001, then-MIT Ph.D. student Andrew "Bunnie" Huang got an XBOX game console from his fiancée for Christmas. He immediately decided to take it apart. He eventually cracked the security scheme and published what he'd learned in a paper and a book [51,172]. He also keeps a Web site devoted to XBOX hacking (http://hackingthexbox.com).

The XBOX is essentially a low-cost PC running a version of Windows. Like a PC, it contains an x86 CPU, 64 MB of cheap RAM, northbridge and southbridge chips, IDE controllers, and so on. Here is a sketch of the system (adapted from reference [51]), where we've left out any uninteresting (to us) subsystems:

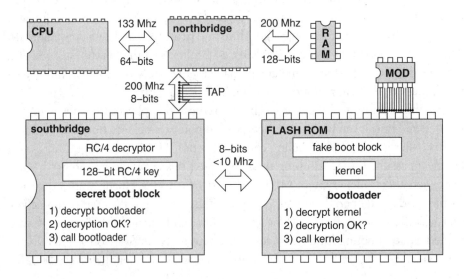

(The "TAP" and MOD chip we'll get to later—they're part of the attack, not the defense.) Hardcoded in the ASIC southbridge chip is an RC/4 decryptor, a 128-bit key, and a secret boot block. On system start-up, the boot block executes and then decrypts, verifies, and jumps to the bootloader, which is contained in FLASH ROM. The bootloader, in turn, decrypts, verifies, and jumps to the OS kernel, which is also in FLASH. This is reminiscent of the TPM-enabled trusted boot process you saw in Section 11.2▶670.

The designers put a fake boot block in the FLASH ROM. Whether this was done intentionally to throw off potential attackers, or was the result of a faulty build process as claimed by Michael Steil [335], is hard to know.

Bunnie made two crucial observations. First, the decryption is done by the CPU, and this means that the key will have to travel over at least two busses. Second, the busses between the FLASH and the CPU are high-speed, so the designers thought they'd be safe from prying and decided to keep them unencrypted. As a result, the key will be traveling in cleartext across the open busses.

So the question was which bus to tap. The busses between the CPU and between the northbridge and between the northbridge and the RAM are both prohibitively wide, 64 and 128 bits, respectively. The bus between the south- and northbridge, on the other hand—is just 8 bits wide! BINGO! Bunnie soldered a *tap board* onto the bus and sniffed it as the plaintext secret boot block, including the RC/4 decryptor and key, which he came across on their way to the CPU. Having access to the fake boot block gave him some help in resolving ambiguities, as did pattern matching on the decryption algorithm. Once he'd figured out that RC/4 was being used, he wrote his own version and fed every 16 bytes of the boot block into it in order to find which worked as a key.

Once the key was found and let loose on the Internet, a cottage industry of "XBOX mod-chip" [335] manufacturers sprung up. One design had to be soldered across the 31 pins of the FLASH ROM and contained a complete replacement of the FLASH. Over time, simpler designs emerged that needed less hardware expertise to install. With the access to the key, it became possible to patch the kernel to allow non-authorized software to be loaded, particularly pirated copies of games. It also allowed competing operating systems, such as Linux, to be booted.

11.4.2 Injecting Ciphertext—Dallas Semiconductor DS5002FP

The DS5002FP is a popular microprocessor for use in ATMs, pay-TV decoders, and the like. It does *bus encryption*, which means that it stores code and data in an external SRAM chip and encrypts addresses and data so that neither ever appears in cleartext on the bus. The manufacturer describes it like this [321]:

> ... the secure microprocessor chip incorporates the most sophisticated security features available in any processor. The security features of the DS5002FP include an array of mechanisms that are designed to resist all levels of threat, including observation, analysis, and physical attack. As a result, a massive effort is required to obtain any information about memory contents.

In spite of this, Markus Kuhn [16,17,215] in his diploma thesis [214] describes an attack that is able to completely extract the cleartext of the protected program.

The processor contains a 64-bit key K, a true random-number generator RND, and three cryptographic functions E_K^a (for address permutation), $E_{K,addr}^d$ (for data encryption), and $D_{K,addr}^d$ (for data decryption):

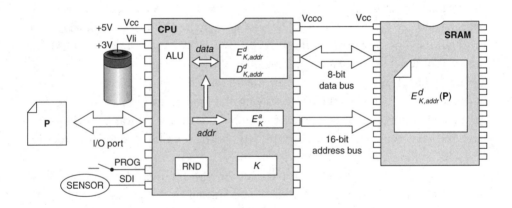

The processor is connected to an SRAM memory chip through a 16-bit-wide address bus and an 8-bit-wide data bus. The SRAM chip is powered by the processor. An external backup battery can keep data alive for more than 10 years.

In terms of defenses, the DS5002FP has a *self-destruct input* (SDI) pin that can be connected to an external tamper-detection sensor. When it triggers (due to changes in light, temperature, pressure, and so on), the processor wipes K and turns off power to the memory chip, effectively erasing all secret code and data. To prevent micro-probing attacks, the DS5002FPM (a variant of the DS5002FP) has an additional top coating layer [321]:

This additional layer is not a simple sheet of metal, but rather a complex layout that is interwoven with power and ground, which are in turn connected to logic for the encryption key and the security lock. As a result, any attempt to remove the layer or probe through it results in the erasure of the security lock and/or the loss of encryption key bits.

When you initialize the processor, it generates a new value for K using the internal random-number generator. You then toggle the PROG pin, which makes the processor read the cleartext program P, encrypt it with $E^d_{K,addr}$, and store the result to the external SRAM chip.

The function $E^d_{K,addr}$ encrypts (and $D^d_{K,addr}$ decrypts) one byte at a time. Encryption is dependent on the key K as well as on the address $addr$ where the byte is stored. This prevents an attacker from manipulating the encrypted program by moving instructions around. Addresses are permuted by the E^a_K function. In other words, to encrypt and store byte b at address z, the CPU computes

$$z' \leftarrow E^a_K(z)$$
$$b' \leftarrow E^d_{K,z}(b)$$
$$\text{SRAM}[z'] \leftarrow b'$$

and to load and decrypt the byte again, it computes

$$z' \leftarrow E^a_K(z)$$
$$b' \leftarrow \text{SRAM}[z']$$
$$b \leftarrow D^d_{K,z}(b')$$

When the CPU isn't accessing memory, it generates random bus traffic to confuse an observer.

Markus Kuhn's attack is intended to exhaustively feed guessed encrypted instructions to the processor and then examine how it reacts to them. Step by step, this allows the attacker to deduce the encryption functions for each memory address. Once he has a few decryption functions figured out, he can craft a small program that dumps the cleartext contents of memory to an output port.

It's a good idea to start by trying to decipher the instruction

```
75 a0 XX        MOV 0xa0 XX
```

that writes the byte XX to the parallel port P2 (located in memory at address 0xa0). This is a clever instruction for the attacker to start looking for, since it's easy to detect when he might have found it: It should make something appear on the parallel port! Moreover, every unique byte XX he tries to write with the MOV instruction should result in a unique byte appearing on the output port. So the search is very simple:

```
for(x=0; x<256; x++)
    nexty:
    for(y=0; y<256; y++)
        E₂← 0
        for(z=0; z<256; z++)
            reset CPU and feed it the code
                a₀+0: x
                a₀+1: y
                a₀+2: z
            p←value read from port P2
            if (E₂(p) is not empty) goto nexty
            E₂←E₂∪{p↦z}
    return (x,y,E₂)
```

This code tries every possible value (x,y) for the first two bytes of the instruction and tabulates all the values that appear on the P2 port in a set E_2 when varying the third byte through all values $0\ldots255$. If all 256 bytes appear, then (x,y) is probably the MOV 0xa0 instruction. At the end of this test, the attacker has collected the following information:

$$
\begin{aligned}
x &= E^d_{K,a_0} \\
y &= E^d_{K,a_0+1} \\
E_2(p) &= E^d_{K,a_0+2}(p), \forall 0 \le p \le 255
\end{aligned}
$$

He's certainly off to a good start, since he has *complete* knowledge of the encryption function for the byte at address $a_0 + 2$!

In the next step, he'll want to similarly deduce the encryption functions for address $a_0 + 3$, $a_0 + 4$, and so on, which we call E_3, E_4, ... He can do this by searching for a NOP-like instruction, which he can insert right before MOV 0xa0 XX, effectively moving it forward by one byte in the instruction stream. Once he has tabulated a few encryption functions, seven is enough for the DS5002FP, he knows enough to generate a small program that traverses memory and writes the contents of each decrypted byte to an output port.

Markus Kuhn's attack is possible because of the small ciphertext granularity. An upgraded version of the DS5002FP, the DS5240/DS5250, encrypts 8 bytes of data at a time rather than one byte at a time. This makes it much more costly to tabulate the encryption functions.

11.4.3 Hacking Smartcards

Smartcards have become ubiquitous as secure storage devices. They are used on mass transit systems, as prepaid phone cards (*stored value cards*), as identification cards, in cellular phones (*SIM cards*), in pay-TV set-top boxes, and in credit cards. Their main strength is that they contain protected memory in which a secret such as a private key can be stored. They also have cryptographic capabilities: They can generate and store public-key key-pairs, perform RSA encryption, compute SHA-1 hashing, and so on. Smartcard manufacturers employ various techniques to protect the cards against tampering, but since they're typically deployed in mass quantities, there's a trade-off between security features and cost.

Smartcards have neither internal power nor a clock. They are entirely passive devices and only work when they are inserted into a card reader, a *card acceptance device* (CAD). As you see from the picture here, the CAD provides power (Vcc) and a clock signal (CLK) to the card and communicates with it over a 1-bit serial link (I/O):

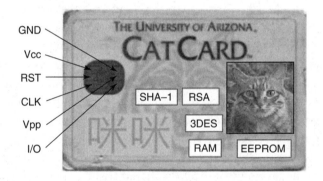

The CAD has no direct access to the internals of the card, including its memory; the only way to access it is through a protocol executed over the serial link. The fact that smartcards are completely dependent on the CAD for power and clock signal makes them particularly easy to attack. For example, as you will see, varying the supply voltage or the clock signal can induce exploitable faults.

As an example, Gemalto's TOP DM GX4 has a JavaCard virtual machine interpreter, 68KB of persistent RAM, 78KB EEPROM, and supports 3DES/AES/RSA encryption, SHA-1 cryptographic hash, and asymmetric key pair generation. Java Card is a standard that specifies a subset of the Java language and standard libraries designed specifically for smartcard programming, along with a virtual machine instruction set optimized for size. When it comes to security, the manufacturer vaguely states [136]:

> the platform implements most advance[d] security countermeasures en-
> forcing protection of all sensitive data and function in the card. ... in-
> cludes multiple hardware and software countermeasure[s] against various
> attacks:
>
> - Side channel attacks
>
> - Invasive attacks
>
> - Advanced fault attacks
>
> - Other types of attack.

In this section, we're going to describe attacks against smartcards, simply because these have been described extensively in the open literature. There's no reason
why the same techniques can't be used against other types of chips that contain secrets, such as the TPM we discussed in Section 11.2►670. The TPM, in fact, has been
described as a "smartcard soldered to the motherboard of a computer." The packaging is different, but the functionality is similar: Both the TPM and the smartcard
contain a secret private key and various cryptographic functions.

Attacks against smartcards are either *invasive* or *non-invasive*. The adversary
starts an invasive attack by physically exposing the bare chip, and then either probes
the surface to extract information or manipulates the chip to make it perform an
unintended function. An invasive attack, by definition, destroys the card, but the
adversary can use the secret code and data that he's collected to clone a new one.
In a non-invasive attack, the adversary doesn't destroy the card but rather extracts
information by monitoring its execution characteristics, such as its power usage,
electromagnetic radiation, execution time, and so on. He can either do this during
normal operating conditions or he can deliberately induce faults to coax the chip
to give up its secrets.

Invasive attacks are useful when an attacker knows very little about the card,
its physical characteristics, or the software it contains. These attacks can take a long
time to perform and may require sophisticated and expensive equipment. However,
once the attacker has gathered enough information about the card, he may be able
to use it to devise a non-invasive attack that's easier, cheaper, and faster to deploy.

Much of the published literature on attacks against smartcards comes out of
Ross Anderson's group at Cambridge. Several of Anderson and Kuhn's papers have
become must-read classics [14,16,17,207], and Sergei Skorobogatov's Ph.D. thesis [328] gives a particularly thorough treatment of attack techniques. This presen-
tation is based in large part on their work.

11.4.3.1 Invasive Attacks   An attacker can find plenty of information in the literature that describes how to launch a physical attack against a smartcard. Other than having different packaging techniques, smartcards and micro-controllers are very similar, and both have been subjected to the same kinds of attacks. The semiconductor industry also uses these techniques to analyze failures in their own chips and to reverse engineer competitors' chips [226,306]. For attackers with insufficient knowledge but sufficient funding, there are companies such as Chipworks that will provide reverse engineering services for a fee (`http://www.chipworks.com`):

> Chipworks can extract analog or digital circuits from semiconductor devices and deliver detailed easy-to-understand schematics that document a single functional block or all the circuits. . . . We decapsulate the chip and analyze the die to locate the circuit blocks of interest. Then, using our Image Capture and Imaging System (ICIS) we generate mosiacs for each level of interconnect. Finally, advanced software and expertise is used to extract the circuits for analysis.

We won't go into details here but rather give a brief overview of the steps that a typical attack will go through. The first step an attacker needs to take is to *depackage* the chip and glue it to a test package so that he can connect it to a circuit board and examine it further [225,301]:[3]

1. Remove the chip from the card itself by heating and bending it.
2. Remove the epoxy resin around the chip by dipping it in 60°C fuming nitric acid.
3. Clean the chip by washing it with acetone in an ultrasonic bath.
4. Mount the exposed chip in a test package and connect its pads to the pins of the package.

For ordinary chip packaging techniques, steps 1 through 4 are known as *decapsulation*.

Next, he'll want to create a high-level map of the chip layout:

5. Use an optical microscope to take large, high-resolution pictures of the chip surface.
6. Identify major architectural features (ROM, ALU, EEPROM, and so on) and/or lower-level features such as busses and gates.

---

3. Don't try this at home; these chemicals are harmful.

7. Remove the top metal track layer by dipping the chip in hydrofluoric acid in an ultrasonic bath.

8. Repeat from 5, for each layer.

Breaking a chip down by stripping away one layer at a time and analyzing each layer is known as *deprocessing*.

The next step is *reverse engineering* the chip, analyzing the information collected during the deprocessing stage to gain an understanding of the behavior of the different functional units of the chip. For complex chips, the attacker may have to revert to automatic techniques that use image processing [44] to reverse engineer the layout, but with some experience he may be able to reconstruct enough of the design directly from the photographs to know where to launch an attack.

The final steps use *microprobing* to read out contents of the smartcard memory. A *microprobing workstation* has an optical microscope and a "cat whisker" probe that can make connection with any part of the chip with great accuracy. The probe can either read out a signal from the chip or induce a signal to the chip. Here are the steps of a *passive* attack:

9. To allow the probe contact with the chip, use a laser cutter mounted on the microscope to remove (patches of) the *passivation layer* that covers the top-layer aluminum interconnect lines.

10. Record the activity on a few of the bus lines (as many as there are probes) while going through transactions with the card.

11. Repeat from 10 until the bus activity trace from all of the bus lines has been collected.

If the attacker is lucky, just passively watching the busses while the smartcard is going through a critical transaction will force it to reveal all the secrets in its memory—all the code, all the stored keys, and so on. If not, he needs to launch an *active* attack:

12. To force the chip to cycle through all instruction addresses, use the laser cutter to disable the chip area that implements branching instructions.

Since the program counter is updated automatically as long as no branches are taken, the chip will produce each instruction on the bus for the adversary to examine.

The steps above are sufficient for older chip designs with large feature sizes. If the feature size of the chip is below that of visible light, the attacker will be forced to turn to more expensive technology. A *Focused Ion Beam* (FIB) workstation can not only produce detailed images of the chip surface but can also etch away connections, drill holes in the chip to access deeper layers, and *deposit* material on the chip surface to make new connections.

Over time, these invasive attacks will become more complex, more expensive, and less accessible to hobbyist hackers. Smaller feature sizes, wider internal busses, more interconnect layers, and more built-in defenses will require increasingly sophisticated tools. For example, many smartcards now use ASIC (Application-Specific Integrated Circuit) technology. In such *glue logic*, there are no obvious building blocks to search for so it becomes close to impossible to manually locate the place to probe or manipulate.

On the other hand, the tools that are necessary to attack such designs will be necessary for chip designers too, in order for them to be able to analyze chip failures. Thus, there will always be a second-hand market of cheaper instruments sufficient for analyzing last generation's chips. An attacker with *some* funding, but not enough to purchase his own equipment, can, for a few hundred dollars per hour, rent time in a state-of-the-art laboratory. And if, like Bunnie Huang and Markus Kuhn, he's a university student, his school may already have access to all the tools he needs.

11.4.4 Non-Invasive Attacks

Non-invasive attacks have many advantages over invasive ones: The attacker doesn't have to expose himself to dangerous chemicals, he doesn't need expensive equipment, and once he has an effective attack against one particular card, he can easily reuse it on another of the same model. Also, since he doesn't destroy the card in the process, he can keep on using it after the attack, with the added benefit that he now knows the secrets it contains.

Non-invasive attacks can be both *active* and *passive*. In a passive attack, the attacker just examines what comes out of the chip, such as electromagnetic radiation, power consumption, or execution time. In an active attack, he feeds carefully (or not so carefully) constructed data, power, or clock signals to the chip and *then* measures the chip's behavior. In Section 11.4.2 ▶697, you saw how Markus Kuhn fed random encrypted instruction bytes to the DS5002FP chip until he found some with the behavior he was looking for. This was an *active non-invasive attack*. Bunnie Huang's attack on the XBOX in Section 11.4.1 ▶696 was a *passive non-invasive attack*, however, since he just watched a bus until the key he was looking for came across.

11.4.4.1 Fault Induction Attacks In a *fault induction attack* (also known as a *glitch* attack), the attacker generates a sharp voltage spike, increases the clock frequency, or subjects the chip to an electric field, all in an attempt to cause an error in the computation. The goal is to force the processor to execute the wrong instruction. Obviously, not every wrong instruction will cause an exploitable fault, so he will have to resort to judicious use of trial and error. As an example, consider this routine that's supposed to write a region of memory to the I/O port:

```
void write(char* result, int length) {
    while (length > 0) {
        printf(*result);
        result++;
        length--;
    }
}
```

If he could force a fault in the light gray code, replacing it with any instruction that doesn't affect the `length` variable, then the loop will cycle through all of memory, dumping it on the port!

11.4.4.2 Timing Attacks The idea of a *timing attack* was first presented by Paul Kocher [205] in 1996. In 1998, Dhem et al. [113] gave a practical attack. The idea is for the attacker to generate a large number of messages (such as, "Please encrypt this file with your secret key"), send them to the smartcard, and then measure the time the operations take. From the timings, he can deduce the key. Assume that the attacker knows that the encryption routine uses this *modular exponentiation* function:

```
s[0] = 1;
for(k=0; k<w; k++) {
    if (x[k] == 1)
        R[k] = (s[k]*y) mod n;
    else
        R[k] = s[k];
    s[k+1] = R[k]*R[k] mod n
}
return R[w-1];
```

Here, x is the w-bits-long private key he wants to recover. The attack deduces one bit at a time. Let's say that he wants to recover bit x_0. He constructs two sets of messages, M_1 and M_2, so that the messages in M_1 should cause the light gray code to execute, while the messages in M_2 should take the dark gray branch. He now asks the smartcard to encrypt all the messages and records their time. Since the light gray code does a multiply but the dark gray code doesn't, the messages in M_1 should take longer to encrypt than those in M_2. If (on average) they do, he can deduce that $x_0 = 1$, otherwise $x_0 = 0$. The smaller the difference in time between the two branches, the more samples he will have to generate. Knowing x_0, he can continue to deduce x_1 in the same manner.

11.4.4.3 Power Analysis Attacks In a *power analysis* attack, the attacker draws conclusions about the internal behavior of the chip from measurements of the power that it consumes. Different instructions consume different amounts of power, and monitoring the power usage as the chip goes through a transaction can reveal which instructions it's executing. Busses also draw power as bus lines change between 0 and 1, which means that it may be possible to estimate the number of bits that changed on the bus by measuring the amount of power consumed.

Power analysis is probably the easiest attack to implement. All the attacker needs is a resistor on the chip's power supply line, a high-resolution, high-sampling-frequency volt meter over the resistor, and a computer to store and analyze the current traces. As with timing attacks, there can be significant noise in the measurements, but he can counter this by averaging over a large number of transactions.

There are two kinds of power analyses, *simple power analysis* (SPA) and *differential power analysis* (DPA). SPA looks directly at a trace of the power consumption and deduces the instructions executed. For example, if he can distinguish the power signature of the multiplication operation in the modular exponentiation routine we showed earlier, the attacker could extract the key material. DPA is a more powerful technique that uses statistical methods to analyze the power consumption over many cryptographic operations. Paul Kocher et al. report that DPA allowed them to "extract keys from almost 50 different products in a variety of physical form factors" [204].

11.4.4.4 Countermeasures There are a variety of ways to protect against these attacks. Judicious use of randomization is probably necessary, for example, generating an internal clock signal by inserting random delays in the external one. Interleaving multiple threads of control is another possibility, but it's difficult to achieve on smartcards with limited computational resources. Environmental sensors are already implemented on most smartcards. It's essential, for example, to detect if an attacker lowers the clock signal in order to more easily monitor the computations.

David Maher of AT&T Labs writes a scathing review [239] against what he considers the scaremongering attack scenarios that you've seen here. He points out, and rightly so, that cryptographic processors don't exist in a vacuum, but rather are one integral part of a complete security architecture. If one minute you're buying groceries in Tucson and the next a Porsche in Beijing, alarms are going to be raised at the credit card company that your card probably has been cloned. Similarly, pay-TV companies know their smartcards will be under heavy attack and architect their systems to detect anomalies and to minimize losses when attacks are discovered. It's important to anticipate attacks (and know that you must anticipate attacks that you can't anticipate!) and to design your system with upgradable security to counter such attacks.

11.4.5 Board-Level Protection

The IBM 4758 cryptographic coprocessor is interesting because, as far as we know, its physical protection hasn't been broken! Also, its design is well described in the open literature [173,370,371]. The 4758 is validated at "FIPS 140 level 4" [174], the U.S. government's highest security standard for cryptographic modules, which states:

- The cryptographic module components shall be covered by potting material or contained within an enclosure encapsulated by a tamper detection envelope (e.g., a flexible mylar printed circuit with a serpentine geometric pattern of conductors or a wire-wound package or a non-flexible, brittle circuit or a strong enclosure) that shall detect tampering by means such as cutting, drilling, milling, grinding, or dissolving of the potting material or enclosure to an extent sufficient for accessing plaintext secret and private keys cryptographic keys or CSPs.

- The cryptographic module shall contain tamper response and zeroization circuitry that shall continuously monitor the tamper detection envelope and, upon the detection of tampering, shall immediately zeroize all plaintext secret and private cryptographic keys and CSPs. The tamper response and zeroization circuitry shall remain operational when plaintext secret and private cryptographic keys or CSPs are contained within the cryptographic module.

In contrast to the rest of this section, where we've shown you how easily hardware can be compromised, the 4758 serves as an illustrative example of what is actually necessary to provide adequate security against both invasive and non-invasive attacks.

The 4758 costs about $4,000, which is quite affordable for its target audience. There are many potential applications. A variety of vending machines now "sell money," for example, by topping off mobile phones, adding money to smartcards used in electricity meters, or printing postage stamps. Since such machines are installed in potentially hostile environments, it's important that they be physically secure. These processors are also used by banks to protect electronic transfers from insider attacks.

The 4758 is delivered as a PCI card that you plug in to a host computer. It consists of a 486-type processor, 4MB of RAM, 4MB of FLASH, 32KB of battery backed RAM, cryptographic facilities (DES, 3DES, and RSA encryption, true random-number generation, SHA-1 cryptographic hash), and a date and time unit:

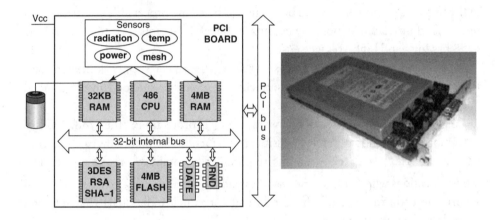

The battery and the PCI bus controller are outside the secure perimeter, and everything else is physically secured.

What's interesting about the 4758 are its tamper-detection and protection facilities. It has both a physical layer of protection to make invasive attacks difficult, and a collection of sensors that detect that tampering is under way. When a tamper-detection sensor triggers, the 4758 turns off power to the battery-backed RAM, zeroing any secret code and data. It then resets the CPU, which stops it from refreshing the RAM, destroying *its* contents.

To protect against invasive attacks, the PCI board is surrounded by a "polyurethane mixture and a film with an imprinted circuit pattern to detect minute penetration and erosion attacks" [173]. Earlier versions used several layers of 40-gauge nichrome wire wound around the device and connected to power and ground. The device would then be embedded in epoxy. Regardless, if an attacker tries to chemically eat through the potting material or drill down to the processor, the wires will either short out and destroy the device or alert the processor that an attack is under way. Earlier versions of the coprocessor were also covered in a metal enclosure with switches that would trigger if the case was opened.

Memory remanence presents a potentially serious attack. The problem is that RAM can hold values even after its power has been turned off. This could allow an attacker to remove the unit from the host computer (thereby powering down any active defenses), drill down to RAM, and extract the secrets. The length of time that the data remains readable can be extended by freezing the memory or subjecting it to X-ray radiation. To protect against such memory imprinting attacks, the 4758 has temperature and radiation sensors.

The card is powered from the host computer. This leaves it open to fault-induction attacks, where the voltage is brought abnormally high or low. As you saw in the previous section, this could be enough to make the processor execute random unintended instructions, possibly causing it to leak its secrets. For this reason, the 4758 has low- and high-voltage sensors.

Finally, to prevent power analysis attacks, the power supply is filtered, and to prevent electromagnetic analysis attacks, the board is shielded inside a metal enclosure, forming a *Faraday Cage*.

There are no known attacks against the physical protection of the 4758. A group at Cambridge has shown that it's possible to extract the DES keys (`http://www.cl. cam.ac.uk/~rnc1/descrack`), but this requires an accomplice on the inside. The type of locations where this coprocessor is installed are also likely to have additional security procedures in place to make it difficult for a single individual to have enough time alone with the device to successfully launch an attack.

Performance for heavily armored processors like the 4758 is a problem. The reason is that the more layers of physical protection you add, the more of the heat generated by the processor will get trapped within the enclosure. In practice, this means that you will have to lower the clock rate to reduce the amount of heat that gets generated.[4] This, in turn, could mean that you need to separate your application into two parts, one security-sensitive part that runs slowly on the armored co-processor, and the remaining part, which runs fast on a standard CPU.

The lesson we can learn from the attacks in the previous sections and the successful design of the 4758 you've seen here is that it's essential to protect against *every* possible attack scenario. *Any* kind of leakage of information, *any* possible way

---

4. For example, the IBM 4764, the current incarnation of the 4758, supports a 266MHz PowerPC, orders of magnitude slower than current processors. The hardware implementations of cryptographic primitives, however, are fast. In other words, general-purpose code will run much slower than on commodity hardware, but the performance of cryptographic code will be competitive.

to physically abuse the processor, *any* way to inject it with faulty or unexpected code or data, *any* way to subject it to adverse environmental conditions—unless every hole is plugged, an adversary will find it and exploit it. The 4758 shows that it's possible to build a reasonably secure device (although, since it's not deployed in vast numbers in situations where any hacker can get a whack at it, it's really hard to say for sure), but so far we haven't seen one that's efficient, secure, *and* cheap.

11.5 Discussion

There are many *disadvantages* of hardware-only or hardware-assisted software protection techniques. First, there are deployment issues. If you were to invent a perfectly secure and non-intrusive system today, it might take a decade before it was shipped on every new PC, and longer before older, nonprotected, PCs had been phased out. In the meantime, you're stuck in a situation where some hardware is protected and some is not. Of course, in special-purpose systems such as game consoles, set-top pay-TV boxes, or military systems, the time from invention to deployment can be much shorter. And some hardware techniques (such as dongles) don't require wholesale modifications to PC internals.

Some hardware-based software protection techniques are more expensive for the software producer. This is true of dongles, for example. Dongles are also cumbersome to use for the customer. What happens if they lose the dongle? They will have to call up the software producer, convince them that they have a legal copy of the software, and wait for the new device to arrive in the mail. In the meantime, they can't use the software they bought legally!

Similar problems occur when a program is tied to a piece of hardware, such as being encrypted for a particular secure CPU. What happens when the user upgrades to a faster CPU? Again, they must prove they own a legal copy of the software and get a new copy tailored for the new CPU. What happens if the software vendor has gone out of business? Any data files produced by the software suddenly become irrevocably unreadable!

What do you need in a cryptographic processor design for it to be completely trustworthy? Well, as you saw in Section 11.4▶695 and Section 11.4▶695, *no information of any kind* can be allowed to leak off the chip, and *not a single bit* of code or data must ever be allowed to be modified or replayed. This means that electromagnetic radiation, power usage, and instruction timings cannot carry any information useful to an attacker. It means that all bus communication must be encrypted, and furthermore, no data or address patterns can reveal any information. It means that no adverse environmental conditions (low power, high power, power spikes, clock spikes, high temperature, X-ray radiation, . . .) can go undetected or cause the processor to get off the intended execution path. It means that freezing or radiating memory won't burn in the data long enough for an attacker to extract it. And it means that the processor chip itself cannot be decapsulated and then probed or modified.

From an engineering perspective, you have to balance these security requirements against processor performance, design complexity, ease of testing, and manufacturing costs. For example, since the yield of microprocessor manufacturing is never 100%, each chip has to be tested prior to shipping. Any on-chip facilities that make such testing easier will also make it easier for an adversary to probe it! It's also likely that the cost of the processor will go up with the number and complexity of its security features. Here's a table with prices we found during a quick Web search of the processors you've seen in this chapter.

Kind	Manufacturer	Model	Price	Comment
TPM	Infineon	SLB 9635 TT1.2	$2.85	quantities of 3,000
dongle	Aladdin	HASP	$23	quantities of 1,000
crypto-processor	Maxim	DS5002FP	$13.56	quantities of 1,000
smartcard	Gemalto	TOP IM FIPS CY2	$36.85	
crypto-processor	IBM	4758	$4,000.00	approximate

Actual costs will vary with quantity, discounts, and so on, but this should give you a general idea. The TPM has (as far as we know) no anti-tampering features that would explain why its so much cheaper than a smartcard. It's also interesting to note that there is a two-orders-of-magnitude difference in price between the smartcard (for which we know many effective attacks) and IBM's 4758 (for which there are no known attacks).

Bibliography

[1] Hofstadter and Douglas R. Basic Books, Godel, Escher, *Bach: An Eternal Golden Braid*, January 1999. ISBN 0465026567.

[2] Sandmark. `www.cs.arizona.edu/sandmark/`.

[3] Zelix klassmaster. `www.zelix.com/klassmaster/index.html`.

[4] D. Abramson and R. Sosic. Relative debugging using multiple program versions. In *8th Int. Symp. on Languages for Intensional Programming*, Sydney, May 1995.

[5] Alfred V. Aho, Ravi Sethi, and Jeffery D. Ullman. *Compilers: Principles, Techniques, and Tools*. Addison-Wesley, 1988.

[6] Alex Aiken. Moss—a system for detecting software plagiarism. `www.cs.berkeley.edu/~aiken/moss.html`.

[7] Alex Aiken, Saul Schleimer, Joel Auslander, Daniel Wilkerson, Anthony Tomasic, and Steve Fink. Method and apparatus for indexing document content and content comparison with World Wide Web search service. U.S. Patent 6757675, June 2004. Assigned to the Regents of the University of California.

[8] Aladdin. HASP4 programmer's guide. ftp://ftp.aladdin.com/pub/hasp/new_releases/docsHASP_Manual_EN.zip, 2007.

[9] B. Anckaert, M. Madou, and K. De Bosschere. A model for self-modifying code. In *8th Information Hiding*, July 2006. Springer-Verlag.

[10] Bertrand Anckaert, Mariusz Jakubowski, and Ramarathnam Venkatesan. Proteus: virtualization for diversified tamper-resistance. In *DRM '06: Proceedings of the ACM Workshop on Digital rights management*, pages 47–58, New York, 2006. ACM Press.

[11] Bertrand Anckaert, Mariusz Jakubowski, Ramarathnam Venkatesan, and Koen De Bosschere. Run-time randomization to mitigate tampering. In A. Miyaji, H. Kikuchi, and K. Rannenberg, editors, *Proceedings of the Second International Workshop on Security*, number 4752, pages 153–168, Berlin, October 2007. Springer-Verlag.

[12] Bertrand Anckaert, Bjorn De Sutter, and Koen De Bosschere. Covert communication through executables. In *Program Acceleration through Application and Architecture Driven Code Transformations: Symposium Proceedings*, pages 83–85, Edegem, Sept. 2004.

[13] Bertrand Anckaert, Bjorn De Sutter, Dominique Chanet, and Koen De Bosschere. Steganography for executables and code transformation signatures. In P. Choosnik and C. Seongtaek, editors, *Information Security And Cryptology—ICISC 2004*, number 3506, pages 425–439, Germany, April 2005. Springer-Verlag.

[14] R. Anderson, M. Bond, J. Clulow, and S. Skorobogatov. Cryptographic processors—A survey. *Proceedings of the IEEE*, 94(2):357–369, 2006. IEEE.

[15] Ross Anderson. Trusted computing frequently asked questions, version 1.1. `www.cl.cam.ac.uk/~rja14/tcpa-faq.html`, August 2003.

[16] Ross Anderson and Markus Kuhn. Tamper resistance—a cautionary note. In *Proceedings of the Second USENIX Workshop on Electronic Commerce*, pages 1–11, 1996. USENIX.

[17] Ross Anderson and Markus Kuhn. Low cost attacks on tamper resistant devices. In *IWSP: International Workshop on Security Protocols, LNCS*, 1997. Springer-Verlag.

[18] Ross J. Anderson and Fabien A. P. Petitcolas. On the limits of steganography. *IEEE Journal of Selected Areas in Communications*, 16(4):474–481, May 1998. Special issue on copyright & privacy protection.

[19] ANSI. Audio recording—compact disc digital audio system, 1999. iec 60908 ed. 2.0 b:1999.

[20] Andrew Appel. Deobfuscation is in NP. `www.cs.princeton.edu/~appel/papers/deobfus.pdf`, 2002.

[21] W. A. Arbaugh, D. J. Farber, and J. M. Smith. A secure and reliable bootstrap architecture. In *SP '97: Proceedings of the 1997 IEEE Symposium on Security and Privacy*, page 65, Washington, DC, 1997. IEEE.

[22] William A. Arbaugh, David J. Farber, Angelos D. Keromytis, and Jonathan M. Smith. Secure and reliable bootstrap architecture. U.S. Patent 6185678, 2001.

[23] M. Atallah, V. Raskin, C. Hempelmann, M. Karahan, R. Sion, and K. Triezenberg. Natural language watermarking and tamperproofing. In *Proc. 5th International Information Hiding Workshop*, 2002. Springer-Verlag.

[24] Mikhail J. Atallah and Chang Hoi. Method and system for tamperproofing software. United States Application 20060031686, February 2006. Assigned to Purdue Research Foundation.

[25] Mikhail J. Atallah, Victor Raskin, Michael Crogan, Christian Hempelmann, Florian Kerschbaum, Dina Mohamed, and Sanket Naik. Natural language watermarking: Design, analysis, and a proof-of-concept implementation. In *IHW '01: Proceedings of the 4th International Workshop on Information Hiding*, pages 185–199, London, 2001. Springer-Verlag.

[26] David Aucsmith. Tamper resistant software: An implementation. In Ross J. Anderson, editor, *Information Hiding, First International Workshop*, pages 317–333, Cambridge, U.K., May 1996. Springer-Verlag. Lecture Notes in Computer Science, Vol. 1174.

[27] David Aucsmith and Gary Graunke. Tamper resistant methods and apparatus. U.S. Patent 5892899, April 1999. Assigned to Intel Corporation (Santa Clara, CA).

[28] Lee Badger, Larry D'Anna, Doug Kilpatrick, Brian Matt, Andrew Reisse, and Tom Van Vleck. Self-protecting mobile agents obfuscation techniques evaluation report. Technical Report 01-036, NAI Labs, November 2001.

[29] Mark W. Bailey and Jack W. Davidson. A formal model and specification language for procedure calling conventions. In *POPL '95: Proceedings of the 22nd ACM SIGPLAN-SIGACT Symposium on Principles of Programming Languages*, pages 298–310, New York, NY, 1995. ACM.

[30] Sundeep Bajikar. Trusted platform module (TPM) based security on notebook PCs—white paper. Technical report, Intel Corporation, June 2002.

[31] Boris Balacheff, Liqun Chen, Siani Pearson, David Plaquin, and Graeme Proudler. *Trusted Computing Platforms: TCPA Technology in Context*. Prentice Hall PTR, Upper Saddle River, NJ, 2002.

[32] Thomas Ball. The concept of dynamic analysis. In *ESEC/FSE-7: Proceedings of the 7th European Software Engineering Conference*, pages 216–234, London, 1999. Springer-Verlag.

[33] Thomas Ball and James R. Larus. Optimally profiling and tracing programs. *ACM Trans. Program. Lang. Syst.*, 16(4):1319–1360, 1994.

[34] Boaz Barak, Oded Goldreich, Russell Impagliazzo, Steven Rudich, Amit Sahai, Salil Vadhan, and Ke Yang. On the (im)possibility of obfuscating programs (extended abstract). In J. Kilian, editor, *Advances in Cryptology—CRYPTO 2001*, 2001. LNCS 2139.

[35] Elena Gabriela Barrantes, David H. Ackley, Stephanie Forrest, and Darko Stefanović. Randomized instruction set emulation. *ACM Transactions on Information and System Security (TISSEC)*, 8(1):3–40, February 2005.

[36] Gareth Baxter, Marcus Frean, James Noble, Mark Rickerby, Hayden Smith, Matt Visser, Hayden Melton, and Ewan Tempero. Understanding the shape of Java software. In *OOPSLA '06: Proceedings of the 21st Annual ACM SIGPLAN Conference on Object-Oriented Programming Systems, Languages, and Applications*, pages 397–412, New York, 2006. ACM.

[37] W. Bender, D. Gruhl, and N. Morimoto. Techniques for data hiding. In *Proc. of the SPIE 2420 (Storage and Retrieval for Image and Video Databases III)*, pages 164–173, 1995.

[38] R. E. Berry and B. A. E. Meekings. A style analysis of C programs. *Communications of the ACM*, 28(1):80–88, January 1991.

[39] Robert M. Best. Preventing software piracy with crypto-microprocessors. In *Proceedings of IEEE Spring COMPCON 80*, pages 466–469, San Francisco, CA, February 1980. IEEE.

[40] Robert M. Best. Crypto microprocessor that executes enciphered programs. U.S. Patent No. 4 465 901, issued Aug. 14, 1984.

[41] Philippe Biondi and Fabrice Desclaux. Silver needle in the Skype. In *Black Hat Europe*, Feb–Mar 2006. www.blackhat.com/presentations/bh-europe-06/bh-eu-06-biondi/bh-eu-06-biondi-up.pdf.

[42] Brian Blietz and Akhilesh Tyagi. Software tamper resistance through dynamic program monitoring. In *Digital Rights Management: Technologies, Issues, Challenges and Systems, First International Conference, DRMTICS 2005*, volume 3919 of *Lecture Notes in Computer Science*, pages 146–163. Springer, 2005.

[43] Manuel Blum and Sampath Kannan. Designing programs that check their work. *Journal of the ACM*, 42(1):269–291, January 1995.

[44] S. Blythe, B. Fraboni, S. Lall, H. Ahmed., and U. de Riu. Layout reconstruction of complex silicon chips. *Solid-State Circuits, IEEE Journal of*, 28(2):138–145, Feb. 1993.

[45] Dan Boneh, David Lie, Pat Lincoln, John Mitchell, and Mark Mitchell. Hardware support for tamper-resistant and copy-resistant software. Technical report, Stanford, CA, USA, 2000.

[46] Bob Boothe. Efficient algorithms for bidirectional debugging. In *Proceedings of the ACM SIGPLAN 2000 Conference on Programming Language Design and Implementation*, pages 299–310. New York, 2000. ACM.

[47] Hans Brandl. Trusted computing: The TCG trusted platform module specification. In *Embedded Systems*, Munich, Germany, 2004. `www.wintecindustries.com/orderdesk/TPM/Documents/TPM1.2_-_Basics.pdf`

[48] Ernie Brickell, Jan Camenisch, and Liqun Chen. Direct anonymous attestation. In *CCS '04: Proceedings of the 11th ACM conference on Computer and communications security*, pages 132–145, New York, 2004. ACM.

[49] Andrei Z. Broder. On the resemblance and containment of documents. In *Compression and Complexity of Sequences (SEQUENCES'97)*, pages 21–29, 1997. IEEE.

[50] H. Bunke and K. Shearer. A graph distance metric based on the maximal common subgraph. *Pattern Recognition Letters*, 19:255–259, 1998.

[51] Andrew "Bunnie" Huang. Keeping secrets in hardware: The microsoft Xbox case study. In *Cryptographic Hardware and Embedded Systems—CHES 2002, 4th International Workshop*, pages 213–227, London, 2002. Springer-Verlag.

[52] Michael G. Burke, Paul R. Carini, Jong-Deok Choi, and Michael Hind. Flow-insensitive interprocedural alias analysis in the presence of pointers. In *LCPC '94: Proceedings of the 7th International Workshop on Languages and Compilers for Parallel Computing*, pages 234–250, London, 1995. Springer-Verlag.

[53] Jan Camenisch. Better privacy for trusted computing platforms (extended abstract). In *ESORICS*, pages 73–88, 2004. Springer-Verlag.

[54] Jan Cappaert, Nessim Kisserli, Dries Schellekens, and Bart Preneel. Self-encrypting code to protect against analysis and tampering. In *1st Benelux Workshop on Information and System Security*, 2006. `http://www.cosic.esat.kuleuven.be/wissec2006/`

[55] Larry Carter, Jeanne Ferrante, and Clark Thomborson. Folklore confirmed: reducible flow graphs are exponentially larger. In *POPL '03: Proceedings of the 30th ACM SIGPLAN-SIGACT Symposium on Principles of Programming Languages*, pages 106–114, New York, 2003. ACM.

[56] Pavol Červeň. *Crackproof Your Software: Protect Your Software Against Crackers*. No Starch Press, 2002. ISBN 1886411794.

[57] Mariano Ceccato, Mila Dalla Preda, Jasvir Nagra, Christian Collberg, and Paolo Tonella. Barrier slicing for remote software trusting. In *SCAM '07: Proceedings of the Seventh IEEE International Working Conference on Source Code Analysis and Manipulation*, pages 27–36, Washington, DC, 2007. IEEE.

[58] Jien-Tsai Chan and Wuu Yang. Advanced obfuscation techniques for Java bytecode. *J. Syst. Softw.*, 71(1-2):1–10, 2004.

[59] Hoi Chang and Mikhail J. Atallah. Protecting software code by guards. In *Security and Privacy in Digital Rights Management, ACM CCS-8 Workshop DRM 2001*, Philadelphia, November 2001. Springer-Verlag, LNCS 2320.

[60] David R. Chase, Mark Wegman, and F. Kenneth Zadeck. Analysis of pointers and structures. *ACM SIGPLAN Notices*, 25(6):296–310, June 1990.

[61] Y. Chen, R. Venkatesan, M. Cary, R. Pang, S. Sinha, and M. Jakubowski. Oblivious hashing: A stealthy software integrity verification primitive. In *5th Information Hiding Workshop (IHW)*, pages 400–414, October 2002. Springer LNCS 2578.

[62] Yuqun Chen, Ramarathnam Venkatesan, and Mariusz H. Jakubowski. Secure and opaque type library providing secure data protection of variables. U.S. Patent Application 20040003278, January 2004. Assigned to Microsoft Corporation.

[63] R. J. Chevance and T. Heidet. Static profile and dynamic behavior of COBOL programs. *SIGPLAN Notices*, 13(4):44–57, 1978.

[64] Shyam R. Chidamber and Chris F. Kemerer. A metrics suite for object oriented design. *IEEE Transactions on Software Engineering*, 20(6):476–493, June 1994.

[65] S. Chow, P. Eisen, H. Johnson, and P. van Oorschot. White-box cryptography and an AES implementation. In *9th Annual Workshop on Selected Areas in Cryptography (SAC 2002)*, 2002.

[66] S. Chow, H. Johnson, P. van Oorschot, and P. Eisen. A white-box DES implementation for DRM applications. In *ACM CCS-9 Workshop (DRM 2002)*, 2002.

[67] Stanley T. Chow, Harold J. Johnson, and Yuan Gu. Tamper resistant software encoding. U.S. Patent 6594761, July 2003. Assigned to Cloakware Corporation (Ontario, CA).

[68] Stanley T. Chow, Harold J. Johnson, and Yuan Gu. Tamper resistant software encoding. U.S. Patent 6842862, January 2005. Assigned to Cloakware Corporation (Ottawa, CA).

[69] Frank Nian-Tzu Chu, Wei Wu, Julie D. Bennett, and Mohammed El-Gammal. Thread protection. U.S. Application 20050278782, December 2005. Assigned to Microsoft Corporation.

[70] Frank Nian-Tzu Chu, Wei Wu, Julie D. Bennett, and Mohammed El-Gammal. Software obfuscation. U.S. Application 20060005250, January 2006. Assigned to Microsoft Corporation.

[71] Cristina Cifuentes and Mike Van Emmerik. Recovery of jump table case statements from binary code. In *IWPC '99: Proceedings of the 7th International Workshop on Program Comprehension*, page 192, Washington, DC, 1999. IEEE.

[72] Cristina Cifuentes and K. John Gough. Decompilation of binary programs. *Software— Practice and Experience*, 25(7):811–829, July 1995.

[73] S. Cimato, A. De Santis, and U. Ferraro Petrillo. Overcoming the obfuscation of Java programs by identifier renaming. *J. Syst. Softw.*, 78(1):60–72, 2005.

[74] F. Cohen. Computer viruses—theory and experiments. In *IFIP-TC11, Computers and Security*, pages 22–35, 1987.

[75] F. Cohen. Current trends in computer viruses. In *International Symposium on Information Security*, 1991.

[76] Frederick B. Cohen. Operating system protection through program evolution. *Computer Security*, 12(6):565–584, 1993.

[77] Frederick B. Cohen. *A short course on computer viruses (2nd ed.)*. John Wiley & Sons, Inc., New York, 1994.

[78] C. Collberg, E. Carter, S. Debray, J. Kececioglu, A. Huntwork, C. Linn, and M. Stepp. Dynamic path-based software watermarking. In *ACM SIGPLAN Conference on Programming Language Design and Implementation (PLDI 04)*, 2004.

[79] Christian Collberg, Edward Carter, Stephen Kobourov, and Clark Thomborson. Error-correcting graphs for software watermarking. In *Workshop on Graphs in Computer Science (WG'2003)*, June 2003. Springer-Verlag.

[80] Christian Collberg, Andrew Huntwork, Edward Carter, and Gregg Townsend. Graph theoretic software watermarks: Implementation, analysis, and attacks. In *Workshop on Information Hiding*, pages 192–207, 2004. Springer-Verlag.

[81] Christian Collberg, Ginger Myles, and Andrew Huntwork. Sandmark–A tool for software protection research. *IEEE Security and Privacy*, 1(4):40–49, 2003. IEEE.

[82] Christian Collberg, Ginger Myles, and Michael Stepp. An empirical study of Java bytecode programs. *Software—Practice & Experience*, 37(6): 581–641, 2007.

[83] Christian Collberg, Jasvir Nagra, and Will Snavely. biànliǎn: Remote tamper-resistance with continuous replacement. Technical Report 08-03, University of Arizona, 2008.

[84] Christian Collberg, Jasvir Nagra, and Fei-Yue Wang. Surreptitious software: Models from biology and history. *4th International Conference on Mathematical Methods, Models and Architectuce for Computer Network Security*, pages 1–21, Sept. 13–15, 2007. Springer-Verlag.

[85] Christian Collberg and Tapas Ranjan Sahoo. Software watermarking in the frequency domain: implementation, analysis, and attacks. *J. Comput. Secur.*, 13(5):721–755, 2005.

[86] Christian Collberg and Clark Thomborson. Software watermarking: Models and dynamic embeddings. In *Conference Record of POPL '99: The 26th ACM SIGPLAN-SIGACT Symposium on Principles of Programming Languages*, 1999.

[87] Christian Collberg, Clark Thomborson, and Douglas Low. A taxonomy of obfuscating transformations. Technical Report 148, Department of Computer Science, The University of Auckland, New Zealand, July 1997. `citeseer.ist.psu.edu/collberg97taxonomy.html`.

[88] Christian Collberg, Clark Thomborson, and Douglas Low. Breaking abstractions and unstructuring data structures. In *IEEE International Conference on Computer Languages, ICCL'98.*, Chicago, May 1998.

[89] Christian Collberg, Clark Thomborson, and Douglas Low. Manufacturing cheap, resilient, and stealthy opaque constructs. In *ACM SIGPLAN-SIGACT Symposium on Principles of Programming Languages, POPL'98*, San Diego, January 1998.

[90] Christian Collberg, Clark Thomborson, and Greg Townsend. Dynamic graph-based software fingerprinting. *TOPLAS*, 29(6):1–67, October 2007.

[91] Christian Sven Collberg, Clark David Thomborson, and Douglas Wai Kok Low. Obfuscation techniques for enhancing software security. U.S. Patent 6668325, December 2003. Assigned to InterTrust Technologies (Santa Clara, CA).

[92] S. D. Conte, H. E. Dunsmore, and V. Y. Shen. *Software engineering metrics and models*. Benjamin-Cummings Publishing Co., Inc., Redwood City, CA, 1986.

[93] Robert P. Cook and I. Lee. A contextual analysis of Pascal programs. *Software—Practice and Experience*, 12:195–203, 1982.

[94] T. H. Cormen, C. E. Leiserson, R. L. Rivest, and C. Stein. *Introduction to Algorithms*. MIT Press and McGraw-Hill, 2nd Ed., 2001.

[95] Patrick Cousot and Radhia Cousot. An abstract interpretation-based framework for software watermarking. In *POPL'04*, Venice, Italy, 2004. ACM.

[96] Patrick Cousot, Michel Riguidel, and Arnaud Venet. Device and process for the signature, the marking and the authentication of computer programs. U.S. Patent 20060010430, January 2006.

[97] I. Cox, M. Miller, and J. Bloom. Watermarking applications and their properties. In *Int. Conf. on Information Technology*, pages 6–10, March 2000.

[98] I. J. Cox, M. L. Miller, and J. A. Bloom. *Digital Watermarking: Principles and Practice*. Morgan Kaufmann, 2002. IEEE.

[99] CrackZ. Dongles—"Faked Hardware Protections." `www.woodmann.com/crackz/ Dongles.htm`, 2007.

[100] Scott Craver, Nasir Memon, Boon-Lock Yeo, and Minerva M. Yeung. Resolving rightful ownerships with invisible watermarking techniques: limitations, attacks, and implications. *IEEE Journal on Selected Areas in Communications*, 16(4):573–586, May 1998.

[101] Gregory Cronin. *Defense Mechanisms*, pages 314–319. Salem Press, 2001.

[102] Saumya Debray Cullen Linn and John Kececioglu. Enhancing software tamper-resistance via stealthy address computations. In *19th Computer Security Applications Conference*, 2003. IEEE.

[103] Larry D'Anna, Brian Matt, Andrew Reisse, Tom Van Vleck, Steve Schwab, and Patrick LeBlanc. Self-protecting mobile agents obfuscation report—Final report. Technical Report 03-015, Network Associates Laboratories, June 2003.

[104] Robert L. Davidson and Nathan Myhrvold. Method and system for generating and auditing a signature for a computer program. U.S. Patent 5559884, September 1996. Assignee: Microsoft Corporation.

[105] Eduard K. de Jong. Application program obfuscation. U.S. Application 20050069138, March 2005. Assigned to Sun Microsystems, Inc.

[106] Eduard K. de Jong. Interleaved data and instruction streams for application program obfuscation. U.S. Application 20050071664, March 2005. Assigned to Sun Microsystems, Inc.

[107] Eduard K. de Jong. Multiple instruction dispatch tables for application program obfuscation. U.S. Application 20050071652, March 2005. Assigned to Sun Microsystems, Inc.

[108] Eduard K. de Jong. Non-linear execution of application program instructions for application program obfuscation. U.S. Application 20050071653, March 2005. Assigned to Sun Microsystems, Inc.

[109] Eduard K. de Jong. Permutation of opcode values for application program obfuscation. U.S. Application 20050071655, March 2005. Assigned to Sun Microsystems, Inc.

[110] Eduard K. de Jong. Rendering and encryption engine for application program obfuscation. U.S. Application 20050069131, March 2005. Assigned to Sun Microsystems, Inc.

[111] Saumya Debray, Benjamin Schwarz, Gregory Andrews, and Matthew Legendre. PLTO: A link-time optimizer for the Intel IA-32 architecture. In *Proc. 2001 Workshop on Binary Rewriting (WBT-2001)*, September 2001.

[112] Saumya K. Debray, William Evans, Robert Muth, and Bjorn De Sutter. Compiler techniques for code compaction. *ACM Trans. Program. Lang. Syst.*, 22(2):378–415, 2000.

[113] Jean-Francois Dhem, Francois Koeune, Philippe-Alexandre Leroux, Patrick Mestré, Jean-Jacques Quisquater, and Jean-Louis Willems. A practical implementation of the timing attack. In *CARDIS*, pages 167–182, 1998. Springer-Verlag.

[114] Paul F. Dietz. Maintaining order in a linked list. In *Proceedings of the 14th Annual ACM Symposium on Theory of Computing*, pages 122–127, San Francisco, CA, May 1982. ACM.

[115] DoD. www.sstc-online.org/Exhibitor/exhibitorlist/OrgList.cfm?Letter=D, 2006.

[116] DoD. Bush comment. www.military.com/Content/MoreContent/1,12044, FL-bushcomment_040301.htm,00.html, 2006.

[117] Stephen Drape. Generalising the array split obfuscation. *Information Sciences*, 177:202–219, 2006.

[118] Eldad Eilam. *Reversing: secrets of reverse engineering*. WILEY, 2005.

[119] Rakan El-Khalil and Angelos D. Keromytis. Hydan: Information·hiding in program binaries. In *International Conference on Information and Communications Security*, pages 189–199. 2004. Springer-Verlag.

[120] Bruce S. Elenbogen and Naeem Seliya. Detecting outsourced student programming assignments. *J. Comput. Small Coll.*, 23(3):50–57, 2008.

[121] W. Elliot and R. Valenza. Was the Earl of Oxford the true Shakespeare? *Notes and Queries*, 38(4):501–506, 1991.

[122] Mike Van Emmerik and Trent Waddington. Using a decompiler for real-world source recovery. In *11th Working Conference on Reverse Engineering (WCRE 2004)*, pages 27–36. IEEE, 2004.

[123] Paul England, Butler Lampson, John Manferdelli, Marcus Peinado, and Bryan Willman. A trusted open platform. *Computer*, 36(7):55–62, 2003.

[124] Ernie. Disk copy protection. http://groups.google.com/group/comp.misc/msg/40908776591692bb, March 1997.

[125] M. Anton Ertl. Stack caching for interpreters. *SIGPLAN Not.*, 30(6):315–327, 1995.

[126] Nick Farrell. Mac Display Eater kills home files. *The Inquirer* (February 27, 2007), 2007. www.theinquirer.net/default.aspx?article=37824.

[127] Robert Fitzgerald, Todd B. Knoblock, Erik Ruf, Bjarne Steensgaard, and David Tarditi. Marmot: an optimizing compiler for Java. *Software—Practice and Experience*, 30(3):199–232, 2000.

[128] Counsel for IBM Corporation. Software birthmarks. Talk to BCS Technology of Software Protection Special Interest Group. Reported in [18], 1985.

[129] Aviezri S. Fraenkel. New proof of the generalized Chinese remainder theorem. *Proceedings of the American Mathematical Society*, 14(5):790–791, October 1963. American Mathematical Society.

[130] Georgia Frantzeskou and Stefanos Gritzalis. Source code authorship analysis for supporting the cybercrime investigation process. In *International Conference on E-business and Telecommunication Networks (ICETE)*, pages 85–92. INSTICC Press, 2004.

[131] Michael L. Fredman, János Komlós, and Endre Szemerédi. Storing a sparse table with 0(1) worst case access time. *Journal of the ACM*, 31(3):538–544, 1984.

[132] Kazuhide Fukushima and Kouichi Sakurai. A software fingerprinting scheme for Java using classfiles obfuscation. In *Information Security Applications*, pages 303–316, 2003. Springer-Verlag.

[133] Dhananjay V. Gadre. Roll your own electronic lock. *Electronic Design*, February 2000. `http://electronicdesign.com/Articles/ArticleID/1154/1154.html`

[134] B. Gassend, G. Suh, D. Clarke, M. Dijk, and S. Devadas. Caches and hash trees for efficient memory integrity verification. In *The 9th International Symposium on High Performance Computer Architecture (HPCA9)*, February 2003. IEEE.

[135] Jun Ge, Soma Chaudhuri, and Akhilesh Tyagi. Control flow based obfuscation. In *DRM '05: Proceedings of the 5th ACM Workshop on Digital Rights Management*, pages 83–92, New York, 2005. ACM.

[136] Gemalto. TOP DM GX4, Product information. `www.gemalto.com/products/top_javacard`, 2007.

[137] Rakesh Ghiya and Laurie J. Hendren. Is it a tree, a DAG, or a cyclic graph? A shape analysis for heap-directed pointers in C. In *POPL'96*, pages 1–15, St. Petersburg Beach, Florida, 21–24 January 1996. ACM.

[138] Jonathon Giffin, Mihai Christodorescu, and Louis Kruger. Strengthening software self-checksumming via self-modifying code. In *Proceedings of the 21st Annual Computer Security Applications Conference (ACSAC 2005)*, pages 18–27, Tucson, AZ, December 2005. Applied Computer Associates, IEEE.

[139] Jonathon T. Giffin, Mihai Christodorescu, and Louis Kruger. Strengthening software self-checksumming via self-modifying code. Technical Report 1531, University of Wisconsin, Madison, September 2005.

[140] Mahadevan Gomathisankaran. Architecture support for 3D obfuscation. *IEEE Trans. Comput.*, 55(5):497–507, 2006.

[141] I. P. Goulden and D. M. Jackson. *Combinatorial Enumeration*. New York: Wiley, 1983.

[142] Torbjörn Granlund and Richard Kenner. Eliminating branches using a superoptimizer and the GNU C compiler. In *ACM SIGPLAN '92 Conference on Programming Language Design and Implementation*, 1992. ACM.

[143] Trusted Computing Group. TCG specification architecture overview, revision 1.4, August 2007. `www.trustedcomputinggroup.org/resources/tcg_architecture_overview_version_14`

[144] Tim Güneysu. CD/DVD copy protection. Technical report, Ruhr-Universität Bochum, December 2004.

[145] Lan Guo, Supratik Mukhopadhyay, and Bojan Cukic. Does your result checker really check? *dsn*, 00:399, 2004.

[146] Jens Gustedt, Ole A. Mhle, and Jan Arne Telle. The treewidth of Java programs. In *4th International Workshop on Algorithm Engineering and Experiments (ALENEX)*, 2002. Springer-Verlag.

[147] Gael Hachez. *A Comparative Study of Software Protection Tools Suited for E-Commerce with Contributions to Software Watermarking and Smart Cards*. Ph.D. thesis, Universite Catholique de Louvain, March 2003.

[148] J. Alex Halderman. Evaluating new copy-prevention techniques for audio CDs. In *Proc. 2002 ACM Workshop on Digital Rights Management (DRM 02)*, November 2002. ACM.

[149] J. Alex Halderman. Analysis of the MediaMax CD3 copy-prevention system. Technical Report TR-679-03, Princeton University Computer Science Department, Princeton, NJ, October 2003.

[150] J. Alex Halderman and Edward W. Felten. Lessons from the Sony CD DRM episode. In *Proc. 15th USENIX Security Symposium*, pages 77–92, Vancouver, BC, August 2006. USENIX.

[151] M. H. Halstead. *Elements of Software Science*. Elsevier North-Holland, 1977.

[152] Frank Harary and E. Palmer. *Graphical Enumeration*. New York: Academic Press, 1973.

[153] Ben Hardekopf and Calvin Lin. The ant and the grasshopper: Fast and accurate pointer analysis for millions of lines of code. *SIGPLAN Not.*, 42(6):290–299, 2007.

[154] Laune C. Harris and Barton P. Miller. Practical analysis of stripped binary code. *SIGARCH Comput. Archit. News*, 33(5):63–68, 2005.

[155] Warren A. Harrison and Kenneth I. Magel. A complexity measure based on nesting level. *SIGPLAN Notices*, 16(3):63–74, 1981.

[156] Kazuhiro Hattanda and Shuichi Ichikawa. The evaluation of Davidson's digital signature scheme. *IEICE Transactions*, 87-A(1):224–225, 2004.

[157] Kelly Heffner and Christian S. Collberg. The obfuscation executive. In *Information Security, 7th International Conference*, pages 428–440. Springer-Verlag, 2004. Lecture Notes in Computer Science, #3225.

[158] L. J. Hendren and A. Nicolau. Parallelizing programs with recursive data structures. *IEEE Trans. Parallel Distrib. Syst.*, 1(1):35–47, 1990.

[159] James Hendricks and Leendert van Doorn. Secure bootstrap is not enough: shoring up the trusted computing base. In *EW11: Proceedings of the 11th workshop on ACM SIGOPS European Workshop*, page 11, New York, 2004. ACM.

[160] Sallie Henry and Dennis Kafura. Software structure metrics based on information flow. *IEEE Transactions on Software Engineering*, 7(5):510–518, September 1981.

[161] Amir Herzberg, Haya Shulman, Amitabh Saxena, and Bruno Crispo. Towards a theory of white-box security. In *SEC-2009 International Information Security Conference*, 2009.

[162] Bert Hill. Dutch firm offers $72.5m U.S. for Cloakware. *Ottawa Citizen*, December 2007. `www.canada.com/ottawacitizen/news/business/story.html?id=5a3af 664-2eb7-47b3-bd1d-d3044dbcd3a9`.

[163] Michael Hind. Pointer analysis: haven't we solved this problem yet? In *PASTE '01: Proceedings of the 2001 ACM SIGPLAN-SIGSOFT workshop on Program analysis for software tools and engineering*, pages 54–61, New York, 2001. ACM.

[164] Michael Hind and Anthony Pioli. Which pointer analysis should i use? In *ISSTA '00: Proceedings of the 2000 ACM SIGSOFT International Symposium on Software Testing and Analysis*, pages 113–123, New York, 2000. ACM.

[165] Fritz Hohl. Time limited blackbox security: Protecting mobile agents from malicious hosts. In *Mobile Agents and Security*, pages 92–113. Springer-Verlag, 1998. Lecture Notes in Computer Science, Vol. 1419.

[166] Thorsten Holz and Frederic Raynal. Detecting honeypots and other suspicious environments. In *Proceedings of the 2005 IEEE Workshop on Information Assurance and Security*, U.S. Military Academy, West Point, NY, June 2005.

[167] Bill Horne, Lesley Matheson, Casey Sheehan, and Robert E. Tarjan. Dynamic self-checking techniques for improved tamper resistance. In *Security and Privacy in Digital Rights Management, ACM CCS-8 Workshop DRM 2001*, Philadelphia, November 2001. Springer-Verlag, LNCS 2320.

[168] William G. Horne, Lesley R. Matheson, Casey Sheehan, and Robert E. Tarjan. Software self-checking systems and methods. U.S. Application 20030023856, January 2003. Assigned to InterTrust Technologies Corporation.

[169] James J. Horning, W. Olin Sibert, Robert E. Tarjan, Umesh Maheshwari, William G. Home, Andrew K. Wright, Lesley R. Matheson, and Susan Owicki. Software self-defense systems and methods. U.S. Application 20050210275, September 2005. Assigned to InterTrust Technologies Corporation.

[170] Susan Horwitz. Precise flow-insensitive May-Alias analysis is NP-hard. *TOPLAS*, 19(1):1–6, January 1997.

[171] Susan Horwitz, Thomas Reps, and David Binkley. Interprocedural slicing using dependence graphs. *TOPLAS*, 12(1):26–60, January 1990.

[172] Andrew "Bunnie" Huang. *Hacking the Xbox: An Introduction to Reverse Engineering*. No Starch Press, San Francisco, CA, 2003.

[173] Ibm pci-x cryptographic coprocessor. `www.ibm.com/security/cryptocards/pcixcc/overview.shtml`, January 2009.

[174] National Institute of Standards Information Technology Laboratory and Technology. Security requirements for cryptographic modules. `http://csrc.nist.gov/publications/fips/fips140-2/fips1402.pdf`, May 2001.

[175] International Organization for Standardization and European Computer Manufacturers Association. Information processing: volume and file structure of CD-ROM for information interchange. International standard; ISO 9660: 1988 (E), ISO, April 1988.

[176] Intertrust. Microsoft settlement. `www.intertrust.com/main/ip/settlement.html`, April 2004.

[177] IOCCC. The international obfuscated c code contest. `www.ioccc.org`, 2007.

[178] Matthias Jacob, Mariusz H. Jakubowski, and Ramarathnam Venkatesan. Towards integral binary execution: implementing oblivious hashing using overlapped instruction

encodings. In *Proceedings of the 9th workshop on Multimedia & Security*, pages 129–140, New York, 2007. ACM.

[179] Mariusz H. Jakubowski and Ramarathnam Venkatesan. Protecting digital goods using oblivious checking. U.S. Patent 7,080,257, July 2006.

[180] Mariusz H. Jakubowski, Ramarathnam Venkatesan, and Saurabh Sinha. System and method for protecting digital goods using random and automatic code obfuscation. U.S. Patent 7054443, May 2006.

[181] Christopher Johnson. Illinois man who distributed illegally copied movies pleads guilty to federal copyright infringement charges. U.S. Department of Justice, Assistant U.S. Attorney, Central District of California, Release No. 04-049, April 2004. www.usdoj.gov/criminal/cybercrime/spraguePlea.htm.

[182] Harold Joseph Johnson, Yuan Xiang Gu, Becky Laiping Chan, and Stanley Taihai Chow. Encoding technique for software and hardware. U.S. Patent 5748741, May 1998. Assigned to Northern Telecom Limited (Montreal).

[183] James A. Jones, Alessandro Orso, and Mary Jean Harrold. Gammatella: visualizing program-execution data for deployed software. *Information Visualization*, 3(3):173–188, 2004.

[184] Rajeev Joshi, Greg Nelson, and Keith Randall. Denali: a goal-directed superoptimizer. *SIGPLAN Not.*, 37(5):304–314, 2002.

[185] I. J. Jozwiak, A. Liber, and K. Marczak. A hardware-based software protection systems–analysis of security dongles with memory. In *ICCGI '07: Proceedings of the International Multi-Conference on Computing in the Global Information Technology*, page 28, Washington, DC, 2007. IEEE.

[186] David Kahn. *The Codebreakers*. Scribner, 1996.

[187] Sampath Kannan and Todd Proebsting. Register allocation in structured programs. In *SODA: ACM-SIAM Symposium on Discrete Algorithms (A Conference on Theoretical and Experimental Analysis of Discrete Algorithms)*, 1995.

[188] Sampath Kannan and Todd Proebsting. Register allocation in structured programs. *J. Algorithms*, 29(2):223–237, 1998.

[189] Yuichiro Kanzaki. *Protecting Secret Information in Software Processes and Products*. Ph.D. thesis, Nara Institute of Science and Technology, 2006.

[190] Yuichiro Kanzaki, Akito Monden, Masahide Nakamura, and Ken-ichi Matsumoto. Exploiting self-modification mechanism for program protection. In *COMPSAC '03: Proceedings of the 27th Annual International Conference on Computer Software and Applications*, page 170, Washington, DC, 2003. IEEE Computer Society.

[191] Yuichiro Kanzaki, Akito Monden, Masahide Nakamura, and Ken-ichi Matsumoto. A software protection method based on instruction camouflage. *Electronics and Communications in Japan (Part III: Fundamental Electronic Science)*, 89(1):47–59, 2006.

[192] Richard M. Karp and Michael O. Rabin. Efficient randomized pattern-matching algorithms. *IBM J. Res. Dev.*, 31(2):249–260, 1987.

[193] Gaurav Kc, Angelos Keromytis, and Vassilis Prevelakis. Countering code-injection attacks with instruction set randomization. In *10th ACM Conference on Computer and Communications Security*, pages 272–280, 2003. ACM.

[194] Thomas A Keaney and Eliot A Cohen. *Gulf War Air Power Survey Summary Report.* 1993. ISBN: 0160419506.

[195] Jack Kelley. Terror groups hide behind web encryption. *USA Today*, February 5, 2001.

[196] B. W. Kernighan and D. M. Ritchie. *The C Programming Language.* Prentice-Hall, Englewood Cliffs, NJ, 1978.

[197] Raymond R. Kiddy. Method of obfuscating computer instruction streams. U.S. Patent 6694435, February 2004. Assigned to Apple Computer, Inc. (Cupertino, CA).

[198] David Kilburn. Dirty linen, dark secrets. *Adweek*, 38(40):35–40, October 1997.

[199] Alexander Klimov and Adi Shamir. A new class of invertible mappings. In *CHES '02: Revised Papers from the 4th International Workshop on Cryptographic Hardware and Embedded Systems*, pages 470–483, London, 2003. Springer-Verlag.

[200] Paul Klint. Interpretation techniques. *Software, Practice & Experience*, 11(9):963–973, 1981.

[201] Donald E. Knuth. An empirical study of FORTRAN programs. *Software—Practice & Experience*, 1:105–133, 1971.

[202] Donald E. Knuth. *Fundamental Algorithms*, volume 1 of *The Art of Computer Programming*, Third Ed., Addison-Wesley, Reading, MA, 1997.

[203] P. Kocher, J. Jaffe, B. Jun, C. Laren, and N. Lawson. Self-protecting digital content. Technical report, Cryptography Research, 2002.

[204] Paul Kocher, Joshua Jaffe, and Benjamin Jun. Differential power analysis. *Lecture Notes in Computer Science*, 1666:388–397, 1999.

[205] Paul C. Kocher. Timing attacks on implementations of Diffie-Hellman, RSA, DSS, and other systems. *Lecture Notes in Computer Science*, 1109:104–113, 1996.

[206] Gina Kolata. Veiled messages of terror may lurk in cyberspace. *New York Times*, October 30, 2001.

[207] Oliver Kömmerling and Markus G. Kuhn. Design principles for tamper-resistant smartcard processors. In *Proceedings of the USENIX Workshop on Smartcard Technology, Chicago, 10–11 May, 1999.*, pages 9–20, 1999. USENIX.

[208] Raghavan Komondoor and Susan Horwitz. Using slicing to identify duplication in source code. In *Proceedings of the 8th International Symposium on Static Analysis*, pages 40–56. Springer-Verlag, 2001.

[209] K. Kontogiannis. Evaluation experiments on the detection of programming patterns using software metrics. *Working Conference on reverse Engineering*, 0:44, 1997. IEEE.

[210] F. Koushanfar, G. Qu, and M. Potkonjak. Intellectual property metering. In *4th Information Hiding Workshop*, pages 87–102, 2001. Springer-Verlag.

[211] Ivan Krsul and Eugene Spafford. Authorship analysis: Identifying the author of a program. Technical report CSD-TR-94-030, Computer Science Deparment, Purdue University, 1994.

[212] Christopher Kruegel, William Robertson, Fredrik Valeur, and Giovanni Vigna. Static disassembly of obfuscated binaries. In *SSYM'04: Proceedings of the 13th Conference on USENIX Security Symposium*, pages 18–18, Berkeley, CA, 2004. USENIX.

[213] Markus Kuhn. The TrustNo 1 cryptoprocessor concept. Technical Report CS555, Purdue University, April 1997.

[214] Markus G. Kuhn. Sicherheitsanalyse eines mikroprozessors mit busverschlüsselung (security analysis of a microprocessor with bus encryption). Master's thesis, Erlangen, Germany, July 1996. (in German)

[215] Markus G. Kuhn. Cipher instruction search attack on the bus-encryption security microcontroller ds5002fp. *IEEE Transactions on Computers*, 47(10):1153–1157, 1998.

[216] Sukhamay Kundu and Jaydev Misra. A linear tree partitioning algorithm. *SIAM Journal of Computing*, 6(1):151–154, March 1997.

[217] Martin Kutter and Frank Hartung. Introduction to watermarking techniques. In S. Katzenbeisser and F. Petitcolas, editors, *Information Hiding: Techniques for Steganography and Digital Watermarking*, pages 97–120. Artech House, 2000.

[218] Mark D. LaDue. HoseMocha, January 1997. `www.cigital.com/hostile-applets/HoseMocha.java`.

[219] M.K. Lai. Knapsack cryptosystems: the past and the future. `www.ics.uci.edu/~mingl/knapsack.html`, 2003.

[220] Robert Charles Lange and Spiros Mancoridis. Using code metric histograms and genetic algorithms to perform author identification for software forensics. In *GECCO '07: Proceedings of the 9th Annual Conference on Genetic and Evolutionary Computation*, pages 2082–2089, New York, 2007. ACM.

[221] James R. Larus. Whole program paths. In *Proceedings of the SIGPLAN '99 Conference on Programming Languages Design and Implementation*, 1999. ACM.

[222] Tímea László and Ákos Kiss. Obfuscating C++ programs via control flow flattening. In *10th Symposium on Programming Languages and Software Tools (SPLST 2007)*, pages 15–29, Dobogókõ, Hungary, June 2007.

[223] Tímea László and Ákos Kiss. Obfuscating C++ programs via control flow flattening. *Annales Universitatis Scientiarum de Rolando Eötvös Nominatae—Sectio Computatorica*, 2008.

[224] Kevin Lawton. Bochs 2.3.7. `http://bochs.sourceforge.net`, 2008. ACM.

[225] Thomas W. Lee. *Microelectronic Failure Analysis—Desk Reference*. ASM International, Materials Park, OH, 3rd ed., 1993.

[226] Thomas W. Lee and Seshu V. Pabbisetty, editors. *Microelectronic Failure Analysis— Desk Reference*. ASM International, Materials Park, OH, 3rd ed., 1993.

[227] Don Libes. *Obfuscated C and Other Mysteries*. Wiley, 1993.

[228] D. Lie, C. Thekkath, and M. Horowitz. Implementing an untrusted operating system on trusted hardware. In *Proceedings of the Nineteenth ACM Symposium on Operating Systems Principles*, pages 178–192, 2003. ACM.

[229] David Lie, John Mitchell, Chandramohan A. Thekkath, and Mark Horowitz. Specifying and verifying hardware for tamper-resistant software. In *SP '03: Proceedings of the 2003 IEEE Symposium on Security and Privacy*, page 166, Washington, DC, 2003. IEEE Computer Society.

[230] David Lie, Chandramohan Thekkath, Mark Mitchell, Patrick Lincoln, Dan Boneh, John Mitchell, and Mark Horowitz. Architectural support for copy and tamper resistant software. In *ASPLOS-IX: Proceedings of the Ninth International Conference*

on Architectural Support for Programming Languages and Operating Systems, pages 168–177, New York, 2000. ACM.

[231] Cullen Linn and Saumya Debray. Obfuscation of executable code to improve resistance to static disassembly. In *Proceedings of the 10th ACM Conference on Computer and Communications Security*, pages 290–299, 2003. ACM.

[232] Chao Liu, Chen Chen, Jiawei Han, and Philip S. Yu. Gplag: detection of software plagiarism by program dependence graph analysis. In *KDD '06: Proceedings of the 12th ACM SIGKDD International Conference on Knowledge Discovery and Data Mining*, pages 872–881, New York, 2006. ACM.

[233] B. Lynn, M. Prabhakaran, and A. Sahai. Positive results and techniques for obfuscation. In *Eurocrypt*, 2004. Springer–Verlag.

[234] Matias Madou, Bertrand Anckaert, Bjorn De Sutter, and De Bosschere Koen. Hybrid static-dynamic attacks against software protection mechanisms. In *Proceedings of the 5th ACM Workshop on Digital Rights Management*. ACM, 2005.

[235] Matias Madou, Bertrand Anckaert, Patrick Moseley, Saumya Debray, Bjorn De Sutter, and Koen De Bosschere. Software protection through dynamic code mutation. In *The 6th International Workshop on Information Security Applications (WISA 2005)*. Springer-Verlag, August 2005.

[236] Matias Madou, Ludo Van Put, and Koen De Bosschere. Loco: an interactive code (de)obfuscation tool. In *PEPM '06: Proceedings of the 2006 ACM SIGPLAN Symposium on Partial Evaluation and Semantics-based Program Manipulation*, pages 140–144, New York, 2006. ACM.

[237] Matias Madou, Ludo Van Put, and Koen De Bosschere. Understanding obfuscated code. In *ICPC '06: Proceedings of the 14th IEEE International Conference on Program Comprehension*, pages 268–274, Washington, DC, 2006. IEEE.

[238] Christopher J. Madsen. VBinDiff 3.0 beta 4—visual binary diff. `www.cjmweb.net/vbindiff`, 2008.

[239] David Paul Maher. Fault induction attacks, tamper resistance, and hostile reverse engineering in perspective. In *FC '97: Proceedings of the First International Conference on Financial Cryptography*, pages 109–122, London, 1997. Springer-Verlag.

[240] Anirban Majumdar., Antoine Monsifrot, and Clark D. Thomborson. On evaluating obfuscatory strength of alias-based transforms using static analysis. In *International Conference on Advanced Computing and Communications (ADCOM 2006)*, pages 605–610, December 2006. IEEE.

[241] Anirban Majumdar, Stephen Drape, and Clark Thomborson. Metrics-based evaluation of slicing obfuscations. In *IAS '07: Proceedings of the Third International Symposium on Information Assurance and Security*, pages 472–477, Washington, DC, 2007. IEEE.

[242] Anirban Majumdar, Stephen J. Drape, and Clark D. Thomborson. Slicing obfuscations: design, correctness, and evaluation. In *DRM '07: Proceedings of the 2007 ACM Workshop on Digital Rights Management*, pages 70–81, New York, 2007. ACM.

[243] J. Marchesini, S.W. Smith, O. Wild, and Rich MacDonald. Experimenting with TCPA/TCG hardware, or: How I learned to stop worrying and love the bear. Technical report TR2003-476, Computer Science, Dartmouth College, December 2003.

[244] Harry Massalin. Superoptimizer—a look at the smallest program. In *Proceedings Second International Conference on Architechtural Support for Programming Languages and Operating Systems (ASPLOS II)*, Palo Alto, CA, October 1987. ACM.

[245] T. J. McCabe. A complexity measure. *IEEE Transactions on Software Engineering*, 2(4):308–320, December 1976.

[246] Jonathan M. McCune, Adrian Perrig, Arvind Seshadri, and Leendert van Doorn. Turtles all the way down: Research challenges in user-based attestation. In *Proceedings of the Workshop on Hot Topics in Security (HotSec)*, August 2007. USENIX.

[247] George H. Mealy. A method for synthesizing sequential circuits. *Bell System Technical Journal*, 34(5):1045–1079, 1955.

[248] Hayden Melton and Ewan Tempero. An empirical study of cycles among classes in Java. *Empirical Softw. Eng.*, 12(4):389–415, 2007.

[249] R. C. Merkle. Protocols for public key cryptosystem. In *Proceedings IEEE Symp. Security and Privacy*, pages 122–134, 1980. IEEE.

[250] Microsoft. Preemptive solutions' dotfuscator will ship with microsoft visual studio 2005. `www.microsoft.com/presspass/press/2004/jul04/07-19preemptivesolutionpr.mspx`, July 2004.

[251] A. Monden, I. Hajimu, K. Matsumoto, I. Katsuro, and K. Torii. Watermarking Java programs, In *Proc. 4th International Symposium on Future Software Technology (ISFST'99)*, pages 119–124, 1999. Nanjing, China: Software Engineers Association.

[252] A. Monden, H. Iida, K. Matsumoto, Katsuro Inoue, and Koji Torii. A practical method for watermarking Java programs. In *24th Computer Software and Applications Conference*, 2000. IEEE.

[253] Akito Monden, Hajimu Iida, Ken ichi Matsumoto, Koji Torii, and Yuuji Ichisugi. Watermarking method for computer programs. In *Proceedings of the 1998 Symposium on Cyptography and Information Security (SCIS'98—9.2A)*, January 1998. (In Japanese)

[254] Akito Monden, Antoine Monsifrot, and Clark Thomborson. A framework for obfuscated interpretation. In *ACSW Frontiers '04: Proceedings of the Second Workshop on Australasian Information Security, Data Mining and Web Intelligence, and Software Internationalisation*, pages 7–16, Darlinghurst, Australia, 2004. Australian Computer Society, Inc.

[255] Scott A. Moskowitz and Marc Cooperman. Method for stega-cipher protection of computer code. U.S. Patent 5745569, January 1996. Assignee: The Dice Company.

[256] F. Mosteller and D. L. Wallace. *Inference and Disputed Authorship: The Federalist.* Addison Wesley, Reading. MA, 1964.

[257] Steven S. Muchnick. *Advanced Compiler Design and Implementation.* Morgan Kaufmann Publishers Inc., San Francisco, CA, 1997.

[258] John C. Munson and Taghi M. Kohshgoftaar. Measurement of data structure complexity. *Journal of Systems Software*, 20:217–225, 1993.

[259] G. Myles and H. Jin. Self-validating branch-based software watermarking. In *7th International Information Hiding Workshop*, 2005. Springer-Verlag.

[260] Ginger Myles. *Software Theft Detection Through Program Identification*. Ph.D. thesis, University of Arizona, 2006.

[261] Ginger Myles and Christian Collberg. Software watermarking through register allocation: Implementation, analysis, and attacks. In *ICISC'2003 (International Conference on Information Security and Cryptology)*, 2003. Springer-Verlag.

[262] Ginger Myles and Christian Collberg. Detecting software theft via whole program path birthmarks. In *Information Security, 7th International Conference*, 2004. IEEE.

[263] Ginger Myles, Christian Collberg, Zachary Heidepriem, and Armand Navabi. The evaluation of two software watermarking algorithms. *Software: Practice and Experience*, 35(10):923–938, 2005.

[264] J. Nagra and C. Thomborson. Threading software watermarks. In *6th International Information Hiding Workshop*, 2004. Springer-Verlag.

[265] Jasvir Nagra. *Threading Software Watermarks*. Ph.D. thesis, University of Auckland, March 2006.

[266] Jasvir Nagra, Clark Thomborson, and Christian Collberg. A functional taxonomy for software watermarking. In M. J. Oudshoorn, editor, *Proc. 25th Australasian Computer Science Conference*, pages 177–186. ACS, January 2002.

[267] Arvind Narayanan and Vitaly Shmatikov. Obfuscated databases and group privacy. In *CCS '05: Proceedings of the 12th ACM Conference on Computer and Communications Security*, pages 102–111, New York, 2005. ACM.

[268] Joseph M. Nardone, Richard P. Mangold, Jody L. Pfotenhauer, Keith L. Shippy, David W. Aucsmith, Richard L. Maliszewski, and Gary L. Graunke. Tamper resistant methods and apparatus. U.S. Patent 6205550, March 2001. Assigned to Intel Corporation (Santa Clara, CA).

[269] Joseph M. Nardone, Richard P. Mangold, Jody L. Pfotenhauer, Keith L. Shippy, David W. Aucsmith, Richard L. Maliszewski, and Gary L. Graunke. Tamper resistant player for scrambled contents. U.S. Patent 6175925, January 2001. Assigned to Intel Corporation (Santa Clara, CA).

[270] Joseph M. Nardone, Richard T. Mangold, Jody L. Pfotenhauer, Keith L. Shippy, David W. Aucsmith, Richard L. Maliszewski, and Gary L. Graunke. Tamper resistant methods and apparatus. U.S. Patent 6178509, January 2001. Assigned to Intel Corporation (Santa Clara, CA).

[271] Gleb Naumovich, Ezgi Yalcin, Nasir D. Memon, Hong Heather Yu, and Mikhail Sosonkin. Class coalescence for obfuscation of object-oriented software. U.S. Application 20040103404, May 2004.

[272] George C. Necula, Scott Mcpeak, S. P. Rahul, and Westley Weimer. CIL: Intermediate language and tools for analysis and transformation of C programs. In *Compiler Construction*, pages 213–228, Grenoble, 2002. Springer-Verlag.

[273] Roger M. Needham and David J. Wheeler. Correction to xtea. Technical report, Computer Laboratory, Cambridge University, England, October 1998.

[274] C. G. Nevill-Manning and I. H. Witten. Compression and explanation using hierarchical grammars. *The Computer Journal*, 40:103–116, 1997.

[275] Diarmuid O'Donoghue, Aine Leddy, James Power, and John Waldron. Bigram analysis of Java bytecode sequences. In *Proceedings of the Second Workshop on Intermediate*

Representation Engineering for the Java Virtual Machine, pages 187–192, 2002. National University of Ireland.

[276] O. Ore. The general Chinese remainder theorem. *American Mathematical Monthly*, 59:365–370, 1952.

[277] John K. Ousterhout. Why threads are a bad idea (for most purposes). Invited Talk at Usenix Technical Conference, 1996. Slides available at www.sunlabs.com/~ouster/.

[278] E. I. Oviedo. Control flow, data flow, and program complexity. In *Proceedings of IEEE COMPSAC*, pages 146–152, November 1980. IEEE.

[279] Pascal Paillier. Public-key cryptosystems based on composite degree residuosity classes. In *Proceedings of EUROCRYPT'99*, volume LNCS 1592, pages 223–238. Springer-Verlag, 1999.

[280] Jens Palsberg, S. Krishnaswamy, Minseok Kwon, D. Ma, Qiuyun Shao, and Y. Zhang. Experience with software watermarking. In *Proceedings of ACSAC'00, 16th Annual Computer Security Applications Conference*, pages 308–316, 2000. IEEE.

[281] Jason R. C. Patterson. Accurate static branch prediction by value range propagation. In *SIGPLAN Conference on Programming Language Design and Implementation*, pages 67–78, 1995. ACM.

[282] Fabien A. P. Petitcolas. Stirmark 3.1. www.cl.cam.ac.uk/~fapp2/watermarking/ stirmark, February 2004.

[283] Fabien A. P. Petitcolas, Ross J. Anderson, and Markus G. Kuhn. Attacks on copyright marking systems. In *LNCS 1525, Information Hiding, Second International Workshop, IH'98*, pages 219–239, Portland, OR, 1998. Springer-Verlag. ISBN 3540653864.

[284] Karl Pettis and Robert C. Hansen. Profile guided code positioning. In *SIGPLAN Conference on Programming Language Design and Implementation*, pages 16–27, 1990. ACM.

[285] John Phipps. *The Protection of Computer Software—Its Technology and Applications*, Physical protection devices, pages 57–78. Cambridge University Press, New York, 1989.

[286] Ugo Piazzalunga, Paolo Salvaneschi, Francesco Balducci, Pablo Jacomuzzi, and Cristiano Moroncelli. Security strength measurement for dongle-protected software. *IEEE Security and Privacy*, 5(6):32–40, 2007.

[287] M. Dalla Preda and R. Giacobazzi. Semantic-based code obfuscation by abstract interpretation. In *Proceedings of the 32nd International Colloquium on Automata, Languages and Programming (ICALP'05)*, volume 350 of *Lecture Notes in Computer Science*, pages 1325–1336, July 2005. Springer-Verlag.

[288] Mila Dalla Preda. *Code Obfuscation and Malware Detection by Abstract Interpretation*. Ph.D. thesis, Dipartimento di Informatica, Universita' di Verona, 2007.

[289] Mila Dalla Preda and Roberto Giacobazzi. Control code obfuscation by abstract interpretation. In *SEFM '05: Proceedings of the Third IEEE International Conference on Software Engineering and Formal Methods*, pages 301–310, Washington, DC, 2005. IEEE.

[290] Mila Dalla Preda, Matias Madou, Koen De Bosschere, and Roberto Giacobazzi. Opaque predicates detection by abstract interpretation. In *Algebraic Methodology*

and Software Technology, 11th International Conference, AMAST 2006, volume 4019 of *Lecture Notes in Computer Science*, pages 81–95, 2006. Springer-Verlag.

[291] Private communication.

[292] Todd Proebsting. Optimizing ANSI C with superoperators. In *POPL'96*. ACM, January 1996.

[293] Todd A. Proebsting and Scott A. Watterson. Krakatoa: Decompilation in Java (Does bytecode reveal source?). In *Third USENIX Conference on Object-Oriented Technologies*, June 1997. USENIX.

[294] Niels Provos and Peter Honeyman. Detecting steganographic content on the Internet. In *ISOC NDSS'02*, San Diego, CA, February 2002. The Internet Society.

[295] William Pugh. The Omega test: a fast and practical integer programming algorithm for dependence analysis. In *Supercomputing*, pages 4–13, 1991. IEEE/ACM.

[296] Ludo Van Put, Dominique Chanet, Bruno De Bus, Bjorn De Sutter, and Koen De Bosschere. Diablo: a reliable, retargetable and extensible link-time rewriting framework. In *Proceedings of the 2005 IEEE International Symposium On Signal Processing And Information Technology*, pages 7–12, Athens, 12 2005. IEEE.

[297] Gang Qu and Miodrag Potkonjak. Analysis of watermarking techniques for graph coloring problem. In *Proceedings of the 1998 IEEE/ACM International Conference on Computer-Aided Design*, pages 190–193. ACM, 1998.

[298] Gang Qu and Miodrag Potkonjak. Hiding signatures in graph coloring solutions. In *Information Hiding*, pages 348–367, 1999. Springer-Verlag.

[299] Gang Qu and Miodrag Potkonjak. Fingerprinting intellectual property using constraint-addition. In *Design Automation Conference*, pages 587–592, 2000. IEEE.

[300] M. Rabin. How to exchange secret by oblivious transfer. Technical report, Harvard Center for Research in Computer Technology, Cambridge, MA, 1981.

[301] R. Raghunathan and D. Davis. *Microelectronic Failure Analysis—Desk Reference*, chapter Chip Access Techniques. ASM International, Materials Park, OH, 4th ed., 1999.

[302] G. Ramalingam. The undecidability of aliasing. *ACM TOPLAS*, 16(5):1467–1471, September 1994.

[303] U.S. Army Research, Development, and Engineering Command (RDECOM). Army fy06.s SBIR solicitation topics—a06-022 software-based anti-tamper technique research and development. `www.acq.osd.mil/osbp/sbir/solicitations/sbir062/army062.htm`, 2006.

[304] Karl Reichert and Gunnar Troitsch. Kopierschutz mit filzstift knacken. *CHIP Online*, May 2002. `http://archiv.chip.de/artikel/Tipp-des-Monats-Audio-Kopierschutz_archiv_17083661.html`.

[305] John R. Rice. Method and system for fortifying software. U.S. Application 20060101047, May 2006.

[306] Richard J. Ross, Christian Boit, and Donald Staab, editors. *Microelectronic Failure Analysis—Desk Reference*. ASM International, Materials Park, OH, 4th ed., 1999.

[307] Hex-Rays SA. The IDA Pro disassembler and debugger. www.hex-rays.com/idapro, 2008.

[308] H. J. Saal and Z. Weiss. An empirical study of APL programs. *International Journal of Computer Languages*, 2(3):47–59, 1977.

[309] Harry J. Saal and Zvi Weiss. Some properties of APL programs. In *Proceedings of Seventh International Conference on APL*, pages 292–297. ACM, 1975.

[310] David Safford. Clarifying misinformation on TCPA. Technical report, IBM Research, October 2002.

[311] Mooly Sagiv, Thomas Reps, and Reinhard Wilhelm. Solving shape-analysis problems in languages with destructive updating. Technical report TR 1276, Computer Sciences Department, University of Wisconsin, Madison, WI, July 1995.

[312] Reiner Sailer, Trent Jaeger, Xiaolan Zhang, and Leendert van Doorn. Attestation-based policy enforcement for remote access. In *CCS '04: Proceedings of the 11th ACM Conference on Computer and Communications Security*, pages 308–317, New York, 2004. ACM.

[313] Reiner Sailer, Xiaolan Zhang, Trent Jaeger, and Leendert van Doorn. Design and implementation of a TCG-based integrity measurement architecture. In *SSYM'04: Proceedings of the 13th Conference on USENIX Security Symposium*, pages 16–16, Berkeley, CA, 2004. USENIX.

[314] A Salvadori, J. Gordon, and C. Capstick. Static profile of COBOL programs. *SIGPLAN Notices*, 10(8):20–33, 1975.

[315] Robert Sather. *The Protection of Computer Software—Its Technology and Applications*, Disc-based protection methods, pages 23–57. Cambridge University Press, New York, 1989.

[316] Saul Schleimer, Daniel Wilkerson, and Alex Aiken. Winnowing: Local algorithms for document fingerprinting. In *Proceedings of the 2003 SIGMOD Conference*, 2003. ACM.

[317] D. Schuler and V. Dallmeier. Detecting software theft with API call sequence sets. In *Proceedings of the 8th Workshop Software Reengineering*, 2006.

[318] David Schuler, Valentin Dallmeier, and Christian Lindig. A dynamic birthmark for Java. *22nd IEEE/ACM International Conference on Automated Software Engineering (ASE 2007)*, 2007. ACM.

[319] B. Schwarz, S. Debray, and G. Andrews. Disassembly of executable code revisited. In *WCRE '02: Proceedings of the Ninth Working Conference on Reverse Engineering (WCRE'02)*, page 45, Washington, DC, 2002. IEEE.

[320] F-secure Inc. Global slapper worm information center. www.f-secure.com/slapper/, 2002.

[321] Dallas Semiconductor. Ds5002fp secure microprocessor chip. http://datasheets.maxim-ic.com/en/ds/DS5002FP.pdf, 2006.

[322] Arvind Seshadri, Mark Luk, Adrian Perrig, Leendert van Doorn, and Pradeep Khosla. Externally verifiable code execution. *Commun. ACM*, 49(9):45–49, 2006.

[323] Arvind Seshadri, Mark Luk, Elaine Shi, Adrian Perrig, Leendert van Doorn, and Pradeep Khosla. Pioneer: verifying code integrity and enforcing untampered code execution on legacy systems. *SIGOPS Oper. Syst. Rev.*, 39(5):1–16, 2005.

[324] Arvind Seshadri, Adrian Perrig, Leendert van Doorn, and Pradeep Khosla. Swatt: Software-based attestation for embedded devices. In *2004 IEEE Symposium on Security and Privacy*, page 272, Los Alamitos, CA, 2004. IEEE.

[325] Adi Shamir and Nicko van Someren. Playing Hide and Seek with stored keys. In *FC '99: Proceedings of the Third International Conference on Financial Cryptography*, pages 118–124, London, 1999. Springer-Verlag.

[326] Claude E. Shannon. Communication theory of secrecy systems. *Bell System Technical Journal*, pages 656–715, 1949.

[327] Zhiyu Shen, Zhiyuan Li, and Pen-Chung Yew. An empirical study of FORTRAN programs for parallelizing compilers. *IEEE Transactions on Parallel and Distributed Systems*, 1(3):356–364, 1990.

[328] Sergei P. Skorobogatov. *Semi-Invasive Attacks—A New Approach to Hardware Security Analysis*. Ph.D. thesis, University of Cambridge, 2005.

[329] Michael P. Smith and Malcolm Munro. Runtime visualisation of object oriented software. In *First IEEE International Workshop on Visualizing Software for Understanding and Analysis*, Paris, France, 2002. IEEE.

[330] Backer Street Software. Rec 2.1—Reverse engineering compiler. `www.backerstreet.com/rec/rec.htm`, 2007.

[331] Mikhail Sosonkin, Gleb Naumovich, and Nasir Memon. Obfuscation of design intent in object-oriented applications. In *DRM '03: Proceedings of the 3rd ACM workshop on Digital Rights Management*, pages 142–153, New York, 2003. ACM.

[332] Eugene H. Spafford. The Internet worm incident page 203, 1990. ESEC '89, 2nd European Software Engineering Conference. Springer-Verlag.

[333] Steven Stark. Why lawyers can't write. *Harvard Law Review*, 97(1389), 1984.

[334] United States federal law. Federal information security management act of 2002. `http://csrc.nist.gov/drivers/documents/FISMA-final.pdf`, 2002.

[335] Michael Steil. 17 mistakes microsoft made in the Xbox security system. In *22nd Chaos Communication Congress*, Berlin, Germany, December 2005. `http://events.ccc.de/congress/2005/`

[336] Julien P. Stern, Gael Hachez, Francois Koeune, and Jean-Jacques Quisquater. Robust object watermarking: Application to code. In *Information Hiding*, pages 368–378, 1999. Springer-Verlag.

[337] Frank A. Stevenson. Cryptanalysis of contents scrambling system. `www.dvd-copy.com/news/cryptanalysis_of_contents_scrambling_system.htm`, November 1999.

[338] Margaret-Anne Storey, Casey Best, and Jeff Michaud. SHriMP views: An interactive environment for exploring Java programs. *9th International Workshop on Program Comprehension (IWPC 2001)*, 2001. IEEE.

[339] Mario Strasser. Software-based TPM emulator for Linux. Technical report, Department of Computer Science, Swiss Federal Institute of Technology, Zürich, Switzerland, 2004.

[340] Frederic Stumpf, Omid Tafreschi, Patrick Roeder, and Claudia Eckert. A robust integrity reporting protocol for remote attestation. In *The Second Workshop on Advances in Trusted Computing (WATC '06)*, November 2006.

[341] H. Tamada, M. Nakamura, A. Monden, and K. Matsumoto. Design and evaluation of birthmarks for detecting theft of Java programs. In *Proc. IASTED International Conference on Software Engineering (IASTED SE 2004)*, pages 569–575, Feb. 2004. IASTED/ACTA.

[342] H. Tamada, K. Okamoto, M. Nakamura, A. Monden, and K. Matsumoto. Dynamic software birthmarking to detect the theft of Windows applications. In *Proceedings of the International Symposium on Future Software Technology*, Oct. 2004.

[343] Haruaki Tamada, Masahide Nakamura, Akito Monden, and Kenichi Matsumoto. Detecting the theft of programs using birthmarks. Information Science Technical Report NAIST-IS-TR2003014 ISSN 0919-9527, Graduate School of Information Science, Nara Institute of Science and Technology, Nov. 2003.

[344] Gang Tan, Yuqun Chen, and Mariusz H. Jakubowski. Delayed and controlled failures in tamper-resistant systems. In *Information Hiding*, 2006. Springer-Verlag.

[345] C. Thomborson, C. He, J. Nagra, and R. Somaraju. Tamper-proofing software watermarks. The Australasian Information Security Workshop (AISWA) 32:27–36, 2004. Australian Computer Society.

[346] Clark David Thomborson, Yong He, Ram Abhinav Somaraju, and Jasvir Nagra. Tamper-proofing watermarked computer programs. U.S. Application 20050050396, March 2005. Assigned to Auckland UniServices Limited.

[347] Frank Tip. A survey of program slicing techniques. *Journal of Programming Languages*, 3(3):121–189, September 1995.

[348] David S. Touretzky. Declaration in Support of Motion for Summary Judgement, in DVDCCA v. McLaughlin, Bunner, et al., case no. cv—786804, November 2001.

[349] David S. Touretzky. Gallery of CSS descramblers. `www.cs.cmu.edu/~dst/DeCSS/Gallery`, 2008.

[350] Alan M. Turing. On computable numbers, with an application to the Entscheidungsproblem. *Proceedings of the London Mathematical Society*, 2(42):230–265, 1936.

[351] Paul Tyma. Method for renaming identifiers of a computer program. U.S. patent 6,102,966, 2000.

[352] Sharath K. Udupa, Saumya K. Debray, and Matias Madou. Deobfuscation: Reverse engineering obfuscated code. In *WCRE '05: Proceedings of the 12th Working Conference on Reverse Engineering*, pages 45–54, Washington, DC, 2005. IEEE.

[353] unknown. Decoys: Tanks but No Tanks. *Time Magazine*, (Monday, Feb. 4) 1991. `www.time.com/time/magazine/article/0,9171,972244,00.html`.

[354] Ramarathnam Venkatesan and Vijay Vazirani. Technique for producing through watermarking highly tamper-resistant executable code and resulting "watermarked" code so formed. U.S. Patent 7051208, May 2006.

[355] Ramarathnam Venkatesan, Vijay Vazirani, and Saurabh Sinha. A graph theoretic approach to software watermarking. In *4th International Information Hiding Workshop*, Pittsburgh, April 2001. Springer-Verlag.

[356] Hans Peter Van Vliet. Crema—The Java obfuscator, January 1996.

[357] Hans Peter Van Vliet. Mocha—The Java decompiler. `www.brouhaha.com/~eric/software/mocha`, January 1996.

[358] Neal R. Wagner. Fingerprinting. In *Symposium on Security and Privacy*, pages 18–22, Oakland, California, 25–27, April 1983. IEEE.

[359] Kelly Wallace and Mike Chinoy. U.S. surveillance plane lands in China after collision with fighter. archives.cnn.com/2001/US/04/01/us.china.plane, 2001.

[360] Chenxi Wang. *A Security Architecture for Survivability Mechanisms*. Ph.D. thesis, University of Virginia, School of Engineering and Applied Science, October 2000. `http://citeseer.ist.psu.edu/wang00security.html`.

[361] Chenxi Wang, Jonathan Hill, John Knight, and Jack Davidson. Protection of software-based survivability mechanisms. *dsn*, 00:0193, 2001.

[362] Jie Wang and Jay Belanger. On the NP-isomorphism problem with respect to random instances. *Journal of Computer and System Sciences*, 50(1):151–164, February 1995.

[363] Xiaoyun Wang and Hongbo Yu. How to break MD5 and other hash functions. In Ronald Cramer, editor, *EUROCRYPT*, volume 3494 of *LNCS*, pages 19–35. Springer, 2005.

[364] Zheng Wang, Scott A. McFarling, Ken B. Pierce, and Ramarathnam Venkatesan. Methods for comparing versions of a program. United States Patent 6954747, October 2005. Assigned to Microsoft Corporation (Redmond, WA).

[365] Peter Wayner. Mimic functions. *CRYPTOLOGIA*, 14(3), July 1992.

[366] Peter Wayner. Strong theoretical steganography. *CRYPTOLOGIA*, 19, July 1995.

[367] Peter Wayner. *Disappearing Cryptography: Information Hiding: Steganography and Watermarking (2nd Edition)*. Morgan Kaufmann Publishers Inc., San Francisco, CA, 2002.

[368] Tim Weber. The Internet is doomed, 2007. `www.bbc.co.uk/blogs/davos07/2007/01/the_internet_is_doomed.shtml`.

[369] Hoeteck Wee. On obfuscating point functions. In *STOC '05: Proceedings of the Thirty-Seventh Annual ACM Symposium on Theory of Computing*, pages 523–532, New York, 2005. ACM.

[370] S. H. Weingart. Physical security for the μABYSS system. In *Proceedings of the IEEE Symposium on Security and Privacy*, pages 52–58, 1987. IEEE.

[371] S. H. Weingart, S. R. White, W. C. Arnold, and G. P. Double. An evaluation system for the physical security of computing systems. In *Sixth Annual Computer Security Applications Conference*, pages 232–243, Tucson, AZ, December 1990. IEEE.

[372] Ruediger Weis, Stefan Lucks, and Andreas Bogk. TCG 1.2—Fair play with the 'fritz' chip? Technical report, Cryptolabs Amsterdam/VU Computersystems, RAI Centre, Amsterdam, The Netherlands, October 2004.

[373] Deborah Whitfield and Mary Lou Soffa. An approach to ordering optimizing transformations. In *PPOPP'90*, pages 137–146, 1990. ACM.

[374] Deborah Whitfield and Mary Lou Soffa. Automatic generation of global optimizers. In *Principles of Programming Languages '91*, pages 120–129, 1991. ACM.

[375] Amy Wimmer. Laptops' removal no mistake, officials say. *St. Petersbug Times*, Aug. 11, 2002.

[376] Niklaus Wirth. Type extensions. *ACM Transactions on Programming Languages and Systems*, 10(2):204–214, April 1988.

[377] Gregory Wolfe, Jennifer L. Wong, and Miodrag Potkonjak. Watermarking graph partitioning solutions. In *Design Automation Conference*, pages 486–489, 2001. ACM.

[378] Wei Wu, Frank Nian-Tzu Chu, Erik Fortune, Julie D. Bennett, Mohammed El-Gammal, and Simon D. Earnshaw. Inhibiting software tampering. U.S. Application 20060005251, January 2006. Assigned to Microsoft Corporation.

[379] Glen Wurster, P.C. van Oorschot, and Anil Somayaji. A generic attack on checksumming-based software tamper resistance. In *2005 IEEE Symposium on Security and Privacy*, pages 127–138, 2005. IEEE.

[380] P. Young and M. Munro. Visualising software in virtual reality. In *Proceedings of the IEEE 6th International Workshop on Program Comprehension*, pages 19–26, June 1998. IEEE.

[381] Jonathan A. Zdziarski. Nes.app 2.0.3—the Nintendo emulator for iPhone. www.zdziarski.com/projects/nesapp, 2008.

[382] Xiangyu Zhang and Rajiv Gupta. Hiding program slices for software security. In *CGO '03: Proceedings of the International Symposium on code Generation and Optimization*, pages 325–336, Washington, DC, 2003. IEEE.

[383] Youtao Zhang, Jun Yang, and Rajiv Gupta. Frequent value locality and value-centric data cache design. In *Architectural Support for Programming Languages and Operating Systems*, pages 150–159, 2000. ACM.

[384] W. Zhu, C. C. Thomborson, and Fei-Yue Wang. Obfuscate arrays by homomorphic functions. *Special Session on Computer Security and Data Privacy*, pages 770–773, May 2006. IEEE.

[385] Xiaotong Zhuang, Tao Zhang, Hsien-Hsin S. Lee, and Santosh Pande. Hardware assisted control flow obfuscation for embedded processors. In *CASES '04: Proceedings of the 2004 International Conference on Compilers, Architecture, and Synthesis for Embedded Systems*, pages 292–302, New York, 2004. ACM.

[386] Xiaotong Zhuang, Tao Zhang, and Santosh Pande. Hide: an infrastructure for efficiently protecting information leakage on the address bus. In *ASPLOS-XI: Proceedings of the 11th International Conference on Architectural Support for Programming Languages and Operating Systems*, pages 72–84, New York, 2004. ACM.

Index

THE ADDISON-WESLEY SOFTWARE SECURITY SERIES

Gary McGraw, Consulting Editor

ISBN 0-321-42477-8

ISBN 0-13-227191-5

ISBN 0-201-78695-8

ISBN 0-321-29431-9

Also Available

ISBN 0-321-41870-0

ISBN 0-321-35670-5

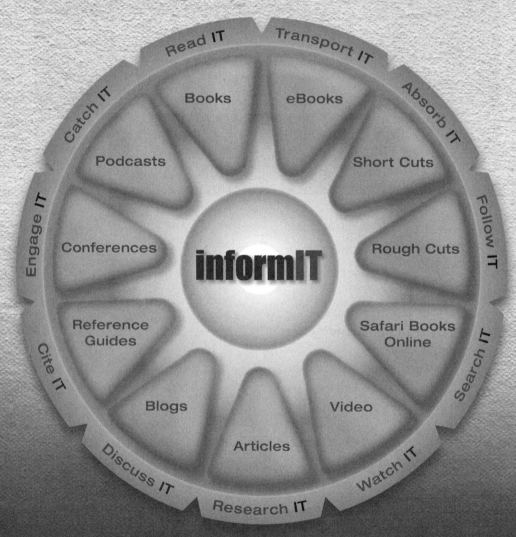

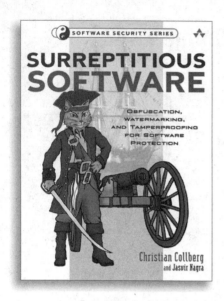